LAUNCHPAD FOR *LET'S COMMUNICATE* HELPS STUDENTS LEARN, STUDY, AND APPLY COMMUNICATION CONCEPTS.

- **An easy-to-use interface.** Ready-made interactive LaunchPad units give you the building blocks to assign instantly as is or customize to fit your course. A unit's worth of work can be assigned in seconds, significantly decreasing the amount of time it takes for you to get your course up and running.

- **LearningCurve offers adaptive quizzing and a personalized learning program.** In every chapter, callouts prompt students to tackle the gamelike LearningCurve quizzes to test their knowledge and reinforce learning of the material. Based on research as to how students learn, LearningCurve motivates students to engage with course materials while the reporting tools let you see what content students have mastered, allowing you to adapt your teaching plan to their needs.

- **Hundreds of LaunchPad videos** help students understand theory and communication concepts in action. These include numerous public speaking clips and full-length speeches.

- **Video tools** make it easy to create video assignments and evaluate student videos using rubrics and time-based comments. Instructors and students can upload videos, embed clips from YouTube, and upload publisher-supplied videos.

"My initial reaction is excitement. The authors differentiate themselves from [authors of] other intro texts with their focused pedagogical approach, combining illustrations with concepts in order to enhance student understanding of concepts."

Brent Kice
University of Houston–Clear Lake

ILLUSTRATIONS, APPLY YOUR SKILLS FEATURES, AND MORE TO HELP STUDENTS UNDERSTAND AND RETAIN CONCEPTS.

Customized illustrations help students understand and retain human communication theories and concepts. The authors and artist worked together to come up with hundreds of illustrations meant to help students understand and retain concepts. Artist Peter Arkle gave the illustrations his trademark style and humor, as he's done for public speaking text *Speak Up!* as well as other outlets, including *Time* magazine, the *New Yorker*, and the *New York Times*.

Beyond the illustrations, *Let's Communicate* uses special features, end-of-chapter pedagogy, and practical advice to help students understand concepts so that they can apply them in real life.

- **The Apply Your Skills feature in** every chapter asks students to use an illustration to extend the concept either to their lives or to other real-life situations.
- **End-of-chapter pedagogy** asks students to respond to the chapter with in-class activities and discussion concepts.
- **Practical advice** helps students know what to do when faced with difficult communication situations, whether it's a job interview, a confusing text message, or a relationship problem.

FRAMING

They NEVER stop and frisk old white guys like me!

RACIAL PROFILING

GUN CONTROL

"STAND YOUR GROUND" = "KILL AT WILL"

TRAYVON MARTIN

FLORIDA'S SELF-DEFENSE LAW

SOME OF THE AUTHORS' FAVORITE ILLUSTRATIONS . . . AND WHY

Douglas Fraleigh: This illustration extends the concept that communication is more than just common sense—it's a skill that students need to build—by showing a new example. It also extends the text by showing this principle in a mediated context. Students will be familiar with this channel (texting) and likely also with the scenario. (From Chapter 1: Introduction to Human Communication)

Katherine Adams:

This illustration helps show that each type of relationship faces its own set of relational maintenance challenges. This illustration helps students by visually comparing and contrasting strategies of a workplace romantic couple. It shows them

maintaining their relationship at home and then doing so at work—making clear that each context requires different maintenance behaviors. (From Chapter 9: Practices for Effective Interpersonal Relationships)

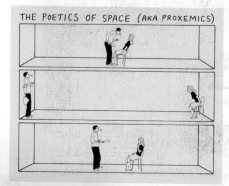

Joseph Tuman: I love the simplicity of this. In this illustration showing proxemics, three panels clearly demonstrate why too close and too far away are not adequate—and how speaking at a reasonable distance works. Showing this contrast makes it memorable. (From Chapter 15: Delivering Your Speech)

LET'S COMMUNICATE PRESENTS STRONG THEORY, UNIQUE CONTENT, AND REAL-LIFE EXAMPLES

Substantive content, with a focus on technology, culture, gender, and social justice. *Let's Communicate* contains all the theories and research that students need to know across all topics of communication: fundamentals (such as perception and listening), important influences on communication (such as culture and experiences), interpersonal, group, public speaking, mass and mediated communication, and interviewing. Within these sections, authors put a special emphasis on their interests: technology, culture, gender, and social justice. With practical, accessible advice, the authors consistently help students adapt their communication style and habits, especially toward communicating in a digital age.

Engaging writing and examples. Each chapter opens with an absorbing vignette that the authors culled from their own lives and interests, while examples throughout show situations from the classroom, workplace, community, and public sphere. Topics range from the collaboration on the recent Star Wars movie (group communication) to online dating (perception) to the differences between Tiananmen Square and the Arab Spring (mass and mediated communication).

"The use of visual stimulation alongside the text is a very good choice. Many of our students today grew up through visual stimulation both in and out of the classroom, so they are predisposed to approach learning from this perspective. I do not feel, in contrast, that other texts on the market currently put emphasis on this style of learning to the extent that this text [does]."

Jason Nado
Blackhawk Technical College

Let's Communicate

AN ILLUSTRATED GUIDE TO
HUMAN COMMUNICATION

Let's Communicate

AN ILLUSTRATED GUIDE TO HUMAN COMMUNICATION

Douglas M. Fraleigh
California State University–Fresno

Joseph S. Tuman
San Francisco State University

Katherine L. Adams
California State University–Fresno

With Illustrations by
Peter Arkle

bedford/st.martin's
Macmillan Learning
Boston | New York

For Bedford/St. Martin's

Vice President, Editorial, Macmillan Learning Humanities: Edwin Hill
Publisher for Communication: Erika Gutierrez
Development Manager: Susan McLaughlin
Senior Developmental Editor: Julia Bartz
Developmental Editor: Kate George
Editorial Assistant: Mary Jane Chen
Senior Production Editor: Peter Jacoby
Media Producer: Rand Thomas
Senior Production Supervisor: Jennifer Wetzel
Marketing Manager: Kayti Corfield
Copy Editor: Jamie Thaman
Indexer: Kirsten Kite
Permissions Editor: Linda Winters
Senior Art Director: Anna Palchik
Text Design: Jerilyn Bockorick
Cover Design: William Boardman
Cover Illustrations: Peter Arkle
Composition: Cenveo Publisher Services
Printing and Binding: LSC Communications

Manufactured in the United States of America.

1   0   9   8   7   6
f   e   d   c   b   a

For information, write: Bedford/St. Martin's, 75 Arlington Street,
Boston, MA 02116   (617-399-4000)

ISBN: 978-1-4576-0601-4

Doug
To my family, the greatest source of happiness in my life.

Joe
For my wife, Kirsten: With every new book, there are more reasons to appreciate your love and patience.

Kathy
To all my students, who teach me more about communication than any textbook ever could.

BRIEF CONTENTS

FUNDAMENTALS OF COMMUNICATION

1 Introduction to Human Communication 3
2 Perceiving Others, Perceiving Ourselves 31
3 Verbal Communication 67
4 Nonverbal Communication 103
5 Listening Skills 131

IMPORTANT INFLUENCES ON COMMUNICATION

6 Culture and Communication 161
7 Mass and Mediated Communication 191

INTERPERSONAL COMMUNICATION

8 Principles of Interpersonal Communication 219
9 Practices for Effective Interpersonal Relationships 251

GROUP COMMUNICATION

10 Principles of Group Communication 283
11 Problem Solving and Leading a Small Group 319

PUBLIC SPEAKING

12 Public Speaking: First Steps 347
13 Speech Content: Research, Supporting Materials, and Ethics 381
14 Organizing and Outlining 415
15 Delivering Your Speech 455
16 Informative Speaking 489
17 Persuasive Speaking 521

Appendix A Job Interviews A-1
Appendix B Sample Speeches A-21

ABOUT THE AUTHORS AND ILLUSTRATOR:

<u>DOUGLAS M. FRALEIGH</u> is a professor and chair of the Communication Department at California State University-Fresno, where he also teaches in the Smittcamp Family Honors College and serves as assessment coordinator for the College of Arts and Humanities. His teaching and research interests include freedom of speech, argumentation, and public discourse. He is coauthor of *Speak Up!: An Illustrated Guide to Public Speaking* and *Freedom of Expression in the Marketplace of Ideas*. Before becoming chair, he was active in speech and debate coaching at Fresno State, Cornell, UC Berkeley, and California State University-Sacramento. He holds a juris doctor from UC Berkeley and a BA from CSU-Sacramento. When not busy teaching, writing, and administrating, he looks forward to running, reading, family time (especially plays and sporting events), and hanging out with his dogs.

<u>JOSEPH S. TUMAN</u> is a professor and former chair of the Department of Communication Studies at San Francisco State University, where he received the Jacobus tenBroek Society Award, a statewide award for Excellence in Teaching. He has also taught at the University of California at Berkeley, the New School, and the University of Paris II, and has published widely in the field of communication studies (including coauthoring *Speak Up!: An Illustrated Guide to Public Speaking*). Joseph has appeared regularly on local and national network television and radio as a political analyst since 1984. He has served on the boards of several nonprofits in Oakland, and in 2014 he was one of the leading candidates in the mayoral race. Currently, he serves as an advisor and expert analyst regarding terrorism and social media for the North Atlantic Treaty Organization. In his spare time, he is an avid triathlete and marathoner.

<u>KATHERINE L. ADAMS</u> has been a professor of communication for over thirty years at California State University-Fresno, where she formerly served as chair of the Department of Communication and currently chairs the Department of Media, Communications and Journalism. Her primary teaching responsibilities include undergraduate and graduate courses in communication theory, interpersonal communication, and small group communication. She also helped create an honors public speaking course and taught in the Smittcamp Family Honors College. A former graduate of the University of Utah, she published her first interpersonal textbook with her mentor and noted small group communication scholar B. Aubrey Fisher. She continued on to publish two textbooks in small group communication. She has held all the major offices in the Western States Communication Association, including its past presidency. She has also completed four AIDS/LifeCycle events to help raise money for the fight against AIDS.

<u>PETER ARKLE</u> is a freelance illustrator who grew up in Scotland and received a BA in illustration from St. Martin's School of Art and an MA from the Royal College of Art (both in London). His clients include magazines (the *New Yorker, Canadian Business, Time,* and the *Harvard Business Review*), newspapers (the *New York Times* and the *Wall Street Journal*), sports brands (Nike and Brooks Running), scientists (the Howard Hughes Medical Institute), lawyers (Kennedys Law), whisky makers (anCnoc Highland Single Malt Scotch Whisky), hotels (Morgans Hotel Group), and other enterprises that keep his life interesting. He just published a book, *All Black Cats Are Not Alike*, with his wife, Amy Goldwasser. To see more of Peter's work, please visit peterarkle.com.

PREFACE

As educators, we have devoted our careers to helping teach our students to communicate more effectively. Communication skills are central to students' ability to thrive in their personal lives, careers, and communities. It's also clear that the books we assign our students are critically important resources in their educational journey. Over the years, we have happily witnessed generations of capable, confident communication students walk across the stage at graduation.

Communication is a broad discipline, and the challenge of developing competence across a range of communication contexts can seem overwhelming to a student, especially in an introductory course. In setting out to write *Let's Communicate*, our aspiration was to craft a text that would engage students' interest in the broader field of communication while also helping them understand fundamental principles of human communication. We wanted to create a book that was both informative and fun to read. In *Let's Communicate*, we believe we have achieved these goals.

Let's Communicate is the first illustrated human communication text on the market. The illustrations are custom-drawn by professional artist Peter Arkle, who lends his trademark style and wit. The illustrations serve as a pedagogical tool to visually explain and reinforce course concepts in ways that make them uniquely different from those offered in traditional stand-alone textbooks. The incorporation of art is a response to the various learning styles present among our students. In an increasingly visual culture, illustrations pull students in and build their interest in reading the text. They also help students better understand and retain course concepts, as evidenced by research on the power of visual representations (Carney and Levin, 2002).

The illustrations go hand-in-hand with the text's substantive introduction to the communication discipline. *Let's Communicate* is a comprehensive text that anchors the three traditional contexts of human communication theory and practice—interpersonal communication, small group communication, and public speaking—within a discussion of communication's central concepts. Chapters provide a strong basis for the fundamentals of communication (perception and self, verbal and nonverbal communication, and effective listening), and cover important influences on communication (culture, mass media, and mediated communication). We introduce major theories and principles of communication in every chapter (identity management, language rules, relational dialectical theory, maintenance models, group socialization, source credibility, social judgment theory, and so on) while providing a unique perspective based on our research interests (technology, culture, gender, and social justice).

By design, the text features an accessible writing style and a reasonable chapter length, so students will be engaged rather than intimidated. We present fundamentals in a clear manner that gets to the heart of each concept, regularly using examples relating to students' lives and experiences in tandem with illustrations that clarify course principles. Aware that our students are communicating in a digital age, we include numerous examples of communication on social media and other mediated channels. Apply Your Skills features appear in each chapter, encouraging students to extend important concepts to their own lives or to other real-life situations.

We are also very excited about the powerful digital tools accompanying the text on LaunchPad. This learning platform contains hundreds of videos, LearningCurve (our adaptive quizzing program), various assessment options, video assignment tools, instructor supplements, and a full e-book.

In sum, *Let's Communicate* is a comprehensive introductory human communication textbook that combines a unique illustrated pedagogy with accessible writing, singular content, and powerful digital tools. We are confident that after exploring this introduction to the field of human communication, students will become more effective communicators in their personal lives, careers, and communities.

FEATURES

Award-winning teachers and scholars Douglas Fraleigh, Joseph Tuman, and Katherine Adams used their decades of experience to create a book that combines strong theory with cutting-edge content. Douglas Fraleigh—professor, writer, and scholar—and Joseph Tuman—writer, political analyst, and award-winning professor—honed their unique approach to writing with *Speak Up!*, the first illustrated guide to public speaking. With this endeavor, they have teamed up with Katherine Adams, a renowned professor and scholar, to carefully create a communication textbook that teaches students the principles of human communication in a way that will keep them interested and eager for more. The authors brainstormed to come up with the hundreds of pedagogically useful illustrations, and artist Peter Arkle (who also draws for *Time* magazine, the *New York Times*, and the *New Yorker*) added his trademark style and humor to capture students' attention.

Substantive content, with a focus on technology, culture, gender, and social justice. *Let's Communicate* contains all the theories and research that students need to know across all topics of communication: fundamentals (such as perception and listening), important influences (such as culture and mass/mediated communication), interpersonal, group, public speaking, and interviewing. Within these sections, the authors put particular emphasis on their interests: technology, culture, gender, and social justice. With their practical, accessible advice, the authors consistently help students adapt their communication style and habits, especially toward communicating in a digital age.

Help students learn and apply skills. *Let's Communicate* uses lively writing, compelling examples, and pedagogical illustrations to help students understand concepts so that they can apply them in real life.

- **The Apply Your Skills feature in** every chapter asks students to use an illustration to extend the concept either to their lives or to other real-life situations.
- **Hundreds of hand-drawn illustrations** help students understand and retain human communication theories and concepts.
- **End-of-chapter pedagogy** asks students to respond to the chapter with in-class activities and discussion concepts.
- **Practical advice** helps students know what to do when faced with difficult communication situations, whether it's a job interview, a confusing text message, or a relationship problem.

Customized illustrations help students understand and retain human communication theories and concepts. The authors brainstormed to come up with each of the hundreds of illustrations included in the text, meant to help students understand and retain concepts. Artist Peter Arkle gave the illustrations his trademark style and humor, as he's done for public speaking text *Speak Up!* as well as for many other outlets.

Engaging writing and examples. Each chapter opens with an absorbing vignette that the authors culled from their own teaching experiences, lives, and interests, while examples throughout show situations from the classroom, workplace, community, and public sphere. Topics range from the collaboration on the recent Star Wars movie (group communication) to online dating (perception) to the differences between Tiananmen Square and the Arab Spring (mass and mediated communication).

LaunchPad

LaunchPad helps students learn, study, and apply communication concepts. Digital resources for *Let's Communicate* are available in LaunchPad, a dynamic new platform that combines a collection of relevant video clips, self-assessments, e-book content, and LearningCurve adaptive quizzing in a simple design. LaunchPad can be packaged at a significant discount with *Let's Communicate*, or it can be purchased separately.

- **LaunchPad has an easy-to-use interface.** Ready-made interactive LaunchPad units give instructors the building blocks to assign instantly as is or customize to fit any course. A unit's worth of work can be assigned in seconds, significantly decreasing the amount of time it takes to get a course up and running.

- **LearningCurve offers adaptive quizzing and a personalized learning program.** In every chapter, callouts prompt students to tackle the gamelike LearningCurve quizzes to test their knowledge and reinforce learning of the material. Based on research as to how students learn, LearningCurve motivates students to engage with course materials while the reporting tools let you see what content students have mastered, allowing you to adapt your teaching plan to their needs.

- **Hundreds of LaunchPad videos** help students understand theory and communication concepts in action. These include numerous public speaking clips and full-length speeches.

- **Video tools** make it easy to create video assignments and evaluate student videos using rubrics and time-based comments. Instructors and students can upload videos, embed clips from YouTube, and upload publisher-supplied videos.

Curriculum solutions: customize for your needs. Get in touch to find your solutions. Go to **macmillanlearning.com/curriculumsolutions** to learn more.

DIGITAL AND PRINT FORMATS

Whether it's print, digital, or a value option, choose the best format for you. For more information on these resources, please visit the online catalog at **macmillanlearning.com**.

LaunchPad for *Let's Communicate*, at launchpadworks.com, combines the full e-book, videos, quizzes and self-assessments, instructors' resources, and LearningCurve adaptive quizzing. LaunchPad can also be integrated into course management systems. To get access to all multimedia resources, package LaunchPad with the print book or order LaunchPad on its own.

***Let's Communicate* is available as a print text.** To get the most out of the book, package LaunchPad at a significant discount with the text. To get *Let's Communicate* plus LaunchPad, order ISBN: 978-1-319-11536-4.

***Let's Communicate* e-book option.** E-books meet students where they already live—online and digital—and *Let's Communicate* is available in a variety of e-book options. Visit **macmillanlearning.com** to learn more about these options.

RESOURCES FOR STUDENTS AND INSTRUCTORS

Resources for Students

For more information on these resources or to learn about package options, please visit the online catalog at **macmillanlearning.com**.

LaunchPad for *Let's Communicate* helps students learn, study, and apply course concepts.
We designed LaunchPad as a resource to help students achieve better results. Our goal was to increase their confidence by providing a place where they could read, study, practice, complete homework, and more. **LaunchPad can be packaged with the book or purchased separately, and can be integrated with course management systems. See more on the inside back cover, or visit launchpadworks.com.**

The Essential Guide Series

This series gives instructors flexibility and support in designing courses by providing brief booklets that begin with a useful overview and then address the essential concepts and skills that students need. Essential Guides cover topics like rhetoric, intercultural communication, presentation software, interpersonal communication, and small group communication, and can be packaged with *Let's Communicate*.

Media Career Guide: Preparing for Jobs in the 21st Century, Tenth Edition
Sherri Hope Culver, Temple University

Practical, student friendly, and revised to include the most recent statistics on the job market, this guide includes a comprehensive directory of media jobs, practical tips, and career guidance for students considering a major in the media industry.

Resources for Instructors
For more information or to order or download instructor resources, please visit the online catalog at **macmillanlearning.com**. The *Instructor's Manual*, *Electronic Test Bank*, and lecture slides are also available in LaunchPad.

Instructor's Manual for Let's Communicate
Jennifer Mullen, Indiana State University

This comprehensive *Instructor's Manual* includes teaching notes on managing a human communication course, organization, and assessment; sample syllabi; chapter outlines; discussion questions; personal writing assignments; classroom activities; media resources; and ready-to-print activities.

Electronic Test Bank for Let's Communicate
Marnel Niles Goins, California State University–Fresno

Let's Communicate offers a complete testing program, available for Windows and Macintosh environments. Each chapter includes multiple-choice, true/false, short-answer, and essay questions. This easy-to-use *Electronic Test Bank* also identifies the level of difficulty for each question, includes the textbook page number where the answer can be found, and connects every question to a learning objective.

Lecture Slides for *Let's Communicate*
These lecture slides can be used in class. They include each chapter's main ideas, plus lots of example illustrations and explanations from the text.

Teaching Interpersonal Communication, Second Edition
Elizabeth J. Natalle, University of North Carolina–Greensboro
Alicia Alexander, Southern Illinois University–Edwardsville
    Written by award-winning instructors, this essential resource provides all the tools instructors need to develop, teach, and manage a successful interpersonal communication course. New and seasoned instructors alike will benefit from the practical advice, scholarly insight, and suggestions for integrating research and practice into the classroom—as well as from the new chapter dedicated to online teaching.

Coordinating the Communication Course: A Guidebook
Deanna Fassett, San José State University
John Warren, Southern Illinois University–Carbondale
    This guidebook offers the most practical advice on every topic central to the coordinator-director role. Beginning with establishing a strong foundation, this professional resource continues on with thoughtful guidance, tips, and best practices on such crucial topics as creating community across multiple sections, orchestrating meaningful assessment, and hiring and training instructors. Model course material, recommended readings, and insights from successful coordinators make this resource a must-have for anyone directing a course in communication.

ESL Students in the Public Speaking Classroom: A Guide for Instructors, Second Edition
Robbin D. Crabtree, Fairfield University
David Alan Sapp, Fairfield University
    As the United States increasingly becomes a nation of nonnative speakers, instructors must find new pedagogical tools to aid students for whom English is a second language. This guide specifically addresses the needs of ESL students in the public speaking course and offers instructors valuable advice for helping students deal successfully with the challenges they face.

Curriculum solutions: customize *Let's Communicate* to your needs.
Get in touch to find your solutions. To learn more, go to **macmillanlearning .com/catalog/preview/curriculumsolutions**.

Macmillan Communication COMMunity
Created by instructors for instructors, this is an ideal forum for interacting with fellow educators—including Macmillan authors—in your discipline. Join ongoing conversations about everything from course prep and

presentations to assignments and assessments to teaching with media, keeping pace with—and influencing—new directions in your field. Includes exclusive access to classroom resources, blogs, webinars, professional development opportunities, and more. Go to **community.macmillan .com/community/communication** to visit the COMMunity.

ACKNOWLEDGMENTS

This project was launched in a meeting at the 2008 National Communication Association Convention in Chicago, and we have had the opportunity to work with many outstanding people on our journey. We would like to thank Joan Feinberg, former co-president of Macmillan Higher Education, and Denise Wydra, former president of Bedford/St. Martin's, for all their support as we planned and developed *Let's Communicate*. We are very grateful for the contributions of Macmillan Learning's vice president of editorial, Edwin Hill; publisher for communication, Erika Gutierrez; and development manager, Susan McLaughlin. Their input and professionalism were highly valuable as we focused on both the big picture and the specific details that led to the publication of *Let's Communicate*.

We were delighted to have the opportunity to collaborate with professional artist Peter Arkle. We looked forward to every new delivery of art from Peter with great anticipation. His ability to take a general idea for an illustration and turn it into a piece of art that is attention grabbing, educational, and fun is without parallel. The illustrations are the signature of our text and central to our pedagogy.

We were very fortunate to work with outstanding editors on this project. Senior editor Julia Bartz devoted countless hours to work with us on every phase of the development and production of this text. Her excellent work in planning our approach to the book, editing our writing, conceptualizing ideas for illustrations, and offering ideas for optimizing the content of the book was all much appreciated. We also owe a debt of gratitude to former senior editor Simon Glick, whose support in the early stages of this project was absolutely vital. We thank editorial assistant Mary Jane Chen for her dedication to the project and her focus on getting every detail right.

We are very indebted to Dr. Marnel Niles Goins of California State University–Fresno for her excellent work on our Nonverbal Communication chapter. Marnel drafted a fantastic chapter in record time, explained concepts in a clear and student-friendly manner, and made great suggestions for illustrations. We also want to thank Marnel for her expert work creating the *Electronic Test Bank*. Many thanks also to Jennifer Mullen of Indiana State University for creating the *Instructor's Manual* and filling it with a wealth of helpful and creative content for instructors to pull from.

We are very thankful to the incredible professionals who guided the production and design of *Let's Communicate*, including senior art director Anna Palchik. Senior production editor Peter Jacoby did outstanding work turning our manuscript into page proofs and ultimately a published text. We especially appreciate his collaboration with us to make sure each illustration was placed at an optimal spot in the text as well as his hard work delivering page proofs under a tight schedule. Along with Peter, senior production supervisor Jennifer Wetzel put in the hard and careful work needed to turn hundreds of manuscript pages with hundreds of illustrations into a finished product.

Beyond producing the book itself, we have been fortunate to work with a crackerjack marketing team. We love working with marketing manager Kayti Corfield, who helped develop our marketing and sales message.

We are also extremely grateful to the many reviewers who gave us feedback on *Let's Communicate* and offered suggestions to make it even better. The invaluable input of our colleagues in the human communication profession offered both validation for what was working and constructive suggestions for improvement. We would like to thank Len Assante, Volunteer State Community College; Barbara L. Baker, The University of Texas at Dallas; Alison Behrman, Iona College; Allison Beltramini, Waubonsee Community College; Ellen Bland, Central Carolina Community College; Lori Britt, James Madison University; Hui-Ching Chang, University of Illinois at Chicago; Sabryna Cornish, College of DuPage; Karen Cristiano, Drexel University; Tasha Davis, Austin Community College; Natalie Dudchock, Jefferson State Community College; Aaron Duncan, University of Nebraska–Lincoln; Karen Erlandson, Albion College; Sarah Fogle, Embry-Riddle Aeronautical University–Daytona Beach; Lysia Hand, Phoenix College; Danielle Harkins, Germanna Community College; Nancy Henschel, Lakeshore Technical College; Hugh Johnston, Barry University; Marisa Jones, Jefferson State Community College; Brent Kice, University of Houston–Clear Lake; James Kimble, Seton Hall University; Shana Kopaczewski, Indiana State University; Chris Lint, Pennsylvania Highlands Community College; Talia Lipton, Rockland Community College; Allyn Lueders, Wayne State College; David McKinney, Jefferson State Community College; Shellie Michael, Volunteer State Community College; Jennifer Millspaugh, Richland College; Jennifer Mullen, Indiana

State University; Jason Nado, Blackhawk Technical College; Gregg Nelson, Chippewa Valley Technical College; Laura Oliver, The University of Texas at San Antonio; Karen Otto, Florida State College at Jacksonville; Deb Pagnotta, Iona College; Lisa Peterson, Boise State University; Jeff Ringer, St. Cloud State University; Ronald Ringer, St. Cloud State University; Rebecca Tiedge, Boise State University; Sherry Tucker, Community College of Baltimore County; Cindy Vincent, Salem State University; Judith Vogel, Des Moines Area Community College; James Wilson, Shelton State Community College; Russ Wittrup, Austin Community College; and Denise Woolsey, Yavapai College.

The three of us were delighted to have the opportunity to coauthor *Let's Communicate*; our connections with one another go back many years. For Joe and Doug, this is their ninth major book project as writing partners, and it is a privilege to continue to work together. Kathy, who joins our partnership in this book, has taught with Doug at California State University–Fresno for twenty-seven years. Doug has always had the greatest respect for Kathy's scholarship and wanted to collaborate with her on a book project. All of us draw from a lifetime of personal experiences and perspectives; this can be seen from the examples you will discover when reading *Let's Communicate*.

Doug would especially like to thank his wife, Nancy; his son, Douglas; his daughter-in-law, Renee; and his daughter, Whitney, for their love and support. He is always seeking their expertise or pitching them ideas for examples and illustrations, and he much appreciates their contributions.

Joe would like to thank his wife, Kirsten; his daughter, Helena; and his son, Nate, for their continued love, support, and, above all else, patience as he worked on yet another manuscript instead of paying more attention to his family. He would also like to thank his fellow faculty in the Department of Communication Studies at San Francisco State University for their suggestions and advice regarding parts of this manuscript.

Kathy is especially grateful to both Doug and Joe for the invitation to be part of this project. She is particularly thankful to senior editor Julia Bartz, whose patience and insight helped turn lengthy first drafts into chapters that engage students without overwhelming them. Her two children, Sebastian and Jackson—who watched her surrender too many hours in front of the computer screen—will always be her inspiration.

CONTENTS

Brief Contents   vii

Preface   ix

FUNDAMENTALS OF COMMUNICATION

1   INTRODUCTION TO HUMAN COMMUNICATION   3

Communication: The Basics   5

Communication Defined   5

Contexts for Communication   5

The Importance of Effective Communication   8

Benefits of Effective
   Communication   8

Gaining Communication
   Competence   12

Principles of Communication   17

Communication Is Transactional   17

Communication Is Symbolic   19

Communication Can Result in Shared
   Meaning   20

Communication Should Be Ethical   20

Misconceptions about Communication   22

Communication Is Not Just Common
   Sense   22

Communication Is Not Always
   Positive   23

Communication Does Not Always End in Agreement   24

Communication Cannot Solve Every Problem   25

Chapter Review   26

FILTER OUT DISTRACTIONS

First one to look at their phone has to pay for dinner!

2 PERCEIVING OTHERS, PERCEIVING OURSELVES 31

Perceiving Others 32
The Meaning of Perception 33
The Role of Perception in Communication 34
The Formation of Perceptions 36

Barriers to Perception and How to
Overcome Them 40
Why Are Perceptions Often Inaccurate 41
Improving the Accuracy of Perceptions 46

Perceiving Ourselves 49
The Nature of Your Self-Concept 49
Sources of Self-Concepts 51
Improving Your Self-Concept 55

Identity Management 57
How We Engage in Identity Management 58
Objectives of Identity Management 59
Ethics and Identity Management 60
Online Identity Management 60

Chapter Review 62

3 VERBAL COMMUNICATION 67

The Nature of Verbal Communication 68
Language Is Rule-Based 69
Language Is Symbolic 70
Language Is Literal and Figurative 72
Language Is Dynamic 72
Language Is Contextual 74

Verbal Communication and the Challenge
of Understanding 75
Language Is an Imperfect Vehicle
for Understanding 76
Problematic Language Exacerbates
Misunderstandings 77

The Effects of Verbal Communication 81
Uses of Language 82
Abuses of Language 85

Guidelines for Verbal Communication   88
Make Your Message Clear   88
Make Your Message Considerate   91
Make Your Responses Respectful   95
Chapter Review   97

4   NONVERBAL COMMUNICATION   103

Influences on Nonverbal Communication   104
Culture   104
Gender   106
Technology   107

Functions of Nonverbal Communication   108
Supplementing   108
Repeating   109
Contradicting   110
Regulating   110
Substituting   112
Accenting   112

Types of Nonverbal Communication   113
Kinesics   113
Facial Expressions   114
Oculesics   115
Haptics   116
Proxemics   117
Physical Appearance   118
Paralanguage   119
Smell (Olfactics)   120
Chronemics   121

Technology and Its Impact on Nonverbal
Communication   122

Guidelines for Communicating Nonverbal
Messages Effectively   125
Chapter Review   126

5   LISTENING SKILLS   131

How We Listen   132
Listening and Hearing   133
Listening Styles   136

Overcoming External Listening Challenges   138

The Culprits Behind Poor Internal Listening   141
Information Overload   141
Distracted Listening   142
Interruptive Listening   143
Agenda-Driven Listening   143
Argumentative Listening   144
Nervous Listening   145

Becoming a Better Listener   146
Filter Out Distractions   146
Focus on the Speaker   147
Show That You Are Listening   147

Helping Others Listen to You   148
Anticipate Ineffective Listening Before You Speak   149
Encourage Active Listening   151

When You Are the Listener   152
Making a Speech Critique   152
Giving Conversational Feedback   154

Chapter Review   155

IMPORTANT INFLUENCES ON COMMUNICATION

6 CULTURE AND COMMUNICATION   161

What Is Culture?   163

Culture and Diversity   164
Race, Ethnicity, and Heritage   165
Gender and Sexual Orientation   166
Age   168

Variations in Culture: How Do They Affect Communication?   169
Uncertainty Avoidance   169
High and Low Context   171
Individualistic and Collectivist
    Cultures   172
Masculine and Feminine
    Cultures   173

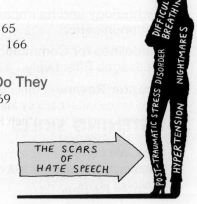

THE SCARS
OF
HATE SPEECH

DIFFICULTY BREATHING
NIGHTMARES
POST-TRAUMATIC STRESS DISORDER
HYPERTENSION

High-Contact and Low-Contact Cultures   174
Power-Distance and Low-Power Distance Cultures   174

Assimilation, Accommodation, and Separation   175
Assimilation   176
Accommodation   177
Separation   178

Challenges to Intercultural Communication   178
Ethnocentrism   179
Prejudice   180
Hate and Hate Speech   181

Constructive Steps For Improving Intercultural Communication   182
Show Awareness of and Respect for Cultural Variations   183
Express a Willingness to Learn about and Participate in Other Cultures   184
Limit Ethnocentrism and Condemn Hate   185

Chapter Review   187

7   MASS AND MEDIATED COMMUNICATION   **191**
Understanding Mass Media   192
Entertainment and News Media   193
Old Media and New Media   197
Free Media and Paid Media   199

Understanding Social Media   201
Effects of Social Media   202
Anonymity, Free Speech, and Privacy Issues   205
Digital Divide and Net Neutrality   206

Media-Centric Criticism   207
Critical Media Theory   207
Agenda-Setting Theory   208

Suggestions for Mediated Communication   211
Become a Critical Consumer of Mass Media   211
Avoid Being Influenced by Media Depictions of "the Other"   212
Be Mindful about How Much Personal Information You Share on Social Media   213
Don't Say Anything Online You Wouldn't Say in Person   213
Consider Taking a Break to Avoid Technology Burnout   214

Chapter Review   215

INTERPERSONAL COMMUNICATION

8 PRINCIPLES OF INTERPERSONAL COMMUNICATION 219

Interpersonal Communication in the Dyad 220
The Benefits of Interpersonal Relationships 221
The Nature and Type of Close Dyads 222

Selecting a Few from the Many 225
The Secrets of Attraction: Noticing 226
The Secrets of Initiating: Opening Moves 229

Capturing Relational Movement 231
The Straightforward Path 232
The Turbulent Path 233

Self-Disclosure and Privacy 236
Social Penetration Theory 237
The Downside to Self-Disclosure 238
Communication Privacy Management Theory 238

Understanding and Managing Dialectical Tensions 241
Dialectical Tensions 241
Managing Dialectical Tensions 244

Chapter Review 245

TASK ATTRACTION

9 PRACTICES FOR EFFECTIVE INTERPSONAL RELATIONSHIPS 251

Relational Maintenance 252
Common Maintenance Behaviors 253
Maintaining Relationships with Technology 254

Maintaining Different Types of Relationships 256
Romantic Relationships 256
Friendships 258
Workplace Relationships 261

Five General Guidelines for Maintaining Relationships 262
Embrace Your Agency 262
Meet Connecting Bids 263

Take Action Based on Knowledge 264
Nurture Mutual Commitment 264
Don't Fear Uncertainty 265

Managing Interpersonal Conflict 265
What Is Interpersonal Conflict? 266
Common Causes of Conflict 266
Benefits of Interpersonal Conflict 268

Styles and Patterns of Conflict 269
Six Conflict Styles 269
Unhealthy Conflict Patterns 271

Staying Respectful, Strong, and Positive in Conflict 274
Accept Cyclical Conflict 274
Monitor Your Emotions 274
Express Criticisms Gently and Respectfully 275
Engage in Conflict with Positive Expectations 276
Keep Positivity in Balance with Negativity 276

Chapter Review 277

GROUP COMMUNICATION

10 PRINCIPLES OF GROUP COMMUNICATION 283

Small Group Characteristics 284
Small Group Communication 285
Types 286
Group size 287

Advantages of Small Groups 291
Diverse Perspectives 291
Multiple Resources 292
Commitment 293

Small Group Dynamics 293
Small Group Roles 294
Group Development 298

Cultural Diversity 300
Individualistic and Collectivist 301
Power Distance 301
Uncertainty Avoidance 302

High and Low Context   302
Masculine and Feminine   303
Mindful Communication   303

Small Group Communication in the Digital Age   305
Technology for Group Meetings   305
Technology for Group Work and Document Sharing   308
Guidelines for Using Technology for Group Work   309

Effective Participation in a Small Group   310
Prepare for Group Meetings   311
Listen Interactively   311
Participate, Don't Dominate   312
Fulfill Your Commitments   313
Use Technology to Your Advantage   313
Encourage a Positive Climate with Politeness
    and Authenticity   313

Chapter Review   314

11 PROBLEM-SOLVING AND LEADING A SMALL GROUP   319

Group Problem Solving   321
Define the Problem   322
Generate Possible Solutions   323
Establish Criteria for Evaluating Solutions   324
Select the Best Solution   325

Tips for Using Problem-Solving Agendas   327
Make Sure Group Members Understand the Task   327
Get Rid of Roadblocks   328
Carefully Observe Your Process   328
Technology and Group Problem Solving   330

Effective Group Leadership   331
Leaders versus Leadership   331
Types of Leadership   332
Leading in Virtual Groups   333
Leadership Challenges   334

Leading Meetings and Managing Conflict   334
Leading Meetings   334
Managing Conflict   339

Chapter Review   342

PUBLIC SPEAKING

12 PUBLIC SPEAKING: FIRST STEPS 347

Introduction to Public Speaking 348
Why Study Public Speaking? 349
A Great Tradition 350
Key Elements of Public Speaking 351

The Speech Preparation Process 353
The Classical Approach to Speech Preparation 353
The Benefits of an Organized Preparation Plan 354

Audience Analysis 355
The Importance of Audience Analysis 355
Analyzing Situational Characteristics 356
Incorporating Demographics 357
Seeking Common Ground 362
Identifying Prior Exposure 364

Topic Selection 365
Developing a Set of Potential Topics 366
Selecting the Best Topic 369
Refining Your Topic 370
Drafting Your Specific Purpose 374
Drafting Your Thesis Statement 374

Chapter Review 376

13 SPEECH CONTENT: RESEARCH, SUPPORTING MATERIALS, AND ETHICS 381

Researching Your Speech 382
Creating a Research Plan 383
Evaluating a Source's Credibility 385
Conducting Library Research 387
Using the Internet 389
Interviewing Experts 393
Presenting Evidence in Your Speeches 394

Selecting and Using Supporting Materials 395
Uses of Supporting Materials 395
Types of Supporting Materials 397
Guidelines for Using Supporting Materials 403

Speech Ethics   403
Communicating Truthfully   404
Acknowledging and Representing
   Others' Work   406
Chapter Review   409

14 ORGANIZING AND OUTLINING   415

Organizing the Body of
Your Speech   416
Selecting Your Main Points   417
Arranging Your Main Points   418
Organizing Your Supporting Materials   422
Using Organizing Words and Sentences   423

Introducing Your Speech   425
Gain Audience Attention   425
Signal Your Thesis   427
Show Your Audience What's in It for Them   427
Establish Your Credibility   428
Preview Your Main Points   428

Concluding Your Speech   430
Transition to Your Conclusion   430
Summarize Your Main Points   430
Finish with a Memorable Clincher   431

Outlining Your Speech   434
Two Stages of Outlining   434

Creating Your Working Outline   437
Outlining the Body of Your Speech   437
Outlining Your Introduction   439
Outlining Your Conclusion   439
Creating a List of Works Cited   440
Inserting the Title, Specific Purpose, or Thesis   440
A Sample Working Outline   440

Creating Your Speaking Outline   445
Formatting Your Speaking Outline   446
Elements of Your Speaking Outline   446
A Sample Speaking Outline   447

Chapter Review   450

15 DELIVERING YOUR SPEECH   455

Selecting the Right Mode of Delivery   456
Reading from a Manuscript   456
Memorizing from a Manuscript   458
Extemporaneous: Speaking from an Outline   460
Impromptu: Speaking without Preparation   461

Using Vocal Delivery Skills   463
Volume   463
Tone   465
Rate of Delivery   466
Projection   467
Articulation   468
Pronunciation   469
Pausing   470

Using Nonverbal Delivery Skills   471
Eye Contact   472
Gestures   474
Physical Movement   475
Proxemics   476
Personal Appearance   478

Presentation Aids   479
Advantages of Presentation Aids   479
Guidelines for Developing Presentation Aids   480
Using Presentation Aids during Your Speech   483

Chapter Review   485

16 INFORMATIVE SPEAKING   489

Techniques for Informing   490
Definition   490
Explanation   492
Description   493
Demonstration   494
Narrative   496

Types of Informative Speeches   498
Objects   498
Individuals or Groups   500
Events   502
Processes   503
Ideas   506

Developing Your Informative Speech   508
Analyzing Your Audience   508
Selecting a Technique   509
Focusing on Your Goal to Inform   511

Clarifying and Simplifying Your Message   511
Move from General to Specific   513
Reduce the Quantity of Information You Present   514
Make Complex Information Seem Familiar   514
Use Presentation Aids   515
Reiterate Your Message   515
Repeat Your Message   516
Chapter Review   516

17 PERSUASIVE SPEAKING   521

The Nature of a Persuasive Speech   522
Persuasive Speeches Attempt to Influence
Audience Members   523
Persuasive Speeches Advocate Fact, Value,
or Policy Claims   523

Tailoring Your Persuasive Message to
Your Audience   525
Adapting to Audience Disposition   526
Accounting for Your Audience's Beliefs   527
Appealing to Your Audience's Needs   527
Connecting to Your Listeners' Values   528
Demonstrating How Your Audience Benefits   528
Acknowledging Listeners' Reservations   529

Building Blocks of Persuasion   530
Ethos: Your Credibility as a Speaker   530
Logos: The Evidence and Reasoning behind Your Message   533
Pathos: Evoking Your Listeners' Emotions   540

Organizing Your Persuasive Speech   544
Criteria-Application Pattern   544
Categorical Pattern   545
Moore's Motivated Sequence   546
Problem-Cause-Solution Pattern   547
Chapter Review   548

APPENDIX A: JOB INTERVIEWS   A-1

Preparing for Your Job Interview   A-2
General Questions   A-2
Take Stock   A-4
Résumé   A-6
Social Media   A-6
Homework   A-9
Practice   A-9
Attire and Appearance   A-10

During the Job Interview   A-11
Levels of Interviews   A-11
Be Prepared   A-13
Act Confident   A-13
Be a Good Listener   A-14
Advocate Honestly   A-14
Wrapping Up   A-14
What to Avoid   A-16

After the Interview   A-18
Exercise Patience   A-18
Thank-You Notes   A-19
Follow Up   A-19
Take Notes   A-20

APPENDIX B: SAMPLE SPEECHES   A-21

Sample Persuasive Speech
Anna Martinez, *Extra Credit You Can Live Without*   A-21

Sample Informative Speech
DJ, *Freeganism: More than a Free Lunch*   A-27

Sample Persuasive Speech
Elijah, *Preventing Cyberbullying*   A-32

Sample Persuasive Speech
David Kruckenberg, *Child Slavery and the Production of Chocolate*   A-37

Notes   N-1
Glossary   G-1
Index   I-1

Let's Communicate

AN ILLUSTRATED GUIDE TO
HUMAN COMMUNICATION

ARTHUR ASHE AWARD FOR COURAGE

This year, I have a lot of experience being part of something a lot bigger than myself. At times, I've felt like I've been living in a massive storm, and I know the storm will end. I'm here tonight to tell you that the lessons I learned about love, respect, and being true to yourself will never leave me...

...To anyone out there, especially young people feeling like they don't fit in and will never be accepted, please know this: great things can happen when you have the courage to be yourself.

LearningCurve can help you master the material in this chapter. Go to **launchpadworks.com**.

INTRODUCTION TO HUMAN COMMUNICATION

OBJECTIVES

- Introduce the study of human communication.
- Explore how communication works, why effective communication is essential, and what makes a competent communicator.
- Build a foundation of knowledge and skills for successful communication of all types.

Michael Sam needed more than athletic ability and a strong work ethic to advance from lightly regarded high school recruit to National Football League draft choice. His communication skills also played an important role. While playing high school football in Hitchcock, Texas, and hoping to become the first member of his family to attend college, he had few scholarship offers. Then a spot opened up at the University of Missouri at the last minute. Head Coach Gary Pinkel insisted on a face-to-face meeting before making an offer. During this conversation, Michael so impressed Coach Pinkel that he received a scholarship on the spot.

When Michael arrived on campus, he stood out—and not in a good way. He had only been a two-star (out of five) recruit, he was small for a lineman, and he read Harry Potter books. At first Michael was intimidated by his larger teammates, but then he began to entertain them with made-up songs that parodied the team's exhausting practices. His creativity and energy helped him bond with his teammates.

Over time, Sam became an increasingly successful player. By his senior year, he exercised another communication skill: leadership. Highly respected by his teammates, Michael provided motivational inspiration to the entire defense and mentored individual teammates off the field. He was voted the team's most valuable player (along with being named the Southeastern Conference Defensive Player of the Year and earning consensus All-American recognition).

As top college prospects began preparing for the 2014 NFL Draft, Michael would come to rely heavily on his public communication skills. In an ESPN interview on February 9, 2014, Michael disclosed, "I am a gay man and happy to be one." When Michael was drafted by the St. Louis Rams, he became the first player to be openly gay while playing in the NFL. Since the interview, Michael has become a public figure, answering questions about why he chose to come out when he did and what advice he would give to other athletes. As a result of the way he presented himself, Michael was given the 2014 Arthur Ashe Courage Award, which honors a person who best exhibits courage in the face of adversity.

Michael Sam's experiences provide a unique example of how effective communication skills can yield valuable benefits in life. But these skills aren't just important for public figures—everyone needs them. Human communication, the subject of this book, is a fundamental activity that we use every day of our lives. It is central to our relationships with friends, family members, and romantic partners. Beyond communicating with other individuals, we also communicate in groups, whether at work or in school. And sometimes we need to communicate by addressing an audience, either at school or in the community.

As evidenced by social media, smartphones, and video-sharing apps, technology is playing an ever-increasing role in communication. According to the Department of Health & Human Services' Office of Adolescent Health, "adolescents (ages eight to eighteen) spend an average of seven and a half hours per day using media," including TVs and computers—and this number doesn't even include talking on the phone or texting![1] Think of your own habits—are you planning to take a study break while reading this chapter to check your Twitter, Instagram, or Facebook account?

This book will help you build communication skills to use in every aspect of your life. After reading this chapter, you will have a better understanding of how communication works, why effective communication is essential in life, and what makes a competent communicator. Then, in Chapters 2–7, you will learn about the foundations for successful communication; finally, in Chapters 8–17, you will see how you can apply the principles you have learned to relational communication, group communication, public speaking, and computer-mediated communication.

COMMUNICATION: THE BASICS

Let's start at the beginning: What do we mean by communication, and how do we use it in our everyday lives?

Communication Defined

Think of all the ways that you communicate every day, with everyone from your favorite barista to your significant other. If asked, you could probably think of a definition for the term *communicate*. However, it wouldn't necessarily match the definitions of the other students in your class. Case in point: an analysis by two communication scholars identified over one hundred unique definitions of the term![2] For this textbook, we have selected a definition that is familiar to most people who teach and research communication.

Communication is the transactional process through which people use symbols to send and receive messages to negotiate, interpret, and create shared meaning. We will go into more detail about this process later in the chapter. For now, it's important to know that communication includes both sharing your ideas with others and receiving the ideas they are sharing with you. This process is **transactional** because all participants continuously send and receive messages. We regularly take part in communication transactions in a variety of ways. Let's examine some of the situations in which communication is used.

Contexts for Communication

Communication takes place in a variety of contexts, each of which presents different challenges and opportunities for participants. Here we will introduce each of the major contexts. Later chapters in this book will consider each of these contexts in depth and provide you with strategies for communicating effectively in each one.

Interpersonal communication. We define **interpersonal communication** as the communication between two people that includes a deeper level of enjoyment and intimacy. These relationships include intimate partnerships and friendships, but they also include professional relationships, particularly those that turn into friendships.

Messages have both a content meaning and a relational meaning,[3] and during interpersonal interactions, relational meanings are especially important. For example, suppose you invite a friend to go shopping and your friend responds, "Sorry, I have to give my dog a flea bath." The **content meaning** of the friend's response is the literal idea expressed by the message, in this case the fact that she will be giving her dog a flea bath. But you may also hear a **relational meaning**, which is what you believe the message has to say about your relationship. You might interpret this message to mean that she must not care too much about your friendship—after all, she'd rather bathe her dog! But as we will discuss later in this book, the relational meanings we interpret might not always be accurate. Perhaps your friend has noticed that her dog is scratching himself silly and needs to help rid him of his condition as quickly as possible.

When you value a relationship with another person, it is important to remember that your communicative behaviors send messages about your views of that relationship.

Group communication. A **small group** is a limited number of people who work toward a common goal and believe that they can achieve more together than acting alone. You will inevitably be asked to participate in a group at some point in your life—whether in the classroom, in your community, or at work. For example, your lab group might be required to present the results of an experiment to your science class, or you might be part of a sales team that is called on to explain the results of your new marketing campaign to coworkers. To work effectively, group members must be aware of **small group dynamics**, or the ways in which members relate to one another and view one another's functions within the group.

Public speaking. **Public speaking** is the delivery of a message by a speaker to an audience. In public speaking, the speaker does most of the talking, and audience members primarily listen. Nevertheless, public speakers receive feedback from audience members during their presentation, and skillful presenters are able to adapt their message to this feedback. Public speaking is a very important skill; at many times in your life you will likely be called on to present your ideas—on campus, in your community, and in your career. You (like plenty of other people) may find the thought of presenting a speech frightening. But fear not: you can learn to master public speaking—just as most people learn to read, ride a bicycle, or keep up with the latest technology.

Public speaking is audience-centered. Good speakers consider what topic would be appropriate for their audience on a particular occasion and develop their message in a way that the audience will find interesting and understandable. Although preparing and delivering a speech may seem an intimidating process, you will discover that it actually consists of a set of manageable steps that are not all that different from experiences in your daily life. If you have a well-organized plan for speech preparation and stick to that plan, you can be a very successful speaker.

Mass and mediated communication. **Mediated communication** consists of messages transmitted through either a mechanical or an electronic medium. When this takes place on a very large scale, we call it **mass communication**. These messages are often conveyed through **mass media** outlets, such as television, radio, print media formats (newspapers and magazines), and, most recently, the Internet. Mass communication channels are increasingly blending due to **convergence**, or the superimposition of one medium on the platform of another medium.[4] For example, many newspapers, magazines, and radio stations now have websites where content can be accessed. Historically, the channels of mass communication have been owned by business entities and other large organizations that have the resources to afford the high cost of producing and transmitting information to vast audiences. However, the growth of the Internet has given individuals and small groups a means of reaching mass audiences through blogs, websites, and social media. However, mass communication is not the only type of mediated communication. Chances are that you also use mediated channels for interpersonal, group, or public communication. For example, a text message to a good friend, a Google Hangout to plan a charitable fund-raising event, a Facebook status update, and a podcast on which you explain how to grow prize tomatoes would all be examples of mediated communication.

Now that you know some basics about communication, let's turn to the elements of effective communication.

COMMUNICATION: THE BASICS

THE IMPORTANCE OF EFFECTIVE COMMUNICATION

The ability to communicate well with others is an important life skill. In this section, we'll expand on the benefits of being a capable communicator as well as introduce the basics of how to communicate competently.

Benefits of Effective Communication

Strong communication skills offer benefits in every area of life where you interact with others. Let's look at some of these areas to see what you can gain through the study of communication.

Communication helps in your personal life. Consider all the different relationships that you value—with friends, romantic partners, family members, and others who are special to you. Effective communication is a key ingredient in maintaining any of these relationships or forming new ones. You want to be able to share your ideas and dreams with others in your life, and you also need to be a good listener in order to understand theirs.

From time to time there will be conflict in even the best relationships, and you'll need to decide how to manage it. When talking about difficult issues, you'll need to be able to use words that are constructive and that show how you continue to value the relationship. Skilled communication is essential to new relationships, too. Have you ever wanted to get to know a casual friend better, or wondered how to introduce yourself to someone smoothly? The way you interact with new people in your life will have an important effect on whether or not a relationship takes hold and grows.

The development of communication technology has created new environments for relational communication. Do you think a text message can convey an apology as well as a face-to-face conversation? Have you ever tried online dating? How would you attempt to learn more about a person from another town whom you met on Facebook? Can the ability to stay in touch with people 24/7 become too controlling and damage relationships? We'll discuss these situations and more in the chapters to come. Just as it is important to become an effective in-person communicator, it is also necessary to know how to communicate well in the virtual world.

BENEFITS OF EFFECTIVE COMMUNICATION: PERSONAL LIFE

Communication helps in your career. If you have a full-time job (or will in the future), you are likely to spend more time with coworkers than with family and friends. Thus, it's no small wonder that communication skills become so important in the workplace! While interacting with others, you'll need to maintain professional relationships and interact productively in order to get things done. At some point you may need to work as an official group or team, which means that having group communication skills will put you ahead of the game.

Many careers also require effective public speaking skills. These include not only obvious fields, such as sales, law, politics, and teaching but also a range of scientific and technical fields.[5] It's not surprising that in the National Association of Colleges and Employers 2015 Job Outlook Survey, verbal communication skills and the ability to work in a team are two of the qualities that employers are most likely to seek in potential job candidates.[6]

Mediated communication skills also play an increasingly important role in various career paths. For example, many businesses and agencies need people who can create and maintain websites and social media for the company. Shel Holtz, an International Association of Business Communicators fellow, worked with two colleagues to identify "thirty-four distinct social and digital media competencies" that are needed in the workplace.[7] Many fields also require mediated presentations or meetings—meaning that if you know how to effectively

BENEFITS OF EFFECTIVE COMMUNICATION: CAREER

plan and execute them, you'll be an even bigger asset to your supervisor or team.

Communication helps you as a student.

Although studying hard is obviously important, making connections on campus with faculty, staff, and fellow students is another key factor in college success.[8] It is important to feel comfortable speaking with your instructors when you have questions, concerns, or interests relating to your classes, or to advocate effectively for yourself when getting a problem solved at the financial aid or student services office. If you're going to a school far from home, you'll need to build a whole new social circle, as well as get along with fellow students and possibly roommates who have very different personalities or backgrounds.

You will also almost certainly be placed in groups for presentations, projects, or work in a lab class. To do well, you will need communication skills to make sure that group members can cooperate and work productively as a team. Many instructors' assignments include oral presentations, and students with strong speaking skills can more effectively present their ideas to the class. A thoughtfully crafted and skillfully delivered presentation makes a better impression on the instructor and the class. Public speaking skills also improve your ability to speak out when you participate in campus clubs or organizations.

BENEFITS OF EFFECTIVE COMMUNICATION: STUDENT

Communication helps you in your community. Suppose the new people in the apartment next to yours are playing music too loud when you are studying for an exam you must take the next morning. What do you do? In order to get your neighbors to turn the music down (without turning *them* into enemies), you'll need a tactful approach. Or consider another situation: If you were in a minor traffic accident and you believe it was not your fault, could you tell your side of the story clearly and convincingly to a police officer? We encounter many people in our everyday lives, and having good communication skills can help us interact with them effectively, regardless of the circumstance.

Communication skills are also important when you want to get involved in your community. If you are active in service organizations, athletic leagues, religious groups, or political committees, you need to be able to get along with other members, work well when grouped with others, and be able to speak effectively when you want to share your ideas at a meeting.

Gaining Communication Competence

Hopefully we've shown you that you need strong communication skills to function effectively when interacting in *all* of life's circumstances—whether you're with friends or loved ones, on the job, at school, or in your community. The aim of this book is to help you increase your

communication competence, or the ability to achieve your communication goals. Effective communicators achieve these goals by "using appropriate communication behaviors selected from their communication repertoires."[9]

Let's break this down further. Gaining communication competence can be divided into three actions: achieving communication goals, building a communication repertoire, and choosing appropriate communication behaviors. We'll discuss each of these in turn.

Achieving communication goals.
If you want to convince your boss to raise your salary, tell that special someone how much you love him or her, or show your younger sister how to change the oil in her car, your goals are motivating you to communicate with others. But as we mentioned earlier, communication is a transactional process in which *all* participants send and receive messages. To communicate effectively, you must be concerned with the goals of your partner(s) as well as your own. If you disregard their needs, the quality of the relationship will suffer—and your efforts to reach your goals could very well fail.

Even when one communicator holds power over another, successful communication depends on the needs of both. For example, military officers, work supervisors, or team coaches need to be sure that others understand their directions. Effective leaders will also get better results

ACHIEVING COMMUNICATION GOALS (**NOT** LIKE THIS)

Oh em gee, peeps, can you, like, totally, um, upload my brain with an ETA on the ending of this here projecteroonie?

from those they direct if they consider their needs along with their own expectations.

Building a communication repertoire. Your **communication repertoire** consists of all the skills you have available for interacting with others, including verbal resources and nonverbal expressions, listening skills, the ability to perceive and empathize with others' perspectives, different communication styles, and channels of communication. You likely use a combination of these to effectively communicate. Your *verbal resources* include all the words in your vocabulary that you might use to express an idea to others. For example, if you want to borrow a friend's car, you could word your request in a variety of ways. When speaking, you also use *nonverbal expressions*, such as hand or facial gestures, eye focus, tone of voice, and proxemics (which means how you use space and distance). While these can reinforce your verbal message, they can also contradict it.

Listening skills are another important resource. To communicate well, you need to understand the messages your communication partner is trying to express. When you merely hear a message, you receive it in a passive way, without carefully considering the content. But if you actively listen, then you process the message to uncover its meaning. You can communicate to your partner that you understand—or, on the other hand, that you need more clarification. You can also respond in a manner that shows interest, both verbally and nonverbally (nodding, eye contact, and so on).[10]

The *ability to perceive and empathize with* others' perspectives is another useful skill. Empathy includes several dimensions: having the best interest of others in mind, understanding what they feel or believe,

and using good judgment to assist them in achieving their communication goals.[11] You can relate better to another person by putting yourself in their shoes, which leads to improved communication. For example, suppose you are working on a group project for a class and one member insists that you don't need to include research sources. Other group members, who have all read the instructor's assignment description, are well aware that sources must be cited and are impatient with this group member. You know that this group member is a parent who works thirty hours a week, takes a full load of courses, and struggles to cope with the stresses of such a demanding life. Instead of taking a hostile stance, you might defuse the tension by noting that maybe this person was at work when the description was posted and didn't have a chance to read it.

There are also a variety of *communication styles* that you can use while interacting with others. You might make your point in an emotional or a forceful manner, or you might decide to use humor. At times you may need to be blunt in stating your position, while at other times you may choose to be more subtle and indirect. While many people have certain styles they turn to regularly, the ability to use diverse styles in an authentic manner provides you with more options.

The *channel of communication* is another important consideration. When dealing with a conflict with a significant other, you may decide that face-to-face conversation or a phone call would be more effective than either a text or a Facebook message. For group interactions, you may decide that the best way to meet is virtually, via a group chat service such as Google Hangout. Today, more than ever, we have a wide variety of ways to get in touch with people—but it can be a challenge to figure out the best choice for a given situation.

This brings us to our final action in gaining communication competence: choosing the appropriate communication behavior.

Choosing appropriate communication behaviors. To reach our communication goals, we must figure out the most appropriate behavior to use in each interaction. This may seem challenging, but it is worth considering several key factors that impact your ability to communicate well.

Experiences. If you have communicated with the same person(s) before, that experience will influence the choice you make. Say you ask a roommate about his new girlfriend and he snaps at you; you may try a less direct approach the next time (or avoid the subject altogether!). If

CHOOSING APPROPRIATE COMMUNICATION BEHAVIORS

a coworker is slow to return an e-mail, you might see if a text message gets a faster response. And if you're working in a small group that tends to get off-track, you may have found that a gentle reminder of the task at hand helps people focus. The same idea applies to past communication experiences. If you have done well in previous job interviews by projecting confidence, you'll be more likely to use that style in future interviews.

Culture. The cultural background of people you interact with also affects your choices. It is important to be aware of the appropriateness of communication behaviors when interacting with people from a culture different from your own.[12] What is the expected way to bargain in a business setting? When might it be acceptable to interrupt the other speaker? Should you get right to the point or spend some time getting to know each other first?

Feedback. While you are communicating with others, they will provide both verbal (words) and nonverbal responses. By paying attention to this feedback, you can help determine whether your interaction is going well or poorly. Suppose you run into a person you met in class at the campus food court and you'd like to get to know her better. If her eyes glaze over every time you talk about the class, you might want to bring up another subject. If she leans in more attentively when you mention the local music scene, you'd probably want to continue talking about that topic. Say she sounds passionate when relating a story about her experiences in a band; it would be wise to listen carefully rather than interrupt to share one of your own musical experiences.

Context. The communication context also provides guidance about appropriate behaviors. If you're appealing a parking ticket in court, you would want to show up on time and respond respectfully to the judge. On the other hand, if you're hanging out with friends, you could choose a more informal and boisterous tone. You would probably speak loudly when giving a presentation in a large classroom, but you'd lower your voice if you needed to speak to someone during a religious service.

To communicate effectively, it is also important to understand how communication works. Let's take a look at the process of communication.

PRINCIPLES OF COMMUNICATION

There are several key characteristics of communication. Communication is transactional, it is symbolic, it can result in shared meaning, and it should be ethical. Here we will break down the meaning of each of these principles.

Communication Is Transactional

Earlier in this chapter, we defined communication as the transactional process through which people use symbols to send and receive messages to negotiate, interpret, and create shared meaning. To understand how this works, let's take a look at a model of this process.

A MODEL OF COMMUNICATION

WE ARE ALL CHANNELS

A person with an idea to express is the **source**, and the ideas that he or she conveys constitute the **message**. The source must **encode** the message, meaning that he or she must use verbal and nonverbal symbols to express the ideas. **Verbal communication** means the exchange of messages using language, whereas **nonverbal communication** means communicating without words.

The source communicates the encoded message through a **channel**, or the medium of delivery. For example, sources could simply use their voices to speak with a small group, rely on a text message to communicate with a friend who is miles away, or perhaps develop an instructional podcast used by their company to train people in diverse locations. These are all types of channels.

Sources communicate their message to one or more **receivers**, who try to make sense of the message by decoding. To **decode**, receivers process the source's verbal and nonverbal symbols to form their own perception of the message's meaning. **Noise** (also called **interference**) is a phenomenon that disrupts communication between source and receiver. Noise may be caused by external sources (for example, when a cell phone ringtone disrupts a conversation). But noise can also originate internally—within the source or his or her listeners. For instance, an employee might not be able to follow his supervisor's explanation of a new policy at work if he's preoccupied by thoughts of a recent argument with a friend or trying to remember where he put his car keys.

Recall that because communication is transactional, participants are continuously sending *and* receiving messages during their interaction.[13] How does this work in practice? Imagine that you're telling a friend about your day. You are sending and she is receiving that story. But as you're speaking, your friend might nod attentively—perhaps to encourage you to add more details. Or she might steal a glance at her smartphone, suggesting that you should wrap up your story. These responses to our messages are called **feedback**.

Our own communication choices are influenced by the feedback that we receive. So in the previous example, if your friend nods, you

PAY ATTENTION TO FEEDBACK

might add extra facts with enthusiasm. On the other hand, if she seems distracted by her phone, you might lose your smile and wrap it up quickly.

The communication process is also continuous. The way that we express our message or understand others' messages is affected not only by the immediate responses we receive but also by our previous communication experiences. For instance, if you have a friend who often exaggerates, you might take the claim "I just had the worst day of my life" with a grain of salt. Conversely, if your friend tends to be very realistic and down to earth, you might respond to the same claim with concern.

Communication Is Symbolic

Another key element of communication is that verbal and nonverbal symbols are used to send and receive messages. It's important to realize that these symbols are *arbitrary*, meaning that there's not necessarily a connection between a word or a nonverbal behavior and the idea it represents. For example, in the English language, the collection of pages you're now reading is called a book (or an e-book if you have accessed it online). There's no logical reason that the b-o-o-k must be used to refer to this object. Other languages have entirely different words for *book*, such as *libro* (Spanish) and *phoo ntawv* (Hmong). The same principle is true for nonverbal behaviors. In some cultures, making eye contact during communication is a sign of interest and respect. In other cultures, the same behavior is considered rude.

Communication Can Result in Shared Meaning

The fact that symbols are arbitrary creates challenges for communicators. Because people do not necessarily attach the same meaning to words or behaviors, misunderstandings can easily result. For example, suppose you list your relationship status on Facebook as "In a relationship"; these words may not have the same meaning to your partner as they do to you. Your friends might have yet other interpretations of what you mean by this phrase.

During the communication process, participants are constantly interpreting the meaning of others' nonverbal expressions. People may come up with their own meanings of symbols as they interact. For example, perhaps on family trips your father used to tell stories from "back in the day." Sitting in the back of the car, you and your siblings may have exchanged a special look that you all understood to mean "Uh-oh, there he goes again."

A goal of many communicators is to create **shared meaning**—a common understanding with little confusion and few misinterpretations.[14] Although achieving this understanding can be difficult, you can improve your ability to express your thoughts and understand the ideas of others. The upcoming chapters of this book will provide many ideas and suggestions on how to do this.

Communication Should Be Ethical

Ethics—rules and values that a group uses to guide conduct and distinguish between right and wrong—should come into play during every stage of the communication process. Ethics are not a new consideration. In the first century C.E., the Roman rhetorician Quintilian argued that parents and teachers should strive to produce "the good person speaking

SHARED MEANING

well." That is, communicators should be virtuous, moral, and focused on the public good.[15]

Today, concerns about unethical communication abound. Research on lying in personal relationships has found that over the course of a week, people admitted to deceiving almost one-third of the people they interacted with on an individual basis.[16] In the public sphere, Americans no longer trust a wide range of institutions—not only the usual suspects, such as corporations and government, but also schools and organized religion.[17] The online world has also led to new modes of unethical communication, such as trolling (posting incendiary comments to get a reaction) and catfishing (misrepresenting one's identity to online contacts).

How do ethical communicators act? The National Communication Association's ethical principles "advocate truthfulness, accuracy, honesty, and reason as essential to the integrity of communication."[18] An important guideline is to communicate with others as you would like them to communicate with you. If a particular communicative behavior upsets you when practiced by others, you should refrain from practicing it yourself. Ethical communicators do not deceive or manipulate others, and they take responsibility for their own communications. They also carefully listen to others' ideas and keep an open mind. A final ethical principle that is especially important in academic work is to properly acknowledge the work of others when you borrow their ideas.

Now that we've spent some time considering what the nature of communication is, let's take a look at what communication is *not*.

MISCONCEPTIONS ABOUT COMMUNICATION

As we've discussed, communication skills can improve the quality of your personal relationships, help you be successful in the workplace and community, enable you to work productively in groups, and help you speak confidently to an audience. But it cannot be said that communication is always easy or effective. Here we'll address some of the common misconceptions about communication.

Communication Is Not Just Common Sense

Some students express surprise that they're required to study communication in college. They may believe that because they communicate every day, successful communication is something that's natural and easy, making the study of this subject pointless. However, just because we communicate does not guarantee that we are doing it effectively. Just as daily singing in the shower does not mean that we'll make it onto

COMMUNICATION IS NOT JUST COMMON SENSE

shows such as *The Voice*, frequent communicating doesn't guarantee that we do it well.

At times, each of us has probably found it difficult to understand others, or to make our thoughts clearly understood. Perhaps we've experienced situations in which we're unable to get others to agree with us. We may have also upset other people with our words, even when that was not our intent. Luckily, by studying the guidelines for effective communication, you can gain skills that make you more effective when interacting with others.

Communication Is Not Always Positive

While communication skills can lead to many beneficial outcomes, there are also types of communication that have negative consequences. People view deceptive communication as the number two harm that can be done to a partner in a relationship (after infidelity),[19] and it can also damage the effectiveness of workplace groups.[20]

COMMUNICATION IS NOT ALWAYS POSITIVE

Deception can be very harmful in public discourse, too. After the publication of a government study commonly referred to as the Pentagon Papers revealed that government officials had told many falsehoods about the Vietnam War, a "credibility gap" developed, making the American public less likely to believe that their leaders are telling the truth.[21] This distrust of public officials continues to this day.

Communication can be used to manipulate others into making decisions that are not in their best interest. For example, a friend might attempt to make you feel guilty unless you hang out with her—even though you have to study for a test the next day. Or a significant other might use threats and manipulation in an effort to get his way ("Unless you let me go to Vegas this weekend, I'm breaking up with you").

Bullying is another form of negative communication that often involves the use of words in an attempt to gain power over others. Some people gain satisfaction by consistently putting down friends or family members. Others use words insensitively, hurting others' feelings when kinder words could have accomplished the same purpose.

Communication Does Not Always End in Agreement

Effective communication often helps people understand each other better. Nevertheless, it can't always guarantee that they'll reach an agreement. Consider the case of two roommates. One loves hip-hop, and the other adores country music. They speak for hours about why they love the music that they do and share some of their favorite songs. Each roommate might patiently listen to the other and come to understand why he or she loves that genre of music. But neither roommate ever changes the other's musical preferences. If beliefs and attitudes are deeply felt, have held up for a long time, or are a major part of a person's culture or identity, even highly effective communication is unlikely to change them.

Communication Cannot Solve Every Problem

Although good communication can often result in benefits for an individual or a society, it doesn't mean that every issue or concern can be fixed through effective communication. If you and a friend have grown apart because you no longer have much in common, talking about this problem may not restore the friendship. If a business is jeopardized during a severe economic slowdown, even the perfect application of group discussion techniques may not produce a plan that can save the company from bankruptcy. The most capable and sensitive diplomats in the world cannot always secure a peace treaty between groups of people who have been in conflict for years or decades.

Why do we note these misconceptions? We believe it's important to understand what communication is—both its possibilities and its limits—in order to know what it can and can't achieve. In the chapters that follow, we'll go deeper into the many ways in which you can use communication for positive outcomes—both for you and for your relationships.

COMMUNICATION DOES NOT ALWAYS END IN AGREEMENT

COMMUNICATION CANNOT SOLVE EVERY PROBLEM

CHAPTER REVIEW

This chapter introduced you to the field of communication. Communication is a transactional process in which two or more people use symbols to negotiate, interpret, and create shared meaning. It takes place in a variety of contexts, including personal relationships, small groups, public speaking, and mass and mediated communication.

The ability to communicate well is a vital life skill. You need to be able to communicate effectively in your personal life, in your career, as a student, and in your community. To do this, you must gain communication competence, meaning you have a good repertoire of communication behaviors and are able to select the ones that will help you achieve your goals each time you interact with others.

There are several basic principles of communication. Communication is transactional, which means that communicators are simultaneously sending and receiving messages. Communication is also symbolic, meaning that we use arbitrary words and nonverbal behaviors to represent something else. An important goal (and challenge) is to use these symbols to create shared meaning. A last important principle is that communication should be ethical. This means that communicators should be truthful, accurate, honest, and reasonable when interacting with others.

Finally, we explored several common misconceptions about communication. Effective communication is a challenge—it is not simply based on common sense. While communication can have many beneficial outcomes, it is not always positive, due to behaviors such as deception and manipulation. Communication doesn't always result in agreement, nor can it solve every problem. Understanding these limitations will allow you to focus on what you can do to improve your communication—a topic we'll direct our attention to in the proceeding chapters.

LaunchPad
macmillan learning

LaunchPad for *Let's Communicate* offers videos and encourages self-assessment through adaptive quizzing. Go to **launchpadworks.com** to get access to:

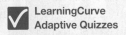 LearningCurve
Adaptive Quizzes

 Video clips that help you understand
human communication

Key Terms

communication 5

transactional 5

interpersonal communication 6

content meaning 6

relational meaning 6

small group 6

small group dynamics 6

public speaking 6

mediated communication 7

mass communication 7

mass media 7

convergence 7

communication competence 13

communication repertoire 14

source 18

message 18

encode 18

verbal communication 18

nonverbal communication 18

◎ channel 18

receiver 18

decode 18

◎ noise (interference) 18

feedback 18

shared meaning 20

ethics 20

Review Questions

1. Define *communication*.
2. Give an example of communication in each of the four communication contexts.
3. What is one way that effective communication skills are beneficial in each of the following contexts: personal life, career, student, and community?
4. Define *communication competence*.
5. What does it mean to say that communication is a transactional process?
6. What are some principles of ethical communication?
7. What are four misconceptions about communication?

Critical Thinking Questions

1. Name one person whom you believe to be an effective communicator. What are the main characteristics that make him or her effective?
2. Consider the following contexts: having a conversation with a friend, working with a group to plan a class project, and delivering a speech to an audience. How are communication challenges similar in each of these contexts? How are they different?

3. What are some circumstances in which mediated communication can be advantageous? What are some circumstances in which face-to-face communication would be more effective?

4. What are some of the approaches in your personal communication repertoire that have worked best for you? Why do you think they have been successful?

5. Suppose your best friend or romantic partner wants you to spend the afternoon together, participating in an activity that you really do not enjoy. You have a paper that is due in a week, but you could finish it on time even if you took the afternoon off. Would it be ethical to tell him or her that you cannot do the activity because you have to write the paper? Explain your answer.

Activities

1. Working in small groups, assign one communication context (interpersonal, group, public speaking, or mass and mediated communication) to each group member. (These contexts are discussed on pp. 6–7.) Have each person come up with a potential communication problem that relates to the context. Share the problems with the group one at a time, and have group members discuss how each problem could be addressed.

2. Make a list of three careers that you can see yourself doing. What are some of the communication skills that people who work in each career would need? Make note of the similarities as well as the differences.

3. Draft a hypothetical letter explaining a significant life decision (change of major, change of career, decision to get married, decision to join the military) to a friend or family member who is important to you. Then try to explain that decision in a 160-character text message. Compare the letter and the text, considering how well you can explain the decision in each medium of communication.

4. Go online and watch a commercial that involves any type of communication interaction. Identify elements of the model that were discussed in this chapter. Be sure to include noise and feedback.

5. In groups, write a brief skit about a situation in which one person misunderstands the meaning of the words used by another person. Have each group present its skit to the class, and discuss how the misunderstanding might have been avoided.

Apply Your Skills

Look at the illustration "Communication Is Not Just Common Sense" on page 23. Then create and illustrate (or write about) three new examples of text exchanges that resulted in a misunderstanding that needed to be resolved. The first should be an example from a personal relationship, the second between two coworkers, and the third between two students who have been paired for a class project. Then rewrite the text messages in a way that could have prevented the misunderstanding.

Study Plan

_____

_____

_____

_____

_____

_____

_____

_____

_____

_____

_____

_____

_____

2

PERCEIVING OTHERS, PERCEIVING OURSELVES

OBJECTIVES

- Understand that our communication with others is based on our perceptions, which are formed either through conscious thinking or through instant mental associations, and therefore may not always be accurate.

- Analyze our perceptions of ourselves—our self-concepts—and how they are influenced by the feedback we receive from others and sociocultural influences.

- Explore ways of improving our self-concepts and managing our identity, both in face-to-face communication and in online settings, while remaining ethical and accurate in what we present to others.

Shoshana was psyched to see that her college planned to start a club basketball team. She had excelled on her high school team, but it was in a small schools division and she hadn't been recruited for college ball. Shoshana missed the excitement of the game and hoped she would be selected for the club, although she was a little concerned that team practices might conflict with her demanding class schedule.

Shoshana attended the sign-up event for college clubs. At the women's basketball table, the new coach was passing out forms. Before Shoshana could say a word, the coach glanced at her and said, "This table is for the *basketball* team."

"I know," Shoshana replied, wondering if the coach didn't think she looked like a player. When Shoshana tried to tell the coach about her high school experience, the woman sneezed and turned to talk to her assistant. Shoshana tried to ask a question about the practice schedule, and the coach said brusquely, "I'll go over that at tryouts tomorrow." The coach then smiled and warmly greeted the (incredibly tall) student right behind Shoshana.

Shoshana left feeling disheartened. That night, she thought long and hard about the coach's seeming lack of interest in her, along with her gruff demeanor. Shoshana had no idea what skill level was required to play in college. Was the coach trying to tell her not to bother trying out? The next day, Shoshana skipped the tryouts.

What Shoshana didn't know was that the coach *hadn't* been insinuating that Shoshana shouldn't try out. Instead, she'd been fighting a cold, distracted by her assistant, and feeling overwhelmed by the amount of students stopping by. She'd also been briefly friendly to the tall student because she knew the student's parents. The miscommunication at the sign-up table had unfortunate consequences for both parties: Shoshana missed out on playing a sport she loved, and the coach missed out on a great player.

As Shoshana's example illustrates, accurate perceptions are very important. They have a major impact not only on how we view and interact with other people but also on how we see ourselves. In this chapter, we discuss steps you can take to improve your perceptions of others, as well as ways you can strengthen your perceptions of yourself. We begin with an explanation of how we perceive other people, followed by a discussion of how we can improve the accuracy of our perceptions. Next, we cover how we perceive ourselves. Finally, we consider how we can manage our identities to influence others' perceptions of us.

PERCEIVING OTHERS

As human beings, we are constantly in the business of perceiving other people. Whenever we communicate with others, we are trying to figure out what they are like and what their behaviors mean. The ability to perceive others correctly is important because this perception creates your view of reality—for example, whether you believe that someone can be trusted, is effective in the workplace, or would make a good friend.

People who are able to read others more accurately are able to employ better social skills, form closer relationships, and generally navigate life more smoothly. To improve our perceptive accuracy, we must first understand the nature of perception. In the following sections, we consider what perceptions are, how they impact communication, and how our perceptions are formed.

The Meaning of Perception

By **perception**, we mean the process by which we come to understand the **stimuli** in our world. Stimuli include any **sensory information**— the information we receive through our senses of sight, hearing, smell, taste, or touch. Many perceptions, such as our inference about the likelihood of rain when we see dark clouds and feel humid air, or our best guess about the contents of a mystery casserole when we smell it wafting through the campus dining hall, are not central to communication with others. However, **person perception** plays a major role in communication. By this term, we mean the process of making judgments about others, "deciding what they are like, predicting what they will do, [and] providing explanations for their behavior."[1]

Perceptions are based on **inferences** from the sensory information that we have. This means that the sensory information we take in about a person provides a basis to make further educated (or, as we will see, often not-so-well-educated) guesses about him or her. In other words, we go beyond the available data and make additional assumptions about an individual's

PERCEPTION

characteristics.[2] For example, imagine that you had to ask each of your new instructors for this term to excuse an absence from class so that you could attend a close friend's wedding in another state. Before doing so, you would consider what you have observed about each instructor and predict how he or she will respond. These predictions would be inferences.

Our inferences and perceptions are not reality—we cannot read other people's minds. Our perceptions of others represent our assessment of who they are and what their communicative behaviors mean—and we're not always correct. For example, suppose you're chatting with a stranger at a party. In the midst of your conversation she pulls out her phone, checks a text message, and starts texting somebody back. You might perceive that this person is rude. Your interpretation could be correct, but it's also possible that there's more to the story. Perhaps she was just notified of an emergency (a break-in, a friend in the hospital) and needed to respond immediately. In this case, your assumptions about her rudeness may not be correct.

The Role of Perception in Communication

Perception influences our decision to communicate (or not communicate) with others. It also influences our choices about how to communicate, the impression we make through our communication choices, and the depth and strength of our interactions. Let's consider each in turn:

Making the right communication choices. Our perceptions help us decide whether to interact with another person in the first place. They play a significant role when we decide whether to trust another person with a secret, suggest a romantic relationship, or ask for advice.[3] We want to know "who will help, harm, or interest us."[4]

These assessments also influence the choices we make when deciding how to communicate. When we interact with others, it is helpful to try to understand their goals and motivations.[5] Our perceptions influence how we attempt to get on another person's good side, maintain a relationship, obtain information, or influence another person's attitudes or actions.[6] Recall a time in your life when you asked a parent or a friend for a favor; you may well have waited until he or she seemed to be in a good mood or was demonstrating favorable feelings toward you.

In the workplace, an ability to infer the feelings of others can improve job performance in a variety of contexts. This skill also assists in negotiations.[7] For example, when you get a job after college and are negotiating salary or working conditions with your boss, your strategy would likely depend on whether he or she seemed old-school or collaborative.

Making a good impression. Your communicative behaviors influence others' perceptions of you. For example, a partner in a close relationship might tell you that he is struggling with a school assignment. In an effort to be helpful, you might offer advice about how to do the assignment well. Your partner might perceive this as a lack of confidence rather than a supportive gesture.[8] Impressions also matter in job interviews. If you find yourself using "like" when talking to others (for example, "I had an internship in the senator's office and, like, learned a lot of skills"), be careful. In one study, interviewers perceived job candidates to be less professional when they injected "like" into their sentences.[9]

Deepening and strengthening our interactions. Perceptions have a unique influence on communication interactions because perception is a two-way process. When you are communicating with others, they know that you are forming perceptions of them at the same time that they are forming perceptions of you. This knowledge influences communication choices. For example, say you've started dating someone who really enjoys texting. Though you don't normally text a lot yourself, you understand that ignoring the texts or sending back brusque messages will do nothing to further your relationship. Therefore, you make the effort to respond in a timely manner—or, if you're not comfortable with the situation, you make sure to explain your texting communication style to your partner. In the same vein, if *you* are the texter, you can let your partner know of this preferred style. He or she may choose to follow your lead or at least explain why he or she prefers to interact in a different way (phone or e-mail). In either case, you come to a deeper understanding of the other person, and your relationship benefits.

Now that we have considered the definition of *perception* and the role of perceptions in communication, let's consider the process by which perceptions are formed.

The Formation of Perceptions

Our perceptions of others are formed through the process of receiving stimuli and assessing the meaning of these stimuli. Sometimes this is a conscious decision; for example, you are likely to carefully consider your perceptions when thinking about a significant other or analyzing your boss before asking to take the weekend off. However, as we learn more about the human brain, we increasingly recognize how often perceptions are formed almost instantly and without our conscious awareness.[10] Let's see how this process works.

Receiving stimuli. Our environment is typically so rich with stimuli that we cannot possibly take in all the available sensory information. Hence, the human mind focuses on a limited amount of stimuli when perceiving others, in a process that is often automatic and unconscious. To some extent, the stimuli we attend to depends on our needs, experiences, and attitudes. We are also drawn toward certain stimuli, such as those that are louder, brighter, or more unusual. But it is important to remember that we are taking in only a limited amount of the available information when we perceive others—meaning that we might miss some significant information.

Using mental associations (schemas) to make sense of stimuli. Once the mind perceives stimuli pertaining to a person, it uses this information to form an idea of his or her attributes, what he or she might do, and the meaning of his or her communicative behaviors. This can be quite a challenge because the actions and expressions of others are often ambiguous.[11] As mentioned earlier, perceptions represent our inferences about another person, not reality. Different people will reach different conclusions about someone who does not make eye contact in conversation, says they have an undeclared major, or asks a lot of questions in class.

How does the mind construct a perspective about others? The key is the **mental associations** (or **schemas**) that stimuli activate. The mind stores vast quantities of information, and when we experience certain stimuli, they trigger responses based on stored information. In other words, our mind makes associations between the stimuli we focus on and other ideas stored in the brain. These associations are often made quickly by the mind, without conscious thought.[12]

To get an idea of how this works, consider what thoughts come to your mind when you think of a grandmother. What is her personality like? Her talents? Her interests? Chances are that you could answer these questions almost instantly, without giving them a lot of thought. This is because your mind contains many associations with the concept of a grandmother, some of which were quickly activated. If you repeat this process for a chemistry major or a member of your school's marching band, you might make significantly different mental associations for each of them.

Your mind stores a wide number of associations with types of people, events, and symbols—ones that you might not even be aware of. When you are exposed to stimuli, some of those links are activated.[13] Your mind does not store these associations "like files in a filing cabinet waiting to be accessed."[14] Instead, the mind works more like a search engine, retrieving a number of associations when a stimulus is noted. As is true with repeated Internet search results for a given term, some mental associations will come up more consistently than others. But as is also true with search engines, the set of associations your mind retrieves will not be exactly the same each time; in other words, mental associations are dynamic rather than fixed. And, just as new information on the web can change search results, your mental associations can change as you encounter new information.

Sources of mental associations. It might be surprising to learn that your mind often makes mental associations without you realizing it. However, this is normal. Our mind is a vast trove of information from which to draw associations. Let's consider some of the main storehouses of knowledge from which mental associations come.

First, our own *life experiences* have a significant influence on the associations we make.[15] Consider what you associate with student athletes, campus police officers, or college Republicans or Democrats. If you have met or observed such persons, those experiences will cause you to associate different personality traits, life goals, and other qualities with each.

Second, *information that people give you* about a category of persons can influence the associations you make, even when you haven't encountered someone in that category. You might hear this information from parents, teachers, or other influential persons in your life.[16] For example, before you played on your first sports team or took your first music lesson, a parent or sibling may have talked to you about what a coach or music teacher is like. This type of information likely helped you get off to a good start in your new activity. Unfortunately, as we will discuss later in this chapter, information about categories of persons can also contribute to harmful stereotypes.

Third, the *media* influences our mental associations. For instance, research has found that watching television news coverage of crime can influence viewers' perceptions of the typical race of criminal perpetrators and victims.[17] Fictional accounts can also influence perception. It is possible to go through life without many interactions with lawyers, detectives, professional athletes, or entertainers. But portrayals in movies and television shows can influence the associations we make. One study found that viewing favorable portrayals of gay men and lesbians on 1990s television shows such as *Will and Grace* positively influenced viewers' general attitudes about gays and lesbians.[18] Current shows in this vein, like *Modern Family*, may well be continuing this trend.

Fourth, *culture* plays a major role in our perceptions. The stories, religious beliefs, rules of law, and artistic works of diverse cultures can easily result in varied understandings of individuals and the meanings behind their behavior.[19] As a result, the thought process a particular stimulus generates can diverge from culture to culture.[20] For instance, those in Western cultures tend to focus on the object of perception, whereas those in East Asian cultures tend to focus on the context or circumstances in which an object is perceived.[21] For example, suppose that a student had ridden a longboard through campus on a walking

THE FOUR SOURCES OF MENTAL ASSOCIATIONS (EXPLAINED ALOUD)

path where riding was against the rules. Westerners would mostly likely focus on the rider—perhaps he or she does not care about the safety of others or likes to defy the rules. Conversely, in a culture that focuses more on context, people might perceive that the student was late for class or unaware of the rules.

BARRIERS TO PERCEPTION AND HOW TO OVERCOME THEM

Since perceptions are often based on instant mental associations and incomplete data, it shouldn't be surprising that they're not always accurate. Fortunately, there are steps you can take to improve the quality of your perceptions. In this section, we expand on some of the reasons perceptions are inaccurate, then present some strategies for perceiving others more accurately.

Why Are Perceptions Often Inaccurate?

Imagine that you and a group of friends are discussing personality traits of firstborn children. You may base your ideas on the experiences of your family and those of others close to you, as well as on your gut feelings about what being a first child means. However, if you were a researcher, you would examine this topic in a very different way. For example, to determine whether firstborn children are more likely to be introverted or extroverted, you would compare large samples of firstborn and later-born persons.[22] Rather than relying on your own experiences and gut feelings, you might use a precise, rigorous questionnaire that had been proven to be a reliable indicator of whether a person has either of these two traits.[23]

Our perceptions are not typically based on such a systematic process; therefore, they can easily be incorrect. We often make inferences about others' personalities and intentions almost automatically, with minimal mental deliberation.[24] For example, people may read someone's face and make a decision to trust or distrust that person in less than one-tenth of a second.[25] These judgments are generally based on limited information,[26] although extra information that might strengthen the quality of the decision is often available.[27] Granted, sometimes our intuitive perceptions can be accurate.[28] There are also circumstances in which it is best to trust your intuition due to potential danger (for example, if you feel a wave of apprehension while walking alone at night). Still, in our day-to-day interactions, we often create perceptions in ways that are neither logical nor systematic[29]—and that can lead to the wrong conclusion. Let's explore some common mistakes that are made when forming perceptions.

First impressions. Although most of us have been warned about jumping to conclusions, people often make judgments about others based on the first information they receive. In addition, they typically devote less mental energy to processing later information relating to that person.[30] People may also "freeze" on their first impression and resist further cues that contradict it.[31]

How does this work? Suppose it is the first day of class, and the room is packed to overflowing. You see a classmate volunteer to give up a seat to another person. From this single event, you might decide that this student is thoughtful and polite. Even if you see later behavior that contradicts this (the classmate texting during someone's speech or

pushing to the front of the line at the bookstore), you will be inclined to stick to your original judgment. A study of college roommates confirmed the power of first impressions. Students who had a favorable initial opinion of their roommate said that their future conversations were more satisfying and that they were better able to resolve later tensions constructively. Conversely, those with more negative first impressions reported less rewarding exchanges and handled conflict less effectively.[32]

Stereotypes. A **stereotype** is an inference that people draw about others simply because they're part of a given social category.[33] These categories may be based on a wide variety of individual attributes, including ethnicity, sex, religion, appearance, physical features, occupation, behaviors, and personality. When people stereotype, they assume that everyone in a category shares certain positive or negative characteristics. For example, they may assume a certain group to be hardworking or lazy, honest or deceptive, cheerful or cranky, generous or greedy. In his renowned 1963 address at the Lincoln Memorial, Martin Luther King Jr. dreamed that one day his children would be judged by the content of their character rather than the color of their skin. Stereotypes block this aspiration because they take a shortcut around the consideration of an individual's character.

DEFYING STEREOTYPES

Stereotypes can easily result in inaccurate perceptions of others. They may be unfounded, or they may be based on the exaggeration of a difference that actually exists between two groups.[34] Societal expectations or conditions may also lead to inaccurate assessment of others. For example, the performance of traditional gender roles in certain communities may cause people in those communities to incorrectly assume that differences between men and women are inherent.[35]

College students are not immune to stereotyping. You might be surprised to learn that a study of college students found that stereotypes about people with tattoos persist, even though this practice is becoming increasingly popular. These stereotypes included statements that tattooed people are "more likely to be irresponsible," "more prone to violence," and "more likely to spread disease." (Interestingly, the study found no significant difference in the GPAs of tattooed and non-tattooed students.)[36] Another study of college students found that common stereotypes of student athletes included beliefs that they were lazy, failed to study, and spent too much time partying.[37]

Fooled by appearances. In this online world, we could well update the proverb "Don't judge a book by its cover" to "Don't judge people by their Facebook picture." Typically, we take note of a person's looks before exchanging a single word—and we use our

observations to make inferences about the person's characteristics.[38] As the popularity
of social media grows, digital
pictures (on Facebook, Twitter,
Instagram, Tumblr, and so on)
may be our first glimpse of
someone new.

Whether online or in per-
son, how reliable are perceptions
based on appearance? Some evidence indicates that people can
judge personality traits such as
"extraversion, emotional stability,
openness, self-esteem, and religi-
osity" based on appearance

alone "with some degree of accuracy."[39] And as we have already noted,
nonverbal behavior is an important means for communicating messages. If
a person looks happy, puzzled, or angry, there's a reasonable chance that
this is precisely how he or she feels.

However, you should never use appearance as the primary way
to form perceptions of others. As previously mentioned, inaccurate
judgments of others based on ethnicity or sex have caused great harm
in society. Even if some aspects of appearance can give us clues about
a person's traits, physical features are not the best evidence. Research
has shown that perceptions based on appearance are a weaker indicator of a person's characteristics than are other social cues that are
typically present. Indeed, using a person's looks as a basis for perception can make judgments less accurate than if appearance was
ignored.[40] What's more, the accuracy of our judgments improves as
we get to know other people and interact with them in different
contexts.[41]

She reminds me of Aunt Minnie (transference). Chances are
that you have met someone who reminds you of another person who
is (or has been) significant in your life. Perhaps this new person smiles
just like your mother does, tells jokes the way your best friend in
high school did, or has a voice that reminds you of your boyfriend
or girlfriend.

Your mind stores a wide variety of characteristics that are associated with the significant people in your life. When you meet a new person who shares a trait with someone important to you, your brain will mentally activate these associations. **Transference** occurs when your mind triggers inferences about the new person based solely on the shared traits.[42] For example, suppose a new classmate has the same confident walk as your older brother and shares his laugh. With very little consideration, you might infer that this new classmate also shares your brother's religious views, athletic ability, optimism, and lack of dance skills. These additional inferences are often incorrect.[43]

Giving ourselves the benefit of the doubt. When we make judgments about other people's behavior, we are much less charitable than when we judge ourselves. This is due to two common and related mistakes. The **self-serving bias** occurs when we attribute our successes to our own favorable personality traits rather than to circumstances. For example, suppose you're taking a history exam on chapters 1 through 5 of your textbook. You spent most of your study time on chapter 5, and—lucky for you—the exam is mainly on that chapter. You earn an A! Applying the self-serving bias, you'd chalk up your grade to your impressive study skills and exceptional writing talents—not the good fortune that your instructor selected questions from the only chapter you focused on.

The **fundamental attribution error** takes place when you over-estimate the impact of others' personal traits and play down the role of circumstances. Let's return to the example of the history exam. Suppose that a classmate had studied the first four chapters far more than you did but was unable to finish studying chapter five because someone pulled the fire alarm and her dorm was evacuated. She received a C–. If you conclude that she received a lower grade due to her poor study skills—and not the bad timing of the dorm evacuation—you would be committing this error.

Improving the Accuracy of Perceptions

From the previous sections, it's clear that our brains constantly and instantly form our perceptions—with sometimes suboptimal results. In the sections that follow, we expand on why and discuss ways to strengthen our powers of perception.

Recognize that perceptions are fallible. It may seem difficult, if not impossible, to wrangle our brain in order to perceive the people and world around us more clearly, but it *is* possible. After forming an initial perception, one way to improve it is by engaging in *correction*. During this process, we consider the input we've taken in and apply logic to make a more reasoned judgment about others' behavior.[44]

Our ability to take on additional information processing may be limited if we are tired, distracted, or pushed for time.[45] We may also fail to recognize the need to consider a correction.[46] Therefore, when making judgments about others, it is important to *always* keep in mind that our impressions may be inaccurate. We can also take the following active steps to improve the accuracy of our perceptions.

Seek additional data. Because first impressions can be misleading, you can strengthen your perceptions by looking for additional information.[47] By continuing to interact with another person before making a judgment, you can gain more feedback about him or her. Unfortunately, when people have negative first impressions of somebody, they tend to limit further communication.[48] This restricts their ability to get a better picture of what the person is like. It's important to make an effort to know someone before passing judgment. The same advice holds true in the opposite direction—it would not be wise to trust

another person with your car keys or your ATM PIN just because the two of you hit it off at a party!

You can also ask a person questions that will allow you to gain a better understanding of his or her traits.[49] For example, suppose you have a group assignment and one member refuses to do library research. You could suspect that this person is lazy and cannot be counted on to do a fair share of the work. But perhaps the real problem is that person's lack of research experience. You might ask, "What if several of us went to the library together?" or even, "Would you like to take the lead on another part of the assignment?" The answers to these questions will give you more insight about whether your classmate is truly not motivated.

First impressions can be misleading. Isn't that right, **kermie**?

Er, yes. You should never judge a **pig**—I mean, a **book**—by its cover.

Differentiate facts and inferences.

Remember that perceptions are inferences that we form from the details we note about another person. These details may be **facts**, which are statements for which there is enough proof to convince almost any reasonable and objective person that they are true. However, an inference is not a fact. Inferences make a mental leap, going beyond the details you have noted and making an educated (or not so educated) guess about what they mean.

For example, suppose that your friend Sabrina never returns your phone calls, but she does respond to your text messages. You might suspect that this means she does not enjoy conversing with you and is trying to avoid spending time on the phone with you. Sabrina's failure to return phone calls and her use of text messages are facts—indeed, wireless provider records could verify when each of you did or did not call or text. However, the belief that Sabrina dislikes talking with you on the phone is an *inference*—you are assuming what she means by her behaviors.

These inferences may be hard to distinguish from facts because they may feel like facts to you. You may be convinced that Sabrina is blowing you off, but only she knows the meaning of her actions. Perhaps she's been especially busy lately, or maybe her workplace doesn't allow her to take personal calls. To find out, you'd need to get more information before drawing conclusions about her behavior.

Check perceptions.   If you are not sure about the meaning of another person's behavior, use **perception checking** to gain a better understanding.[50] Perception checking is a conscious, three-step process that allows you to ask other people about their intentions in a nonthreatening way:

- Describe the behavior that you observed.
- Offer at least two possible interpretations for that behavior.
- Ask the other person to explain what he or she meant by the behavior.

For example, suppose you tell your boss that you would like to work additional hours next week. When the schedule comes out, you note that your hours have actually been reduced. Instead of worrying that your boss may be unhappy with the quality of your work, you could ask the following questions to perception-check:

- I noticed that you reduced my hours for next week even though I had requested more. (*Description*)
- Was this because you were not happy with my work? Or was there some other reason—maybe you had less work for everyone to do next week? (*Interpretations*)
- I wanted to check and see what you were thinking. (*Explanation*)

Your boss can then explain the reason for the decision. Perhaps he or she will affirm that your work is good and offer a different explanation. Perhaps your boss simply forgot about your request and will try to give you more hours the following week. Even if your fears are true and your boss does have a problem with your work, you can find out what is wrong and take steps to improve.

While perception checking, ask your questions in a nonconfrontational manner. Be sure to avoid language that will put the other person on the defensive. For example, if you observed that a romantic partner seemed to be flirting with someone at a party, you might say, "It looked to me like you were paying a lot of attention to Kayla" rather than "Your flirting with Kayla was so over the top."

So far in this chapter we have focused on how we perceive the communicative behaviors of others. This is certainly a project in which we can and should invest considerable mental energy. But there is another important target of perception that commands our attention: ourselves. The second half of this chapter focuses on the opportunities and challenges of self-perception.

PERCEIVING OURSELVES

Consider how you act with your friends, family members, professors, or boss. Chances are that each person sees a different you. How do you reconcile all of these "yous" into a single person?

Each of us has a **self**—our own personal construction of who we are. We share elements of our self (or perhaps who we *wish* we were) in a number of diverse contexts, such as the classroom, social events, online networking sites, and job interviews. The information we share offers clues about the way we view ourselves. But only *you* know the whole picture of how you see yourself.

The Nature of Your Self-Concept

Your **self-concept** includes all your perceptions of yourself. It reflects "our attempt to explain ourselves to ourselves" and includes abilities, accomplishments, personality, preferences, and characteristics.[51] In addition to individual attributes, your self-concept includes an **extended self** that focuses on your perceptions of yourself as a participant in a relationship (for example, sister, son, or friend) or as a part of a group (for example, African Americans or Christians).[52] Self-concepts have a past, present, and future dimension;[53] for example, you may identify yourself by your intended career in addition to your current major.

Attributes of self-concepts.

Your self-concept is *unique*. This means that it characterizes you and no one else in the world. Consider the person who you think is the most like you, perhaps a best friend or sibling. Even if the two of you have much in common, there are probably many differences you can point to as well.

Your self-concept is also *dynamic*, meaning that some of its elements can change over time.[54] Take the example of Alexis. As a college student, the most important terms she used to describe herself were *soldier*, *daughter*, *enthusiastic*, *athletic*, and *hardworking*. Several years later, she had completed her military service, become a mother, and begun her career as an emergency medical technician. *Parent* and *EMT* now topped her list.

Although its particular elements can change, your self-concept is *relatively stable*.[55] A person's self-concept is most likely to change in adolescence, as the social and physical changes of the teenage years take effect.[56] Researchers note that stability increases as we move through late adolescence and into the adult years.

ATTRIBUTES OF SELF-CONCEPTS

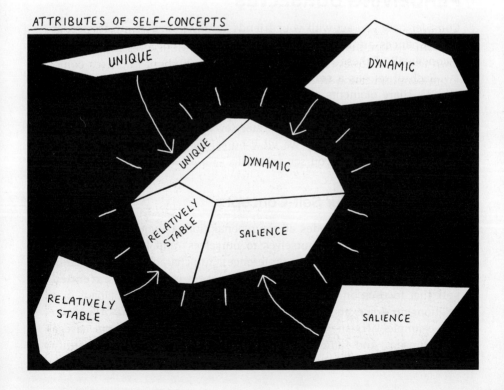

The *salience* of self-concept attributes varies from person to person, meaning that these attributes do not have equal importance among people considering their self-concept.[57] Thus, if a number of people perceive themselves as hard workers, some will view this work ethic as a major part of their identity, while others will consider the trait less relevant.

Self-concept and self-esteem. Your self-concept includes both a *descriptive* and an *evaluative* dimension. The descriptive dimension is your perception of who you are—in other words, how you would describe yourself. The evaluative dimension refers to what you think of that description. This can also be referred to as **self-esteem**, or your evaluation of the person you visualize when you describe yourself. Your **global self-esteem** reflects your overall self-evaluation, and your **domain-specific self-esteem** reflects your self-assessment on a specific trait, such as honesty, fitness, or test taking.[58]

Sources of Self-Concepts

Communication plays a central role in the development of self-concept. To some extent, individuals create a picture of themselves through their own analysis. However, much of what we learn about ourselves comes from communication in diverse contexts.

Reflected appraisals. Our self-concepts are significantly influenced by the feedback we receive about ourselves from others, called **reflected appraisals**. This term is based on the metaphor of a *looking-glass self*—the feedback allows you to "see" your characteristics, much as a mirror enables you to see a visual image of yourself.[59] If you are often told that you are smart, friendly, honest, lazy, or slow, you are likely to include those assessments in your image of yourself. Think of words that others have used to describe you; chances are that some of these have influenced your perspective of who you are.

While we're not born with a self-concept, most toddlers begin to describe themselves between eighteen and thirty months of age.[60] If you ask your relatives, they may remember a time in your early years when they tried to help you with something and you asserted your own capability—"I can do it!"

REFLECTED APPRAISALS

The feedback of parents plays a key role in the development of a child's self-concept, particularly for younger children.[61] One noteworthy study of the effect of parental feedback was provided by researchers Betty Hart and Todd Risley, who investigated the impact of poverty on academic growth. They observed interactions in forty-two families over a two-and-a-half-year period and projected that by age four, children in working-class families hear 100,000 more instances of encouraging feedback than discouraging comments. Conversely, in poor families, children hear 125,000 more instances of discouraging feedback.[62] Another recent study found that girls who felt encouraged by their mothers to do well in math and science had greater motivation to succeed in these courses.[63]

In adolescence, other sources of feedback begin to play an increasing role. Reflected appraisals from peers become particularly important,[64] and many of these can be quite negative. Books such as Rosalind Wiseman's *Queen Bees and Wannabees* (the first edition of which helped inspire the movie *Mean Girls*) and Rachel Simmons's *Odd Girl Out* show how high school peers threaten others' self-concepts.[65] In a study of over six hundred high school students, 90 percent provided hurtful accounts of communication tactics used to reject them from their peer group.[66] Students today also have to contend with cyberbullies, who take advantage of the limited adult supervision, anonymity, and 24/7 nature of the web to hurt others. This form of aggression is particularly harmful to its victims and can do a lot to damage self-concepts.[67] On the bright side, teens can strengthen their self-concepts by having reliable and supportive friends.[68] Research shows that self-esteem is higher among adolescents who identify with a group of friends.[69] Siblings are also an important source of support and constructive feedback.[70]

When people of all ages construct a self-concept from reflected appraisals, their sources of information may not be considered equally. Generally, we don't act like researchers attempting to determine how a cross-section of society truly perceives us. Instead, we may focus on the feedback received from members of an **in-group**, or a social group we feel affiliated with and respect.[71] Conversely, we're more likely to reject negative statements from an **out-group** that we don't feel a part of.

Sociocultural contexts.
A variety of constructs influence our self-concept, including "gender, ethnicity, religion, and national origin."[72]

Messages from a wide variety of sources in society, including families, friends, educators, and media sources, socialize us to believe what it means when we declare ourselves as a Latino, Lutheran, lesbian, or any other dimension of self.[73]

Culture can have a particularly important influence on self-concept. From an early age, members of your culture communicate "culturally

THE POWER OF UBUNTU (THE BOND THAT CONNECTS ALL LIVING THINGS)

At the end of Apartheid rule, South Africans adopted a national anthem that included lyrics in the five most widely spoken official languages of their nation. Lyrics were included from both the anthem of the African National Congress (which led the movement against Apartheid) and the Apartheid-era national anthem.

N'kosi sikelel'i Africa... (XHOSA)
Yizwa imithandazo yethu... (ZULU)
Morena boloka setjhaba sa heso... (SOTHO)
Uit die blou van onse hemel... (AFRIKANS)
Sounds the call to come together... (ENGLISH)

RUGBY WORLD CUP, JOHANNESBURG, SOUTH AFRICA, 1995
SOUTH AFRICA 15   NEW ZEALAND 12
(THE FIRST MAJOR SPORTING EVENT PLAYED IN
SOUTH AFRICA FOLLOWING THE END OF APARTHEID)

important beliefs, values, and preferences."[74] You internalize these cultural attributes as part of your conception of yourself. For example, among the speakers of Bantu languages in Africa, an important principle is *botho* or *ubuntu*.[75] Archbishop Desmond Tutu characterizes *ubuntu* as "the essence of being human," or a belief that the humanity of each person is intertwined with that of others.[76] The idea of living within a collaborative society focused on "care, compassion and solidarity," rather than living only for oneself, contributes to a Bantu speaker's sense of identity.[77]

Despite increasing acceptance of more egalitarian gender roles in society, conventional expectations still hold some influence on self-concepts. While a study of college students found that both men and women consider higher education most important to their self-concept, it also showed that parenthood mattered more to women. Still, this gendered difference has been decreasing over time.[78] Advocates from Betty Friedan (author of the 1963 classic *The Feminine Mystique*) to Facebook CEO Sheryl Sandberg (whose 2013 book *Lean In* encouraged women to achieve their full career potential) have contributed to a continuing shift in traditional gender roles.

Improving Your Self-Concept

Despite these sources of self-concepts, you are not fated to be shaped wholly by your family, culture, and surroundings. You can take positive steps to shape and strengthen your self-concept. These actions involve positive self-talk, personal growth, reappraisal, and support networks.

Positive self-talk. When you consciously engage in **self-talk**, you essentially talk to yourself. This can be literal (talking out loud) or figurative (thinking to yourself). Positive self-talk builds you up, addressing your capabilities, positive traits, and worth as a human being. Thus, before a difficult science test, you might say, "I studied hard for this, and I'm going to kick butt!" If you are trying to get up the nerve to talk to somebody new, you might say, "I'm a likable person—I've made lots of friends in the past." If you don't get a job you were qualified for, you might say, "This job would have been great, but I'm not taking it personally, and there are a lot of other opportunities out there."

Positive self-talk can increase your self-confidence and improve your ability to succeed.[79] For example, a recent study of college students enrolled in a research methods and statistics course found that those who had engaged in encouraging self-talk were more likely to report positive feelings after a class. On the other hand, students whose self-talk placed pressure on themselves were more likely to report negative feelings and increased anxiety after the class.[80]

Make sure that your self-talk does not set you up for a negative **self-fulfilling prophecy**. This occurs when you expect a particular outcome to occur, which causes you to behave in a way that makes the outcome more likely. For example, suppose that you are really fired up about an issue on campus, so you decide to run for the student senate. As you work on your campaign, you begin to worry about your chances of winning the election. If you start telling yourself that you're a lousy candidate and that other students won't respond well to your message, you may change the way you run your campaign. Maybe you'll put less effort into meeting other students ("They won't like me anyway") and getting your message out ("Why make a campaign poster if nobody will like my ideas?"). Obviously, these actions could negatively affect your campaign—perhaps causing you to lose an election you might have won. Conversely, positive self-talk could encourage you to enthusiastically campaign, perhaps leading to a favorable self-fulfilling prophecy.

SELF-FULFILLING PROPHECY

Personal growth. **Personal growth** refers to the process of strengthening your self-awareness and trying to live a life consistent with your values and capabilities.[81] College can be a unique opportunity for personal growth, as you are likely meeting new people, hearing different ideas and perspectives, and contemplating your future career.[82]

Spend time in college considering your goals. What would you like to achieve in terms of your academics and career preparation? Your social life? Your health and well-being? Realistically assess your available time for these goals, and make an action plan to achieve them. You may also want to talk to mentors, counselors, friends, and others who can advise you. Monitor your progress, and be sure to celebrate your achievements along the way. Having pride in your personal growth will undoubtedly boost your self-esteem.

Reappraisal. When you are feeling down on yourself, a good way to improve your outlook is to view the situation from a different perspective. **Reappraisal** occurs when you change your interpretation of something that happened in your life.[83] Suppose that you were a finalist for a scholarship, but another student received the award. You might initially feel disappointment and despair, figuring that the scholarship committee was not impressed with your qualifications and that the winner is a much better student than you. To reappraise, you could shift your perspective, telling yourself that you were a finalist, after all, and that next time the winner could easily be you.

Support networks. Spending time with understanding people can have a major influence on our lives and well-being. Friendships provide an important source of support.[84] A good friend will be sympathetic when you're going through a hard time, build you back up after a failure, and help you realize when you are wrong. These types of friends have your best interest at heart, and just being around them can help you feel good about yourself.

IDENTITY MANAGEMENT

All of us have both a private and a public self. Your **private self** is known only to you—nobody else truly knows the whole picture of how you see yourself. Your **public self** is the self that you represent to other people.

When we present ourselves to others, we may act strategically. In other words, the self that you represent may differ, depending on the context. Consider how you would present yourself if you were meeting someone interesting at a party. You would probably present yourself differently than you would if you were participating in a job interview, working with a group in class, or hanging out with close friends or family members.

The process by which people "present information about themselves in order to appear as they wish others to perceive them" is known as **identity management** or **impression management**.[85] Let's take a look at how this process works and how it might help us obtain our goals.

How We Engage in Identity Management

We regularly apply identity management when interacting with others, although our message and strategy change depending on the situation.[86] People are likely to purposefully try to manage impressions of themselves when the stakes are high—for example, if you are trying to convince a romantic partner of your commitment to the relationship or persuade your boss that you are worthy of a promotion. At other times, identity management is instinctive. You may successfully use a self-presentation behavior many times in your life in a given circumstance, even getting to the point where you employ it almost automatically, without thinking.[87] For example, if you have often been able to fit in with new acquaintances by projecting a casual and laid-back attitude, you may instinctively adopt that personality in future interactions with new people.

Most people have a limited number of personas they use when presenting themselves to others.[88] When choosing a self-presentation strategy, the target of the effort is a key consideration. The principles and beliefs of the person or audience in question influence the identity management strategies that you employ.[89]

Another important consideration in identity management is **self-disclosure**, or the intentional revelation of important information about ourselves that others are not likely to know. Self-disclosure has long been considered important to the impressions we make on each other during relationship development. For example, to build trust, we might decide it is important to open up about ourselves. We will elaborate on considerations relevant to self-disclosure, as well as the management of our privacy, in Chapter 8.

WHO HAS HIGHER EMOTIONAL INTELLIGENCE?

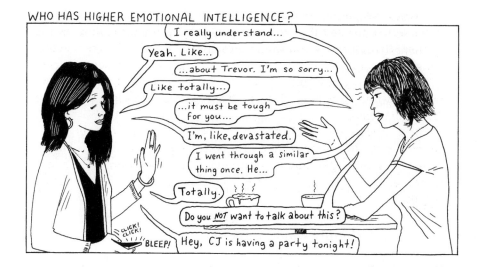

Emotional intelligence, or the ability to understand one's own and others' emotions, is another key factor. People who have this capability are better able to select sound identity management tactics.[90] For example, if you have a good understanding of your employer's concerns and values, your self-presentation can emphasize these attributes, such as a strong work ethic, loyalty, or creativity.

Objectives of Identity Management

There are a number of goals that we may try to achieve through identity management, and they are typically accomplished through different communication strategies, including ingratiation, self-promotion, exemplification, supplication, and intimidation.[91] Let's take a look at what each of these strategies involves:

- **Ingratiation** is used when a person hopes to be liked. For example, during a meeting at a client's office, a sales representative might point to a picture of the client with his or her spouse and kids and say, "You have such a lovely family."

- **Self-promotion** is employed to make an individual appear capable. For instance, a candidate for office in a sorority or campus club might emphasize her experience and expertise in leadership roles.

- **Exemplification** is applied to show that the person has a high moral character. This occurs when a politician asserts his or her honesty and strong religious convictions.
- **Supplication** is exercised when an individual wishes to demonstrate helplessness or dependence on others. A student who begs to retake an exam because he or she was confused when taking the original test is employing this strategy.
- **Intimidation** involves the user trying to convince others that he or she is dangerous, using threats or other statements that cause discomfort. A coworker using this tactic might insult or yell at you if you are unwilling to take his Saturday shift.[92]

Ethics and Identity Management

At first glance, identity management can seem like an unseemly activity—creating an impression of ourselves to gain a personal advantage. However, we inherently reveal some aspects of ourselves during interactions with others. Unless those who interact with us are willing to listen to the whole story of our lives, we cannot reveal our entire self-concept. So picking and choosing which elements of ourselves to reveal is inevitable.

Thus, the ethical issue is not whether or not you engage in identify management; rather, it is the accuracy of the information you present when doing so. Researchers have found that although people sometimes try to create false impressions, they often present truthful information that helps other people know them better.[93] Truth-telling is an important societal norm. We expect it when interacting with others, and it is one of four maxims underlying a cooperative conversation.[94] If impression management is based on false information or intended to manipulate others (for example, lying about your work experience during a job interview), then it would be wrong.

Online Identity Management

Social media provides us with new and unprecedented opportunities for identity management. Whether editing profiles, uploading pictures, joining groups, or announcing what we're up to, we may be broadcasting information about ourselves to a vast audience (depending on our privacy settings). Self-presentation in the online world offers a unique opportunity for us to consider how we would like to present ourselves, and which parts of us to share. However, it also comes with challenges. One issue is that people can more easily misrepresent themselves, posting information that others may not be able to verify; some people may even present themselves as an entirely different person. Another issue is that once something is posted, it will likely be viewed by many people at different times. This makes it much more difficult to adapt impression management strategies to any particular person who looks at your profile or site.[95] Consider also that employers routinely check potential employees' Facebook pages, along with their LinkedIn and Twitter profiles (one study notes that over half of employers do so).[96] Therefore, it's important to think carefully before you post anything that could be seen as offensive, hurtful, or misleading.

Beyond these issues, online identity management can bring up questions that constitute more of a gray area. Consider the ultimate virtual test of identity management: online dating. Daters need to find ways to stand out to potential partners but not seem too outside the norm. They must also do this in a confined number of words. It's not an easy task—which is why there have been hundreds of articles (if not more) written to help daters make the perfect profile.

IDENTITY MANAGEMENT: ETHICS

Many online daters are aware that other people's profiles may not be 100 percent accurate—though the degree of truthfulness can vary. For example, someone saying he's an inch taller than his true height is different from someone claiming to be ten years younger than she actually is. In order to learn more, prospective daters may employ interactive strategies, such as talking on the phone or actually meeting up in person, along with more passive ones, such as checking a series of messages for consistency or researching prospective dates via Google or another search engine.[97]

CHAPTER REVIEW

Throughout our lives, we actively perceive others. Through this process, we attempt to make sense of the stimuli in our world, particularly (for the purposes of this chapter) the communicative behaviors of others. Perceptions often come from instant mental associations that form when we note a stimulus, although they also may be formed through conscious thinking about the meaning of the stimuli we have received.

Our perceptions may be inaccurate due to faulty mental associations based on first impressions, stereotypes, appearances, or transference. However, we *can* improve the accuracy of perceptions. The first step is to recognize that our perceptions can be erroneous. Therefore, before we can be confident about the meaning of another person's behavior, it is important to do the following: seek additional data, keep the difference between facts and inferences in mind, and actively check perceptions.

In addition to perceiving other people, we are consistently forming perceptions about ourselves. Your self-concept includes all your perceptions of yourself. It is unique and relatively stable, although it can change throughout your life. Your self-esteem is based on how you evaluate the person you visualize when you ask the question, "Who am I?"

Self-concepts are significantly influenced by communication with others. Reflected appraisals give us information about ourselves through feedback provided by others. Sociocultural factors such as culture and gender also influence self-concept. We can strengthen our self-concept in a number of ways, such as through positive self-talk, personal growth, reappraisal of our beliefs, and building positive support networks.

Self-concept may influence our identity management—a process we always engage in, whether we're aware of it or not. While identity management can have several objectives, it's important to be ethical and therefore accurate when presenting information about ourselves to others. While self-disclosure can lead to closer relationships, we must be careful about this online, when our audience may be vast and varied.

LaunchPad
macmillan learning

LaunchPad for *Let's Communicate* offers videos and encourages self-assessment through adaptive quizzing. Go to **launchpadworks.com** to get access to:

 **LearningCurve Adaptive Quizzes**

 Video clips that help you understand human communication

Key Terms

perception 33
stimuli 33
sensory information 33
person perception 33
inferences 33
mental associations (schemas) 37
stereotype 42
transference 45
self-serving bias 45
fundamental attribution error 46
facts 47
perception checking 48
self 49
self-concept 49
extended self 49
self-esteem 51
global self-esteem 51
domain-specific self-esteem 51

reflected appraisals 52
in-group 53
out-group 53
self-talk 55
© self-fulfilling prophecy 56
personal growth 57
reappraisal 57
private self 57
public self 57
identity (or impression) management 58
© self-disclosure 58
emotional intelligence 59
ingratiation 59
self-promotion 59
exemplification 60
supplication 60
intimidation 60

Review Questions

1. Define *perception*, and explain the perception-forming process.
2. Explain how our perceptions influence our communication.
3. Identify four sources of mental associations.
4. What are some reasons why perceptions can be inaccurate?

5. Define *self-concept* and *self-esteem*.
6. What are some of the sources of our self-concept?
7. What are the five objectives of identity management?

Critical Thinking Questions

1. Compare and contrast the ways that we form perceptions of ourselves and form perceptions of others.
2. Which do you think is more accurate—your self-perception or your perception of a person whom you know well (such as a sibling, parent, or friend)? Why?
3. Identify a person who created a favorable (or unfavorable) first impression but for whom your impression changed over time. Why do you think your first impression was inaccurate? What information caused you to change your mind?
4. Identify ways that your culture, gender, or past experiences have influenced your perceptions of other people. Include one or two examples.
5. Create a brief description of yourself that you would send to a potential employer. Then, compare it with one of your social media pages, like Instagram, Twitter, Snapchat, or Facebook. What similarities and differences do you see? Compare how a future employer would perceive you versus how your friends and family perceive you.
6. What are some of the reasons that online identity management differs from "in real life" identity management?

Activities

1. Watch a movie or television show that you have not seen before. Choose one of the characters, and write down your first impression of that character. At the end of the movie or show, write down your impression of that character again. Has your impression changed? If so, what factors caused it to change?
2. Go online and watch a five- to ten-minute speech by a politician or another public figure that you support. Write down your perception of his or her character. Compare your perception to the perception of others by reading the comments under the video and by doing an online search. Is your perception similar to or different from the perceptions of others? Why do you think this is the case?

3. Working in groups, prepare a two- to three-minute skit in which a key character has to make a difficult decision. Perform the skit in front of the class, but stop just before he or she makes the decision. Have other members of the class guess what your character will decide and explain how they made that inference. Then finish the skit (as planned) so class members can see if they made the correct inference.

4. Working in groups, have each member privately write down his or her self-concept at age ten. Then have group members say what they think each person was like when he or she was ten. See how well the group member assessments match up.

Apply Your Skills

THE FOUR SOURCES OF MENTAL ASSOCIATIONS (EXPLAINED ALOUD)

Go to the illustration "The Four Sources of Mental Associations (Explained Aloud)" on page 40. Then provide an example of a person for whom your initial perception changed over time. Explain how your first impressions were influenced by life experiences, information that people gave you, the media, and your culture. Then explain why your perception changed. Did you use any of the strategies for improving the accuracy of perceptions (discussed on pp. 46–49)? Were there other reasons why your perception changed?

Study Plan

_____

_____

_____

_____

_____

_____

_____

3

VERBAL COMMUNICATION

OBJECTIVES

- Understand that because language is imperfect and because words have different meanings for different people, we must work to achieve a shared meaning.
- Examine the ways that language can accomplish various objectives and also be impeded by negative forms, such as biased language or hate speech.
- Identify methods of communicating ethically, effectively, and respectfully.

Robert and Fernando had been best friends since eighth grade. They were a perfect match for each other—they laughed at the same corny jokes and could finish each other's sentences. They shared similar interests and had similar life goals. After being accepted to the same college, they found an apartment near campus and jumped into the college experience. Their first year was going great, but then a serious problem arose.

The problem began with finances. Robert and Fernando's monthly bills were automatically deducted from Fernando's checking account. Robert was to give Fernando a check for half of the expenses at the beginning of each month. Unfortunately, after Robert's check bounced in December, it took him over a month to get his share of the expenses to Fernando. Then in February, Robert asked Fernando if he could cover the apartment costs until March. At that time, Robert promised him that he would have the money for February and March.

Fernando needed to have an adult conversation with his best friend. He barely had enough money in his account to cover all the expenses for February. He was also not sure that he ought to be bailing Robert out month after month—even though they were best friends, Fernando began to fear that Robert might be taking advantage of him.

Fernando also needed a tactful way to request more information from Robert. If his friend was in a serious financial bind, he would try to be more flexible. But Robert was very proud and might be reluctant to admit he was having financial problems. Fernando was also well aware that Robert had found a "special someone" and had been going out rather frequently. If Robert's rent money was being diverted to extravagant nights on the town, then Fernando needed a diplomatic way to tell Robert that he needed to take care of his half of the expenses first.

If you were in Fernando's shoes, what would you say? Fernando needed to find just the right words to have an honest conversation with Robert. He would need to watch his language carefully so that he could express his concerns honestly without showing disregard for his best friend's feelings. He really didn't want to lose his best friend, but he knew they needed to resolve their financial issues.

Fernando needed effective verbal communication skills. By **verbal communication**, we mean the exchange of messages using language. Like Fernando, we all encounter many situations in which we need to find just the right words when we interact with others.

In this chapter, we offer guidelines to help you communicate with other people in a manner that is more understandable, respectful, and authentic. By honing these skills, you will improve your interactions with others. This chapter begins with a discussion of the nature of verbal communication, followed by an analysis of the challenges presented when we try to understand each other's words. Next, we discuss some of the useful effects of verbal communication along with the potentially negative consequences words can have. Finally, we consider some tips for the effective use of words.

THE NATURE OF VERBAL COMMUNICATION

As we have noted, verbal communication involves the use of language to exchange messages. A **language** is a standardized use of words that is shared by a community of people. This community may be large and transcend national boundaries, as is the case with English and Spanish speakers. It may also be a small group; for example, Yurok (an indigenous language used by people living along the Klamath River and Pacific coast in Northern California) was historically spoken by about twenty-five hundred people.[1] It may also be a community that communicates in the virtual world—for example, people who communicate through text messages or Twitter.

Let's consider a few key principles about languages that have important considerations for verbal communication.

Language Is Rule Based

A language that is used to communicate with others must have a standardized method for using words that is understood and followed by members of that language community. If speakers used words at their own whim rather than in a commonly understood manner, "the result would be chaos rather than communication."[2] Let's take a look at three key language rules.

SEMANTIC RULES

Semantic rules. Semantic rules govern the meaning of words. When you see the words *yellow, yoga, yes,* or *young,* you have a general understanding of what these terms mean. No language community can effectively communicate without some common understanding of how words are defined. However, this does not mean that every person has an identical understanding of the meaning of all terms in any language. For example, there would undoubtedly be a difference of opinion in your class about the age at which a person is no longer "young" and whether one's status as "young" refers to a chronological age. Later in this chapter, we elaborate on the reasons why language cannot create identical understandings of meaning.

Syntactic rules. Syntactic rules regulate the order in which words are organized into sentences. To see how word order makes a difference, consider two sentences that contain the same words: the statement "I can go to Jamba Juice with you when my biology lab is finished at noon" has a different meaning than "when my Jamba Juice is finished at noon, I can go to biology lab with you." English, Spanish, and Arabic are examples of languages in which the primary order of a sentence is subject-verb-object, such as "I studied chemistry." Other languages, including Korean, Basque, and Sanskrit, primarily use a subject-object-verb format.

Pragmatic rules. Pragmatic rules apply to the use of language to achieve goals, adapt to different communication contexts, or engage in particular types of communication (such as telling a joke or texting). For example, a parent trying to get a young son to clean his room might try to achieve this objective by saying, "Clean your room now," "If you clean your room, I'll take you out for ice cream," or "If you do not clean your room, you won't get your allowance."

Different pragmatic rules would apply for this same parent when choosing words in another context, such as asking an employee to finish a project at work. They would also lead to different word choice if the task was being assigned in a written note to the employee rather than explained in a face-to-face conversation.

Language Is Symbolic

The words we use to communicate are **symbols**, meaning that the words are used *arbitrarily* to represent something else. The word(s) used to

PRAGMATIC RULES

represent something (an object, a living organism, a concept, an action, or anything else that we can consider) have no inherent connection to the entity that they represent. The word *duck* does not "look like a duck, walk like a duck, or quack like a duck."[3] Nevertheless, English speakers have learned to connect the sound made by saying "duck" with that particular web-footed bird.

Symbols help us communicate efficiently—it would be more difficult and time-consuming to indicate that you were referring to the web-footed critter we call a duck if you had to rely on a description rather than that single word.[4] To see why this is true, think of a variation on the game Pictionary (a game in which one player selects a card containing a word and then draws a picture representing the word while teammates try to guess the word). Your word is *duck*, and rather than drawing a duck, you must describe the picture you would draw as the audience tries to guess the word. It would take a good number of words to describe a drawing of a duck so that your team would guess "duck" rather than, say, "swan" or "goose." The common understanding among English speakers about the meaning of the word *duck* provides a much faster way to refer to this creature.

The symbol used to refer to a given concept can vary greatly from language community to language community. The letters g-r-e-e-n are not the only way to refer to that typical color of grass, a Mountain

Dew bottle, and the T-shirt many people wear on St. Patrick's Day. That color is equally well represented by the term *verde* in Spanish or *midori* in Japanese. Although *green, verde,* and *midori* have very different pronunciations and use different combinations of letters (or characters in the Japanese writing system), speakers of each language have no problem understanding the color being referenced. If a language community came to use *zot* or *zag* to represent the color known as green in English, those terms would work equally well for that group of speakers.

The same language can also use different words to refer to the same idea. Changes in English slang are one example—what is *off the chain* or *fly* to many current students was *groovy* to their parents and *swell* to their grandparents. But this phenomenon is not limited to slang. After the invasion of Britain by the Normans from France in 1066, the Middle English word *inwit* (knowledge within) came to be replaced by the term we know as *conscience*.[5]

Language Is Literal and Figurative

Words can have two very different kinds of meanings. The **denotative meaning** is a word's exact, literal definition (or *definitions* in the case of words with multiple literal meanings, such as *duck* or *run*). Words also have a **connotative meaning**—sometimes more than one. These meanings represent the associations that come to mind when you hear or read a word. A word's connotative meaning may have little resemblance to its denotative meaning. For example, when someone says that a stock is "a dog," that term connotes a poor investment opportunity. This meaning has little in common with the literal meaning of the term *dog*. When communicators have a common understanding of a word's connotative meaning, it can make communication more descriptive or powerful. For example, if a friend says that a new indie pop musician's video "went viral," that term better represents the dynamic impact of the video than the phrase "got many views online."

Language Is Dynamic

There is no fixed form of any given language; instead, "human languages are in constant flux."[6] There are few (if any) cultures in which a person living now would be able to understand those who were born a thousand years ago.[7] Languages change for many reasons. One is that no two people acquire or use language in exactly the same way. Some words and usages gain in popularity, and others become less common (most people say "sofa" or "couch" rather than "davenport" nowadays). Another is that new inventions and experiences require new words.[8] Think of the new vocabulary that resulted when social media platforms were created and their use became widespread—for example, "I friended her on Facebook." A person returning from living on a desert island for twenty years with no human contact would have no understanding of the nature of Facebook. He or she would also be unfamiliar with the use of "friended" as a verb.

Language communities also interact with one another through migration or trade. One result of this is **borrowing**, which refers to words or other features of one language community being adopted by another language community.[9] Many words in modern English do not trace back to Old English; rather, they come from a multitude of languages, including

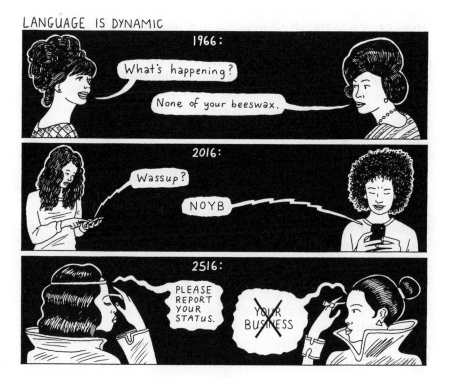

Dutch, Spanish, Latin, Greek, or French.[10] English-speaking foodies use loanwords from a variety of cultures—*curry* (India), *bagel* (Yiddish), *enchilada* (Spanish), and *kimchi* (Korean).[11] In Latin America, Spanish speakers borrowed many words from indigenous languages. Thus, Ecuadorians use the Quechua word *papa* rather than the Spanish word *patata* (which, by the way, is the source of the English word *potato!*).[12]

Language Is Contextual

The meanings of words are **context dependent**. This means that the same word can have different meanings, depending on the circumstances in which it is used. The statement that "words have different meanings" has two different senses in which it is true. First, words often have "semantically unrelated meanings."[13] For example, a word may function as different parts of speech (such as nouns, verbs, and adjectives) or have multiple meanings when used as the same part of speech. Consider the previous example of the word *duck*. As a verb, it could refer to lowering oneself ("Duck under the branch") or evading ("Duck the difficult question"). As a noun, the word could refer to the flying web-footed creature that quacks, a student or an alumnus of the University of Oregon (or a member of the Anaheim hockey team), or a stack of rocks left to mark the correct route for hikers and backpackers. If someone's behavior is a bit strange, we might say he or she is "an odd duck."

A word can also have different meanings even when we understand the semantic sense in which it is being used. This is because words are **ambiguous**—they have no precise meaning that is understood by all. Two people may have very different ideas about what constitutes going out on a *date*, even though both understand that the word is being used to refer to a social activity with potential romantic implications, not the day on the calendar or the food found on a palm tree. How fast does someone have to be moving to be *running* rather than *jogging*? When you are starving and your food server tells you that the order will be *right up*, how long will it be until you get your food? You and your instructor may disagree about what constitutes a *good* grade on an assignment even though you both understand that *good* is a positive term. You can undoubtedly think of many more terms that have ambiguous meanings.

Because words may have a number of meanings, we rely on context when trying to determine which meaning is intended. Words used in

LANGUAGE IS CONTEXTUAL

conjunction with any given word may supply the context needed to improve understanding. The words that accompany a discussion of hiking, hunting, or hockey will usually clarify which type of duck a speaker is referring to. An invitation to a coffee date has more of a casual "let's be friends" connotation, whereas an offer of a date at a fancy French restaurant probably signals a more serious and romantic interest. The relational context can also help us understand the meaning of words. When a romantic partner says, "You are looking good today," you would interpret it very differently than if your doctor used the same words after a medical exam.

VERBAL COMMUNICATION AND THE CHALLENGE OF UNDERSTANDING

As we noted in Chapter 1, a goal of effective communication is the creation of shared meaning, in which the participants in a communication interaction come to a common understanding with little confusion and few misinterpretations. When we engage in verbal communication, language is the vehicle we use to express the ideas that we want to share and to understand the ideas of others. However, words do not transport ideas from one person to another. By considering the nature of a language and the manner in which we come to learn it, it is easy to see why this is true.

Language Is an Imperfect Vehicle for Understanding

Verbal communication would create shared meaning if all humans could be programmed with futuristic language software. A source would have an idea to express, and the software would select the words that represent that idea. Then the receiver would hear or see those words, and the software would stimulate the source's meaning in the receiver's mind.

However, the analogy between futuristic software and the actual process of using language breaks down on two levels because languages are not like software, and humans do not learn languages by being programmed. Software directs a computer to operate in the same way every time it is called into action. But as you learned in the first section of this chapter, language is symbolic, dynamic, and ambiguous—that is, the words used to refer to any entity are arbitrary, words and rules are constantly changing, and the meaning of words is open to interpretation. Despite the best efforts of our teachers, most of our language learning does not occur in a common, systematic manner. Beginning at a very young age, children learn the meanings of words and the rules of language experientially by interacting with adults,[14] developing their own unique linguistic range.[15] We work out meanings of ambiguous words on our own, based on how words seem to be used in our daily environment.[16] No person knows all the words and rules of the language(s) he or she speaks.[17]

You have surely experienced misunderstandings in your own life. Think of times when another person took your words the wrong way. Perhaps you thought that a classmate's speech was excellent, and you said, "That was your best speech of the semester." Rather than thanking you, your classmate said, "What was wrong with my other speeches?" Maybe you complimented a friend's trendy clothes, but your friend thought you were making a critical statement about his or her tendency to follow the crowd and conform to social trends. Conversely, there are

SEMANTIC TRIANGLE

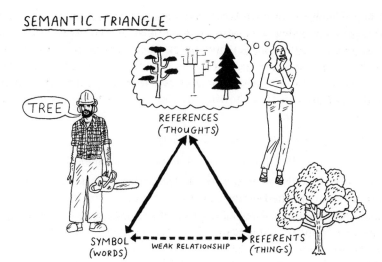

probably times you can recall when you may have misinterpreted a statement made by a friend, family member, or coworker.

A shorthand explanation communication scholars use to refer to this phenomenon is that *meanings are in people, not in words.*[18] When you have a thought in your mind, you can select the words that you believe will accurately represent your idea. However, when others see or hear your words, those words may not represent the same idea to them. Linguistic scholars C. K. Ogden and I. A. Richards used the triangle of meaning (or semantic triangle) to show how a person's thought and the symbol(s) he or she uses to represent that thought are correct to him or her. However, there is no direct relationship between the thought and the symbol (word) he or she is using to represent that thought. Thus, the use of that symbol is unlikely to stimulate the communicator's precise meaning in the receiver's mind. The receiver assumes that the speaker is using the words in the same manner that he or she would use them, which may not be the case.[19]

Problematic Language Exacerbates Misunderstandings

Although accurate communication is generally possible because our meanings for words are similar to others' meanings,[20] there are a number of reasons why verbal communication can lead to misunderstandings. Let's consider some common factors.

Abstract language. **Abstract words** refer to an entity in very general terms. The word(s) do represent the idea that the speaker intends to express, but they are so broad that they encompass many other possible ideas. Use of these words can be confusing and ambiguous to your audience. In contrast, **concrete words** are specific and suggest exactly what you mean. Following are four possible statements a friend might make to you:

- Let's hang out this summer. (abstract)
- Let's get together and play our guitars this summer. (less abstract)
- Let's get together at my house and play our guitars next Tuesday afternoon. (more concrete)
- Let's get together at my house and play our guitars next Tuesday at 1:00. (most concrete)

Only the third and fourth statements give you a good idea of both the proposed activity and the suggested time, and the fourth statement is most helpful for informing you of the precise proposal. The time frame in the second statement is far too general for you to make plans. The

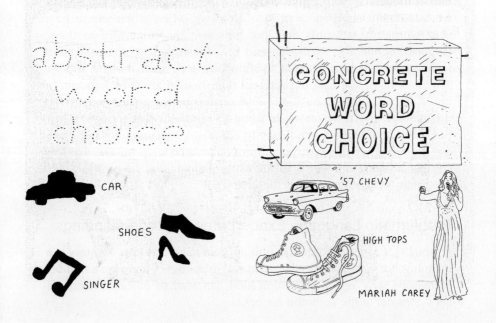

first statement may not even be perceived to express a sincere desire to get together. (Statements such as "Let's hang out" or "Let's do lunch" are sometimes used to express a lack of interest in seeing somebody without using blunt language.)

Jargon. **Jargon** consists of specialized or technical words or phrases familiar to people in a specific field or group. Jargon can include technical terms as well as abbreviations, acronyms, and other esoteric expressions. For example, people in the field of telecommunications use jargon extensively—including expressions such as *FTTP* (fiber to the property), *3G* (third-generation telecommunication network), *CapEx* (capital expenditures), and *first-tier ops* (telecommunication operators with the largest market share). Cell biologists are familiar with terms such as *ribosomal DNA* and *anaerobic cellular metabolism*, but the average person will not understand what they mean.

Misunderstanding is one problem when unfamiliar jargon is used. For example, use of medical jargon by physicians has been identified as

a leading communication problem in the medical care system.[21] A second problem is that the use of jargon can be perceived as exclusionary. This can be illustrated by terms from the business world, such as *bandwidth*, *freemium*, and *metric*. People in a business meeting who are unfamiliar with these terms may feel like outsiders and be reluctant to risk their credibility by asking for clarification.

Improper use of words. **Improper word choice** occurs when a communicator uses a word that *does not* have the meaning that he or she intends to express. This error commonly takes place when two similar-sounding words have different meanings and the communicator uses the wrong word.

For example, the words *elicit* (draw out or provoke a reaction) and *illicit* (illegal) are often confused. It would be improper to say, "If our group included a joke in our presentation, we would illicit laughter from the class." One student speaking about the grunge music movement in Seattle accused the late Kurt Cobain (Nirvana's lead vocalist) of *immortal* behavior. Surely he did not intend to say that Cobain would live forever. If you are going to use specialized terms, it is important to understand the proper definition. For example, it would be incorrect to use the terms *recession* and *depression* interchangeably to describe economic conditions because the terms have different economic meanings.

Equivocal language. Shared meaning is unlikely when **equivocal language** is used. This means that the speaker uses word(s) with a range of meanings, perhaps in a deceptive manner. Here, the communicator makes a strategic decision not to express his or her thoughts with precision. Sometimes this word choice has good intentions—for example, you might tell your partner the white lie that his new fashion-challenged sweater "is really something," without stating that you think the sweater will attract negative attention. At other times, equivocal language constitutes an unethical deception. Suppose your team leader at work calls for a meeting on Saturday, and one team member says, "I'm with that idea 100 percent." Based on that comment, your team would expect her to show up for the meeting. However, she has no intention of showing up on Saturday. Here, she is intentionally using deception in a manner that will harm the remainder of the team; thus, equivocation cannot be justified.

THE EFFECTS OF VERBAL COMMUNICATION

Language has powerful effects on our lives. Consider something that someone said to you that has had the greatest influence on your life. Helpful advice or positive reinforcement may have encouraged you to make good decisions in your life. You are likely to have a favorite song, with lyrics that are especially meaningful to you. Thoughtfully crafted words or poetry may help you share your feelings with a person who is special in your life, and articulate answers to interview questions may help you land the job of your dreams.

Verbal communication plays a key role in every human communication context discussed in this text. The words you use influence others' perceptions of you. Words can bring greater understanding or conflict to an interpersonal relationship, help keep a group on track, inform others about a new discovery, and persuade or inspire people. Language can be a force for good—Abraham Lincoln's Gettysburg Address and Martin Luther King Jr.'s "I Have a Dream" speech expressed the highest aspirations of the American people. Conversely, words can also cause great pain, whether in an interpersonal or a public context. In this section, we first consider some helpful uses of language and then provide some cautions about harmful word choice.

Uses of Language

Whether expressed as the functions of language or as the objectives of a communicator,[22] theorists and philosophers of language have noted a number of language uses. Each time we use words to communicate, we are likely to be accomplishing one or more of the following purposes. After reading about these purposes, check the illustration on p. 84 to see how many uses you can identify.

Sharing information. In our interactions with others, we often provide information about ourselves and our world or learn such information from others. When you are getting acquainted with someone, you might share some of your likes or dislikes in order to find common ground and launch a new friendship. At work, you may be asked to explain the details of a particular job to a new employee. Some shared information can be life changing. For example, research by the Pell Institute showed that providing prospective first-generation college students with information about the college admissions process, the steps involved in applying for financial aid, and stories of successful role models had significant impact on students' decision to apply to college and subsequently enroll.[23]

Influencing others. Verbal communication can also be used for **persuasion**, which is the effort to influence people's beliefs, attitudes, or actions. Whether you hope to convince your friends to believe that a smoothie has more calories than a cheeseburger, agree that the new Thai restaurant near campus has the best food in town, or help you move to a new apartment, you are engaged in persuasion. Conversely, you are also a constant target of persuasion—consider the number of advertising messages you see every time you travel to school or access the Internet.

Words play an important role in persuasion. Much as mental associations made when observing other people lead to perceptions (recall Chapter 2), words can activate mental associations through thoughts and emotions, affecting how people perceive a given issue.[24] Political consultants carefully consider the exact words that are used to express an idea. They may assess the instant responses of focus-group members who are exposed to a variety of words that might be used to discuss the same basic idea and recommend optimal word choices for their clients. Thus, advocates of reducing the budget deficit by raising taxes on high-income-earning Americans may refer to such proposals as a *millionaires tax*, whereas opponents of the increase may call the proposal a tax on *job creators*.

Words are not just used to sell products and candidates. Throughout history, effective use of language has had a profound effect on social change. The Declaration of Independence's proclamation that governments derive their power from the consent of the governed heralded a new philosophy of government that was diametrically opposed to the divine right of kings. Frederick Douglass moved audiences with his graphic description of life under slavery and proved a powerful advocate for the equality of all people, regardless of race or gender. In the twenty-first century, new forums for the effective use of language have evolved. Wael Ghonim's memorial Facebook page used the captivating title "We are all Khaled Saeed" (in tribute to a young Egyptian who was murdered while in police custody) to draw in hundreds of thousands of followers, providing a significant inspiration to the Tahrir Square protesters in Egypt.[25] Lina Ben Mhenni, a linguist and activist, created a blog called *A Tunisian Girl*. As one of a small number of Tunisians willing to condemn that nation's government before the Jasmine Revolution, she provided some of the "most revealing and scathing criticisms" of Tunisia's authoritarian government.[26]

Expressing feelings. Language has a powerful ability to express humans' emotional states. Have you ever told a special person in your life exactly how much he or she means to you? Chances are that you carefully considered every word you were going to say, trying to find just the right words. If you have the aptitude for it, perhaps you expressed your words in a poem or a song. Even if you are not inclined to author a creative work, you can probably think of others' lyrics or poetry that expresses what you are feeling at any given time. Whether you prefer country, hip-hop, rock, alternative, or some other genre of music, you can undoubtedly think of songs that convey love, patriotism, anger, hope, and many other emotions.

Special occasion speeches are intimately connected with important human events and often evoke emotional responses, such as laughter, tears, joy, or pride. A good speaker will highlight the values shared by members

CAN YOU PICK OUT THE **FIVE** USES OF LANGUAGE?

① I'm truly very frustrated: ever since I watched *Game of Thrones*, I am *TERRIFIED* of humans.

② There's an old movie called *Jaws* that I highly recommend you watch. It might help you overcome your fear.

③ I heard that it didn't have a very happy ending, but...

④ ...I could envision myself being terrifying again with the right inspiration.

That's the spirit, old chap.

⑤ I will download it as soon as I get back to my cove.

I wish you luck, Mr. White.

Thank you, Doctor Flippy!

SOCIETY OF DOLPHIN THERAPISTS

CHOOSE FROM THESE: accomplishing actions, sharing information, imagining, influencing others, and expressing feelings.

① _____   ④ _____
② _____   ⑤ _____
③ _____

of the audience and select language that is appropriate for the event being commemorated. For example, at the memorial service for South African president Nelson Mandela, his great-granddaughter Phumla Mandela used the following words to inspire the people who had gathered to celebrate the president's life: "You are lodged in our memories. You tower over the world like a comet, leaving streaks of light for us to follow."[27]

Imagining. When using language to imagine, we use words to deal creatively with our experiences or fantasize about how the world might be.[28] Storytelling is one common way of using language creatively. Rhetorician Walter Fisher referred to humans as *homo narrans*, or storytelling beings, because stories or narratives are central to our effort to make sense of the world and share our ideas with others.[29] Perhaps you enjoy creative writing or even filmmaking. Eduardo Sánchez and Daniel Myrick were recent graduates of the University of Central Florida's film school when they wrote and directed the highly successful independent horror film *The Blair Witch Project*. Tara Stone, a senior at John Paul the Great Catholic University (located near San Diego), was the screenwriter for a film titled *Red Line*, a fictional account of the interactions of the survivors of a Red Line subway crash. The film was produced primarily by students, and most scenes were shot on campus.[30]

Even if you do not have time to create such works, chances are that you are a consumer of them. U.S. publishers reported revenue of almost $28 billion in 2014,[31] and there were over 1.2 billion movie admissions in the United States and Canada in that same year.[32] We also use language to imagine in everyday conversation. Have you and a friend ever discussed an ideal life partner or job? What life would be like if you had children (or what the world will be like when your children grow up)? What you would do if you won the lottery? These conversations and many others involve using words to imagine.

Accomplishing actions. Another important function of words is to perform actions.[33] This means using speech to do something—for example, to apologize, assert, approve, or advise. When we do this, we use words that express the action we are doing. For example, you might say any of the following:

> "*I am sorry* that I forgot your birthday."
>
> "*I am sure* that there is gas in the car."
>
> "*You did the right thing* by helping the homeless person."
>
> "*I recommend that* you eat more vegetables."

The italicized words are ways to verbally represent, respectively, the acts of apology, assertion, approval, and advice. There are also words that we use to promise, compliment, threaten, or accomplish thousands of other acts. We could not perform many of these deeds without the words that are understood to refer to the actions we are taking.

Abuses of Language

Language is not inherently positive or negative; its effects depend on the choices that communicators make. When used in an ethical and effective manner, language can bring delight into our lives and facilitate a more just world. However, just as words have the power to accomplish great good, words can also have negative consequences.

Biased language. **Biased language** is the use of words that suggest prejudice or preconceptions about a group of people based on shared characteristics. Such language often makes negative judgments about **immutable characteristics** (those that are impossible to change or deeply ingrained in one's culture), such as race, ethnicity, gender, sexuality, religion, or mental or physical ability. When biased language intensely attacks individuals based on their membership in such groups, it is sometimes referred to as **hate speech**. The use of these terms threatens the self-concept of members in the targeted group and erodes the mutual respect that is important for a healthy communication. Such words have been likened to a verbal slap in the face, and once they have been uttered, "it is unlikely that dialogue will follow."[34] For example, one student lost credibility with his audience for using biased language while speaking about law-enforcement techniques. He repeatedly referred to the officers as the "guys" on the job, and his reference to efforts by the police to "handle certain neighborhoods where residents won't cooperate" was viewed as a thinly veiled reference to socioeconomics or race.

Some of the consequences of biased words are psychological. Professor Charles Lawrence III has testified to his own reaction to the use of the n-word: "I feel powerless before this word and its minions. In a moment's time, it has made me an other. In an instant it has rebuilt the wall between my friend's humanity and my own, the wall that I have so painstakingly disassociated."[35] Although these words may seem innocuous to the speaker, evidence shows that they have "a powerful impact upon the psychological well-being of marginalized groups."[36] Targets of hate speech suffer consequences, including apprehension, nightmares, anger, and loss of self-esteem. These effects can be particularly harmful to children.[37]

There are also physical effects on the targets of biased language. For example, anti-gay harassment has particularly adverse consequences when directed to teens and young adults, including a uniquely high rate of suicide among LGBT youth.[38] Research has also identified a link between the use of homophobic language and aggressive acts directed against gay and lesbian students, such as bullying.[39] Race-based hate speech has been associated with a number of effects on its targets, including headaches, high blood pressure, drug use, and depression.[40]

Biased language can also create or reinforce social inequality. The words that we use in our discourse "construct the social reality in which people live."[41] For example, the use of gendered language can serve as a barrier to equality between the sexes.[42] Thus, the use of generic masculine terms to refer to both men and women (such as "a judge must

be sure that *he* is fair to both sides") makes it more likely that receivers will perceive that the language applies only to males.[43] The use of masculine-gendered wording in job announcements can discourage women from applying for such jobs even if they have the skills and aptitude required to do well in that field.[44]

Inflammatory language. Sometimes a communicator's words are so harsh or offensive that they create a barrier to continued interaction and prevent the creation of shared meaning. In a relationship, sometimes a partner expresses a criticism in such a negative or insensitive manner that it causes the other partner to experience **flooding**. This feeling, especially likely to be triggered in heterosexual males in a romantic relationship, is marked by an intense physiological fight-or-flight response. This means that the target of the criticism has such an "intense, overwhelming" reaction that he or she will "do almost anything to terminate the interaction."[45]

For example, suppose that a couple is discussing how to pay for a child's education. The husband has been out of work for a year and is very sensitive about the job loss. During the discussion, his spouse says, "If you had managed to keep your job, we would have plenty of money for tuition." The husband is so hurt that he walks out, making further dialogue impossible. Alternatively, he may even respond with a hurtful comment directed back at his partner, making successful communication even less likely.

GUIDELINES FOR VERBAL COMMUNICATION

Now that we've discussed both the positive and the negative effects of verbal communication, let's turn to some ethical guidelines you can use when communicating effectively with others. These include making your message clear, making your message considerate, and making your responses respectful.

Make Your Message Clear

Recall that misunderstandings can happen because language is an imperfect vehicle for communicating ideas from one person to another. Words that are clear to you may not necessarily be understood in the same manner by others, and certain terms may not be familiar to a listener

FLOODING (VIA *AUGUST: OSAGE COUNTY*)

or reader. Following are some suggestions to help ensure the accuracy of verbal communication.

Consider your listeners or readers. In most situations, the best way to ensure that you're using understandable language is to choose words that are likely to be in the vocabulary of the person or people interacting with you. Their educational background can suggest a general vocabulary level, and their life experiences can help you predict what terms are likely to be understood. Take care in deciding when to use jargon—most college students who have tried to add a class after the term has begun would recognize the term *crashing a course*, whereas people who have not attended college (or graduated years earlier) might think you had more violent intentions. As a general rule, if you can make a point in plain language, do so. If you need to use more technical or obscure terms to express your idea, explain what these terms mean.

Use concise language. The use of **concise language** is another way to improve the clarity of your message. This means that you use the fewest words necessary to express an idea. You may occasionally want to add words or phrases to incorporate color, eloquence, or humor into your message. However, you should have a good reason for inserting such extra words. The term for unnecessary words is **verbal clutter**—extraneous words that make it hard for others to follow your message. The sentence "Regardless and notwithstanding of your love for Thai cuisine, it would be more economical to cook dinner at home" would be much less cluttered if you simply said, "Although you love Thai food, let's save money and cook dinner at home."

USE CONCISE, NOT FLOWERY, LANGUAGE:

Perhaps it could be that this moment presents itself as an appropriate opportunity for the dynamic duo that we are to withdraw henceforth with the chief goal of satisfying the desires of our digestive systems via the timely partaking of wholesome and suitable victuals provided to us by a culinary establishment in this vicinity.*

* Let's go out for dinner.

Focus on concrete terms. Recall that concrete words are specific, whereas abstract terms are more general. If you use concrete terms, others are more likely to understand your message. For example, you may create an issue in your relationship if you text your partner the abstract statement "Going out with some people after class." He or she is likely to wonder where you will be going out and fear for the worst (a club?) and also question just who "some people" are (could that include your ex?). And which class are you referring to? (It better not be that night class that ends at ten!) If you use a concrete statement instead, such as "My group and I are going to Quiznos for lunch after our presentation in speech class," your message will be clear—and also less threatening.

Check for understanding. If you express an important idea, you can double-check to see if your message was understood. Rather than simply stating your point and moving on, you might ask your audience what they thought you said. How might this work? Suppose you are discussing an upcoming group presentation at work. You are willing to create the Power-Point slides but do not expect to be responsible for presenting the slides, too. You might say, "I'll take care of the PowerPoint." If the other members think that's great, but nobody else jumps in to volunteer, you might ask, "Does everybody understand that I am creating the slides but that someone else will need to deliver the presentation?"

Make Your Message Considerate

We have already noted the powerful negative effect that biased language can have on its targets. As an ethical communicator, you need to carefully consider the impact of words that are likely to have a painful impact. Following are some principles to keep in mind in order to avoid bias in your message.

Avoid stereotypes. As we noted in Chapter 2, stereotypes are inferences drawn about others because of their membership in a particular social category, and these beliefs are often inaccurate. Indeed, many members of a given social category simply do not have the traits that are

(FAILURE TO) CHECK FOR UNDERSTANDING

alleged to apply to their group.[46] When used in verbal communication, not only are stereotypes offensive to the people being labeled, but they also hurt the credibility of the person who is inaccurately assuming that all members of any group have some particular characteristic.

It is especially important to avoid stereotypes when discussing topics that are loaded with the potential for controversy. For example, if you oppose affirmative action policies, do not make claims that women or people of color are less qualified for certain jobs. Instead, you might say that race or gender should play no role in any hiring decision. Or you could acknowledge that there is discrimination in society but claim that affirmative action is not the best policy to remedy discrimination.

Use gender-neutral terms.
Recall that the use of masculine pronouns when referring to groups that can include men or women can reinforce gender-based stereotypes. Therefore, it is important to avoid bias when using pronouns and choose a **gender-neutral term** (a word that does not suggest a specific gender) when possible.

The use of "he or she" is one way to avoid implying that a group applies to only men or women. Another option is to use plural terms when they fit the idea you are conveying. For example, rather than saying, "A good department chair keeps his or her meetings organized," you might say, "Good department chairs keep their meetings organized." If a single reference is more appropriate to your speech, you might alternate references to "she" and "he" from paragraph to paragraph or example to example. Thus,

USE GENDER-NEUTRAL TERMS

POLICE OFFICER
(NOT POLICE MAN)

MAIL CARRIER
(NOT POSTMAN)

FIRE FIGHTER
(NOT FIREMAN)

in a speech about hiking, you might say, "When the leader of a hike takes a water break, *she* should make sure that all group members are well hydrated." For the next main point, you might say, "When the leader notes that some hikers are falling behind, *he* should slow down the pace."

Also avoid gender-specific nouns or noun phrases, such as *poetess, chairman, cleaning lady,* or *aviatrix.* These terms suggest that a position is only appropriate for a man or a woman—or, in the case of terms such as *aviatrix,* imply that women who hold a given position are somehow different from men who hold the same job. Use neutral words, such as *poet, chair, housekeeper,* and *pilot* instead.

Make appropriate references to ethnic groups. To show respect, carefully consider the noun or phrase that members of an ethnic group prefer when referring to that group. Sometimes different members of an ethnic group use more than one term to refer to themselves—for example, *Latino/Latina* and *Chicano/Chicana.* If you are uncertain about which term to use in such a case, ask friends or classmates who are members of that group which name they prefer. If you are communicating with a person who indicates which term he or she prefers, it is important to honor that person's request.

When ethnicity is relevant to the point you are making, be sure to refer to ethnic groups correctly. Not all persons from Laos are Hmong. A visiting professor from Nigeria is not African American. When a language uses different masculine and feminine forms, pay attention to those forms. For example, author Ana Castillo is a Chican*a*, not a Chican*o*.

Avoid unnecessary references to ethnicity, religion, gender, or sexuality. When a person's ethnicity, religion, gender, or sexuality is not relevant to a point you are making, there's no need to mention it when referring to that person. If you say "the *Chinese American* judge," "the *Jewish* baseball player," "the *male* first grade teacher," or "the *lesbian* CEO," listeners may believe that you find it odd for people with those backgrounds to do that job. On the other hand, if you were discussing the history of baseball great Jackie Robinson, it would probably be appropriate to refer to his African American heritage. When Robinson joined the Brooklyn Dodgers in 1947 and became the first African American to play in the major leagues in the modern era, he was subjected to many forms of racism. His enduring legacy stems as much from his experiences as an African American as it does from his talent as a ballplayer. In this case, it would be relevant to acknowledge his race during your speech.

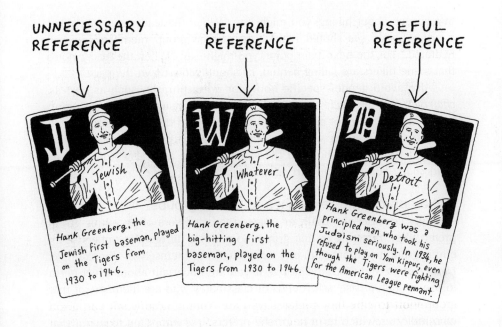

UNNECESSARY REFERENCE

Hank Greenberg, the Jewish first baseman, played on the Tigers from 1930 to 1946.

NEUTRAL REFERENCE

Hank Greenberg, the big-hitting first baseman, played on the Tigers from 1930 to 1946.

USEFUL REFERENCE

Hank Greenberg was a principled man who took his Judaism seriously. In 1934, he refused to play on Yom Kippur, even though the Tigers were fighting for the American League pennant.

Appropriate language and political correctness. The distinction between appropriate language and politically correct speech can make it even more difficult to know exactly how communicators should avoid bias. The rationale for using appropriate language is that biased words can cause great pain, particularly when somebody's identity is threatened.

On the other hand, some critics have argued that efforts to encourage appropriate language have gone too far. These critics claim that principles of appropriate language limit other people's freedom of expression by establishing strict standards of *political correctness*—social expectations that language must reflect a politically and socially liberal view.

The best way to avoid the debate over appropriate language and political correctness entirely is to be certain that you can substantiate any claim you make with sound evidence and reasoning. Otherwise, those who hear you are likely to perceive you as prejudiced. Saying something like "We all know that the Americans with Disabilities Act puts an unfair burden on employers" would instantly reveal a bias and lack of thought about this issue. To rationally discuss the effects of this act on businesses, you would need to have sound evidence and examples to back up any claims you were making.

APPROPRIATE LANGUAGE

Make Your Responses Respectful

In addition to carefully considering your word choice when you are a message source, it is important to be a good receiver. This requires both a serious effort to understand what other people are trying to express through their verbal messages and respect for the perspectives that are being expressed (even if you disagree).

Work for accurate understanding. In this chapter, we have noted that verbal communication can easily result in misunderstanding. This occurs because meanings are in people, not in words. Thus, when communicating with others, it is important to work to ensure that you understand the meaning that they are trying to express. Effective listening (the subject of Chapter 5) is a starting point for this effort.

Once you have heard (or read) a message, decode it with care. Humans are not experts in reading the minds of others. You should not assume that you know what another person is trying to say. For many people, it is natural to react defensively when confronted with words that may threaten their self-concept. If a friend in your carpool says, "You got us to school very quickly today," your first thought might be, "She is criticizing my driving by implying that most days I am slow." If you take that as her intended meaning, a frosty conversation may easily result. In a similar manner to perception checking (Chapter 2), it is a better idea to discuss the issue with your friend. You might simply ask, "Do you think that I drive too slowly on some days?" If your friend was not trying to be critical (perhaps she had hoped to speak with her instructor before class and was simply happy to arrive at school early), then you do not have an issue. If your friend does have a concern about your driving, then you can now try to resolve the issue in a friendly manner.

Respond with respect. It is also necessary to recognize that we will not always agree with people when we interact. When there is disagreement, it is important to treat others' viewpoints with respect. It is appropriate to express your differing perspective and to explain in candid terms why you do not agree. However, when these differences are expressed as a personal attack, productive communication is unlikely. Suppose group members or coworkers have a scheduling conflict. If one member tells another, "You are always trying to get out of doing your fair share," a hostile response is likely, and the group will be pulled away from resolving the issue. By remaining focused on the issue—how to resolve the scheduling problem in an equitable way—the group is more likely to find a solution.

Take ownership of your feelings. You control your response to the words of others. If you feel that another person's language shows disrespect or a disregard for your feelings, it is tempting to use "you make me feel" language in response. For example, if a partner has criticized you for devoting too little attention to your relationship, you might respond, "You always make me feel so inadequate when

RESPOND WITH RESPECT

you criticize me." That statement is almost certainly inaccurate. Your partner's language did not cause you to feel inadequate; you decided to let those words affect your self-concept. It is more honest and more productive to say, "I feel inadequate when you criticize me."

CHAPTER REVIEW

Fernando and Robert's story at the beginning of this chapter illustrates a key feature of verbal communication: at many times in our lives, we need to find just the right words to use when interacting with others. Verbal communication is the exchange of messages using language.

We covered several key features of language—it is rule based, it is symbolic (the words we use to express ideas are arbitrary), it is literal and figurative, it is dynamic (ever-changing), and it is contextual. Meanings are in people, not in words; thus, the words one person uses to express an idea may be understood differently by the receiver(s) of the message. Because of these factors, it can be a challenge to achieve shared meaning when using words to communicate with others.

Language is a powerful means of communication. We use it to share information, influence others, express our feelings, imagine, and accomplish actions. When used effectively, language can achieve great things in our own lives and in society. However, language also has the power to hurt. Biased or inflammatory language can seriously harm the targets of these words and create barriers to productive communication and productive relationships.

There are several guidelines you can follow to communicate verbally in an effective and ethical manner. These include making your message clear when you are communicating, making your message considerate of others, and making your responses to the ideas of other people in a respectful manner.

LaunchPad
macmillan learning

LaunchPad for *Let's Communicate* offers videos and encourages self-assessment through adaptive quizzing. Go to **launchpadworks.com** to get access to:

 LearningCurve Adaptive Quizzes

 Video clips that help you understand human communication

Key Terms

verbal communication 68
language 68
semantic rules 69
syntactic rules 70
pragmatic rules 70
symbols 70
denotative meaning 72
connotative meaning 72
borrowing 73
context dependent 74
ambiguous (words) 74
abstract words 78

concrete words 78
jargon 79
improper word choice 80
equivocal language 80
persuasion 82
biased language 85
immutable characteristics 86
hate speech 86
flooding 88
concise language 90
verbal clutter 90
gender-neutral term 92

Review Questions

1. Define *verbal communication* and *language*.
2. Explain the five key principles of language.
3. Why is language an imperfect vehicle for understanding?
4. List four factors of verbal communication that can lead to misunderstanding.
5. Name five primary uses of language.
6. Define *biased language* and *hate speech*.
7. What are three guidelines for improving your own verbal communication?

Critical Thinking Questions

1. Make a list of some of the phrases and words that you believe are unique to your family or friends. Then try saying them to someone who is not a part of your family or friendship group. Were they understood? Explain why you think they were or were not.
2. Think of a time when you tried to talk with another person about a problem or concern and your discussion did not go well. How could you have changed the words you used to make your conversation more productive?
3. Briefly review Chapter 2 on perception. How is forming a perception of others similar to understanding a verbal message? In what ways are these two processes different?
4. Take a look at the last three text message conversations you've had. Using some of the key terms in the chapter, describe the verbal communication that was used. For example, were the denotative and connotative meanings of the messages understood? Did you use more concrete or abstract words? Was jargon used? Were any terms equivocal?
5. How do you think communication would change if everyone could speak a common second language? Would it improve? What barriers (if any) to successful verbal communication might remain?

Activities

1. As a group, look up five words that have been added to the dictionary in the past three years. Have any of your group members ever used

these words? Does each word enable more efficient or more accurate communication? Explain.

2. Get together in small groups. Each member should write down his or her favorite color without showing the other group members. Take a few minutes to look up how to say the color in two or three different languages. Share your favorite color with your group members in the other languages, and see if they can guess what it is. Finally, discuss the similarities and differences between the words.

3. Make a list of at least three phrases that you remember your parents, grandparents, or primary caregivers saying as you were growing up. Write down the denotative and connotative meanings of the phrases. Do you say any of these phrases now? Explain why or why not.

4. Modify the job description below. Rewrite each reference to the successful candidate in a gender-neutral manner, and correct any improper word choices, jargon, and abstract words. Compare your revised job description with that of a classmate.

STORE MANAGER

- She must have a degree in business or management; it is preferred that her college minor be a good one.
- She must have many years of experience in a management position; it is preferred that she has worked somewhere nice.
- She must have an ability to work well with a diverse work-force and customer base in order to move the needle and complement our team.
- She must demonstrate good written and oral communication skills.
- She must be able to be a part of the swim lane of our team.
- Her letters of recommendation must have been written recently, and she should be able to start work soon.

Apply Your Skills

Review the illustration "Flooding (via *August: Osage County*)" on page 89, which provides an example of how flooding can occur during an interpersonal exchange. Think of a time when you experienced flooding. Did you experience any of the symptoms depicted in the illustration or any other symptoms of stress? Review the "Guidelines for Verbal Communication" section in this chapter (pp. 88–97). Could any of these guidelines have made the interaction less stressful?

Study Plan

_____

_____

_____

_____

_____

_____

_____

_____

_____

_____

_____

_____

DANIEL DAY-LEWIS AS ABRAHAM LINCOLN IN *LINCOLN*

DANIEL DAY-LEWIS AS JOHN PROCTOR IN *THE CRUCIBLE*

DANIEL DAY-LEWIS AS CHRISTY BROWN IN *MY LEFT FOOT*

NONVERBAL COMMUNICATION 4

Daniel Day-Lewis spent a year studying the life and behavior of Abraham Lincoln for his role in the movie *Lincoln*. Even when he wasn't filming, he spent a lot of time practicing Lincoln's high-pitched voice and vocal intonation, or paralanguage. This wasn't the first time Day-Lewis had immersed himself in an acting role; he believes that imitating the nonverbal behavior of a character may be even more important than learning the script for his movies.

Day-Lewis is a method actor, which means that he plays new roles best when he learns how to talk and move like the character he is portraying—to the extent that he actually feels like he *is* the character. For example, he didn't take a shower during the entire filming of *The Crucible*![1] He wanted to feel (and smell) what it was like to be a seventeenth-century farmer. A *New York Times* article reports that he refused to leave his wheelchair and insisted on being fed by the film crew when he played a man with cerebral palsy in *My Left Foot*.[2] The crew even had to carry him to places on the set that weren't wheelchair accessible.

Day-Lewis has won an Oscar for best actor three times, making him one of the world's most recognized actors. The months, and even years, spent studying for different acting roles has paid off, even though he is usually exhausted after filming is over—so much so that since the filming of *Lincoln*, he has reportedly taken off five years from acting to live on a farm.[3] Day-Lewis's method acting shows just how important nonverbal behavior is when communicating. Audience members believe Day-Lewis's characters are based on how well he becomes those characters. Similarly, people believe the messages of others based not only on what they say but also on their nonverbal messages.

Nonverbal communication refers to any type of communication besides the words themselves. In other words, nonverbal communication is *how* you communicate a message, not what you actually say. In an early study, nonverbal communication scholar Albert Mehrabian found that tone and facial expression represented 93 percent of the message when people were communicating about feelings.[4] While researchers argue about the exact percentage, most agree that at least two-thirds of messages are communicated nonverbally. This means that every message you send is influenced much more by your nonverbal communication than the words you speak.

This chapter addresses the importance of nonverbal communication. We discuss how culture, gender, and technology influence nonverbal communication, as well as its different functions and types. At the end of the chapter, we offer suggestions for improving nonverbal behaviors so that you can become a more effective communicator—in this case, making your nonverbal behavior support your verbal message.

INFLUENCES ON NONVERBAL COMMUNICATION

Many things can influence how you understand or misunderstand a nonverbal message. In this section, we discuss three primary influences: cultural, gender, and technology. Each of these affects how you both interpret and send nonverbal messages.

Culture

In previous chapters, we've discussed how culture affects communication. The term *culture* is often used to describe racial and ethnic groups, but it can include different religious and regional groups as well. (See Chapter 8 for more information about communication and culture.) Culture plays a strong role in how we send and receive both verbal and nonverbal messages. In general, cultural groups exhibit similar behaviors and have similar beliefs, but it is important to recognize the diversity within these groups and avoid making generalizations and assumptions about nonverbal (or even verbal) behaviors.

While some nonverbal behaviors are **cross-cultural**, meaning they exist in more than one culture, there are others specific to particular cultural groups. For example, crying is generally regarded as a cross-cultural nonverbal behavior representing sadness. In news coverage of a tragic event, those being interviewed are often sad and weeping, regardless of their physical location in the world. Similarly, people attending a funeral will often cry out of grief.

However, nonverbal behaviors at funerals can differ based on culture. In the United States, for instance, it is common to wear black to funerals to symbolize sadness and grief. By contrast, Hindus wear white to funerals because to them it represents purity and spirituality, which are especially important at a funeral. If you were to wear black to a Hindu funeral, it would be considered offensive.

It's important to use care when interpreting the nonverbal behaviors of others, no matter where you are in the world. We should also understand that our own nonverbal behaviors are not always cross-cultural.

INFLUENCE ON NONVERBAL COMMUNICATION: CULTURE

As a matter of fact, many of the nonverbal behaviors that we take for granted may be interpreted differently by those from cultures other than our own. In the next section, we discuss how gender, another aspect of culture, affects nonverbal communication.

Gender

Gender is another significant cultural influence on nonverbal communication. We often think of gender as simply "male" and "female" or "man" and "woman." But as we discussed in previous chapters, gender is fluid. Though there are men who exhibit masculine behaviors and women who exhibit feminine behaviors, both males and females have the ability to exhibit the behaviors typically associated with the other gender. (See Chapter 8 for more information on communication and gender.)

These same behaviors affect nonverbal communication. For example, researchers have found that traditionally feminine behaviors place greater emphasis on empathy, affection, and closeness.[5] Thus, when engaged in conversation, women tend to sit or stand closer to each other than men do. Women hug each other, smile more, and often take up less space than men by crossing their legs and arms.[6] Two female friends may greet each other with a hug and a kiss, whereas two male friends may greet each other with a fist bump or a slap on the back. This is because masculine behaviors emphasize competition and toughness. Men are also expected to cry less than women, and when sitting and standing, men take up more space than women by widening the stance of their legs.[7]

Males and females are often ostracized (or worse) if they engage in nonverbal behaviors that run contrary to gender norms. In 2014, two transgender women in Atlanta were harassed and assaulted on a subway because of the way they were dressed.[8] According to the women, two male passengers began taking pictures of them with their cell phones, asking them if they were men or women. The women asked the men to stop taking pictures. The men then attempted to violently undress the women. No passengers intervened, though cell-phone footage of the incident has appeared on social media. The men were later arrested and charged with assault.

The women defied nonverbal expectations of what it means to be a man and what it means to be a woman based on their physical appearance. As a result, they were physically assaulted. This horrific event points to a much broader national and international problem: gendered expectations

TRADITIONALLY "GENDERED" BEHAVIORS CAN BE FLUID

of nonverbal behaviors are often steeped in prejudice and tradition. A number of organizations are fighting against these types of acts, including the National Organization for Women (NOW),[9] Equality Now,[10] and the National Center for Transgender Equality.[11]

Technology

In addition to culture and gender, technology influences nonverbal communication. **Computer-mediated communication**, or CMC, refers to communication that occurs using electronic devices, including computers, tablets, cell phones, and smartphones. With the increase of how much we rely on CMC, it is important to note its impact on nonverbal messages. Have you ever sent a friend a text message that was misinterpreted? There may have been a misspelled word or an accidental autocorrect, or you may have forgotten to add "lol." It's easy to misinterpret an e-mail or a text message because it's challenging to include nonverbal messages in your communication.

However, there are ways you can try to replicate nonverbal communication when using technology. You might use ALL CAPS to show the importance of your message (or yell) or include various emoticons to show that you are angry or laughing. Similarly, if you were sending a text message, you might add "!!!!!!!!" or "☺" to supplement the words you communicate.

INFLUENCE ON NONVERBAL
COMMUNICATION: TECHNOLOGY

Though messages can still be easily misinterpreted when using technology, companies are taking note. In 2014, the Huffington Post reported that more than 250 new emojis, or pictures one can send via text, were released by the Unicode Consortium to be used in text messages and e-mails. These include a left writing hand, a middle finger, and even a spider-web.[12] Imagine using the spiderweb emoji to indicate that you're feeling tied up, ill, or bothered. Nowadays, users—particularly teenagers—are even combining two or three emojis to send messages with no words at all included in the content.[13]

These three influences on nonverbal communication—culture, gender, and technology—frame our understanding of nonverbal communication. As we discuss the different types of nonverbal communication later in the chapter, we will include additional examples of communication behaviors based on these three influences. Next, let's explore the different functions fulfilled by our nonverbal communication.

FUNCTIONS OF NONVERBAL COMMUNICATION

Can your friends tell what kind of mood you're in without you saying a word? This is because your nonverbal behaviors function in a variety of ways. A purposeful smile can supplement a message, just as a glare can substitute for a message. Even though up to two-thirds of a received message is based on nonverbal behavior, this behavior is not always easy to notice. In this section, we discuss the different functions of nonverbal communication, which will help explain how and why we use it. After reading through this section, you should be able to note the specific functions being acted out by your classmates, friends, and family members.

Supplementing

Nonverbal communication **supplements** verbal communication, meaning that it adds to or enhances the words you speak or write.[14] For

example, imagine that you're meeting up with a friend to get coffee after your math class. If you just received an A on your midterm, you might say to your friend, "I got an A!" Most likely, your words would be accompanied by nonverbal communication that showed just how happy you are. You might smile, laugh, hug your friend, or even jump for joy. Even if you just mentioned this to your friend on the phone, he or she could probably hear the excitement in your voice.

If you failed the exam, however, your admission to your friend would be much different. Your voice might sound sadder. You might mumble, "I failed," or perhaps barely get the words out. Your eye contact with your friend would probably suffer, and you might avoid his or her face by looking at the ground or rolling your eyes. You might even shrug to show that you are giving up. In these ways, your nonverbal behaviors are supporting, or supplementing, your verbal communication.

Repeating

In addition to supplementing, it is possible to **repeat** verbal messages with your nonverbal messages.[15] For example, if you place your finger over your lips and say, "Shh, be quiet!" to the person next to you in a movie theater, your message is being repeated. Similarly, saying, "I don't know" and shrugging your shoulders repeats the message that you are unsure. When nonverbal behaviors repeat verbal messages, the message is emphasized and is more likely to be believed by the person receiving the communication, since the same content is being presented in two different ways.

Contradicting

Nonverbal messages also have the ability to **contradict** verbal messages.[16] Consider Ellen, who is giving her friend Jazmine directions to the auto supply store. "Once you leave the apartment complex, take a *left* onto Girard Avenue," Ellen stated, making big gestures to the *right* side of the room. "The store will be two blocks down, on the right side of the road." After Jazmine got in her car and drove out of the apartment complex, do you think she turned left or right?

Interestingly, most of us would probably turn right (if we didn't have the ability to look up the directions on our smartphones). This occurs because nonverbal communication tends to have a greater influence on how we understand messages than does verbal communication. Although Ellen told Jazmine to turn left, she gestured to her right. When nonverbal and verbal messages contradict, people tend to believe the nonverbal messages.

Have you ever had a bad day but tried to smile anyway? Sometimes this is difficult to do without someone knowing that you're feeling a bit down—especially someone who knows you well. Even if you say, "I'm OK. Everything is fine," your nonverbal behaviors—such as a disingenuous smile, sad eyes, or slouched shoulders—can show that you're not actually fine. Nonverbal behaviors are harder to regulate than are verbal behaviors; thus, they often reveal how people truly feel.

Regulating

Nonverbal communication can also **regulate** verbal behaviors.[17] Nonverbal messages can indicate a person's desire to continue or stop a conversation. Imagine speaking to a friend when you are in a rush to get to class. Besides saying "I have to get going," you might begin to make less eye contact, check the time on your phone, or physically move away from the person, indicating that you are no longer interested in the conversation and that it should end soon. Many other types of nonverbal communication are used to regulate conversations, including touch, pointing, and even hand gestures. If you're debating where to go for lunch with a classmate, you might point or gesture toward the person after you've offered your suggestions—indicating that it's his or her turn to talk.

Your instructors probably use a lot of nonverbal communication to regulate their messages. Watch the interaction in the classroom the next time one of your instructors asks a question. If several students raise their hands, your instructor may turn his or her body toward one student and gesture or look in that direction, indicating that the student may answer. When the student has answered the question, the instructor may turn toward another student who has her hand up and make eye contact with her, showing that it is now her opportunity to answer the question. Nonverbal behaviors like eye contact and body movement are imperative for regulating conversations.

REGULATING

Substituting

On some occasions, nonverbal communication can **substitute** for verbal communication.[18] During these times, there are no verbal messages, just nonverbal messages. In a movie theater, you might wave to your late-arriving friend to indicate where you are sitting. Or you might look across the room and smile at a classmate whom you have a crush on to show your interest. These behaviors substitute for verbal messages, meaning that they are the messages themselves. Many nonverbal behaviors—such as waving hello, blowing a kiss, shrugging your shoulders, and even giving someone the middle finger—can substitute for verbal communication.

Accenting

Nonverbal communication can also **accent** verbal communication.[19] Accenting is different from supplementing because accenting highlights one portion or word of a message. Let's say that you are uncertain of your partner's commitment to your relationship. He responds with, "I love you," and points to you. The pointing of his finger highlights "you" and is his attempt to show you that it is *you* whom he loves. Accenting verbal messages places emphasis on a particular part of the words that are spoken. Accenting can be done by employing a variety of nonverbal messages, such as changing the intonation of your voice or leaning forward in a conversation.

ACCENTING

As you can see, nonverbal communication is powerful. With it, you can supplement, repeat, contradict, regulate, substitute, and accent verbal communication. Note that it is possible for nonverbal communication to function in more than one category at a time (for example, your message could both regulate and substitute a nonverbal message). Your challenge is to use this information to look at the interactions occurring around you and try to identify the different functions of nonverbal communication.

TYPES OF NONVERBAL COMMUNICATION

Now that we've discussed the functions of nonverbal communication, let's focus on the types of nonverbal communication. Suppose you have an interview tomorrow for an internship. The clothes you wear, the handshake you give, and even your cologne or perfume are all types of nonverbal communication that will play a role in how you are perceived by the organization. Though we may pay attention to some types more than others (falsely believing that there are only two or three), there are actually many types of nonverbal communication. In this section, we discuss body movement, facial expressions, eye contact, touch, space, physical appearance, vocal intonation, smell, and time.

Kinesics

Kinesics is another term for the study of body language. It includes hand movements, body shape, and even how you walk. Have you ever recognized a friend from far away based on how he was walking or by the movement of her hands? That's because nonverbal communication has a personal element to it, meaning that each person uses unique body movements. You may even notice that family members exhibit similar body movements. A father and son may have a similar walk, or two siblings may make the same facial expression when laughing. Some people say that couples who have been together for a long time even begin to exhibit similar body language.[20]

We use our bodies to communicate messages to others. Before we even learn to talk, we learn to use body movement to communicate. For example, studies have found that babies often use their hands and fingers to point to what they want before they can actually say the words.[21] As we grow older, we learn to use our body to communicate more complex messages. For example, to emphasize a point, you might lean your body

COUPLES THAT HAVE BEEN TOGETHER FOR A LONG TIME EXHIBIT SIMILAR BODY LANGUAGE

1966   2016

closer to the person you are speaking with. Or to show disdain, you might turn your body away from the other person. To show that you're interested in a job, you give a firm handshake at the beginning and end of the interview. According to researchers, firm handshakes are a cross-cultural behavior that represents honesty, especially when negotiating with a person from a different culture.[22]

Facial Expressions

In addition to body movement, **facial expressions** are one type of nonverbal communication that people notice immediately. The face has forty-three muscles, so it has the capacity to portray a large number of expressions. A smile can show happiness, a frown can show sadness, and a furrowed eyebrow can show anger. Facial expressions have the power to show what you really feel, even if words contradict them. This is why, during negotiations, Ethiopians prefer face-to-face meetings—so that they can discern the subtle facial expressions that would not be noticed in a phone or an e-mail conversation.[23]

Based on your facial expression, others are making character judgments about you, even if you think you're being pretty neutral. In 2013, Taylor Orci created a video spoof that claimed that people often think she is angry because she has a mean resting face, meaning that her normal facial expression makes her look upset or hostile.[24] The idea has since gone viral, and others—including a number of celebrities—began making the same claim. It goes to show that we must be careful when attempting to discern the meaning of others' facial expressions.

Oculesics

The study of eye contact, or **oculesics**, refers to a form of nonverbal communication that is sometimes overlooked. Yet think of all the emotions you can portray with your eyes. To illustrate this point, take a picture of only your eyes showing each of the following expressions: happiness, sadness, anger, and surprise. Then, show the pictures to a friend and see if he or she can guess which expression portrays each emotion. Chances are, your friend will get most of them correct. That's because the emotions you portray with your eyes are more difficult to control than even your facial expressions. With just your eyes, you can flirt, start a fight, show disinterest, or look annoyed.

In the United States, direct eye contact is usually appropriate. A person who lacks eye contact is seen as shy or even untrustworthy. For a job interview, experts stress the importance of making eye contact with the interviewer to demonstrate confidence and honesty. Similarly, public speakers are judged as being more competent when they make eye contact with their audience.[25] Eye contact is so important that it's taught to certain populations in order to help improve confidence, including adults who stutter and children with autism.[26]

OCULESICS

HAPPINESS

SADNESS

ANGER

SURPRISE

FLIRTING

FIGHTING

BORED

ANNOYED

Outside the United States, making direct eye contact with another person can be viewed as disrespectful or even insubordinate. Ethiopians, for example, don't make much eye contact when engaged in business.[27] Researchers have found that Japanese make very little eye contact with superiors, including bosses, elders, and teachers, though they will make more eye contact with their friends.[28] Thus, we see that just as important as eye contact is the ability to avert your gaze.

Haptics

The study of touch—another type of nonverbal communication—is often referred to as **haptics**. Through touch, you can show affection and sexual interest. In one study, researchers found that among heterosexual couples, men initiate touch more during courtship, whereas women initiate touch more during marriage.[29] In addition to affection, touch has the power to heal. Scientists believe that touch is instrumental in helping premature babies develop.[30] Touch can also serve as a source of comfort for nursing home residents.[31]

But just as touch has the power to heal, it also has the power to hurt. Physical violence is a type of haptics that is harmful. In an earlier example, we discussed the transgender women who were assaulted in Atlanta. Similarly, domestic violence and elder abuse are both examples of the power touch has to harm.

Touch also demonstrates the type of relationship we have with each other. For example, if you greet someone with an extended kiss on the lips, it will be assumed that you two are partners. If you high-five someone, perhaps it's because you're on the same team. If you pick someone up at the airport and greet him with a long hug, it means that you probably haven't seen him for a long time and missed him. Just as with the other types of nonverbal communication, we must be aware of how we touch others.

Proxemics

Did you know that men take up more space than women do? This refers not just to body size but also to personal space. Women cross their legs and arms more often than men do, particularly in public spaces. The study of space, or **proxemics**, looks at a type of nonverbal behavior that is significantly impacted by gender as well as culture.

Nonverbal behavior scholar Edward T. Hall coined four levels of distance that are used in the United States: intimate (0 inches to 18 inches), personal (18 inches to 4 feet), social (4 feet to 12 feet), and formal (12 feet or more).[32] A couple in love might stand mere inches apart, or a person might attempt to intimidate an enemy by standing very close to him, representing what Hall refers to as intimate distance. Good friends might sit next to each other on the subway or in a movie theater, portraying Hall's classification of personal distance. In the United States, people enjoy their space so much that scholars can accurately predict which seat at a table, urinal in a restroom, and space in an elevator will be chosen first.[33] This is because people usually want as much social distance as possible.[34] Formal space can be seen when a public figure is giving a speech from behind a podium to a large audience.

Of course, these distances change as the context changes. Two angry group members might sit as far apart as possible while still remaining in a group meeting. The immediate context of a situation affects the expectation of personal distance as well. You would expect to sit very close to a fellow football fan at an NFL playoff game. A rush-hour subway ride in New York City might result in strangers sitting so close that they're touching.

Conversely, some countries have little expectation of large personal space. In São Paulo, Brazil, there is an expectancy of closeness.[35] In Cairo, Egypt, strangers may brush against each other in passing without saying "excuse me" or acknowledging the closeness.[36] Take the bus in Jamaica or India and you'll notice that passengers squeeze next to each other to fit. This is because culturally, individuals in both countries expect closer human interaction than do people in the United States.

THE POETICS OF SPACE (AKA PROXEMICS)

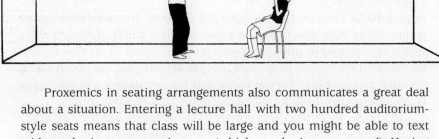

Proxemics in seating arrangements also communicates a great deal about a situation. Entering a lecture hall with two hundred auditorium-style seats means that class will be large and you might be able to text without the instructor seeing you (which we don't recommend). Having dinner at a friend's house where the parents sit at separate ends of a long dining-room table may mean that the family is formal or traditional. In a conference room, the person sitting at the head of the table during a meeting is expected to take the lead, so take care with your seat choice the next time you attend a group meeting.

Physical Appearance

Physical appearance is a form of nonverbal communication in which the harshest judgments are made. Physical appearance includes the colors and clothing we wear, our choice of hairstyle, and the **artifacts**—like tattoos and nose rings—we decorate our bodies with to help define ourselves. From appearance, we make judgments about peoples' gender, race, class, sexuality, education, occupation, religion, and personality. For example, you might assume that a woman in exercise attire likes to work out. Or you might guess that a man with unwashed hair and tattered clothes is homeless.

Yet many times the judgments we make are unfair and incorrect. Student evaluations show that female professors are judged on their attire more than are their male counterparts.[37] African American females who wear their hair in its natural state are often encouraged to chemically straighten their hair in order to get a good job.[38] Many companies even have policies that limit men from having facial hair.

Obviously, physical appearance is a cultural phenomenon, meaning that it is influenced by one's culture. In the United States and abroad, there are varying cultural norms related to religious expression. You may notice some Muslim women wearing a hijab, or headscarf. A Jewish male may wear a yarmulke, or skullcap. A Christian girl may wear a cross on a chain around her neck. In essence, what you wear gives insight into various layers of your culture.

Paralanguage

Paralanguage is slightly different from the other types of nonverbal communication we've discussed. It's not a movement of the body or a look; rather, **paralanguage** refers to the tone, pitch, accent, and volume of your voice, and the study of it is referred to as **paralinguistics**. In Chapter 3, we noted that verbal communication refers to the exchange of messages using language. Paralanguage does not include the *what* of the message, as in verbal communication; instead, it refers to *how* the words are actually said.

Females typically have higher-pitched voices than males, yet females with lower pitches are usually seen as confident, whereas males with higher pitches tend to be viewed as weak. The tone of a person's words

can display seriousness, humor, anger, and excitement. To ask a question, it is standard practice to use a higher tone at the end of the sentence. However, research has shown that although females have traditionally used higher tones at the end of sentences, a new type of speech is emerging called vocal fry.[39] Vocal fry became popular with the Kardashians and other female celebrities and is characterized by a lower pitch at the end of a sentence, along with a creaky, laryngitis-like quality.[40]

You are likely to change your voice depending on your mood and your relationship to the person with whom you are speaking. People around you can understand the change in your voice, too. For example, a study found that strangers could determine if a person was talking to a friend or a romantic partner based only on the intonation of his or her voice.[41] Interestingly, vocal change occurs among Tanzanians when conducting business negotiations, during which they speak very loudly, even cutting each other off.[42]

Smell (Olfactics)

One of the more understudied forms of nonverbal communication is that of smell, referred to as **olfactics**. Smell has the ability to both attract and disgust us, and it also influences our assumptions about others' personalities. Cologne, for example, is intended to make a man smell good. You may assess a man wearing a cologne favorably or unfavorably depending on whether you like the smell—and how strong it is. Olfactics goes beyond products, too. One study found that people could correctly assess anxiety, depression, nervousness, and instability based on a person's scent.[43]

In the United States, men and women take great care with their personal hygiene in an effort to display confidence and likability.

Names of men's scents tend to include words that portray strength and toughness, such as "Cool Rustic," "Forest," "Mountain Spring," and "Black Thunder." Women's scent names tend to be more delicate: "Baby Powder," "Cucumber Melon," "Fresh Orchid," and "Sexy Amber." In general, men and women are expected to smell clean and fragrant. To accomplish this, people in the United States normally take showers at least once a day, brush their teeth twice a day, and wear freshly washed clothes.

Other countries, however, think people in the United States care too much about personal hygiene. One guide given to immigrants and new U.S. citizens says that people living in the United States are overly concerned with smell.[44] The guide includes such examples as showering every day, wearing deodorant, and using cologne and perfume. Although these types of activities may seem normal to those living in the United States, to others, they are a waste of money, water, and time.

Chronemics

The last type of nonverbal communication we will discuss is **chrone-mics**, or the study of time. In the United States, we tend to have a high concern for time because we are a monochronic culture. Edward T. Hall defines **monochronic** as doing one task at a time.[45] In practice, this focus on time expresses itself as careful scheduling and time management. For example, if you have a doctor's appointment at 12:45 p.m., you would make sure to arrive a few minutes early so that you don't miss your time slot. If you never arrive on time to your 10:00 a.m. class, your teacher will make a note of it. If you're meeting a friend at a restaurant and you're going to arrive late, you will most likely text your friend to let her know. Time is especially important when considering Internet communication and cell phones. People expect others to respond to their e-mails within twenty-four hours—and even less for their text messages.[46]

Yet many cultures have a much looser expectation of time and prefer to do several tasks at once. These are considered **polychronic** cultures. Barbadians, Liberians, and Italians, for example, prefer relationships to timeliness. So if you were in Italy and were on your way to your 2:30 p.m. business meeting but were stopped by a friend for a chat, it would be acceptable to arrive late. That's because in Italy, spending time talking with a friend is typically considered more important than business.

CHRONEMICS

In this section, we covered many types of nonverbal communication: kinesics, facial expressions, oculesics, haptics, proxemics, physical appearance, paralinguistics, olfactics, and chronemics. It's no wonder that nonverbal communication accounts for at least two-thirds of the messages we send. In the next section, we discuss another important influence on nonverbal communication: technology.

TECHNOLOGY AND ITS IMPACT ON NONVERBAL COMMUNICATION

As suggested earlier, it's more challenging to communicate nonverbal messages using computer-mediated technology, but it is possible. The most common forms of CMC are e-mail and texting, though there are other forms, such as instant messaging. With the absence of certain types of nonverbal communication in CMC, such as kinesics, facial expressions, haptics, paralinguistics, and olfactics, researchers have studied how nonverbal communication can still function across various technological platforms—with fascinating results.

With CMC, there are greater expectations of immediacy and response. Love him or hate him, LeBron James has millions of followers on Twitter and Instagram, resulting in fans and foes feeling as if they know the "real" LeBron. The sense of immediacy increases because communication is potentially occurring two ways: LeBron posts comments or pictures, and you can comment or "like" the pictures. With technology, the public and personal space (or proxemics) that we discussed earlier diminishes with celebrities, as well as with our friends, family, and acquaintances. As a result, our expectations of time change. We want and expect faster responses to e-mail and text messages. While we are waiting, time often seems to move more slowly than normal. Something to keep in mind is that we don't always know what the other person is doing at the time; thus, they might be unavailable—driving, in class, sleeping, and so on.

Consider Jermaine, who has a crush on Nicole, a woman he met in one of his general elective classes. The two had known each other for three weeks and had even studied for their first test together. Though Jermaine had Nicole's phone number, it took some time for him to muster the courage to ask her for a date. After much contemplation, he texted her: "Hey! Got dinner plans? I'd love to take you out. ☺" His hands were a little clammy, but he hit "send" anyway.

Two hours later, Jermaine still hadn't received a response. "I shouldn't have added the smiley face at the end," he told himself. "She's probably not interested in me at all. Or maybe I waited too long to ask her out." Seconds later, Nicole responded, "Sure! Sorry for the late reply, just got outta class. What time? I'm free after 6." Jermaine smiled and breathed a sigh of relief. Those two hours had felt like an eternity.

The use of technology also allows us to be creative when supplementing, repeating, substituting, and accenting nonverbal messages. We mentioned the new emojis that were released in 2014. Before emojis became popular, people used the symbols on their keyboards to create additional meaning. For example, < 3 represents a heart, :) means a smiley face, :-I represents a serious face, and ;P suggests someone winking and sticking a tongue out in mock seriousness. These basic symbols have become so popular that many computer systems automatically turn them into their corresponding symbolic heart or face. Today, there are even apps available that allow people to create emojis that look like them (see Bitmoji). The use of gifs—animated images often taken from movies and television to express emotions—has also become widespread.

However, there are several issues that emerge with the increasing use of emoticons, emojis, and gifs. CMC emoticons are rarely used to

EMOJIS CAN HIDE THE SENDER'S TRUTHFULNESS

regulate conversation, as you would be able to do with face-to-face inter-action. It's also difficult for emoticons and emojis to contradict the actual words used. A study by Dresner and Herring called this a "paradox."[47] The authors state that with face-to-face communication, facial expressions are often unintentional and hint to the emotion of the person (which is why it's sometimes hard to hide sadness or anger through facial expressions). But emoticons are intentional. With emoticons and emojis, the sender of the message determines how he or she wants the receiver to interpret the message. This is also why it's easy to deceive someone using CMC. Receivers don't have the cues that they would normally use to determine the truthfulness of the message through face-to-face interaction.

With the increasing use of technology as a substitute for face-to-face communication, it's especially important to be mindful when sending and interpreting messages. If you are unsure of what a message means or if you think that a message you are sending can be easily misinter-preted, consider calling or meeting with the receiver of your message.

This way, he or she can take note of your nonverbal communication and more accurately decode your message.

GUIDELINES FOR COMMUNICATING NONVERBAL MESSAGES EFFECTIVELY

Though our nonverbal behaviors may become second nature, we shouldn't assume that we are always effective communicators; there is always room for improving how we send nonverbal messages—whether in a public or a private setting. Here are some recommendations for effectively expressing nonverbal messages:

- Avoid interpreting another person's nonverbal messages through your own lens. Remember, culture and gender greatly influence nonverbal communication. As much as possible, try to understand and respect the nonverbal message of the sender.

- Be careful in expressing your own nonverbal messages. You can't undo nonverbal messages once they are communicated. A hurtful look or screaming match will not be easy to forget.

- Do not use nonverbal communication to harm or malign. Nonverbal communication should not be used to mentally, emotionally, or physically provoke another person.

- If you don't understand a nonverbal message, ask the sender to explain. Rather than potentially misunderstanding instructions or a conversation, asking "What do you mean?" provides instant clarification and understanding.

- When preparing to communicate publicly with an audience, spend as much time practicing your nonverbal communication as you do writing the words you intend to say. Your audience will judge the quality of your speech not just on your verbal communication but also on your nonverbal communication, including eye contact, body movement, and the intonation of your voice.

- When using technology to send messages, try to be as clear as possible in your language. In addition, be intentional about your use of emoticons or emojis to clarify or highlight something you are saying with words. If the conversation is especially sensitive, a phone call or a face-to-face conversation may be best, so that the paralanguage, eye contact, and body expressions can be seen and heard.

DON'T INTERPRET NONVERBAL MESSAGES THROUGH YOUR OWN LENS

- Understand that even with practice, there is still the potential for misunderstanding nonverbal communication. Perfect communication is unrealistic. Instead of attempting to *perfect* your nonverbal behaviors, your goal should be to *improve* them.

While there are more specific ways to improve each type of nonverbal communication, these guidelines should aid you in improving your nonverbal skills in any environment.

CHAPTER REVIEW

In this chapter, we defined *nonverbal communication* and discussed its nature, as well as how it is influenced by culture, gender, and technology. Nonverbal communication serves a number of functions that can assist another person in understanding your verbal message. These functions include supplementing, repeating, contradicting, regulating, substituting, and accenting nonverbal messages.

Nonverbal communication can include kinesics, facial expressions, oculesics, haptics, proxemics, physical appearance, paralanguage, olfactics, and chronemics. However, with our increasing use of technology—particularly computer-mediated communication—our use of nonverbal communication has both decreased and changed; thus, we must be thoughtful when creating and interpreting nonverbal messages that are sent using text messages, e-mail, and instant messaging.

Since nonverbal communication plays such a major role in how our messages are understood, improving your own use of nonverbal messages is important. It's also important to be mindful of cultural, gender, and technological influences on the nonverbal messages that you receive. Hopefully, your increased knowledge of nonverbal communication will make you a more effective communicator.

LaunchPad
macmillan learning

LaunchPad for *Let's Communicate* offers videos and encourages self-assessment through adaptive quizzing. Go to **launchpadworks.com** to get access to:

✔ **LearningCurve Adaptive Quizzes**

▶ **Video clips that help you understand human communication**

Key Terms

nonverbal communication 104
cross-cultural 105
computer-mediated
   communication 107
supplement 108
repeat 109
contradict 110
▶ regulate 110
substitute 112
accent 112
▶ kinesics 113
facial expressions 114

oculesics 115
▶ haptics 116
▶ proxemics 117
physical appearance 118
artifact 118
▶ paralanguage 119
paralinguistics 119
olfactics 120
chronemics 121
monochronic 121
polychronic 121

Review Questions

1. Define *nonverbal communication*, and explain the importance of culture in understanding the nonverbal behaviors of others.
2. Explain how CMC can affect nonverbal communication.

3. What are the six functions of nonverbal communication?

4. What is another term for the study of body language? Provide an example of what kinds of nonverbal communication are studied in this area.

5. Name a country where direct eye contact is usually preferred. Name a country where direct eye contact may be viewed as disrespectful.

6. What is the study of space called? Who uses more personal space, men or women?

7. Define *olfactics*, and explain why some countries think the United States may be overly concerned with it.

Critical Thinking Questions

1. There are many functions of nonverbal communication. Can a nonverbal message serve two or more functions? Explain your answer.

2. In the United States, eye contact is preferred in many social situations. What is one situation in which an averted gaze would be appropriate?

3. Describe the four types of distance. Which type of distance— intimate, personal, social, or formal—would be acceptable when meeting your potential boss during an interview?

4. What are some nonverbal messages people send to indicate that their personal space has been violated?

5. In the chapter, *nonverbal communication* is defined as anything except for the words themselves. How would you redefine *nonverbal communication* to make it applicable to the deaf community?

Activities

1. Take an amateur stab at method acting, like Daniel Day-Lewis. Think of a celebrity you are familiar with and attempt to imitate him or her. Write down what changes you made to your nonverbal behaviors.

2. Video-record yourself talking on the phone to a friend or family member for three to five minutes. Once the conversation has ended, review the video, and make note of how you used the various types of nonverbal communication. What did you notice about your own nonverbal communication that you didn't know before?

3. Imagine that you're creating an online dating profile. Since nonverbal communication is reduced in CMC, write down some things that you could do to make yourself more attractive to others on the site. Consider the fact that potential mates who are viewing your profile won't be able to hear your laugh, smell your cologne or perfume, or see your walk.

4. Earlier in the chapter, you were asked to take pictures of your eyes communicating various emotions. Repeat this task, but this time, try to portray more complex emotions with your eyes: confusion, love, flirting, kindness, and impatience. See if your friend can correctly guess the emotions you are portraying.

5. With a friend, practice saying the following phrase: "I love you." Taking turns, each person should emphasize a different word. Write down how each emphasis changes the meaning of the phrase, and explain how paralinguistics affects how you understand the phrase.

Apply Your Skills

Look at the illustration "Emojis Can Hide the Sender's Truthfulness" on page 124. Create your own guidelines for using emojis appropriately. Based on your own experiences, come up with a list of dos and don'ts for using emojis in text messages and in social media. Pair these guidelines with pictures of emojis, if you'd like.

Study Plan

_____

_____

_____

_____

LISTENING SKILLS 5

OBJECTIVES

- Learn how we listen and the different learning styles we use.
- Understand the external and internal challenges that keep us from being effective listeners.
- Identify strategies to become better listeners and to help others listen to us.

Suzanne and Ben met at work, and developed a friendship that eventually became a romance. After only six months of dating, they decided to get married. In a very short time they had come to know each other so well that friends and family members joked that they could read each other's minds.

After only a few months of marriage, however, the couple hit a rough patch in their relationship. They argued constantly—often in front of other people. Ben was increasingly frustrated that Suzanne listened only to as much of whatever he said as was necessary to argue with him. For example, when the two were having a discussion about the bills they jointly owed, Ben said, "These bills haven't been paid yet. Can you write checks tonight for your share of the rent and the power and water bills?" But all that Suzanne focused on, according to Ben, was the first part of the statement: "These bills haven't been paid yet." Suzanne felt like Ben was criticizing her for always being late, instead of recognizing that he was really asking her to be responsible for her half of their expenses.

For her part, Suzanne complained about Ben as well—saying that he possessed an annoying habit of constantly interrupting her and finishing her sentences, instead of just listening to what she was trying to say. The imperfect ways that both Ben and Suzanne listened to each other impacted their willingness to talk—and threatened the quality and longevity of their marriage.

As Suzanne and Ben's story reveals, listening is a vital skill in human communication. Yet there is a significant difference between *listening* and *hearing* what someone else is saying. Anyone who has ever experienced a relationship conflict with a family member or friend may have heard the complaint: "You just don't listen to me!"

If you're not particularly skilled at listening, you're not alone—many people have a similar difficulty. Yet you can learn how to strengthen your listening skills, and this chapter offers helpful guidelines. In the pages that follow, we explore the importance of listening in human communication, the ways in which listening and hearing are different, the dominant listening styles we make use of, the barriers and obstacles to effective listening, and steps you can take to improve your listening skills.

HOW WE LISTEN

Listening plays a key role in multiple aspects of human communication, including how you communicate in school settings; how you communicate in organizations and the workplace; and, most assuredly, in the way you communicate with family, friends, loved ones, and even (or especially) those with whom you experience interpersonal conflict. For example, salespeople who interact with potential customers understand that a needs-based sales strategy depends on being able to listen to what a client or prospective client has to say.[1] Likewise, health-care workers comprehend the significance of listening to their patients when assessing their needs and treating their afflictions.[2] And just as students spend most of their time in class listening to their teachers,[3] so, too, do teachers need to be good listeners for their students.[4]

To understand the significance of listening, we begin by examining the specific differences between listening and hearing.

Listening and Hearing

Listening and hearing are two very different activities, and research affirms the importance of listening—versus merely hearing—in human communication. Several studies have suggested that people can miss virtually all the content of oral messages when they only hear, rather than listen (imagine the droning teacher's voice in Charles Schulz's *Peanuts* cartoons).[5] **Hearing** means merely receiving messages in a passive way. **Listening**, on the other hand, means actively paying attention to what you're hearing; it involves both processing the message to decide on its meaning and retaining what you've heard and understood.

To further explain this distinction, let's briefly consider how both science and communication researchers define *listening* and *hearing*. Cognitive scientists—those who study the mind—consider listening to be a conscious mental process that includes the following components:[6]

- Selection (attention, perception)
- Organization (interpretation)
- Integration (storage recall)

Communication researchers define *listening* in a slightly different manner —with terms that describe it as a step in the communication process:

- Sensing
- Interpreting
- Evaluating
- Responding[7]

Both cognitive scientists and communication researchers agree that hearing is a passive, physical activity: the act of sound waves reverberating against the eardrums, triggering messages that are sent to the brain.[8] Though listening is possible once hearing begins, listening is an altogether more complicated process.[9] Take the acts of watching television versus reading a book. Whereas watching television is a passive activity (like hearing),[10] reading is a learned activity that requires information processing (like listening).[11] Listening can be further broken down into two main aspects: processing and retaining.

Processing what you've heard. When you engage in **processing**, you're actively thinking about a message you're receiving from someone else—not only the words but also the nonverbal cues. For example,

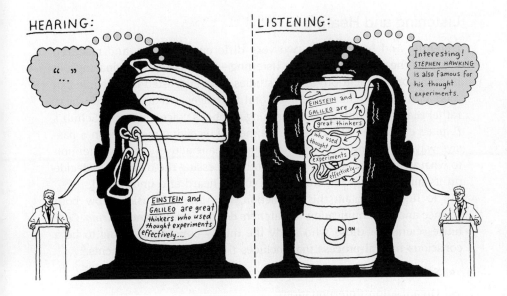

suppose you're a small-business owner who's meeting with Jeff—a salesperson for eLogic, a business-software developer. You want to decide whether eLogic's software for tracking and fulfilling orders is right for your business. As Jeff describes the product, you consider the implications of what he is saying, how using the software will affect your bottom line, and whether Jeff represents a reputable company. You observe his attitude and body language (confident and knowledgeable or nervous and inept?). You may even jot down notes. You then mull over a series of questions: "Can my business afford this investment? Will I need to provide extensive training to help my workers learn the new software? Are there other programs that would deliver similar advantages but are easier and cheaper to use?" By weighing these matters —that is, by processing the information in your mind—you stand a better chance of making a smart decision for your business.

Retaining what you've processed. The more carefully you process what you're hearing, the more you will engage your powers of **retention** —your ability to remember what you've heard. In fact, one of the authors of this textbook joined in a ten-year study of listening patterns and found that poor retention of a speech was directly related to audience attentiveness during the presentation.[12] This study also found that individuals with poor attention habits remembered only a fraction (25 percent or

THE ATTENTIVENESS CURVE

TIME OF SPEECH

less) of what was said in a speech. Worse, what they *could* recall was often inaccurate or confused with something else they had in their heads at the time of the presentation. Among people who fail to process what they're hearing, the ability to accurately recall what was heard decays over just three to six hours after the original communication.

The study also revealed a recurring pattern of attentiveness—called "the Attentiveness Curve"—in people who did not listen well. At the beginning of a presentation, poor listeners tended to pay little attention. However, their attention quickly improved as the presentation continued —perhaps because they realized they *should* have been paying attention —but then just as quickly fell to a very low level, only to rebound near the end of the speech. Clearly, their sporadic levels of attention made it much harder for these listeners to process messages; it is no wonder, then, that they retained very little.

To further see the connection between processing and retention, consider your own listening behavior as a student. How much information do you retain if you pay little attention to your instructors in class? If you take notes during lectures, how accurate are they? How much do you remember from lectures in which you did not process what you were hearing? There's no doubt about it: the more carefully you process messages, the more likely you'll remember what you heard—and retain it accurately.

In the next section, we analyze listening behavior further by examining the different types of listening styles.

Listening Styles

Research over the last several decades has demonstrated that people listen in different ways and that the best listeners often modify or alter their listening behavior depending on the context or situation.[13] In general, however, most people usually default to a specific style out of habit[14] and are reluctant to switch from the style of listening they usually use,[15] even if doing so might make them better at receiving and retaining information. In fact, it appears that most people will default to a traditional style of listening out of habit.[16]

Learning about the different learning styles—*action-oriented listening, content-oriented listening, people-oriented listening,* and *time-oriented listening*[17]—is the first step to using them to your advantage. Let's consider each of these in turn.

Action-oriented listening.
People who use this style of listening usually focus on getting to the meaning of a message and determining what response is required. **Action-oriented listeners** often prefer messages that are direct, concise, and error-free; as such, they are easily frustrated by those who ramble and take a while to get to the point. Unsurprisingly, while this style of listening may be effective in crisis situations or in the fast-paced business world, it can spell trouble in relationship communication between friends, family, or lovers.

Content-oriented listening.
In contrast to action-oriented listeners, **content-oriented listeners** favor depth and complexity of information and messages. They are willing to spend more time listening, pay careful attention to what's being said, and enjoy discussing and thinking about the message afterward.

People-oriented listening.
Like content-oriented listeners, **people-oriented listeners** are willing to invest time and attention to a conversation or discussion, yet they are differentiated by their interest in being supportive of friends and strengthening relationships. These listeners notice the mood and body language of the person talking, and express more empathy toward him or her.

Time-oriented listening.
The major identifying element of this listening style is time—or, more precisely, a concern with managing time. **Time-oriented listeners** see time as a precious resource to be conserved and protected. Thus, they often exhibit impatience or direct people to hurry through and get to the main points of a conversation or presentation. Consequently, their interactions with others are often rushed—and begin with warnings about how much (or how little) time they have to spend listening.[18]

Did you recognize any of these styles as your default? Using one or two of them more often doesn't mean you can't embrace other styles and use them in appropriate contexts.

Do you have a friend with personal problems who needs someone to talk to? Most likely, a people-oriented approach is best. Did a fellow student ask you to critique an oral report he plans to deliver in class? Consider a content-oriented approach. Conversely, is your own time limited because of a pending deadline—and in spite of this, a colleague has asked for your advice on a problem? If so, take a time-oriented approach, explaining your time constraints and setting reasonable expectations about what you are able to listen to.

OVERCOMING EXTERNAL LISTENING CHALLENGES

In an ideal world, everyone would be able to focus fully while listening, no one would ever interrupt another person, and everyone would be able to remember every part of a conversation or presentation afterward. As you probably realize, this is rarely the case! The good news is that by examining common listening challenges, you can learn to overcome them.

In the next two sections of the chapter, we discuss two types of challenges: **external**, which refers to those coming from the outside world, and **internal**, those coming from within us. We cannot always control external factors, but we do have a degree of control over internal factors. However, in both cases, there are ways to minimize barriers to listening.

In this section, we will discuss external factors. These include a speaker's rate of delivery, time of message and time of day, and physical location of the listening situation, and external noise surrounding the listening environment.

EXTERNAL FACTORS THAT AFFECT LISTENING: TIME

Rate of Delivery

A speaker's **rate of delivery** refers to how fast or how slow an individual speaks; both can impact how and whether people listen. Rates that are too fast are difficult for people to listen to and track. One study indicated that listening comprehension "significantly decreased" when the rate of words spoken and listened to exceeded a threshold of 250 words per minute.[19] To some extent, listening comprehension suffers because the processing is too difficult to keep up with—but it is also true that articulation and pronunciation suffer as speakers increase their rate of delivery, making it difficult to identify or recognize what is being said. Conversely, when a speaker's rate is too slow, listening can suffer simply because listeners have to work too hard to stay interested. Slow speech can be as little as 120 words per minute.[20]

If you think you may be susceptible to poor listening because of someone's rate of delivery, try these suggestions. When an individual speaks too fast, attempt to focus on what is being said and filter out any outside distractions or inner extraneous thoughts. Literally focus on each word and then internally summarize to see how all the parts of the message fit together. And remember: in many situations (e.g., a conversation or a small-group presentation), you can ask the speaker to slow down! Also, be reassured that while comprehension may decline at rates in excess of 250 words a minute, it's possible to train yourself to listen to faster rates of delivery. At high school and college debate competitions, for example, judges and audience members can listen to and process debater information considerably in excess of the above stated amount—but only with note taking and lots of practice.

Time

As a concept, **time** can cut two ways in its impact on effective listening: the actual time it takes to listen to a message, and the time of day or week with respect to the listener's internal body clock. First, the longer it takes to get a message across, the less attentive we become. And failure to pay attention translates into diminished retention of the message (as mentioned earlier). This can occur in individual conversations as well as larger presentations.

It's equally true that listening is implicated by body clock. Depending on the time of day, you may be more or less alert, tired, or hungry. For example, you likely feel differently in a class that starts at 10 a.m. than you do in a class that starts at 1 p.m. A late-morning class usually finds you rested and, assuming you had breakfast, nourished and perhaps caffeinated. A 1 p.m. class, by contrast, could find your blood sugar levels starting to spike, dropping, and leaving you with an overwhelming feeling of the need to sleep. Experts in the field of training have observed this phenomenon when evaluating worker attentiveness in training sessions.[21]

As listeners, we can combat some of the issues presented by time by following the guidelines for active listening discussed later in this chapter. We should also eat more small meals and keep our blood sugar fairly level—which will avoid dramatic spikes and sleepiness. And if we're speaking to a group of people, we should plan the meeting, conversation, or presentation at a time of day when they will be most attentive.

Physical Location

The **physical location** of the communication event also has a significant impact on listeners. Are you in a place where you can listen comfortably? Are there distractions within this location? If so, is it possible to control these distractions and focus? If necessary, can you alter the communication forum and move it altogether?

External Noise

Related to location, **external noise** in the environment surrounding the communication situation—anything from street noise to a flashy visual

EXTERNAL NOISE

aid left up during a presentation to chattering audience members—can make it very difficult to hear or pay attention. These external distractions often negatively affect retention of the message. One study blended speech and excessive road traffic noise and found that external noise impaired retention, recall of speech text, and semantic memory.[22]

As listeners, we aren't always able to control our environments—but as participants in a conversation, audiences to a speech, or members of a group, we can seek quiet environments when possible.

THE CULPRITS BEHIND POOR INTERNAL LISTENING

As mentioned earlier, beyond external challenges to listening, there are also *internal* challenges—those caused by the personal behavior of you or your communication partner(s). These behaviors can be divided among several culprits of poor listening, including information overload, distracted listening, interruptive listening, agenda-driven listening, argumentative listening, and nervous listening. Later in this chapter we also discuss defeated listening and superficial listening.

Information Overload

More than fifty years ago, George Miller of Harvard University suggested that there was a threshold limit for how much information the human brain could meaningfully process at the same time.[23] Although

INFORMATION OVERLOAD

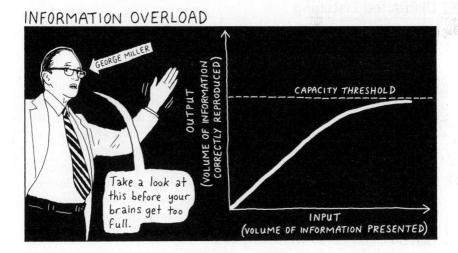

Miller settled on the number seven to make his case about such a limit, his larger point was that humans could potentially face **information overload**—a condition in which we're no longer capable of effectively processing new information.

Miller came up with a graph to illustrate information overload. As you can see from the image, the horizontal axis refers to the volume of information an individual receives, while the vertical axis plots the amount of information the same individual is capable of processing. The dotted line represents the threshold capacity—a point of saturation beyond which point the same individual can no longer absorb and meaningfully process new information. Beyond this threshold, as represented in the diagram, processing simply flattens out.

Modern communication and information technology have greatly expanded the number of possibilities we have for staying connected, sharing information and messages, and integrating these into our lives and work. Many of us—especially those who grew up using different forms of information technology—embrace the concept known as **multitasking**, which means attending to multiple tasks at one time. However, studies have found that multitasking can drastically reduce productivity.[24] And with regard to listening, taking in too much—and too complex—information at one time can negatively impact how we listen.[25] How can we counteract this listening barrier? When listening to others, minimize the other information you're taking in. The most effective way to do this may well be to turn off your cell phone or put it out of view.

Distracted Listening

People who engage in **distracted listening** simply do not pay attention to what they're hearing. For example, if you're overly interested in the questions you're going to ask during a conversation, you won't be attuned to what the other person has to say in response. In a lecture, you are likely to engage in distracted listening if you are more focused on your own thoughts about the subject than on what your instructor has to say. Not surprisingly, distracted listening prevents you from processing another person's message—and therefore keeps you from retaining it.

Often, these listeners are distracted by **internal noise**—thoughts or emotions that make it hard to concentrate. Internal noise can include anxiety, ego, and preoccupation—for example, worrying about how well you're doing in class, thinking about a movie from the night before, or pondering aspects of your personal life. These can color the way we

ONE LISTENER EXPERIENCING INTERNAL NOISE

process the words of one another. Measuring these distracting emotions or thoughts with precision can be challenging,[26] but most individuals possess a general awareness of them. If you catch yourself being a distracted listener, imagine yourself putting your thoughts or worries aside—and know that you can always pick them up again when your conversation, class, or meeting is over.

Interruptive Listening

With **interruptive listening**, one person consistently interrupts another. In a public speaking situation, you may have seen or heard instances of interruptive audience members, shouting things like "Yeah, right!" or blurting out questions before the speaker is ready to entertain them. The same applies in conversational speaking when one person constantly interrupts and interjects his or her own commentary or questions on another before the person can finish his or her sentence. Individuals who do this are likely to miss critical aspects of what was originally being said in the conversation. Worse, they often come across as rude and arrogant, thus losing the respect of others involved in the conversation.

Agenda-Driven Listening

On occasion, individuals may demonstrate **agenda-driven listening**. In a conversational context, this occurs when one member of the communication dyad is focused on learning or hearing certain information and completely uninterested in—and therefore oblivious to—everything

else. In truth, such an individual is not really listening so much as looking for confirmation or affirmation of his or her own agenda—and ignoring anything else that is said.

This listening challenge can also show itself when a speaker (giving a presentation) has to accommodate questions and comments from audience members. For example, as audience members raise questions and offer comments during the speech, the speaker thinks only about his or her next point. Perhaps the speaker scans his or her notes while a listener asks a question or provides monosyllabic and overly brief responses—revealing that he or she is not really listening to audience members. Whether in conversation or in public speaking situations, this behavior can annoy others and damage credibility.

Argumentative Listening

People who feel in conflict with individuals they are listening to may display **argumentative listening**, or selective listening—listening to only as much as they need to fuel their own arguments. Argumentative listening can also afflict people who feel personally attacked by questions in a conversation. Because they hear only part of what a questioner has

asked, they can't respond to the question in a thoughtful, informed way. This hurts their credibility.

People can also fall victim to argumentative listening during an interview if they disagree with the interviewee's opinions or ideas. Here, they may focus more on their own views and miss out on everything the other person has to say.

Nervous Listening

People who fall victim to **nervous listening** feel compelled to talk through silences because they're uncomfortable with a lapse in the conversation. This occurs often in interpersonal situations. For example, imagine that you've just met an attractive person with whom you're trying to strike up a conversation. When he or she takes a long moment to respond to a question, you start filling in the silence with nervous chatter—making it even more difficult for the person to respond.

In the realm of interpersonal communication—like a job interview—nervous listening can cause just as much havoc. If an interview subject takes a long time to answer a question, a nervous listener might ask more questions or blurt out a string of comments; thus, the

NERVOUS LISTENING

interviewee would never have any opportunity to answer, and the interviewer would end up with incomplete research. The same is true in a speech context. Imagine giving a speech introduction in which you ask a provocative question in an attempt to engage the audience. If no one in the room responds to your question, you might get thrown off and feel compelled to say something—anything—to get the speech moving again. You might fill in the silence with a random joke or comment, only to see confused or annoyed looks on your listeners' faces (see Chapter 15 on delivery).

Nervous listening—in any context—can damage your ability to gather and interpret information that you need to effectively communicate. If you feel twinges of nervousness, collect yourself and wait a few beats before continuing.

BECOMING A BETTER LISTENER

Along with overcoming specific culprits of poor listening, you can improve your listening skills by focusing on **interactive listening**. In interactive listening, you filter out distractions, focus on what the other person or people are saying, and show that you are listening.

Filter Out Distractions

As previously described, there are potentially countless distractions in any speaking situation, both external and internal. If you are an audience member, filtering out distractions means avoiding nonlistening activities, such as gazing around the room or surfing online. If you are giving a speech, filtering out distractions during presentations or question-and-answer sessions means focusing on reactions or questions from audience members rather than looking ahead to your next point. As a participant in a conversation, filtering out distractions means avoiding distractions by keeping your gaze on the other person. This means that unless you need your phone or other device to look up something that's pertinent to your conversation, it's best to put it away.

Focus on the Speaker

In any listening situation, keep your mind on what the speaker is saying, not on what you may be about to hear or what you're going to say next. Ask yourself, "What does this statement that I've just heard mean? Do I agree or disagree with it? Do I have questions or comments of my own about it—or even a different point of view? How might other people think or feel about this comment or issue?"

Show That You Are Listening

As a responsible listener, you should show the speaker that you are listening by using your attending skills, which means focusing on the other person and using a combination of nonverbal and verbal cues (see Chapters 3 and 4). Look at the other person while he or she is speaking *and* as you are responding. Indicate nonverbally—perhaps with alert posture and a smile or nod of your head—that you are paying attention.

When the opportunity presents itself, you can also verbally communicate that you are listening. For example, you can ask thoughtful

questions or even comment appropriately at a particular moment in your conversation. As a public speaker, you can paraphrase questions asked by audience members both to show that you understand and to allow them to correct any misinterpretation.

HELPING OTHERS LISTEN TO YOU

Despite your best efforts, you may occasionally find yourself talking to people who do not listen well. For example, while paying attention to another person's nonverbal and verbal responses as you speak, you may notice that the person acts as if he or she is listening, but you can tell that he or she is not. The good news is that there are several strategies you can use to help people listen more effectively to your words. In this section, we outline several steps that you can take to both anticipate and deal with listening challenges.

HELPING OTHERS LISTEN TO YOU

Anticipate Ineffective Listening before You Speak

Advance preparation is key to ensuring that someone will truly listen to your message. It's even more important when you are giving a speech or presentation, and need to consider all of your audience members. Whether one person or two hundred, consider audience needs as well as outside factors, and plan your communication accordingly.

Consider your listener's attention and energy levels.
As suggested previously, time of day can affect listening ability. Having a conversation with someone at 8:30 on a Monday morning will likely be trickier than having the same conversation at 11:00 a.m. on a Tuesday. The person may be tired from the weekend, may not have adjusted to the new week, and will probably have a limited attention span. Therefore, avoid speaking as if you were delivering a monologue at such times. Instead, make your points concisely, and allow time for your listener to respond.

Assess your audience's knowledge and abilities.
If the person or people you talk to know little about the subject of your conversation, they may become confused when faced with unknown jargon or too many technical details. To avoid that, explain concepts and define key terms. Also, consider any barriers to understanding, such as whether everyone has a similar capacity with the English language or whether

HAMMER HOME YOUR MAIN MESSAGE AT THE BEGINNING AND AT THE END

anyone has problems with hearing. Then adjust your word choice or volume level as needed. (See Chapter 12, pp. 355–65, for a discussion on audience analysis in speechmaking.)

Front- and back-load your main message. Listeners tend to pay the most attention just after the beginning of an oral communication and just before the end. For this reason, plan ahead of time in the following way: front-load your main message—that is, present it early in your points. Then use your conclusion to give listeners another opportunity to process and retain your message. (See Chapter 14, pp. 425–34, for specific information on writing introductions and conclusions in speechmaking.)

Use presentation aids strategically. In a public speaking situation, presentation aids can help you capture audience attention and thereby encourage listening (see Chapter 15, pp. 479–84, for more on presentation aids). Therefore, plan to space these aids throughout your presentation in order to maintain interest. Also, don't incorporate a given presentation aid until you want your audience to see or hear it. When you are finished with it, put it away, outside your listeners' view or hearing range.

Encourage Active Listening

When you are ready to talk, be sure to focus on what you see in the other person. Pay particular attention to whether—and how—the other person is listening to you, and be prepared to make adjustments as you go.

Tailor your delivery. As you speak, pay attention to factors that affect a person's ability to listen: voice, volume, fluency, projection, rate, and timing. Speaking too quietly can inhibit listening, as may poor fluency, fast delivery, or excessive pausing. Be sure to maintain eye contact and avoid obtrusive gestures (such as pointing) or turning your back as you speak (see Chapter 15 on Delivering Your Speech for more information on this subject).

Watch out for argumentative listeners. As discussed earlier in this chapter, argumentative listeners will attend to only as much of your words as they need to build up their own case. To improve your chances of keeping their attention, acknowledge their viewpoints early (e.g., "I know you may not think having tattoos will affect your career") and repeatedly press your main message.

Watch out for defeated listeners. You might also notice a conversation partner who has tuned you out. Such **defeated listening** often occurs when listeners feel overwhelmed by your message and find it too difficult to follow, perhaps because the subject you are discussing is too technical or detailed and beyond easy comprehension. Defeated listeners may avoid eye contact or work on something else while you speak.

You can prevent defeated listening by pausing occasionally to ask the listener questions—such as whether he or she understands what you have said so far, or if they can think of an example or application of what you have just said. By doing so, you can test the person's comprehension and processing while assessing whether he or she is really following along. If you cannot engage the person, back up and repeat your message, using simpler language and different examples.

Watch out for superficial listeners. Some people who pretend to pay attention but who are in fact distracted by internal or external noise (such as wandering thoughts, cell phones, newspapers, or conversation) are engaged in **superficial listening**. To prevent it, request that people

DEALING WITH
ARGUMENTATIVE LISTENERS

DEFEATED LISTENERS

SUPERFICIAL LISTENERS

turn off cell phones and resist checking for messages on handheld devices or laptops during a presentation or an important conversation Also, be sure to use direct eye contact with people who you sense are listening superficially (they will pay more attention if they see that you are watching them), and go ahead and ask them questions—or invite them to ask you some.

WHEN YOU ARE THE LISTENER

When you are on the receiving end of a conversation or speech, listening not only helps you retain the other speaker's message but also enables you to provide the speaker with critical feedback on the conversation or an informed **speech critique**—written or oral feedback offered after a speech presentation. Critiquing is an essential component of public speaking classes because it helps speakers learn from their experiences; likewise, offering feedback in a conversation is a good way to demonstrate that you have been listening and to help you be certain that you have understood what your conversation partner has been saying. In the following section, we offer suggestions for both public speaking situations and conversations.

Making a Speech Critique

Your instructor will likely specify what you should cover in a critique. The following can give you additional guidance.

- *Take notes.* While listening to a presentation, jot down your thoughts about the speaker's delivery and message. By recording

GOOD FEEDBACK:

Great eye contact, voice could be louder, be careful not to turn back to audience, speak a bit slower...

BAD FEEDBACK:

Irrelevant! Makes no sense, I am bored, your hairstyle is distracting, who cares? Whatever...

your impressions as you form them, you'll be able to access your thoughts when it comes time to offer your critique.

- ***Identify main points.*** As you take notes, begin to distinguish what you think are the speaker's main points—these are the two or three most important ideas that the speaker wants you to remember (speechwriters sometimes call these "takeaways," or the "take-home message"). You can identify main points by listening carefully to the introduction; most speakers will preview main points during that part of the speech. You can also listen for signaling language in the transitions of the speech. Finally, effective speakers often restate their main points in their conclusion, giving you one more chance to retain them.

- ***Consider the speaker's objectives.*** To provide **constructive criticism**—feedback a speaker can use to improve his or her skills—strive to understand what the presenter is trying to accomplish. Identify the speech's general rhetorical purpose—to inform, persuade, or mark a special occasion (see pp. 371–72)—as well as the speech's specific purpose. Next, evaluate how well the speaker achieves his or her goal.

- ***Support your feedback with examples.*** Offering an overly general comment such as "good eye contact" or "work on your organization" is not particularly useful to a speaker. Support generalizations like these with specific examples, such as "You made eye contact with people on every side of the room" or "You had a good preview, but I found the organization of your main points difficult to follow." Specific comments help speakers know which behaviors to do more of during their next speech and which to avoid.

- **Be ethical.** Be courteous in your critique, and treat the speaker the same way you hope and expect to be treated when it's your turn to receive feedback. During the speech, avoid prejudging the speaker or topic. Think critically about the message you're hearing, and make sure that you hold the speaker accountable for his or her words. If you are offended by or disagree with something in the speech, tell the person while providing your critique. But do so courteously, and avoid making your comment sound like a personal attack. Explain why you disagree, and offer examples.

Giving Conversational Feedback

While a conversation is less formal than a speech, there are still ways you can maximize the interaction, whether it be with a friend, significant other, family member, or coworker (to name a few).

- **Carefully assess whether the other person just wants to be heard or expects feedback.** On occasion, you will have conversations with people who ask broad rhetorical questions ("Can a person who committed infidelity in his last relationship ever be trusted?"), want to get something off their chest ("I cheated on my driving test!"), or need to vent their feelings about something ("I am soooo done with this job and this boss"). They may not expect you to solve their problems or answer their questions. Mostly, they just want to speak—and sometimes think out loud in the presence of

SOMETIMES PEOPLE JUST WANT TO BE HEARD

I don't need you to fix this. I just need you to hear me out.

another person. In these situations, it is important that you listen and wait to comment or provide feedback only when you are sure that is what they are seeking. Try asking, "Would you rather that I just listen to you now, or would you like me to offer my thoughts about what you said?" If feedback is what they seek, they will tell you.

- ***If feedback is desired, be sure you understand what the person has said before commenting.*** Nothing will lose you credibility with the other person faster than making comments or asking questions that only demonstrate you were NOT listening. If you are not sure you understand what has been said, try summarizing and ask for clarification of points that are still unclear. More questions can serve as evidence that you are affirmatively working to understand and process what has been said. These questions also serve the function of giving your conversation partner a chance to respond and expand on what has been said, in a now-interactive way.

- ***Seek to demonstrate empathy in your feedback.*** Empathy is different from sympathy. The latter term refers to expressions of sorrow for someone else's grief or difficult situation. By contrast, empathy references an expression of understanding, usually informed by personal experience. Empathy can be useful in feedback as a way of letting the other person know that others (in this case, you) have been through the same experience. It can also shed light on possible outcomes or solutions for problems. At the level of human engagement, it also allows you to emotionally connect with the other person, who will now feel that he or she has not only been heard but also, and more important, been *understood*.

- ***Seek to be honest and ethical in your feedback.*** To put it simply: someone who has trusted you enough to speak openly with you deserves an honest and truthful response when you are called on to comment or provide feedback.

CHAPTER REVIEW

In this chapter, we discussed a major contrast: hearing noises, sounds, and words versus listening to them. *Hearing* refers to passively receiving these stimuli; *listening* refers to how one processes and retains them.

Listening can be broken down further into different styles, including action-oriented listening, content-oriented listening, people-oriented listening, and time-oriented listening.

Listening challenges can be divided into two types: external (coming from the outside world) and internal (coming from within us). External factors include a speaker's rate of delivery; time of message and time of day; the physical location of the interaction; and any external noise, such as street sounds or a visual aid left up too long. The culprits behind poor listening are the internal factors caused by the personal behavior of you or your communication partner. These include information overload, distracted listening, interruptive listening, agenda-driven listening, argumentative listening, nervous listening, defeated listening, and superficial listening.

The chapter offered several tips for becoming a better listener—including filtering out distractions, focusing on the speaker, and showing that you are listening—as well as ways to help others listen to you. In addition, it suggested ways to offer feedback as a listener in both public speaking situations and conversations. When critiquing a speech presentation, listeners should offer constructive criticism by considering the speech's objectives, supporting feedback with examples, and keeping appropriate ethical guidelines in mind. When giving conversational feedback, listeners should carefully assess whether the person actually expects feedback. If feedback is desired, the listener should be clear on what the person has said before commenting, demonstrate empathy in his or her feedback, and be honest and ethical.

LaunchPad
macmillan learning

LaunchPad for *Let's Communicate* offers videos and encourages self-assessment through adaptive quizzing. Go to **launchpadworks.com** to get access to:

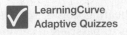 LearningCurve
Adaptive Quizzes

 Video clips that help you understand
human communication

Key Terms

hearing 133
listening 133
processing 133
retention 134
action-oriented listeners 137
◉ content-oriented listeners 137
people-oriented listeners 137
◉ time-oriented listeners 137
external 138
internal 138
rate of delivery 139
time 139
physical location 140
external noise 140

information overload 142
multitasking 142
distracted listening 142
internal noise 142
interruptive listening 143
agenda-driven listening 143
argumentative listening 144
nervous listening 145
interactive listening 146
defeated listening 151
superficial listening 151
speech critique 152
constructive criticism 153

Review Questions

1. What is listening? How does it differ from hearing?
2. What two steps make up the listening process? Explain each one.
3. Name the four listening styles.
4. What are four external factors that can affect your ability to listen?
5. Define *interactive listening*.
6. Explain four ways you can encourage active listening when you are the speaker.
7. What is a speech critique, and why is it important for the speaker?

Critical Thinking Questions

1. Review the four listening styles. How might the context or uniqueness of a situation determine which listening style you use?
2. What are some strategies a speaker can use to combat external noise, such as road traffic or loud talking in the hallway?

3. Consider the internal barrier nervous listening. Instead of speaking during extended pauses, what are some things you can do to help with any discomfort you may feel during moments of silence?

4. Is it possible to multitask and still be an interactive listener? Explain your reasoning.

5. How can good listening skills help you give a constructive critique to a classmate?

6. Does the increase in the use of technology negatively or positively affect one's ability to listen? Explain your answer.

Activities

1. Reflect on your own listening skills by writing down the details of a recent conversation you had with a friend. Which of the four listening styles did you use, and why?

2. Watch a monologue from a late-night talk show. After viewing it once, write down a summary of the monologue, then watch it again with notes in hand to see how much you remembered. You can try doing the same activity with a cooking program or a sports show. If you try both variations on this activity, are the outcomes any different? If so, what is different, and why?

3. For one class period, view your communication instructor as a speaker trying to keep an audience (the class) engaged in effective listening. Write down the strategies he or she uses to keep the audience listening and reduce ineffective listening. How could your instructor encourage more effective listening?

4. During one of your other classes, take notes on how students around you are listening to the instructor's lecture. What specific behaviors do you observe? Are your classmates distracted or interactive listeners?

5. In groups of three or four, share what you did over the past weekend in as much detail as possible. Without taking notes, have each group member verbally summarize what the group member said he or she did. How accurate were your summaries? What external or internal noise got in the way, if any?

Apply Your Skills

Take a look at the illustration concerning nervous listening on page 146. How might the man in the illustration respond to show that he is actually listening to what has been said?

Study Plan

CULTURE AND COMMUNICATION

6

OBJECTIVES

- Understand and articulate a meaning for *culture* and *intercultural communication*.
- Describe the most typical variations in culture and how they affect communication.
- Develop a mindful approach to intercultural communication.

After being paired up as lab partners in a chemistry class, college students Christine and John began dating and soon became exclusive. Early on in the relationship, John knew there was one person Christine needed to meet: his mother, Turan.

Whereas Christine's family of German and Scottish descent had been in San Francisco for several generations, John's family had immigrated to the United States in the 1950s from Iran. Like many first-generation immigrant families in the United States, John's family shared a close bond. John cherished his mother's opinion on any subject, especially about potential mates. So, with Christine's excited but nervous assent, he arranged an afternoon meeting for the two women at Christine's apartment.

As the day approached, Christine worried about her ability to make a good impression on John's mother. John reassured her and also told her that because of Iranian custom, Turan would probably prefer tea to coffee. Christine accordingly bought some tea and cakes.

161

The next night, after Christine and Turan had met, John stopped by his mother's place to see how it had gone.

"Well, you know, she's nice," Turan said. "But . . ." She let the last word trail off, making a face.

"But what?" John insisted.

"I didn't want to say anything." Turan shrugged.

"What?" John asked. "Tell me."

Turan paused before answering. "When I got to her apartment, she poured tea."

"Which was very considerate," John noted.

"But she didn't give me any." Turan shook her head sadly. "That was very rude."

John called Christine to find out what had happened. He was surprised to find that Christine thought it had gone well.

"Did you give her tea?" he asked.

"I offered her a cup of tea, but she declined," Christine replied. "So I poured myself one, sat down, and we started our conversation."

John instantly realized what had happened. In Persian culture, it is considered impolite to immediately accept an offer of something from someone. This cultural custom derives from the Farsi expression *Ta a'rof*, which means "to stand on ceremony." In this case, the ceremony or custom dictates that a person decline an offer two or three times before accepting.

Christine did not know this cultural reference—and how could she? As a product of Western culture—specifically American culture, which prides itself on directness in communication—she naturally assumed that when Turan said, "No, thank you," she meant just that. **Intercultural communication** is the communication that occurs between people of different cultural backgrounds. As this story illustrates, miscommunication —even among those with the best of intentions—can and does occur. The United States is increasingly becoming a nation of people from a myriad of cultural backgrounds; indeed, recent census data indicates that the country is on a gradual path to becoming a "plurality nation" in which "no group is the majority."[1] More than ever, we must be able to communicate with one another—especially because many of us come from different backgrounds. To that end, it's important to understand our own cultural makeup, which can comprise multiple, overlapping parts. If we're aware of our own tendencies and potential cultural biases, we can make an effort to overcome them and become better communicators with anyone we might meet.

In this chapter, we address the definition of *culture*; the ties between culture and diversity; variations in culture; assimilation, accommodation, and separation; challenges to intercultural communication; and constructive steps for improving intercultural communication. Let's begin with a closer examination of the term *culture*.

WHAT IS CULTURE?

What do you think of when you hear the word *culture*? This English word originally referenced a tendency toward "natural growth," but evolved to reference that which was elevated, precious, and uncommon in society.[2] Like the word *art*, it reinforced a sense of human value.

In the nineteenth century, certain philosophers used the word when contrasting wealthy elites (high culture) with people of lower socioeconomic position (low culture). By the twentieth century, anthropologists had embraced the term to reflect *all* of human existence, collectively, by groups of people. Today, most people define **culture** as *the sum of knowledge, beliefs, values, and patterns of behavior shared by members of a group*.

There is general consensus that culture is not something you are born with (such as your height or the color of your eyes) but rather something you must be *taught*—and, if it takes root, something you *learn*. The term **enculturation** is the process by which we learn about the culture we are born into—everything from its values to its mores and traditions, as well as its language and its history.

As mentioned earlier, culture can have a large influence on our lives and the ways we communicate. But the opposite is also true: how we communicate affects our culture—by reinforcing it or, in some cases, by slowly questioning and changing it.

If someone says that he or she belongs to a certain culture, it could mean a variety of things. The person may be talking about geographical boundaries (Parisian culture), religious affiliations (Jewish culture), or any other type of group with specific patterns of behavior (hacker culture). People may belong to multiple **co-cultures**—cultures that exist within a larger culture. For example, even if you consider yourself a part of American culture, you might also belong to other co-cultures—say, if you're Chinese American, LGBTQ, or a twenty-something.

WHAT IS CULTURE?

(USING SCOTLAND AS AN EXAMPLE)

KEY: 1. WHISKY (NOT WHISKEY) 2. THE LOCH NESS MONSTER 3. KILTS 4. HAGGIS 5. THE FLAG 6. SEAN CONNERY 7. SCOTTISH TERRIER 8. SHEEP 9. THISTLE SYMBOL 10. BAGPIPES 11. ROBBIE BURNS 12. DEEP-FRIED MARS BARS 13. GOLF 14. RAIN 15. HILLS 16. MEDIEVAL ART 17. DIALECT 18. ARCHIE GEMMILL'S GOAL IN THE 1978 SOCCER WORLD CUP

When individuals from one culture live within or come into contact with other cultures, opportunities to learn about the other cultures (or perhaps the larger, dominant culture) arise. This learning process for co-cultures is referred to as **acculturation**. Later in this chapter we describe how acculturation is sometimes complemented or complicated by the accompanying phenomena of assimilation, accommodation, and separation.

CULTURE AND DIVERSITY

You've likely heard the word *diversity* in reference to a variety of different types of people. Indeed, **diversity** refers to the differences stemming from traditional categories like race, ethnicity, gender, age, sexual orientation, disability, and religion.[3] And how does the idea of diversity relate

to culture? To examine this, imagine diversity as a horizontal plane, containing all the general differences that can exist among people. Now imagine culture as a vertical line, showing the depth and richness of these various categories—specifically, their values, beliefs, and norms. In the past, certain groups may have been defined by society's constructs (for example—prior to 1920 in the United States—women being told they couldn't vote simply because they were women). Nowadays, people have more agency to make choices about what groups they belong to—as well as to decide what those groups mean to them.

In the following section, we explore some of the larger traditional categories through a cultural lens.

Race, Ethnicity, and Heritage

Today, many people consider themselves part of a culture based on familial or geographical origins. This can provide a sense of identity

CELEBRATING THE NEW YEAR AROUND THE WORLD:

LEÓN, MEXICO

ST. PETERSBURG, RUSSIA

NEW YORK, USA

GLASGOW, SCOTLAND

(see Chapter 2), a connection to others, and a means of keeping certain customs alive. These ideas are usually divided into two categories: **race**— a commonality based on genetically shared physical characteristics of people in a group—and **ethnicity**—cultural background that is usually associated with shared religion, national origin, and language. However, these words are rather controversial, mostly because they lack some kind of inherent or precise meaning.[4] Thus, some modern usages are derogatory (e.g., prejudice and hate speech), whereas others are meant to empower. When people consider themselves part of a culture, they are making an active choice—which is a far cry from accepting other peoples' labels.

Another way to view this more positively is through the term **heritage**, which refers to the traditions, achievements, and beliefs that are part of the history of a group or nation.[5] People can choose to which degree they would like to remember and honor their heritage—whether that means celebrating certain holidays, learning their ancestors' language, or even making recipes that have been handed down through generations.

Gender and Sexual Orientation

Diversity also includes within its spectrum the term **gender**, referring to both cultural and behavioral traits related to one's biological sex. To be sure, sex and gender, while related, are not the same. Up until the 1960s, it was commonplace to categorize individuals by their biological sex (male or female) and their gender (masculine or feminine). This automatic and imposed labeling reinforced the use of gender stereotypes about feminine and masculine traits.[6] It also ignored those who didn't identify with their biological sex (transgender people).

In more recent years, a combination of sexuality studies, second-wave feminism, and masculinity studies have challenged these earlier ideas and begun to dismantle the concept of gender as binary (two choices: male or female). People are now questioning the degree to which traditionally "masculine" or "feminine" traits are the products of genetics, and what portion of them are socially constructed—from how we're raised to how we're shaped by social interactions.

Just one example of shifting ideas about gender roles is how men and women navigate the workforce. More women work than ever before, and more families now consist of two income-earning parents. Men are also entering fields that were traditionally dominated by women. For example, census data report that a rising number of men (more than tripling since the 1970s) are becoming nurses.[7] Unfortunately, the more things change, the more some issues remain the same. The same data indicated that male nurses on average were earning more than their female counterparts!

A separate but related culture is that of one's sexual orientation. While our culture has historically been mainly **heteronormative**—which says that heterosexuality is the normal or preferred sexual orientation—this outdated mode of thinking is beginning to shift. A growing number of the U.S. population supports gay rights, to a degree that might have been surprising just ten years ago.

ENGINEER

NURSE

MINISTER

BABY BOOMER   GENERATION X   MILLENNIALS   GENERATION Z

Age

Today, we are also more aware than ever of the differences between people based on age. **Age identity** usually slices two ways: by chronological age and by generational association.[8] Though people may identify with others of similar chronological age (for example, people in their early twenties), this can be a moving target. Since we all get older, we must update our identities accordingly—from identifying as twentysomethings to reaching "the big 4-0" and beyond. By contrast, identifying with people on the basis of generation involves an identity that never really changes because it is fixed with those who were born around the same time. Examples include baby boomers, Gen Xers, and the group known as millennials.[9]

Most research indicates that younger people tend to self-identify by chronological age, but as they get older, they disassociate themselves from their age group and instead emphasize their connection to their generation.[10] As individuals reach retirement age, most will completely disassociate themselves from their chronological age because of the negative stereotypes associated with being old—such as being confused, feeble, and fragile. Interestingly, although young people typically perpetuate these stereotypes, the elderly are also guilty of perpetuating them about themselves.[11] However, these stereotypes might be shifting. Fueled by better health care and more devotion to lifelong exercise, the baby-boomer population has found that they can work longer and later into their lives, and be physically active to a much later age. For example, it is not at all uncommon to find men and women competing in triathlons and marathons into their late eighties.

VARIATIONS IN CULTURE: HOW DO THEY AFFECT COMMUNICATION?

We've taken a look at some of the diverse cultures that people can be a part of within a larger community. But what about those larger communities themselves—how do whole countries and parts of the world differ from each other in communication practices? Many scholars have studied and identified these larger cultural communication variations,[12] which explain some of the differences in how people interact. These variations include *uncertainty avoidance; high- and low-context cultures; individualistic and collectivist cultures; masculine and feminine cultures; high- and low-contact cultures;* and *level of power distance.* Let's consider each of these in turn.

Uncertainty Avoidance

The term **uncertainty avoidance** refers to a society's willingness to tolerate ambiguity or uncertainty. Consider your own tolerance level here: How comfortable are *you* with uncertainty? For example, when you are driving to an unfamiliar location, do you get anxious when the directions you have get you lost? Are you the kind of person who would use a map—or better, an app—to guide you with precision all the way? Or are you comfortable with wandering and finding your way, occasionally stopping to ask for directions if you need them?

Individuals in certain cultures have a **high uncertainty avoidance**, which means they prefer planning and following a process. They follow rules and directions, and at times can be quite formal, rigid, and inflexible. By contrast, individuals in cultures with **low uncertainty avoidance** are much more casual, informal, and relaxed. Those with high uncertainty avoidance show resistance to change, whereas those

UNCERTAINTY AVOIDANCE

with low uncertainty avoidance show only moderate resistance to change.[13] Germany is one country that shows a high uncertainty avoidance, whereas Singapore and Denmark both adhere to low uncertainty avoidance.

High and Low Context

Anthropologists and intercultural experts Edward T. Hall and his wife, Mildred R. Hall, discovered that cultures can differ along a scale of low to high context. When a culture shows preference for low-context communication, it means that people focus mainly on the spoken word—and that the words directly communicate the message.[14] In other words, people don't rely as much on the context or situation in which the words are spoken. If the words lack specificity, people will ask questions to clarify. Individuals in **low-context cultures** often experience anxiety and discomfort over vagueness and ambiguity. Examples of low-context cultures include Australia, Sweden, and the United States.

In **high-context cultures**, people rely on information from the situation to help interpret the message. Very little verbal information needs to be coded or included, and people will understand because the context for the message is already plain to them. Think of the example in the introduction

with John, Christine, and Turan; since Turan is from a high-context culture, she expected Christine to act in a certain way because of the situation. High-context cultures include Mexico, Japan, and Taiwan.

Individualistic and Collectivist Cultures

Another cultural variation involves orientation toward the *individual* versus orientation toward the greater group, or *collective* community. In other words, which does a culture value more: the individual or the collective group? People who live in **individualistic cultures** (those that value the individual over the group) typically privilege anything associated with preserving individual freedom and personal autonomy; thus, they value privacy and control, choice, and the freedom to express themselves.[15] Examples of individualistic cultures include Australia, Sweden, and especially the United States.

COLLECTIVIST vs. INDIVIDUALISTIC

LE COLLECTIF
THE COMMUNITY DINING EXPERIENCE THAT'S GOOD FOR THE ENVIRONMENT
THIS IS THE ONLY MENU WE HAVE
NO SUBSTITUTIONS, NO SPECIAL REQUESTS, AND ABSOLUTELY NO COMPLAINING

Good for you!   Good for all!

PRIX-FIXE MENU

FIRST COURSE:
Locally sourced wild foraged but totally sustainable green salad

MAIN COURSE:
Grass-fed heritage beef stew accompanied by roasted seasonal vegetables and fairly traded spiced quinoa

DESSERT:
The best chocolate pudding <u>ever</u>

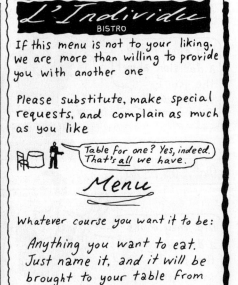

L'Individu
BISTRO
If this menu is not to your liking, we are more than willing to provide you with another one

Please substitute, make special requests, and complain as much as you like

Table for one? Yes, indeed. That's <u>all</u> we have.

Menu

Whatever course you want it to be:
Anything you want to eat. Just name it, and it will be brought to your table from anywhere in the world.
It's up to you!

Collectivist cultures (which value the group over the individual) prefer harmony, cooperation, tradition, loyalty, and togetherness.[16] For example, in such cultures, considerations about a meal might mean providing a menu that's best for the group, instead of focusing on everyone's individual dietary preferences. Individuals who inhabit a collectivist culture are also conditioned to control the expression of their emotions—certainly more than those who live in individualistic cultures.[17] Expressing emotion can be seen as championing individual feelings, which are usually withheld. Collectivist cultures include most of the nations in Asia and all of South America.

Masculine and Feminine Cultures

Earlier in this chapter we examined the diversity element known as gender, which can divide in terms of the ways in which different cultures view *masculinity* and *femininity*. The idea of masculinity and femininity can also apply to cultures, often in fairly traditional and even stereotypical terms. Research has found that traditionally **masculine cultures** embrace such values as ambition, assertiveness, decisiveness, and independence. They also champion differentiated gender roles (often favoring general male dominance), economic growth, money and material acquisition, and sympathy for achievers.[18] Masculine countries have been observed to "strive for a performance society,"[19] meaning that they privilege performance by stressing effectiveness and merit. Cultures that reflect predominantly masculine values include Mexico, the United States, and Japan.

Feminine cultures tend to value benevolence, caring, gender equality and fluid gender roles, interdependence, intuition, an avoidance of hierarchy, high quality of life, and sympathy for those less fortunate.[20] In contrast to masculine countries, feminine countries are generally more permissive and tend to favor compromise and negotiation. Feminine countries often "strive for a welfare society,"[21] meaning that they privilege the collective and desire to nurture and take care of all. Countries that are associated more with feminine culture include the Netherlands, Sweden, and Chile.

It's important to note that the labels "masculine" and "feminine" apply to societies as a whole—including all men and women within them. For example, in a masculine culture, an individual might bargain for a significant pay increase without worrying whether others doing comparable work would receive a similar increase (or any increase at all). By contrast, in a feminine culture, an individual would be more likely to be in a labor union, in order to make pay equitable for everyone.

High-Contact and Low-Contact Cultures

Another cultural variation is the degree to which individuals feel comfortable expressing themselves verbally and nonverbally, and their preferred level of physical closeness and contact. These cultures can be broken down into two types: **high-contact cultures** and **low-contact cultures**.[22] In moderate- to high-contact cultures, people often move or stand closer to one another, touch more frequently, and are willing to express themselves nonverbally. In low-contact cultures, the reverse is true: individuals generally stand farther apart, touch with much less frequency, and are more likely to be emotionally distant and reserved.[23]

Countries that are classified as high-contact cultures include all of those near the Mediterranean, in the Middle East, and in eastern Europe, as well as those in central and South America. The United States, Great Britain, and Australia are believed to be moderate- to high-contact cultures. Most Asian countries and, to a lesser degree, countries in northern Europe are often thought to be low-contact cultures.[24]

High-Power-Distance and Low-Power-Distance Cultures

Another cultural variation involves **power distance**, or the extent to which a culture recognizes and tolerates power—specifically, the distribution

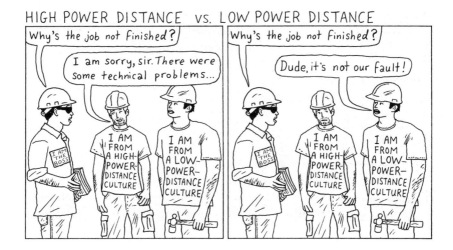

of power among individuals. Power distance can take many forms, including political, legal, economic, financial, and social.[25]

In **high-power-distance cultures**, those in superior positions (for example, the wealthy or politically connected) have considerably more power than those in subordinate positions. They will also maintain an emotional and psychological distance from one another. High-power-distance cultures accept the hierarchy that exists between superiors and subordinates (for example, employers and employees, or teachers and students) and even rationalize it as legitimate, traditional, and customary.[26] The United States and Germany are both countries with a high power distance.

In **low-power-distance cultures**, superior and subordinate relationships are close, rather than distant, and more egalitarian. Rather than being hierarchical, these cultures build in expectations that relations between superiors and subordinates will be friendly and accessible.[27] Low-power-distance countries include India and China.

ASSIMILATION, ACCOMMODATION, AND SEPARATION

When thinking about different cultures, it's important to remember that they don't exist in a vacuum. Indeed, the world is increasingly interconnected as technology, competition for resources, trade, education, and mobility shrink the distances (real or socially constructed) between us. Recall the term *co-cultures*, which refers to cultures that exist within the presence of other, larger cultures. While people can often balance different co-cultures (for example, being a part of football culture within the larger American culture), there are also times when co-cultures and cultures may affect each other.

Assimilation

One example of this is **assimilation**,[28] or when one takes on the characteristics of a dominant general culture. This can be voluntary. Consider Hakizimana, a young man who moves from Egypt to go to school in London. Hakizimana might decide to take on English characteristics, such

as dressing like the other students, speaking in English, and perhaps even taking on a nickname to make it easier for Americans to pronounce and remember his name. In voluntary assimilations, the person often seeks acceptance from the dominant culture—in other words, he or she wants to fit in.

Assimilation can also be forced upon a co-cultured individual to varying degrees, usually to meet some external objective more important for the dominant culture than the individual. For example, in 2004 France enacted a law prohibiting the wearing of religious symbols in public schools, including Christian crosses, Jewish yarmulkes, Sikh turbans, and a variety of Muslim headscarves.[29] The latter of these proved to be a flash point in French politics, as many viewed it as an assault on Islam, forcing conformity with the dominant French culture. The French government defended its actions by pointing out that separation of church and state had been the law in France since 1905. Forcing this rule on the dress code for students in a public school, officials argued, met the law for everyone and produced a kind of sameness or solidarity for all students.

Accommodation

Some co-cultures reject assimilation and instead seek **accommodation**, meaning that the co-cultured individual or group retains its core cultural identity while remaining within the dominant general culture. Unlike assimilation, which may alter and shift one's core cultural identity, accommodation keeps the core culture intact. What occurs instead is more of an "adjustment of the existent self definition" of core cultural identity.[30] In other words, the individual or group doesn't give up its core cultural identity but rather acknowledges the adding of another cultural layer.

By means of example, consider the presence of a Chinatown within a large city like New York, San Francisco,

MANHATTAN

CHINATOWN

or even Oakland, California. These are typically merchant districts as well as inner-city residential areas housing a large number of Chinese Americans and Chinese immigrants with U.S. visa status. These business districts, open to everyone, are frequented by Americans not of Chinese ancestry. Likewise, the merchants, business owners, and property owners pay taxes and obey the laws of the surrounding city. Thus, the original identity of Chinese culture remains intact, while an accommodation with the external dominant (in this case, Western) general culture is made.

There is also a middle ground between assimilation and accommodation. Some people mostly assimilate to the dominant culture but also work strenuously to preserve their culture. For example, Judaism promotes the idea of its preservation by encouraging *bar* and *bat mitzvahs*—coming-of-age rituals for boys and girls, which serve as their transition to adulthood and membership in the larger Jewish community. Many families choose to embark on these rituals, which involve rigorous study of the Torah and its 613 laws, in order to maintain their connection to their culture.

Separation

Beyond assimilation and accommodation, another option exists: that of **separation**, or leading a separate existence while in the midst of the dominant culture. While these co-cultures may overlap with the larger culture in terms of laws and physical proximity, they interact almost exclusively with one another and minimize contact with the dominant general culture. In the United States, obvious examples of this include the Amish and, in some cities, Hasidic Jews.

CHALLENGES TO INTERCULTURAL COMMUNICATION

In a world that's growing more interconnected and interdependent economically, politically, and technologically, we will all be exposed to people of different cultural backgrounds. As mentioned earlier in the chapter, it's important to be able to communicate with all types of people. One important aspect of this is to realize our own tendencies and potential cultural biases. Taking it a step further, some people might see "different" as threatening, which can lead to more serious problems. The following sections explore these challenges, which include *ethnocentrism*, *prejudice*, and *hate* and *hate speech*. Let's address each of these in turn.

Ethnocentrism

When people are biased against and frequently intolerant of other cultures—especially a culture they see as subordinate to their own—they often exhibit what is known as **ethnocentrism**—the tendency to perceive one's own culture as important and superior to other cultures.[31] Thus, being ethnocentric often influences people to have a positive view of their own culture while seeing other cultures in negative contexts. One of the benefits to ethnocentrism is that it signals loyalty and positive commitment to other members of one's own culture. There is a price for this, however: ethnocentrism encourages marginalization of other cultures; reinforces isolation of one's own culture; and contributes to misunderstanding, ignorance, and prejudice.

A simple example of this can be observed in the way that the United States has stubbornly refused to give up its measurement system—one that was based on the English measurement system of inches, feet, yards, and miles—even though almost the entire rest of the world (including Great Britain!) has converted to and uses the metric system. The metric system is easier to remember, is easier to perform

ETHNOCENTRISM

In the USA I am five feet, ten and a half inches tall.

Yes, but in almost* every other country in the world you are 1.79 meters tall.

Sure, but what does *THAT* mean?

☐METRIC   ■IMPERIAL

*LIBERIA AND MYANMAR/BURMA ARE ALSO NON-METRIC

equations on, and makes more sense for dealing in an international world. Why is the United States different? Certainly not because it makes sense; more likely, it is because our own ethnocentrism makes us see ourselves as the place that others should work to conform to— not the other way around.

Prejudice

A larger manifestation of ethnocentrism is **prejudice**—the act of show-ing negative and illogical bias toward that which is different. Prejudice is related to the word *prejudge*—meaning to make a judgment or form an opinion before all the facts are discovered or known. Thus, these kinds of judgments and opinions are not based on reason (logic) or experience.

For example, the United States used to be a heteronormative cul-ture, but opinion is shifting, as explained earlier in this chapter. In recent years, political discourse has pushed issues such as same-sex marriage to the surface. In 2015, the Supreme Court legalized same-sex marriage. Now, a majority of Americans support gay marriage.[32] What caused this shift in public opinion? Certainly the hard work of LGBTQ advocates, but also a growing knowledge and acceptance of gay and lesbian couples.

Traditional political opposition to equal rights for LGBTQ individu-als shifted as more children of elected officials came out publicly about their sexuality; for example, the daughter of former vice presi-dent Dick Cheney is open about being a lesbian. Her father, a con-servative Republican, helped lobby for marriage equality.[33] Those who opposed same-sex marriage were often reminded about gay and les-bian couples they personally knew—and who were affected by a law that treated them as unequal. Without this information and experi-ence, however, the prejudice would remain and manifest itself in any number of ways.

Prejudice is, at its root, the product of *ignorance*—the state of not know-ing; the absence of facts, data, logic, or experience. When we are ignorant of people who are different from us, we not only act in a way that is preju-diced but also behave and communicate in a way that is *bigoted*—which is to say, intolerant of those differences. Prejudice, ignorance, and bigotry can all have negative consequences and can lead to even more extreme reac-tions, such as hate speech (addressed in the next section).

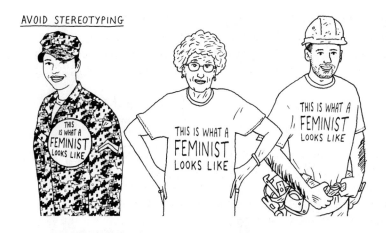

Prejudice requires maintenance, and one of the ways people perpetu-ate these negative challenges to intercultural communication is through a process known as **stereotyping**. When we stereotype, we make broad generalizations about people based on limited, exaggerated, or even false information about individuals. In this way, stereotyping is like inductive reasoning (that is, what is true of the individual must be true of the group). This kind of logic is frequently fallacious—and, in the cultural context, potentially damaging and dangerous. Some make use of stereo-types in order to refute them. For example, consider the meme of people wearing "This is what a feminist looks like" T-shirts in order to refute the idea that all feminists look a certain way (or even that all feminists must be female!).

Hate and Hate Speech

Hate is the feeling of intense, even hostile, aversion to someone or something. In a cultural framework, **hate** is intense aversion to and bias against individuals solely on the basis of their membership in a cultural grouping. Examples of hate include racism, sexism, anti-Semitism, ageism, intense ethnocentrism, and homophobia. People with these extreme biases target victims not only because of their membership in a group but because of the characteristics they share with members of that group (for example, skin color). Often these characteristics are immutable—meaning the individual does not pos-sess any control over them.

When hate is expressed, we often refer to it as **hate speech**. This can consist of insults, slurs, or epithets directed to a group of people or a person within a perceived group.[34] Hate speech can produce extremely damaging results for the victims, including self-hatred,[35] low self-esteem, and a diminished ability to enter into relationships—both with members of other groups and with members of their own group.[36] Victims of hate speech may also suffer physiological reactions, including difficulty breathing, nightmares, post-traumatic stress disorder, hypertension, and even suicide.[37]

Not one bit of this is particularly constructive or helpful with intercultural communications. And in the United States, such speech is often protected by the First Amendment to the Constitution.[38] Therefore, we must take personal responsibility and become more sensitive and careful about how we communicate between cultures.

CONSTRUCTIVE STEPS FOR IMPROVING INTERCULTURAL COMMUNICATION

In her landmark book *Communicating across Cultures*,[39] Stella Ting-Toomey suggests that culturally based conflicts in communication might be avoided if individuals are willing to practice **mindful intercultural communication**. In Ting-Toomey's calculus, being *mindful* means embracing a willingness to learn more about other cultures and to think outside our own cultural biases. It also means demonstrating respect for another culture by voluntarily adapting the culture's style of communicating as a way to avoid conflict.[40] This mindfulness approach informs the following constructive steps we recommend for addressing intercultural communication challenges:

- *Show awareness of and respect for cultural variations.*
- *Express a willingness to learn about and participate in other cultures.*
- *Limit ethnocentrism and condemn hate.*

Let's consider each of these in order.

Show Awareness of and Respect for Cultural Variations

Recall the variations we discussed earlier in the chapter—including high and low uncertainty avoidance, high- and low-context cultures, individualistic versus collectivist cultural orientation, approaches to masculinity and femininity, comfort (or the lack thereof) with human contact, and understanding of power distance. As you encounter people from other cultures, it's important to look for information about the types of variations each person follows.

For example, in the introduction to this chapter we discussed a young American woman meeting the Persian mother of her boyfriend. Have you determined which variation was in play here? The problem in their communication exchange owed to the difference between high- and low-context culture. Christine is a product of American culture, which is low context, meaning that communication exchanges must often be explicitly stated. When Turan, the mother, declined the first offer of tea, Christine assumed that her answer was literal. Turan, by contrast, comes from the more high-context Persian culture. In Iran, her refusal (and subsequent refusals) would be culturally understood as being polite—and an invitation for the other party to insist that she accept the tea.

Becoming aware of cultural variations can definitely improve communications. But it is equally important (if not more important) to be clear about one's *own* cultural variations. Explore this by asking yourself the following questions: How comfortable are you with uncertainty? If you were to assess yourself, how would you rate your cultural awareness of high- or low-context information and understanding? Do you consider your culture oriented more toward individuals or more concerned for all (collective)? How do you think about masculinity and femininity (if you think about them at all)? Do you feel comfortable being physically close to people, or do you maintain a distance? How do you think of power and of those who wield or lack it?

Express a Willingness to Learn about and Participate in Other Cultures

Your learning should not end with cultural variations in communication. Indeed, the more you familiarize yourself with other cultures, the less likely you will be to end up ignorant or prejudiced about others. This is especially true if you are willing to spend time immersed within another culture.[41] Don't be afraid to learn some new words in a language or to try eating new foods. Be open to different customs. Many things that at first seem foreign to us demonstrate how similar we are in the end. For example, there are certain group dances at weddings that involve dozens and even hundreds of people holding hands, while a person at the front of the line pulls it along, weaving and bobbing, for what can be twenty minutes at a time. You can find

these same dances in wedding celebrations for individuals from all three of the world's largest religions: Judaism, Christianity, and Islam. These and other discoveries will remind you that the world is a smaller place than you think. The Internet can provide a wealth of information about different cultures around the world—just be sure to use credible websites.

Limit Ethnocentrism and Condemn Hate

Although ethnocentrism is inevitable (we all see things through our own cultural lens) and helpful for the purpose of building inner-group cohesion, its external impact vastly outweighs any gains to the group. Ethnocentrism promotes more than ignorance—it also fosters misunderstanding. Such an outcome makes conflict resolution between groups, people, and countries difficult—sometimes impossible. It can also strain existing relations to the breaking point. Unfortunately, the solution is not to simply say, "I will not be ethnocentric," because the reality is, we are all biased to a degree.

Instead, the more realistic solution is to limit and control ethnocentrism by acknowledging that there are aspects of other cultures, groups, and countries that you simply may not understand. Rather than try to comprehend them by comparing them to our own norms or values, begin this process by acknowledging the need to *learn more before evaluating*. Let your reactions to a group—or the group's reactions to you—be a guide when looking for biases in the way you approach them. When asking questions about another culture, think like an anthropologist and look for both *meaning* (information about life experiences, thoughts, cognitive views, and perspectives) and *function* (how do they "live out" their beliefs on a daily basis?). In these simplest of ways, you will begin to limit how much your own ethnocentric bias colors the way you see the rest of the world.

For example, many of us in the United States cringe at news reports out of China that explore the difficulties faced by successful Chinese women who reach the age of thirty and are deemed undesirable for marriage.[42] This follows the observed phenomenon of Chinese men in larger Chinese cities indicating a preference to marry women who are "less successful" than they are. In this culture, the men fear being made to look bad in comparison to women who have achieved more—hence, their preference for a wife who may be less educated and accomplished

LIMIT ETHNOCENTRISM

in the workplace. As Americans, most if not all of us look with disapproval at a culture that punishes women for trying to get ahead and rewards men for building themselves up by selecting partners who seem less by comparison. And while there may be little dispute about the correctness of our judgment, the fact remains that we are viewing another culture through our lens and judging its morality based on our ethics. This is not to suggest we should approve of the practice; rather, we should acknowledge our own bias and attempt to understand the other cultural practice.

With regard to the more serious crime of hate speech, we strongly urge you to avoid and condemn it in all its forms. This practice, which targets victims on the basis of shared group characteristics, does more than foster division; it can emotionally, spiritually, and psychologically scar its recipients with a wound that cannot be seen from the surface.

CHAPTER REVIEW

In this chapter, we explored the complex world of culture and what happens when people of different cultural backgrounds interact and communicate. While we defined culture as the sum of knowledge, beliefs, values, and patterns of behavior shared by members of a group, we also explored its connection to the idea of diversity, along with some of the most common categories, such as race, ethnicity, and heritage; gender and sexual orientation; and age. In terms of cultural variations, we examined the following: high- and low-uncertainty-avoidance, high- and low-context cultures, individualistic and collectivist cultures, masculine and feminine cultures, high- and low-contact cultures, and high- and low-power-distance cultures. To view how various cultures and co-cultures can exist in one space, we looked at the various possibilities, which include assimilation, accommodation, and separation. Finally, we examined the problems posed by ethnocentrism, prejudice, and hate and hate speech. We also offered some constructive steps for improving intercultural communication, which include the following: show awareness and respect for cultural variations, express a willingness to learn about and participate in other cultures, and limit ethnocentrism and condemn hate.

LaunchPad
macmillan learning

LaunchPad for *Let's Communicate* offers videos and encourages self-assessment through adaptive quizzing. Go to **launchpadworks.com** to get access to:

 **LearningCurve**
Adaptive Quizzes

 Video clips that help you understand human communication

Key Terms

intercultural communication 162
culture 163
enculturation 163
co-cultures 163
acculturation 164
diversity 164
race 166

ethnicity 166
heritage 166
gender 166
heteronormative 167
age identity 168
uncertainty avoidance 169
high uncertainty avoidance 169

low uncertainty avoidance 169
◉ low-context cultures 171
◉ high-context cultures 171
◉ individualistic cultures 172
◉ collectivist cultures 173
masculine cultures 173
feminine cultures 173
◉ high-contact cultures 174
◉ low-contact cultures 174
power distance 174
◉ high-power-distance cultures 175

◉ low-power-distance cultures 175
◉ assimilation 176
accommodation 177
separation 178
ethnocentrism 179
prejudice 180
stereotyping 181
hate 181
hate speech 182
mindful intercultural
    communication 182

Review Questions

1. What is intercultural communication?
2. How is culture different from diversity?
3. How are the terms *sex* and *gender* related? How and why are they different?
4. What is the meaning of *uncertainty avoidance*?
5. Define *separation*, and provide an example of a culture in the United States that separates itself from the dominant culture.
6. Why would people exhibit ethnocentrism?

Critical Thinking Questions

1. Have you ever experienced a cultural variation—different from your own sense of culture—in your own community? How did you process and react to this experience?
2. What do you think is the best way to learn about another culture? The least effective way?
3. Review the definition of *assimilation*. Is it ever acceptable to force a person or group of people to assimilate into another culture? Why or why not?
4. Many people in the United States read, write, and speak only English—even though we are a very culturally diverse country. Is this an example of ethnocentrism? Explain your answer.
5. Do you have any biases? If so, what are they—and why do you possess them?

Activities

1. In a group, share your race, ethnicity, or heritage. Have each group member share something about his or her culture. What are some things that you learned about your group members that you didn't know? Discuss. Think about your own cultural heritage. Write down any traditions that you take part in (such as a rite of passage, holiday, or special meal). Why are these traditions significant to you?

2. Review your school's policies on student conduct to see if there are any rules about bias, hate speech, or bigotry. What are the rules, if any? Do you think that students follow these rules?

3. Ask your friends and classmates how they would feel about a military draft being reinstated in the United States. In particular, ask how they would feel about the draft being extended to *both* males and females, beginning at age eighteen. Ask them why they feel the way they do.

Apply Your Skills

Go to the illustration regarding challenging stereotypes on page 181. Using these people as models, think of at least one other stereotype that could be challenged if they had different words on their shirts.

Study Plan

_____

_____

_____

_____

_____

_____

MASS AND MEDIATED COMMUNICATION

7

OBJECTIVES

- Understand mass media, including its different forms, emerging technologies, and critical theories.
- Learn the nature and effects of social media.
- Explore media-centric criticism and two theories behind the creation of media.
- More effectively engage in mediated communication.

A quarter century ago, the world watched limited TV news coverage of student-led pro-democracy demonstrations in China's capital, Beijing. Video footage and photo stills poignantly captured the Tiananmen Square protests and subsequent government crackdown, in which Chinese troops opened fire on civilians. The government's careful control of the news media made further coverage from inside China difficult, but one individual was able to smuggle out photos and video of the confrontation. One haunting, now-famous image shows a single man facing down a column of Chinese T-80 tanks. These materials shocked the world and defined the conflict in stark, unambiguous imagery.[1] People within China also managed to send out reports through a still obscure but increasingly used form of technology: the Internet.

Due to the government's restriction on information, an official death toll for the protests has never been released.[2] Even today, the Chinese government continues to control the flow of information on the protests. On its anniversaries, the Chinese government censors online searches that include terms like *candle* and *never forget*. Still, activists in China are finding ways around government control—for example, by putting out a call on social media to wear black or light a candle in honor of those killed.[3]

As a testament to the ongoing influence of the Internet and computer-mediated communication, social media was hugely influential in another wave of protests known as the Arab Spring. Beginning in 2010, these democratic revolutions swept through North Africa and the Middle East, including Tunisia, Libya, Egypt, and Syria. Facebook, Twitter, and especially YouTube provided up-to-date accounts of demonstrations and government responses—not only informing the outside world but also connecting individuals within each country.[4] For example, in the week before Egyptian president Hosni Mubarak's resignation, tweets from Egypt concerning political change in the country expanded tenfold, from approximately 23,000 to 230,000 per day.[5]

Both the Tiananmen Square protests and the Arab Spring protests illustrate the significant social and political contributions of mediated communication. In effect, **mediated communication** is any communication transmitted through a channel, whether television, the Internet, or even a cell phone. In this chapter, we explore two converging types of mediated communication: mass communication and social media. The contrast between China's ongoing control of news and social media, and the Arab Spring's explosion of news *through* social media, shows that this topic is rapidly evolving.

How often do you find yourself checking your text messages, scrolling through Facebook, or idly watching a commercial? Mass and mediated communication is often all around us, but we may not take the time to think about its effects. This chapter will help you understand how these systems work and how to use them both ethically and effectively. To that end, we begin by examining mass media, before moving on to social media and social networking. After that, we focus on two theories for media criticism, before closing with some suggestions on how to most effectively use mediated communication.

UNDERSTANDING MASS MEDIA

Mass media can be defined as mediated communication on a very large scale. Communication scholar Richard Campbell further describes it as "the cultural industries—the channels of communication—that

MASS MEDIA IS PERVASIVE

produce and distribute songs, novels, newspapers, movies, Internet services, and other cultural products to large numbers of people."[6] Clearly, mass media plays a huge role in transmitting information about culture (not to mention politics, science, and other types of information) to the world.

Campbell's definition is useful because it shows that mass media comes in a variety of forms. Whether we're watching a big screen movie or reading a blurb on a news aggregator site, we're taking part in a cultural exchange—one that individuals, groups, and societies use to make sense of their lives and to articulate values and ideals.[7] Another aspect of mass media is that it is **pervasive**, meaning that it is everywhere and available at all times. It can also become overbearing by its ability to constantly and continuously demand our attention.

In the next section, we explore the concept of mass media further by examining some of its dichotomies: entertainment and news media, old and new media, and free and paid media.

Entertainment and News Media

Mass media has two main purposes: to entertain and to inform. **Entertainment media** includes novels and short stories, movies, and TV shows. Conversely, **news media** includes newspapers and magazines, journals, news-oriented websites, and broadcast and cable news. These

PEOPLE OF ENTERTAINMENT MEDIA

JIMMY FALLON   LUPITA NYONG'O   JENNIFER LAWRENCE   STEWIE

types diverge in several important ways. Since people expect entertainment media to provide escape and recreation, they usually understand that the content will not necessarily be factual or literal. Even when addressing real-world events and issues—as can be seen with reality-based TV shows like the still-popular *Survivor*, or with movies based on real events, such as *American Sniper* or *The Theory of Everything*, consumers understand that the content has been modified to package the broadcast or film as entertainment. In addition to shaping content through editing, filmmakers take a certain amount of license with real-life events to make a story more compelling.[8]

News media, by contrast, operate under an admittedly risky assumption that outlets are presenting information that's factual and can be trusted or taken literally. In contemporary America, journalism is the process by which news information is gathered and presented as stories in various print, online, and broadcast formats. Journalism has cast itself in the role of providing important information, facts, and ideas to assist citizens in making decisions about their lives and to help them decide how to vote and otherwise exercise their rights in a democracy.

Consumers of news media are not always aware of why certain news stories are chosen or emphasized. Sometimes the medium affects these decisions. For example, print media like newspapers and magazines can often include more in-depth articles, whereas TV and radio broadcasts are bound by having to provide a more succinct version of a story (or may have to avoid longer and more complex stories completely).

PEOPLE OF NEWS MEDIA

DON LEMON   ANDERSON COOPER   BILL O'REILLY

KATIE COURIC   RACHEL MADDOW

In visual mediums, however, video can bolster the amount of information shared, even with a relatively brief televised news story.

Both print and broadcast news media follow another tradition of American journalism by framing stories about important issues in terms of *conflict*. This includes conflict between ideas (Palestinian statehood versus Israeli security and sovereignty), entities (the United States government versus the government of Iraq), or individuals (candidates in an election campaign). Sometimes, in showing two sides, news media create an illusion of balanced reporting but are actually generating conflict to make the story more compelling. The writer Ishmael Reed has said that "all fiction is friction"—meaning that conflict is the key to drawing readers in and sustaining their interest. While this is a natural tendency, it can be an issue when news sources exaggerate or misrepresent stories to garner more readers or page views.

A related issue arises when news sources, in a rush to appear to be covering both sides equally, give weight to arguments or sides that are not factually accurate. Consider the issue of climate change. The 2013 Intergovernmental Panel on Climate Change (IPCC) report noted that there's 95 percent certainty that people are the main cause of global warming.[9] Despite this and numerous other studies, many media outlets continue to pair reports of global warming with naysayers who have no reliable scientific proof to support their claims. In an even greater media failing, a widely publicized climate change debate on *Meet the Press* featured Bill Nye and Congresswoman Marsha Blackburn[10]—neither of whom are climate scientists. Editors and other media disseminators may argue that consumers of news should be able to make up their own minds about what is factual or accurate—but this is difficult to accomplish with unestablished claims or even outright misinformation.

While entertainment and news media differ in many ways, they also share points of **convergence**, or situations in which they meet. Convergence can occur both within a media type (for example, in entertainment media, when a rap star crosses over to making TV sitcoms or movies) and across media types (for example, when news media stories cross over and become entertainment media in the form of books or movies). It is through this practice that a series of newspaper stories in the *Washington Post* about the Watergate break-in could later become a best-selling nonfiction book (*All the President's Men*) and eventually an Oscar-winning movie. The focus of conflict that is common to both entertainment and news media allows for this convergence, as does the fact that being a high-profile story, author, or performer in one kind of medium can help generate popularity for a work that appears in a different medium.[11]

The lines between entertainment and news media have been further blurred by the success and popularity of comedy programs such as *The Daily Show* (originally with Jon Stewart and now with Trevor Noah). This popular program, whose audience includes many young viewers, is formatted as a news talk show. It shows segments about real news events and features real newsmakers—including elected officials—as guests. But Noah, like his predecessor Stewart, is a comedian, and his program pokes fun at these events (and sometimes at his guests!). So, is the show news or entertainment? The answer is, a little of both.

CONVERGENCE

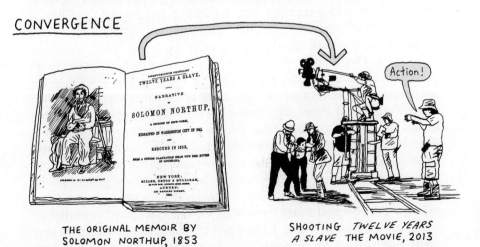

THE ORIGINAL MEMOIR BY
SOLOMON NORTHUP, 1853

SHOOTING *TWELVE YEARS
A SLAVE* THE MOVIE, 2013

Old Media and New Media

Twenty years ago, most people got their news and entertainment through a few standard mediums: TV, radio, film, books, magazines, journals, and newspapers. These products were offered on a set schedule (daily, weekly, monthly), and while some broadcasts were live, the majority of them were preplanned.

Today, all that has changed. While we still have **old media** (traditional forms of mass communication), we also have **new media** (mass communication via newer forms of technology, such as the Internet). In a relatively short period of time, personal computers have become commonplace for the majority of American households—as common as owning a television used to be.[12] Today, millions of individuals or households in the United States are connected in one form or another to the Internet. People go online to research, read the news, buy things, share information, and even find potential mates. Because it is largely unregulated by state or federal government entities (in the United States), the Internet is also a place where information about politics, campaigns, and governance can be posted, shared, and exchanged.

FROM OLD MEDIA TO NEW MEDIA

The Internet's emergence has affected how news media is created and how it may be accessed and consumed. Consider the following ways the Internet has affected news coverage:

- **Formatting of news.** In the 1940s, TV news emerged and eventually replaced print media (newspapers and magazines) as the chief form of media people used to get information about the world. One of the effects of this trend was that news sources had to reduce stories according to time allotments rather than word counts and column space. Of course, given that a TV news story contained visual messaging (videos and occasional photographs), it could be argued that the stories were still in-depth due to their nonverbal messages. The rise of news via the Internet has also had effects on format. Internet users are in the habit of quickly digesting a short news story and then moving on to other stories, or multitasking and using other forms of media while consuming the news. We might compare this to tasting different small samples of food instead of ordering and consuming a whole dish of something. Time is at a premium, and stories must be easily digestible. Slate.com is so conscious of this that it even has a "minutes to read" feature attached to its stories so that readers will know in advance how long it will take to read a specific article.[13]

- **Events unfolding in real time.** Twenty-four-hour cable TV news channels like CNN and the proliferation of satellites that beam stories around the globe have made it possible for emerging stories to be covered 24/7. Still, the Internet's rising influence, particularly with regard to social media, has raised the stakes—with both positive and negative results. For example, the mass protests in Iran (2009–10)—sometimes called the Twitter revolution—generated wide coverage in the Western media, even though there weren't many Western reporters in the region at the time. Instead, locals sent out information via Twitter and Facebook. In the end, it was not enough to energize a revolution to topple Iran's repressive government, but it was effective in providing access to a globally significant news event *in real time*, with perspectives offered by Iranians who were on the scene.[14] Real-time news can also lead to more problematic coverage. For example, early online reports concerning shooting deaths at the Sandy Hook Elementary School in Newton, Connecticut, misidentified an innocent man as the shooter in a rush to provide up-to-the-minute news. CNN, the

Huffington Post, and Slate.com all rushed to judgment, even showing the individual's Facebook page in the story.[15]

- **Increased interactivity.** Today, many people feel as though they
  are more a "part" of the news—and that they can now take a larger
  role in the making or sharing of actual news. Some online news
  sources now include tweets from people who were on the scene of a
  breaking news story. People can often comment on news stories, adding their own opinions about the topics at hand. Sometimes people's
  social media musings can actually *become* the news, meaning that
  they're affecting editorial choices about what to cover. For example,
  the Huffington Post regularly publishes the "Trending 20" tweets
  from Twitter, which are chosen based on "interesting, informative
  and hilarious tweets from worldwide Twitter trending topics."[16]

Free Media and Paid Media

Consider the tremendous media coverage that the Academy Awards generate each year: videos and articles on the best (and worst) red carpet
looks, celebrity banter and interviews, highlights, fiascos, and, of course,
who takes home the Oscar. While the Academy is not paying news outlets to cover the ceremony, this coverage does promote the event—and
the films nominated.

This example demonstrates **free media**, or a message communicated
by the news media in a manner that is practically free for the original
messenger. In order to generate content, news and entertainment outlets
often promote certain individuals, organizations, or products, such as
movies and books. It's a symbiotic relationship that isn't always readily
apparent. And sometimes the relationship doesn't always run smoothly.
Alec Baldwin may be the most notorious example of a celebrity who has
turned against the media, publicly making complaints against various
reporters and news sources.

On the other hand, **paid media** is simply paid advertising in any
form. For a new movie release, this could include billboards, previews
at theaters, TV ads, bus ads, websites, and Twitter campaigns. The
expense for this kind of mass media can be considerable—but, targeted
carefully, it can greatly assist in placing filmgoers in a theater on opening night or movie buffs at the cinema on opening weekend. From that
point forward, of course, reviews and the all-critical word of mouth are
key to a film's long-term prospects—but these, too, may be incorporated
into future attempts at advertising. Newspaper ads, for example, typically

EFFECTS OF THE INTERNET ON THE NEWS:

trumpet (and often quote out of context) film reviewers' comments, while TV ads often feature individual sound bites from audience members. Since these ads are paid for by the studios, audience members' comments are naturally positive and affirming.

There are often crossovers between free and paid media. Just one example is American politics. Candidates with low name recognition (voters don't know who they are) must spend huge amounts of money just to introduce themselves to voters. Sadly for candidates, raising money to spend on this introductory advertising is difficult because campaign donors usually prefer to give to candidates with high name recognition. First-time candidates often contact news reporters in an attempt to get

CONTINUED ON P.48

mentioned in stories, since these can reach a large number of readers or viewers. Candidates know they can't control what a journalist writes about them—but then again, even negative coverage promotes name recognition.[17] This makes the candidate more credible and increases his or her chances for funding.

Now that we've explored mass media, let's turn to a type of media that allows people to create, interact with, and consume information: social media.

UNDERSTANDING SOCIAL MEDIA

Do you have a Facebook profile? Do you check it more than five times a day? If so, you're not alone—23 percent of Facebook users do.[18] Social media, in forms like Facebook, Twitter, Snapchat, Instagram, Tumblr, YouTube, and Pinterest, has certainly infiltrated our lives, as well as the way we communicate. Before we go further, let's define **social media**: "forms of electronic communication . . . through which users create online communities to share information . . . and other content."[19] When people interact through social media, we call that **social networking**.

THE FOUR Cs

The general goals and characteristics of social media and social net-working are what scholars Hoffman and Novak (2011) have called the four Cs: **connect**, **create**, **consume**, and **control**.[20] This means that social media creates opportunities for people to *connect* with each other and *create* conversations. It also allows people to *create* and *consume* content, and to *control* its dispersion. These four goals distinguish social media from traditional mass media, which is normally a one-way communication path from a sender to a receiver. However, as we mentioned earlier, mass media is becoming ever more interactive, making the line between mass and social media less defined. For example, think of someone who makes a YouTube video that then goes viral and is watched by millions of people—is that social media or mass media? In our view, it's both.

Effects of Social Media

The growth and popularity of social media in this country and around the world have had profound effects on the ways that large numbers of people communicate with one another. Consider the following effects:

- **A new way to effect change and raise consciousness.** In 2014, global outrage exploded after a terrorist group called Boko Haram kidnapped three hundred girls from a boarding school in northern Nigeria. The girls, who ranged in age from fifteen to eighteen, were to be auctioned off for $12 each to become "wives of the militants."[21] A Twitter campaign, built around the hashtag #bringbackourgirls, succeeded in raising international consciousness about the incident. Sadly, it did not result in the release of the girls.

- **Access to more information.** The Internet has undoubtedly changed the way students search for information—including offering online search engines and academic article databases to help students find sources for papers and projects. But another big change is that students can access actual instruction from well-qualified experts on a variety of topics. Programs like Khan Academy,[22] for example, offer free courses in a variety of subjects. These courses are available on YouTube and are widely praised for making subjects more accessible to a wider audience.[23] Similarly, TED (Technology, Entertainment and Design) talks offer engaging lectures that last no more than eighteen minutes.[24] Free and accessible to anyone with an Internet connection, TED talks have acquired a global audience.

- **Easy and constant connections to people.** Social networking sites like Facebook, Instagram, and Snapchat can enable you to make contact and connections with literally thousands of people. Your friends may live in proximity to you or be all the way around the world, but on these sites, they're only a click away. Of course, these friendships take place in a virtual space, which may mean that you may not be regularly interacting in an F2F (face-to-face) way. While many who use social networks benefit from being connected to a greater number of people, the quality of interactions will likely be different and possibly less fulfilling than interacting with people in real life. Online, it's easier for people to construct identities for themselves, suggested by the photographs they post, the sentiments they share, and the postings from others they approve with a "like" or "favorite." Often, these constructions are only a limited presentation of the person inside. That veneer can be even more pronounced when the social networking site is an online dating site. While sites like OkCupid and Match.com enable busy people to meet others, this meeting may not be as effective as an F2F interaction. For example, online communication lacks many of the cues and features that build attraction—like touching.[25] Individuals may also be dishonest about their age, weight, height, income, and marital status.[26] (This can become painfully obvious when people actually meet in person.) Still, dating sites can facilitate lasting real-life relationships. One study estimates that one-third of married couples in the United States met online.[27]

Still, there are some who would argue that computer-mediated communication (CMC) has advantages over traditional F2F exchanges. In 1996, communications scholar Joseph Walther developed what he termed a **hyperpersonal model** for interpersonal communication through CMC. This model suggests that CMC exchanges between participants allow hyperpersonal communicators to strategically develop and edit the sense of themselves they present to one another—all in a way that optimizes how they are received and perceived. When combined with other forms of social media, this allows CMC users as a group to achieve a greater sense of unity, liking, and intimacy than otherwise might be possible in an F2F exchange.[28]

EFFECTS OF SOCIAL MEDIA

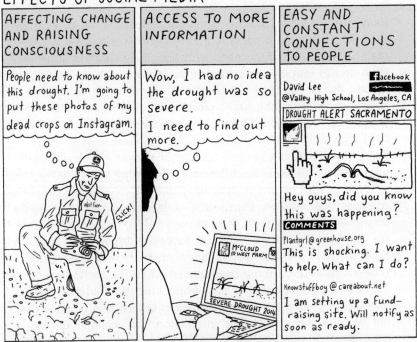

Anonymity, Free Speech, and Privacy Issues

The relatively quick growth of the Internet and social media has led to some fascinating issues that we face every time we go online. One of these is **anonymity**—the state of being unknown. Some feel that anonymity protects freedom of speech, since people can post anonymous comments or responses without any fear of repercussions. An extreme example of this is "hacktivist" groups like Anonymous. In 2012, members of Anonymous chose to become involved with a Steubenville, Ohio, rape case, blaming the local authorities for not investigating the case thoroughly.[29] The group planned rallies and uncovered evidence, but it also posted private files that didn't have anything to do with the case. While Anonymous's actions did lead to several indictments of those involved, some disagreed with the group's methods and claimed that it invited unwarranted online abuse.

An unquestionably negative consequence of anonymity is **trolling**: the posting of anonymous comments, sometimes via false, constructed identities, solely to stir up controversy and discord. "Trolls" post comments not to advance any truths but solely to amuse themselves. For this reason, sites such as the Huffington Post have established policies that ban anonymous posts.[30]

Another growing issue related to anonymity is privacy. Many users don't realize that virtually everything they post—words, photos, videos—is essentially posted forever. Elaborate programs track not only what we post but also how and where we post it. In other words, the very idea of online privacy should be questioned. For those applying for jobs, this is especially relevant. Companies often Google potential employees—and may well pass over any candidates with compromising information or inappropriate photos.

Social media platforms often track and use data from their users—to the point where they have been publicly chastened. For example, in 2013, Instagram changed its policy language after a backlash from users in response to a "terms of use" change that appeared to give the company freedom to use any photos that users had uploaded on the site.[31] Companies like Facebook (which owns Instagram) and Google use algorithms to discover trends and human behavior, *especially* with respect to how, why, where, and when we spend our money. And revelations about the National Security Agency sparked public outrage when, in 2013, government contractor Edward Snowden leaked documents that showed government surveillance over private phone and Internet use.[32] In 2014,

Snowden started a "Reset the Net" campaign, which calls for a strengthening of privacy rights online.[33]

Digital Divide and Net Neutrality

As indicated in previous sections, new media in the form of the Internet and CMC offer great opportunities for vastly expanding the ways in which we communicate. Unfortunately, however, not everyone in the world—or the United States—enjoys access to this technology. A so-called **digital divide**—the gap between those with access to the Internet and those without access—exists in the United States. According to U.S. Census Bureau information, less

RESET THE NET

EDWARD SNOWDEN

than three-fourths of all U.S. households have access to the Internet. By contrast, many countries in Europe enjoy much higher numbers—including the Netherlands, where 95 percent of all households have access.[34]

This divide can be observed in the different access levels in rural areas versus metropolitan areas. But even in big cities like Detroit, Oakland, or Miami, there are large gaps between those with access and those without. The latter group is typically populated by those living in poverty—and for many big cities, this may disproportionately affect minorities. This is a tragedy of no small significance. Access to the Internet not only facilitates communication but is essential for education, housing, access to social services—and especially looking and applying for a job. Closing the digital divide is one of the solutions to fighting poverty and unemployment.

One way to help decrease the digital divide is for the government to pass laws and enact policies to protect **net neutrality**—in which Internet service providers allow equal access to all sites, without enacting "fast lanes" for those who pay more. The government has met with great resistance from providers, which want to charge for access to the Internet—and charge a premium for fast broadband access. In early 2015, the FCC voted to reclassify broadband under Title II of the Communications Act in an attempt to preserve net neutrality. It remains to be seen how these policies will play out over the coming years.

MEDIA-CENTRIC CRITICISM

Now that we've discussed what mass and social media are and how we use them, let's turn to another question: Who is creating this media that so permeates our lives, and to what effect? For our purposes, we examine two theories that attempt to answer these questions: critical media theory and the agenda-setting theory. In the following sections, we examine the central ideas and assumptions underlying both theories.

Critical Media Theory

According to **critical media theory**, those who own mass media in its various forms (a newspaper chain, a movie studio, a television network) purposely influence the content of mass media messages. This influence allows them to dominate and marginalize others.[35] Critical media theory has its origins in several different schools of thought, including **cultural criticism**, which examines mass media for potential bias and discrimination.

Theorists of cultural criticism, including Edward Said, have related it to concepts of "**the Other**." This concept suggests that people create intergroup identity by focusing on how they're different from other people or outside groups. This builds group cohesion and a sense of group identity. However, it also leads to negative stereotypes and false patterns of representation of those designated as the Other.

One example Edward Said provides is how Muslims and Arabs are often portrayed in Western popular culture "as oil suppliers or potential terrorists."[36] Similarly, we could consider how often American TV news and dramas have focused on crime stories—and how often the alleged perpetrators are depicted as African American males. These patterns of representing African American males as criminals or Others perpetuate negative stereotypes.[37]

Critical media theory asserts that certain forms of mass media (for example, print, broadcast, or online) may purport to be neutral, objective, and independent of outside influence, when in fact they may be directly or indirectly exactly the opposite.[38] A common complaint about critical media theory is that it does not acknowledge the positive effects of mass media on society—both in providing information that may benefit or help

CRITICAL MEDIA THEORY

people (such as stories about better nutrition) and in increasing participation in the democratic process (such as sharing information from unbiased political sites like OnTheIssues.org, which offers information on politicians' voting records and public statements).[39] Certain experts also fault critical media theory for its failure to acknowledge the various types of mass media available, which represent a wide variety of perspectives and ideologies.[40] Particularly with the advent of the Internet, there are many opportunities to find opposing or dissimilar viewpoints online.[41]

But though there may be more sources available, it's important to remember that many people still rely on "traditional" and trusted sources for news (CNN, the *New York Times*, the *Wall Street Journal*). In the last few decades, there's been an unprecedented amount of **conglomeration**, in which major corporations buy other companies, putting them all under the same umbrella of ownership. In 2011, a popular graphic traced the vast majority of media (90 percent) to just six sources (GE, News-Corp, Disney, Viacom, TimeWarner, and CBS).[42] The fact that so few companies disseminate so much of our media has troubled many. It also makes the theory we discuss in the next section even more important to consider.

Agenda-Setting Theory

Almost ninety years ago, noted journalist Walter Lippmann argued that ordinary life was too full of competing information and priorities for the average person to know all of the details and issues of the day. Said

Lippmann: "We are not equipped to deal with so much subtlety, so much variety, so many permutations and combinations. And all together we have to act in that environment, we have to reconstruct it on a simpler model before we can manage it."[43] The result, he suggested, was that an entity— mass media as news media—had to prioritize these issues for us. And that it did—by selecting what issues would make compelling news stories for us to read, listen to, observe, and discuss. In 1972, researchers Maxwell McCombs and Donald Shaw named this concept, labeling it as **agenda-setting**.[44] The label took hold and became a common reference for understanding how news media tells the public "what to think about."[45]

Agenda-setting occurs because of the unique constraints of mass media, previously discussed. First, public consumption requires a now constant refilling of news content. Second, formats are limited by time and space—such as the number of minutes available for a TV broadcast or the word count limits for a newspaper. Even with the addition of new media content on the Internet, there are still some limitations about how many stories or entries can be provided (with the expectation that they will be read) and the degree to which people are willing to read them. Historically, these kinds of constraints have forced reporters and editors to make choices about what is newsworthy. The act of choosing one story over another means that certain stories and issues will not receive coverage. It also means that the issues that are covered acquire a certain level of public importance and, inevitably, public focus.

Agenda-setting occurs at two levels. The first level involves the aforementioned choice of what editors decide to cover. The second level focuses on the complexity of each issue—and which part of it is emphasized in the telling of the story. By featuring a certain attribution of an issue or a story, or **framing** it in a certain way, those in the media are telling us that it has particular significance.[46] In practice, a frame emphasizes certain attributes by defining a problem, explaining its potential causes, making moral judgments, and suggesting possible remedies for problems or effects.

Consider this example. In February 2012, a Neighborhood Watch volunteer in Sanford, Florida, named George Zimmerman shot and killed an unarmed seventeen-year-old boy named Trayvon Martin. Zimmerman claimed he shot Martin in self-defense because of a scuffle between the two of them that left him feeling threatened and in fear for his life. He was taken into custody but later released without charges being filed. In early March, this was still predominantly a local story in Florida news, but by mid-March, the story had gone national, with coverage from the

Atlantic,[47] *Crimesider* from CBS News,[48] and the *New York Times.*[49] Most coverage initially focused on Florida's "stand-your-ground" self-defense law. Only the *New York Times* focused on the fact that Martin was African American and questioned whether race was involved in the case.

Over time, the framing of this tragedy shifted more broadly to a discussion of race. This led to an investigation by the U.S. Department of Justice, an investigation by the local grand jury, and a protest by the NAACP. The framing of the story around race also moved into a public dialogue about the hoodie that Martin had worn that night—in particular, how his clothing revealed a racial stereotyping of young black males. In protest and solidarity, various people donned hoodies—including LeBron James and members of the Miami Heat, who posed for photos wearing their team jackets with the hoods up.[50] African American members of the House of Representatives, the U.S. Senate, college students, and church congregants did the same.

In April 2013, Zimmerman was charged with second-degree murder. In the aftermath of the trial, the framing of the story continued to evolve, focusing on the nature of Neighborhood Watch programs, general

FRAMING

questions surrounding gun control, the future of Florida's self-defense law, and the meaning and fairness of Zimmerman's charges. Zimmerman was acquitted in July 2013, sparking public outrage over a process that people believed provided no justice for Trayvon Martin or his family. This tragedy played out for the better part of a year, dominating both TV and newspaper coverage. Often, news sources published multiple stories devoted to different frames of the event within the same broadcast or newspaper section. The inclusion of all these stories naturally meant that on those days, there wasn't time or space for other news stories—and, as a result of their exclusion, their salience for the public was diminished.

Most agree that the news media's agenda-setting of issues through framing and general coverage has influenced what the public sees as important events and issues. This public agenda-setting along with public opinion eventually influences and shapes the government's policy agenda.[51]

SUGGESTIONS FOR MEDIATED COMMUNICATION

We have gone over the definitions and effects of mass media and social media, and have shown the importance of awareness in media consumption. We now offer additional suggestions for effectively navigating the mediated communication in your life.

Become a Critical Consumer of Mass Media

There are almost endless sources of content for mass media—especially for news. Rather than accepting everything you see or read as true, be vigilant about asking questions and challenging what is presented. Remember that consuming mass media is like consuming food—meaning that a healthy diet is a well-balanced diet. Instead of limiting yourself to a certain news program or newspaper, diversify and try multiple forms of media. Also, be willing to look across an ideological spectrum. If you usually listen to NPR, try checking out something from another perspective, like the *Wall Street Journal*. Different sources and content providers may give you different perspectives—all of which enhance the depth of your understanding.

A WELL-BALANCED MASS MEDIA DIET

Avoid Being Influenced by Media Depictions of "the Other"

As suggested in the section on critical media studies, the media often tends to represent people in ways that feed ethnocentrism, stereotypes, and even racism. These patterns of representation may reinforce how people in a dominant group feel toward one another (loyalty, support, privilege), and may also encourage them to keep other kinds of people outside their group. Dominant cultures often use "the Other" to rationalize their behavior, including actions like slavery, colonization, or military invasion.[52] Be aware of these patterns of representation and the effect they can have on promoting ethnocentrism (see Chapter 6). You can also counter this by supporting programs and media that provide a more diverse perspective.

Be Mindful about How Much Personal Information You Share on Social Media

One of the most enjoyable features of social media is the ease with which we can share comments, photos, and videos. However, as we mentioned earlier, you should know that once you post these, they exist forever. Even with apps like Snapchat (where photos that you post disappear after a certain amount of time), it's easy enough for others to take a screenshot, saving your image forever. You never know where this information might turn up. And other people—including potential employers—might be able to find it with a simple Google search. So, be smart. We aren't suggesting that you should censor everything you say; we're simply reminding you that if you think your posts are private and will never be seen by anyone outside a network—think again. Post information or photos only if you don't mind that others may come across them in the future.

Don't Say Anything Online You Wouldn't Say in Person

In the same vein, remember that once you post your thoughts online (on Facebook, Twitter, or other platforms), you can't take those thoughts back. Many a person has regretted something they've said online—and sometimes their thoughtless or offensive remarks can even lead to public condemnation. In late 2013, one PR executive who made a racist remark on Twitter before boarding a plane launched such a Twitter backlash that she was fired by the time she landed.[53]

Obviously, one should never make racist remarks, but even jokes and sarcasm can be misunderstood and taken the wrong way. A 2013 study showed that social networks can affect people's self-esteem and cause them to have lower self-control while interacting.[54] We don't yet know the full effects of social media and how it may change our behavior. But if you ask yourself whether you would say the same thing in a face-to-face interaction with others, that's a good indication of whether it's appropriate online.

Consider Taking a Break to Avoid Technology Burnout

Information technology, telecommunications, social media, and social networking are pervasive—and potentially addictive. A 2013 Internet trends report claimed that between March 2013 and March 2014, the number of "mobile addicts" (defined as those who check their phones sixty or more times a day) grew 123 percent, from 79 million to 176

million.[55] This may seem hard to believe, but how many people do you see on campus or walking down the street relating more to a smartphone than to the people or the environment around them? We feel connected to others through media and technology, but these connections are not literal or physical so much as virtual. Because of this, we urge you to occasionally take a break and unplug from your computer laptop, tablet, or smartphone. Being physically present can encourage being emotionally and intellectually present. It can also foster better listening and, with it, better understanding among those around you.

CHAPTER REVIEW

In this chapter, we explored the effects of mass and mediated communication, and how they have changed over time. We began by comparing the secreted photos and video from the Tiananmen Square protests to the tweets and YouTube videos from the Arab Spring. To explore mass media, we looked at its dichotomies: entertainment and news media, old and new media, and free and paid media. In this section, we also examined convergence, both within and across media types.

In the section on understanding social media, we discussed its characteristics and general goals (to connect, create, consume, and control). Social media's major effects include affecting change, offering more access to information, and providing constant connection to others. Social media's rise has led to new issues concerning anonymity, free speech, and privacy.

The next section examined media-centric criticism through two theories: the critical media theory and the agenda-setting theory, which includes the idea of framing. Finally, we offered several suggestions for using mediated communication, from becoming a critical consumer to taking a break to avoid technology burnout.

LaunchPad
macmillan learning

LaunchPad for *Let's Communicate* offers videos and encourages self-assessment through adaptive quizzing. Go to **launchpadworks.com** to get access to:

 **LearningCurve Adaptive Quizzes**

 Video clips that help you understand human communication

Key Terms

mediated communication 192
mass media 192
pervasive 193
entertainment media 193
news media 193
convergence 196
old media 197
new media 197
free media 199
paid media 199
social media 201
social networking 201
four Cs: connect, create,
   consume, control 202

hyperpersonal model 204
Ⓞ anonymity 205
Ⓞ trolling 205
digital divide 206
net neutrality 206
critical media theory 207
cultural criticism 207
the Other 207
conglomeration 208
Ⓞ agenda-setting 209
framing 209

Review Questions

1. What is mass media?
2. How are entertainment media and news media similar—and how are they different?
3. What is paid media? How is it different from free media?
4. Define *agenda-setting*. How does framing relate to agenda-setting?
5. What is meant by the term *the Other*?
6. When does media convergence occur?

Critical Thinking Questions

1. Have you ever used an Internet search engine to jump-start your research for a paper? Why would you trust or distrust the information you find there?
2. Have you or a friend ever used an online dating site to meet someone? If so, was the person the same as the one described online? If the person was different, explain how.
3. Think about the last time you watched or read the news. What was your news source, and what type of agenda-setting was used? For example, what stories were covered more prominently? What stories were given less coverage?

4. Online news sites like the Huffington Post have banned anonymous posts due to trolling. What are the pros and cons of these types of bans?

Activities

1. Make a list of all the television shows you watch. Then determine if they fall into the entertainment media or news media category. Why do you prefer one category over the other? Do any of these shows fit into both categories?
2. If you are a member of a social networking site like Facebook, examine the page of a close friend, family member, or partner. How much of what is posted accurately represents who you know that person to be?
3. On one of your social networking pages, consider how much of your personal privacy you are compromising with each post or photo you share. Take a look at your privacy settings, and determine who can view your profile. Can a prospective love interest, potential in-law, or future employer see some or all of what you've posted?
4. Spend fifteen minutes online reading articles on a news website. Take note of the following: What types of articles drew your attention? Did you read the articles in their entirety? How much time did you spend reading each article?

Apply Your Skills

Go to the illustration on framing with the example of Trayvon Martin on page 210. Now imagine that the news story was broader than this example—and was now about the Black Lives Matter movement. How might this illustration look different with respect to the individual frames of the story?

PRINCIPLES OF INTERPERSONAL COMMUNICATION

8

OBJECTIVES

- Learn why interpersonal communication, particularly in the dyad, is so important to our personal and social lives.

- Understand why we are attracted to others and how these personal relationships can change over time.

- Explain the value and challenges of privacy management in personal relationships.

- Understand how relational partners manage the everyday tensions of opposing desires.

Kelley and Terri met in high school in the Philippines. Both had fathers in the American military, though Terri's family had arrived two years after Kelley's. Kelley would never forget the first day that Terri showed up in her biology class. Terri was confident, outspoken, and fluent in Italian, since she'd lived in Italy until recently. Intrigued, Kelley asked Terri if she needed someone to show her around. That day, a friendship was born.

Kelley and Terri remained good friends through high school and decided to attend the same college in California. They took classes together, became sorority sisters, and offered honest, sometimes painful feedback on the quality of each other's dating choices. After graduation, Kelley got a job offer in New York, while Terri made plans to stay in San Francisco. It was difficult to say good-bye, but they promised to stay in close touch.

Through the years, their friendship continued, though in many different forms. Sometimes they were extremely busy with careers and families, and months would pass without contact. They reconnected at high school reunions, where they were surprised to find how easy it was to pick up where they'd left off. And even during periods when they weren't in close contact, Kelley and Terri still kept each other updated on major life events. When Kelley got married, Terri was a bridesmaid. Years later, when Terri's mother passed away, Kelley flew in from New York to help Terri with the arrangements and to comfort her during that difficult time.

Now both women are in their sixties and are still friends. Kelley recently attended the wedding of Terri's son, Jake. Over cake and champagne, the guests marveled over the number of years that Kelley and Terri had known each other. Jake and his friends vowed to continue their friendships through the decades, too.

Kelley and Terri's story shows an example of an **interpersonal relationship**—a special one-on-one connection that can last and change over long periods of time. We explore some of the benefits of this type of relationship, and then look at how these relationships form and change. We also look at how concepts like self-disclosure and privacy contribute to the quality of our interpersonal communication. We end by examining the contradictory forces that constantly push and pull at our relationships.

INTERPERSONAL COMMUNICATION IN THE DYAD

Think of all the people you casually talk to in a given day. This could include a classmate who asks to see your notes, a professor you need to talk to in order to clarify an assignment, or a barista taking your coffee order. These interactions are likely automatic and standard—in other words, *im*personal. More *inter*personal interactions maximize "the presence of the personal"—meaning that you and the other person enjoy each other's company on a deeper level.[1] **Interpersonal communication** occurs in the interactions between people who find each other unique and irreplaceable.

This type of communication can happen between any number of individuals; however, the **dyad**, or the two-person social unit, offers the most potential for it. The dyad's small size allows people greater opportunities for **intimacy**—access to more information about each other and richer insight into the other person.[2] The reality, though, is that the dyad is the most fragile social unit: it takes two to create and only one to break. In the following section, we explore interpersonal communication within the dyad.

The Benefits of Interpersonal Relationships

In her nonfiction book *Committed: A Sceptic Makes Peace with Marriage*, author Elizabeth Gilbert notes that "To be fully seen by somebody, then, and to be loved anyhow—this is a human offering that can border on the miraculous."[3] There are multiple benefits to connecting with another person, and they often center on **self-expansion**, or the opportunity to deepen and broaden one's personal identity.[4] For example, studies have shown that the number of words a person uses to describe his or her "self" increases in romantic relationships and declines toward a relationship's end.[5] Let's take a look at the four main benefits of interpersonal relationships:[6]

Belonging. One of humans' top needs is to belong.[7] Whether in person or online, most people seek out others to find acceptance for who they are.[8] Facebook and other social networking sites have exploded due to this need to be connected—and they provide the chance to do so on a constant basis. People add friends on Facebook to demonstrate that they're connected to a larger social group, both directly through friends and indirectly through friends of friends.[9]

Emotional, Psychological, and Physical Well-Being. Interpersonal relationships help our emotional life in several ways: they give feedback for us to help judge our experiences, they guide our actions, and they help us learn how to act in a socially appropriate manner. Additionally, research has linked strong social connections to a plethora of health-related bonuses: a reduction in stress,[10] higher overall happiness,[11] and a stronger immune system.[12]

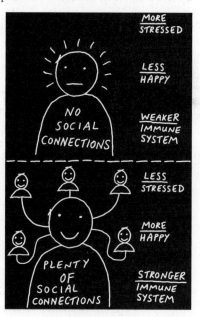

Self-Expression. Enjoying friendships means that we're able to partake in an important and often enjoyable pastime: talking about ourselves. People post about themselves 80 percent of the time on social media.[13] When sharing our thoughts and talking about our lives, we activate the region of our brain that is associated with our sense of satisfaction—the same region activated by sex, food, and money.[14]

Reciprocal Altruism. The exchange of favors between non-blood relations is called **reciprocal altruism**. Scholars have long considered this the defining aspect of friendships.[15] It simply feels good to help those we're close with.[16] The absence of reciprocal altruism—say, after a close coworker transfers to another office—may highlight the ways in which both parties once tried to make life easier for the other.

The Nature and Type of Close Dyads

While dyads can technically be any two-person unit, we're going to focus on intimate dyads in order to examine interpersonal communication. Intimate dyads are voluntary; both people choose to take part in them and, over time, come to share an **interdependence**, or a reliance on each other. In the following sections, we explore the most common forms of close dyads, including friendships, work peers, and romantic relationships.

Note that we don't include family. This relationship often contains close bonds and interdependence; however, it doesn't include the notion

RECIPROCAL ALTRUISM

OWEN

MZEE

(VISIT www.owenandmzee.com FOR THEIR WHOLE STORY)

of choice (at least for biological family members). Due to the uniqueness of family dynamics, family relationships are often studied in a field of their own.

Friendships. A **friendship** is a close dyad defined by strong affinity, warmth, and affection.[17] Friendships can be found across culture, gender, and sexual identity lines.[18] A central feature of friendship is the assumption of a shared balance of power.[19] Friends also accept both the good and the bad attributes of each other.[20] When they do give judgment, it is usually thought to come from a place of caring.[21] Friends offer and receive emotional, psychological, spiritual, and physical support. In certain traumatic situations, such as being rejected by parents when coming out as gay, people often turn to their friends as safe support for their identities.[22]

Both male and female American college students report valuing similar levels of closeness in their friendships, yet they express it differently.[23] Females as well as androgynous males find validation for their emotional lives in their friendships.[24] Traditional males more often connect through the camaraderie of activity, or situations in which they can offer practical help as a way to show they care.[25] Friendships also differ across cultures. In the south of Spain, for instance, both men and women seek intimate closeness from their same-sex friends rather than from their spouse.[26]

Work Peers. Consider all the television shows about people who become close while working together—from *Workaholics* to *Mad Men* to *Silicon Valley*. Given that we often spend the majority of our days with coworkers, it makes sense that friendships arise, especially if we work

VIRTUAL WORK PEERS

in organizations that foster respect and civility.[27] Work relationships can offer support and enjoyment—if the friends can avoid the threatening dynamic of competition.[28]

Work friendships can fall into a few categories. **Professional peers** work side by side, giving each other practical as well as personal support.[29] **Collegial peers** are friends who also happen to be coworkers—say, if you helped a friend get a job at your current place of employment. A **special peer** denotes a coworker who becomes similar to a best friend at work. Special peers exhibit the most friendship, trust, and emotional support. **Virtual peers**, or coworkers, communicate through mediated communication (such as those in different geographical locations), and their closeness depends on how much they interact.

Romantic Relationships.
Romantic relationships, while not always easy, reflect humans' deep desire to seek out a life partner. Interestingly, in spite of reports that marriage for Americans may be becoming a less preferred choice, most Americans do get married at least once, according to a March 2015 report of current census data.[30]

Romantic relationships have characteristics not found in other types of close dyads. For example, they include a higher level of social access—meaning that the two people involved have to plan their time and even their futures around the other—as well as physical access. Romantic relationships require a level of commitment not found in most other dyads—one that is often a better predictor of sustaining a romantic relationship than reported love alone.[31] Finally, these relationships contain a **negotiated permanence**—meaning that the people involved often assume that they will continue to stay together. This may be why partners choose to stay in romantic relationships even if they are not especially happy.

NEGOTIATED PERMANENCE

I take you to be my life partner, companion, and friend. With you I look forward to facing all that life has to offer...

Beyond these typical characteristics, there is a surprising diversity to romantic relationships. For instance, more and more married couples are choosing to live in separate residences, not because of their careers but because they can better sustain their relationship that way.[32] Cohabitation, once taboo, is now the preferred option (as opposed to marriage) upon the discovery of an unplanned pregnancy.[33] Certain people choose to have open marriages, in which the spouses can date other people. Rarely discussed romantic triads involve a committed pair who bring in a third person to share their relationship, often due to the illness of one partner.[34] Although diverse in nature, their commonality lies in negotiating the same issues of love, longing, and commitment.

SELECTING A FEW FROM THE MANY

Think back to your first few days at college—and particularly all the people you interacted with. Could you, if asked, make a list of all of them now? Most likely not. Still, some of those people are probably now close friends and perhaps even romantic partners. But how did that process happen—of selecting a few out of a larger group?

Initially, we constantly scan our environment and draw assumptions about those around us based on what we see and hear. We make note of people's appearance, how they dress, and how they behave. Due to today's technological world, we often gather information from more than just in-person cues. College students report using a combination of face-to-face interaction, calling, texting, e-mail, and social networking sites to compile information about others.[35]

We continue to move in closer perceptually (see Chapter 2) and make our selections based on things like the roles we place others in ("Is she a jock?") and our interpretations of their nature ("Hmm, he was a little rude to the waiter"). Once we've whittled down the pool, we need to stay connected long enough to foster any potential close relationships. In the following sections, we explore the two major steps—attraction and opening moves—that show how new relationships begin.

The Secrets of Attraction: Noticing

Selecting friends begins with attraction to another person—both when you notice someone *and* when you want to get to know that person better. This initial stage is composed of three potential types of attraction: physical, social, and task. **Physical attraction** means just what it sounds like. Due to our visual nature, we tend to connect more with those who are most like us in terms of physical attractiveness across all types of interpersonal relationships.[36] **Social attraction** means aligning ourselves with others who we believe are like us—for example, if you are a calm person, you may seek out others who are similarly laid back.[37] **Task attraction** refers to being drawn to others who complete jobs in ways we value and agree with. If you have ever worked on a project with a friend, only to find out that you have very different ways of working, be grateful you were friends first. Task-wise, at least, you wouldn't have been attracted to each other.

Interestingly, our online activity can affect how we judge (and are judged on) these three types of attractiveness. Your task and social

PHYSICAL ATTRACTION   SOCIAL ATTRACTION   TASK ATTRACTION

attractions get a boost when your friends post positive comments about you on Facebook. Posts from friends regarding drinking and sexual activity increase physical attractiveness for males but have the opposite effect for females.[38] The judged physical attractiveness of your friends' Facebook pictures can affect your own judged attractiveness. Even your number of Facebook friends can affect perceptions of attractiveness. Currently, social attractiveness drops to its lowest when your number of friends is below one hundred. It also drops when you exceed three hundred friends— showing that moderation leads to higher perceived social attractiveness.[39]

Whereas these three types of attractiveness describe *how* we notice people, *why* do we notice them in the first place? There are three under-lying and interconnected sources of attraction: brain chemistry, proximity, and similarity.

Brain Chemistry. Attraction is a distinct emotion rooted in the brain's nerve circuitry and chemistry.[40] The chemistry of attraction is most

pronounced in brain hormones like acetylcholine and phenylethylamine, which has led some scholars to argue that romantic love is actually caused by hormones.[41] This physical experience may be why people use terms like "falling in love," "crazy love," and "lovesick" to denote being consumed and overtaken by feelings for another.

Proximity. Think of the movie *Silver Linings Playbook*. The main protagonist, Pat, meets Tiffany after moving back in with his parents, when he meets her while out for a run. Tiffany further encourages their proximity by asking Pat to work on a dance routine with her—meaning that they'll see each other nearly every day. Due to the time they spend together, their relationship grows.

It's perhaps unsurprising that people we live, work, and socialize near are easier to connect with. However, proximity alone does not lead to automatic attraction. Close contact can actually hinder a potential relationship if the individuals don't share similar interests and values.[42] Attraction is a mix of proximity and the other factors we share (discussed in the next section).

The Internet—and particularly online dating—is changing traditional assumptions about the role of proximity in attraction. While some online daters choose to interact only with those who live close geographically, the platform does allow people in different states (or even countries) to form relationships. People use *social comments* online—such as

PROXIMITY THEN AND NOW

personal questions, validating comments, and personalized phrases (like nicknames)—to reduce the feeling of distance and increase their sense of connection.[43]

Similarity. The different types of attraction (physical, social, and task) show that we're generally drawn to those we think are similar to us. However, we often assume that others (even those we meet online) *are* like us, regardless of whether or not they actually are.[44] We're especially inclined to assume similarity when attracted to someone, focusing on the ways in which we are alike. These assumptions validate our own interests and values. Interestingly, perceived similarity is just as powerful to attraction. Studies have shown that spouses who *think* they are similar have an even greater degree of satisfaction than spouses who actually are.[45]

We often think that similarity is the secret to attraction and are therefore delighted to find people with whom we share a lot in common. However, we are no more attracted to people who are similar to us than we are to those who are dissimilar to us—at least when given the chance to interact with them.[46] When we take the time to get to know someone, we're able to view that person as a fully realized human being instead of simply a list of personal characteristics. Through interacting, we can discover what we do have in common—and better understand our differences.

The Secrets of Initiating: Opening Moves

In the movie *Pitch Perfect*, Beca reluctantly begins an internship at a radio station and meets fellow freshman Jesse. While he's immediately attracted to Beca, she will have nothing to do with him romantically (at least at first). You may also have experienced the situation of being drawn to someone who's initially a stranger. Noticing someone directs your focus, yet you have to decide whether you are going to make any opening moves. These moves are critical for testing out whether there is a mutual interest between the two of you. Let's look at three processes that play a role in initial interactions.

Introductions. Imagine you're entering a party or another event where you don't know anyone. Does the idea make you feel anxious? If so, you're not alone. Cortisol, the stress hormone, increases when we meet a stranger. This is because we are aware of being assessed by another person while *we* are also making choices about future contact.[47]

Yet introductions—what some experts call safe, "ritualistic openers"[48]—are necessary to ignite potential relationships. Unsurprisingly, people prefer to be introduced rather than introducing themselves. By orchestrating an introduction, the mutual friend can help the two strangers figure out how to act by providing information and common ground that may exist between them.[49]

Introductions are daily occurrences but incredibly sophisticated dances, especially when we're anxious about impressing the other person. We have to express our attraction through smiles, physical movement, eye contact, and scripted greetings—all while providing information to help identify ourselves socially. Introductions can also quickly go awry. Have you ever made the mistake of forgetting that you'd already been introduced to someone? Or been introducing two people and forgot one (or both) of their names? Due to these potential faux pas, introductions can be nerve-racking. If you do make a mistake, it's usually best to acknowledge it—and perhaps joke about your faulty memory!

Managing First Impressions. Some have claimed that you can tell the outcome of a relationship within the first few minutes, or even seconds, of interacting.[50] Whether or not this is actually true, we do know that first impressions set a tone for future interactions.[51] Chapter 2 showed that if you label someone with positive (or negative) characteristics, you will continue to see the person that way, even if he or she acts in a way that suggests otherwise. The opposite is also true. If you make a bad first impression, it can be difficult to shake.

Luckily, first impressions do not anchor forever. Further interactions can lead to more realistic perceptions of others; thus, it's often wise to place impressions on hold until you have a chance to meet with people more than once.[52] Last impressions are also important. If you believe you're not maximizing your chance to impress, consider ways to part on an especially friendly or positive note.

Small Talk. In this initial stage, it's likely that you'll engage in **small talk**, or polite and usually superficial conversation. Small talk is something most of us are taught to do, but despite the name, it's anything but small.[53] Making small talk allows people to cautiously connect while avoiding potential rejection that might come from revealing too much personal information. While some people may claim that they

CIRCUS SMALL TALK

hate small talk (or don't have time for it), it's an important step in building relationships. Pushing for a relationship prematurely can backfire—and giving it up too quickly may prevent you from discovering a new friendship.

What happens after these initial stages? Typically, nothing; in most cases, we choose to remain strangers and acquaintances. These "weaker ties" allow us to meet and interact with people who have different views than us (which doesn't threaten us to the degree that differences in closer relationships could). These acquaintances also help us extend our social networks and the resources they provide us.[54]

In the next section, we discuss what happens when we do want to become closer with our chosen few.

CAPTURING RELATIONAL MOVEMENT

Anniversaries are so important in Western culture that Hallmark has provided a modern anniversary gift guide (including clocks, desk sets, and textile furs) in addition to the more traditional guide (paper, wool, and lace). Anniversaries are noteworthy because they mark the passage of time in relationships. All of us have our own stories depicting **relational movement**, or how and why our relationships move through time as they do. Scholars have also come up with different explanations for how and why relationships progress. We discuss two kinds of these relational paths: straightforward and turbulent.

The Straightforward Path

Earlier depictions suggest that relationships move in a straight line toward a certain destination—usually intimacy—and then tread water.[55] If something disrupts the movement, it's seen as needing to be resolved or removed to avoid relationship failure.

Knapp's staircase model, with five steps moving toward intimacy (initiating, experimenting, intensifying, integrating, and bonding) and five steps moving away from intimacy (differentiating, circumscribing, stagnating, avoiding, and terminating), is one of the most common of the straightforward models. All of these stage models capture relationship movement in a linear A-B-C-D-E pattern:[56]

- People meet for the first time, getting acquainted through socially prescribed rules of small talk.
- Increased interdependence leads to a buildup in intimacy.
- Partners begin coordinating their lives through spending time together, sharing more personal information, and perhaps even labeling the relationship. At this point, they "tread water," remaining in this established phase.
- If the relationship runs into problems, it undergoes a deterioration, in which the partners feel distanced and spend time apart.
- Unless the partners resolve their problems, the relationship ends.

Identifying stages is very appealing and offers us ways to assess where we think we should be in our relationships. We know that some friendships move from superficial talk to more personal conversation, yet they might not necessarily include more intimate behavior, such as sharing secrets or spending a lot of time together.[57] A major reason for this is that people have different definitions of friendship. While some might expect to hang out with a friend multiple times a week (or even every day), others might think that texting and an occasional meet-up suffices.

The straight path also implies that once a relationship ends it is effectively over—in other words, the partners separate completely. However, many partners continue interacting with each other for all kinds of reasons.[58] Divorced partners may continue to co-parent their children, and some romantic partners find value in creating a friendship even when they're no longer together.[59]

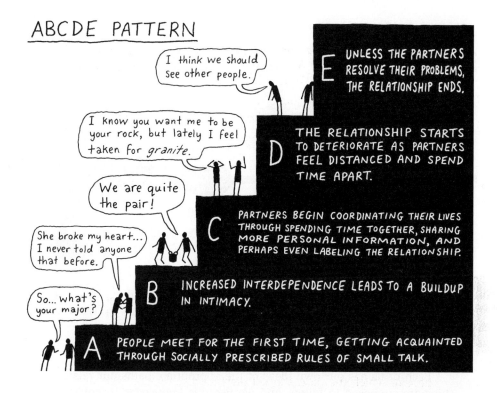

The Turbulent Path

Over time, consensus has emerged that relationships don't necessarily progress in a straightforward and linear way. They're often much more messy and involve cycles of change. We explore this concept by focusing on two of the more popular turbulent models: imagined trajectories and cyclical tensions.

Imagined Trajectories. Honeycutt's **imagined trajectories model** states that relationships are mainly composed of periods of stability that are occasionally disrupted by critical events. These critical events (say, a first kiss or a serious fight) are turning points that bring about change, resulting in partners becoming either closer or more distanced.[60] Critical events are not marked by the relevant stage but by the partners themselves. For example, a couple with strong family ties might not find parental introductions to be a huge deal. However, for others—maybe those who are less close with their parents—this would be a momentous (and perhaps stressful) occasion.

IMAGINED TRAJECTORIES *(PERIODS OF STABILITY THAT GET DISRUPTED BY CRITICAL EVENTS)*

BRAD PITT and ANGELINA JOLIE meet on the set of *Mr. & Mrs. Smith.*

PITT and JOLIE pose for *W* magazine "Domestic Bliss" photo shoot.

PITT says that he and JOLIE will marry...

...when everyone else in the country who wants to be married is legally able.

EVENT 1 SUMMER 2004 | EVENT 2 JANUARY 2005 | EVENT 3 JULY 2005 | EVENT 4 JANUARY 2006 | EVENT 5 OCTOBER 2006 | EVENT 6 AUGUST 2014

PITT divorces then wife Jennifer Aniston.

JOLIE confirms to *People* magazine that she is pregnant with her first child with PITT.

PITT and JOLIE get married in France.

Each of us has our own ideas of the appropriate paths our relationships are supposed to follow, and we use this knowledge to guide our expectations and actions. However, these differences can sometimes lead to awkward situations. Imagine that you ask a coworker out for coffee simply to get to know him or her better. You later find out through other coworkers that he or she viewed your invite as a date!

Our assumptions allow us to decipher the quality of our relationship at different points in time. Our background regarding relationships can also affect our views of our current relationships. For example, people with more romantic relational experience develop more realistic ideas about how relationships move forward, relying less on cultural stereotypes to ground their expectations.[61]

Understanding our own thoughts about relational movement can allow us to step back and judge the meaning certain events have in our relationships. The idea of turbulence also helps us accept that occasional disruptions (both good and bad) can and should be expected.

Cyclical Tensions.

The **cyclical tensions model** offers a view of constant and cyclical states of change filled with messy starts and stops, rather than a pattern that holds steady. Due to opposing forces in the relationship (discussed later in the chapter), partners are consistently adjusting in these periods of calm and upheaval.[62] Consider actor Samuel L. Jackson and his wife, LaTanya Richardson (also an actor), who have been married since 1980. Their three-plus decades of marriage have likely endured rough patches—common in all marriages, not just those in Hollywood—but they have remained together through periods of both calm and upheaval.

People feel these cycles—a sort of waxing and waning—even within different aspects of one relationship. For example, recorded conversations between college peers becoming friends do not show a gradual increase in opening up to each other. These potential friends, following their own rules for when and where to give personal information, were more personal in private and less so in public. Throughout this process, they cycled through periods of small talk in public and more personal talk in private.[63]

Through these different depictions of movement, we've explored the nuances of relational movement—which, rather than simply progressing in a straightforward manner, is often quite turbulent and cyclical. The processes of movement are also very personal and dependent on the meanings both partners bring to events in their relationships. Seeing real-life relationships as more messy and imperfect can give you the freedom to enjoy whatever moment you happen to be in.

In the next section, we discuss the ways that people in relationships learn to navigate another potentially challenging but often rewarding aspect of relationships: vulnerability.

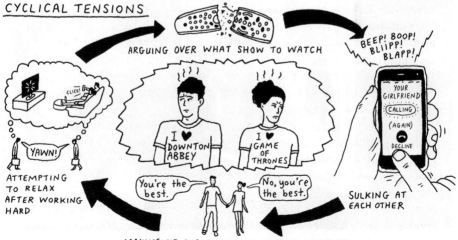

CYCLICAL TENSIONS

ARGUING OVER WHAT SHOW TO WATCH

BEEP! BOOP! BLIPP! BLAPP!

YOUR GIRLFRIEND CALLING (AGAIN) DECLINE

CLICK! YAWN!

I ♥ DOWNTON ABBEY

I ♥ GAME OF THRONES

ATTEMPTING TO RELAX AFTER WORKING HARD

You're the best.

No, you're the best.

SULKING AT EACH OTHER

MAKING UP AND ENJOYING A HAPPY WEEKEND

SELF-DISCLOSURE AND PRIVACY

You're interested in a woman you've been sitting next to in class who has yet to open up to you about anything beyond schoolwork. On another occasion, you sit down next to a stranger at a diner counter and, within minutes, hear his complete life story, down to the pet dog (Skippy) he had as a child. Both of these examples show different ends of the spectrum in terms of **self-disclosure**, meaning what we reveal about ourselves to others (and what they reveal to us).

One way to think about self-disclosure is the **Johari window**, which describes the different degrees of what we know about ourselves and what others know about us.[64] The Johari window breaks this up into four quadrants: open, blind, hidden, and unknown.

Communication and psychology scholars have long explored the role self-disclosure plays in explaining why we grow closer together.

JOHARI WINDOW

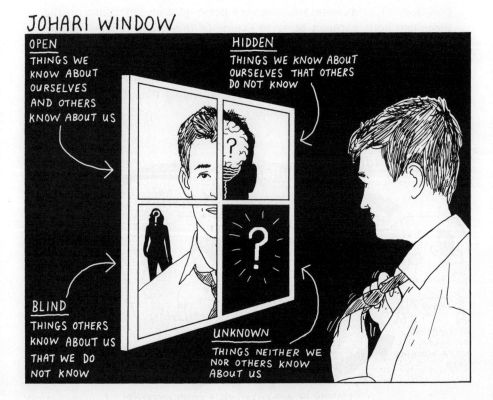

OPEN
THINGS WE KNOW ABOUT OURSELVES AND OTHERS KNOW ABOUT US

HIDDEN
THINGS WE KNOW ABOUT OURSELVES THAT OTHERS DO NOT KNOW

BLIND
THINGS OTHERS KNOW ABOUT US THAT WE DO NOT KNOW

UNKNOWN
THINGS NEITHER WE NOR OTHERS KNOW ABOUT US

They especially became interested in the "hidden" pane of the Johari window—those disclosures that reveal private or personal information about ourselves. This kind of self-disclosure has become *the* explanation for relationship movement.[65] The social penetration theory, discussed next, posits self-disclosure as the reason we grow closer over time.

Social Penetration Theory

Social penetration theory explains that our close relationships are the result of "penetrating" the more hidden informational layers of the other person, as if peeling away the layers of an onion.[66] You may start with more superficial conversation and then talk about more intimate topics as time goes on, often reciprocating or exchanging similar information with each other.[67] Researchers have shown that appropriate use of self-disclosure is critical to creating and keeping relationships.

We often find that self-disclosure and liking another person go hand in hand, and self-disclosure can be a sign that you trust someone with your disclosure.[68] However, this is not the whole story. A "more disclosure is better" policy is not always prudent.

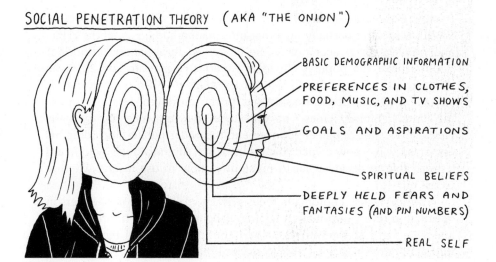

SOCIAL PENETRATION THEORY (AKA "THE ONION")

BASIC DEMOGRAPHIC INFORMATION

PREFERENCES IN CLOTHES, FOOD, MUSIC, AND TV SHOWS

GOALS AND ASPIRATIONS

SPIRITUAL BELIEFS

DEEPLY HELD FEARS AND FANTASIES (AND PIN NUMBERS)

REAL SELF

The Downside to Self-Disclosure

Self-disclosure does not always lead to liking.[69] Imagine that your best friend just revealed that he or she has started dating your recent ex. This disclosure might forever alter the friendship. Even worse, you may have experienced a situation in which someone passed your private information along to others without your permission. As uncomfortable as it is to imagine these situations, this paradox of taking a risk to gain trust—which *requires* trust—is inherent in all relationships.

Self-disclosure is not necessarily a good or a bad thing in itself. Rather than indiscriminate self-disclosing, we can use theories of privacy management to decide how to figure out the best self-disclosure for different relationships.

Communication Privacy Management Theory

The **communication privacy management (CPM) theory** is built on two ideas: first, that we "own" our information, and second, that we have the right to control access to it. Communication experts use a boundary metaphor to explain this control of private information.[70] Safe information is enclosed by a thinner boundary, while more private information has a thicker boundary. For example, you might easily share your name and occupation with someone you just met (thin boundary). However, if you had a family secret, you might not share that with even a close friend (thick boundary).

Our **boundary insiders** are those with whom we share information. We allow them to partially own that information and enjoy all the rights and privileges that accompany the co-owned information.[71] Consider Robin Thicke, the popular Canadian American singer. In late 2014, he dropped a bombshell during legal proceedings by openly admitting his struggle with drug abuse. He said that for the entire year he was promoting his hit "Blurred Lines," he was under the influence during interviews.[72] With his public announcement, the wider public—including his estranged wife—now owned that information. All individuals who heard it were able to decide what to make of it, how to use it, and whether to tell others.

Partners must coordinate their privacy management. The person deciding to reveal information is often caught between a desire to share and a fear that sharing might prove harmful. The person receiving the information has to decide how to react to the information. For example,

COMMUNICATION PRIVACY MANAGEMENT (CPM) THEORY

one of the authors once received a phone call from his or her father, ready to reveal a secret that had long burdened him. Initially, he could not make himself share the secret and said, "If I tell you, I feel like I will die." Clearly, the fear and emotion of telling was so great that crossing the thick boundary felt lethal. Still, the man did share the secret. Upon hearing it, the receiver then had to immediately figure out how to receive this revelation and how to respond appropriately.[73]

Negotiating privacy is a complicated process that involves both creating privacy rules and responding to privacy violations.

Privacy Rules. Everyone makes up his or her own set of "privacy rules" to regulate how and when to share private information. The five factors influencing these rules are personality, biological sex, motivation, culture, and the relationship of the person one is disclosing to.[74] For example, someone who has seen a great deal of harm come from disclosures in his or her family might be less inclined to reveal private information to a friend or romantic partner.

Sex and culture are interesting factors influencing privacy rules. Female boundaries are slightly thinner than male boundaries because females are taught to judge the risk of their privacy choices differently than are males. Males, for instance, tend to consider more negative ramifications to disclosure than women, perhaps due to being taught greater control over privacy risks.[75] Different cultures may make privacy rules that surprise Western readers. For example, in collectivist cultures (see Chapter 6) in which family may take precedence over the individual, such as in Lebanese culture, doctors may not directly tell a patient a diagnosis but instead share it with the family. The family then decides whether or not to tell the patient.[76]

Privacy Violations. Think of issues that arise when someone is uncomfortable sharing a secret, or when his or her boundary insider doesn't realize it's a secret in the first place. In the movie *Her*, Theo learns that Samantha, his personal operating system, is not his exclusive love interest. She talks to 8,316 other people and loves 641 of them, too! While she has no problem sharing this revelation, Theo is devastated. These sorts of privacy violations are a common reason for **boundary turbulence**, or the friction that occurs when privacy rules are threatened or broken.[77]

When a dyad experiences privacy violations, it often has to modify its privacy rules in order to adapt to the turbulence. One kind of privacy violation romantic partners face is **relational embarrassment**, which occurs when a relational partner acts inappropriately toward the other partner in front of others.[78] Romantic pairs count on a private space to buffer them from the public world, which gives the relationship the chance to grow. When they do things publicly that violate this private space—such as tease their partner in front of other people—the resulting boundary turbulence can threaten the relationship.

Privacy management is also challenging because people often assume that a desire for privacy denotes a desire to pull away. It may be hard to separate the two thoughts, but relationships always involve the need to be both connected and separate. Privacy maintenance is not only normal but absolutely necessary for a functional relationship. We discuss this concept further in the next section.

UNDERSTANDING AND MANAGING DIALECTICAL TENSIONS

Moving from acquaintances to friends or lovers is a big step—and though these types of interpersonal relationships are vital for our health and well-being, they come with a new set of challenges. Often we may think something is wrong when we feel torn between two things—like wanting to share our lives with someone and also wanting our space, or enjoying the safety of routine while also longing for something new. Something that many people may not realize is that relationships inevitably contain these contradictory forces that push and pull the partners in opposing directions.[79] Simply realizing that these contradictions exist may help ease anxiety and allow us to have a sense of control in our relationships.

Dialectical Tensions

These contradictory forces are called **dialectical tensions**, which are the result of both **centripetal forces** pushing us together and **centrifugal forces** pulling us apart.[80] Centripetal forces include openness, stability, loyalty, warmth, respect, and caring, whereas centrifugal forces may mean distance, betrayal, coldness, disrespect, and ambivalence. All relationships contain these forces working "in tension" together.

Friends and romantic partners, for instance, are pushed and pulled by both loyalties and betrayals. For example, you might find that remaining loyal to a friend necessarily means betraying a romantic partner.[81] Or you might find yourself feeling torn between spending time with a significant other and spending time with friends. In the following sections, we explore some of the most common dialectical tensions people face in close relationships.

Connection/Separation. The most common dialectical tension in our personal relationships is the one between connection and separation.

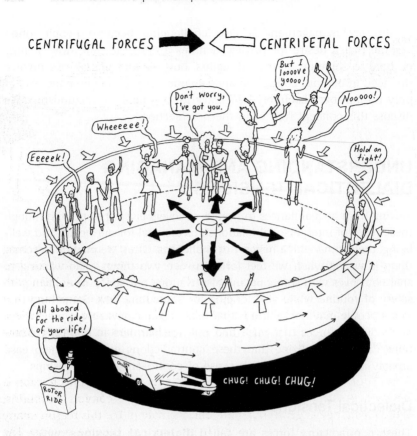

It may come as an unpleasant surprise to find that you crave some space after spending a lot of time with a beloved friend or after the honeymoon period in a burgeoning relationship. But relationships contain more than just these two extremes. Consider that a little separation can even strengthen relationships by allowing the partners to miss each other. Although it may seem contradictory to want to be both connected and separate—and though it may even make us feel caught in between these two places—it is a completely normal and even healthy place for a close relationship to be.

Openness/Closedness. The second most common dialectical tension is between openness and closedness. Many believe that the mark of a good relationship is complete openness and honesty with the other person—in other words, no secrets. But in the messy reality of relationships, people often regulate what and how much they share. For

instance, in new relationships, most people do not reveal everything about their lives and personalities, in order to put their best foot forward and impress the other person. Ironically, when couples have been with each other for a long time, they may maintain a level of privacy not because they are withholding information but because they believe there is nothing left to tell—that is, that their partners already know everything about them.[82]

Predictability/Novelty. The third most common dialectical tension is between predictability and novelty. While there is comfort in routine, there's also the danger of boredom and stagnation. For this reason, many couples plan date nights—though these, too, can become routine! The key is to maintain the "routine" of date night while planning new and

exciting activities.[83] For instance, some couples turn their routine into a game, challenging each other to come up with new and exciting ways to spice up their date nights.

Managing Dialectical Tensions

These and other dialectical tensions are found in any interpersonal relationship, though different tensions may deepen at different times. There are a variety of options that people can choose to navigate these tensions.[84]

Separation. The most common management strategy is separating one opposing force from the other in certain situations or when dealing with particular topics. Special peers at work may decide to be open about all

sorts of job-related issues but still avoid sharing information about their request for raises. Romantic partners may agree to go on separate vacations once a year while also deciding that they'll spend holidays together.

Selection. When partners use selection strategies, they select or value one opposing force while ignoring the existence of the other. For example, if two friends spend all their free time together, they may be exhibiting connection to the denial of separation. Over time, this strategy can prove to be unsustainable, especially for managing connection/separation and predictability/novelty.

Balance. People who use a balance strategy keep both opposing forces in mind but try not to give too much weight to one or the other. For example, consider a long-distance couple that is planning a visit. They may feel the need to talk about the status of their relationship but also want to fully enjoy the time they'll have to spend together. One way to come to a happy medium might be deciding to talk about the relationship in person while also limiting the amount of time they will spend on this topic so that they can focus on the moment and each other.[85]

Reframing. Though this strategy is rare, some partners decide to recognize and rethink the dialectical tensions between them—and tell themselves they're not necessarily contradictory. One study found that women who have partners with Alzheimer's are able to feel more connected to their spouse by focusing on their own lives, believing that this is what their spouse would have wanted for them.[86]

CHAPTER REVIEW

In this chapter, we focused on interpersonal communication, which happens between people who find each other unique and irreplaceable. We explored this type of communication within dyads— two-person social units. People enter into dyads in order to self-expand, whether that's through belonging, overall well-being, self-expression, or reciprocal altruism. The most common forms of intimate dyads are friendships, work peers, and romantic relationships.

After exploring the nature of interpersonal relationships, we turned to the opening stages of relationships. These include noticing another and feeling attraction (caused by brain chemistry, proximity, and similarity, among other factors). In order to initiate an interaction with someone, we need to engage in opening moves, such as introductions, as well as manage first impressions and make small talk. In our study of continuing relational movement, we looked at the straightforward and turbulent paths of relationships. The now more widely accepted turbulent path can be further separated into the imagined trajectories model and the cyclical tensions model.

Next, we explored how opening up the self to another person is central to intimacy. We continually decide what, when, and to whom we wish to share private information as ways to build trust and closeness. While the social penetration theory suggests that more disclosure is always good, this is not always the case. The communication privacy management theory explains how we can control the amount of information we share—and reminds us that we make up our own privacy rules within relationships. When we invite people to become boundary insiders, boundary turbulence may arise.

Partners who have strong interpersonal relationships are able to recognize and manage the natural dialectical tensions that arise from centrifugal and centripetal forces. The most common pairs are connection/separation, openness/closedness, and predictability/novelty. People can use various strategies to navigate these forces, including separation, selection, balance, and reframing.

LaunchPad
macmillan learning

LaunchPad for *Let's Communicate* offers videos and encourages self-assessment through adaptive quizzing. Go to **launchpadworks.com** to get access to:

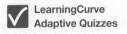 LearningCurve
Adaptive Quizzes

 Video clips that help you understand human communication

Key Terms

interpersonal relationship 220
interpersonal communication 220
dyad 220
intimacy 220
self-expansion 221
reciprocal altruism 222
interdependence 222
friendship 223
professional peer 224
collegial peer 224
special peer 224
virtual peer 224
negotiated permanence 225
physical attraction 226
social attraction 226
task attraction 226

small talk 230
relational movement 231
Knapp's staircase model 232
imagined trajectories model 233
cyclical tensions model 234
self-disclosure 236
Johari window 236
social penetration theory 237
communication privacy
 management (CPM) theory 238
boundary insiders 238
boundary turbulence 240
relational embarrassment 240
◉ dialectical tensions 241
centripetal forces 241
centrifugal forces 241

Review Questions

1. How is interpersonal communication defined?
2. Describe the benefits of self-expansion.
3. Explain the role of small talk in the opening moves between people.
4. What are the stages of linear models of relationship development?
5. How are self-disclosure processes and privacy management the same? How are they different?
6. What is a boundary insider? How would privacy rules explain any privacy violations between yourself and another person?

Critical Thinking Questions

1. Review the benefits of self-expansion in dyads. What are some ways you interpersonally communicate these benefits to others? Which benefit is most important to you, and why?
2. Think about the different types of work peers discussed in the chapter. How would your expectations differ for each? For example,

which type of work peer is most likely to have your cell phone or landline number? Why?

3. Consider one of your close relationships. Which relational path (straightforward or turbulent) better describes this relationship? Make a timeline of the relationship that clearly shows critical events or stages.

4. Consider an initial meeting with a stranger that didn't go well. What happened in either the introduction or small talk phase (or both!) that went wrong? What could you have done—or what could you do now—to try to repair the interaction?

5. Of the three most common dialectical tensions, choose one that you and a partner are managing well in your relationship. How does this management affect other dialectical tensions in the relationship?

Activities

1. Look through some popular "relationship" magazines (*O, Maxim, Men's Health, Cosmopolitan, Latina, Seventeen, Essence*) for articles offering advice on how to meet new people to date. Summarize key themes from the advice, and look to see if they match the processes of attraction: brain chemistry, proximity, and similarity. What are the popular culture messages about these sources of attraction?

2. Create your own Johari window. In each pane of the window (open, blind, hidden, and unknown), place examples of the information relevant to that pane. Are some panes harder or impossible to fill in? If so, write down why this might be the case.

3. In a small group, come up with a scenario in which a friendship or relationship contains a dialectical tension (connection/separation, openness/closedness, predictability/novelty). Write three short scripts that show the different strategies for dealing with this tension, and act them out in front of the class.

4. Explore the lyrics of two songs for their hidden privacy rules. Examples include "Secrets" by OneRepublic, "Honesty" by Billy Joel (later covered by Beyoncé), and "Love the Way You Lie" by Eminem and Rihanna. Make a list of the messages in the songs about how to best manage privacy with others. Compare your list with a classmate's.

Apply Your Skills

Review the illustration about managing dialectical tensions on page 244. Consider two different types of personal relationships in your life. For each, write down examples of the ways that you manage dialectical tensions with that partner (selecting, framing, balancing, and/or separating). Compare the two relationships. Do you use one management style more than the others? Which styles, if any, are not used? Do you use the styles differently in each relationship? Do these similarities or differences say anything specific about the nature of each relationship?

Study Plan

_____

_____

_____

_____

_____

_____

_____

_____

_____

_____

_____

PRACTICES FOR EFFECTIVE INTERPERSONAL RELATIONSHIPS

OBJECTIVES

- Learn the importance of maintaining a variety of relationships through daily behavior and through use of technology.
- Explain the dynamics of interpersonal conflict and its impact on the health of relationships.
- Identify common styles of conflict and unhealthy conflict patterns.
- Understand the constructive ways we can use conflict.

Darin kicked off his fiftieth birthday with a party he called Darinpalooza, inviting his guests to come dressed as musicians. The resulting pictures on Facebook showed Darin dressed as Bruno Mars and his wife, Marcie, grinning in an outlandish Lady Gaga wig—proof that the couple could still have fun after being married for years. Marcie explains the key to their longevity and satisfaction this way: "We're willing to negotiate our expectations with each other."

Since Marcie is a pilot, she's often away from home. To combat the separation, Marcie and Darin check in with each other nightly. In the past, they called each other, but now they often text. They generally send casual messages, but if one of them wants to talk about something more serious, he or she uses the code, "Are you free to talk?" This negotiated communication has helped the couple stay close through their years together.

Marcie and Darin also negotiate their expectations when conflict occurs. Early in their marriage, Marcie found herself giving Darin the silent treatment when they were fighting. Darin finally explained that he found this offensive. He understood that she might not want to talk at that moment but asked that she still treat him respectfully. This led them to start taking some time apart during a conflict in order to process their feelings about whatever was the source of their disagreement, agreeing to discuss the issue later. They also established a pattern of troubleshooting conflict by brainstorming future scenarios and talking candidly about how they would feel and act if, for instance, one of them had an affair, or if they ran into financial trouble.

Marcie and Darin's situation shows that relationships aren't automatic —they require consistent care, attention, and maintenance. Chapter 8 introduced you to the complicated, often messy terrain of relationships, and in this chapter, we take a closer look at how to maintain them. To enjoy successful relationships, we must be active participants in them—being mindful of their dynamics and willing to communicate with our partners during both peace and conflict. In this chapter, we focus on two critical areas that can affect the quality of relationships. First, we look at ways to nurture and maintain relationships on a daily basis (think of Marcie and Darin checking in with each other every night). Second, we explore the conflict that inevitably occurs—and how, surprisingly, we can use conflict to actually strengthen relationships.

RELATIONAL MAINTENANCE

Perhaps you are used to staying in touch with old friends from high school through Facebook and e-mails. Or maybe now that you are in college, you remember to call your mom on her birthday. Possibly you are someone used to checking in with your partner to talk about how to improve your relationship (something you think about a lot, and something he or she doesn't typically consider). There are probably lots of actions you take to maintain your relationships. We associate stable relationships with desired levels of mutual control, trust, liking, and commitment—which are common characteristics of the types of relationships addressed in Chapter 8. **Relational maintenance** refers to the actions we take to *sustain* these desired levels in our relationships.[1]

Let's take a closer look at what those relational characteristics mean. *Mutual control* is feeling that your benefits match your contributions. When you feel as though you are giving more than you're getting, you may experience distress in the form of anger and depression.[2] *Trust,* when questioned or lost, can lead to suspicion between partners. Betrayal is reported as one of the most common reasons for ending friendships.[3] While love is central to personal relationships, another essential element is *liking,* which grows out of affection and respect.[4] **Commitment**— investment in the relationship—is a better predictor of stability than are feelings of love.[5] We're motivated to maintain our desired levels of these traits, and we act to protect them if they are threatened.[6]

In the following sections, we first discuss our most common daily maintenance actions and the impact of technology on those choices. We then show how the uniqueness of different types of relationships can influence our maintenance efforts. Finally, we offer some general guidelines for you to consider in your efforts to sustain your personal relationships.

Common Maintenance Behaviors

Our relational lives are filled with routine actions that serve to keep them moving along. Some relationships, for instance, find their sense of stability in humor and jokes shared over time. Others feel closer to each other trading texts during the day. Still others find their glue in sharing

activities like rock climbing or gaming. Many of our relational maintenance behaviors can be grouped into six categories of the "prosocial"
(as opposed to antisocial) choices we make.[7]

- **Positivity:** Being nice, cheerful, affectionate, and hopeful.
- **Openness:** Being direct, sharing private thoughts and feelings,
  giving advice, listening, and discussing the future.
- **Assurances:** Encouraging, comforting, and meeting needs.
- **Social Networks:** Leaning on friends and family for support.
- **Sharing Tasks:** Doing chore-like tasks together.
- **Sharing Activities:** Spending time enjoying each other's
  company.

We will go into these in more depth later, to show how one can
use them to maintain different types of relationships. But for now, know
that these maintenance behaviors are typically routine, daily actions
we use to bond with others. Some are strategic, like the planned use
of e-mail between grandparents and grandchildren in their efforts to
stay in touch.[8] These behaviors, whether routine or strategic, vary
across relationship types and communication channels (for example,
face-to-face and mediated).

Maintaining Relationships with Technology

Technology is changing many areas of our lives (see Chapter 7),
including our relationships. Consider this: we've attached our cell
phones to our personal identities so strongly that if separated from
them, our bodies respond as if we've been separated from a good
friend.[9] We often use e-mail and social media to maintain both our
offline and our online relationships.[10] Long-term couples report the
key role the Internet plays in their relationships, while those between
the ages of eighteen and twenty-nine report an even higher significance.[11] We also use technology to reconnect with old friends, stay
in touch with family, and publicly display our romantic relationships. While "sexting" is most often associated with single people,
committed partners also engage in it.[12] For the seven million couples
currently in long-distance relationships,[13] those who use technology
to maintain their relationship report higher levels of love compared
to those who don't.[14]

We publicly share our relationships with Facebook friends, with Twitter followers, and through interactions that take place on all platforms. Technology allows us to give "more relational maintenance bang for the message-sending buck," allowing an unprecedented amount of public viewing of our maintenance efforts.[15] E-mail, texting, instant messaging, and "gramming" (Instagramming) are also cheaper and more efficient compared to using the postal service—we can even send gifts to people through social media. The Internet and social media impact our relational communication, the plans we make with each other, and the ways we become close with one other. Some partners even report using the Internet to manage a fight that felt hard to deal with in person.[16]

Technology offers us the advantage of speed when communicating, something that prior generations didn't enjoy. Consider someone hard at work crunching numbers for his boss—he can quickly take a break from work and send a Gchat message to his girlfriend.[17] Twitter is another convenient way to keep up our relationships, allowing us to quickly spread news, share our thoughts about everyday events, and connect with partners—all while carefully choosing our audience through accepting or rejecting followers.[18]

All of our close relationships involve behaviors that help us reach our desired levels of mutuality, trust, liking, social support, and commitment. At the same time, the very things that make our relationships different require that we use different behaviors for each.

MAINTAINING RELATIONSHIPS WITH TECHNOLOGY

MAINTAINING DIFFERENT TYPES OF RELATIONSHIPS

Managing close relationships well requires being able to figure out the best behavior to use for each type.[19] All six types of maintenance—positivity, openness, assurances, social networks, sharing tasks, and sharing activities—are generally helpful in your relationships. However, some types of relationships require more of these specific behaviors than do others. In this section, we discuss the common maintenance behaviors in romantic relationships, friendships, and workplace relationships, followed by general guidelines to consider for maintaining all types of relationships.

Romantic Relationships

Relationships bring us love and happiness, but they also come with boredom and irritation. Here's a surprising (and perhaps heartening) statistic: 44 percent of couples report being really annoyed with each other on a daily basis.[20] As mentioned earlier, it's not enough for us to just enter into romantic relationships—we must actively maintain them or they will deteriorate.[21] The good news is that there are commonly accepted ways to do this in romantic relationships, regardless of ethnicity or sexual orientation.[22]

Positivity and Assurances. Partners who link their happiness to being positive report that the top two behaviors they use to maintain their relationships are positivity and assurances.[23] Some ways to do this are bringing fun and playfulness into a relationship, as well as supporting a partner with surprise gifts. Daytime TV guru Dr. Phil and his wife came up with a way to increase their positivity: the "first four minutes" rule. Instead of meeting each other at the end of long workdays with a list of frustrations and complaints, they spend the first four minutes telling funny stories, speaking with a positive tone, and even sharing why they missed the other person.[24]

Partners also get a boost when they make assurances about each other and their relationship. Assurances increase the level of commitment and trust between two partners. Behaviors like flirting with other people while keeping silent about how much you care about your partner are not reassuring.

ROMANTIC RELATIONSHIPS:
POSITIVITY AND ASSURANCES, SHARING TASKS, SOCIAL NETWORKS, TECHNOLOGY.

Sharing Tasks. Asking partners if they need help, giving them rides, and working together on household chores are all forms of sharing tasks, or doing things together. Sharing tasks is regarded as the most frequently used maintenance behavior for romantic partners, regardless of how serious both consider their relationship. These kinds of tasks play an important role in partner satisfaction.[25]

Social Networks. Close relationships don't exist in isolation; their survival relies on the approval of their social network[26]—especially for gay and lesbian and interethnic couples.[27] Partners often invite their friends and family to do things with them. They can also turn to their respective social network for help and advice.

Gay and lesbian couples use social networks to help support them being out as a couple. They also report a need to publicly comment on their relationship to others in their effort to have it recognized as an equally valid relationship.[28] Overall, though, their maintenance patterns are similar to those of opposite-sex couples, relying on shared tasks for connection.

Technology. Military spouses often report using e-mail to manage their spouses' deployment, relying on its speed and generally private nature to stay in touch.[29] Facebook offers a public space where partners can display their relationship in pictures and posts, show each other support, craft expressions of affection, and coordinate schedules. Seventy percent of college students post their relational status on social media.[30]

Sharing tasks and getting support from our social networks make more sense when experienced face-to-face, yet these maintenance behaviors also occur online.[31] When couples display their relationship on social media, this is considered "sharing" the task of showing that they are together. Partners who have been together for a while report a higher tendency to share digital tools—including passwords, e-mail accounts, and even calendars—to give them a sense of continuity and togetherness.[32]

Social media allows couples greater access to information about each other—and also makes it easier for them to monitor each other. Online monitoring of romantic partners, while considered spying and a trust violation offline, is more accepted as normal online.[33] While social media has opened up ways to gather large amounts of information about romantic partners, it can also cause jealousy, something we'll address later in the chapter.

Friendships

Friends can sustain their commitments with less contact than those in romantic relationships, but they, too, must actively maintain their relationship so that it survives over time and distance. The following behaviors may overlap with romantic relationship behaviors, but they also contain important differences.

Positivity. Friends find pleasure in shared humor and doing things that bring happiness to each other. In the 2015 movie *The End of the Tour*, based on true events, journalist David Lipsky joins writer David Foster Wallace during the last few days of his massive tour for *Infinite Jest*. The two men quickly bond over their writing careers, joking banter, and shared affinity for Alanis Morissette. In real life, Lipsky eventually wrote a best-selling memoir about the interview and the short but intense relationship between himself and Wallace.

Sharing Activities. Friendships are built on sharing activities—this is one of the main ways that friends connect and get close to each other.[34] But this can be a challenge when geographic separation or a lack of time gets in the way. Friends can combat this, however, by developing expectations that they will always be there for each other.[35] Just take it from pop singer Ariana Grande, on traveling for her career: "The best part about having true friends is that you can go months without seeing them and they'll still be there for you and act as if you'd never left! Of course I miss my friends but they're very understanding and I know they'll always be here for me!"[36]

While separations do complicate sharing activities, social media allows people to overcome that separation. Before social media, e-mail was the first technological tool friends used to maintain a connection. As its use drops off, the closeness friends feel toward each other is dramatically affected.[37] Current means like Skype and Facebook are popular tools for helping friends remain connected, getting reacquainted with high school buddies, and staying connected with friends met offline in school.[38] Studies show that college friends use social media more for connecting with old high school friends and keeping up with current friends than they use it for maintaining their romantic relationships or beginning new friendships.[39]

Openness. Another cornerstone to friendship is simply catching up or sharing personal information.[40] Both friends and romantic partners can do this online or on social media via private messages.[41] Young boys and girls show a similar desire to confide in and trust their closest friends. However, by late adolescence, many males show less interest in opening up, bending to sex role stereotypes.[42]

Cross-Sex Friendships: Special Considerations. Cross-sex friendships, while confusing at times, can be very emotionally rewarding.[43] Males often use this type of friendship for emotional support

CROSS—SEX FRIENDS

that might be missing in their same-sex friendships, and females value the male perspective. Most cross-sex friends try to remain platonic mainly because they think that anything more would threaten the friendship. Less frequently, they do so to avoid upheaval in their social network or because they are simply not attracted to the other person.[44] When friends are platonic to protect the friendship, the relationship is often open, positive, and assuring, and includes shared activities. When friends are attracted to each other, they can use a policy in which they take a break from each other whenever romantic feelings arise.[45]

If either friend is dating or married, he or she faces the challenge of managing the competing interests of the friendship and the romantic relationship.[46] Being open about the friendship with a romantic partner helps to normalize its presence in their lives and reassure the other partner.

Friends with Benefits: Special Considerations A reported 60 percent of college students have been in at least one friends-with-benefits (FWB) relationship.[47] FWB means a commitment-free sexual relationship with a trusted person. The ambiguity of such a relationship poses some interesting maintenance challenges. FWBs rarely turn into exclusive romantic relationships—mainly because the friends worry that the sex will hurt their friendship.

FRIENDS WITH BENEFITS

Relatively few people in FWB relationships are directly open about their ground rules; instead, they actively avoid discussing what to call the relationship, its status, and its future.[48] Yet FWB partners still maintain their relationship with emotional and communication rules that they personally monitor. By doing this, they're able to tell if they're becoming emotionally attached to their FWB partners. If this happens, partners typically make plans to stop or put the relationship on hold.[49]

Workplace Relationships

While there's more research available about maintaining friendships and romantic relationships, we're beginning to find out more about workplace relationships. Workplace peers, whether collegial or special (see Chapter 8), can thrive if both partners can handle the stress of job competition and work demands.[50] Some of the most-used maintenance actions are combinations of positivity (to offset the often stressful environment) and assurances (to make it clear that you value a work friend as more than just a colleague).[51]

Some other behaviors include being open with each other and being able to find support outside work. On Fox's popular comedy *Brooklyn Nine-Nine*, Detective Jake Peralta insists that he is more than just work friends with Sergeant Terry Jeffords—who does not see their friendship extending beyond the precinct. Yet after Peralta helps the sergeant through a personal problem, Jeffords finally accepts Peralta as his "friend-friend."

Workplace romantic relationships, once seen as forbidden, are more common now and are even seen as contributing to a positive workplace environment.[52] However, romantic partners are advised to act professionally

at work—both with each other and toward others.[53] While partners may have access to computers and e-mail at work, they should keep in mind that workplace computers can be monitored.[54]

FIVE GENERAL GUIDELINES FOR MAINTAINING RELATIONSHIPS

Maintaining relationships involves two parts: how you think about others, and how you behave toward others.[55] The following guidelines offer a combination of attitudes and behaviors that should help you sustain your close relationships.[56]

Embrace Your Agency

In Chapter 2, we suggested that people aren't passive participants, tossed around by circumstances over which they have no control. Instead, people make decisions to act based on their interpretation of what's going on around them. Imagine that your friend has had to cancel two lunch engagements in the last couple of weeks. The last time she did this, you were already at the restaurant. Seeing her behavior as irresponsible, you might post a snide remark on her Facebook wall. Alternatively, you might see your friend as being really busy and simply trying to manage as much as she can and choose to privately reach out to her. Either way, it's your choice to make, and it could well affect the future of your friendship.

Meet Connecting Bids

Ecstatic that the movie script you've been working on for months is finally getting a read by a major studio, you share your news with your partner. The response you get is, "That's good news. Hey, did I tell you I got two three-pointers at the pickup game at the park?" as your partner looks at an incoming text.

Connecting bids are those daily overtures of connection we make to our partners.[57] Whether deep or superficial, verbal or nonverbal, direct or indirect, they are critical to maintaining our relationships. There are three possible responses to any connecting bid. In the movie script example, your partner reacted with a **turning-away response**, in which he or she

CONNECTING BIDS

TURNING AWAY:

CQLLEGE

I got an A on my chemistry exam!

That's *great*. There's no way I'm going to get an A on my exam tomorrow. I'm not prepared at all.

TURNING AGAINST:

CQLLEGE

I got an A on my chemistry exam!

Can you keep it down? I'm trying to study for **MY** exam tomorrow.

TURNING TOWARD:

CQLLEGE

I got an A on my chemistry exam!

Congratulations! You studied for that exam for a week. You deserve it.

recognized your bid and then quickly shifted to self-centered interests. A **turning-against response** is one of annoyance and aggression ("Whatever, I'm sick of hearing about the script—you've been going on about it for months!"). A **turning-toward response** demonstrates how much he or she values and understands you ("Wow! I know you've put so much time and effort into that script—I'm so glad your dream is coming true").[58]

Meeting every connecting bid you receive is not practical; however, you want to avoid falling into harmful patterns of turning away and turning against.[59] During divorces, husbands turn away from their wives' connecting bids 82 percent of the time. Spouses in healthy marriages show very little turning away.[60] Consistently turning away from a partner's connecting bids may discourage the partner from ever trying again.

Take Action Based on Knowledge

One of the top myths about relationships is that it's best to hold back feelings when you're upset with your partner rather than to engage in conflict.[61] We discuss the consequences of avoidance in conflict later in the chapter, but for now, know that those who choose to avoid rather than engage are more stressed and unhappy. Worse, when these partners finally do say something, it is usually less than constructive.

We learn the rules and values of relationships through our caregivers, the media, popular culture, books, our social networks, and our own experiences. The knowledge we gain deeply guides our inferences (see Chapter 2) and actions in our own relationships—but this knowledge is only helpful if it is grounded in reality. Make sure you bring *informed* knowledge into your close relationships. This knowledge may come from experience, from a trusted counselor or therapist, or from a relationship-based course—including this one.

Nurture Mutual Commitment

As mentioned in Chapter 8, healthy relationships require mutual commitment. When you perceive that you are putting in and receiving about the same amount as the other person, you will be more motivated to maintain the relationship.[62] "Is she as into this relationship as I am?" "Why am I doing all the work?" "Why do I always let him have his way?"—answers to questions like these can reveal how satisfied (or dissatisfied) we're feeling with our relationships. Our interest in relationships can ebb and flow—that's to be expected. But overall,

both partners should offer the same commitment level, or be able to restore an imbalance.

Don't Fear Uncertainty

Dialectical theory (Chapter 8) teaches that there are no beginnings, middles, or ends to these ever-transforming relationships—only sustained possibilities.[63] Indeed, the single best guiding principle for maintaining relationships is to understand that people and relationships continually transform over time.[64] Partners who are able to appreciate uncertainty and ambiguity in relationships are less likely to try to control their relationships out of fear.

Now that we've explored the ways we maintain our relationships, let's move on to the topic of conflict. The reality of close relationships is that they can also breed frustration and disagreement. But as we will see, this is not necessarily a bad thing, as conflict can also be used to strengthen our relationships.

MANAGING INTERPERSONAL CONFLICT

Krystan and Bailey were best friends who shared an apartment while attending school. One day Krystan asked Bailey, "What is the matter with you?" Bailey, taken aback, replied, "Nothing." But Krystan wouldn't let it go: "I *know* something is bothering you; you've been quiet all week." Finally, Bailey replied, "You know, I work hard to keep the kitchen clean, and I hate it when you let your dirty dishes pile up in the sink!" Feeling defensive, Krystan shot back, "You're the one who demands that our kitchen be spotless. It's crazy! You need to relax."

Conflict happens between close partners (including roommates) who daily gripe, deceive, complain, disappoint, tease, and embarrass each other.[65] It can also happen between those who are more often satisfied and positive. In other words, conflict is inevitable—along with being chaotic and messy.[66] What starts out as a simple disagreement over dishes in the sink can lead to hurt feelings and a laundry list of other issues.

Many of us see conflict as a win-lose battle and, for that reason, usually try to avoid it.[67] Nevertheless, it's natural for individuals with unique thoughts, feeling, needs, and goals to clash. Accepting this reality, let's now focus on how to best manage these episodes of conflict.

What Is Interpersonal Conflict?

Interpersonal conflict is a struggle that occurs when partners reveal what they see as incompatible interests.[68] Let's take a closer look at this term through the example of Krystan and Bailey. First, Bailey initially hid her annoyance—it didn't become interpersonal until she revealed it to Krystan.

Second, the conflict occurred because the two are interdependent on each other. Living together, they have come to rely on each other, both for emotional support and for sharing a living arrangement. And finally, each woman saw the other as blocking her interests. If Krystan and Bailey didn't care about who did the dishes—they just wanted them to get done—then this would have been just a disagreement. However, Krystan saw Bailey's behavior as disrespectful toward her efforts to keep the kitchen clean. This was at odds with the respect she thought she deserved for the work she did do in the kitchen.

In the next section, we explore the most common causes of conflict, ranging from specific behaviors to personality traits.[69]

Common Causes of Conflict

Partners struggle over all sorts of issues. "I can't get her to listen to me." "Every time I come home, my in-laws are over." "She keeps telling our friends about every little fight we have." The causes behind conflicts can typically be sorted into three categories.

Behavior. Conflict can arise over specific actions or inactions of partners. These behaviors—from not responding to an e-mail to flirting with someone other than your partner—can be numerous and varied. The most common triggers are being critical, rebuffing the other person, and making unreasonable demands.[70]

Online behavior can both help with maintenance and cause conflict. For instance, married and committed couples report that partners are distracted by their cell phones.[71] Jealousy may arise when partners "like" or comment on the posts of attractive friends, pose with pictures of them, or "friend" former partners. Increased jealousy is especially dangerous, as it can make one increase negative behavior and lessen more positive behaviors.[72] On Twitter, partners who fight publicly show an increase in relationship problems.[73]

Relational Rules. As mentioned earlier, we make our own rules for relationships based on our experiences, the people in our lives, and other outside influences. When our partners don't mold to our expectations, conflict may ensue. Partners can also find themselves in conflict over various forms of rule breaking, such as cheating, telling others private information about their partners, being overly critical, gossiping, or deceiving.[74]

Personality. Personality conflict centers around a partner's perceived characteristics.[75] In other words, people mired in personality conflict

RELATIONAL RULES

blame the conflict on their partner's personality (for example, being lazy, inconsiderate, or cruel). In turn, these perceptions influence how they choose to deal with their partners. Studies show that unhappy couples are not very charitable when it comes to interpreting their partner's actions. They often attribute the other's bad behaviors to personality defects, holding the partner responsible for those behaviors.[76]

Benefits of Interpersonal Conflict

Some romantic pairs report one to three conflicts a week, and "distressed" couples report even more.[77] However, in spite of what you might think about conflict, it has important benefits; for example, expressing conflict can be cathartic, release tension, and energize a relationship.[78]

Constructive conflict can improve both our understanding of our partners and our relationship with them. During periods of conflict, partners can hear each other's perspective and possibly change their behavior.[79] For instance, working through the issue of whether your work peer really has your back can reveal times when he or she felt your lack of support. This might lead to changes in your own actions.

We also use conflict to regulate our relationships.[80] For example, conflict can expose unmet expectations, unrealistic obligations, and unfair judgments. Seeing these, partners can decide to reassess their assumptions and even the rules that guide how they act.[81]

BENEFITS OF INTERPERSONAL CONFLICT

STYLES AND PATTERNS OF CONFLICT

Research suggests something surprising: there is no apparent link between the number of arguments a married couple has and their marital happiness.[82] What does affect happiness is how partners manage their conflict. Behavior can be broken down into a range of styles, from destructive to constructive.

Six Conflict Styles

Six styles occur in interpersonal conflict.[83] Each varies according to how direct partners are in expressing their struggle and their willingness to be cooperative.

Competitive Fighting: *Direct and Uncooperative.* Competitive fighters take control to get what they want. They do this by accusing, blaming, joking in a hostile manner, and calling their partner names.[84] Unsurprisingly, these behaviors appear to lead to dissatisfied partners.[85] But while competitive fighting is generally harmful, it can be helpful when partners are direct but not aggressive.[86] If partners are going through a more dramatic conflict, such as if one breaks a major trust, then they may need to be more direct—particularly if one partner doesn't want to discuss the issue.

Collaborating: *Direct and Cooperative.* Collaborators work toward a solution that's beneficial to both partners. Common attributes include focusing on partner behaviors instead of personality, being accountable, and seeking each other's feelings and opinions. Collaborators can be considered interpersonally competent, and in fact, parents who model this style can benefit their children.[87]

Compromising: *Moderately Direct and Moderately Cooperative.* "You win some and you lose some" is the common refrain of compromising. Consider a couple who argues about the amount of time one of them spends with friends. Although the partner in question refuses to stop seeing her friends on the weekends, she agrees to see them just one day of the weekend, rather than both. In this case, both partners get some of what they wanted. Compromise is quicker than collaboration and common in American society, which often teaches people to give a little to get what they want. While most of us see this style as fair and reasonable, we should still exercise some care with this method. If partners perceive the result as unfair or think their needs are never being met, compromise can result in dissatisfaction.[88]

Yielding: *Indirect and Cooperative.* Often we find ourselves admitting that our behavior might be unfair, unreasonable, or even wrong; in these cases, yielding is appropriate. A common phrase to describe this is "picking your battles" for the good of the relationship. Imagine that Tanuja becomes annoyed when her wife's mother buys them an expensive crib without consulting them. Eventually she decides to let go of her annoyance and accept the gift graciously. While this method is effective for keeping the peace, if it is used too often out of fear or a sense of powerlessness, it can put a chill on the relationship.[89]

Avoiding: *Indirect and Neutrally Cooperative.* Avoiding is not yielding—it's the refusal to confront the other partner. Roommates and college-age romantic partners, for instance, often prefer to hold back complaints.[90] Even happy marital pairs will sometimes avoid issues.[91] We observed earlier that a common myth of relationships is that partners should hold back their feelings of distress. In reality, though, avoiding has its place.[92] Avoidance may prevent potential aggression and harm in abusive relationships. By contrast, in generally positive relationships, partners may decide that certain issues are just not that important. More skilled communicators can choose to "agree to disagree" rather than enter a direct confrontation with each other.

Indirect Fighting: *Indirect and Uncooperative.* Indirect fighting refers to using passive-aggressive tactics. For example, you might accept your friend's annoying new friend into your circle but then post inappropriate pictures of her partying on Facebook. This type of fighting also occurs when you invalidate your partner's concerns ("You always make such a big deal about that"), make sarcastic comments ("Yeah right, you want to stay together"), complain that he or she won't leave you alone, leave in a huff, and give your partner the silent treatment. These are all ways of indirectly protecting your own goals at the expense of the other.[93] Indirect fighting can be particularly dangerous to relationships; it may even be more destructive than competitive fighting because of its indirectness.[94]

Conflict choices vary across people, contexts, and relationships. We all learn conflict styles that feel appropriate, often from our family. A cooperative conflict style is ideal, yet research has shown that people

SIX CONFLICT STYLES

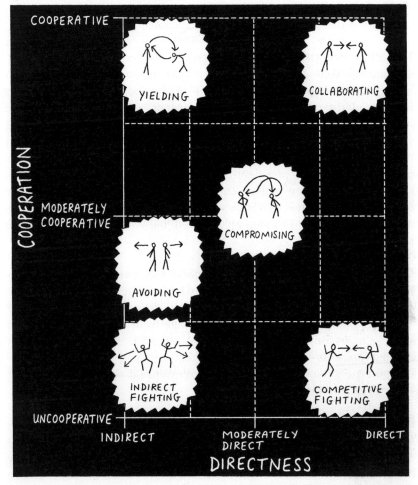

generally use the more indirect and competitive behaviors than the direct, cooperative ones.[95] Being aware of the more negative conflict patterns can help you identify which ones you now use and which of the more beneficial patterns you could switch to.

Unhealthy Conflict Patterns

Beyond conflict styles, partners also engage in different **conflict patterns**. These are the ways that partners react to each other—and how these reactions affect the conflict. For example, if two partners counter each other's complaints with more complaints, then the negativity and conflict is likely to escalate.[96] Four of the most common unhealthy patterns of conflict are discussed in the following sections.

Negative Reciprocity. When negativity (for example, name calling, accusations, yelling, and dismissals) triggers more negativity, the result is **negative reciprocity**. This is one of the most damaging patterns between partners.[97] It's especially prevalent when partners perceive hostile intentions behind each other's behavior.[98] For example, partners who unload grievances or use third parties (such as mutual friends) to make a case against their partner can easily be seen as hostile. This pattern of hostility is prevalent among dissatisfied couples and is especially obvious among violent couples.[99] Within healthy relationships, responding to negative behavior with positive communication—such as answering calmly or bringing up a shared joke—can offset the negative pattern.[100]

Common Couple Violence. The pattern of **common couple violence** involves violence and emerges when partners believe they have no control in the relationship, feel ignored, or want to vent their anger but don't know how.[101] Behavior can range from throwing objects and shoving to beating or using a weapon. Although most couples report isolated incidents of this pattern (for example, a partner throwing something on the ground), whereas others experience it on a regular basis,[102] violence in any form is unacceptable.

Demand-Withdraw. The **demand-withdraw** pattern can often be seen in competitive and indirect fighting. This occurs when one partner demands a change while the other partner, benefiting from the way things are, withdraws. The partner's withdrawal is an attempt to keep the balance in his or her favor. This pattern is damaging to relationships and is often hard to break.[103] A common withdrawal strategy is the silent treatment.[104] Unfortunately, this strategy can increase hostility and prevent partners from finding a solution. It can even affect the mental health of children who are exposed to it.[105]

Cascading Negativity. Psychologist John Gottman's Four Horsemen of the Apocalypse model describes a harmful long-term conflict pattern: a cascading sequence of negativity.[106] With **cascading negativity**, couples move from complaints, to contempt, to defensiveness, and then to

DEMAND—WITHDRAW

stonewalling. While complaints are not uncommon, they can cause contempt when partners make them personal: "You are so condescending" as opposed to "I don't like it when you brag after winning a match." These personal complaints tend to trigger a partner's *contempt*.

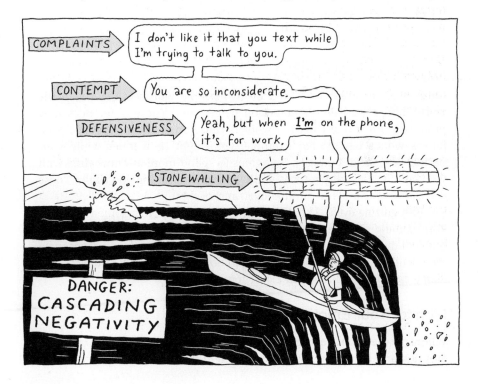

Contempt is poisonous because it leads to people exaggerating the negative aspects of partners at the expense of seeing their good.[107] *Defensiveness*, a natural response to feeling attacked, follows. For example, "You never consider me when you plan our future; you just do what you want to do!" This overgeneralizing and assuming isn't fair or helpful.[108] *Stonewalling*, or withdrawing, happens when a partner feels attacked and moves to protect him- or herself. Stonewalling typically leads to the demand-withdraw pattern.

STAYING RESPECTFUL, STRONG, AND POSITIVE IN CONFLICT

Negative conflict patterns show that our actions, emotions, *and* perceptions act in unison as we deal with conflict.[109] If we want to find ways to better manage conflict, we must attend to all three.

Typically, people don't respond well to hostility.[110] However, making the choice to act constructively can change the direction of conflict. Remaining positive in the face of conflict can encourage our partners to do the same, and can bring trust and satisfaction to our relationships. With that in mind, let's turn to some specific considerations.

Accept Cyclical Conflict

Close relationships are created by two people who see and act in the world differently (see Chapter 2 on perception). These differences may produce conflict that can't be "won" because one person is right or even knows what's best.[111] For example, you might be a loner while your partner is a social butterfly. He agrees to spend more at-home time with you, but he eventually returns to old patterns, upsetting you again. These cyclical conflicts can resurface over and over.

Recognizing cyclical conflict allows you to accept that some issues will keep coming up over time.[112] It doesn't mean that you didn't solve the problem the first time—it's normal to face these issues and then renegotiate them as they resurface. If you're able to do this constructively, the renegotiating can actually bring you closer together.

Monitor Your Emotions

When partners notice incompatible goals or think that their partners are blocking their interests, they may feel hurt and even angry. When

ACCEPTING CYCLICAL CONFLICT

those emotions become intense enough to trigger a fight, flight, or freeze response, there could be harmful effects. **Emotional flooding** occurs when a person's heart rate and blood pressure skyrocket, his or her muscles tense, breathing is difficult, and it is hard to think. Whining, defensiveness, and contempt can all trigger emotional flooding.

Men flood sooner than women in conflict and take longer to return to their normal heart rates.[113] The cycle can be broken with positive responses, such as well-placed humor or affection. It's smart to know your own base heart rate so that you can monitor any flooding and engage in conflict only when you have calmed down. Research shows that taking three deep breaths can significantly help in reducing stress.[114]

Express Criticisms Gently and Respectfully

Leading marriage experts have found kindness to be the key to marital health.[115] Healthy couples develop a

HOW TO DEAL WITH EMOTIONAL FLOODING

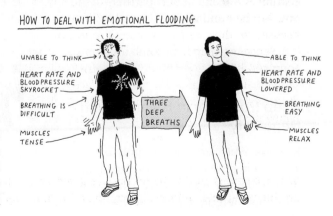

EXPRESS CRITICISMS GENTLY AND RESPECTFULLY

I know you were just trying to be helpful, and I appreciate that. Next time, let me take care of it.

habit of looking for things in their partners to appreciate rather than to be annoyed by. Kindness is particularly hard during conflict, but it's possible to remain kind while also expressing your anger or hurt. During a conversation (or disagreement), pause so that you can choose how to express these emotions—ideally in a way that shows respect for your partner.

Engage in Conflict with Positive Expectations

The reasoning you attach to your partner's behaviors dramatically influences how you interpret them. For example, John forgets to take the trash out, and his partner, Mira, believes it is because he is neglectful, not realizing that he was up all night with the baby. When couples are distressed, they rarely give each other a break. Instead, they assume their partner has negative intentions.[116] To add insult to injury, the perception that John is not attentive will shape Mira's future perceptions of him. She might focus on other "uncaring" behavior toward her, or dismiss any of his behavior that contradicts this perception.[117] Seeing your partner in a positive light and giving him or her the benefit of the doubt constitute one difference between happy and unhappy couples.

ENGAGE IN CONFLICT WITH POSITIVE EXPECTATIONS
(NOT LIKE THIS)

Why didn't you respond to any of my texts ?!? You're always ignoring me.

But... I was making you dinner.

Keep Positivity in Balance with Negativity

Partners who are able to pull themselves out of the moment in conflict have a unique opportunity. They can note their interpretations, decide how to react, and work on fixing negative patterns. Even if they don't get it right every time, they can attempt to balance their negative behaviors with positive ones. John Gottman is famous for his claim that one negative behavior needs to be counterbalanced with five positive ones.[118]

MEDIA CAN HELP US PROCESS RELATIONSHIPS

Most couples generally have a good sense of their issues and sensitivities. With this knowledge, partners can share how they interpret each other's actions and the impact those interpretations might have. Research shows that couples who watch movies about relationships (like *Blue Valentine* or *Trainwreck*), and then reflect on the movies by discussing them, show marked improvement in their behavior toward each other.[119] Talking about relationships that we see among family and friends, as well as in the media, can help us process our own relationships.

CHAPTER REVIEW

In this chapter, we focused on the two ways to sustain personal relationships: maintaining them and dealing with conflict. We maintain different types of relationships in different ways. Romantic relationships, friendships, and workplace relationships have unique qualities that influence the tactics we may use. We suggested five specific guidelines for maintaining relationships: embrace your agency, meet connecting bids, take action based on knowledge, nurture mutual commitment, and don't fear uncertainty.

With regard to interpersonal conflict, we discussed its common causes and showed the benefits that it can bring to healthy relationships. We highlighted six conflict styles that vary according to directness and a person's willingness to be cooperative. The most direct and most cooperative style is collaborating, while the least direct and least cooperative style is indirect fighting. Competitive fighting, compromising, yielding, and avoiding fall between the two extremes.

Conflict is natural in relationships, yet too often partners get caught up in negative, damaging patterns. Negative reciprocity, common couple violence, demand-withdrawal, and cascading negativity can all damage healthy relationships. To close, we offered five suggestions for successfully managing conflict: accepting perpetual conflict, monitoring your emotions, expressing criticisms gently and respectfully, engaging in conflict with positive expectations, and keeping positivity in balance with negativity.

LaunchPad
macmillan learning

LaunchPad for *Let's Communicate* offers videos and encourages self-assessment through adaptive quizzing. Go to **launchpadworks.com** to get access to:

 LearningCurve
Adaptive Quizzes

 Video clips that help you understand human communication

Key Terms

relational maintenance 252
commitment 253
positivity 254
openness 254
assurances 254
social networks 254
sharing tasks 254
sharing activities 254
connecting bids 263
turning-away response 263
turning-against response 264
turning-toward response 264
interpersonal conflict 266

competitive fighting 269
collaborating 269
compromising 269
yielding 270
avoiding 270
indirect fighting 270
conflict patterns 271
negative reciprocity 272
common couple violence 272
demand-withdraw 272
cascading negativity 272
emotional flooding 275

Review Questions

1. Define *relational maintenance*.
2. Explain each of the six relational maintenance behaviors, using examples from your experience.
3. What are some of the challenges to maintaining romantic relationships, friendships, and workplace relationships?
4. What are the five guidelines for effective relational maintenance? How does each one promote the relationship?
5. Explain each of the three components of interpersonal conflict.
6. List the three common causes of conflict, providing an example for each.
7. How is conflict beneficial personally and relationally?
8. Compare each of the six conflict styles.
9. What are the characteristics of each of the unhealthy conflict patterns?
10. How do each of the five healthy conflict behaviors help you stay respectful, strong, and positive in conflict?

Critical Thinking Questions

1. You learned about six typical relational maintenance behaviors. These are prosocial rather than antisocial. What are some ways relational partners use antisocial behaviors (for example, spying on their partner or asking others to share information about their partner) to maintain their relationships? Are these helpful? Harmful?
2. People talk quite frequently about how technology helps them maintain their relationships. What is your experience with social media and relational maintenance? What are the most helpful and the least helpful aspects of it, and why?
3. Consider the challenges of long-distance relationships. Which maintenance behaviors do you believe are used the most often, and why? Which ones do not make any sense in this context, and why?
4. Conflict involves believing that your partner is somehow standing in the way of something you want. When you consider the three causes of conflict, what is being interfered with in behavioral, relational rule, and personality conflicts?

5. What are the central themes running through the four destructive conflict patterns? How do the five suggestions for constructive conflict management help address these themes?

Activities

1. Look through popular magazines (list these) that address how men and women can maintain their romantic relationships. List the suggestions, and categorize the areas most often discussed (sexual relations, listening, support, and so on). Compare and contrast the advice in these magazines, and consider how popular media "teaches" you about relational maintenance. How does this knowledge influence your own actions in romantic relationships?

2. Connecting bids are central to helping us sustain an emotional connection with someone. Create a matrix with three columns. Label each column "Turn Away," "Turn Against," and "Turn Toward." Now consider one close relationship (friendship or romantic). Considering this relationship, list as many verbal and nonverbal examples of each that you typically display. Ask your partner to do the same. Now compare your lists. Any similarities? Are there any behaviors that are seen differently by yourself and your partner? Do these patterns help illustrate the positive or negative challenges in your relationship?

3. Write a script between two friends, a dating couple, or special peers at work that depicts a conflict in which the pair exhibit the collaborating style of conflict. Then alter some of the verbal or nonverbal actions that would turn the interaction from collaborating into each of the remaining styles. Discuss the type of actions you chose to illustrate each style.

4. Select a movie about the ups and downs of marriage—for example, *Mr. & Mrs. Smith* (2005), *While We're Young* (2014), *Blue Valentine* (2010), *Unfaithful* (2002), or *Who's Afraid of Virginia Woolf?* (1996). Select your favorite conflict episode and, based on what you saw, offer specific advice that might help improve the interaction.

Apply Your Skills

Go to the illustration about cascading negativity on page 273. Write two scripts. In one, show two partners exhibiting negative behaviors that lead to more and more negativity. In the second script, show the same partners reaching a critical place in the pattern in which one attempts to redirect the negativity. Use the principles of effective conflict to write about the redirection and defend why you believe it would alter the course of negativity.

Study Plan

_____

_____

_____

_____

_____

_____

_____

_____

_____

_____

_____

_____

_____

_____

PRINCIPLES OF GROUP COMMUNICATION

10

OBJECTIVES

- Demonstrate the importance of small groups to our lives.

- Explain the central role of communication in small group dynamics.

- Explore several guidelines for improving small group communication in both face-to-face and mediated contexts.

Early in the semester, Tamika, Chantal, Isaac, Haley, and Roderick were assigned to work together on a group project in their small group communication course. Their assignment: to create a campaign for a presidential candidate. The project included an in-class presentation and a "media day" on the campus quad, complete with candidate buttons and brochures.

The five students didn't know each other and were a little anxious the first time they met to discuss the criteria for the project. But quickly, all five found they had something in common: they wanted to choose a celebrity who had demonstrated savvy in an endeavor unrelated to his or her profession. They agreed on Angelina Jolie because they liked her international work—not to mention her movies.

Team Jolie discussed meeting on a regular basis. To accommodate their schedules, Chantal suggested they set up a wiki group so they could share their written work and meeting agendas. Isaac took charge of figuring out when everyone could meet face-to-face.

At the first meeting, the team ran into a roadblock: coordinating everyone's different opinions. All offered ideas, but no one seemed willing to summarize them and move the group along. Roderick suggested they stop and set some ground rules, like assigning key roles to members and respecting everyone's input.

As the team climate improved, the group members began to see the benefits of working in a small group. Through spirited and respectful discussions, each member was able to offer valuable ideas. At the end of the semester, the group's classroom presentation and their "Vote for Angie" booth in the quad were resounding successes—earning them even more votes than their most charismatic opponent: Team Clooney. As this example illustrates, learning to work effectively in a group is a valuable life skill. The small group has been identified as the single most important social formation we encounter, and it affects every level of our lives—from the personal to the professional.[1] Although group interactions are sometimes challenging, you will likely encounter them in the classroom, in your community, and at work. Your success hinges on understanding that effective groups are formed through thoughtful and reflective participation rather than good circumstance. This chapter introduces you to the types, forms, purposes, and dynamics of small groups. The discussion continues in Chapter 11, in which we explore leadership, decision making, and working in small groups to solve problems and attain goals.

SMALL GROUP CHARACTERISTICS

A **small group** is a limited number of people who work toward a common goal and who believe that, together, they can achieve more than any one of them acting alone. A popular term for a small group is a *team*, which often refers to groups with clearly defined member responsibilities, rules, and goals. For our purposes, we use the terms interchangeably because the dynamics of each are the same.[2] The most common characteristic of a small group is that members work interdependently toward a collective goal—that is, team members rely on one another to succeed.[3]

Small groups offer important advantages over individual efforts. Group members often have unique experiences, perspectives, and talents

ADVANTAGES OF WORKING IN SMALL GROUPS

to offer. With this pool of resources, groups can tackle problems any one person would find overwhelming. The group can also divide up a project so that each member takes responsibility for the portions of the job he or she is best suited for. And by sharing their ideas, members can spot potential problems or improvements in a plan that an individual working alone might miss.

Small Group Communication

Small group communication is at the heart of group dynamics and involves the constant efforts of group members to influence one another. These efforts are normal and necessary to create an effective group. If we want to be sensitive to small group communication, we can't just focus on who is sending us messages and when—we must remember that *everyone* simultaneously processes, interprets, and shares messages (recall this from Chapter 1). Any time we're interacting with others, they can (and often will) perceive our words and actions in any number of ways—even those that we didn't intend.

As we also discussed in Chapter 1, any message between two or more people carries two simultaneous meanings—its *content* and its *relational* meaning. It's no different in small group communication. Imagine that a person from your volunteer committee says to you, "Hey, where are the minutes from the last meeting?" The message's content— what it literally says—is a request for a record of the last meeting. But perhaps what catches your attention is the message you interpret about your relationship with the individual making the request. Is this a request from a friend or a demand from an intrusive acquaintance or overbearing leader? The verbal and nonverbal cues (along with your thoughts and experiences of the person) will affect your interpretation.

This example shows that while small groups have end goals, they must also focus on how the people within the group communicate with each other as they strive to meet those goals.

Types

Take a moment to write down every small group you've ever belonged to. Note the variety of groups, which likely reflect a wide range of purposes across multiple contexts (educational, professional, cultural, religious, political, and personal). A **primary group**, such as our families or our friends, helps us with our need to both be cared for and connect with others, as well as teaching us how to socialize in groups.[4] A **secondary group** is a task- or work-oriented group that we form to help influence others and solve problems. We'll focus on these groups in the following two chapters. Some of the most common types are as follows:

- **Learning groups** are popular throughout our lives and offer us a way to understand our world. Movies and TV shows may depict student study groups or learning cohorts (such as the interns in *Grey's Anatomy*). Effective learning groups are associated with higher student achievement.[5]

- **Committees** can be found in professional organizations such as schools, government agencies, legislatures, and corporations. Committees serve their larger organization whether they're a permanent fixture (for example, a budget committee) or have been created for one special task, after which they'll be disbanded (for example, a university faculty search committee). A few special types of committees include **task forces**, which are composed of

members with the skills and knowledge necessary for the particular assignment, and **quality control circles**, whose goal is to find a way to better their company's performance.

- **Self-managed work teams** have emerged over the years as a result of employees gaining more autonomous control of their work. In these teams, skilled peers oversee their own schedules and work policies within the boundaries of their parent company—with little supervision.
- **Top management teams**, or **TMTs**, are a result of organizations decentralizing and appointing multiple managers to lead different units.[6] TMTs are composed of upper-level managers who focus less on production and more on improving leadership within the organization.

Group Size

What is the ideal size for a "small" group? The general rule of thumb is to create a group with the smallest number of people needed to reach its purpose. Groups are considered too big when members have a hard time keeping track of everyone's contributions.[7] In most situations, three- to six-member groups have the best chance of working effectively and reaching their goals.[8] Five is typically a good number because members can contribute and share enough information within reasonable time limits without becoming overwhelmed.[9]

Size and Complexity. We are constantly moving in and out of different communication contexts. After spending all day in a small work group (group communication), we might have a quiet dinner with a good friend (interpersonal communication). The next morning, we might deliver a presentation to a large audience (public speaking). We often make these shifts without conscious notice, but the resulting changes in our communication are important to consider.

While it may seem subtle, the number of people in a group changes the degree of effort and coordination needed to communicate well. Group members communicate with certain others in the group or the group as a whole, revealing patterns of information flow. These patterns are called **networks**. As the size of a group grows, these networks become more complex. Networks can differ in their level of centrality— meaning whether information flows from a central person or flows more evenly among members. The more centralized the network, the less other members talk to each other and the group as a whole; instead, they spend their time listening to the central person.

The number of potential relationships (meaning the different possibilities of interaction) within groups increases their psychological and social complexity. Consider, for instance, that in a five-person rock band, there are seventy-five possible ways for group members to interact! Clearly, this band has to establish roles (like who writes the lyrics) and

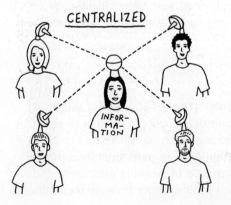

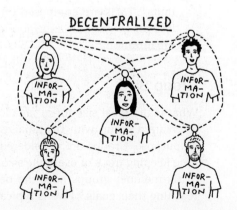

CENTRALIZED

DECENTRALIZED

goal activity (perhaps coming up with enough songs for an album) to better coordinate these relationships. Groups of this size must also manage the number of member contributions, the likelihood of sub-groups arguing over ideas, increased difficulty reaching agreement, and overall member satisfaction with the complexity of the process.

Size and Stability.

Groups have a potential for stability that two-person relationships lack (see Chapter 8). Should a group lose one member, it can still carry on. This is especially evident in groups like committees, many of which stay in existence for long periods of time. Group stability is also a function of the specific roles members can take on. These roles, discussed later in the chapter, have clear functions that a group must include to run smoothly. Compared to pairs, groups more overtly define, discuss, and debate their goal and their roles as they try to balance their individual desires with a shared group responsibility.

When new members appear in a group, both the new member and the established group go through **group socialization** as they adapt to

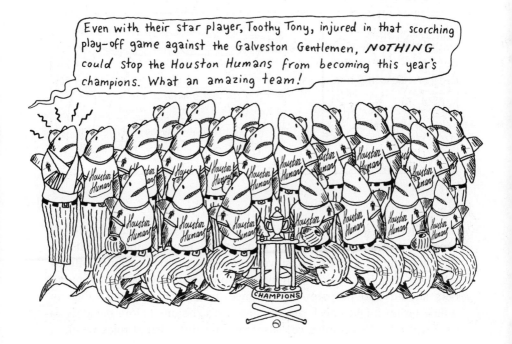

SOCIALIZATION

these changes.[10] This process requires all members to exhibit open and sensitive communication. Before integrating a new member, established members should develop a positive attitude toward the possibility offered by a new member and develop ideas around what to expect. New members should also prepare—for instance, those considering joining an online group might check out the group discussions before deciding to get involved.[11] Newcomers can also consider the existing roles within a group (perhaps by asking questions of people already in the group). New members find themselves fully integrated when they feel comfortable with the group, and vice versa. Although groups can survive the loss of a member, the loss may still have an impact. When this happens, group members should talk openly about why the person left and how it's affected the group.

ADVANTAGES OF SMALL GROUPS

Groups can be voluntary or involuntary. In the workplace, you may not have a choice; for example, many American corporations believe that small groups play a fundamental role in good decision making and employee commitment.[12] Beyond this, we can choose to join hundreds of small groups throughout our lives, such as book clubs, running groups, and volunteer organizations. Doing so fulfills our desires to grow, to belong, and to contribute to something larger than ourselves.

Individuals are great problem solvers, but groups can sometimes surpass an individual's ability—for example, when the task at hand does not have a clear answer, or when there is limited time allotted to tackle the problem.[13]

Let's consider the advantages of groups that allow us to make the most of their potential, whether they're voluntary or mandatory.

Diverse Perspectives

Working with others allows us to draw on everyone's unique experiences and perspectives. Group members with different ideas can tackle complex problems by offering up, weighing, and trying out multiple solutions. For example, consider the challenges of ensuring effective health care for all. During the spring of 2014, fifteen female senators formed a bipartisan group calling for the use of women and minorities in clinical drug trials. This was in response to reports that both groups were being woefully underrepresented. The group's letter to the U.S. Food and Drug Administration led to formal calls for increased diversity in these trials.[14]

Greater group **heterogeneity**, or member difference (as compared to **homogeneity**, or member similarity), is not without its challenges. In groups that are highly heterogeneous, group members may find themselves having to provide more background information for their ideas,

DIVERSE PERSPECTIVES

and are more likely to disagree with each other. But while homogeneous groups may run more smoothly, heterogeneous groups that find ways to coordinate multiple perspectives perform more productively.[15] In other words, a group with diverse perspectives that *values* all of those perspectives and is able to use them effectively has the best chance of reaching its goals.

Multiple Resources

Groups have the distinct advantage of being able to gather and share more information than an individual working alone. Often, more than one person can gather information while others can assess it. In the process of sharing information, group members can ensure checks on reasoning, encourage new ideas, and help spot potential problems. This advantage is especially important in the health care industry. For example, teams of medical specialists often provide better recommendations to patients than their primary care physician alone.[16]

In the process of sharing information, group members tend to pay more attention to information they believe everyone knows or agrees with.[17] Members with different or contrary ideas may avoid speaking out for fear of being labeled disruptive to a group consensus. One way to confirm that members are all sharing information

MULTIPLE RESOURCES: A MEDICAL TEAM

is to make sure everyone presents what they know before the group makes any decisions.

Commitment

Working together on a challenging problem increases each member's commitment to the group's solution—even more so than if they were working to solve it alone.[18] After all, no one understands a potential solution better than the group who worked together to develop it, and no one will work harder to ensure its success. As an example, consider Fresno's Lowell Neighborhood Association, an organization dedicated to improving the lives of neighborhood residents by involving those residents. With the help of the association, residents identify their neighborhood issues and figure out ways to address them. In 2014, the group tackled slumlord accountability by creating a short video called "Slumlords in Our Community" to raise awareness in the community.

SMALL GROUP DYNAMICS

Have you ever joined or been assigned to a group that just didn't click? What about the opposite—a group that got along well and seemed as though it could tackle any problem? Both of these outcomes were likely

due to **small group dynamics**—all the ways members communicate with one another, both verbally and nonverbally. In order for a group to work together well, members must know what to expect from one another. More specifically, they must know what roles their fellow group members play.

Small Group Roles

Small group dynamics are a balancing act between what individual members want and what the group as a whole wants. To this end, members take on roles that serve various functions. These roles may be classified as work, social, or selfish in nature.[19] Work and social roles are helpful, whereas selfish roles are unproductive and should be avoided.

Work Roles. In a group in which members are fulfilling **work roles**, you'll likely see people asking good questions, supplying valuable information, and synthesizing that information. Work roles encourage verbal messages that have to do with the task at hand or procedures to be followed, such as, "Let's talk about our next move" or "The common theme of Jesse and Noel's position is . . ."

Typically, there are nine work roles for small groups:

- *Initiators* suggest the group's goal and offer new ideas or propose new solutions.
- *Information providers* offer facts—based on researched evidence or personal experience—relevant to the issue under discussion.
- *Information gatherers* ask other members to share facts they know, and seek out supplemental information from other sources.

INITIATORS

INFORMATION
PROVIDERS

INFORMATION
GATHERERS

ELABORATORS

CLARIFIERS

EVALUATORS

SYNTHESIZERS

RECORDERS

PROCEDURAL
GUIDERS

- *Elaborators* add supporting facts, examples, or ideas to address or support a point that someone has raised during the discussion.
- *Clarifiers* attempt to make the meaning of another member's statement more precise.
- *Evaluators* offer their own judgments about the ideas put forward.
- *Synthesizers* identify emerging agreements and disagreements among the group as a whole, noting relationships among ideas.
- *Recorders* take notes during meetings, tracking major decisions and plans made by the group. They also distribute those notes and ensure proper follow-up and additional meetings.
- *Procedural guiders* suggest new ways to accomplish a task as well as remind the group of the procedures they need to follow in order to get the job done.

Social Roles. **Social roles** help sustain and strengthen interpersonal relations within a small group. When members perform social roles effectively and monitor how they talk to other members, groups are more likely to work together comfortably, support one another, and present findings or recommendations that reflect group consensus. With social roles, communication focuses on the relationship or communication between group

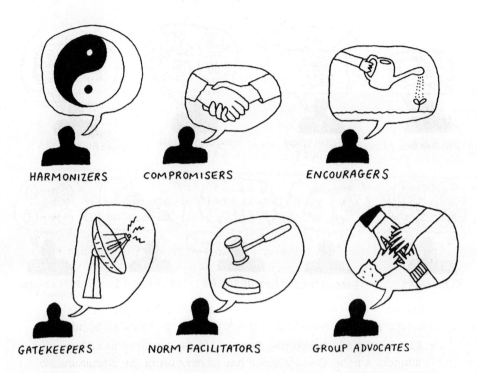

HARMONIZERS   COMPROMISERS   ENCOURAGERS

GATEKEEPERS   NORM FACILITATORS   GROUP ADVOCATES

members: "Tom, I respect your position, yet have you considered . . ." or "Brandon, we have not heard from you yet, what are you thinking?"
  Typically, there are six social roles:

- *Harmonizers* decrease tension in the group—whether by infusing humor at just the right time or by making positive and optimistic comments.

- *Compromisers* attempt to find common ground between adversaries within the group, offering solutions that appeal to those on both sides of the conflict.

- *Encouragers* inspire other group members by complimenting their ideas and work.

- *Gatekeepers* facilitate the exchange of information among group members.

- *Norm facilitators* reinforce healthy group norms and discourage unproductive ones.

- *Group advocates* show solidarity by focusing their behavior on promoting and valuing the group itself.

BLOCKERS   WITHDRAWERS   DOMINATORS   DISTRACTERS

Selfish Roles. In small groups, members also sometimes assume **selfish roles**; these roles accomplish little for a group because they're motivated by the self-centered, obstructive ends of individual members. Groups with members in these roles may experience incomplete findings, infighting, and dissension.

Typically, there are four selfish roles:

- *Blockers* stop the group from moving toward its objective—either by refusing to accept decisions the group has made or by rejecting other group members' ideas or opinions.

- *Withdrawers* refuse to make any contribution or participate in the discussion. They may feel out of their element in the group or have difficulty following other members' comments and ideas.

- *Dominators* usually monopolize group interactions, interrupt others, argue for the sake of arguing, and insist on having the last word. This behavior may stem from feelings of insecurity or an aggressive personality.

- *Distracters*—the exact opposite of *harmonizers*—send the group in irrelevant directions by making off-topic comments or engaging others in extraneous conversation. They may also mock other members' serious attention to the work, feign helplessness, or demand constant help.

Your group role is dependent on two things: your abilities and what the group expects from you. Through a trial-and-error process in which the group either supports or ignores your attempts, you will settle into a role. However, this is not to say that you will play the same role all the time in every group you are in. Different groups will bring out different roles in you. Consider Nick, who joins his college's debate team. A fledging comedian, Nick uses humor to relieve tension when two teammates

ROLE CONFLICT (AS SEEN IN *THE WALKING DEAD*)

argue in front of the group. The other debaters appreciate Nick's jokes, and he finds that over time he regularly defuses situations with humor—making him the group's harmonizer. In other groups, though, Nick finds himself in different roles—for example, as an information provider at the mentoring organization he helped found.

Members can play more than one role in a group and even bring in roles from other groups they participate in. Sometimes, though, these roles can clash, producing **role conflict**. For example, Jordan manages a coffee shop and also goes to school part time. She feels conflicted between her managerial role and her membership in a group at school. During one group meeting, she decides that she simply can't research information that weekend because she has to be at work training a new employee. This situation demonstrates that people will select the role of greatest importance to them.[20]

For your group to be as successful as possible, match your strengths with your group's expectations. As a group, be sure to balance the necessary work and social roles with those members who are most capable. Be careful not to assume, for instance, that only females should fill the social roles, or that because a member was a great initiator in a previous group he or she will be successful as an initiator in the current group.

Group Development

Groups go through different stages of development—just like personal relationships do (see Chapter 8)—as they seek their goal. A common

TUCKMAN'S MODEL OF GROUP DEVELOPMENT

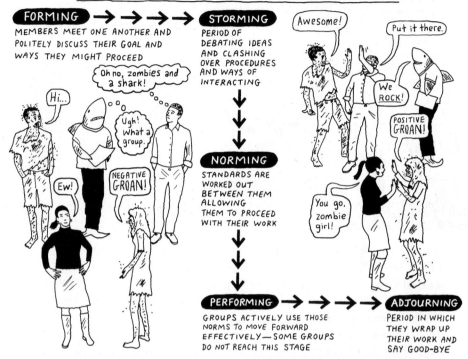

FORMING → → → →

MEMBERS MEET ONE ANOTHER AND POLITELY DISCUSS THEIR GOAL AND WAYS THEY MIGHT PROCEED

STORMING

PERIOD OF DEBATING IDEAS AND CLASHING OVER PROCEDURES AND WAYS OF INTERACTING

NORMING

STANDARDS ARE WORKED OUT BETWEEN THEM ALLOWING THEM TO PROCEED WITH THEIR WORK

PERFORMING → → → →

GROUPS ACTIVELY USE THOSE NORMS TO MOVE FORWARD EFFECTIVELY — SOME GROUPS DO NOT REACH THIS STAGE

ADJOURNING

PERIOD IN WHICH THEY WRAP UP THEIR WORK AND SAY GOOD-BYE

way to capture these changes is described in **Tuckman's model**, which helpfully uses five rhyming terms to describe the different stages: forming, storming, norming, performing, and adjourning.[21] These terms cover all the stages of group development, from members getting acquainted with one another, to becoming more comfortable with one another, to saying good-bye.

Some small group scholars, however, believe that this linear model oversimplifies group development. These scholars propose alternative models to better capture the unpredictable ways groups develop. Connie Gersick developed **Gersick's two-phase model** from observing work groups in real time.[22] She found that no matter how long groups are working on a task, a major turning point occurs at the midpoint of the project.

According to this model, groups typically take rather long periods to set up a project, talk about how to tackle the task, and gather necessary information. It's only at the midpoint that they take action to actually follow through on the plan.

GERSICK'S TWO-PHASE MODEL

TUE 1	WED 2	THUR 3	FRI 4	SAT 5	SUN 6	MON 7	TUE 8	WED 9	THUR 10
Phone all team members	**START PROJECT**	THINK	5pm HAIRCUT	Watch season finale: THE WALKING DEAD	Phone Mom & Dad	PRO-CRAST-INATE	DILLY-DALLY	Stare into space	TALK TALK TALK BUT NO ACTION
FRI 11	**SAT 12**	**SUN 13**	**MON 14**	**TUE 15**	**WED 16**	**THUR 17**	**FRI 18**	**SAT 19**	**SUN 20**
THINK MORE	THINK WHILE HAVING PEDICURE	Buy onions	Skype all team members	REALLY START PROJECT	DAY OFF	PICK UP DRY CLEANING	Remember to buy onions	CON-CEN-TRATE	AAAGH!
MON 21	**TUE 22**	**WED 23**	**THUR 24**	**FRI 25**	**SAT 26**	**SUN 27**	**MON 28**	**TUE 29**	**WED 30**
Buy more onions	VERY SERIOUS TEAM MEETING	PANIC	YAWN!	REALLY PANIC	:)	LAST EDITS MEETING	BUY COFFEE	Final team meeting	**PROJECT DUE!**

Often this occurs because group members realize they are running out of time and pause to assess what they still need to do. More effective groups make the necessary adjustments to their task in order to meet the deadline. Groups that miss opportunities early on to establish effective procedures or that fail to make proper adjustments at the mid-point usually run out of time.

CULTURAL DIVERSITY

Recall that in Chapter 6 we defined diversity as the differences stemming from traditional categories like race, ethnicity, gender, age, sexual orientation, disability, and religion. You may see diversity in your school or personal communication—and you will likely also experience it when you are employed. The twenty-first-century workplace involves greater diversity than ever before. Interestingly, groups that don't value diversity believe there are much sharper differences between members than do groups that do value diversity.[23]

Cultural diversity—encompassing differences in attitudes, motives, beliefs, opinions, and skills—can be a valuable asset for a team, but only if members recognize and appreciate it as such. Working with group members who are more similar to us is often easier and undemanding; however, such groups are not able to achieve the same degree of accomplishment as more heterogeneous groups.[24] Recall from Chapter 6 the idea of **ethnocentric bias**—meaning that we use our own culture to interpret and evaluate the behaviors of others. Dispelling this bias will help us move toward a more positive **synergy**, or a collective level of performance greater than that created by any single member. It will also help avoid negative synergy—patterns of interactions that lead to tension, inattention, and grasps for control.

In Chapter 6 we discussed the main cultural variations that impact communication. Here we focus exclusively on how these variations can impact small group communication.

Individualistic and Collectivist

Individualistic and **collectivist** variations reflect the degree to which a culture values individual versus group needs and rights. More individualistic members (for example, those from North America) value clarity over the nuance of expression valued by collectivist members (for example, Latin and Asian Americans). Effective groups balance the amount of input from each member—meaning that everyone should feel comfortable speaking and share equally with the group. A study showed that in groups composed of European American and Japanese students, the European American students took more turns speaking than did the Japanese students,[25] which led to unbalanced member input.

Individualism and collectivism is not an either/or variation, as it ranges differently between generations or even within one culture. For example, Japanese students have shown individualistic communication in their group communication with their peers as compared to their communication with their parents.[26]

Power Distance

Cultural groups can also differ regarding how much **power distance** is emphasized. Low-power-distance cultures (for example, Israel and Denmark) work to limit inequality and expect that individuals of lower power should be able to speak up. In high-power-distance cultures (for example, Iraq and India), hierarchical values are more emphasized—for example, they may expect more centralized networks (discussed earlier), in which a group leader is in control. In small groups, this cultural value relates to the idea of **conformity** (behaving according to certain standards) and its impact on group dynamics. Low-power-distance cultures may expect less conformity among group members, especially in relation to the group's more powerful members. High-power-distance cultures may be put off by the encouragement of equal participation.[27]

DIRECT vs. INDIRECT COMMUNICATION

Uncertainty Avoidance

Given the amount of information processed by a group, **uncertainty avoidance** is particularly relevant to small group dynamics. Group members from such cultures as Great Britain and Hong Kong tolerate a greater amount of uncertainty or ambiguity and have more patience with risk taking and dissent. Members from cultures like the United States and Greece prefer norms that promote clarity and value structure, so that everyone knows what to expect. When groups are composed of both types, members can feel uncomfortable or fearful because they're not sure what will be expected of them.[28]

High and Low Context

High- and low-context communication is related to individualistic-collectivist and uncertainty avoidance because it deals with the large amount of verbal and nonverbal messages shared within a group. Low-context cultures (for example, the United States and Germany) value the explicit meaning of messages, whereas high-context cultures (for example, China) prefer to read between the lines of a message and pick up on the subtle cues of what is *not* being said. Discussing and debating ideas in a mixed group of these values can lead to members accusing each other of either being too direct or avoiding the topic at hand.

Masculine and Feminine

Cultures that value dominance over nurturing differ in **masculine** and **feminine** preferences. Members from more masculine cultural countries (for example, Mexico and Austria) value more direct leadership in a group. Those from more feminine cultures (for example, Thailand and the Netherlands) tend to encourage the social aspects of group work and more participatory communication, often paying closer attention to the relationship aspect of messages (how things are said) than to the actual content. These values, based on stereotypical ideas of masculinity and femininity, may also affect who gets pressured into taking particular task and social roles in a group.

Mindful Communication

How can group members work toward recognizing and valuing the benefits of these differences? One way is to consider the practice of **mindful communication**, which is characterized by thoughtful reflection, openness, and a willingness to bridge differences. This type of communication has been proven to help diverse members work together.[29] The payoffs in terms of creativity, effectiveness, group communication, and enjoyment are tremendous for groups that can effectively use mindful communication:[30]

- **Creativity.** Ethnically and racially diverse groups can produce greater numbers of new ideas compared to more homogeneous groups. However, group procedures must encourage expression of ideas from everyone.

- **Effectiveness.** If group members focus on treating one another with mindfulness and respect, heterogeneous groups can be more effective than homogeneous groups.[31] Groups can also increase effectiveness by exploring the ways members are the same and focusing on a goal everyone can agree on.[32]

- **Group Communication.** We noted earlier that heterogeneous groups offer great payoffs if members are able to meet the challenge of using their diverse perspectives and experiences for group work. Individual group members who prefer the value of collectivist orientations communicate with more respect and cooperation (regardless of age, gender, or ethnicity) than those who prefer individualistic values.[33] Their communication also serves to encourage others to contribute. In addition, although members who see themselves in the minority in a diverse group tend to socialize more with each other, this does not typically influence communication when focused on the task at hand.[34]

- **Enjoyment:** In one study, majority Caucasian groups were compared to minority-dominated groups to see how individuals in the different groups assessed their level of enjoyment with the group experience. Everyone, both Caucasians and ethnic minorities, enjoyed working in minority-dominated groups more, and at no cost to their work.[35]

The exact nature of the impact of diversity on group dynamics is hard to pin down. Keep three things in mind to effectively manage group diversity. First, the influence of cultural values may not be seen early

on, when members of the group are getting to know one another, but may take on a larger role later in the process.[36] Second, if a group is diverse, it does not automatically mean that it will have more problems than a less diverse group. Third, people are diverse in many ways, so avoid making assumptions about people based on their cultural backgrounds. Diverse membership is not a cure-all—the benefits emerge from mindful communication that fosters cooperation and respect.

SMALL GROUP COMMUNICATION IN THE DIGITAL AGE

New technology has impacted every aspect of our lives, including small group work. Depending on your class schedule and career plans, you may be asked to participate in a group that's mainly (or all) remote—meaning you're not all in the same place at the same time. Consider Janelle, who met both online and face-to-face with her classmates for group projects in her hybrid psychology course, or Dylan, who for his job at a design firm was asked to hire and meet with several freelancers across the country remotely. One conclusion is certain: the issue is no longer *whether* to use technology for small group work but rather to what *degree*. The table on the next page helps compare what you gain and lose with each form.

In general, people do prefer face-to-face communication. However, while challenging, it is possible for mediated communication to approach the immediacy of face-to-face communication. This depends on how comfortable people are with communicating through the digital medium.[37] Let's take a look at some of the ways a small group might use technology.

Technology for Group Meetings

A particular challenge for any group, whether face-to-face or virtual, is getting everyone together for a meeting. Groups have a growing number of technological options for planning.

E-mail. This form allows group members to reach one another remotely. Members can use e-mail to announce the details of a meeting or even to allow a member to participate in a meeting. If members use e-mail formally for group work, they should send thoughtful messages if they want them to be taken seriously by others.[38] A few simple rules will help: Write short and simple messages with an informative subject line

Medium	Advantages	Disadvantages
Face-to-Face	• Rich in both content and relational meaning • Members adapt to one another easily • Sense of connection immediate	• Emotions can get in the way of what is being said • Members can more easily push each other away • Speaking up in difficult situations may not be easy
Mediated (computer, phone)	• Promotes content meaning • Members can think about messages before sending • Information can be stored for future use • Members can feel more free and less inhibited to contribute	• Social connection takes longer to build • Group feels less cohesive initially, more sterile • Fewer verbal and nonverbal cues to help in interpreting others' messages

to alert group members to the importance of the message. Before you send a message, make sure to review it, note who it is being sent to (and cc'd), and check that you included attachments (if necessary). As a group, you can decide the level of informal language, abbreviations, and emoticons you wish to allow for group business.

Text messaging. This form is also popular, yet not all mobile phone users have text data plans (and certain members may not have a cell phone). Check with your group to make sure all members have access to this medium. Texting is best used for brief and routine messages.[39] If you're using it for more businesslike exchanges with group members, avoid slang and verbal shortcuts. Also, avoid texting during face-to-face group meetings unless you're being asked to text another group member concerning group business.

Instant messaging (IM). This form is more rapid than e-mail or even voice mail. Immediate exchanges begin with a click on another's user handle. If you are IM'ing individual group members during a meeting,

SMALL GROUP COMMUNICATION
IN THE DIGITAL AGE

know that this will likely reduce how much you remember of the meeting. For example, Rachel and Jay used Google Chat (GChat) through a virtual sales meeting to give each other short, quick feedback on the sales negotiations. However, after the meeting, when asked to summarize those comments, they had both forgotten some key points.[40]

Video and Audio Conferencing. Videoconferencing, via services like Skype and Google Hangout, is easy to implement and allows groups to meet online or mix their face-to-face and online interaction. All it requires is a computer, the Internet, and a webcam. Groups can hold entirely remote meetings with this technology, or use it to include members who are not able to be physically present at a meeting. Audio conferencing, such as using a conference call number, is also a possibility if members have access to phones but not necessarily computers. Usually members dial in, enter a code, and are then placed in the audio conference. This form can also be used if certain members are not able to be physically present.

Meeting Applications. These are abundant for all Apple and Android platforms (mobile phones and notepads). Meeting Application, MeetingMinutes, GoToMeeting, and Fuze, for example, are all apps dedicated to helping groups host online meetings. Members are able to connect with one another, set up events, track meetings, show and record an agenda and minutes, conduct video and audio discussions, and share and store content.

Electronic Bulletin Board Services (BBS) and Instant Relay Chat (IRC). These are available not only in the previously discussed meeting applications but also as part of learning platforms used by instructors across the country. Groups use these for more detailed discussions across several remote locations. Members can share perspectives, reflect on ideas, and monitor participation, so that everyone can be part of the discussion. Use the BBS services if your discussions will involve critical consideration of ideas as opposed to a more freewheeling generation of ideas.[41] BBS allows you to send messages back and forth to one another with time in between (asynchronously), so that you can think about your message and edit it if need be. These services are helpful for task work, but less so for social interaction.

IRC allows members to send messages at the same time (synchronously), so that group members feel as if they are talking in real time. It is best for when groups want to brainstorm several ideas at once. If you use IRC, be careful that discussions do not veer off topic. Should you choose to use either service, make sure all members know how to access it, and use a moderator to help ensure balanced interaction as well as positive, courteous messaging.[42]

Technology for Group Work and Document Sharing

Learning platforms like Macmillan Learning's own LaunchPad, along with more general ones, such as Google +, Wiggio, and EnterTheGroup, offer computer assistance for every aspect of group work. These platforms often come with calendars for group meetings and assignment due dates, e-mail lists of members, file sharing for group research, survey capabilities, assignment tracking, and more. Wiggio has the capability to hold virtual meetings and conferences. EnterTheGroup provides users with actual video resources on project management and group conflict-resolution strategies.

Another technology-related consideration is document sharing. File-hosting services like Wikispace, Google Docs, and Dropbox allow group members to work on the same documents from different locations. Members can create, write, analyze, and edit documents online for future use. One of the authors of this book used Wikispace to produce a departmental review. Several groups of students and instructors stored documents (including meeting agendas, meeting minutes, and summary assessments) on this free web hosting service. As a result, every member had access to the documents and could edit and integrate them as needed.

Guidelines for Using Technology for Group Work

Now that we have shown some of the many ways groups can use technology for group meetings, let's turn to some general guidelines. Since you'll likely need to use technology for group work, keep the following three suggestions in mind.

First, figure out which type of technology is the most useful for your purposes. All forms have drawbacks, and it's important to be aware of both the benefits and the limitations. For example, as we saw with Rachel and Jay, IM'ing may be useful in meetings because it allows immediate feedback between participants; however, members can't always retrieve the content for future reference.[43] Use audio conferences for simpler information sharing. If your meeting requires thorough discussions of group issues, you may want to consider videoconferencing, in which you can see and hear one another.[44] In a similar vein, be aware that technological mishaps can happen. To avoid this, test all necessary equipment beforehand. Ensure that everyone can see and hear one another, and use names to clarify who is being addressed.

Second, remember that although computer technology seems widespread, not everyone has access to it or is comfortable using it. Make sure all group members have the same access to the technology you'd like to use. If they're uncomfortable using it, consider showing them how.

Third, try to imitate or facilitate face-to-face immediacy whenever you can. Even an e-mail can contain personal references ("How are you?"). If computers are the primary way your group interacts, mix in face-to-face meetings whenever possible. If this is not possible, find other ways to bring more personal touches to your task-oriented messages.

TRY TO FACILITATE FACE-TO-FACE IMMEDIACY

Simply using Skype or FaceTime for meetings allows members to see and talk with one another as if they were all together. If group members are comfortable with it, they can also bring an emotional dimension to their e-mails and texts with the use of emoticons or emojis. This works best when members are of a similar age and—if working together—at a similar level. For example, you would not send messages with emoticons to your boss—unless he or she has done so first!

EFFECTIVE PARTICIPATION IN A SMALL GROUP

Rules are particularly important to group participation. Think of the chaos that would result if group members decided to ignore the meeting time—or left whenever they wanted! Rules provide a road map for small group inter-action. Sets of actions that clash—for instance, members engaging in too many selfish roles or attempting unguided virtual group discussions—are counterproductive. The following instructions will help sharpen your aware-ness of how to act respectfully and effectively in groups. Remember: your group's success depends on it.

EFFECTIVE PARTICIPATION IN A SMALL GROUP

Prepare for Group Meetings

Poorly run meetings cost corporations millions of dollars, affecting their bottom line and damaging employee health and emotional well-being.[45] Yet groups tend to forget the significance of a welcoming environment in which everyone is well prepared and understands the aims of the meeting.[46]

Preparation for a meeting is actually easy. If you are leading the meeting, make sure everyone knows the time and place (consider using scheduleonce.com, an online meeting tool). Make and distribute an agenda beforehand so that members will be able to think about the topics to be discussed in advance. Microsoft Word and other software programs offer templates for agendas that you can easily adapt for your purposes. At the actual meeting, remember to bring anything you need (handouts, presentation aids) with you. If you are just an attendee, you can still prepare yourself: read any agenda or materials sent out beforehand, and be prepared to discuss the mentioned topics.

Listen Interactively

To avoid situations in which people might feel as though they're not being heard, practice effective and interactive listening (see Chapter 5).

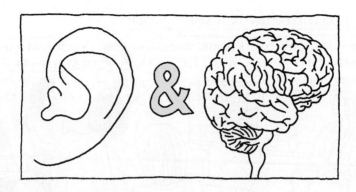

As other members of your group share their ideas and comments, show you are listening through nonverbal cues (nodding, eye contact, *not* looking at your phone) as well as verbal ones (asking questions or agreeing with what they've said). When challenging a point, show you understand it by first repeating the point, or respond first to something he or she said that you *do* agree with.

Listening is important throughout all the group processes, from early creative brainstorming to later critical analysis of how to arrive at the best solutions. Listening is also crucial as a group negotiates diversity. You can help facilitate listening by offering reasons why group members should listen to your point (will it help you meet your goal date more quickly?), by linking your ideas to other ideas in the group, or by directing your message to specific people in the group.

Participate, Don't Dominate

The key ingredient to good group work is full participation by all members. However, full participation doesn't just happen; it requires an environment that supports participation—meaning that *all* members must encourage it.[47] To facilitate the expression of ideas, members must also actively monitor the discussion.

When you have a relevant point to make—especially when it's about something you have expertise or experience with—you should be sure to share your idea. At the same time, be careful not to monopolize the discussion. If you find yourself speaking a disproportionate amount of the time, take a break and let other members contribute. In virtual groups, managers can use a chart to map who talks and how much to help distribute participation. Programs such as IRC allow members to think about what they are going to say, which can equalize participation.

Fulfill Your Commitments

When you make commitments, the rest of your group will rely on you to fulfill them. If you don't fulfill your commitments, you could adversely affect the entire group. As in a personal relationship, broken trust can be hard to recover, so make sure you complete your tasks on time, every time.

Use Technology to Your Advantage

As mentioned earlier, not everyone has the same skill level for using computers, online social networks, or videoconferencing, nor do they place the same value on its use. If these are necessary for group work, be sure that all group members have easy access to computers with webcams and reliable Internet connections. Discuss how everyone feels about communicating remotely for group work before deciding on it. For example, if certain group members have trouble logging into Skype, work in advance to help them figure out how to do it, or perhaps decide on another way to meet. Ideally, the technology used should simplify, not complicate, your group's progress.

Encourage a Positive Climate with Politeness and Authenticity

There is an ancient Native American tale about two wolves that live in our hearts and vie for our attention. One is the wolf of anger and defensiveness, and the other is the wolf of kindness and support. The wolf we choose to feed is the one that guides our hearts.

This tale is applicable to how we choose to interact with others in a group setting. A group's **climate**—its emotional or relational atmosphere—depends on how members communicate with one another. Groups that have grown close actually show more willingness to disagree with one another, since they share a climate of trust.[48]

Being polite helps facilitate a positive climate. Politeness begins with being on time for a group meeting (or at least informing the group if you will be late). Some other suggestions: Turn off your cell phone unless it will be used for group business. During the discussion, listen respectfully to others, even when you disagree with their views. Focus on issues when disagreeing rather than people and personalities. Most people prefer group mates who act in ways that demonstrate that others' interests are important.[49]

When group members feel they can be authentic, this creates a safe space for people to express diverse perspectives. Let honesty, not personal or political interests, guide considerations of problems and solutions. If you have an idea that you believe is important, mention it—even if you're worried about how others might perceive it. And if you have concerns about another member's suggestion, explain your reservations to the group. You should balance candor with tact when questioning a peer's idea, taking care to clearly critique the idea, not the person. We talk more about group conflict in Chapter 11.

CHAPTER REVIEW

The adage "Several heads are better than one" reflects the idea that people often make better decisions when they share and discuss their ideas. In school, the workplace, and your community, you will likely join small groups that will make use of multiple perspectives and others' talents to solve a variety of problems. Group members engage in small group communication in order to influence one another and achieve group goals. The groups we belong to may be primary or secondary (which includes learning and work groups).

Group size affects the coordination of ideas and stability of information flow. The number of people in a group changes the degree of effort and coordination needed to communicate well. Networks (patterns of information flow) vary in their degree of centralization. Groups can remain stable even if a member leaves. When new members appear, a group must go through group socialization.

Groups have several advantages over the individual: they provide more diverse perspectives, multiple resources, and a greater level of commitment. We explored small group dynamics, or the ways in which group members relate to one another and understand everyone's function in the group. Effective members focus on work and social roles and avoid selfish ones. They actively share their ideas, consider one another's viewpoints, constructively participate, and help the group reach decisions in a supportive climate. Group development models include Tuckman's model (linear) and Gersick's two-phase model.

Cultural variations (such as individualistic and collectivist) can impact small group communication. Mindful communication provides large payoffs for groups who recognize and value their diversity in terms of creativity, effectiveness, group communication, and enjoyment.

Technology can also benefit groups, depending on which mediums are chosen and why. All group members are responsible for fostering the climate of a small group and should follow guidelines for effective participation to benefit the group.

LaunchPad
macmillan learning

LaunchPad for *Let's Communicate* offers videos and encourages self-assessment through adaptive quizzing. Go to **launchpadworks.com** to get access to:

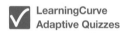 **LearningCurve**
Adaptive Quizzes

 Video clips that help you understand
human communication

Key Terms

small group 284
small group communication 285
primary group 286
secondary group 286
learning groups 286
committees 286
task forces 286
quality control circles 287
self-managed work teams 287
top management teams (TMTs) 287
networks 288
group socialization 289
heterogeneity 291
homogeneity 291
small group dynamics 294
work roles 294

social roles 295
selfish roles 297
role conflict 298
Tuckman's model 299
Gersick's two-phase model 299
ethnocentric bias 300
synergy 301
individualistic-collectivist 301
power distance 301
conformity 301
uncertainty avoidance 302
high- and low-context 302
masculine-feminine 303
mindful communication 303
climate 313

Review Questions

1. What are the distinguishing characteristics of a group, and how do we determine whether a group is "small"?
2. How does size impact a group's complexity and stability?
3. What are the stages that tell the story of group socialization?
4. What do small groups offer compared to an individual when facing problems?
5. Define *small group communication*.
6. How do work, social, and selfish roles differ from each other?
7. What are typical stages any work group passes through?
8. How do key cultural values impact small group communication?
9. What are significant considerations when using computer technology for group work?
10. List six guidelines for effective group participation.

Critical Thinking Questions

1. Groups are not a simple collection of individuals who happen to share one goal. What must happen between members for a "group" to emerge? If you were forming a group, at what point would that group be too large, and why?
2. Consider previous groups you have been involved in. Which work roles tend to be most prominent? How does the absence of the other work roles impact the group? Which social roles are easiest to play? Which ones take more effort, and why? Of the list of selfish roles, which ones are the most detrimental to a group?
3. Consider the stages of group socialization and your own experience coming into a group or leaving one. Generate a list of rules groups should establish to help them adjust to fluctuating membership.
4. Review the six guidelines for effective small group participation. Develop two more that you believe need to be added to the list, and explain why they should be added.

Activities

1. Gather ten people and select one goal, like planning an end-of-the-year party for the class. Select two of the ten people to observe the

group discussion. Begin your discussion with three people, adding one person every twenty minutes until all eight people have been able to talk about the party. Have the observers share how the increased size influenced the group discussion. Then ask participants to share how they felt during the discussion and at which point they thought there were too many people in the group.

2. Create two groups of five members each. Assign each group a task with no clear answer. Give each member one or two roles to play in the group, including one or two of the selfish roles. Have each group role-play the discussion, acting out the assigned roles. After the discussions, talk about the experience of each of those roles in terms of the climate that arose in the group.

3. Create a group of five members. Assign them a socially relevant issue to discuss for thirty minutes while seated in a circle. Select five other individuals and place them around the circle. Prepare a rubric that allows evaluation of the following: preparation for meetings, courteous listening, participation, authenticity, effective technology use, and climate guidelines. While watching the discussion, the five observers should use the rubric to comment on the group's discussion. After the discussion, allow the five observers to share their findings with the group, being sure to include examples.

Apply Your Skills

Look at the illustration about socialization on p. 290. Describe your own socialization into a recent work group, either at school or in your community. Go through each phase of socialization and offer examples of what happened at each stage. Did you skip any stages? Did this affect how the group accepted you? Now, consider being in a group in which you experienced a new group member. Considering the stages of socialization, were there any stages the group handled particularly well? Were there any stages the group could have handled more effectively? Did it make a difference in the new member being accepted in the group? If so, how?

PROBLEM-SOLVING AND LEADING A SMALL GROUP

11

OBJECTIVES

- Explore the different characteristics small groups must consider when identifying a problem.
- Identify the various ways members can effectively problem-solve as a group.
- Distinguish types of leadership in groups, including virtual groups.
- Examine tips for leading meetings and managing conflict effectively.

In 2012, Star Wars series creator George Lucas set off a firestorm of opinions when he sold Lucasfilm to Disney. Kathleen Kennedy, famed producer of the Indiana Jones films, soon announced that the company would produce a trilogy sequel featuring the original crew: Harrison Ford, Carrie Fisher, and Mark Hamill.[1] Kennedy faced an almost impossible task to "reboot $4 billion worth of . . . intellectual property." She set out to do it by gathering together a group of people that she refers to as the Lucasfilm story group.

This "creative brain trust" of talented screenwriters and writer-directors included both those with experience on the original films and those who brought a new set of eyes to the project. They began the task of creating a new trilogy with nothing in place: no story, no script, no director, no plan. J. J. Abrams, well known for co-creating the television show *Lost* and for directing the latest *Star Trek* films, signed on to direct the new Star Wars movie. He suggested a goal for the group in this new project: to create a film with less computer-generated special effects and more of the true spirit of the original films (and to boldly go where no director had gone before—just kidding!). The group had less than two years to accomplish this—an extremely tight deadline for a high-profile and complex film that had yet to have a story.

Working under the incredible pressure of fan expectations, the group generated a multitude of outlines and ideas, yet no one coherent story emerged. Abrams stepped in and took to the task of writing the story with Lawrence Kasdan, who had helped write two of the original films. As Abrams's schedule took him across continents, they continued to work, logging hours of conversations about the project, while other members of the team worked on preproduction details in London. Finally, after a lengthy conversation with Kasdan in a Paris café, the script emerged.

Amid the built-up anticipation and excitement of lifelong fans, *Star Wars: The Force Awakens* opened in December 2015 to an audience eager to continue the Star Wars story line. But the movie would never have even been made if Kathleen Kennedy hadn't formed a group to come up with the concept and J. J. Abrams hadn't successfully led the team that developed it. In this chapter, we focus on the concepts of group problem-solving, effective group leadership, and managing group conflict. As discussed in Chapter 10, groups can be broken down into primary and secondary groups. Primary groups, which include our friends and family, help us with our need to both be cared for and connect with others. Secondary groups are task- or work-oriented groups that we form to help influence others and solve problems.

The group involved in resurrecting the Star Wars series was one of the latter. While primary groups are very important, it is work groups that allow us to collectively manage all sorts of problems we encounter on a daily basis. Although we do tackle some problems individually, many problems require us to work with others—often people we may not initially know. In order to define the problem and find a workable solution with others, we must draw on our knowledge and skills. In this chapter, we explore the process of group problem-solving, tips for using problem-solving agendas, characteristics of effective leadership, and ways to effectively lead groups and manage conflict.

GROUP PROBLEM-SOLVING

Early in the school year, you are assigned to be part of a group for a large class project. Once assembled in the group, you and the other members introduce yourselves, feeling a bit awkward as you read over the course assignment together. The next two meetings go smoothly enough, as members begin to feel more comfortable and the project gets underway, but just weeks into the project, problems arise. Some members do not show up regularly, you take over more work than you want, and meetings turn into gossip sessions—that is, if people manage to look up from their phones. You suggest a plan to get back on track, only to be met with resistance from a classmate who's intent on being right all the time—though she's also not willing to take the lead.

If you've ever run into problems in a group setting, you know that group problem-solving can be challenging. However, when group members work together successfully, the rewards can be huge. When a group is faced with a **problem**, or the realization that reality doesn't match with what's desired (for example, you don't have a class project but you need to create one), its members must determine how to solve the problem. Together, members must seek, evaluate, and coordinate input from everyone in the group. The challenge is that these contributions often clash at first. Therefore, the group must consolidate everyone's input into a clear statement of the problem, along with an idea of how to best proceed.

WHAT IS A PROBLEM?

When working in groups to solve problems, we recommend employing a multistep procedure to help get the work done in a focused and effective way. The ordered procedure helps group members make more responsible choices as they define the problem, lay out solutions, select a solution, and move to implement it.[2]

An **agenda**, or a standardized problem-solving plan, helps groups coordinate their work. Chapter 10's rules for effective group participation (for example, preparing for meetings and fulfilling commitments) focused on written agendas for meetings. When talking about agendas in this context, we are referring to the formal steps a group performs to manage its work. This type of agenda, although varied, focuses on four steps:[3]

1. Define the problem
2. Generate possible solutions
3. Establish criteria for evaluating solutions
4. Select the best solution

If any of these steps is missing or rushed, it could affect the group's ability to work effectively and successfully. Let's consider each of these steps in depth.

Define the Problem

Group members must know exactly what problem must be solved or what objective is to be achieved before they can choose a course of action. As mentioned, problems arise because there are obstacles standing in the way between what's occurring and what's desired.[4] For example, let's say that you are editor in chief of your college newspaper, and hundreds of editions of the paper are left in distribution boxes each cycle and must be collected. You and the other editors are concerned that many students do not appear to be reading the newspaper. Your editing team could meet to investigate what is causing this unpopularity (the obstacle) so that you can come up with a solution to improve your readership (your desired goal).

During initial discussions, everyone might have an opinion about the nature of the problem. Imagine that out of the debate, two different and distinct potential problems emerge. One attributes the low readership to distribution of the paper—meaning that the newspapers are being placed in low traffic areas. If the newspaper team can't get the newspapers to students, then students obviously can't read them. The other potential problem is that students are just not that interested in news, particularly school-based news.

DEFINE THE PROBLEM

Defining the problem impacts everything a group does afterward, including the identification of possible solutions. If the problem is one of distribution, then any remedies must focus on getting the paper into the hands of students. If it's one of low interest, then better distribution will not matter; students have to want to read the paper in the first place.

Group problem-solving can look a little crazy compared to someone working alone on a problem. In this stage, group members often jump around from topic to topic and grab on to what is commonly known, avoiding unique perspectives on the problem. It's important to pause at the beginning and map out what's facing the group while listening to one another's perspective so that a *group* perspective becomes possible. This kind of thoroughness lays the groundwork for your next phase of work: coming up with possible solutions.

Generate Possible Solutions

After you've defined the problem, the next step is to create a list of potential solutions to the problem. Ideally, these solutions should overcome

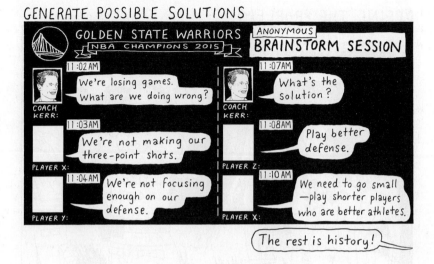

GENERATE POSSIBLE SOLUTIONS

anything standing in the way of achieving your goal. Groups often tend to jump right to a solution without thoroughly talking about what they hope to achieve and why. The quality of your solution, however, rests on the work you do early in the process, as well as what you do later on. Proposing and approving solutions *before* the group has discussed the desired goal and potential obstacles can lead to failed solutions, with potentially more problems to follow.

Brainstorming, discussed in Chapter 12, is one of the most effective techniques for creatively building a list of solutions. Remember that during brainstorming, the goal is to generate as many ideas as possible without judging them. Scholars have learned that it's best to allow group members to list their solution ideas alone before sharing them with the group.[5] Electronic brainstorming (EBS) is particularly useful for this because members submit their ideas anonymously online, so that all ideas are displayed for everyone to see. Members feel less judged for their ideas using EBS compared to face-to-face brainstorming.[6]

Establish Criteria for Evaluating Solutions

Once your group has generated possible solutions, you can now talk about the factors you'll use to evaluate them. Using factors or **criteria** to make decisions is something you likely do all the time, although you may not refer to it in these terms. For instance, you and a few friends might be hungry and decide to get something to eat nearby. The good and bad news is that there are dozens of places around your apartment complex from which to choose. Possible criteria you might use to decide include how much you wish to spend, what type of food you're craving, how much time you have to eat, and whether you've been to the place before.

In class, your criteria might come from the requirements of your assignment— such as the kind of problem you're working on and how much time you have. In the job field, employers might ask their research and development teams for a new product that must fall within certain dimensions and budgets. Kathleen Kennedy, from our opener, asked her Lucasfilm team to write a story appealing to the childlike magic of the original films.

A.S. ASSOCIATED STUDENTS
UNIVERSITY OF PENICUIK, NEBRASKA

CRITERIA FOR SPENDING
ANNUAL FEES

* Essential service or program (child care/health/legal resources)

* Program involves max number of students

* Program exemplifies values set out in university charter

* Program links school to community

* Program generates income

Criteria also emerge from your analysis of the problem and why it exists in the first place. If, for instance, a shortage of teaching faculty results in the failure of a department to meet the needs of its majors, workable solutions need to address the hiring of additional faculty. In the end, each proposed solution will have its own strengths and weaknesses, and your criteria will help you select the best *overall* solution.

Select the Best Solution

Once you and your group have defined the most important criteria, you can use it to evaluate the advantages and disadvantages of your list of solutions. You and your dinner-bound friends might end up going to Pieology because, after discussion, it is the quickest (criterion) and cheapest (criterion) place to eat. Groups must carefully apply the chosen criteria to each solution in order to find the one that best meets *all* the criteria, so that you can reach your desired goal.

In Fresno, California, the city council presented a Water Conservation Act as the best solution to the Central Valley's historic drought. Staff selected this solution instead of others because it best met the following criteria: flexibility for city personnel and homeowners, financial resources targeted to areas of greatest need, and financial incentives provided for conservation.[7]

Actively considering which solution is the best shifts your problem-solving analysis to one of decision making. A **decision** occurs any time you make a choice between alternative solutions. While voting is a common way to make decisions, there are several options a group may use. For example, a group could decide to base its choice of solutions on group **consensus**, meaning a decision that everyone can support, whenever possible. Although it can be hard to achieve consensus, it is also very rewarding because it increases a group's commitment to its decisions.

If you're in a group that finds itself at a stalemate (meaning the group is unable to come to a decision), you can also consider **arbitration**, which means asking an outside person to make a decision for your group, or **mediation**, which means asking an outside person to suggest another alternative. A fourth option is to allow your leader to decide without group input. Groups often use a combination of decision types.

We've shown that the four-step problem-solving agenda is an effective way to find the best solution to a group's problem. But simply following an agenda is not enough for effective problem-solving—you must also be aware of *how* you follow it. In the next section, we discuss tips for maximizing the potential of your agenda.

TIPS FOR USING PROBLEM-SOLVING AGENDAS

Some groups prefer to charge ahead quickly, hoping to figure out a solution so that they can reach their goal. Unfortunately, such groups often find themselves in trouble later in the process. Good group work involves both knowing what your steps are and thoughtfully following those steps. Members must pay attention to the process of working through their problem-solving agenda; this is why task and social roles (see Chapter 10) are so crucial to productive group discussions.[8] A group has a far better chance of success if its members are interested, motivated, capable, and respectful, and if it has the resources it needs. The following three tips will help groups get even more out of their problem-solving agendas.

Make Sure Group Members Understand the Task

Don't assume that everyone sees the problem the same way or understands what it is—even if it was written down and distributed to all members. Initially, group members often share the information they believe everyone has about the problem. This often creates a false sense of commonality and ignores the unique information members may have about the problem.[9] This tendency also makes it harder for members to share different ideas. They may not want to be seen as rocking the boat for fear they may lose their credibility or be seen as unsupportive.[10] Different perspectives—which are often beneficial—need to be actively sought out.[11]

In addition to encouraging members to share unique thoughts and information about the problem, you and your group may want to ask the following questions:

- What parameters will we have to work within to address the problem?
- How difficult is our problem to solve?
- How many of us are really interested in the problem?
- What does each member know about the problem?
- Does our problem call for few or many solutions?
- Have we phrased our problem clearly without mentioning any solutions?

These questions can help you explore all the facets of your task.

MAKE SURE ALL GROUP MEMBERS UNDERSTAND THE TASK

Get Rid of Roadblocks

A problem will not be solved if groups aren't able to recognize and communicate with one another about obstacles. For example, not only are group members more willing to share commonly known information about a problem, but they also (unsurprisingly) favor their own solutions.[12] Consider these questions: Are we talking about solutions too early without having discussed the problem? Are fellow members beginning to lose interest in the project? This is important to note, as interested members happily contribute their ideas and want to share in group decision making.[13] Removing these roadblocks helps groups move forward and feel satisfied.

Carefully Observe Your Process

In Chapter 10 we talked about how groups develop over time, growing and changing throughout the process. Often they move along seemingly slowly, only to hit a sudden burst of activity.[14] For example, group members may plod along on a project for the first half of a semester until

CAREFULLY OBSERVE YOUR PROCESS

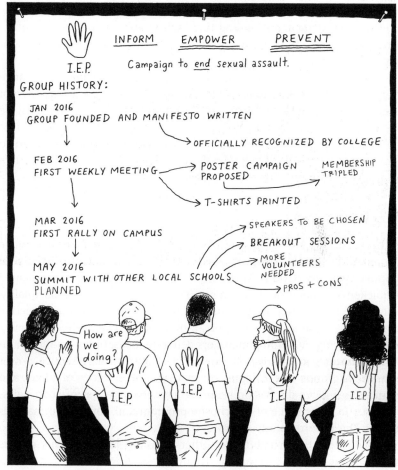

they suddenly realize that they have only four more weeks to finish their project. (Does this sound familiar?) In order to avoid this rush, it's important to assess your work often enough that you won't want or need to drastically change it later. Effective groups consistently pause and reflect on their process and make appropriate adjustments.

Effective groups are also willing to review what has been accomplished *during* the group process—and not just when it's over. Group members should be both participants in the process and active observers of the process. They should ask themselves if they've skipped any crucial steps—and if so, how that impacted their problem-solving. Members should also be willing to help the group make adjustments to its procedures, even if it means spending time going over some items. In other words, never be afraid to reconsider decisions and make changes if they're necessary.

A failure to be vigilant about group work or to be willing to change procedures can lead to more problems. Groups in this situation may not be able to solve their problem—and, in some cases, may not even be able to identify their problem—resulting in a frustrating waste of time and effort. It's always better to reconsider and change course than to reach the end with a poor decision. Technology, an ever-present resource for groups, can help with this vigilance.

Technology and Group Problem-Solving

Whether working face-to-face, online, or both, groups can take advantage of numerous **group support systems (GSS)** and **group decision support systems (GDSS)**. These are computer-aided programs, designed to quicken the pace of problem-solving without sacrificing its quality. Groups use these when they want real-time discussion without meeting face-to-face. These systems support, rather than replace, effective group problem-solving by helping members generate ideas, organize and evaluate information, and arrive at a decision. They can also reduce power distance in groups (see Chapter 6), increase the number of ideas, and organize and focus discussion sessions. The effectiveness of such a system rests on acceptance of the chosen program and how well it matches the way the group already interacts.[15]

In Chapter 10 we highlighted other technological tools that groups can use: e-mail, text messaging, instant messaging, video- and audio-conferencing, meeting applications, and electronic bulletin board services. These will only become more widely used, since virtual groups are becoming more commonplace in business and education.[16] One challenge these groups face is not feeling as connected to one another as they would face-to-face. When groups interact online 90 percent or more of the time, members begin to feel less positive about the group and its effectiveness.[17] Virtual group members, compared to their face-to-face counterparts, experience more difficulty carrying out those group social functions (discussed in Chapter 10) that are necessary for creating a cohesive climate.[18]

For effective group interactions, it's important to create a space for members to be social, such as special chat rooms. Members must also know and understand the technology that makes their virtual work possible, and also have a chance to meet face-to-face if possible. If not, then some form of video-conferencing can help. In terms of problem-solving, members need to ensure that all group documents are easily accessible to all members.[19] Laying out your problem and keeping track of all the resources needed to solve it require coordinated group work, whether virtual or face-to-face. This coordination is not possible without effective, insightful leadership.

EFFECTIVE GROUP LEADERSHIP

Whether one is the coach of a gold medal–winning Olympic team, the leader of a Nobel Prize–winning medical research team, or the director of a successful play, that individual is garnering recognition for being a successful leader. Successful groups always depend on capable participation by every group member, including those seen as leaders in the group.

Leaders versus Leadership

While groups may function effectively without a leader, they will not succeed without leadership. A **leader** acts in ways that move the group toward its goal, while **leadership** is behavior that does the same. All the task and social behaviors we discussed in Chapter 10 are leadership behaviors, meaning that everyone in a group can exhibit leadership over the course of a project.

Typically, one group member emerges as someone who consistently guides the group toward its goal and is able to facilitate similar actions from others. This person organizes group meetings, keeps the group focused, encourages all members to participate, facilitates problem-solving, and mediates conflict. Unless agreed to by the group, the leader does not have total control; rather, he or she helps members reach decisions and achieve goals. The following section describes the means by which groups find their leaders.

Types of Leadership

Group members can be labeled as leaders in two ways. Sometimes an external authority selects a **designated leader** to help the group move quickly forward with its task. For example, a governor may appoint a blue-ribbon committee to investigate ways to install a mass transit system statewide and designate an outside expert to guide the inquiry. Designated leaders have the benefit of legitimacy, since they've been appointed. When group members accept designated leaders, this provides early stability because the group doesn't have to spend time and energy deciding who is going to lead.[20]

Frequently, a group will have an **emergent leader**, or one who comes to be seen as a leader by the group over time. While not officially elected or even named as such, these individuals have to rely on their ability to communicate, their expertise in either the problem at hand or group dynamics, and their likability, since they cannot rely on the power of an official title.

LEADER | LEADERSHIP

Once recognized by the group, emergent leaders who are able to participate productively and assess the group's dynamics can help the group improve. This willingness and ability to coordinate member contributions, along with the ability to communicate effectively about the task, are two key reasons people emerge as leaders.[21] As it turns out, seeing yourself as a leader can help you be seen that way by others. Those who act on positive self-images of themselves as leaders get recognized more often as leaders than those who believe they are not very good at leadership.[22]

Leading in Virtual Groups

Interestingly, virtual groups with no designated leader are able to easily identify their emergent leader. In fact, members of virtual groups often show more agreement on a leader than face-to-face groups with a designated leader. These individuals, like their face-to-face counterparts, communicate to others more than other members, are well liked, and encourage members rather than order them around.[23] Compared with face-to-face groups, emergent leaders in virtual groups carry more legitimacy than a designated leader.

Leadership Challenges

Both types of leaders can face challenges leading a group, and being labeled a leader does not guarantee leadership behaviors. Designated leaders can be influential because of their title, but they must gain the respect and acceptance of group members. If they're unable to do this, they'll have a much harder time being effective and helping the group accomplish its goal. In this type of situation, other informal leaders may emerge.

Since emergent leaders have no designated title to make them influential, they begin on the same footing as everyone else. They must be skilled communicators, but if they dominate other group members through the sheer force of their personality or level of experience, they will leave less room for other voices and ideas.

LEADING MEETINGS AND MANAGING CONFLICT

In order to be a good leader, one must listen to group members and make them feel comfortable presenting their ideas and concerns. Two of the major responsibilities of a leader include leading group discussions during meetings and helping the group manage its conflict.

Leading Meetings

Effective leaders conduct meetings in ways that enable members to work together productively, contribute their ideas, and make well-informed decisions. These leadership concerns apply in both face-to-face and virtual environments. If you're the leader of a group, consider these tips for facilitating meetings.

Address procedural needs. Procedural questions a leader should consider include the following: Where and when will meetings take place? What is the purpose of the meeting? Who will start meetings and record notes? How will notes be circulated to members who could not attend a particular meeting? Archiving meeting notes is particularly important for virtual groups. As mentioned in Chapter 10, Wiggio is an example of a free online tool kit for groups of every kind. This type of electronic tool kit provides ways to manage group meetings whether face-to-face or online.

Model the behavior you expect. There are many ways to exhibit the behavior you'd like all team members to follow. For example, avoid interrupting others or dismissing their questions or comments. Show up on time (and be prepared) for meetings. Make group members feel they can interact comfortably with you. Resist any urge to dominate discussions or decisions. Take the initiative to show you value active participation. Communicate actions of trust, openness, and fairness.

Virtual groups, some of whom might never see their leader, can easily identify good and bad leadership behaviors.[24] Online, leaders can show members how to interact with one another by carefully

MODEL THE BEHAVIOR YOU EXPECT

I want you all to be DELIBERATE and CONCISE. Which reminds me of a funny story from my own life. I was born in a log cabin, and when I was five, I wanted a dog more than anything else in the world. And I didn't mind which sort of dog: big, small, smooth, shaggy, black, or...

YAWN!

What is she going on about?

GROUP LEADER

monitoring their own contributions, modeling effective use of the technology (for example, planning conference calls), and avoiding misreads of nonverbal behaviors (for example, reading silence as intentional rather than a signal delay).

Facilitate discussion. Constructive and open group discussion does not automatically happen—leaders have to facilitate it. One way is to make sure that all members of your group have the opportunity to participate in each discussion. Equal participation is not the goal here— *perceiving* equal opportunities to participate is. If some group members are not speaking during a meeting, strive to bring them into the discussion ("Jessica, what do you think?" or "That's a good point, Ben—you've clearly researched this carefully. But let's also give Ilana a chance to share her ideas").

Remember to direct comments to the group as a whole in addition to individual members. Too many comments to individual members can make the group feel fractured instead of collective. If using an electronic tool kit like Wiggio, Google +, or even a GSS program, you can see a checklist of who has already participated and use that to manage and increase participation.

Keep members on task. If the discussion begins to stray from the topic under consideration, keep members on task in a friendly way. For example, you might say, "I agree with Shane that our department's holiday party is going to be a blast. But let's talk about how we're going to tackle reserving the space for the event." It's often helpful to share summaries of the group's discussion so that members can hear their progress or lack thereof.

In virtual meetings, group members must face the challenge of a lack of verbal and nonverbal cues. It is important that virtual leaders focus on facilitating a sense of togetherness that comes more naturally in face-to-face meetings.[25] This group cohesion helps the group focus more effectively on its goal. To enhance cohesion, leaders can do simple things—like asking people to share personal stories during meetings, personalizing messages to members, and even making sure that members introduce themselves and use names throughout the meeting. Of course, virtual leaders have to balance these social aspects with the tasks at hand, yet it serves virtual leaders well to carve out some amount of social space.

KEEP MEMBERS ON TASK

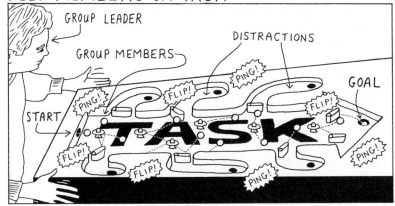

Help members avoid groupthink. Groupthink is a group's tendency to uncritically accept ideas and information because of strong feelings of loyalty or single-mindedness within the group.[26] Critical analysis of the United States' invasion of Iraq has revealed how groupthink can dramatically impact U.S. foreign policy.[27] As discussed earlier, groups tend to lock on to decisions early on without sufficient analysis. Simply put, group members do not like to share ideas and opinions that are counter to what they believe the rest of the group thinks.[28] Agreement and disagreement are a fact of life in groups; however, groups engaging in groupthink display much higher levels of agreement than disagreement.[29]

These groupthink tendencies erode the lively and open exchange of ideas necessary for informed decision making.

How do you know if your group is exhibiting groupthink? Imagine that one person advocates a course of action in your group and everyone else nods in agreement. Instead of moving the group toward making a final decision you could try to broaden the discussion. For instance, you might ask a particularly insightful participant if he or she can think of any potential risks to the proposed plan. If nobody is willing to offer any reservations, consider raising some concerns yourself ("I like San-geeta's idea, but let me play devil's advocate for a minute"). Create and support a climate that promotes considering the pros *and* the cons of the proposed options before selecting one. Groups leaning toward group-think—especially those dealing with time pressures and a decision of high importance—can change course with good leadership.[30]

Facilitate decisions. When it seems as though members of your group have creatively and critically discussed the issue at hand, help them come to a decision. As a leader, you will participate in the final decision, but your leadership role does not entitle you to make the deci-sion for the group. In other words, avoid using your power to manipulate the group. Leadership is critical to a productive group, and you must decide how best to enact that leadership—are you going to coordinate with others or tell them what to do without listening? Generally, group members who feel they're being bossed around tend to be dissatisfied with the group's leadership.

FACILITATE DECISIONS

Helping groups reach a thoughtful consensus is challenging work.[31] Good leaders know this. If agreement comes too easily, leaders look for groupthink. Should members become too attached to their positions, leaders help them consider alternatives. Leaders treat stalemates between members as an opportunity to explore next best possibilities, or perhaps as a chance to integrate multiple ideas. Finally, even toward what appears to be the end of the group project, good leaders ask members to critically look for any flaws in their decision before members build the final case for it.[32] Once the decision has been made, they ensure that it is recorded and then move the group on to the next issue.

Assess meeting-to-meeting effectiveness. In Chapter 10, we talked about how expensive poorly run meetings can be for the group and for the larger organization. Leaders play a role in evaluating how well a group meets its goals for a particular meeting. Those who review past minutes, take and review their own notes, and make critical adjustments in future meetings are often seen as good leaders.[33]

Leadership, essential in any group, is the responsibility of all members. It requires watching, assessing, and doing those things necessary to move the group forward. However, even with the best leadership, a group might run into **conflict**, or express struggle between members who see each other as getting in the way of goals, resources, values, and beliefs. In the next section, we discuss the reality of conflict and how strong leaders can help members manage it.[34]

Managing Conflict

Conflict can be found at all levels of groups and organizations. Take, for example, the case of a president of a large organization who was rumored to be considering completely restructuring his company in order to keep two vice presidents apart—all because they refused to talk to each other. While conflict is unavoidable, leadership can determine whether a group falls apart from it or grows.

Importantly, constructive conflict can draw members closer together, release tension, and help members better understand the issues facing them.[35] Effective leaders face conflict in their groups with the understanding that figuring out the cause will help the group manage it productively. The following guidelines can help leaders use conflict to the benefit of the group.

Refer to ideas by topic, not by person. Conflict can be caused by personality clashes—in which people's differing outlooks cause

REFER TO IDEAS BY TOPIC, NOT BY PERSON

disagreements. These can either prevent work on the task or derail the group if members are already working on the task.[36] To help avoid clashes, leaders should focus on the content of a suggestion rather than the person expressing the suggestion. This puts the focus on the contribution, not the person it's coming from.

For example, suppose you're part of a group that's trying to get your candidate elected president of the university's student body. Monique advocates a mass e-mail campaign to build support for the candidate, but Tim thinks that leafleting would be better. An effective leader will refer to these ideas as "the e-mail plan" and "the leafleting plan," rather than "Monique's idea" and "Tim's suggestion." When ideas get associated with an individual, that person may develop a feeling of personal investment in that option. He or she may then become defensive if the proposal is criticized—even if it has real shortcomings.

One way to manage an existing personality clash may be to discuss the problem in private, rather than airing the conflict in front of the entire group. If there is a member who gets along well with the people experiencing the conflict, he or she may be able to help them find a way to manage their disagreement. Sometimes helping group members find common ground will help de-escalate conflicts that can appear impossible to solve.

Manage conflicts respectfully. Small group conflict is inevitable. Avoiding conflict or deflecting it means a group is not dealing with it; this is extremely counterproductive. *How* groups manage their conflict is the key—and it is here that groups often fall into problems. If a conflict between group members becomes distracting, effective leaders should manage it in a timely and sensitive way. This is a better option than allowing it to continue or repressing it.

It's often helpful to give disagreeing members an equal opportunity to explain their perspectives. In this case, leaders can let each person speak without interruption and then ask other members for their views. If both ideas have merit, perhaps you can help the group find a solution that draws the best from each perspective. While you may ultimately need to offer your opinion or vote in order to break a deadlock, you should try to give the other group members an opportunity to speak before injecting your opinions.

For example, picture a small church choir that always selects one or two new songs for each Sunday service. One Sunday, conflict erupts over which songs should be selected. One choir member wants a special song to celebrate her mother's birthday, but the rest of the choir believes the songs should speak to everyone present. The choir director listens to both requests and finally suggests "The Best Day" by Taylor Swift, which was written for a mother but which could also refer to a Creator's love.

Good leaders help the group create rules and a climate of mutual respect (see Chapter 10). If a group has a positive climate, it will affect how group members perceive the value of conflict as well as how they will handle it when it emerges.[37]

Focus on tasks, not disagreements. To help members concentrate on the task at hand rather than any simmering interpersonal tensions, leaders can focus on changes in behavior rather than criticizing individuals. For example, consider the difference between these statements by a leader to group members in disagreement: "Let's get back to discussing our project," instead of "Jon, your answers to Hollis's questions are always so sarcastic." It's also smart to discuss work logistics and tasks early on because struggles over these can often lead to clashes.[38]

Manage disruptive emotions. Conflicts over personal issues can spark intense and disruptive emotions within a group. Even after a conflict has been worked through, members may still feel angry, upset, or embarrassed, and they may withdraw from the discussion. If this happens, leaders can bring reluctant members back into the discussion by inviting their input on important issues. Leaders should focus on promoting positive behaviors and stressing the importance of each member in the group.

CHAPTER REVIEW

Effective group problem solving and leadership does not simply happen—group members must facilitate it. In this chapter, we focused on group problem-solving, tips for using problem-solving agendas, effective group leadership, and how to lead meetings and manage group conflict. First, groups must use some kind of problem-solving agenda as a guide. Essential steps to any agenda include defining the problem, generating possible solutions, establishing criteria for evaluating solutions, and selecting the best solution.

Getting the most out of a problem-solving agenda requires thoughtful work with the agenda. Members can help by taking the time to make sure everyone understands the task at hand, watching for and removing roadblocks, and observing the process and occasionally readjusting how the group is proceeding based on a reassessment of the work. Technology aids a group's problem-solving efforts, regardless of whether the group is virtual, face-to-face, or a mix of the two.

Leadership is essential to successful group problem-solving. While single members may be designated or emerge from the group, all members can practice leadership qualities. The challenges of both facing the task at hand and coordinating all the talent in the group require vigilance and attention to meetings and managing conflict.

Group meetings can be successful with good leadership. Good leaders model to others what is expected while attending to several key responsibilities. They lay out how the group will go about its problem-solving efforts, helping everyone contribute and stay focused on the task at hand. Good leaders conduct thoughtful discussions and avoid any movement toward groupthink. Over the course of meetings, leaders evaluate how well the group is moving along, making any necessary changes to procedures.

Group conflict—whether between members, over procedures, or over the task at hand—is an inevitable occurrence in groups. Good leaders recognize that it's important to deal with conflict effectively rather than avoid it. Effective leaders help keep members focused on the issue at hand while also avoiding personality clashes. Successful leaders also understand that conflict managed respectfully can be productive to a group.

LaunchPad
macmillan learning

LaunchPad for *Let's Communicate* offers videos and encourages self-assessment through adaptive quizzing. Go to **launchpadworks.com** to get access to:

 LearningCurve
Adaptive Quizzes

 Video clips that help you understand human communication

Key Terms

problem 321
agenda 322
criteria 324
decision 326
consensus 326
arbitration 326
mediation 326
group support system (GSS) 330

group decision support systems (GDSS) 330
leader 331
leadership 331
designated leader 332
emergent leader 332
groupthink 337
conflict 339

Review Questions

1. What are the four steps of group problem-solving?
2. What is the difference between arbitration and mediation?
3. State three tips for using problem-solving agendas.
4. Explain the difference between a leader and leadership.
5. What is a designated leader? What is an emergent leader?
6. List the seven guidelines for leading effective meetings.
7. What are four ways to manage small group conflict?

Critical Thinking Questions

1. Any work group has to follow some sort of procedural order when solving its problem. Based on your experience and considering the four steps we recommend, which steps tend to get missed? Explain your answer.
2. Refer to the definitions of *mediation* and *arbitration*. Under what circumstances would a mediator or an arbitrator be appropriate for a work group in a classroom setting?
3. How would you rank order the seven guidelines for effectively leading group meetings? What are your justifications for those rankings?
4. What are the dangers in assuming that small group conflict should be stopped instead of managed?
5. What challenges can occur when moving a personality conflict into a productive conflict?

Activities

1. Consider any topic (for example, farming, veterans' affairs, automobile safety, or music piracy). Interview three or four people and ask them to discuss an issue connected to your topic. Based on the answers you receive and the recommendations from the chapter, define a problem related to your topic. How easy or difficult was it to include all the ideas you received in the definition of your problem?
2. Watch an episode of a popular police television drama. Prepare a note sheet with the four stages of problem-solving and the three tips

for problem-solving. As you watch the show, take notes on when and how the group approached each step of problem solving and how well. Were any steps missed? Were any revisited? How well did the group follow the three tips?

3. A group member comes to you with issues about another member. This person believes the other member is lazy and distracts the group with insulting remarks about the group project and group members. In a group of three or four, lay out specifically how the four guidelines for managing conflict could help you handle this situation. Then write a brief script that details what you would say to the problematic group member.

4. Recall the leader of a recent group in which you participated and write down your experience. Was the leader emergent or designated? Was he or she effective in leading group meetings and managing conflict? Based on the recommendations in the chapter, explain your answers and compare them with those of a classmate.

5. In a group of four or five, review the definitions of group support systems and group decision support systems and then research one of these types of platforms (Moxtra, Google Hangout, Skype). List some of the benefits and drawbacks of the program. Would you use it in a work group? Why or why not?

 ## Apply Your Skills

Review the illustration "Keep Members on Task" on page 337. Poll the class (or a group within your class) and find out which behaviors class members find most exemplify being "off task." Select the class's top five behaviors. Now list the most common ways the class has experienced leaders trying to change these behaviors. Which ones do class members believe are the most effective? Least effective?

MIYA GETS A SPEECH ASSIGNMENT

PUBLIC SPEAKING

FIRST STEPS

OBJECTIVES

- Learn how public speaking is a unique form of communication that everyone uses—in jobs, school, civic engagement, and everyday life.
- Identify the steps in the speechmaking process, which effective speakers consider and revisit when preparing a speech.
- Understand that speeches are audience-centered, which affects how appropriate topics and thesis statements are chosen.

The moment of truth had arrived for Miya in her Human Communication course. The class had finished with group communication and was beginning a unit on public speaking. In four short weeks she would need to present an informative speech to her class. The speech presentation was only one of Miya's concerns. She would also need to submit an outline of her speech, cite information from at least four credible research sources, and prepare at least two presentation aids to supplement her message.

Miya had many questions about this assignment: What should I talk about? What does my instructor expect in an outline? How do I know if a research source is credible? Where am I going to find presentation aids? She also had questions about finding the time to work on her speech: How can I do all this work when I have papers and exams looming in other classes and a boss who keeps scheduling me for the most inconvenient hours?

Nevertheless, Miya was determined to do well on this speech assignment. As she read her textbook and listened to her instructor, Miya came to realize that speech preparation is not an insurmountable task. The process could be broken down into a series of manageable steps, many of which were related to things she'd done in her life. Miya had chosen topics that would be interesting to herself and others when starting conversations, researched in the library for other courses, organized her family's annual camping trip, and practiced getting ready for dance performances and soccer games.

Miya worked out a schedule to complete each step of the speech preparation process on days and times that fit her schedule, stuck to her plan, and practiced speaking in front of her roommates. When the big day arrived, she was ready. Her classmates and instructor listened attentively and cheered when her speech concluded.

Miya's story is not unique. Throughout our teaching careers, we have seen literally thousands of students (many of whom initially had some doubts about their ability to prepare and deliver a successful speech) develop into successful public speakers. Part 5 of this book (consisting of Chapters 12–17) focuses on public speaking and provides advice that can help you craft and deliver an effective presentation.

Chapter 12 is the starting point for your journey into the field of public speaking. After reading this chapter, you will learn the answer to the big-picture questions about this craft: What is public speaking, and why is it important? and What is the process for preparing and delivering an effective speech? You will also discover the answer to key questions about the first two steps in this process: How do I analyze my audience? and How do I select my speech topic? Let's take a look at each of these questions in order.

INTRODUCTION TO PUBLIC SPEAKING

You are about to embark on the study of a subject that has fascinated people for over twenty-five hundred years. The following sections explore the benefits you will gain from studying public speaking, the rich traditions of this field, and some key elements of this form of communication.

Why Study Public Speaking?

Communication involves sharing your ideas with others in a variety of contexts. You have learned about two of these contexts—interpersonal and small group settings. At other times in your life you will be called to present your ideas in front of a larger audience, and you will want to be prepared. Let's take a look at some of the settings where you will need to use public speaking skills.

In the workplace. A knack for public speaking is one of the most important assets you can possess in the workplace. According to the National Association of Colleges and Employers 2016 Job Outlook Survey, verbal communication skills are one of the top qualities that employers seek in potential job candidates.[1] Employees agree that communication skills are important. In the survey "Making the Grade? What American Workers Think Should Be Done to Improve Education," 87 percent of the 1,014 U.S. adult workers surveyed rated communication skills as very important for performing their jobs.[2]

The need to address an audience effectively in a job is not limited to obvious fields such as sales or training. A police officer may need to calm an angry crowd, a librarian may be called on to defend the addition of a controversial book to the collection, a firefighter may need to explain fire prevention to a community group, and the director of a charity bicycle race may need to inform volunteers about how to ensure safety along the route.

In school and community settings. Your school and community are other contexts for public speaking. A wide variety of courses require oral presentations, and participation in campus activities may include presentations to students, faculty, or administrators. Outside school, you may be asked to take a leadership role in service organizations, sports teams, clubs, religious institutions, or political groups. In any of these endeavors, you may find yourself wanting to address your group, or you may be asked to speak for the group before other members of the community.

On special occasions. You could also find yourself speaking at any number of celebrations, such as weddings, award ceremonies, or a colleague's promotion. And sometimes you may be asked to speak when

WHO NEEDS PUBLIC SPEAKING?

you least expect it—for example, if you find out at the last minute that you and your siblings will be saying a few words at your mother's retirement dinner.

As you become a public speaker, you will be participating in a great tradition. For centuries, people around the world have studied the art and practice of public speaking and used public address to inform, influence, and persuade others.

A Great Tradition

As far back as the fifth century B.C.E., adult male Athenians were expected to participate in self-government and speak out in the assembly. The ancient Greeks were the first people to teach rhetoric formally as a subject, and the scholar Aristotle wrote *Rhetoric*, a systematic analysis of the art and practice of public speaking. Ancient Romans added to the discussion, with Cicero writing on the craft of public speaking and Quintilian emphasizing the ideal of an ethical orator—the good person speaking well. Across the globe, for two centuries the Chinese enjoyed an intellectual climate that rivaled that of ancient Greece,[3] with scholars passionately advocating for diverse economic and political philosophies.

Public speaking has also played a key role in American history, beginning with powerful oratory that fueled the drive for independence. The antislavery movement relied on public speaking to propel social change, fueled by speakers like Sojourner Truth and Angelina Grimké. In 1963, about 250,000 people gathered near the Lincoln Memorial in Washington, D.C., to hear Dr. Martin Luther King Jr. deliver his "I Have a Dream" speech,[4] an address that instantly excited the imaginations of people around the world.

Speakers have increasingly been able to reach international audiences. For example, President Reagan spoke at the Brandenburg Gate in

Berlin to challenge Russian leader Mikhail Gorbachev to "tear down this wall" in 1987. In recent times, Pakistani youth Malala Yousafzai has been vocally advocating for girls' education—since she was ten years old! Even a 2012 assassination attempt did not deter Malala from speaking out. While recovering in a British hospital, she announced the establishment of a new charitable organization, the Malala Fund.

Key Elements of Public Speaking

Although public speaking might seem like a new challenge, it shares similarities with other communication contexts that you have studied. For example, in any communication context, you must be able to express your thoughts understandably, as well as present ideas in an ethical manner. Still, there are several characteristics that make public speaking a unique discipline.

Public speaking features communication between a speaker and an audience. In public speaking, the speaker does most of the talking and the audience primarily listens. Audience members do send verbal and nonverbal messages, such as smiles, frowns, words of encouragement, or expressions of disagreement. However, any interjection is usually brief, and for the majority of the time, the speaker has the floor.

Public speaking is audience-centered. Public speakers choose their message with the audience's interests and needs in mind. Good speakers consider what topic would be appropriate for their audience on a particular occasion and develop their message in a way that their audience will find interesting and understandable.

Public speaking emphasizes the spoken word. The core of a public speaker's message is verbal expression, reinforced by appropriate nonverbal communication. Speakers can supplement their message with presentation aids, such as pictures, videotapes, objects, or even live demonstrations. However, most of the speech time is used to *speak* to the audience.

Public speaking is generally a prepared presentation. The best speakers strategically plan what they are going to say and practice their delivery well in advance of the occasion. It is very difficult to simply walk up to the front of an audience and make up a high-quality talk as you go.

YOU ARE NOT A PUBLIC SPEAKER WHEN

YOU ARE A PUBLIC SPEAKER WHEN

THE SPEECH PREPARATION PROCESS

Successful speakers do not achieve great results by accident. Dr. Martin Luther King Jr. was a gifted public speaker who won his first oratorical contest at age fifteen.[5] Nevertheless, he would write multiple drafts before delivering important speeches and would spend as many as fifteen hours preparing a Sunday sermon.[6] He diligently prepared his 1963 "I Have a Dream" speech,[7] which won renown among speech scholars as the greatest oral presentation of the twentieth century.

Preparation is also essential for success in classroom speeches. In our experience, we have found that students who are most effective in public speaking come up with a well-organized plan for speech preparation, and budget enough time to accomplish each step in that plan.

The Classical Approach to Speech Preparation

We have noted that public speaking has a rich tradition, which informs the speech preparation process that we explain here. Underlying this process are principles of rhetoric that have been studied and applied by public speakers for twenty-four hundred years. Today's scholars call these concepts, introduced by ancient Greeks and expanded on by the renowned Roman orator Cicero, the **classical canons of rhetoric**. Each of these five canons is important to consider when you are developing a speech.

- **Invention** is the generation and selection of ideas for use in your speech. This requires analyzing your audience—what are their interests, backgrounds, and opinions with respect to your topic? It also includes researching your topic and considering your own ideas about the subject, generating a large number of ideas for possible use. Then you select the best ideas for accomplishing your purpose with your particular audience in an ethical manner.
- **Arrangement (organization)** refers to the structuring of your main ideas and the material that supports them in a manner that will make your message clear and memorable to your audience.
- **Style** is the choice of language that will express your ideas to your audience in a clear, interesting, and ethical manner.
- **Memory** refers to the preparation and practice needed to get ready for your speech, so that you will be in command of the

material while you are presenting. This canon originally placed emphasis on the use of memory, but contemporary speeches are generally not memorized. Instead, speakers use limited notes that remind them of key ideas while enabling them to develop the ideas conversationally.

- **Delivery** refers to the effective use of verbal and nonverbal communication skills when presenting your speech. The effective use of voice, gestures, eye contact, and movement can make a powerful impression on your audience.

The Benefits of an Organized Preparation Plan

To craft an effective presentation, it is important to select your topic and begin researching for your speech shortly after receiving the assignment. Set up a schedule for completing each major step of the process, and stick to it. By breaking your work into smaller steps, preparation becomes more manageable and less intimidating. And the earlier you prepare your speech outline, the more time you'll have to refine your speech and polish your delivery. In the public speaking chapters that follow, we explain each step and show you how to make good choices at each stage of the process.

Now that we have considered the importance of having a good plan for preparing your speech, we can begin considering the individual steps of speech preparation.

PICK 8 TOPIC ✓ ~~DOGS~~ ~~CATS~~ PETS✓	RESEARCH 9 Who keeps records?	RESEARCH 10 Survey? Visit vet?✓ online?	RESEARCH 11 Rules✓ Library✓	12 READ ✓	13 Buy onions Make outline
STOP 14 PROCRAS- TINATING! ~~PRACTICE~~	Lilly's 15 birthday ~~~~ PRACTICE	REVISE✓ 16 MORE ✓ PRACTICE	YET 17 MORE PRACTICE + GET HAIRCUT	REST 18 + RELAXATION	THE -19 BIG - DAY	Ha ha 20 ha! You did it!!!

EARLY PREPARATION IS KEY

AUDIENCE ANALYSIS

When you need to ask a parent or an employer for a favor, or find a way to break the ice with a person you'd like to know better, chances are you carefully consider the words you use to give you the best chance of achieving your goal. To select the right message, you need to understand the person's point of view—that is, what values, concerns, and beliefs are most important to him or her. With that information, you can relate your message to that point of view. These same communication principles apply when considering your audience in public speaking.

The Importance of Audience Analysis

A speech is given for the benefit of your audience, and its success (or failure) is measured by its effect on audience members. Therefore, one key principle of effective speaking is that the audience drives the message. This does not mean that you simply tell the audience whatever you think they want to hear—especially if that means saying something you don't believe or that's unethical. It *does* mean that when you choose from among the many possible topics you would feel comfortable developing, you make this choice with the audience in mind.

Speakers who tailor their message to listeners create enormous value for their audience and themselves:

- First, listeners become much more interested in and attentive to the speech.

- Second, listeners experience positive feelings toward the speaker when he or she has made an effort to understand their concerns.

- Third, listeners open their minds to the speech because it targets their specific needs, interests, and values.

In order to determine how to tailor your message to your audience, you need to use **audience analysis**, which is the process of learning about an audience's interests and background. Audience analysis can be broken down into a number of different factors that warrant consideration.

Analyzing Situational Characteristics

Situational characteristics refer to factors in a specific speech setting that you can observe or discover before you give your speech. These include audience size, time, and location (forum).

Audience size. The size of your audience affects how you will craft and deliver your message. The smaller the group, the greater the opportunity you will have to interact with audience members and to tailor the message to the needs of a few people. The larger your audience, the harder you will have to work to craft a generally accessible message.

Time. There are two dimensions of time that you should consider when planning your speech. The first is **presentation time**, or the length of time that is available for your presentation. Not only is it rude for a speaker to exceed his or her allotted presentation time, but you will likely lose your audience's attention and favor if the length of your presentation exceeds their expectations.

The second dimension of time is **body clock time**—the time of day or day of the week when you will be presenting. It is more challenging to draw the audience's attention to your speech early on a Monday morning, close to lunchtime, or near the end of the day. Nevertheless, you can still deliver an effective speech at such times—for example, by blending humor or brief stories into your speech to accompany more serious ideas.

Location (forum). The setting where the audience will listen to your speech can vary widely, including classrooms, conference rooms, auditoriums, or outdoor venues. You need to check out the location in advance of your speech. Stand where you will be presenting, and position yourself where the audience will be sitting. Consider how well audience members will be able to see and hear you. Will you need to use a microphone? Will audiovisual equipment be available, and if so, will the presentation

NOT CONSIDERING BODY CLOCK

CONSIDERING BODY CLOCK

aids you plan to use be accessible to the audience? If possible, practice speaking with a microphone and displaying any presentation aids before your audience arrives. You want to be sure that the volume of your voice is not too loud or too quiet and that all audience members can see any graphs, charts, or other items you plan to display.

Incorporating Demographics

Audience **demographics** refers to listener characteristics, such as age, gender, and ethnicity. Demographic information is often used in the world of public relations and marketing to tailor messages to

TAILOR YOUR MESSAGE TO LISTENERS

Getting a job after graduation might be the first thing on many of your minds these days...

Yep, I'm listening.

Fortunately, there are several growth industries that are hiring recent grads right in our backyard.

Sweet—some information I can really use.

Health care is the fastest growing sector in the city, and it's a career that can suit lots of different skills and passions.

Hmmm, health care wasn't on my radar before, but maybe it could be worth checking out...

particular audiences.[8] You can see examples of this phenomenon by comparing the advertisements in different types of magazines, such as *Cosmopolitan*, *Time*, and *Sports Illustrated*.

Demographic information about your audience can help you select ideas that will be most relevant and interesting to the people who will be listening to your speech. It can also be used to ensure that the content of your speech is inclusive of the diverse social groups that constitute your audience.

However, it is important to remember that demographics only provide information about the tendencies of any group—they do not tell you the interests and beliefs of any individual group member. When you have specific information about the members of your audience, use those facts to plan your speech content. Furthermore, as mentioned in Chapters 2 and 6, it's essential that when you are considering demographic factors you are sure to avoid stereotypes, or inferences that people draw about others simply because they're part of a given social category.

Age. The age of audience members can influence their response to your message. Older audience members are less likely to understand references to popular hip-hop artists, rock bands, or late-night comedians. Conversely, a younger audience may not get references to the popular culture or political leaders of earlier generations. When making a reference to a person or an event that may not be familiar to all generations represented in the audience, be sure to provide context for them.

Gender composition. The gender composition of your audience—*mixed* (male and female) or *single gender*—affects how listeners will respond to your speech. Some stories, illustrations, or examples may resonate better with one gender grouping than another. Car sellers, for example, pay close attention to differences in buying patterns. In recent years, marketers in the automotive industry observed that more women were buying cars, and that sales pitches aimed at men did not work so effectively with female customers. Minh, a former student of ours and an automotive salesperson, told a story that shed light on this development. In his experience, effectively selling Volvo station wagons to men and women required two different approaches.⁹ To appeal to men, Minh emphasized the car's turbocharged engine, high-performance tires, and special detailing. To capture women's interest, he stressed features related to safety, reliability, and fuel economy. Though Minh aimed the same broad message at all shoppers—"You'll want to buy this wonderful car"—he tailored the specifics of the message to each gender.

While consideration of gender is a valid component of audience analysis, you must never assume that you know an individual audience member's views based on gender (or any other demographic characteristic, for that matter). The views of countless men and women cut against the grain of traditional ideas of **gender stereotypes**—oversimplified and often distorted views of what it means to be male or female. Likewise, ethical speakers should never resort to **sexist language**, or language with a bias for or against a given gender.

Race and ethnicity. The U.S. population is increasingly diverse, with the Census Bureau noting that racial and ethnic minorities (currently over one-third of the population) are likely to constitute a majority of the population in 2043.¹⁰ On a recent *National Geographic* map displaying the most common last names in the United States, Jones, Smith, and Anderson are prominent, as are Garcia, Martinez, Nguyen, and Kim.¹¹ This increasing diversity is likely to be represented in your audience.

As discussed in Chapter 6, the term *race* usually refers to a commonality based on genetically shared physical characteristics of people in a group. This can affect how listeners respond to a speaker's message, especially in situations in which racial issues are sensitive, affecting people throughout their lives. Ethnicity—cultural background that is usually associated with shared religion, national origin, and language—is also important to consider. It can shape beliefs, values, and attitudes of audience members. When preparing and delivering a speech, it is essential to be sensitive to your listeners' diverse backgrounds and speak to their varied interests.

Consider the following example. After graduation, Jenny got a job as program director for a nonprofit organization that focused on developing a love of reading in young children. One part of her job was to give presentations in an effort to recruit volunteers from local colleges, congregations, and service organizations to read with children in after-school programs. Most of her volunteers and the students they would serve came from neighborhoods that were rich in ethnic diversity. During her presentations, Jenny used examples of books that could be shared with the children as presentation aids, including books by authors representing many of the ethnic groups that lived in the area.

Sexual orientation.
Another demographic characteristic is the **sexual orientation** of your audience members. A speaker must not assume that all audience members are heterosexual. Since speakers have a responsibility to all members of their audience—not simply those in the demographic majority—ignoring LGBT listeners excludes and alienates members of many audiences.

Acknowledging sexual orientation can be accomplished both overtly and passively. A speaker can explicitly include reference to LGBT persons—for example, using examples of gay or lesbian couples along with examples of heterosexual couples in a speech on conflict in relationships. You can also offer passive acknowledgment through word choice when referencing sexual or relational orientation—for example, referring to "loving partners" rather than "married couples."

Religious orientation.
In the United States alone, there are as many as twenty-three hundred religious identifications—including Baha'is, Buddhists, Christians, Confucians, Hindus, Jews, Muslims, and Zoroastrians, to name just a few. Religious orientation may exert a significant influence on your audience members' views on a wide range of social issues, including abortion, gender roles, poverty, and environmental concerns. Therefore, it is important to consider this demographic when crafting your speech.

On September 7, 2010, then Secretary of State Hillary Clinton spoke at the State Department's Iftar, the traditional meal eaten by Muslims during the holy month of Ramadan after fasting from dawn to sundown. Her remarks showed respect for both the Muslim members of her

audience and the persons of diverse faith traditions who were present or who would read or view her message later:

> The Holy Month of Ramadan is a time when Muslims around the world fast and pray, and strive to do good things. It's also a time for reflection and introspection, for charity and for compassion. Ramadan teaches and reinforces values that are honored by millions and tens of millions of people from other faiths and beliefs. So tonight, while we celebrate together, let us consider how we can build broader and deeper bonds of mutual understanding, mutual respect and cooperation among people of all faiths in the year to come.[12]

Seeking Common Ground

You can bond with your audience by identifying **common ground**— beliefs, values, and experiences that you share with your listeners. Consider Andy, a first-year student who had served in the military for eight years before enrolling in college. For the first speech assignment,

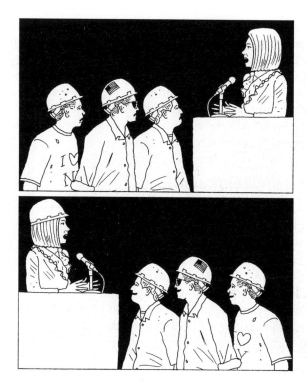

students were being asked to introduce themselves and tell the class something about who they were. Andy was somewhat reluctant to present this speech; he was several years older than most of the other students and had not had much interaction with them—either in or out of class. And although his military service was central to his identity, Andy was not sure if his fellow classmates—few of whom had probably served in the military—would find the topic interesting.

Andy thought about what he did have in common with his classmates. All had experienced the same long lines and struggles to add classes—these were legendary on this crowded campus. To introduce himself, Andy began, "I am a combat veteran, and after three tours of duty, I felt ready for any challenge that college might present. But I have to tell you—after struggling to get the classes I need and standing in endless lines for financial aid, maybe I would rather re-enlist." His classmates responded with smiles, nods, and laughs. Andy then felt very confident as he explained what his military service meant to him. The next speaker began her speech by thanking Andy for his service.

Some speakers attempt to communicate common ground nonverbally. For example, a candidate for national political office might don a cowboy hat while addressing voters in Texas or a sports cap bearing the name of a local team. The mere act of putting on a hat does not prove that you share common ground with an audience, and it can backfire if the audience does not view you as an authentic cowboy or a sincere fan of the home team. This technique should only be used when you have a genuine shared identity with your listeners.

Identifying Prior Exposure

Do you remember hearing the same (unconvincing) lecture from your parents multiple times? Or perhaps an ad slogan that sounded weak the first time you heard it and only more so each subsequent time? This can be a problem for public speakers, too. Therefore, you need to gauge audience members' **prior exposure**—the extent to which they have already heard ideas relating to your topic and their reaction if they did. This information will help you decide whether to include particular points or to craft something new. When assessing prior exposure, there are several questions to ask.

Has my audience heard this message before? If the answer is no, then you can use any ideas that you expect the audience to find interesting or convincing. However, you may need to explain relevant issues and concepts in more basic terms. If the answer is yes, then you need to move on to the next question.

POOR ASSESSMENT OF PRIOR EXPOSURE

Has my audience responded positively to the message? If the audience liked what they heard the first time they were exposed to the ideas in your message, then you'll want to push the envelope in your next speech. You could give the audience new or more in-depth information about the topic. If you are attempting to persuade the audience, you could ask them to become more involved in the issue under discussion. If the audience did not respond favorably, then you need to ask a third question.

Why did the previous message fail? If ideas you intend to present were not successful with your audience, assess what went wrong. Perhaps they needed more proof of the claims that were made, or they did not find the information relevant.

If you find that a message you planned to use has already failed, look for new or different information that may be more effective with your audience.

Once you know about your audience, this information can help you with one of the most important decisions in the speech preparation process: selection of your topic.

TOPIC SELECTION

Selecting the topic for your speech can seem like a challenging task. But as the chapter-opening story of Miya noted, you likely choose topics many times each day. When you start a conversation with a friend, a family member, or the student standing behind you in one of the inevitable long lines on campus during the first week of school, you need to figure out what to talk about. Generally, you select a topic that is likely to be of interest to you and to the other person. In a public speaking class, the same considerations apply—you want to choose a topic that interests you, that is likely to be relevant to your classmates, and (of course) that your instructor considers appropriate for the assignment.

In this section, we present a process for selecting and refining your topic, including developing a list of possibilities, choosing the most promising one from the list, and narrowing that topic so that it meets your speech's objectives and can be covered in the time available for your presentation.

Developing a Set of Potential Topics

Possible speech topics are as varied as human experience. Depending on the assignment, your topic could be lighthearted (raising a goldfish) or serious (how water shortages affect agriculture), address ancient history (Mayan civilization) or current events (the effect of state budget cuts on financial aid), or relate to professional interests (teaching children with autism) or recreational activities (rock climbing).

Often it is the speaker's responsibility to select a topic, though in some instances you may be assigned a topic by your instructor, your employer, or those who have invited you to speak. When you are called on to choose a topic, you can follow a specific process to find the best one. The first step is to develop a diverse set of possibilities using these strategies: research, brainstorming, word association, and mind mapping.

Research. Research is often an effective way to begin your topic selection process. Newsmagazines and newspapers include articles on current events, science, geography and culture, famous people, and the arts.

These sources of information are also increasingly available in an online format. A recent magazine or newspaper will provide ideas for speeches on topics that are new to audience members, or offer new perspectives on more familiar topics. Most libraries keep recent periodicals and newspapers in easily accessible locations, and you can also find some of these on websites or through online indexes.

Brainstorming. Through **brainstorming**, you list every idea that comes to mind without evaluating its merits. Your goal is to develop a sizable list of topics quickly. Do not censor any idea at this point in time; just let your thoughts flow.

There are a variety of categories you can consider when brainstorming. These include your interests and experiences, issues you care about, organizations you belong to, people you admire, places you have been, and lessons from life that you have found important.

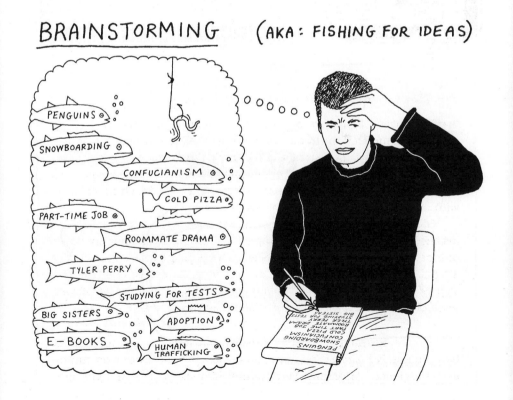

Word association. Another strategy for generating ideas is **word association**. This process begins by listing a single topic, or idea. Then write down whatever comes to mind when you think about that idea. The second idea may suggest yet a third one, and so on. As you do when brainstorming, write down every idea that comes to mind without stopping to evaluate how good (or not good) it is.

Word association enables your mind to function somewhat like a search engine. Your brain (rather than the World Wide Web) is your database, and when you write down a word or phrase, your mind "searches" for other terms that you associate with the original idea. If you use word association for every topic idea you generated while brainstorming, your set of options will grow even more.

Mind mapping. To use **mind mapping**, write down a word or phrase in the middle of a large piece of blank paper, and then surround it with words and images representing other ideas that come to you.

THIS IS MIND MAPPING

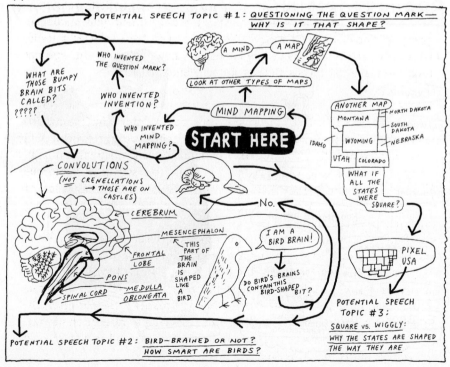

Here are some tips for mind mapping:

- Use images (sketches, doodles, symbols) in addition to words.
- Start with a word or sketch at the center of the page, then work outward.
- Print rather than write in cursive.
- Use different colors to indicate associations and make ideas stand out.
- Use arrows or other visual devices to illustrate links between ideas.
- Jot down new ideas as they occur, wherever they fit on the paper.[13]

The use of multiple colors, pictures, and symbols to create a mind map stimulates your thinking process.[14] You use both sides of your brain and generate additional—and more creative—topic ideas.

Selecting the Best Topic

Once you have generated a list of topics, the next step is to select the best one. To make your choice, consider the assignment, your audience, and your knowledge and interests. And once you have selected a topic, stick with it. The following guidelines can help you pick the optimal topic from the list of possibilities you've generated.

Consider the assignment. For a class assignment, it is important that the topic you select meets your instructor's criteria for the assignment. For example, in most classroom speeches, your instructor will require references to research. This will require you to ensure that quality research sources are available for the topic you select. A humorous speech about your experiences as a food server or a demonstration of how you make your favorite fruit salad would probably fail to meet your instructor's expectations.

Certain topics crop up in public speaking classes every semester, such as marijuana, the drinking age, steroids in sports, and capital punishment. Rather than selecting an obvious and overused topic, it is better to try to get *ahead of the curve* when choosing a topic. For example, rather than talking about an existing phone product, consider researching the next generation of phone products. Picking a fresh or an innovative topic will be more interesting not only for you and your audience but for your instructor as well.

Consider your audience. Your audience members will devote valuable time to listening to your speech. In return, you owe them a presentation that they will find engaging and relevant.

This is where your audience analysis can point you in the right direction. Determine your listeners' priorities and backgrounds, and then use that information as a guide. The topic you select should meet one or more of the following criteria:

- It will interest your audience.
- It is something your listeners need to know about—for their own or society's benefit.
- It will likely inspire, entertain, or emotionally move your audience.

Consider your knowledge and interests. Among all the potential topics you have accumulated, which ones are you most interested in and knowledgeable about? When you choose a topic you're familiar with and passionate about, you'll give a more fluent and enthusiastic presentation. One of our students captivated his audience with a speech on Legos (even though his classmates had not played with toys for years) because his enthusiasm for the subject was so infectious. Conversely, a student who appeared totally uninterested in her speech on job interviews failed to connect with her listeners, even though the subject was highly relevant to them.

Choose a topic and stick to it. Once you have selected a topic, stick with it. In our experience, students who agonize over their topic selection for days or waver back and forth among several possibilities lose valuable preparation time. But don't just take our word for it. An analysis of more than one thousand speech diaries maintained by public speaking students revealed a consistent difference between strong and weaker speeches. The more successful speakers carefully considered their topic choices, but then they efficiently made a decision and stuck with it. Less successful speakers spent days trying to settle on an acceptable topic.[15]

Refining Your Topic

Once you have selected a topic, it's time to refine it. There are two parts to this process: deciding your rhetorical purpose and narrowing your topic to match your purpose and fit the available time.

Determine your rhetorical purpose. Your intended effect on the audience constitutes your **rhetorical purpose**. In a public speaking class, your instructor will often assign your purpose for each speech assignment. Outside class, your purpose may be assigned by an employer or dictated by the context of a special occasion (such as a wedding or a memorial service).

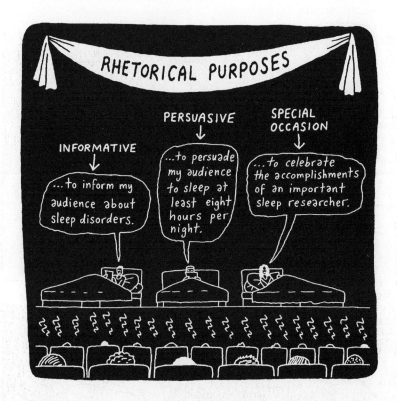

There are three primary rhetorical purposes for speeches:

- **Informative.** When your purpose is informative, the message is educational and your objective is to increase the audience's understanding or awareness of your subject.
- **Persuasive.** When your purpose is persuasive, you seek to convince audience members to consider or adopt a new position or belief, strengthen or weaken an existing position or belief, or take a particular action.
- **Marking a Special Occasion.** When your purpose is to mark a special occasion, you seek to honor an occasion by entertaining, inspiring, or emotionally moving your audience.

Narrow your topic. It is impossible to cover all aspects of most topics in a single five- to ten-minute speech, so you need to select which ones you will focus on. This is an important decision for a speaker. As mentioned earlier, whether you are speaking in the classroom or in your community, it is inconsiderate to exceed the time allotted for your

presentation. You also need to give focus to your speech. New speakers tend to select overly broad topics, making it difficult for the audience to process the message. For example, when discussing a specific sport, such as rugby, a novice speaker might try to cover the setup of the field, the rules, techniques for playing well, and the history of the sport. This is far too much information for a speaker to cover or an audience to remember.

How should you narrow your topic? Many of the same techniques that you used to select your topic can also help you narrow it. You also need to consider which ideas about your topic will best accomplish your rhetorical purpose.

- *Remember your audience.* Which aspects of your topic will be most interesting or relevant to your listeners?
- *Draw on your interests and expertise.* Do you have special expertise or a unique perspective on an aspect of your subject area? Which aspects of your topic interest you the most?
- *Review your rhetorical purpose.* Which aspects of your topic will be most relevant to the purpose of your speech?

Drafting Your Specific Purpose

After you've identified your rhetorical purpose and narrowed your topic, your next step is to determine your **specific purpose**—the objective of your speech—and express it in a concise phrase.

To write your specific purpose, start with a phrase expressing your rhetorical purpose ("to inform," "to persuade," or "to mark a special occasion"). Then follow these words with language indicating what you want to accomplish in your speech. For example:

- To inform my audience about the events at a Portuguese festa
- To persuade my audience members to drink milk produced by our state's dairy farms
- To honor my hero, Graça Machel, for her leadership in the campaign against pediatric AIDS

Use your specific purpose to guide the selection of ideas you will develop in your speech. Each main idea that you choose should help you accomplish that purpose; those that are not relevant to your purpose should be excluded.

Drafting Your Thesis Statement

Once you have determined your specific purpose, create your **thesis statement**: a single sentence that captures the overall message you want to convey in your speech. This statement conveys the bottom line of your speech—the ultimate message that all the facts and ideas in your speech support. If audience members can remember your thesis statement, they should be able to recall the essence of your speech.

In this book, we use the term *thesis* to mean the main point of any type of speech. Some speech instructors may prefer using the term *thesis statement* for a persuasive speech and the term *topic statement* when a speech intends to inform or mark a special occasion. Your instructor will let you know if he or she prefers this alternative usage.

Here are some examples of thesis statements:

- The Hmong New Year includes many culturally distinct features.
- Our college makes significant accommodations for students who are called into military service.
- The dark web can be used to enhance online privacy.
- You should sign up for a service-learning course.
- Today we will honor the volunteers who helped our campus food pantry make such a big difference in the community.

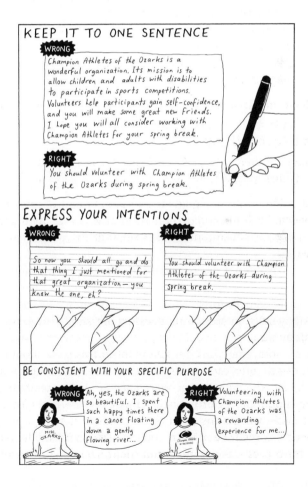

KEEP IT TO ONE SENTENCE

WRONG

Champion Athletes of the Ozarks is a wonderful organization. Its mission is to allow children and adults with disabilities to participate in sports competitions. Volunteers help participants gain self-confidence, and you will make some great new friends. I hope you will all consider working with Champion Athletes for your spring break.

RIGHT

You should volunteer with Champion Athletes of the Ozarks during spring break.

EXPRESS YOUR INTENTIONS

WRONG

So now you should all go and do that thing I just mentioned for that great organization — you know the one, eh?

RIGHT

You should volunteer with Champion Athletes of the Ozarks during spring break.

BE CONSISTENT WITH YOUR SPECIFIC PURPOSE

WRONG Ah, yes, the Ozarks are so beautiful. I spent such happy times there in a canoe floating down a gently flowing river...

RIGHT Volunteering with Champion Athletes of the Ozarks was a rewarding experience for me...

Here are some guidelines for ensuring that your thesis statement conveys your purpose and topic to the audience efficiently and accurately:

- *Keep it to one sentence.* Make sure that your thesis statement consists of a single sentence that conveys the bottom line of your speech.

- *Express your intentions.* Ensure that your thesis statement clearly conveys what you hope your audience will know, do, or feel after listening to your speech.

- *Be consistent with your specific purpose.* Because your specific purpose guides how you research and prepare your speech, make sure that your thesis statement communicates the same idea as your specific purpose. That way, you will avoid the all-too-common problem of presenting a thesis statement in your speech introduction that differs from the content of the body of your speech.

CHAPTER REVIEW

In this chapter, you embarked on the study of public speaking. Gaining skills in this subject can lead to many benefits, whether it be at school, in a career, and in your personal life. In the first part of this chapter, we considered the rich history of public address, along with the special features of public speaking that differentiate it from other communication contexts.

Next we considered the process you should follow when preparing a speech. The process is inspired by the classical canons of rhetoric—invention, arrangement (organization), style, memory (preparation), and delivery. Many steps in speech preparation are similar to experiences in your everyday life.

Begin by analyzing your audience. To do this, you should consider situational characteristics such as audience size, presentation and body clock time, and the location of your speech. Audience demographics, common ground, and prior exposure must also be taken into account when planning your message.

After analyzing your audience, the next step is selecting and refining your topic. Begin by developing a large set of potential topics and then select the best one based on the assignment, your audience, and your knowledge and interests. Then refine your topic by determining your rhetorical purpose (informing, persuading, or marking a special occasion) and narrowing your topic to fit the available time. Finally, craft your specific purpose and write a one-sentence thesis statement that characterizes the essence of your speech.

 **LaunchPad**
macmillan learning

LaunchPad for *Let's Communicate* offers videos and encourages self-assessment through adaptive quizzing. Go to **launchpadworks.com** to get access to:

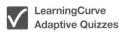 **LearningCurve Adaptive Quizzes**

 Video clips that help you understand human communication

Key Terms

classical canons of rhetoric 353
invention 353
arrangement (organization) 353
style 353
memory 353
delivery 354
audience analysis 356
presentation time 356
body clock time 356
demographics 357
gender stereotypes 360
sexist language 360

sexual orientation 361
common ground 362
prior exposure 364
brainstorming 367
word association 368
mind mapping 368
rhetorical purpose 371
informative 372
persuasive 372
marking a special occasion 372
specific purpose 374
thesis statement 374

Review Questions

1. Name and explain three ways in which becoming a competent public speaker can have an impact on your life and career.
2. What are four characteristics that distinguish public speaking from other communication contexts?

3. Name and define each of the five classical canons of rhetoric.

4. Define *demographics*, and note five demographic characteristics a speaker can consider when analyzing an audience.

5. Define *common ground*, and explain how it can strengthen your credibility as a speaker.

6. Name and define four strategies for generating possible topics.

7. Name and define three rhetorical purposes of speeches.

Critical Thinking Questions

1. Consider a career of interest to you. How could oral communication skills help you in that career?

2. Name one person whom you believe is an effective public speaker. What are the main characteristics that make him or her effective?

3. What are some risks speakers take if they make assumptions about audience members based on demographics? As a speaker, how can you use demographic information appropriately?

4. Suppose that your classmates will be your primary audience for a speech. How can you use your class time to perform informal audience analysis? How might the timing of your speeches over the course of the semester affect your knowledge of your audience? For example, what might you know about your audience at the end of the semester that you didn't know at the beginning?

5. If your analysis reveals that most audience members disagree with the thesis of your persuasive speech, why would it be inappropriate to simply change your thesis to match the audience's viewpoint? Are there any changes to your thesis that would be appropriate?

6. How would your topic selection differ if you were delivering a speech to a club, team, or organization to which you belong rather than to students in a public speaking class?

Activities

1. Think back on any awards programs you like to watch (for example, the Oscars, Grammys, ESPYs, or Video Music Awards) and the ways in which different winners approach their acceptance speeches. Is it obvious when a winner has prepared a speech beforehand? Is it obvious when he or she has not? Have any speakers made comments

that you thought were inappropriate for this type of event? Explain your answers.

2. In groups, have each member find an advertisement in a different genre of magazine (news, popular culture, sports, women's, automotive, and so on). Bring the ads to class and discuss among yourselves which demographic groups are targeted by each ad. Are there other demographic groups that might have a negative reaction to the ad?

3. Next time you are in a crowd—on the bus, at the mall, in a coffee shop, or in class—take a look at the people around you. If you had to address that crowd as a speaker, what common ground could you find? What beliefs, values, or experiences might you share with the members of that crowd?

4. Think of a disagreement you had with a friend or family member when you were unable to change his or her mind. What were the (unsuccessful) reasons that you provided? How might you change your message if you were to discuss the issue with him or her again?

5. Select and read a letter to the editor of an op-ed column in a newspaper or newsmagazine. Can you identify the author's thesis statement?

6. Working in a group, have each member list three potential speech topics. Have each member present their list, one at a time. When a member presents his or her list, the other group members should decide which of the three topics they would find most interesting. Then they should identify which aspects of the topic they would most like to learn about.

 ## Apply Your Skills

Look at the illustration on mind mapping on page 368. Then create your own mind map of potential speech topics for either an informative or a persuasive speech. Be sure to follow the guidelines for mind mapping on page 369, and write down any mental associations that come to mind as you develop your map.

13

SPEECH CONTENT
RESEARCH, SUPPORTING MATERIALS, AND ETHICS

OBJECTIVES

- Learn how to research your speech and cite evidence in your presentation.
- Understand how to use supporting materials to develop main ideas and pull audience members into your speech.
- Recognize the importance of speech ethics.

Roberto selected a topic for his persuasive speech assignment that seemed sure to interest his classmates—avoiding rip-offs when buying products that come with rebates. He had purchased a new phone that cost $99 up front, but the price could be offset by a $30 mail-in rebate. However, Roberto lost the proof-of-purchase bar code, and the company refused to pay the rebate (even though he had a receipt). Roberto prepared a speech that harshly criticized the wireless company and presented some tips for avoiding rebate rip-offs. He had found the tips on a website, but he did not mention that in his speech.

When Roberto showed his instructor a draft of the speech, her feedback disappointed him. She told him that his criticism of the wireless company was "a great rant" but lacked evidence that the issue occurred often enough that audience members should be concerned. He also hadn't provided information on other potential problems with rebates.

381

Finally, Roberto had engaged in *plagiarism* by presenting the tips he had researched without crediting the author, thereby violating his school's honor code and putting his college career at risk.

Following his instructor's advice, Roberto headed to the library to do more research and document his sources of information. In doing so, he found statistics indicating how often consumers are denied rebates. He also discovered examples of other problems with mail-in rebates, such as the fact that some companies use the information on the application to target consumers for telemarketing. Roberto made sure to write down his research sources and the authors' credentials so that he could include them in his speech.

Roberto revised his speech, carefully citing a source each time he used material that he had researched. As it turned out, his speech was very successful. One student commented, "I could have found a much better rebate if I'd heard your speech before buying a new printer."

As Roberto's story illustrates, research may not seem necessary but, in reality, it is central to effective speech preparation. In fact, it leads to good decision making in many areas of life. If you were buying a smartphone or looking for a place to eat dinner, you would not just Google "smartphone" or "Mexican food in [your city]" and go with the first search result. You would want to read reviews by knowledgeable and unbiased people before spending your hard-earned money. That same kind of careful consideration is important when you are deciding what to say in your speech.

Fortunately, there are plenty of quality research sources for nearly any speech topic. You just need to be willing to invest the time and know where to look. After reading this chapter, you will understand how to make and follow a research plan that produces credible information. You will also see how to use that material to support your main points in an effective and ethical manner.

RESEARCHING YOUR SPEECH

Research improves the quality and effectiveness of your speech. By researching, you learn more about your topic and have a greater stock of ideas and main points to consider for inclusion in your speech. You can use **evidence**—information gained from research sources—to support claims in your speech. If audience members are uncertain about a point you are making, evidence can convince them to accept your claim.[1] By presenting evidence, you can also gain **credibility** as a

CREDIBLE EVIDENCE CONVINCES AUDIENCES

speaker—the perception of your audience that you are qualified to speak on your topic.[2] Audience members will see that you are well prepared and more likely to know what you are talking about because you have taken the time to research.

Creating a Research Plan

Good researchers develop a strategy for locating and recording the information they need. The following steps will help you formulate a

research plan—a strategy for finding and keeping track of information to use in your speech.

Inventory your research needs. Decide what objectives you need to accomplish with your research—for example, questions you need answered or specific areas of the topic for which you need more information.

Find the sources you need. Next, analyze where to look for information. A library is a great place to start. Discuss your topic with **research librarians**—career professionals who are hired to assist students and faculty because they are experts at tracking down information. You can also consult library indexes (often available online) and find sources by searching for keywords related to your topic. The Internet also contains vast information resources; however, as we discuss later in the chapter, you need to carefully consider the credibility of Internet sources.

Keep track of your sources. As you gather useful sources, you need to accurately record full source citations. A **citation** contains information about the author of your evidence and where your evidence can be found. It is the academic equivalent of a map to your source. Furthermore, your instructor will expect you to properly cite all sources used; check with him or her to find out what format is required. The following

MAINTAIN ACCURATE RECORDS OF YOUR SOURCES

information is likely to be needed, some for your speech and all for your works cited page:

- Name of the author and his or her credentials
- Title (article or book chapter)
- Source (name of the book, periodical, or newspaper)
- Date of the publication
- Volume number (for periodicals)
- Publisher and city of publication (for books)
- Page number where the evidence appears
- URL for Internet sources

Please note that for Internet sources, the URL alone is not sufficient; you also need to record the name of the author of the information, his or her credentials, and the date of the information.

Evaluating a Source's Credibility

As you find information on your topic, you should select the most **credible sources** for inclusion in your speech. Credible sources are those that can be reasonably trusted to present accurate, objective information. Using credible sources increases the likelihood that audience members will accept your claims.[3] There are several factors to consider when assessing credibility.

Expertise. A source with **expertise** has the knowledge necessary to offer reliable facts or opinions about the topic in question. An expert source has education, experience, and a solid reputation in his or her field. For example, a professor of economics would be well qualified to assess the impact of a higher minimum wage on

WHOM WOULD YOU GO TO FOR MEDICAL ADVICE?

Don't worry, it's definitely NOT skin cancer.

Don't worry, it's definitely NOT skin cancer.

THREE REASONS FOR BIASED SOURCES

ECONOMIC SELF-INTEREST:

The bank bailout was great for the U.S. economy.

COMPANY PROFITS

$

THE NEED TO PLEASE SUPERIORS:

The Defense Department needs a lot more funding this year.

ASSISTANT SECRETARY OF DEFENSE

EGO INVESTMENT:

It's clearly *RIDICULOUS* to claim that the world is shaped like an orange!

PRESIDENT

FLAT EARTH SOCIETY

the U.S. economy, and a veteran backpacker would be well suited to describing how to prepare for a long hike through the mountains.

Objectivity. Sources who demonstrate **objectivity** do not have a bias—prejudice or partisanship—that would prevent them from making an impartial judgment on your speech's topic. Audience members are unlikely to accept the point you are trying to prove if your source is biased.[4] Sources may be biased for several reasons. One common reason is economic self-interest, meaning that a desire to make money may cause them to slant facts or explanations. Another reason is the need to please superiors, as in the case of a government worker who defends a boss's poorly conceived policy. Still others have an ego investment, meaning they are so wrapped up in a theory or a cause that they are unable to evaluate it with an open mind.

Observational capacity. A person with **observational capacity** is one who witnessed a situation him- or herself. For example, a person who

OBSERVATIONAL CAPACITY: MORE AND LESS

witnessed child labor in cocoa fields would have more credibility to comment on that practice than one who watched a television report about the subject. Sources with training and experience also make more credible observers.

Recency. Credible sources are also characterized by **recency**, or timeliness. Generally, newer evidence is more reliable than older evidence because many aspects of life tend to change. For instance, in 2000, one in four 18- to 34-year-olds lived with their parents or in-laws.[5] However, around 2010, good jobs became more difficult to find, and student loan debt significantly increased. As a result, the number of 18- to 34-year-olds living at home has been about one in three,[6] and in 2015, 45 percent of college graduates lived at home.[7]

With these criteria for source credibility in mind, let's now look closely at three major strategies for researching your speech: conducting library research, using the Internet, and interviewing experts.

Conducting Library Research

Libraries remain one of the best resources for researching your speech. Despite the Internet's increasing popularity as a research tool, the library still offers you convenient access to the broadest range of credible sources.

Books. Books are one of the best systems that humans have ever developed for storing and conveying information. Many are written by people with extensive expertise in their subject, although you should always check each author's credentials using the four criteria noted earlier. Books are longer than most other information resources; thus, they are likely to provide extended and broad analysis of the topics they cover. To find books related to your topic, start by researching your library's electronic catalog by subject. Such catalogs are usually available online, allowing remote access. You can even check books out from the library using your digital e-reader. Checking out e-books combines the quality of book evidence with the ease of an online search.

Periodicals. **Periodicals** are publications that appear at regular intervals—for example, weekly, monthly, or quarterly. They include scholarly journals as well as news and topical-interest magazines. Often the most credible information on your topic will come from articles in scholarly journals, generally written by people with expertise on a subject. Articles in these journals are subject to **peer review**—that is, an editor decides to publish only those articles that are approved by other experts in the field.

To locate appropriate periodicals, consult general periodical indexes, which list articles on a wide variety of topics. Most college and public libraries have subscriptions to online indexes, which are particularly helpful because they contain full-text sources for each entry or at least an abstract—a summary of the article's contents. You may also wish to use specialized periodical indexes, which focus on specific subject areas and are increasingly available online.

Newspapers. Newspapers are another useful source, especially when you need very current information. Newspapers are sometimes said to produce "a first draft of history" because their articles represent journalists' views of current events as those events are unfolding. Most newspapers now have websites, many of which allow you to search for articles. In addition, your library may offer access to full-text articles from newspapers that restrict content to subscribers.

Government documents. If your topic relates to government activities, laws, or regulations, government documents can provide useful information for your speech. It is important to check the source of these

ONLINE INDEXES OFFER THE BEST OF BOTH WORLDS:
THE QUALITY OF LIBRARY MATERIALS AND THE SPEED OF THE INTERNET.

materials. Many are written by experts who are hired based on their advanced education and credentials, and they hold their jobs whether Republicans or Democrats are in power. Others may be written by persons motivated by political objectives, placing their objectivity in question.

To find government documents, consult the Catalog of U.S. Government Publications (catalog.gpo.gov/F), the Federal Digital System (www.gpo.gov/fdsys), or CQ Electronic Library (available through many college libraries).

Using the Internet

The Internet has become the go-to research option for many college students. According to a report by the Pew Internet and American Life Project, 73 percent of college students said that they use the Internet more than the library.[8] Furthermore, their online searches often miss the better Internet sources that are available.[9] These research habits can be hazardous to the typical student's academic progress. One study found that higher grades are associated with more frequent use of the library.[10] Another determined that as hours of Internet use increased, exam performance of college students in an introductory economics course decreased.[11]

Whereas libraries emphasize quality research sources, searching the web can be a bit like sending an untrained dog out to retrieve the morning newspaper. He might come back with the paper, but he could just as easily end up digging in your flower bed or eating a neighbor's chicken. In other words, you can't always be certain that your search will generate the information you need. Thus, it is important to understand the benefits *and* limitations of Internet research.

Benefits of Internet research. Internet research allows you convenient access to information on nearly any topic from any location. As noted, many libraries offer access to full-text periodical and newspaper indexes from remote locations; such indexes are among the most likely sources of credible evidence, and we recommend that you focus on them when the convenience of researching from your own computer is important.

The Internet also offers speed—enabling you to track down a news report or a research finding almost instantly, from anywhere in the world. In addition, the Internet places an ever-increasing volume of information at your fingertips. A decade ago, University of California researchers estimated that the volume of information on the World Wide Web was about seventeen times that of all the print collections in the Library of Congress.[12] A Dutch researcher estimated that in March 2016, over 4.7 billion web pages were indexed by search engines.[13] With careful searching online, you may be able to find information that simply does not exist in your own library.

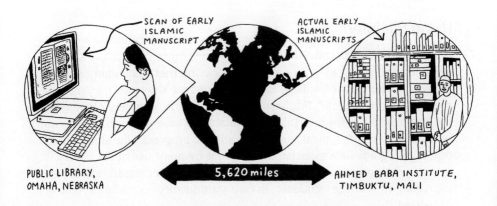

SCAN OF EARLY ISLAMIC MANUSCRIPT

ACTUAL EARLY ISLAMIC MANUSCRIPTS

PUBLIC LIBRARY, OMAHA, NEBRASKA

5,620 miles

AHMED BABA INSTITUTE, TIMBUKTU, MALI

Disadvantages of Internet research. Despite the web's vastness, most of the world's knowledge is still contained in printed works. Authorities in many fields publish their works primarily in books and scholarly journals. And many of these works are copyrighted, so they most likely won't be available on websites that a typical search engine would lead you to.

Moreover, you can't assume that information you find online is credible, since most of it is not vetted in the same way that books and periodicals are. There are literally millions of websites created by individuals, advocacy groups, clubs, and businesses that may contain incorrect and biased information.[14] (In the next section, we discuss how to effectively evaluate the credibility of online sources.)

Consequently, many Internet sources found by students do not have the quality that is expected by their instructors. Too many students yield to the temptation to accept the first results that come from a basic search rather than take advantage of advanced search capabilities and carefully consider the relevance and quality of the sites that turn up.[15] Professor Wendy Lerner Lym of Austin Community College compares Internet research to fast food: sources can be quickly obtained, but they are not good for your academic health.[16] For example, a team headed by Professor Chuanfu Chen of Wuhan University, China, evaluated 2,814 web pages found through keyword searches on popular search engines for topics such as genetically modified foods. The

DANGERS OF INTERNET RESEARCH

researchers concluded that 11 percent of the websites were very weak and 45 percent were weak. Only 11 percent were rated as excellent or good.[17]

Participatory (social) media, in which users both create and access information, is a particularly unsuitable research tool. There is no review of information before it is posted, making it difficult to determine if the site is credible.[18] *Wikipedia*, a site on which any user can modify the content, is a primary example of an often-used source with uncertain credibility. One study found that this source "suffers less from inaccuracies than omissions," reflecting "the limited expertise and interests of contributors."[19]

Furthermore, the quality of a website cannot be assessed based on the **top-level domain**—the designation at the end of a web address that indicates the site sponsor's affiliation (for instance, .com, .org, or .edu). For years websites have been given the choice to register as .com, .net, or .org without restriction.[20] And as of 2013, organizations that can afford the $185,000 application fee may create their own top-level domain.[21]

Evaluating the credibility of online sources.

Evaluating the credibility of websites can be particularly difficult. Many sites fail to identify authors or dates of publication, and sites that identify authorship may not provide the writer's credentials. Therefore, it is essential for you to verify the credibility of a website before citing it in a speech. If the author's name is noted, you can do a search for him or her online or by checking periodical indexes, such as Academic Search Premier, to see if the writer has other credible publications. (Be sure your search has found the correct person, particularly if it is a common name.)

If no author is provided, try to research the credibility of the organization that sponsored the site. An analysis of the organization's purpose or its leaders may indicate whether a political or economic bias exists.[22] A website established to teach legal professionals about online research offers the following indicators as evidence of credibility:

- If websites linked to and from that site are credible
- If another credible source provides similar information
- If a site weighs both sides of an issue
- If a site does not contain advertising[23]

Interviewing Experts

You can also learn about your topic by interviewing people with expertise on your topic. Here are some tips for getting the most out of your interviews.

Prepare for your interview. Begin by deciding what you want to learn from an interview, then decide whom to interview. The person you ask should be an expert on the subject—for example, a faculty member who teaches in the area of your topic. Off-campus sources, including government agencies, nonprofit entities, and businesses, may also prove useful.

Set up your interview. If possible, contact potential interview subjects in person. It is much easier for a busy person to say no to an interview request via e-mail or over the phone than face-to-face. Identify yourself, explain that you are preparing a speech, and describe what you hope to learn from the interview. Be willing to accommodate the person's schedule if he or she agrees to be interviewed.

Plan your interview questions. Next, you should decide which questions to ask. Prepare focused questions that your subject is in a unique position to answer, rather than general ones that you could answer through your own research. If you want the interviewee to elaborate on a topic, formulate open-ended questions that require more than a yes or no answer. For example, instead of asking, "Would you support a federal balanced budget amendment?" ask "What are the risks and benefits of adopting a balanced budget amendment?" If you need to ask a candid question that your subject might prefer to avoid, be sure to phrase the question professionally. If you are too confrontational, you will put your interviewee on the defensive and may cause him or her to clam up.

Conduct the interview. Arrive on time for your interview and dress professionally, unless the occasion warrants different attire (for example, an interview on a farm). Keep the following considerations in mind:

- *Start with friendly, easy-to-answer questions.* These will allow you to establish rapport before you move to more challenging questions that may require extended answers.
- *Stay focused.* If the interviewee digresses, politely steer the discussion back to the topic.
- *Maintain eye contact with your subject.* Only glance down if you need to check your questions or take some notes.
- *Be open to new information.* If your subject brings up a fresh perspective on your topic that you want to explore, you may shift from your planned questions and extend your discussion of that perspective.
- *Listen carefully.* To ensure you're hearing your subject's actual answers, paraphrase key responses back to the person.
- *Tape the interview if your subject gives permission.* Recording an interview secretly is a serious breach of ethics.

Presenting Evidence in Your Speeches

For evidence to be effective in a speech, it is essential that the audience understands that you are presenting evidence and that the source is credible.

When you are using evidence, begin by clearly presenting the full citation, identifying the author, his or her credentials, the publication, and date. This cues the audience that you are about to use evidence. For example, in an informative speech about wheelchair tennis, you could cite a source this way: "According to Paul Sindall of the University of Salford (UK) School of Health Sciences, in the *International Journal of Sports Medicine*, May 2014 . . ."

Then present the information you have researched. Either quote the author directly, word-for-word, or **paraphrase** (restating the idea in your own words) accurately. When paraphrasing, it is unethical to misrepresent your source's point of view.

Once you have completed your research, you need to decide how to select and use the materials you have found to effectively develop your topic.

SELECTING AND USING SUPPORTING MATERIALS

Supporting materials are the different types of information that you use to develop and support your main ideas. These materials, discovered through your research, become the building blocks that you use to construct a successful speech.

Selecting the best supporting materials for each main point is a key step in the preparation process, similar to choosing the right mix of ingredients for a special meal you're preparing. They should fit together to help listeners better understand your message and capture their interest. Consider a class period in which you learned a lot about the subject. Chances are that the instructor defined unfamiliar terms, used examples to clarify the concepts and make the subject relevant, and compared new ideas to familiar information. You can use the same strategies to craft a successful speech.

Uses of Supporting Materials

Supporting materials serve several important objectives in your speech:

- *Building audience interest.* If you want audience members to actively listen to your speech, you must motivate them to focus on the message. By selecting supporting materials that appeal to your listeners' interests, you sweeten the odds that they will pay attention to you. The inclusion of supporting materials that make

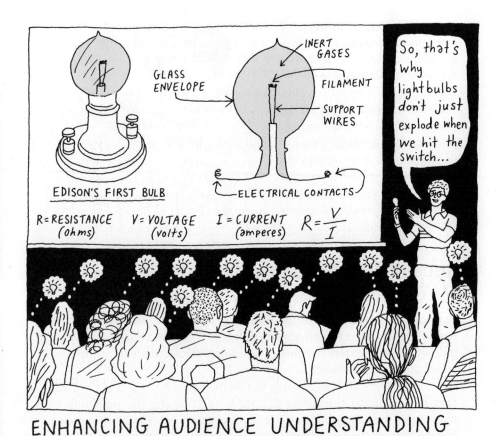

ENHANCING AUDIENCE UNDERSTANDING

audience members laugh or touch their emotions also increases the chance that they will listen to what you are saying.

- *Enhancing audience understanding.* When you present new information to audience members, they may have difficulty understanding your topic. For example, a speech on string theory could be difficult for an audience of mostly liberal arts students to process. You could use definitions of technical terms, such as *superstring*, and brief examples to help them grasp the basic concept of strings and form mental images of them.

- *Strengthening audience memory.* Supporting materials provide hooks for audience members, which help them remember your ideas.[24] For example, if you merely stated that the Incan culture used groups of strings and knots called *khipu* (key-poo) to keep records,[25] listeners may quickly forget what *khipu* are. However, if you show the audience the word and have them pronounce it with you, explain how *khipu* means "knot" in the Inka language, and show a picture depicting how the knots were positioned to store information, you have given the audience several hooks to remember what *khipu* are and how they were used.

- *Winning audience agreement.* Audience members may be skeptical of a point if they've never heard it before, if it strikes them as counterintuitive, or if it contradicts their worldview. If you quote an expert, present a demonstration, or provide examples to illustrate your point, you give your audience reasons to agree with you.

- *Evoking audience emotion.* Factual information greatly enhances any speech, but you'll capture more audience members' attention and interest if you also touch their emotions. For example, an effective speaker might use humor to warm up her listeners or give them a mental break from a slew of sobering statistics.

Types of Supporting Materials

There are many types of supporting materials you can incorporate into a speech. Here we take a look at some of the more common ones: examples, definitions, testimony, statistics, narratives, and analogies.

Examples. **Examples** are samples or instances that support or illustrate a general claim. **Brief examples** are a set of short instances

EXAMPLES OF THREATS TO PRIVACY

(usually a single sentence each) used to support or illustrate your claim. The following excerpt shows how brief examples can be used to support the claim that Americans' privacy is at risk:

- Evolving technology is "making it cheaper and easier for employers to read your e-mails, check out what you've been looking at on the Internet, [and] track where you go with a company car."[26]
- Criminals are illicitly purchasing bugs that allow them to access personal information on your computer.[27]
- "Technologies such as motion-activated video cameras or global positioning systems (GPS) make it increasingly difficult to keep one's location private."[28]

Extended examples provide details about the instance being used, giving your audience a deeper and richer picture of your point. For instance, a speaker might describe a new threat to the privacy of a person who is shopping for a low-cost flight online:

> Suppose you were hoping to get home for Thanksgiving or travel for spring break on a tight budget. Before you can get an online quote, you are asked to provide personal information, including your profile, credit card information, and travel history. If you refuse, you are offered a higher fare. This is exactly what is likely to happen to you under a new policy being adopted by many airlines.[29]

Definitions. When you introduce new information to audience members, you may well use terms unfamiliar to them. For example, few nonscientific audiences would know the meaning of quantum mechanics, and those without a deep understanding of history would not get a reference to the Hittite *pankus*. If you don't take time to define these terms, your listeners may have difficulty understanding your message.

For terms that are specific to the field of your speech, an *expert definition* from a credible source of information on that topic is a good choice. A *functional definition*, which explains how something is used or what it does, is another good way to aid audience understanding. For example, you might explain that the *pankus* was an assembly that decided legal issues in the Hittite kingdom (located in modern-day Turkey).

Testimony. **Testimony** is information provided by other people. Typically you obtain testimony from the sources you research at the library, online, or through interviews. **Expert testimony** consists of statements made by credible sources who have professional or other in-depth knowledge of the topic. (The criteria for evaluating the credibility of an evidence source are discussed in the previous section of this chapter.) **Lay testimony** consists of statements made by persons with no special expertise in the subject they are discussing. Because they lack expertise, lay sources should generally not be used to prove factual claims the audience may not accept. However, lay testimony can help you show how a particular person has been affected by your topic.

Statistics. **Statistics** are information (or data) presented in numerical form. They can help your audience understand how often a situation occurs. While other types of supporting materials can help audience members understand a single instance, statistics can help them see the big picture. For example, in a speech on the rising cost of college textbooks, you might present this statistic: "The College Board estimates that the average cost of books and other course materials was $1,298 at public four-year colleges in 2015–16."[30]

Though useful, statistics can also be disadvantageous. As your use of statistics increases, so does the chance that audience members will perceive your topic as being overly complicated.[31] A long string of statistics may bore or confuse listeners if they are struggling to figure out what "all those numbers" mean. To present statistics effectively to your audience, apply the following guidelines:

- *Limit the number of statistics you present.* Of all the statistics you could offer, select the best few.

- *Use presentation aids to explain your statistics.* For example, you could use a bar graph to illustrate increases in textbook costs.

- *Establish context.* Explain how statistics relate to your listeners. For example, you might note that at a cost of $1,298, a student earning $9 per hour would need to work for about 144 hours to pay for one year's supply of books and course materials.

Narratives. **Narratives** are anecdotes (brief stories) or somewhat longer accounts that can be used to support your main points. Narratives stimulate your listeners' interest because humans (by our very nature) love a good story.[32]

Here is an example of an anecdote that a speaker could use in an informative speech about the development of Google Glass:

> Lead designer Isabelle Olsson thought the camera attached to the glasses looked too bulky. When an engineer told her it could get no smaller, she took matters into her own hands and used a belt sander to grind away plastic until the device looked like "a tiny, two-tier cake." The slimmed-down camera continued to get the job done![33]

Stories like this one are great for capturing audience attention or illustrating a point. And using a quick anecdote is also a good strategy for reenergizing an audience after tackling a complex or technical idea.

Analogies. An **analogy** is a comparison based on similarities between two phenomena—one that is familiar to the audience and one that is less familiar. Analogies can be *literal*, meaning that two entities in the same category are compared. For example, a speaker might describe a

THIS IS A NARRATIVE

new indie band by explaining similarities to the Arctic Monkeys or another well-established band. Analogies can also be *figurative*, which means that the two entities are not in the same category, but the characteristics of one (which is familiar) can help the audience understand the characteristics of the other (which is unfamiliar). This type of comparison helps listeners use their existing knowledge to absorb new information.[34]

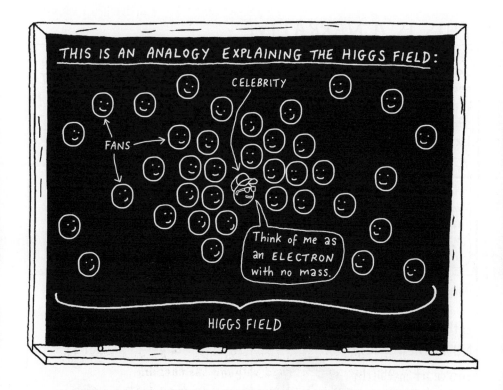

Here's how Dean Lee, a physicist from North Carolina State University, used an analogy during a talk at the North Carolina Museum of Natural Sciences. He was discussing recent research at the Large Hadron Collider in Europe that provided evidence of the existence of the Higgs field (and the Higgs boson, often referred to as the "God particle" in the media). In the paraphrased text that follows, Lee explained what this field does:

> The Higgs field gives mass to other particles. Without the Higgs field, an electron would have no mass. Think of a celebrity as an electron with no mass. He or she walks through a crowded room and is suddenly surrounded by fans who want his or her autograph. The celebrity has effectively formed a crowd with a lot of mass. That is sort of what the Higgs field is doing. It surrounds particles and gives them mass.[35]

Guidelines for Using Supporting Materials

As we have noted, supporting materials can serve a variety of purposes in your speech. In the Internet era, it is not difficult to find mass quantities of information on most topics. How can you be sure you select the best supporting materials? The following guidelines can help:

- *Choose the most credible proof.* Give priority to supporting materials that are backed by credible evidence.
- *Use a variety of supporting materials.* If you use the same type of supporting material over and over—be it personal examples, analogies, or statistics—your effectiveness will be reduced as fatigue sets in with your audience.
- *Appeal to different learning styles. Active learners* learn best by "doing something active" with the material being presented, whereas *reflective learners* "prefer to think about it."[36] *Visual learners*, by contrast, tend to "remember best what they see," whereas *verbal learners* tend to "get more out of words—written and spoken explanations."[37]
- *Avoid long lists.* People usually find it difficult to understand and remember long strings of facts, examples, or statistics, especially when they are not presented with any elaboration.
- *Consider your audience.* Be sure that the supporting materials you select will be effective, given your audience members' knowledge and interests.

When you build the content of your speech by researching and selecting supporting materials, one important consideration is whether the content you have chosen will help you achieve your rhetorical purpose (see Chapter 12). An equally important consideration is whether the ideas you select will achieve your purpose in an ethical manner, a subject we turn to next.

SPEECH ETHICS

At the beginning of this chapter, we learned about Roberto, a student who prepared a speech on product rebates. He had not realized that it was an ethical violation to present information from his research sources without citing them in his speech. Fortunately, he showed his instructor the speech in advance and was able to fix this problem before delivering his presentation.

Many students may be unaware of the appropriate standards for **speech ethics**, the principles and values that should guide your conduct when preparing and delivering a speech. For example, is there an ethical problem if a speaker fails to cite a source of information while delivering a speech, but includes the source in a bibliography at the end of his or her outline? What if a speaker has evidence to support a point made in a speech, but is aware that most credible sources disagree with that point? What if a speaker tells the audience a lie, but he or she honestly believes that the false information will encourage audience members to live a healthier life?

In this section, we discuss principles for the development and delivery of an ethical presentation. Though making ethical choices in public speaking can sometimes be difficult, we will help you develop a responsible system for doing so. The key word here is *responsibility*; whenever you give a speech, you wield power—over what your listeners think, how they feel, and what actions they will end up taking. Thus, you're responsible for the audience's well-being. And making sound ethical decisions as you develop and deliver your speech constitutes one important way to shoulder that responsibility.

Communicating Truthfully

The most basic ethical guideline for public speaking is this: *tell your audience the truth.* How do you feel when someone has lied to you or intentionally misled you? If you're like most people, you resent it and feel manipulated. Once a speaker has deceived an audience, it will be very difficult for him or her to regain credibility. That being said, the word *truth* is fairly subjective and eludes precise definition. It is easier to describe truth in public speaking by examining what is not truth.

Lying. Public speakers who lie are intentionally seeking to deceive their audience, perhaps fearing that the audience would not be understanding or supportive if they knew the truth. For example, consider a student who fabricated his identity as a military veteran when giving a speech about gun safety, believing it would give him more credibility on the topic. Not only would the audience have probably found him credible if he had told

the truth—which was that he had earned a gun safety certificate, but by lying about his background, he risked losing listeners' trust.

Half-truths. When a speaker makes a statement that includes true facts mixed with false information, he or she is telling a **half-truth**. In practice, a half-truth has the same damaging impact as a lie—it deceives the audience. For example, suppose a campus official said, "I have consistently supported preschool and child-care programs on our campus." If, in reality, that official had supported an on-campus preschool but done little to promote child-care services, the statement would constitute a half-truth.

False inference. When speakers make statements with an intent to lead listeners to an incorrect conclusion, they are encouraging a **false inference**. For example, in a presentation titled "UFOs, Extraterrestrials, and the Supernatural," one student described a series of events that occurred in a Midwestern town: an increase in babies born with birth defects, a rise in kidnappings, and a jump in the amount of farmland seized by the federal government. The student did not come out and say these events were all part of a government conspiracy to cover up the presence of aliens. However, he attempted to create that impression. In reality, there was a logical explanation for each of the three events, but the speaker had arranged the message in a way that suggested that the government was trying to conceal the presence of aliens.

Omission. One source of false inference, an **omission**, occurs when a speaker misleads the audience by making a true statement that omits relevant information. For example, suppose a politician said, "I support full funding for the public universities of our state." However, the legislator failed to note that the proposal she intended to advocate would provide for full funding by significantly increasing tuition to make up for reductions in government funds for education. The politician's silence about the tuition increase would constitute an omission.

To communicate truthfully and therefore ethically, do not lie, tell half-truths, encourage false inferences, or omit key facts. There are always alternatives to these actions; for example, you could do more research to discover stronger supporting materials to use in your speech. You could also acknowledge some valid concerns about the ideas you are proposing but make the case that the benefits outweigh the risks. If you fear what the audience might think if they knew the truth, consider the opposite: how will they react if they learn that they have been deceived? In most situations, listeners will react to a lie much more negatively than to an unwelcome truth.

Acknowledging and Representing Others' Work

Instructors typically want students to use a mix of their own ideas and information they have researched from credible sources during a presentation. As noted, when using material that you have researched, you must ethically incorporate and acknowledge the ideas of others. The following pages present some guidelines that you should follow.

Avoid plagiarism. Presenting another person's words or ideas as if they were your own is called **plagiarism**, and it is always unethical. If you plagiarize, you mislead your audience by misrepresenting the source of the material you've used. Equally important, when you plagiarize, you are stealing the ideas and words of another person.

Extreme forms of plagiarism include simply taking an article or other material you have researched, a speech already presented by another student, or a purchased speech, and representing the work as your own. But suppose that rather than blatantly copying another author's entire work, a speaker takes only a couple of paragraphs or even just a few lines and represents the work as his or her own. Would that still constitute plagiarism? Yes. Whether you lift two pages or a single sentence, you are still stealing the author's words and ideas.

Plagiarism is particularly common among students who research their speech online. A student might copy a quotation from a source and paste it into a speech outline without writing down any citation information. When the speech is later due to be presented, he or she will probably not even remember what had been copied and pasted, let alone the citation. To avoid the risk of plagiarism, it is critical to keep track of any information you have cut and pasted and to write down the citation at the time you do your research.

Though plagiarism is always wrong, people sometimes have difficulty discerning the line between plagiarism and appropriate use of researched material. To illustrate why, let's consider two other ethical issues: quoting from a source and paraphrasing the work of others.

Properly quote from sources. Any time that you directly quote information from a source, you need to attribute that material to the source in your speech and outline. When quoting, you present the author's original idea word-for-word and place it in quotation marks.

Here is how a speaker would present a quotation in a speech about Maya art:

> As Samir Patel, associate editor of *Archaeology*, wrote in the January/February 2009 issue, "Maya blue, the brilliant and long-lasting paint that graces scores of Maya sites, is one of just a handful of man-made pigments known to the ancient world."

The quotations you select may not be taken out of context. **Out-of-context evidence** quotes the author's words selectively to support a claim that the author did not make. Take the example of a recent courtroom argument that a chimpanzee that was kept in a small, dark cage should be considered a legal person and allowed to use New York law to argue that his right to liberty had been denied.[38] Suppose the speaker claimed that the judge agreed with the attorneys advocating on behalf of the chimpanzee, quoting the following:

> Your impassioned representations to the court are quite impressive. . . . I will be available as the judge for any other lawsuit or wrongs that are done to this chimpanzee, because I understand what you are saying. You make a very strong argument.[39]

The material that the speaker omitted through the use of ellipsis dots (. . .) shows that this evidence was taken out of context. The judge had also stated: "The court will not entertain the application, will not recognize a chimpanzee as a human or as a person."[40] In other words, although the judge was impressed with the attorneys' arguments, he was not willing to go so far as to rule that chimps are legal persons. The speaker unethically misrepresented the judge's decision.

Acknowledge others' work when paraphrasing. Whenever you use information that you have researched, you need to acknowledge the source of that information in your speech. This is true whether you have directly quoted the author or paraphrased his or her material.

The idea remains the author's, even if you have restated it in your own words. If you do not cite the author, you create the impression that it is your idea instead, which is not ethical. Here is an example of how you might acknowledge and accurately paraphrase the judge's decision in the chimpanzee case, discussed in the previous section:

According to contributing writer Charles Siebert in the *New York Times Magazine*, April 27, 2014, the judge was sympathetic to the chimpanzee's plight and impressed with the attorneys' arguments. Nevertheless, he ruled that a chimpanzee was not a legal person.[41]

Whether you are developing your own ideas in a speech or presenting information you have obtained from research sources, adherence to ethical principles is a fundamental responsibility of public speakers.

CHAPTER REVIEW

The content of your speech will have a major impact on the effectiveness of your presentation. In this chapter, we considered how successful speakers research their topic, make sound decisions about the information they will use to craft their message, and adhere to the ethical responsibilities of public discourse.

Research will significantly improve the quality of your speech. When you use evidence obtained from credible sources, audience members will be more likely to perceive you as a credible speaker and accept the claims you make. Credible evidence—obtained from sources with expertise, objectivity, observational capacity, and recency—can be discovered by researching at the library (or on library websites), on the Internet, or through interviews with experts on the topic. Because much Internet information is not subject to quality-control review before being posted, you need to carefully assess its authors before you use it in a speech.

Supporting materials, the information you use to develop and support main ideas, are the building blocks used to construct a successful speech. They can be used to build interest, enhance understanding, strengthen memory, win agreement, and evoke emotions. Diverse supporting materials, such as examples, definitions, testimony, statistics, narratives, and analogies, should be used to develop your message. When selecting supporting materials, be sure that they are supported by credible proof, represent a variety of types, appeal to different learning styles, are presented in ways other than long lists, and relate to audience members' knowledge and interests.

Speech ethics are the principles and values that should guide your conduct when preparing and delivering a speech. A key ethical principle is to communicate truthfully—this means avoiding not only lies but also half-truths, false inferences, and omissions. Proper acknowledgment of material taken from research sources is another key principle and essential for avoiding plagiarism. Whether you directly quote authors or paraphrase their words, you may not use the words or ideas of another person without properly citing that source in your outline and presentation. When paraphrasing the work of others, it is essential that your words are consistent with the author's message.

LaunchPad
macmillan learning

LaunchPad for *Let's Communicate* offers videos and encourages self-assessment through adaptive quizzing. Go to **launchpadworks.com** to get access to:

✓ **LearningCurve**
Adaptive Quizzes

▶ **Video clips that help you understand human communication**

Key Terms

evidence 382
credibility 382
research plan 384
research librarians 384
 citation 384
credible sources 385
expertise 385
objectivity 386
observational capacity 386
recency 387
periodicals 388
peer review 388
participatory (social) media 392

top-level domain 392
paraphrase 395
supporting materials 395
examples 397
brief examples 397
extended examples 398
testimony 399
expert testimony 399
lay testimony 399
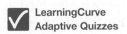 statistics 399
narratives 400
 analogy 400
speech ethics 404

half-truth 405

plagiarism 406

false inference 405

out-of-context evidence 408

omission 406

Review Questions

1. What are the three main steps involved in creating a research plan?

2. What are four key characteristics that determine a source's credibility?

3. Identify the benefits and disadvantages of Internet research.

4. Identify six types of supporting materials. Provide an example of each type of supporting material that you could use in a speech on the topic of your choice.

5. Name five guidelines for using supporting materials in a speech.

6. Define *speech ethics*.

7. Define *plagiarism*, and explain the importance of properly citing your sources.

Critical Thinking Questions

1. Identify speech topics for which each type of the following library research sources could be especially helpful: books, periodicals, newspapers, and government documents.

2. How can you determine the credibility of information presented on a website? Are there any red flags that immediately make you question a site's integrity? What characteristics are likely to make you trust an Internet source?

3. Some television ads during political campaigns offer personal narratives—stories about a candidate's life. Do you think these ads present enough evidence to allow you to cast an informed vote? What other kinds of evidence would you require before making a voting decision?

4. The "shark" drawing on page 405 does not include false inference or evidence taken out of context. What might the shark or the person say if either were committing those two ethical violations?

5. How are students' learning experiences compromised if they plagiarize a speech that was created by another person? How are you affected if your classmate gets away with plagiarism on an assignment?

Activities

1. Go to your campus library and find three sources on a topic you are considering for your next speech. Then ask a research librarian for recommendations on where to search for information on that topic, and consult those sources. Did you find additional useful information in the materials suggested by the librarian?

2. Use an index for scholarly sources, such as Academic Search Premier or JSTOR, to find three articles on a topic of interest to you. Then find three websites that cover that topic. Compare the credibility of the scholarly sources with that of the online sources, as well as the content of the information.

3. Watch an episode of a news personality program on CNN, Fox News, or MSNBC. Then watch *The Daily Show*, *The Nightly Show*, or *The Minority Report*. Is there any difference in the credibility of evidence offered by the hosts or their guests to support the claims that they make? What type of person would be a credible source of information about those claims?

4. Consider the "Dangers of Internet Research" illustration on page 391. Redesign the illustration to show the dangers of failing to research your speech.

5. Review your school's policy on plagiarism. How clear is the definition of plagiarism? Do you think that the guidelines provide clear rules for citing others' work? What is the penalty for stealing someone else's words or ideas?

6. Pay a visit to Factcheck.org, a nonpartisan group that investigates claims made by politicians, news organizations, and interest groups to determine how truthful they are. Select any issue of interest, and read the group's analysis. Identify the types of ethical violations that were uncovered.

Apply Your Skills

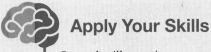

Go to the illustration on page 405, which provides examples of unethical communication (lies, half-truths, and omissions) in an imaginary interaction between a shark and a diver. Create your own scenario in which two communicators create these violations while interacting. Then either illustrate these three violations or write about what they would look like.

Study Plan

ORGANIZING AND OUTLINING

OBJECTIVES

- Understand how to organize main points and supporting material into the body of your speech.
- Learn how to effectively develop introductions and conclusions for your speech.
- Be able to create working and speaking outlines.

Carly stood at the lectern and began her speech. After telling a joke about a leading fashion magazine, Carly indicated that her speech would be about magazines targeted at women and teenage girls and then launched into the topic. She showed her listeners several magazine advertisements featuring gaunt models and explained how listeners could help friends struggling with anorexia and bulimia. One of the ads was for cosmetics, and Carly presented evidence showing how testing of cosmetics on animals was harmful. She also noted several magazine articles with titles she found silly, such as "What His Kitchen Tells You about Him," "Are You Ready for Neon Hair?," and "How Much of a Katniss Are You?"

Carly concluded her speech with a plea for audience members to cancel their subscriptions to women's magazines. Then she sat down, feeling confident that she had scored a success with her audience. During the discussion of her speech, however, many of her classmates said that they had trouble following her presentation. Some admitted that they found her ideas downright confusing. Surprised and upset by their feedback, Carly didn't realize that she had made an all-too-common mistake: failing to organize her speech clearly.

Carly's story reveals the importance of organization in developing a successful speech. When you organize your ideas clearly, you help the audience see how the different ideas in your presentation fit together, improving the understanding of your message.[1] Audience members know what to listen for because your organization provides cues to indicate the main ideas. Good organization is particularly important in oral communication because listeners do not have the luxury of reviewing printed information to understand your message, as they do when reading a message in a book, in a magazine, or online. When you organize your speech clearly, you also enhance your credibility. Effective organization shows that you have taken the time to prepare your talk.[2]

Organizing a speech is not merely a matter of applying an arbitrary set of rules. Rather, a well-organized presentation imposes order on the set of points that you present in your speech by showing the relationship *between* ideas. The organizational pattern you select can communicate essential information to the audience: What are the most important ideas? What evidence and supporting materials are you providing to back up your claims?

There are three main steps for preparing a well-organized speech. In this chapter, we begin by focusing on organizing the **body** of your speech—the part where you present your main points and back them with the evidence and supporting materials discussed in Chapter 13. Next, we discuss the introduction and conclusion of your speech. Just as a movie's opening and closing elements powerfully influence the quality of your theater experience, the beginning and end of your speech play crucial roles in the audience's reception of your message. Finally, we discuss how to **outline** your speech. Outlines provide a written structure for your speech that enable you to visualize the sequence of your main ideas and the points that support them.

ORGANIZING THE BODY OF YOUR SPEECH

When you organize the body of your speech, you begin by deciding what your main points will be and their order of arrangement. Next, you organize the materials that support each main point. Finally, you incorporate organizing words and sentences that reveal the speech structure to your audience at strategic points in your presentation.

Selecting Your Main Points

The body of your speech should be structured around your **main points**—those few ideas that are most important for your listeners to remember. The body also contains **supporting points**—materials designed to prove or substantiate your main points. When your speech is organized around main points with corresponding supporting points, listeners can make sense of the details in your presentation. By contrast, if you present randomly ordered ideas about your topic (as Carly did), your audience will have trouble determining what is most important and understanding the information you are presenting.

How should you select your main points? The following guidelines can help.

Consider your specific purpose. In Chapter 12 we discussed your *specific purpose*, a concise phrase that expresses the objective of your speech. Each main point you select must relate to the specific purpose of your speech. If a potential main point is unrelated (or only weakly related) to your purpose, it should be excluded.

Take your audience into account. As we also noted in Chapter 12, *the audience drives the message*. Therefore, it's important to choose main points that will offer the most useful information and prove most interesting to your listeners. For example, if you were

AUDIENCE ANALYSIS

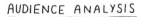

speaking about backpacking tips for an audience of beginners, you would choose basic main points, such as selecting the right pack and remembering all the essential equipment. For an audience of experienced backpackers, you would need more original and advanced information. Your main points might include coping with extreme elevation changes, selecting food for optimal nutrition, and choosing equipment that can survive in subzero temperatures.

Select an appropriate number of main points. In most situations, effective speeches present two to five main points. It is difficult for audience members to remember more than that. Here are some tips for whittling them down to a manageable number:

- See if any related main points can be combined into one broader category.
- Exclude main points that are less likely to resonate with your audience.
- Select the main points that are most important to developing your topic or thesis.

If you find that you have only one main point, that point can be the thesis of your speech. You can then divide your supporting information into two to five key ideas, which will become your main points.

Arranging Your Main Points

Once you have settled on your main points, you'll need to decide the order in which they will be arranged. There are different patterns that you can use depending on the type of information that is covered in each point. Here we take a look at several common organizational patterns. In Chapter 17 on persuasive speaking, we consider a few additional patterns that are specific to that type of speech.

Spatial pattern. In a **spatial pattern**, the main points represent important aspects of your topic that are adjacent to one another in location or geography. Thus, this approach is effective when your topic can be broken down into specific parts that are related spatially. You take the audience from one part to the next—much as a museum guide ushers a group from exhibit to exhibit, or an anatomy professor lectures about parts of the human skeleton from head to toe. For example, a

SPATIAL PATTERN

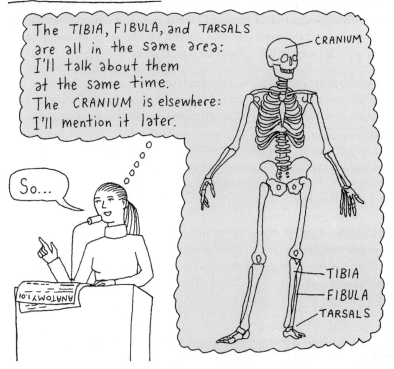

geologist might use a spatial pattern to discuss seismic zones in the continental United States.

Chronological pattern. In a **chronological (temporal) pattern**, you present the information in a time-based sequence, from beginning to end. Each main point covers a particular point in the chronology. If you are discussing a subject that follows a sequence, such as a historical event or a process, this pattern can help your audience keep track of what you're saying. For instance, a speech discussing the decline and rebound of bald eagles in the lower forty-eight states could benefit from a chronological pattern.

Causal pattern. If your speech is explaining a cause-and-effect relationship, a **causal pattern** will help your audience understand the link between particular events and their outcomes. If several major causes exist for the situation or phenomenon you are discussing, each main point can cover one of the causes, as in a speech about fashion trends.[3] Alternatively, if there is a chain of events between cause and effect, each main point can become one link in the chain, as in an explanation as to why e-commerce has grown in significance.

Comparison pattern. A **comparison pattern** organizes a speech around major similarities and differences between two events, objects, or situations. Each main point discusses an important similarity or difference. This pattern can help your audience learn about a new subject by comparing or contrasting it to a subject with which they are familiar. To illustrate, you might compare recent scientific discoveries about planets outside our solar system (exoplanets) with certain characteristics of our own solar system.[4]

Categorical pattern. Another option for organization is a **categorical (topical) pattern**. This pattern is effective when you have a diverse set of main points to support the thesis of your speech. Each main point emphasizes a different but important aspect of the topic that you want the audience to understand.

THIS IS A CATEGORICAL PATTERN

A, B, AND C ARE SUBPOINTS

1. Leonardo da Vinci's art had many impacts.

    A. Leonardo's artistic technique was unprecedented.

    B. Leonardo's technique influenced future artists.

    C. Leonardo's art has generated many controversies.

1, 2, AND 3 ARE SUB-SUBPOINTS

C. Leonardo's art has generated many controversies.

1. Who was the model for the *Mona Lisa*?

2. Who is to the right of Jesus in *The Last Supper*?

3. Is the *Vitruvian Man* a geometrical algorithm?

Organizing Your Supporting Materials

After you select and arrange your main points, you need to develop (explain and prove) each one. In Chapter 13 we discussed evidence and other types of supporting materials that can be used to develop each main point. Now we consider how you can organize your supporting materials to help audience members follow your speech.

Subordination and coordination.

The principle of subordination is the key to a well-organized speech. Using **subordination** means creating a hierarchy of points and their supporting materials in your speech. Main points are the most important (or highest) level of subordination, and supporting materials used to develop a main point (called **sub-points**) are subordinate to that main point. There should be at least two subpoints to support each main point. In the same way, materials that support subpoints are called **sub-subpoints**, and these sub-subpoints are subordinate to their corresponding subpoint. Each subpoint must be relevant to the main point that it is supporting, and each sub-subpoint must be relevant to the subpoint that it is supporting. A well-organized speech also features **coordination**, meaning that each main point is coordinate with—or at the same level of significance as—other main points, just as subpoints are coordinate with other subpoints, and so on.

WHEN A SUBPOINT DOESN'T FIT

When a subpoint doesn't fit. In developing a speech, you may discover that some of the supporting materials you have researched do not relate to any of the main points you selected. Nevertheless, you believe that these materials would improve your speech. What should you do? One option is to reword the main point to encompass the subject of the additional materials. A second option is to create an additional main point to include the supporting materials in question. If you choose the second option, make sure that you have enough material to develop the new main point and that the new main point relates to your topic or thesis statement.

Using Organizing Words and Sentences

As the author of your speech, you will know what your main points are, when you are moving from one point to the next, and what part of the speech you are delivering at any point in time. However, without assistance from you, your audience will have difficulty keeping track of your organization.

To make the structure of your speech easy for others to follow, insert organizing words, phrases, and sentences throughout your presentation. This language offers the audience clear signals that will help them identify your main points and navigate your supporting information. The primary types of organizing language include transitions, signposts, and internal previews and summaries.

Transitions. A **transition** is a sentence that indicates you are moving from one part of your speech to the next. A good transition includes two elements:

* Language summing up the content of the main point you have finished and introducing the new one you are beginning.

- Phrases to signal that one main point is done and the next is beginning.

Both of these elements are used in the following transition:

> *You have learned* about Joan of Arc's military strategies; *next* we will consider the impact of her spiritual beliefs.

This transition makes it clear to the audience that the main point about Joan of Arc's military strategy has ended and the speaker is moving on to discuss her spiritual beliefs.

Signposts. **Signposts** are words or phrases within sentences that help your audience understand your speech structure. Signposts in a speech serve the same function as their counterparts on a road. Just as highway signs tell drivers what direction they are traveling in and where they are going, speech signposts inform audiences about the direction and organization of a presentation.

You can use signposts to show that you are at a specific place in your speech (for example, "my third point is" or "in summary"). You can also use signposts to indicate that you are about to cite research ("according to") or to indicate that a key point is coming ("if you remember one idea from this speech, I hope it will be that . . ."). In addition, signposts help your audience understand the structure of your subpoints (for example, "one cause is . . . , another cause is . . . , and a final cause is . . .").

Internal previews and internal summaries. In crafting your speech, you may have selected a main point that needs several different points of support or requires considerable detail to develop. To help the audience follow your explanation of such a complex point, you may want to use an **internal preview**—a short list of the ideas that will follow. Or to help the audience remember what you have said about the main point, you might use an **internal summary**—a quick review of the key elements of a main point.

Once you have determined your main points and selected the content that you will use to develop them in the body of your speech, it is time to work on the introduction and conclusion.

INTRODUCING YOUR SPEECH

Your introduction creates a first impression of you as a speaker *and* of your message. Both classical and contemporary scholars have recognized the importance of an introduction as a way to set up your speech and build a bond with the audience.[5]

A good introduction must accomplish many purposes: gaining audience attention, signaling your topic and purpose, showing the audience what's in it for them, establishing your credibility, and previewing your main points. It must also be efficient and not overwhelm the body, which is the core of your speech. For a five- to ten-minute speech, you must accomplish all these objectives in about one minute. Let's look at each of the objectives your introduction must achieve.

Gain Audience Attention

Start your speech with an **attention-getter**—material intended to capture your audience's interest. People listening to a presentation may have other matters on their minds. You need to help your listeners redirect their focus from these other matters to you and your message. Following are some strategies for gaining your audience's attention.

I'm sure you're all wondering why I'm sitting on this giant bull. Well, that's a funny story...

Tell a story or anecdote. Most people love a good story, so opening with one can be a compelling yet comfortable way to begin your speech. If you begin your speech with a story, be sure that it relates to your message, takes a limited amount of time (remember, your entire introduction should only be one minute long), and comes across as believable. Do not make up a story to open your speech unless you note that it is a hypothetical example.

Offer a striking or provocative statement. A compelling fact or idea pertaining to your topic can immediately pull the audience into your speech. For example, you might present a surprising statistic or make an ironic statement. This type of attention-getter is particularly effective if you incorporate vivid language into your statement.

Build suspense. Begin your attention-getter by inviting the audience to consider a question or a problem. Build audience curiosity and anticipation before you reveal your topic. The audience will be pulled in to your speech as they contemplate possible answers or solutions and wait for you to reveal your topic.

Let listeners know you're one of them. Another option is to highlight similarities or shared interests between you and the audience. When listeners believe that a speaker is like them, they tend to see him or her as more credible—something that encourages them to pay close attention to your speech. However, to make this type of attention-getter effective, be sure to assert *genuine* common ground. False assertions of common ground can hurt your credibility.

Provide a quotation. A stimulating quotation that illustrates your topic can be an effective attention-getter—especially if you're quoting

someone your audience likes and respects or if the quotation is thought provoking or counterintuitive. You might look to an expert in the field or a layperson to provide a fitting passage.

Signal Your Thesis

Once you've riveted your listeners' attention, your next step is to indicate the thesis of your speech. Providing this information early in your speech answers a question many audience members are asking themselves—"What will this speech be about?"—and helps focus listeners' attention on your message rather than forcing them to figure out what your speech is about.

Your thesis statement should clearly convey the topic and purpose of your speech. You can use your topic statement for this purpose (see Chapter 12) or other language that clearly conveys the bottom line of your speech and alerts your audience to the fact that your topic is being revealed. Your word choice should make it clear that you have finished your attention-getter and are now revealing your topic.

Show Your Audience What's in It for Them

Once you have revealed your thesis, you need to generate audience interest and motivate their active listening. It is a common human tendency to assume that a topic that interests us will naturally be important to others; in truth, however, you need to build that interest. Our former

WHAT'S IN IT FOR ME?

colleague Dr. Gail Sorenson referred to this as WIIFM ("whiff-em"), or "What's in It for Me?" In this part of your introduction, you clarify why your message is relevant and important to your listeners. Just give listeners enough to whet their appetite (one or two sentences), since you will be providing more detail in the body of your speech.

Establish Your Credibility

Once audience members know why your topic relates to them, the next question is, Why should they believe you? In other words, what makes you a credible source on this topic? You build your own credibility by showing that you have relevant experience and education, or that you have thoroughly researched the subject area of your speech. You gain even more credibility when your listeners see you as trustworthy and perceive that you have their best interest at heart.

To establish credibility, explain how you've gained knowledge about your topic. In one or two sentences, emphasize your most relevant credentials (resist any urge to go over your entire résumé or life history), making sure to adopt a modest, unpretentious tone. For example, in a speech about judging ice skating, a speaker could simply note that she had won a number of awards in skating competitions and served as a judge for two years after retiring from competition.

Preview Your Main Points

A **preview** is a brief statement of the main points you will be developing in the body of your speech. It lets your audience members know what main ideas to expect and helps them visualize the structure of your speech—that is, the sequence of ideas you'll present. Your preview should consist of no more than one sentence per main point. To differentiate the main points in your preview, include *signposts* (for example, *first*, *next*, and *finally*) as you mention each main point. The following preview does this clearly:

> Today we'll look at *three major topics* about judging competitive ice skating: *first*, we'll look at rules for judging the event, *followed by* tips that you can use to score the performance yourself, and *finally*, controversies in the judging at previous Olympics.

CONCLUDING YOUR SPEECH

Your conclusion should sum up the message you developed in the body of your speech and leave a memorable impression in your audience members' minds. Conclusions are not the place to develop new ideas; instead, highlight content that you have already presented. A good conclusion generally takes one minute or less (few sins of a speaker are worse than saying "in conclusion" and then continuing to speak for several minutes). The conclusion should contain a transition, a summary of your main points, and a clincher—a memorable idea. We cover these in order.

Transition to Your Conclusion

After presenting your final main point, insert transitional language that signals that you are ready to wrap up your presentation. For example, a speech encouraging students to volunteer at the college food pantry might offer this transition to the conclusion:

> Today *we have seen* how important it is for everyone on campus to help out at our college food bank.

The use of the phrase *we have seen* signals that you're finished with the body of your speech and ready to move on to the ending.

Summarize Your Main Points

After making a transition to your conclusion, present a **summary**, which is a brief review of your main points. A summary has a similar purpose to the preview in your introduction, except that here you are reminding the audience of what you have already said. You may summarize in a single compound sentence that covers each main point, or restate each main point in a complete sentence.

Here is how a speaker might summarize her main points during the conclusion of her speech about judging ice skating:

> Today *we have covered* three major topics about judging competitive ice skating. First, we considered the main rules for judging ice skating. Then, we considered some tips for you to use if you want to score at home. Finally, we considered controversies in judging at previous Winter Olympics.

DON'T REGURGITATE YOUR WHOLE SPEECH... SUMMARIZE IT WITH QUICK BULLET POINTS

Note how the speaker made a clear reference to each main point and used the past tense to help the audience recognize that she was reviewing her points rather than developing new material.

Finish with a Memorable Clincher

End your conclusion with a **clincher**, content that leaves a lasting impression of your speech in your listeners' minds. A clincher should take up only about thirty seconds in a typical speech. Rock musicians have been known to smash their guitars at the end of a show in order to leave a lasting impression. We would not recommend such mayhem in a speech, but there are a number of less destructive strategies you can use to make your speech memorable.

Tie your clincher to the introduction. If you began your speech with a compelling anecdote or example, consider extending it in your clincher. One speech asking students to serve as volunteer tutors began with the story of a twelve-year-old boy who was at risk of dropping out of school because he had fallen behind. The clincher moved back to that opening anecdote, noting that a college student had become the student's tutor and role model, and today, the student was maintaining a B average in high school and applying to colleges.

End with a striking sentence or phrase. There may be a single sentence or phrase that effectively sums up your speech. Advertisers and political campaign managers often use this technique because the words are easy to remember. Although we do not recommend ending your speech with a trivial phrase or catchy tune, you can consider using memorable, relevant phrasing to conclude your speech.

A speech about Hmong history effectively concluded with a theme that had been evident in each main point:

> The name Hmong means "free." And no matter what continent we are living on, that is what we will always be—a free people.

Highlight your thesis. Rather than summing up your speech in a single sentence, you may decide to use a few lines to reinforce the heart of your message. Consider the example of Sally Ride, the first American woman in space. After concluding her career as an astronaut, Dr. Ride became an advocate for math and science education for kids. Here is how she concluded her speech "Shoot for the Stars":

> When I was a little girl, I dreamed of flying in space. And amazingly enough (I still cannot believe it to this day), that dream came true for me. Now it is up to all of us to ensure that this generation of students in school today has access to a high-quality education so the boys and the girls can build the foundation that will enable them to reach for the stars and achieve their dreams too."[6]

Conclude with an emotional message. Recall a speech or presentation that ended by touching your emotions. If you're like most people, that speech left more of an impact on you than a speech that included only cold, hard facts. A clincher that delivers an emotional charge makes a speech particularly memorable, especially in a persuasive or commemorative presentation. Here is how one speaker wrapped up a speech about rehabilitation from brain injuries:

CONCLUDE WITH AN EMOTIONAL MESSAGE

I want you to remember that running is social; you might run individually, but you do it together, as a group. Remember that as you run, you carry with you the memory of everyone who trained with you. You run with them, too.

SNIFF!

To me, the advances in treatments that help people recover from brain injuries are not just material for a speech topic. My brother was severely injured in Afghanistan, suffering from serious memory loss and struggling with speech. But after three years of some of the therapies that we have considered today, I am happy to tell you that he has recovered well enough to join me in college next year.

End with a story or anecdote. A brief story that illustrates the message of your speech can make an effective clincher. Consider this anecdote about Albert Einstein that was used to conclude a speech on preventing dropouts:

> Over one hundred years ago, a boy's teachers said that he was mentally slow and adrift in foolish dreams. The boy's father was told not to worry about his son's career because "he'll never make a success of anything."[7]
>
> Who was that hopeless student? Believe it or not, his name was Albert Einstein. We must never give up on the mind of a child. Educators must convince every student that he or she is valued and capable of learning. Even one dropout is unacceptable.

OUTLINING YOUR SPEECH

Now that you have learned the principles for organizing the introduction, body, and conclusion of a speech, it is time to turn your attention to how you put that organization into practice. This is typically accomplished through your speech **outline**—a written method of organizing a speech using sentences, phrases, or key words.

An outline allows you to clearly show the hierarchy of ideas in your speech—what your main points are and what material supports each of these points. By using an alphanumeric system of headings (beginning with roman numerals for main points and working down to capital letters, numbers, and so on) and a system of indentation, you can present all of your points and evidence, and clearly show how each point is supported.

Two Stages of Outlining

Many speech instructors suggest that you prepare two types of outlines when preparing your speech. The first is a more detailed outline that you will turn in when you present your speech, and the second is a briefer outline that you can use as a reminder when delivering your speech.

The working outline. A **working outline** (also called a detailed or preparation outline) is a thorough outline used to craft your speech. It should be relatively detailed to include your entire speech, from

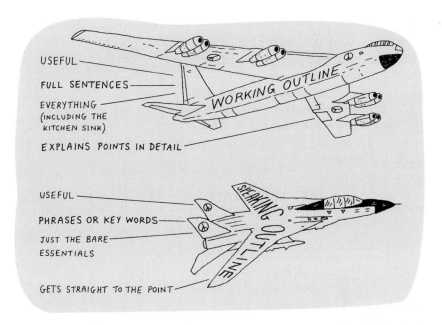

USEFUL

FULL SENTENCES

EVERYTHING
(INCLUDING THE
KITCHEN SINK)

EXPLAINS POINTS IN DETAIL

WORKING OUTLINE

USEFUL

PHRASES OR KEY WORDS

JUST THE BARE
ESSENTIALS

GETS STRAIGHT TO THE POINT

SPEAKING OUTLINE

attention-getter to clincher, with each idea written down in full sentences or detailed phrases (depending on your instructor's preference). If you were to wake up with laryngitis on the day of your speech, another classmate should be able to use your working outline to present your speech for you.

A working outline is helpful to both you and your instructor. It helps you assess the content organization of your speech, ensure that your thesis and main points are well supported, and create smooth transitions between the ideas you present. Your instructor may use the working outline to evaluate your preparation effort; thus, it should clearly show that you have included all required sources, cited all research sources properly (check with your instructor to see what format he or she requires), developed your ideas in sufficient detail, and organized all of your information thoughtfully.

The speaking outline. A **speaking outline** is a shorter outline that expresses your ideas in brief phrases or key words. This is the outline you will use when you actually deliver your speech. It provides quick notes that you can refer to when needed. A speaking outline facilitates

FULL SENTENCE:

> The study showed that even
> a large spider, on a good day,
> makes only 1.5 mg of silk.

DETAILED PHRASE:

> Study — large spider on
> good day makes 1.5 mg
> silk

BRIEF PHRASE / KEYWORD:

> Study: Best = 1.5 mg silk

extemporaneous delivery. As we discuss in Chapter 15, this form of delivery requires that you speak with limited notes; you do not attempt to read a speech word-for-word from a manuscript or memory. Your limited notes are there for reference—you can use them as a reminder of what idea comes next—but you trust yourself to present the details of your speech spontaneously, so that your speech is fresh and conversational.

CREATING YOUR WORKING OUTLINE

A working outline includes three main sections: the introduction, body, and conclusion. As you create your working outline, label each of these parts ("Introduction," "Body," and "Conclusion") in bold so that you can more easily see the speech's structure.

The body of your speech is the heart of your presentation—it is where you develop all of your main ideas. Therefore, many speech instructors recommend that you outline the body first and then draft the introduction and conclusion, which set up and wrap up the content you present in the body.

Outlining the Body of Your Speech

There are several practices that you need to follow to ensure that the body of your outline clearly expresses the content and organization of your speech.

Use proper labeling and indentation. Start each main point at the left margin of your working outline, and indicate each new main point with a roman numeral. Label your subpoints with capital letters and indent them. If you further develop a subpoint with two or more supporting ideas, indicate each of these sub-subpoints with arabic numerals, and indent the sub-subpoints another step beneath the subpoint they support. Typically, you'll want to include between two and four subpoints for each main point, and a similar number of sub-subpoints for each subpoint.

Use full sentences or detailed phrases. In your working outline, express main ideas, subpoints, and sub-subpoints in complete sentences or detailed phrases (each instructor will have his or her own preference for the level of detail required). Recall that your working outline should be detailed enough that another person could deliver your speech from it.

Check for subordination. As previously noted in this chapter, supporting materials must relate to the main point or subpoint that they support. How can you tell if your supporting materials show appropriate subordination? Complete the following sentence for each of your supporting materials: "This supports the point I am making because . . ."

IN A WORKING OUTLINE, NEVER LEAVE THE READER GUESSING

If you cannot come up with a logical way to complete this sentence, you may need to reword a main point or subpoint so that it covers the idea you want to present. You could also consider developing a supporting example or explanation into an additional main point.

Include full information for citations, quotations, and other evidence.
When you use evidence to support a claim in your working outline, you need to include a full citation for the source of your evidence—the author, his or her qualifications, the source publication or web page, and the date of publication. And if you are quoting a source's exact words rather than paraphrasing, be sure to present the information word-for-word and enclose the information in quotation marks. As we discuss later in the chapter, your instructor may also require you to include a works cited list in your outline. *However, the inclusion of your works cited does not substitute for the proper citation of research sources at the places in your outline where you use their ideas* (see Chapter 13 for more information on properly citing sources).

Insert transitions.
As previously noted, transitions are a key element of a well-organized speech. At a minimum, include them between the introduction and the body, when you move from one main point to the next, and between the body and the conclusion. In your outline, indicate a transition by labeling it and placing it in brackets, as shown in the following example:

[TRANSITION   We have considered the physical skills needed to become a Navy Seal; next, let's turn our attention to mental abilities.]

INCLUDE FULL INFORMATION FOR CITATIONS, QUOTATIONS, AND OTHER EVIDENCE

II. Innovations in tracking animals
   A. "Barcode" scanners to monitor zebras;
   Jacob Aron, technology reporter, *New Scientist*, April 7, 2011;
   "Ever thought that the zebra's black-and-white striped markings resemble a biological barcode? Well now a team of U.S. computer scientists and biologists have come up with a scanner, allowing them to identify individual animals from a single still photo."

Outlining Your Introduction

We have noted that there are five main purposes to an introduction. Each of these purposes provides the basis for one part of the introduction. When you have prepared them, the structure should look like this:

INTRODUCTION
   I. Attention-getter
   II. Thesis statement
   III. Connection with the audience
   IV. Speaker's credibility
   V. Preview of main points

In your working outline, each of these five elements should be expressed in complete sentences or detailed phrases, so that a reader will understand what you are planning to say for each part.

Outlining Your Conclusion

Once you've finished outlining your introduction, do the same for the conclusion of your speech. After inserting a transition, outline the summary and clincher, indicating each with a roman numeral. The structure of your outline should look like this (with each part expressed in complete sentences or detailed phrases):

CONCLUSION

I. Summary of main points
II. Clincher

Creating a List of Works Cited

Your instructor may require you to include a list of all the research sources that you cited in your speech. The **works cited list** should not include sources that you did not read or quote in your speech. Some colleges consider including unused sources in a works cited page to be academic dishonesty.

If a works cited list is required, use a complete and proper citation for each source that you used. Your instructor will likely require you to use a particular style for documenting sources; three of the most common styles are those recommended by the American Psychological Association (APA), the Modern Language Association (MLA), and the *Chicago Manual of Style*. Recall that even if you have a works cited page, it also remains your ethical obligation to properly attribute all information you have borrowed from a source each time such information is used in your outline or speech.

Inserting the Title, Specific Purpose, or Thesis

Some instructors may also ask you to write the title, specific purpose, or thesis of your speech at the top of your outline.

A Sample Working Outline

Josh Betancur of Santiago Canyon College developed a speech titled "Invisibility: Science Fiction No More!" In his presentation, he informed the audience about recent scientific developments in the field of invisibility. In this section, we show the full-sentence working outline of his speech, with updated evidence, along with annotations highlighting key concepts covered in this chapter.

INVISIBILITY: SCIENCE FICTION NO MORE!

SPECIFIC PURPOSE   To inform my audience about advances in the science of invisibility

INTRODUCTION •

I. After surviving a cosmic storm, comic book heroine Susan Storm was amazed that she was still alive and even more amazed that she had gained the power to become the Invisible Woman. By creating a force field, she was able to bend the light waves around her so as not to be seen. Now this may sound like science fiction, which it is—for now.

II. Today we will take a look at advances in the science of invisibility.

III. These developments have the potential to affect every aspect of our lives, from aesthetics, architecture, and entertainment, to the military, telecommunications, and transportation. •

IV. After conducting library research and interviews with professors on campus, I have been amazed to learn about the process of invisibility.

V. To understand this exciting new use of technology, it is necessary to first consider the physical science of invisibility, then review experiments attempting to render objects invisible, and finally have a better look, so to speak, at the tremendous potential impacts of this technology on our lives in the future.

[TRANSITION. Let's begin by considering what it takes to make an object invisible.] •

I. Invisibility has been associated with both magic and science.

A. Fiction writers have depended on magical properties. •

1. In Greek mythology, the Cyclops gave Hades an invisibility helmet to give him an advantage when battling the Titans.

2. British science fiction writer H. G. Wells wrote of a magic elixir that one could drink to become invisible.

3. J. K. Rowling imagined an invisibility cloak for Harry Potter.

B. Rather than focusing on science fiction, researchers have focused on scientific principles.

• Anecdote from comic book as attention-getter

• Introduction includes the five components: attention-getter, thesis, connection with the audience, credibility, and preview

• Transition from introduction to body

• Subpoints and sub-subpoints are indented properly

1. Visibility depends on light. In a personal interview on February 10, 2007, Professor Craig Rutan, physics chair at Santiago Canyon College, explained that in order to make something appear invisible, you must find a way to transport light around the object. For example, for the blackboard in this room to be visible, light must travel toward it. If something blocks that light, the board will become invisible. •

2. This effect explains how you see a mirage on a hot summer road. In the November 2006 issue of *Discover*, Senior Editor Josie Glausiusz reports on Duke University physicists David Smith and Dave Schurig, who explain that "when light rays from the sky hit the hot, thin air just above the surface of the asphalt, they bend. . . . Rays once headed from the sky to the ground are redirected to your eye, making the road shimmer like water. In effect, the mirage is cloaking the (now invisible) road behind an image of the blue sky."

• Full citation of research sources

[TRANSITION.   Now that we know what is required for invisibility, we'll take a look at scientific efforts to make objects invisible.]

II. Invisibility research is progressing well. •

• Experiments presented in chronological order

A. Research began with microwaves.

1. According to Glausiusz, the Duke physicists used microwaves instead of light waves because they have a "substantially longer wavelength, which makes the cloaking effect considerably easier to achieve."

2. The same source indicates that the physicists used specially created metamaterials, which "possess an ability, not found in nature, to bend light at extreme angles." They placed rings of these materials around a small cylindrical object and were able to "bend microwaves to flow around the cylinder like water flowing around a pebble in a stream." •

• Use quotation marks when quoting a source word-for-word

[SHOW VISUAL AID OF THIS PROCESS]

B. More recent trials have cloaked objects from visible light.
1. An experiment led by Professor Xiang Zhang of the University of California, Berkeley, was reported in *Nano Letters*, May 2011. The researchers used a "carpet cloak device made of silicon nitride." [SHOW VISUAL AID OF CARPET CLOAK] •The authors concluded that this work "makes actual invisibility for the light seen by the human eye possible."

• Note where presentation aids will be used

2. A team of scientists in the United Kingdom took a different approach. According to Gary Boas, contributing editor of *Photonics Spectra*, August 2012, a "space-time 'event' cloak . . . adds the dimension of time. While spatial cloaks divert light around an object, thus rendering the object invisible, the space-time cloak would slow down and speed up the illuminating photons to create a dark interval where events can take place undetected."

C. How long will it take until an invisibility cloak that can shield larger objects from sight becomes feasible? In an article by Richard Lovett in *National Geographic News,* November 20, 2008, Ulf Leonhardt, a visiting professor at the National University of Singapore, states that "it's a question of the will and the money put into this field."

[TRANSITION. Although we have seen that more work needs to be done, it is also clear that invisibility technology could impact our lives in ways that we can now only imagine.] •

• Transition shows movement from one main point to the next

III. Invisibility technology has many practical applications.
A. First, an invisibility cloak can improve our visual environment. Ian Sample, science correspondent for the *Guardian*, stated in a March 18, 2010, article: "some scientists believe cloaking materials could be used to hide unsightly

buildings or high-security facilities." Could you imagine covering eyesores like air conditioners, power lines, or dumpsters?

B. Second, invisibility technology has medical benefits. George Soukoulis, a senior physicist at Ames Laboratory, explains in the January 9, 2007, *Science Daily* that metamaterials may lead to the development of a "superlens" that can capture "details much smaller than one wavelength of light to vastly improve imaging for materials or biomedical applications, such as giving researchers the power to see inside a human cell or diagnose disease in a baby still in the womb." •

- The words
first, *second*,
third, and *finally*
signpost the four
applications

C. Third, satellite connections may become more efficient. Jim Kerstetter, senior editor for CNET News, wrote an August 21, 2012, article on the CNET News site about Intellectual Ventures, a new company that has received funding from investors including Bill Gates. The company has patented metamaterials technology that would eliminate the need for the heavy and expensive equipment planes now used to stay connected with satellites. The technology, about the size of a laptop, could even be used to create a "personal satellite hot spot."

D. Finally, invisibility research is being extended to shields that protect us from other types of waves. Adam Piore, contributing editor for *Discover* magazine, wrote in the July–August 2012 issue that scientists are now exploring how sound waves might be cloaked to reduce noise pollution, seismic waves could be cloaked to protect buildings, and ocean waves could be deflected from ships.

- Transition
from body to
conclusion

[TRANSITION: Today we have ventured into the unseen world of invisibility.] •

CONCLUSION

I. First, we examined the science of invisibility. Second, we looked at current research into the process of making objects invisible. Finally, we looked at the tremendous impacts that this new technology could have on all our lives. •

II. Now, you may not be able to run out tomorrow and purchase a cloak, but in the not-too-distant future, we will see benefits to diverse fields, including national defense, medicine, and communications. Furthermore, individuals like Susan Storm as the Invisible Woman may no longer just be comic book characters. •

• Efficient summary of main points

• Clincher ties conclusion back to introduction

Works Cited

Boas, G. "True Invisibility Remains Elusive: But Research Moves Toward Practical Applications of Cloaking Technology." *Photonics Spectra* 46 (August 2012): 58. •

Glausiusz, J. "How to Build an Invisibility Cloak." *Discover* 46 (November 2006): 54.

Kerstetter, J. "Remember Invisibility Cloak Tech? It's Useful for Talking to Satellites." CNET NEWS, August 21, 2012. http://news.cnet.com/8301-11386_3-57497129-76/remember-invisibility-cloak-tech-its-useful-for-talking-to-satellites.

Lovett, R. A. "Invisibility Cloak 'Feasible Now.'" National Geographic News, November 20, 2008. http://news.nationalgeographic.com/news/2008/11/081120-invisibility-cloak.html.

"Metamaterials Found to Work for Visible Light." *Science Daily*, January 9, 2007. www.sciencedaily.com/releases/2007/01/070104144655.htm.

Piore, A. "How to Make Anything Disappear." *Discover* 33 (July–August 2012): 70.

Rutan, C. Personal interview, February 10, 2007.

Sample, I. "Cloaking Device Makes Objects Invisible—to Infrared Light Anyway." *Guardian*, March 18, 2010. www.guardian.co.uk/science/2010/mar/18/cloaking-device-objects-invisible-infrared.

Zhang, X., et al. "A Carpet Cloak for Visible Light." *Nano Letters* 11, no. 7 (May 2011): 2825.

• Full citation of sources in works cited list (check with your instructor about his or her preferred citation format)

CREATING YOUR SPEAKING OUTLINE

Your speaking outline is a briefer version of your working outline. By limiting your notes to brief words or phrases, you prevent yourself from reading the speech word-for-word and allow yourself to improvise, choosing fresh words as you speak. This outline provides reminders of your main and supporting points for your reference and can include notes to aid in your delivery.

Formatting Your Speaking Outline

Prepare your speaking outline on 5" × 7" note cards or on regular 8½" × 11" paper. Because you will refer to this outline as needed while delivering your presentation, make it easy on the eyes. If you use a word processor to create the outline, double-space and select a large font size. If you handwrite it on note cards, write neatly and leave space between each line.

Follow the basic structure of your working outline when you set up your speaking outline. Use roman numerals, capital letters, and numbers to identify main points, subpoints, and sub-subpoints, indenting subordinate points. Be sure to number each note card or page of your outline. Your instructor may have specific requirements about the form and length of your speaking outline—be sure that your outline meets those requirements.

Elements of Your Speaking Outline

Your speaking outline should be a condensed version of your working outline that retains all of your main points, subpoints, and source quotations. Indicate each of your ideas in no more than a single sentence, and trust yourself to develop these ideas conversationally while delivering your speech. Include the following elements in this outline:

IF YOU NEED TO CHECK YOUR NOTES DURING YOUR SPEECH... WHICH OUTLINE WOULD YOU PREFER TO READ?

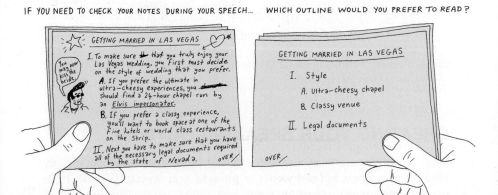

- *Main points.* Write each main point as a brief phrase, single sentence, or a few key words.

- *Subpoints and sub-subpoints.* Write just enough to remind yourself of the key idea.

- *Abbreviations.* To condense your outline, use abbreviations whenever possible. However, be sure to use abbreviations that you will recognize.

- *Evidence.* When providing evidence for your claims in your speaking outline, include necessary citation information. If you are directly quoting the author, this is one place in a speaking outline where you need to include the information word-for-word.

- *Difficult words.* If you'll be using words that are difficult to pronounce or remember, include them in your speaking outline. You may want to spell hard-to-pronounce words phonetically.

- *Transitions.* Include a brief reminder for each transition in your speech. They should not be written word-for-word, but they should include signposts that show you are done with one idea and are moving on to the next. Consider using brackets to set your transitions apart from your points.

- *Delivery notes.* In the margin, consider jotting down **delivery reminders** for handling speaking challenges effectively. For example, write "SLOW DOWN!" in places where you tend to rush, or "LOOK UP!" if you often read from your notes. Consider writing "EMPHASIZE!" to remind yourself to use inflections or gestures to highlight an important idea. To make these reminders stand out, use a different color of ink or highlight them on your outline.

A Sample Speaking Outline

INTRO

Look up—eye contact •

    I. Susan Storm anecdote: bent light waves, became invisible, sci-fi for now.

    II. Advances in sci. of invis.•

    III. Affect many aspects of lives

• Include all five parts of intro, limited to key words

• Abbreviate *science* as *sci.*

Emphasis!

IV. Research and interviews

V. Phys. sci., review experiments, future impact

Pause

[TRANSITION   Begin with what it takes to make object invis.] •

• Remember to include transitions

BODY

I. Invis. assoc. magic + sci.

   A. Fiction—magic •

     1. Hades' invis. helmet

     2. HG Wells's magic elixir

     3. Harry Potter's invis. cloak

   B. Researchers focus sci. principles

     1. Visibility depends on light. Interview with Prof. Rutan, Feb. 10, 2007: Must transport light around object. To be visible, light must travel toward blackboard. Block that light, board invisible. •

     2. Effect like mirage. Sr. ed. Josie Glausiusz report on Duke physicists David Smith and Dave Schurig, *Discover,* Nov. 2006, **"when light rays from the sky hit the hot, thin air just above the surface of the asphalt, they bend. . . . Rays once headed from the sky to the ground are redirected to your eye, making the road shimmer like water. In effect, the mirage is cloaking the (now invisible) road behind an image of the blue sky."**

• Note anecdotes; trust yourself to explain in your own words

• Include citations for all evidence sources

Slowly

[TRANSITION   Now know what is required, look at sci. efforts.]

II. Invis. research progressing well

   A. Began w/ microwaves

     1. Glausiusz, Duke physicists used microwaves because **"substantially longer wavelength, which makes the cloaking effect considerably easier to achieve."** •

     2. Same source: used spec. created metamaterials, **"possess an ability, not found in**

• All word-for-word quotations go in quotation marks

nature, to bend light at extreme angles."
Placed rings of metamat. around cylinder to
"bend microwaves to flow around the cylinder like water flowing around a pebble
in a stream."

Show VA •
    B. More recent trials cloak from visible light
        1. Experiment by Prof. Zhang et al., Cal,
        Nano Letters, May 2011, used "carpet
        cloak device made of silicon nitride."
        Concluded "makes actual invisibility for
        the light seen by the human eye pos-
        sible."

• Reminders to display presentation aid

Show VA •
        2. UK sci. diff. approach. Gary Boas, contrib.
        ed., *Photonics Spectra*, August 2012, "a
        space-time 'event' cloak . . . adds the
        dimension of time. While spatial cloaks
        divert light around an object, thus ren-
        dering the object invisible, the space-
        time cloak would slow down and speed
        up the illuminating photons to create a
        dark interval where events can take place
        undetected."
    C. How long until cloak can shield large objects?
    In Lovett, *National Geographic News*, Nov. 20,
    2008, Ulf Leonhardt, visiting prof., Natl. U. of
    Singapore: "it's a question of the will and the
    money put into this field."

[TRANSITION   Have seen how research proceeding, next
            how impact lives]
III. Many practical apps. •
    A. Improve visual environ. Ian Sample, sci. cor-
    resp., *Guardian*, March 18, 2010, "some scien-
    tists believe cloaking materials could be used
    to hide unsightly buildings or high-security
    facilities."
    B. Med benefits. George Soukoulis, sr. physi-
    cist, Ames Lab, *Science Daily*, Jan. 9, 2007,

• Abbreviate terms you know well

metamat. may lead to **"superlens,"** capture **"details much smaller than one wavelength of light to vastly improve imaging for materials or biomedical applications, such as giving researchers the power to see inside a human cell or diagnose disease in a baby still in the womb."**

C. Satellite connections. Jim Kerstetter, sr. ed., CNET News, Aug. 21, 2012, Intellectual Ventures (investors incl. Gates) patented metamat. tech. that elim. heavy and expensive equipment on planes. Tech. is laptop sized, could create **"personal satellite hot spot."**

D. Protect us from other waves. Adam Piore, contrib. ed., *Discover*, July–Aug. 2012, cloak sound, seismic, and ocean waves.

[TRANSITION   Ventured into unseen world of invis.]

CONCLUSION

• Briefly note main points to summarize

Look up! •

I. Sci. of invis., current research, future impacts

II. Soon see benefits to defense, medicine, communications. Susan Storm as Invis. Woman no longer fiction.

CHAPTER REVIEW

In this chapter, we focused on the importance of a well-organized speech and presented strategies for organizing your message. Good organization begins with the body of your speech. Select an appropriate number of main points and arrange them in a pattern that will best convey your ideas to the audience. Then organize supporting materials to back up each main point. Finally, insert organizing words and sentences that help the audience keep track of where you are in your speech.

After preparing the body, turn your attention to drafting the introduction and conclusion. A good introduction (which should take about one minute) has several purposes, including gaining audience attention, signaling your thesis, showing your audience what's in it for them, establishing your credibility, and previewing your main points. Your conclusion should summarize your main points and end with a clincher that leaves a lasting impression on the audience.

The organization of your speech is reflected in your outline. There are two types of outlines—working outlines and speaking outlines. Your working outline shows the structure of your speech (including transitions), the subordination of supporting materials, and the evidence you cite. This outline is detailed—another person should be able to use it to deliver your speech. The second outline is a speaking outline. It is a briefer outline, presenting key words and phrases. It can be used as a reminder if you lose your place; however, its limited detail allows you to present your speech conversationally—conveying ideas in your own words and maintaining eye contact.

LaunchPad
macmillan learning

LaunchPad for *Let's Communicate* offers videos and encourages self-assessment through adaptive quizzing. Go to **launchpadworks.com** to get access to:

✓ **LearningCurve**
Adaptive Quizzes

▶ **Video clips that help you understand human communication**

Key Terms

body 416
outline 416
main points 417
supporting points 417
◎ spatial pattern 418
◎ chronological (temporal) pattern 419
◎ causal pattern 419
comparison pattern 420
◎ categorical (topical) pattern 420
subordination 422
subpoints 422
sub-subpoints 422
coordination 422
◎ transition 423

signposts 424
internal preview 425
internal summary 425
attention-getter 425
◎ preview 428
◎ summary 430
◎ clincher 431
outline 434
working outline 434
speaking outline 435
◎ extemporaneous delivery 436
works cited list 440
delivery reminders 447

Review Questions

1. Why is good organization essential for developing a successful speech?
2. Name and define five organizational patterns for arranging main points.
3. What are the five major objectives of a good introduction?
4. What are the three main parts of a good conclusion?
5. Explain the difference between a working outline and a speaking outline.
6. What are the main elements of a working outline? A speaking outline?

Critical Thinking Questions

1. How is organizing a speech similar to organizing a piece of written work? How is it different? Are there any organizational tools that a writer can use that a speaker cannot? Does a speaker have options that a writer does not?
2. Visit a website such as American Rhetoric (AmericanRhetoric.com) or Gifts of Speech (gos.sbc.edu) and choose a speech. How could you change the main points or use different language to make the organization of the speech easier to understand?
3. In the illustration on page 423, the speaker puts on a tall hat whenever he makes a main point. While this is clearly an exaggeration, how could a speaker use nonverbal cues or presentation aids to help the audience understand the organization of his or her speech? Could these nonverbal cues or presentation aids still work with a disorganized speech?
4. Which attention-getting strategies could be most effective for a persuasive speech? For an informative speech? For a speech commemorating a somber occasion? For a celebration?
5. How might you use subordination in a conversation with a friend? In a written assignment? When explaining a process to a coworker? What does this lead you to believe about the importance of subordination in communication?

Activities

1. Working individually or in a group, consider how you could improve the organization of Carly's speech, described at the beginning of the chapter.

2. In groups, choose a topic for a speech. Using three organizational patterns, write three to five main points on the topic that fit into each pattern.

3. Watch the beginning of three political speeches on the Internet. Does each speaker begin with an attention-getter? If so, identify which strategy each speaker is using and decide whether it is likely to pull audience members into the speech.

4. Select a speech topic of your choice. Use three different attention-getting strategies to develop possible beginnings for a speech based on the topic.

5. Open one of your textbooks from another course, and outline a chapter based on the headings, subheadings, and key terms that appear in boldfaced or colored text. Do these elements show a hierarchy of ideas? Could you summarize the chapter using only the outline?

Apply Your Skills

Check out the illustration on page 421 that contains subpoints and sub-subpoints in a speech about Leonardo da Vinci. Then create your own similar illustration and corresponding outline. The top panel should include a main point and at least three subpoints. The bottom panel should include one of these subpoints and at least three sub-subpoints. Be sure that your subpoints are subordinate to the main point they support and that your sub-subpoints are subordinate to the subpoint they support.

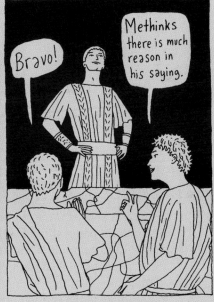

15

DELIVERING YOUR SPEECH

OBJECTIVES

- Learn the pros and cons of the main modes of delivery.
- Understand how to use both vocal delivery skills and nonverbal delivery skills to more effectively deliver a speech.
- Consider how presentation aids might enhance your speech.

Helen, a student in an urban politics class, just finished delivering an oral presentation advocating gardening on unused public land in different U.S. cities. An experienced writer, she had structured her speech clearly and concisely. In just ten minutes, she commented on a wide range of issues—including funding for unused public land, composting, building box gardens, and promoting seed exchanges for growing food. She had carefully outlined her speech and delivered it using a small stack of note cards. She also used several helpful visual aids, such as charts detailing the inadequate supplies of fresh fruit and vegetables for poor people in the inner cities.

Though Helen had worked hard to develop a well-organized speech, she received only a B from her instructor on the presentation. When she asked why, her professor explained that while the content of the speech was excellent, her **delivery**—the combination of vocal and non-verbal communication skills used to present the speech—was less than

455

ideal. The instructor explained that Helen spoke too fast and in a mono-tone, and she fussed too much with her note cards. In addition, she had turned her back on her audience while pointing to and discussing her visual aids.

Helen's experience reveals a major lesson for all public speakers: *how you say something can be as important as what you say*. Why is effective delivery so crucial in public speaking? It helps make your speech compelling and memorable. In an age when audience members may be easily distracted by their many responsibilities, even the most carefully researched and clearly organized talk may not be enough to hold their attention. Speakers today need every advantage they can get to capture—and keep—their listeners' interest. Skillful delivery can give you that edge. In fact, delivery is what comes to mind for most people when they think about speechmaking. Though audience analysis, research, preparation, and practice all play vital roles in public speaking, it's how you deliver your speech that determines whether you find success with your audience members.

In this chapter, we discuss speech delivery, focusing on the various ways you can present a speech as well as the vocal and nonverbal skills you need to deliver a powerful, evocative, and exciting presentation.

SELECTING THE RIGHT MODE OF DELIVERY

Imagine yourself standing before an audience, preparing to make an address. How will you actually deliver your speech? Will you read from a manuscript? Recite from text that you've memorized? Speak extemporaneously from an outline?

In most classroom settings (as well as many settings outside class), speaking extemporaneously from an outline will allow you to achieve the best possible results. This delivery mode enables you to adopt a natural, conversational style that audiences appreciate. Yet there are certain situations in which you may want to read from a manuscript, recite your speech word-for-word from memory, or speak in an impromptu setting. We examine each of these delivery modes in turn, beginning with reading from a manuscript.

Reading from a Manuscript

In this delivery mode, you give your speech by reading directly from a **script**—a typed or handwritten document containing the entire text of

READING FROM A
MANUSCRIPT

MEMORIZING FROM A
MANUSCRIPT

SPEAKING FROM AN
OUTLINE

your speech. As you read, you typically do not ad-lib or deviate from your script.

Although most people using this delivery mode read from a printed script, it has become increasingly popular for speakers to use teleprompter devices when addressing large audiences. From the audience's perspective, teleprompters are clear, appearing as small glass screens around the speaker; from the speaker's perspective, however, they display lines of text, which advance in time with the speech. Having more than one teleprompter allows the speaker to appear to shift his or her gaze toward different parts of the audience while continuing to read the text from the prompter. Although teleprompters might seem ubiquitous—they are used by news anchors, politicians, presenters at award ceremonies, and so on—the technology is not available in most public speaking situations. Thus, for the purposes of our discussion, reading from a script means reading from a printed or handwritten manuscript that the speaker holds in his or her hands.

Delivery from a script is appropriate in circumstances in which speakers (or speechwriters) need to choose their words very carefully. The word-for-word manuscript delivery ensures that listeners hear *exactly* what you want them to. For example, public speakers often use this mode of delivery in press conferences. Imagine a lawyer approaching the microphone to make a statement to the press about his client, a professional athlete accused of wrongdoing. The lawyer reads directly from a carefully prepared manuscript to ensure that his exact words are heard and reported in the news, with no deviations and no surprises. By closely controlling his message, he stands a better chance of controlling what journalists say about him or his client—and therefore influencing public perception.

ONLY SPECIFIC, FORMAL SITUATIONS CALL FOR MANUSCRIPT DELIVERY

Dear valued customers,
As a father of two, I know nothing is more important than the safety of children.
Quality and safety have always taken highest priority at ACME PLASTIC ANIMALS INCORPORATED. It is therefore with great regret that I must announce the total recall of our GREAT WHITE SHARK, model number 884A. During the manufacturing process an error was made...

Still, reading from a script has its disadvantages. To begin with, the script itself becomes a **prop**—something you can hide behind as you read. And like other props, it can limit your eye contact with the audience.

In addition, when you read from a script, you tend to speak in more of a monotone rather than sounding as though you're conversing with your listeners. Some listeners may find the resulting impersonal quality dull, whereas others may find it condescending. Consider the words of one student about a fellow classmate: "To tell you the truth, I almost found it insulting. If all [the speaker] wanted to do was read to us, he could have just given us the notes and let us read them ourselves."

Memorizing from a Manuscript

To recite a speech memorized from a script, you learn your script word-for-word and deliver it without looking at any text, notes, or outline. You behave like an actor on the stage or the screen who memorizes dialogue and recites the words as part of a *performance*. When would you want to deliver a speech by memorizing from a script? Memorization is only advisable when you are called on to deliver a precise message and you are already trained to memorize a great deal of text and deliver it flawlessly.

This delivery mode does offer some advantages over reading from a script. Specifically, there's no physical barrier between you and your audience, so you can maintain eye contact with listeners throughout your speech. This allows you to be more natural with your gestures and in your use of visual aids. And like reading from a manuscript, you can control your word choice by precisely repeating what you've memorized. Memorization was a key feature of classical rhetorical training; in contemporary thought, however, it is no longer considered the best form of speech preparation and delivery in most situations.

The reason? This mode of delivery has distinct disadvantages. For one thing, memorized presentations often come across as slick and pre-packaged—or *canned*. Listeners may view the speech as a stale performance delivered the same way every time, regardless of the audience. As a result, they may take offense or lose interest.

Memorizing is also very challenging—especially with a lengthy speech. In addition, people who speak from memory are typically wedded to their text; the presentation can grind to a halt if the speaker forgets so much as a single word or sentence.

MEMORIZED DELIVERY CAN COME ACROSS AS SLICK... AND NOT IN A GOOD WAY

...but then, the most famous line, one of the most famous lines in all of Shakespeare's plays, comes when Brutus...er... I mean Mark Antony... addresses the, er... ...citizens... in the, er... Forum! He takes the pulpit and says: 'Friends, Romans, countrymen, lend me your eyes...' Aaagh! I mean __ears__! Sorry!

This leads me to my next point, which is... er.................. Um........Aaaagh! Well... er..... .... Sorry!

ANOTHER DOWNSIDE OF MEMORIZATION

Because this delivery mode's disadvantages outweigh its advantages, we recommend avoiding it unless you have a specific background in memorizing large bodies of text (as a trained actor, for example) *and* your speech situation requires it.

Extemporaneous: Speaking from an Outline

In this mode of delivery—the preferred mode in most speech situations—you deliver your speech by referring to a brief outline that you prepared in advance. Typically, you will want to prepare and practice with a full-sentence working outline. Next, you'll want to condense the working outline into a briefer speaking outline (complete with delivery cues) recorded on sheets of paper or note cards (for more information on outlines, see Chapter 14). You should be able to glance at this brief outline and instantly remember what you want to say. And if you've made the note cards easy to read (for example, by using large print and spaces between lines), you can maintain eye contact with your audience.

Using this brief outline to deliver your speech will allow you to speak *extemporaneously*, meaning you will write the outline ahead of time, learn the material in the outline, and then speak spontaneously in the presentation with only the outline available for reference.

Speaking from an outline offers the best aspects of reading from a script and memorizing your speech while avoiding their disadvantages. You can glance at the outline just long enough to spur your memory, so there's no barrier between you and your audience, and your eye contact does not suffer. Also, you don't have to worry about forgetting your place because the outline is at hand to remind you.

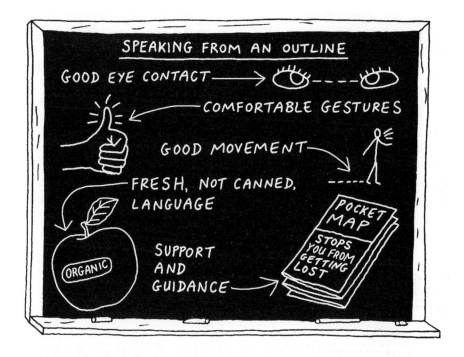

Equally important, when you speak from an outline, your delivery becomes more *conversational*. You sound as if you are talking with your listeners instead of reading a speech *at* them. Finally, with this delivery mode, you choose your words flexibly; thus, you can adapt your message as needed to the audience at hand. For instance, if you notice that a listener looks confused, you can provide further explanation for the point you're discussing.

Of course, speakers need to practice delivering from their outlines to give the best possible presentation. This practice is extremely beneficial in more than one way; research indicates that practice and preparation can lessen the anxiety that speakers feel when it is time to present.[1]

Impromptu: Speaking without Preparation

In different situations, you may be called on to speak unexpectedly. **Impromptu delivery** means that you are generating your speech content in the moment, without time to prepare in advance. These kinds of speeches are both quite common and very challenging for inexperienced speakers. They occur with regularity in a variety of situations: you might be called on to speak at a meeting at the last minute, to comment in a class, or to offer a spur-of-the-moment toast at a wedding or party. You also use impromptu delivery when fielding unexpected questions after a presentation.

Although such situations can seem terrifying for new speakers, it is possible to handle them effectively if you follow a few simple guidelines for impromptu delivery. The key is to remember that even in a spontaneous speaking situation, you can still speak from a mental outline that you draft quickly and keep in your mind, just as you would with a physical outline in an extemporaneous situation. (Or, if you have a few moments to collect yourself, you might try to jot down your main points.) You can pull together a mental outline by quickly asking yourself the following questions:

- **What is the question or topic?** Begin by thinking carefully about the precise nature of the question or topic you have been asked to address. In speech parlance, this is sometimes referred to as *thinking about the call of the question/topic.* Ask yourself, "What

is the specific topic to speak about, or question to answer?" Be precise here.

- **What is my answer or view?** As you are developing a mental outline, consider what you think about the topic, or what you think the answer to the question is.

- **How do I support my position?** Consider what reasons support your view or your answer.

Your answers to these questions should quickly yield a precise topic or thesis statement, as well as a preview of the organization and body of the speech. This entire process can actually occur in just a matter of seconds.

Since this is an impromptu speech, people will not expect a carefully prepared introduction; thus, a direct one will suffice (for example, "I'm delighted to tell you what our division has been developing this year"). Your conclusion need only summarize your points and restate your position (for example, "So, that's what we've been working on this year; I hope you're all as excited about these new products as we are").

USING VOCAL DELIVERY SKILLS

To deliver a high-impact speech, you need to think about more than just your mode of delivery; you need to draw on a variety of speaking skills, both vocal and nonverbal. In this section, we examine the importance of **vocal delivery skills**—that is, the effective use of your voice when delivering a speech. Developing vocal delivery skills involves careful consideration of the use of volume, tone, rate of delivery, projection, articulation, pronunciation, and pausing.

Volume

Volume refers to how loud or soft your voice is as you deliver a speech. Some speakers are not loud enough, whereas others are too loud. A guiding rule for volume: be loud enough that everyone in your audience can hear you, but not so loud as to drive away the listeners positioned closest to you.

Most speakers' biggest challenge is speaking loudly enough. Since audience members don't have the option of turning up the volume, you will need to provide that volume yourself when there is no

microphone available. If you speak too softly and don't project enough, your listeners may have trouble hearing you, and they may even see you as timid or uncertain—which could damage your credibility.

Yet speaking too loudly presents a different set of problems. A student named Jazmin once gave an informative presentation in one of our classes. During her speech, many listeners in the front row began leaning back in their chairs. She was speaking so loudly that her listeners were trying to put some distance between themselves and her.

When you begin preparing your delivery, think about your volume level. How loud is your natural speaking voice? If you aren't certain, ask some friends or relatives to give you an assessment. Then consider your audience for the speech presentation, as well as your speaking forum. How will the size of the audience or the room affect you? Finally, focus on visual cues from your audience while delivering your speech to help you determine whether your volume level is appropriate, and adjust it as needed.

Tone

The **tone** of your speaking voice derives from *pitch*—the highs and lows in your voice. If you can mix high and low tones and achieve some tonal variety, you'll add warmth and color to your vocal delivery. By contrast, if your tone never varies (called speaking in a **monotone**), listeners may perceive your presentation as bland, boring, or even annoying (in the case of a relentlessly high-pitched voice).

How much tonal variety should you aim for to make your voice interesting and enticing? Follow this guiding rule: use enough tonal variety to add warmth, intensity, and enthusiasm to your voice, but not so much

TONAL VARIETY ADDS WARMTH AND COLOR

HIGH   MEDIUM   LOW

RATE OF DELIVERY

I............
Speak........
.........too....
... slowly.

I speak so fast no one can follow my speech.

I speak at just the right speed.

variety that you sound like an adolescent whose voice is cracking. As you practice your speech, try dropping your pitch in some places and raising it in others. If you're not sure whether you're achieving enough tonal variety, practice in front of a trusted friend, family member, classmate, or colleague. Then solicit his or her feedback.

Additionally, consider using **inflection**—raising or lowering your pitch—to emphasize certain words or expressions. For instance, try a lower pitch to convey the seriousness of an idea, and end on a higher pitch if you are posing a question. Like italics on a printed page, inflection draws attention to the words or expressions you want your audience to notice and remember.

Rate of Delivery

Your **rate of delivery** refers to how quickly or slowly you speak during a presentation. As with other vocal delivery skills, going to one extreme or another (in this case, speaking too quickly or too slowly) can hurt your delivery.

Consider the example of Lou, a student at Harvard University who had a very slow rate of delivery. While giving a talk during a seminar on music theory, he noticed that many of the students (as well as the teacher) seemed inattentive. He also became aware that those listeners who *were* paying attention began interrupting him—not with questions about the content of his speech but with queries about his next point. Clearly, they were trying to move him along, which probably meant they were irritated and distracted.

Do you fall into the "slow speaker" category? Do people tend to finish your sentences for you—during conversations or while you're delivering a public address? Although people who try to finish your statements may seem rude, their behavior sends an important signal that you need to step up your rate of delivery. Fail to catch that signal, and you risk losing your audience's interest and appreciation.

Of course, swinging to the other extreme—talking too fast—presents the opposite problem. Overly fast talkers tend to run their words together, particularly at the ends of sentences, preventing their audiences from keeping up with what they're saying. Listeners often have a difficult time following fast talkers not because they are disinterested or impatient but simply because they cannot comprehend what is being said. In the worst-case scenario, potentially interested audience members may transform into defeated listeners because of a fast talker's vocal onslaught (see Chapter 5).

The guiding rule for achieving an appropriate rate of delivery is this: speak fast enough to keep your presentation lively and interesting, but not so fast that you become inarticulate. You can also ask a friend or relative to listen to you and give you feedback about your rate of delivery. Finally, resist any temptation to speed up your delivery to fit an overly long speech into the allotted time. Instead, shorten the content of the presentation.

Projection

Have you ever observed someone singing without a microphone and wondered how the person's voice managed to reach people near *and* far? What about actors on a stage who speak their lines quietly yet can still be heard by everyone in the theater? These individuals use **projection**—"booming" their voices across their speaking forums to reach all audience members.

To project, use the air you exhale from your lungs to carry the sound of your voice across the room or auditorium. Projection is all about the mechanics of breathing. To send your voice clearly across a large space, first maintain good posture: sit or stand up straight, with your shoulders back and your head at a neutral position (not too far forward or hanging

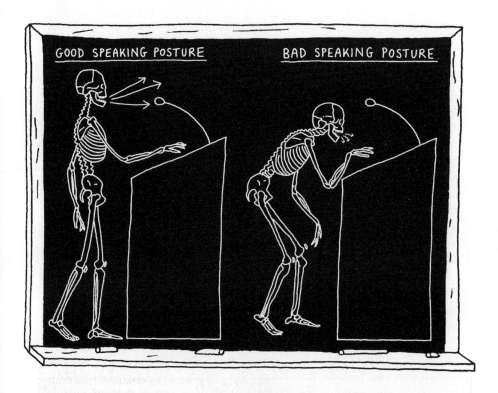

back). Also, exhale from your diaphragm—that sheet of muscle just below your rib cage—to push your breath away from you.

Articulation

Articulation refers to the crispness or clarity of your spoken words. When you articulate, your vowels and consonants sound clear and distinct, and your listeners can distinguish your separate words as well as the syllables in your words. The result? Your audience can easily understand what you're saying.

Articulation problems are most common when nervousness increases a speaker's rate of delivery or when a speaker is being inattentive. Whatever cause of your articulation issues, focus on this rule to get better results: when you deliver a speech, clearly and distinctly express all the parts of the words in your presentation. This advice applies to the vowels and consonants of your words as well as each syllable. Also, make sure not to round off the ends of words or lower your voice at the ends of sentences.

Pronunciation

Pronunciation refers to correctness in the way you say words. Are you saying them in a way that has been commonly agreed on? If you pronounce terms incorrectly, your listeners may have difficulty understanding you. Equally troublesome, they may question your credibility.

Elizabeth, a banking professional, related the following story about the problems that can arise when a speaker mispronounces words:

> In my job I was required to work with lawyers because they drew up the trust documents for their clients. I worked with lawyers, but I was no lawyer myself. Sometimes they can be a little arrogant about their position, thinking that if you didn't go to law school, you shouldn't be working in a law-related field. I worked hard to

earn their respect. But I noticed that when I used some legal terms in front of them, they would occasionally look at one another and smile, like they were sharing a private joke. One such word was *testator*. That's the person who creates a testament like a trust or a will. Whenever I used that word, I always said, "TES-tah-tore," so that it would rhyme with "matador." And the lawyers would smirk—but nobody ever corrected me. Some time later I was embarrassed to learn that the word is pronounced "tes-TAY-ter."

It is especially important to take special care when pronouncing proper names. Taking the time to find out how to properly pronounce an unfamiliar name (be it that of a person or a place) will strengthen your credibility. On the other hand, mispronouncing such names can damage your credibility or even offend your audience. A student named Gabriel learned this lesson the hard way when he pronounced the last name of Supreme Court justice Sonia Sotomayor as "SOTE-a-MAY-or" (as in the mayor of a city) instead of "So-to-my-ORE." Students in Gabriel's class concluded that Gabriel hadn't cared enough to pronounce Sotomayor's name correctly; several pointed out that he could have easily found out how to say it by watching news reports or asking one of his Spanish-speaking classmates.

How can you ensure that your pronunciation is accurate? The guideline here is simple: if you're not certain how to pronounce a word you want to use in your speech, find out how to say it *before* you deliver your presentation. For names of public figures (like Sotomayor), search for radio or television interviews with the subject to find out the preferred pronunciation. For other words, you can ask for guidance from instructors, classmates, coworkers, or friends who might be familiar with the term. Better still, refer to a reputable dictionary, which will provide phonetic spellings for each word as well as a general guide to pronunciation. Many online dictionaries and other resources provide useful audio clips that demonstrate proper pronunciation.[2]

Pausing

Used skillfully, **pausing**—leaving gaps between words or sentences in a speech—affords you some significant advantages. Besides enabling you to collect your thoughts, it reinforces the seriousness of your subject because it shows that you're choosing your words carefully. Pausing can help you create a sense of importance as well. If you make a statement and then pause for the audience to weigh your words, your listeners may conclude that you've just said something especially important.

To get the most out of pausing, use it judiciously—every so often rather than after every sentence. Otherwise, your listeners may wonder if you're having repeated difficulty collecting your thoughts—or they may think you're being melodramatic. In either case, your audience will begin to take you less seriously.

When pausing during a speech, it's best to fill those pauses with silence rather than verbal fillers or vocal tics. A **verbal filler** is a word or phrase, such as *you know* and *like*, that speakers use to fill uncomfortable silences. Here's an example of what vocal fillers do to a speaker's delivery:

> *And so*, the dorm cafeteria was closed . . . *you know*. But I had to study somewhere. *But* . . . I didn't get to study there, *and* . . . *but* . . . I had to go somewhere . . . *but* . . . *and* . . . I tried the Espresso Cafe. *And, like* . . . it was so noisy there, too, *you know*?

A **vocal tic** is a sound, such as *um* and *ah*, that speakers use when searching for a correct word or when they have lost their train of thought:

> *Um* . . . the purpose of my speech is . . . *ah*, to . . . *um* make you see how . . . *um* . . . dangerous this action . . . *ah* . . . really is.

Everyone uses fillers or tics at some point while giving speeches—it's hard *not* to. But using them too often can distract your listeners or make them wonder if you're tentative or ill-prepared. The best way to avoid overusing fillers and tics is by learning to be more aware of when you do use them. How? Try speaking in front of a friend who is holding a clicker or some other low-level noisemaker; have your friend use the noisemaker every time you use a filler or a tic. At first you may be surprised by how often you do so, but with some practice, you will develop better awareness and better habits.

USING NONVERBAL DELIVERY SKILLS

In addition to vocal delivery, you will need to consider your nonverbal behavior as part of the delivery of your speech. **Nonverbal delivery skills** involve the use of physical behaviors to deliver a speech. In this section, we discuss how specific elements of nonverbal delivery—eye contact, gestures, physical movement, proxemics, and personal appearance—can help you connect with your audience and leave a lasting, positive impression.

Eye Contact

To understand what **eye contact** is, you may find it helpful to think first about what it is not. Eye contact is not you looking at your audience members while they look at something else. Nor is it the audience looking directly at you while you stare at your notes or nervously gaze at the ceiling for some divine guidance about what to say next. Rather, with true eye contact, you look directly into the eyes of your audience members, and they look directly into yours.

Eye contact enables you to gauge the audience's interest in your speech. By looking into your listeners' eyes, you can discern how they're feeling about the speech (fascinated? confused? upset?). Armed with these impressions, you can adapt your delivery if needed—for example, by providing a few more juicy details about a particular main point if your listeners look fascinated and hungry for more, or by reexplaining a key point if listeners look confused or overwhelmed.

Eye contact also helps you interact with your audience. For instance, by glancing at a particular listener, you may notice that he or she seems eager to ask a question, thus prompting you to stop and field queries from the audience.

Finally, eye contact helps you compel your audience's attention. Father Paul, a wise Episcopalian priest, once confided a secret of his effective sermonizing technique: "When I speak, I look right at my congregation. And when I do that, I make them look at me, too. And it is harder not to listen to me when I do that . . . precisely because of that!"[3] When you and your audience establish eye contact, it becomes difficult for listeners to look away or mentally drift as you're talking.

From the audience's perspective, eye contact is critical for another reason entirely: in Western cultures, many people consider a willingness to make eye contact evidence of a speaker's credibility—especially truthfulness. An old saying holds that "the eyes are the windows to the soul," meaning that our eyes can betray who we really are or what we really think or believe. Of course, just because someone makes eye contact doesn't necessarily mean that he or she is telling the truth. Likewise, a speaker's failure to look directly at the audience may stem from causes other than

dishonesty, such as nervousness or shyness. Still, as long as people *believe* that the eyes reveal the soul, they will associate a lack of eye contact with deception. To communicate honesty, expertise, and confidence, maintain frequent eye contact with your audience.

How you use eye contact depends on the size of your audience. With small audiences, try to establish and sustain direct eye contact with each listener at various points in your speech. With large audiences, this isn't practical. Therefore, you'll need to use a technique called **panning**. To pan your audience, think of your body as a tripod, and your head as a movie camera that sits atop the tripod. Imagine yourself "filming"

everyone in the group by moving your "camera" slowly from one side of your audience to the other. With this technique, you gradually survey all audience members—pausing and establishing extended eye contact with an individual listener for a few moments before moving on to do the same with another listener.

Panning with extended eye contact gives your audience the sense that you're looking at each listener, even if you aren't. And it still enables you to gauge your audience members' interest, hold their attention, and interact with individual listeners if needed.

Gestures

Gestures—using hand, head, or face movements to emphasize a point, pantomime, demonstrate, or call attention to something[4]—can add flair to your speech delivery, especially when your gestures seem natural rather than overly practiced.[5] At the same time, be aware that gestures can also backfire. For one thing, not all your listeners will interpret the same gesture—a clenched fist, an open palm, a raised forefinger—in the same way.[6] For example, some people see a fist as a symbol of violence, while others consider it a show of forcefulness or determination. If an audience member interprets a particular gesture differently from what you intended, you may inadvertently send the wrong message to that person.

Another consideration is that gestures may communicate a message that appears to contradict your verbal speech message. For example, a student named Lucinda had a habit of extending the index finger of her right hand when speaking, usually when intending to draw people's attention to something on a visual aid or to limit questions until she was done with what she was saying. Written feedback from her classmates, however, indicated that many students interpreted the gesture as aggressive pointing and jabbing, as if Lucinda were calling out some audience members or accusing them of something. Clearly, repetitive use of the gesture was sending the wrong message.

In addition to ensuring that your gestures reinforce your spoken message, avoid using distracting gestures born of nervousness—such as stuffing your hands in your pockets; jingling keys or change in your pockets; or fiddling with a watch, ring, or pen. These behaviors can distract audience members to the point that they'll start focusing more on your gestures than on your speech.

To get the most from gestures, follow these guidelines:

- Use gestures deliberately to emphasize or illustrate points in your speech.
- Remain aware that not all audience members may interpret your gestures in the same way.
- Make sure your gestures reinforce your spoken message.
- Avoid nervous, distracting gestures.

Physical Movement

Physical movement describes how much or how little you move around while delivering a speech. Not surprisingly, standing stock-still (sometimes referred to as the "tree trunk" approach) isn't very effective, nor is shifting or walking restlessly from side to side or back and forth ("pacing") in front of your audience. A motionless speaker comes across as boring or odd, while a restless one is distracting and annoying.

Instead of going to either of these extremes, strive to incorporate a reasonable amount and variety of physical movement as you give your presentation. Skillful use of physical movement injects energy into your delivery *and* signals transitions between parts of your speech. For example, when making an especially important point in your presentation, you can take a few steps to the left in front of your audience, then casually walk back to your original spot when you shift to the next major idea. One useful tip is to combine moderate movement with the panning approach to eye contact, discussed earlier.

How much physical movement, if any, is right for you? Move as much as necessary to invigorate your speech (even if you must come out from behind a lectern or podium), but not so much that you confuse or distract your audience.

Finally, a brief note about speaking from a lectern or podium. Although the lectern might make you feel somewhat more comfortable, it usually acts as a barrier between you and your listeners. Thus, unless you must be at the lectern because of a microphone, we recommend that you come out from behind it at least part of the time in order to interact more fully with your audience. When you are at the lectern, be sure to avoid gripping the sides or top tightly with your hands; such a grip adds tension to your body and will be clearly visible to audience members.

Proxemics

Proxemics—use of space and distance between yourself and your audience—is related to physical movement. Through proxemics, you control how close you stand to your audience while delivering your speech.

The size and setup of the speech setting can help you determine how best to use proxemics. For example, in a large forum, you may want to

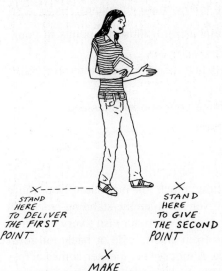

MOVEMENT EMPHASIZES TRANSITIONS AND ENGAGES LISTENERS

X--------   X
STAND HERE TO DELIVER THE FIRST POINT   STAND HERE TO GIVE THE SECOND POINT

X MAKE CONCLUSION HERE

come out from behind the podium and move closer to your audience, so that listeners can see and hear you more easily. Moving toward your audience can also help you communicate intimacy;[7] it suggests you're about to convey something personal, which many audience members will find compelling. Research has also shown that audiences perceive a strong association not only between closeness and intimacy but also between closeness and attraction,[8] and see closeness as an indication of the immediacy/remoteness of the speech message.[9]

Of course, people have different feelings about physical proximity. Whereas some welcome a speaker's nearness, others consider it a violation of their personal space or even a threat. Culture can also influence a person's response to a speaker's proximity. In some cultures, people consider physical closeness downright offensive or invasive.[10] In others, people consider it essential to positive relationships.

To determine how much space to put between you and your listeners, consider your audience's background, the size and setup of your forum, and your ability to move around the forum. When speaking, move close enough to your audience to interact with them and allow them to see and hear you, but not so close as to violate any listener's sense of private space.

THE POETICS OF SPACE (AKA PROXEMICS)

Personal Appearance

By **personal appearance**, we refer to the impression you make on your audience through your clothing, jewelry, hairstyle, and grooming, and other elements influencing how you look.[11]

Personal appearance in a public speech matters for two reasons. First, many people in your audience will form their initial impression of you *before* you even say anything—just by looking at you. Be sure that your appearance communicates the right message about you. Second, studies show that this initial impression based on appearance can be long lasting and very significant.[12] If you make a negative first impression because of a sloppy or an otherwise unappealing appearance, you'll need to expend a lot of time and effort to win back your audience's trust and rebuild your credibility.

The rule for personal appearance is to do what is appropriate for the audience you are addressing, given the occasion and the forum. If you're addressing a somber and formally dressed audience while eulogizing the life of a fallen friend, don't show up in brightly colored casual garb and loud jewelry. Likewise, if you're delivering a presentation to a

IT'S NOT JUST WHAT YOU WEAR, IT'S <u>WHERE</u> YOU WEAR IT   IT'S NOT JUST WHAT YOU WEAR, IT'S <u>HOW</u> YOU WEAR IT

potential client in an industry known for its relaxed and playful corporate culture, consider dressing down for the occasion rather than donning a blue pin-striped suit and power tie.

But in any speaking situation, you should always strive to look presentable through good grooming (tidy hair, nails, makeup, and so on) and an overall tidy appearance (avoiding holes in clothing, clothes that are inappropriately revealing, and the like). That way, you show respect for the audience, the situation, and yourself.

PRESENTATION AIDS

Speech communication experts have long believed that listeners are much more likely to grasp spoken facts and concepts if presenters also provide visual and other nonverbal cues.[13] Indeed, as early as the 1950s, studies showed that the use of audio and visual aids in a speech could increase learning by as much as 55 percent.[14] A **presentation aid** (a.k.a. an *audiovisual aid*) is anything beyond your spoken words that you employ to help your audience members understand and remember your message.

Advantages of Presentation Aids

Savvy use of presentation aids can help you gain several important advantages:

Presentation aids can make your speech more interesting. A colorful and attractive presentation aid can help you spice up any presentation, especially one on a slightly dry topic. For instance, a financial services salesperson giving a talk on retirement savings might display a photo of an older couple looking relaxed, happy, and healthy. The salesperson could also provide graphs that show the makeup of sensible investments.

Presentation aids can simplify a complex topic. If you are giving a speech on a technical or complicated topic, a presentation aid can help you simplify your message so that your listeners can better understand you. For example, a student giving a presentation on how to skydive could show a drawing of a simplified parachute, with labels highlighting each part of the equipment.

Presentation aids can help your audience remember your speech. Many individuals find visual information much easier to recall than spoken information. Thus, the right presentation aids can help ensure that you leave a lasting impression on your listeners. For example, a speaker sharing a lengthy list of reasons for changing the entrance requirements at a community college might hammer home his message by displaying a bulleted list of his main points at the end of his speech.

Guidelines for Developing Presentation Aids

Effectively developing your presentation aids—that is, figuring out exactly what aids to use, how they should appear, and the best way to organize them—is crucial to reaping their potential benefits, from making your speech more interesting to simplifying your topic to helping your audience remember your speech.

Consider the forum. It's important to discuss the location, or **forum**, as you're mulling over which presentation aids to use. Where will the

MAKE SURE YOU CHECK OUT THE FORUM BEFORE YOUR SPEECH

audience listen to your speech? Is the forum equipped to handle presentation aids?

Consider your audience. When choosing appropriate aids, ask yourself, "Of all the possible aids for this speech, which one or which combination would work best with this audience?"

Think about the *demographics* (see Chapter 12) of your audience. Demographics—such as listeners' age, gender, and heritage—can easily predetermine audience members' response to a particular audio or visual aid.

Make sure your aids support your points. Can your points be enhanced by specific images or sounds? For example, if you're giving a speech on a particular city's infrastructure, a map would strongly support your message. A recording of a song about that same city would be less relevant to your speech.

Keep your aids simple and clear. Consider the following suggestions for making your presentation aids simple and clear:

- *Keep your aids simple.* A presentation aid works best when audience members can simply glance at it or hear it once and quickly grasp what you're trying to communicate.
- *Test the size of visual aids.* Make sure each visual aid is large enough to be seen by everyone in your audience.
- *Create contrast.* On visual aids, contrast increases readability. To create contrast, place dark colors against a light background or light colors against a dark background.
- *Test the legibility of visual aids.* Be sure to check whether all the numbers, letters, words, sentences, and graphics in your visual aids are legible—that is, easily distinguished at a distance.
- *Test the volume and clarity of audio aids.* Be certain that your audio aids will be loud enough *and* clear enough (that is, free of static or other noise) for all your listeners to hear.

Use technology wisely. Digital presentations, which may include **presentation software** (which enables users to create, edit, and present information, usually in a slide-show format), have become extremely widespread. Whether in business settings, in communities across the world, or on campuses (maybe even this class), it's useful to know how best to use these. Some specific guidelines include the following:

- *Use technology to unify a mixed-media presentation.* If you have many different styles of aids (pictures, data graphs, lists, video, and audio), consider using presentation software to unify them and keep your audience focused on your message.
- *Remember, content is king.* Don't let your speech be eclipsed by technological bells and whistles. Your speech should be solid enough to deliver without any aids at all.
- *Don't let the software steal the show.* Remember that you need to be the center of attention—not your technology. Help your listeners focus on you and your message: avoid reading from slides, move around as you speak, maintain eye contact with listeners, and limit the amount of text on your slides.

Rehearse with your presentation aids. We strongly advocate that you create your aids while developing your speech—and then practice

using them as you rehearse your presentation. Don't put yourself in the risky position of needing to create aids on the fly while delivering your speech.

Using Presentation Aids during Your Speech

Skillful development of your presentation aids isn't enough to ensure a successful speech. You also need to use the aids correctly during your presentation. Otherwise, you risk making all-too-common mistakes, such as distracting your audience by keeping aids displayed after you're finished with them, or losing eye contact with your listeners while discussing an aid. The following strategies can help you exert maximum impact with your presentation aids.

Make sure everyone can see and hear your aids. Position stereo speakers so that all listeners can hear the audio recordings you're playing. In the same vein, position a computer screen so that everyone can see it. Place a printed graph, chart, or picture prominently on the wall or flip chart, so your entire audience can view it.

Control audience interaction with your aids. To avoid distracting your audience unnecessarily, do not show or play an aid until you are ready for listeners to see or hear it. Then, when you're finished presenting the aid, put it away or shut it off. This strategy keeps your audience's

attention focused on you instead of your aids—and helps ensure that listeners don't miss important parts of your speech.

You can control audience interaction with your aids in several ways. For example, if you are using an audio recording, cue up the desired track ahead of time so that you can play it promptly when you're ready. Avoid playing background music (from an MP3 player or a cell phone) during your speech. If you plan to tape or pin a chart to the wall, do so in advance, but fold half of the display over the other half and tape or pin it down. That way, you'll block the audience's view until you are ready to refer to the chart in your speech, at which point you'll undo the tape or pin.

Use the same technique when displaying a series of images on successive sheets of a flip chart. Insert blank sheets between each sheet containing an image. When you finish with one image, flip the page so that all your audience sees is a blank page.

This technique also works well with overhead transparencies, slide shows, and computer images or video in a PowerPoint presentation. Remove each image after you've discussed it, leaving a blank screen, or turn the equipment off and refocus the audience on you.

Remember the purpose of your aids. Treat your presentation aids as tools that supplement your speech—not the main vehicle for delivering your speech. Your presentation contains your message, and you are the messenger. The best speakers understand that presentation aids support a speech—not the other way around.

CHAPTER REVIEW

As Helen's story at the beginning of the chapter shows, how you deliver your speech and the vocal and nonverbal skills you use while making your presentation can spell the difference between success and failure. In this chapter, you learned the pros and cons of four modes of delivery— reading from a manuscript, reciting from a memorized text, speaking extemporaneously from an outline, and speaking in an impromptu setting—and that extemporaneous delivery is preferred in most contemporary settings. You also discovered how to use many different elements of vocal delivery—volume, tone, rate of delivery, projection, articulation, pronunciation, and pausing—to create more impact in your speeches.

We also discussed how to use elements of nonverbal delivery—eye contact, gestures, physical movement, proxemics, and personal appearance—to further captivate and engage your audience. Finally, you learned about presentation aids, and how they can enhance your speech. By using the right delivery mode as well as the right blend of vocal and nonverbal skills, you can get your message across to your listeners—and leave them wanting more.

 **LaunchPad**
macmillan learning

LaunchPad for *Let's Communicate* offers videos and encourages self-assessment through adaptive quizzing. Go to **launchpadworks.com** to get access to:

 LearningCurve
Adaptive Quizzes

 Video clips that help you understand human communication

Key Terms

delivery 455
script 456
◎ prop 458
impromptu delivery 461
vocal delivery skills 463
◎ volume 463
tone 465
◎ monotone 465
inflection 466

rate of delivery 466
projection 468
articulation 468
pronunciation 469
pausing 470
◎ verbal filler 471
vocal tic 471
nonverbal delivery skills 471
eye contact 472

panning 473

gestures 473

physical movement 475

proxemics 476

personal appearance 478

presentation aid 479

forum 480

presentation software 482

Review Questions

1. What are the four modes of speech delivery?
2. List the advantages and disadvantages of reading from a manuscript when delivering a speech.
3. What are the benefits of speaking from an outline?
4. What are the seven elements of vocal delivery?
5. Explain what is meant by nonverbal delivery, and describe the five elements.
6. Define *eye contact*.
7. When giving a speech, what should be considered when determining how much space to put between you and your audience?

Critical Thinking Questions

1. How can you make decisions about how to pronounce proper names that you've read but never heard? What about proper names that have more than one accepted pronunciation (Kirsten, Louis)?
2. What is the difference between a verbal filler and a vocal tic? During a speech, is it possible to fill a pause with a combination of both? Explain your answer.
3. How can a speaker learn to change his or her rate of delivery? For example, what strategies would you tell a friend to use if he or she spoke too fast or too slow during a speech?
4. Some actors are known for their unique vocal qualities (Samuel L. Jackson, Kevin Spacey, Kathleen Turner, Johnny Depp, Sofia Vergara, Jack Nicholson). What makes these performers' voices so unique? What kinds of vocal delivery skills do they employ when they speak?
5. What should you take into account about your audience when making decisions about the gestures you use during your speech? Can gender, culture, age, and other factors affect the way particular gestures are perceived? If so, how?

Activities

1. In small groups, watch a few political impersonations from *Saturday Night Live* (Will Ferrell's George W. Bush, Fred Armisen's Barack Obama, Tina Fey's Sarah Palin, Amy Poehler's Hillary Clinton, or Larry David's Bernie Sanders). Pay close attention to how some delivery habits are exaggerated—for example, Palin's winking and Obama's frequent use of the word "look." Then watch a few videos of the real politicians giving speeches. Has your perception of their delivery style changed? Explain your answers.

2. Without practicing, make a brief recording of yourself explaining a simple and familiar task—for example, providing directions from your home to campus. Then make another recording of yourself describing a less concrete concept, such as why you really like a specific song. Take note of how often you use verbal fillers and vocal tics in each case. Do you think you would have used them as often if you had prepared an outline and rehearsed? Try it, and compare your results.

3. Check out a few stand-up comedy performances online. Take note of how the comics use nonverbal delivery skills—such as eye contact, gestures, and movement—to engage with their audiences. Which comics are most effective at using nonverbal delivery skills? Why?

4. In groups of three or four, take turns giving impromptu acceptance speeches for being awarded a Grammy. Discuss the pros and cons of each member's tone, rate of delivery, articulation, and use of pauses.

 Apply Your Skills

Look at the illustration concerning pronunciation and mispronunciation on page 469. Can you identify another word that is commonly mispronounced? (For example, many people say "libary" instead of "library.") What might this illustration look like with your example?

INFORMATIVE SPEAKING

OBJECTIVES

- Learn about the different techniques for conveying information.

- Understand the different types of informative speeches, from those on specific objects, to those on individuals or groups, to those on events, processes, and ideas.

- Identify strategies for developing an informative speech and clarifying your message.

Suppose you have a work-study job at the campus health center. In the interest of campus health, your school has arranged for free influenza inoculations to be administered to students on campus in the coming weeks. The center director has asked you to deliver a brief presentation at the student union to inform students about the program.

An **informative presentation** teaches the audience something and increases listeners' understanding of, awareness of, or sensitivity to the topic. Your speech might include information about the way the flu spreads, its symptoms, and the dangers it poses, particularly in people under the age of twenty-four. It would be helpful to talk about simple measures students can take to prevent the spread of the flu, especially among students who live in dense campus housing, as well as those who commute from homes shared with young children or

489

pregnant women. You could also present information about the vaccine itself: whether it is a live virus or a dead one, how it is administered (an injection versus an inhaler), and any potential side effects. Finally, you'd need to go over the logistics of your school's program: where and when the shots will be given, what information students will need to provide to the professionals administering the shots, and how to go about getting an appointment.

Your goal should be to provide all the information students will need to decide whether or not they want to get the shot, as well as how to go about getting it if they decide to do so. Though the presentation is primarily informative, it may also contain a bit of persuasive power. You are, after all, pressing what you believe to be an important health concern, and hoping that students, armed with good information, will opt to take advantage of the program.

In this chapter, we take a close look at informative speaking. First, we examine specific techniques for informing. Next, we consider the common types of informative speaking. Then, we address how to develop an informative speech, including strategies for analyzing your audience and, finally, how to simplify complex information in your presentation.

TECHNIQUES FOR INFORMING

Most informative speeches rely on one of the following techniques for conveying information: definition, explanation, description, demonstration, or narrative. While some topics may lend themselves best to one of these techniques, you will most often use a blend of techniques in your informative presentation.

Definition

Through **definition**, you break something down by its parts and explain how those parts add up to identify the topic. In short, you explain the essence, meaning, purpose, or identity of something. That "something" could be any of the following:

- An object—for example, "What is a lever?"
- A person or group—for instance, "Who are the Hutus?"
- An event—such as, "What was the Diet of Worms?"
- A process—for instance, "What is bookkeeping?"
- An idea or a concept—for example, "What constitutes indecency?"

There are five types of definitions. An example of each is shown in the table below, which demonstrates how you might use each of the five types to define the word *indecency*.

TYPES OF DEFINITIONS

Type	Explanation	Example
Dictionary	The meaning of a term as it appears in a dictionary; also referred to as **denotative meaning**—the exact, literal dictionary definition	*Merriam-Webster's Collegiate Dictionary*, Eleventh Edition, defines *indecency* as the "quality of being indecent." It defines *indecent* as "grossly improper or inappropriate."
Expert	Comes from a person or an organization that is a credible source of information on your speech's topic	According to Justice Stevens of the U.S. Supreme Court in the 1978 case *FCC v. Pacifica Foundation*, indecency refers to "nonconformance with accepted standards of morality."
Etymological	Understanding a word or concept by tracing its roots in the same or other languages	The word *indecency* may derive from the Latin words *in* (meaning "not") and *decentum* (meaning "fitting" or "proper").
Association	Also known as **connotative meaning**; here, people see the word and immediately make an association that is typically socially constructed and agreed upon but not necessarily the literal meaning of the word	Indecency can include profanity—also known as *cursing*, or using curse words. The literal meaning of *curse* is a statement intended to invoke a supernatural power to inflict harm/punishment on a person or thing. When used in our culture, however, curse words usually refer

(*continued*)

TYPES OF DEFINITIONS (*continued*)

Type	Explanation	Example
		to swearing—using words that are commonly agreed to be inappropriate in most settings, often to express anger or frustration.
Functional	Defining a concept by examining how it is applied or how it functions	In practice, American law recognizes indecency as something vulgar, profane, or socially inappropriate. Though to a lesser degree than obscenity, it is functionally on the same path and capable of restriction by the government. It can include profanity and exhibition of bodily parts.

Explanation

Through **explanation**, you provide an analysis of something for purposes of clarity and specificity by tracing a line of reasoning or a series of causal connections between events. In this process of interpretation, you may also offer examples to illustrate the information you're sharing. Explanation works well when you're giving a speech about a process, tracing the emergence of an important event, or explaining how an interesting object works. For instance, you might use explanation to help your audience understand any one of the following:

- The most common causes of running injuries
- How a bill becomes a law in the U.S. Congress
- What events and decisions led up to the outbreak of World War II
- How the engine in a hybrid car works
- The five stages of grieving and loss
- How photosynthesis works

Description

When you use **description**, you use words to paint a mental picture for your listeners, so that they can close their eyes and imagine what you are saying. If you provide sufficient information and detail, your audience may be able to experience vividly what you describe—and through multiple senses. For example, you might decide to use description to help your audience understand one of the following:

- What the aurora borealis looks like
- What it's like to march on Washington, D.C., for a cause you believe in
- What the people you see (every day) on public transportation look like
- How you felt when you got your driver's license
- What the call of a blackbird sounds like
- How your city would look if people stopped littering
- What it's like to attend the Burning Man festival in Nevada

- What it looks like when humpback whales breach
- What a freshly applied tattoo feels like

You can exert maximum impact through description by using vivid language; presentation aids; and details that evoke the senses of sight, sound, smell, touch, and taste. This can be especially effective if you use it as a subpoint to engage listeners' imaginations and place them in the middle of what you're describing.

Demonstration

You might choose to provide a **demonstration** of a topic if your goal is to teach your audience how a process or a set of guidelines works. Demonstrations often call for both physical modeling and verbal elements as you lead the audience through the parts or steps of whatever you are demonstrating. Your audience learns by watching your modeling and listening to your words. Because physical modeling often requires the use of props and visual aids, be sure to practice using these aids before giving your speech. And since you'll be teaching your audience, you need to be confident that you know your topic thoroughly.

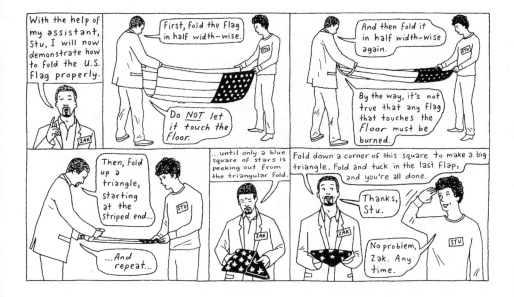

Demonstrations could be helpful for a wide range of informative speeches. For example, you might use a demonstration to show your listeners how to do one of the following:

- Take apart and rebuild a computer
- Care for a bonsai tree
- Create paper origami sculptures
- Start an Etsy shop
- Milk a goat
- Breakdance
- Practice self-defense
- Properly display and store an American flag

For some of these demonstrations, you could bring the needed props to your speech forum. For instance, to demonstrate how to fold an American flag, you could easily bring in a large flag and—with an assistant—show the proper way to fold it for storage in accordance with military custom.[1] You could also improvise, asking members of your audience about the flags they've seen in advertising, used as decoration in dorm rooms, or printed on T-shirts and other clothing, before noting that such seemingly patriotic displays are actually violations of the U.S. Flag Code.[2]

Demonstration coupled with repetition of the speech message has proven especially effective as a learning and memory-enhancement tool. For example, an organization called Per Scholas provides job training for low-income individuals. This program has been spectacularly effective with helping train computer-repair technicians who have little or no previous formal education. The practice of demonstrating the repair process and repeating the message has been key to the success of this program.[3]

Narrative

A **narrative** is a story. When you use a narrative in an informative speech, the story enables you to both share information and capture the audience's attention. The story itself can take the form of a personal remembrance, a humorous anecdote, or perhaps a serious account of an event that happened in someone else's life—all told in a way that informs the audience about your topic. Used skillfully, narratives can help "humanize" a speaker for listeners and thus enhance the speaker's credibility, or ethos. You might choose to use narrative in an informative speech whenever you want to get your point across in an engaging, memorable way. For example, you could use narrative to do the following:

- *Open a speech on the drama and dangers of competitive sports, specifically those with little or no equipment to protect the body.* A poignant introductory story about Kevin Ware, the Louisville shooting guard who severely broke his leg during the 2013 NCAA tournament, could help win your listeners' attention and stir up their emotions right from the start.

- *Emphasize the importance of communication in sustaining intimate relationships.* An entertaining narrative about a misunderstanding that you and your romantic partner ultimately cleared up through skillful communication could help you get the point across in a lighthearted but meaningful way.

- *Help your listeners appreciate the need for careful preparation before a job interview.* A story about how your friend failed to research the background of the employer he was about to interview with and thus missed the fact that his interviewer was an alumnus of the same school could leave a lasting impression on your listeners.

- *Reveal the difficulty of making an appeal from prison.* A story that follows and tracks the appeal process undertaken by someone who was convicted of a crime, incarcerated, and later found innocent could raise audience awareness.

Using narrative effectively takes careful thought and preparation. You need to choose a story that supports your message, rather than just throwing in a narrative simply to entertain or captivate your audience. Thus, select stories—and the details that go into them—based on audience analysis. To illustrate, if you were giving a speech about the 2013 NCAA tournament to an audience composed of people who had little knowledge of college basketball, you might need to explain who Kevin Ware is and why he was so important to the Louisville team and fans. Even if you know the elements of the narrative well, you may also want to research background information and specific details of the story and weave the information you find into the speech.

Finally, remember that telling a compelling story in a way that also informs and educates your audience is a bit of an art. You want to come across as casual and natural (rather than overrehearsed) but also authoritative, which requires extensive preparation and practice. It's almost as if you have to carefully practice acting unrehearsed. In fact, using narrative in a speech can be a risky call, but if you pull it off well, it offers you and your audience genuine rewards. (For more on narrative, see Chapter 13.)

TYPES OF INFORMATIVE SPEECHES

Informative speeches seek to share information, explanations, or even ideas with an audience. Unlike persuasive speeches, which seek to make an argument and therefore confirm or alter an audience's beliefs or actions, informative speeches are meant to give audience members knowledge they might not have possessed before the speech. Informative speeches can be about a wide range of topics: specific objects, individuals or groups, events, processes, and ideas. In this section, we take a closer look at each of these types of informative speeches.

Objects

If you're giving an informative speech about an object, you have a virtually unlimited range of possibilities to choose from. The one thing all objects have in common, though, is that they're not human. The following table

TYPES OF OBJECTS SUITABLE FOR AN INFORMATIVE SPEECH

Type	Examples
Mechanical/ Technological	heart rate monitor blender cell phone weapons system
Natural	flowering plant river mongoose planet
Cultural	painting building poem gourmet dish
Personal	jacket driver's license ice skate necklace

shows just a small sampling of the much larger universe of possible objects your speech could address.

In giving an informative speech about a particular object, you could use a number of techniques. For example, suppose you're preparing a presentation about the benefits of chocolate—which is a food and therefore an object. In this case, you could easily use description to inform your audience. You might, for instance, describe the smooth, creamy texture and sumptuous flavor of a high-quality chocolate truffle and the feeling of well-being that can come from eating it.

Depending on the purpose of your speech, you could also use one or more of the other techniques. For example, you might use

- *definition* to clarify what chocolate is and how it differs from other consumable products derived from cacao beans;
- *explanation* to trace the process by which chocolate bars are made;
- *demonstration* to show how you might bake a chocolate cake; or
- *narrative* to convey chocolate's popularity as a romantic gift.

Finally, note that an informative speech about an object may also have elements of process in it—especially if that object has moving parts.

For instance, to deliver a presentation on how a motorcycle operates, you might explain how the bike's fuel and transmission systems work together to create the process of acceleration.

Individuals or Groups

Giving an informative speech about an individual or a group offers an equally wide range of possibilities. People can't help being fascinated by others, as we can clearly see from the popularity of celebrity-focused magazines, reality television, and personal memoirs. Thus, human subjects with extraordinary physical or emotional characteristics or compelling life stories can make for engaging informative topic material. Groups, likewise, are collections of people with whom your audience can identify; these can include famous politicians in the same party or musical performers who capture tremendous amounts of attention. To illustrate, you could focus your talk on one of the following:

- *A famous politician, entertainer, sports star, explorer, or artist.* For example, you might give a speech about Shirley Chisholm, the first African American woman elected to the U.S. Congress (in 1968) and a candidate for president in the 1972 Democratic primary, nearly four decades before Barack Obama or Hillary Clinton.

- *An unsung hero*—a person or group who did something great but never won recognition for the accomplishment. For instance, you could tell your audience about members of a small tribe in the forests of Burma who survived persecution by the ruling junta.

- *A tragic figure whose life provides a cautionary tale.* For example, you might discuss Amy Winehouse's untimely death from alcohol poisoning after two successful and critically acclaimed albums.

- *An influential political party, artistic movement, sports team, or musical group.* For instance, you might discuss the adversities and triumphs of the college baseball team from the University of California, which managed to advance to the 2011 College World Series even though earlier in the season university officials had announced cancellation of the baseball program due to inadequate funding.

As with objects, you could easily use description to deliver your informative speech about an individual or a group. For example, if your

EARHART, Amelia

BORN IN ATCHISON, KANSAS (1897)

SHE FELL IN LOVE WITH FLYING IN HER LATE TEENS AT A STUNT-FLYING EXHIBITION.

SHE NAMED HER FIRST PLANE "CANARY."

IN 1928, SHE BECAME THE FIRST WOMAN TO FLY ACROSS THE ATLANTIC. THE TRIP TOOK 21 HOURS.

DURING THE LAST LEG OF HER 1937 FLIGHT AROUND THE WORLD, SHE DISAPPEARED OVER THE PACIFIC OCEAN.

speech focused on aviator Amelia Earhart, you could describe her youth and personal qualities along with her famed accomplishments. You might also use narrative to tell a story about the defining experience that led her to become a pilot (namely, attending a stunt-flying exhibition in her late teens). Or you could use explanation to trace the events that led her to attempt her biggest challenge: flying around the world.

Remember that although you will never be able to describe all of a person's life experience in a single speech, you can use life events to make a larger point about a person's character—what kind of person he or she is. You can even support such claims by using narratives supplied by the person's family, friends, associates, and even critics or enemies.

A presentation on a person or group might effectively incorporate information about an object or a process as well. Consider a talk on renowned inventor Thomas Edison. To convey Edison's innovative spirit, you could discuss not only the life experiences that led to his great achievements but also several of his most famous inventions—objects such as the lightbulb and the phonograph. Or you could describe the process by which he developed one of his best-known inventions, including how he resolved problems that surfaced while designing it.

Events

An event is a notable or an exceptional occurrence, either from the present time or from some point in the past. Here are just a few examples of events on which you could focus an informative speech:

- The signing into law of the Twenty-Sixth Amendment, which lowered the voting age to eighteen years
- The discovery of a new planet or species
- The outcome of a high-profile murder trial
- The publication of an important new book
- An underdog's surprising victory over the front-runner in a sporting event
- The emergence in the business world of a new and different kind of company
- The unearthing of new evidence suggesting the origins of humankind
- A wedding, funeral, or religious ritual in your family
- The Republican or Democratic National Convention
- The Billabong Pipe Masters at Banzai Pipeline
- A commemoration at the Tomb of the Unknowns
- Your town's extraordinary Fourth of July celebration
- Fashion Week in New York City

How do you decide what event would make a good topic for an informative speech? Look for events that your audience will consider exciting, newsworthy, historically important, or interesting because they are unfamiliar or surprising.

In delivering an informative speech about an event, you could easily use narrative to tell the story of how the event unfolded. You could also use description to explain how the event affected a group of people. Or you could employ a blend of both narrative and description. For instance, suppose you were presenting a speech about the day you became an American citizen. You might begin with a narrative about your experience as an immigrant, including anecdotes about your travels from your home country and your family's struggle to establish itself in America. You might then detail the process of applying for citizenship. Finally, you might describe your naturalization ceremony and how it felt for you to take the citizenship pledge.

BLENDING NARRATIVE AND DESCRIPTION

Processes

Imagine that you're filing a tax return, changing a tire, planting a vegetable garden, or giving a friend a haircut. Or maybe you're thinking about how two countries resolve a border dispute, how Major League Baseball owners and the players' union negotiate the baseball salary cap for each team, or how marriages are arranged in a particular culture.

Each of these is a process—a series of steps or stages that lead to a particular outcome. You can detect processes both at the level of something localized and simple, such as changing a tire, and at a much broader level, such as the ways in which changes in labor and immigration laws and trade policies affect the cost of automobiles (including those same tires!) in different countries and markets. Thus, we sometimes suggest that processes can be seen at both the micro level and the macro level (that is, the view of a process from fifty feet or from five thousand feet). Many of the informative presentations you will experience in a speech class will lean toward the micro level, something easier to explain and grasp; but that shouldn't discourage you from trying a

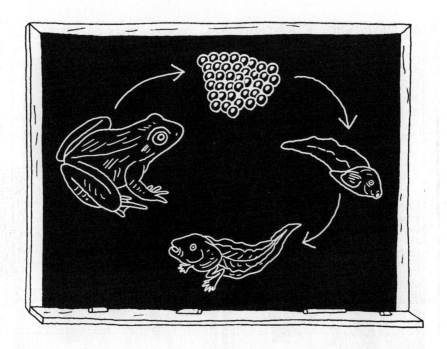

macro-level topic, such as the ways in which global warming occurs. When presented as a process, even larger topics can be digestible for most audiences.

Remember that some topics do not lend themselves well to a discussion of process, simply because of their sheer technical nature (for example, a speech about how changes in the tax code affect the concept of the alternative minimum tax). Does this mean you should avoid a technical topic? No, but it does mean that if you are selecting a topic because it *is* process oriented, focus on subject matter that is within your audience's level of understanding, and try to break down the topic into smaller parts before showing how those parts work together as part of a larger process.

When you deliver an informative speech about a process, you will probably want to walk your listeners through the steps that make up that process, explaining how those steps are carried out and in what order. Depending on your goal, use a variety of techniques to inform your audience about a particular process. For example, if you want listeners to understand how a particular object is made or how it works, you might use explanation to clarify what each step is and how it leads to the creation of the object.

By contrast, if your goal is to teach audience members how to perform the process themselves, combine both explanation and demonstration—that is, verbally and physically model the steps of the process. To illustrate, suppose you're giving a presentation on cake decorating. You'd probably want to explain what tools are needed and what kinds of icings are appropriate for particular styles of decoration. You might also demonstrate by showing the actual techniques used to produce a certain decoration—for example, a basket-weave design—through enlarged photographs or a video. If you are in a relatively intimate environment, you might even ice a cake as part of your presentation.

In deciding which process to focus on in an informative speech, take care to avoid overused topics—such as how to make the perfect PB + J sandwich. Instead, think about processes that would be interesting and fresh for your listeners. Also, consider how you might discuss the impact of an important process. For instance, suppose you're informing your audience about how social networking can assist in getting a job after college. You could add interest to the topic by using a narrative to convey how joining a network such as LinkedIn allows you to create a profile and résumé for work, makes informational interviewing possible, and creates opportunities for jobs.

Ideas

An idea is a theory, a principle, a belief, or a value. Ideas are relatively abstract compared to other informative speech topics, such as an object, a person, or a process. For example, it's harder to describe the notion of "freedom of speech" than it is to explain what the aurora borealis looks like or how a heart rate monitor works. The idea of freedom of speech is more difficult to explain for two reasons: first, it's an idea and not a physical object or process; second, there are limits to freedom of speech—indeed, this concept has several subtleties that restrict its application in many situations (for example, it is illegal to incite certain kinds of violence or to threaten to kill another person).[4]

Some ideas are also loaded because people have difficulty agreeing on their meaning. Consider the notion of "terrorism." Its meaning seems obvious to many after the 9/11 attacks and their repercussions. But are all violent acts against civilians or noncombatants terrorism? Are nation-states guilty of terrorism when their troops accidentally kill civilians? Why do people say things like "One man's terrorist is another man's freedom fighter?" Like freedom of expression, terrorism is a more complex and abstract notion than it may initially appear.

Here are some additional ideas that may constitute topics for an informative speech about an idea:

- Family values
- Truth-telling
- The economic impact of global warming
- Murphy's law ("Anything that can go wrong, will go wrong")
- The advantages of organic farming
- "It's better to give than to receive."
- The separation of church and state
- Saving for retirement even if you are young

Because ideas are so abstract, it's important to select an idea carefully as you consider topics for an informative speech. Otherwise, you may fail to connect with your audience during your presentation. Be sure to consider your audience's interests and level of education while weighing potential ideas to discuss in your speech. For example, if you want to inform your listeners about the economic impact of globalization, think about how much your audience already knows about the topic. If their knowledge is scanty, you'll need to provide more background

IDEAS FOR SPEECHES ABOUT... IDEAS

on globalization during your speech, or you may decide to select another topic with which your listeners are more familiar.

Also ask yourself whether your audience members have had prior exposure to the idea you want to discuss in your presentation. If they have—and did not find the idea compelling—you may want to consider selecting a different topic.

Finally, consider how you might make particularly abstract ideas more understandable to your listeners during your presentation. In a talk on the impact of globalization, for example, you could draw the following analogy: "Globalization is like agriculture. In agriculture, the more evenly you spread seeds across a large field, the more certain you can be that crops will grow in every corner of that field. Likewise, the more you allow commercial activity to flourish across many countries, the more you'll encourage economic well-being among the world's populations."

Most informative speeches about ideas require the use of definition or explanation, both of which enable you to clarify the meaning of the idea you're discussing and examine its various ramifications. For instance, while the meaning of *terrorism* is hotly debated in academic and political circles, most people define it as some form of calculated violence (or the threat thereof) against civilians or noncombatants, all for the purpose of creating mass anxiety and panic while publicizing a political or social agenda.[5] An informative speech on terrorism might *begin* with that definition. But to further *clarify* the idea of terrorism for your audience, you could separate each part of the definition and explain it individually. For instance, to clarify what "publicizing a political or social agenda" means, you could offer several examples of groups that have committed violent acts and then used the resulting publicity to advance their causes.

DEVELOPING YOUR INFORMATIVE SPEECH

To develop an informative speech, you use the same strategies described in earlier chapters, such as analyzing your audience's background and needs, deciding which supporting materials to include, and determining how to organize your content. In this section, we focus on how to analyze your audience, how to select a technique for organizing your speech, and how to focus on your goal to inform. Appropriate audience analysis, organization, and focus help ensure that you prepare a solid foundation and structure for your speech.

Analyzing Your Audience

As with any type of public presentation, audience analysis is essential for developing a successful informative speech. Yet analyzing your audience for an informative presentation raises unique challenges. Specifically, you'll want to focus on where and how your audience is situated for the presentation, your audience's specific demographics, and especially any common ground between you and your audience.

To analyze your audience, start by considering the characteristics of your speaking situation. If you are presenting an informative speech in class, note any requirements for the topic, format, and content of the presentation. If you're planning to deliver your speech outside class, consider the occasion for your speech. Also note the forum (the setting where you will be speaking), the time of day intended for your presentation, the size of your audience, and the expected length of your speech.

Next, remember to examine audience **demographics**—particularly those most likely to influence your listeners' interest and disposition toward your topic. These may include political affiliation, group membership, occupation or academic major, race, ethnicity, gender, sexual orientation, socioeconomic status, age, religious affiliation, and family status. Also look for common ground you might have with your audience—such as shared values, interests, and experiences. By noting common ground while developing an informative speech, you can incorporate strategies to strengthen your credibility, or ethos. (For more on audience analysis, see Chapter 12.)

Selecting a Technique

Your audience analysis also informs your choice of technique—or organizational pattern—for delivering your informative speech. Which technique would *most* help you inform your audience about your topic: definition, explanation, description, demonstration, narrative, or a combination of these? Your choice of technique is crucial because it helps you decide how you'll develop and organize the main points and supporting materials in your presentation.

For example, suppose you were considering using demonstration to present your informative speech. In this case, you would want to ask yourself the following questions:

- *Forum:* "Where will the audience be situated—and will there be ample space for me to move around as I give my demonstration?"
- *Audience size:* "How many people will be in my audience—and will they all be able to see and hear my demonstration?"

SELECTING A TECHNIQUE TO INFORM

You should also consider audience size and details of the speaking forum when planning presentation aids for your informative speech. If you anticipate a small audience and cramped space, a PowerPoint presentation may be unnecessary; showing objects or offering simple handouts might create a more intimate setting. In a bigger forum with a large audience, you may be best served by projecting PowerPoint slides onto a large screen—or even several large screens—combined with adequate amplification of your voice. When speaking in such situations, make sure you plan carefully where you will stand; you may want to stand in the center of the room, directly in front of the screen or screens, and control the audience's interaction with the presentation aids by making the screen go blank after each point is made.

Conversely, let's say you were considering using explanation or description to deliver your speech. In this case, you would focus more on demographics to analyze your audience. Look for anything in your listeners' backgrounds and characteristics that may make it difficult for them to understand the explanation or description you're planning to offer in your speech. For instance, if you're planning to describe a

Hmong wedding ceremony and your listeners have no knowledge of Hmong culture, you'll need to provide more details in your description. Or if you're planning to explain the events leading up to the assassination of U.S. president John F. Kennedy and your listeners are too young to have lived through the event, you'll want to provide a fuller explanation than you would for an older audience. Of course, cultural background and age are not exhaustive examples of demographics. You'll need to consider other characteristics as well to develop an effective informative speech.

What if you're thinking about using narrative to present your speech? Common ground becomes particularly important in this case. To tell a story that will interest and move your listeners, it helps if you have had some of the same life experiences or share some of the same values. When you and your audience have common ground, listeners will find it easier to believe you and identify with the narrative you're presenting.

Focusing on Your Goal to Inform

When developing an informative speech, it's particularly important to remain focused on your rhetorical purpose—to inform—at every phase. If you know your subject well, be sure to establish your own credentials—noting, for example, "As someone who played lacrosse in middle school, high school, and college, I am fairly well schooled in the rules of this game." You should also bear in mind that it's your responsibility to remain objective; if you find yourself choosing evidence to support a particular point of view, you are going beyond informing. Remember that it's easy to remain objective on some subjects (such as knitting or explaining how an engine works), while others will invariably wander into more persuasive territory (defining *terrorism* or *freedom of speech*). We discuss persuasion further in Chapter 17. In this next section, we expand on our discussion of organization in Chapter 14 to cover informative speeches.

CLARIFYING AND SIMPLIFYING YOUR MESSAGE

As you prepare your informative speech, focus on clarifying and simplifying your message as much as possible. It will help your audience understand and thus retain your message. Clarity is something you'll want to

ORGANIZING YOUR INFORMATIVE SPEECH

Organizational Pattern	Pattern Description	Example
Spatial	Describes or explains elements or events as they occur geographically	A speech to explain the trajectory of a meteor that may come dangerously close to Earth
Temporal (Chronological)	Moves from the beginning to the end by referencing points in time	A speech that describes a negotiation process, breaking down each of the bargaining steps as they occur in time
Causal	Explains the roots of a phenomenon or process	A presentation that explains how plate tectonics causes earthquakes and tsunamis
Comparison	Presents major similarities and differences between two items	A speech that compares the global reach and power of the United States with that of ancient Rome
Criteria-Application	Presents the topic as a condition (or series of conditions) that must be met for a conclusion to follow	A speech to explain how the U.S. Patriot Act might be repealed once certain criteria or benchmarks are met
Narrative	The speech as story, with characters and plot	A speech to describe how a life was saved (rescued from drowning) by the speaker
Categorical (Topical)	Main points constitute separate topics, each of which supports the thesis	A presentation to explain running a marathon, breaking it down into separate categories for training, nutrition, technique and style, and mental preparation

strive for in every informative speech, no matter what your topic is or who your listeners are. If you present a message that's confusing or use words that have vague meanings, it will be hard to connect with your audience.

In addition to clarifying your message, your audience analysis will help you decide how much to simplify your informative speech. For example, if listeners have little knowledge of your topic—and the topic is complex—simplicity will be vital. A student named Maria once gave an informative presentation on a complex experimental genetic treatment doctors and research scientists could use to fight cancer. Her audience was made up of students in her speech class—few of whom had sufficient background to follow the technical details in her speech. Maria wisely simplified things by reducing the treatment to "gene therapy." She then further simplified her topic by describing a simple three-step process for introducing genes into cells to prevent disease.

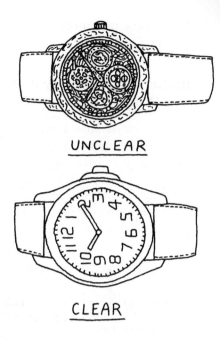

UNCLEAR

CLEAR

Consider the following techniques to clarify or simplify complex messages.

Move from General to Specific

Ask yourself, "At a minimum, what do I want my audience to take away from my speech? What basic message should the audience carry away?" Your answer can help you narrow down a general or

COMPLEX

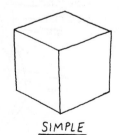

SIMPLE

broad topic to a specific, simpler one—as in Maria's speech on gene therapy.

Reduce the Quantity of Information You Present

An informative speech may contain a tremendous amount of information for the audience to hear, process, and remember. An old adage still rings true here: "Less is more." Look for ways to pare down the details you present. Obviously, a speech about gene therapy could contain huge volumes of information. Maria effectively reduced the quantity of information she presented by boiling the details down to a three-step process.

Make Complex Information Seem Familiar

You can further clarify a complex message by using definition to explain difficult-to-follow terms and ideas. You can also avoid **jargon**—technical or insider terminology not easily understood by people outside a certain group or field. (See Chapter 3 for more about jargon.) In addition, you can draw analogies between complex ideas and things your listeners are already familiar with.[6] For example, Maria could have made an analogy between gene therapy (a new concept for her audience) and a vaccine against polio (something probably familiar to her audience).

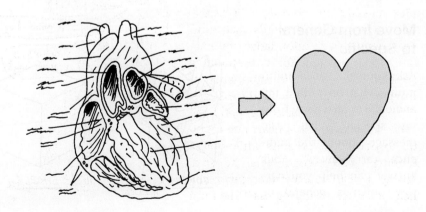

Use Presentation Aids

Presentation aids can also help you clarify and simplify your message. For instance, a diagram of the three-step gene-therapy process Maria described could have enabled her listeners to better envision the process and thus remember it. Likewise, if you were giving a speech on various birdcalls, you could play a recording of a particular call instead of relying only on lengthy descriptions or demonstrations of what the call sounds like. For more discussion of presentation aids, see pages 479–84 in Chapter 15 on delivery skills.

Reiterate Your Message

Through *reiteration*, you clarify a complex message by referring to it several times, using different words each time. For example, in an informative presentation about training for a triathlon, a speaker referred to the importance of using a heart rate monitor three times. The first time he made the point, he said, "It's vital to use a heart rate monitor to track your progress while you're training." The second time, he said, "Using a heart rate monitor can really help you track your progress." The third

time, he said, "The more you use the monitor, the more information you'll have on how you're progressing." By reiterating key points, you help your audience remember your message.

Repeat Your Message

Conveying a key point several times using the same words can also help ensure that your audience understands your message. For example, while introducing the gene-therapy process, Maria could have said something like, "This three-step process offers the best hope for treating cancer in the future." Then, in the conclusion of her speech, she could have said, "Let me repeat: this three-step process offers the best hope for treating cancer in the future."

CHAPTER REVIEW

As the opening example about the speech on influenza vaccines suggested, informative speaking is about teaching your listeners something and increasing their awareness of your topic. You probably use informative speaking many times during a typical day—whenever you're defining, explaining, describing, demonstrating, or telling a story. Whether you're speaking informatively in everyday situations or delivering a formal presentation to a class or some other type of audience, you can greatly enhance your effectiveness by applying the key practices presented in this chapter.

First, know how and when to use the five techniques for informative speaking: definition, explanation, description, demonstration, and narrative. Second, decide on the type of informative speech you want to give—whether it will be about an object, an individual or a group, an event, a process, or an idea. Third, use audience analysis to decide which technique you should use to organize your speech and how much to simplify your message. And fourth, stay focused on informing and maintaining an objective viewpoint.

When you apply these practices, you improve the odds of achieving your purpose in giving an informative speech—that is, you enable your audience members to learn something new and important, and you hone their understanding, awareness, or sensitivity to your topic.

LaunchPad
macmillan learning

LaunchPad for *Let's Communicate* offers videos and encourages self-assessment through adaptive quizzing. Go to **launchpadworks.com** to get access to:

 LearningCurve
Adaptive Quizzes

 Video clips that help you understand human communication

Key Terms

informative presentation 489
◎ definition 490
denotative meaning 491
connotative meaning 491
explanation 492

◎ description 493
◎ demonstration 494
narrative 496
demographics 508
jargon 514

Review Questions

1. Name and explain five techniques for informing.
2. What five types of subjects for informative speeches are offered in the chapter?
3. Name the types of objects that are ideal for an informative speech.
4. What basic steps must be considered as you develop your informative speech?
5. What are seven patterns for organizing your informative speech?
6. Name six basic techniques that you can use to clarify and simplify your informative message.

Critical Thinking Questions

1. Are there any subjects on which you could give an informative speech based on your experience or previous knowledge? How would you establish your credibility without outside evidence?

2. Have you ever felt that someone who claimed to be informing you was in fact pushing a personal agenda? What about the speaker's presentation tipped you off to a potential personal agenda? Did this feeling make you more or less receptive to the information he or she was presenting?
3. Is it possible to define and describe a complex idea, such as terrorism or freedom of speech, without becoming emotionally involved? Can an informative speech be emotional without becoming persuasive?
4. Review the section on audience analysis, and then analyze your class as the audience for your next informative speech. Based on your findings, would it ever be OK to use jargon in your speech? Explain your answer.
5. If you had to give a speech informing your classmates about influenza vaccines, what presentation aids would you use? Would a slide show be more beneficial than a handout? Why or why not?

Activities

1. Take a look at any persuasive speech (choose one from Appendix B, or search at the library or online for any political campaign speech). Edit it so that the focus of the speech is only on informing. How much of the speech is left?
2. Review the types of objects that are suitable for an informative speech. In a small group, choose both a speech topic and a particular object that would be acceptable to use in class for each object type.
3. Consider a subject on which you believe you are well informed (a sport you play, a television show you follow, or a hobby or skill that you have). Do you think you could prepare a fifteen-minute informative presentation on the subject without any research? Create a quick outline showing how you would do it.
4. Look up a "how-to" topic at the library or online (how to make compost, play blackjack, file your taxes). What kinds of sources did you find? Which ones did you find most helpful—and credible—and why?
5. Returning to Maria's informative speech on gene therapy, what type of definition would you suggest she use when explaining gene therapy to the class? Are there other techniques for conveying information that she could use? Write down examples, and share them in a small group.

Apply Your Skills

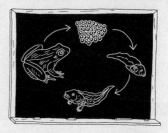

Review the illustration regarding processes on page 504. What is another example of a process that could be demonstrated in a circular and cyclical style? What might your illustration look like?

Study Plan

_____

_____

_____

_____

_____

_____

_____

_____

_____

_____

_____

_____

17

PERSUASIVE SPEAKING

OBJECTIVES

- Learn about the nature of persuasive speeches.
- Understand how to adapt a persuasive message to your audience, and how to use ethos, logos, and pathos to craft a compelling and ethical speech.
- Understand how to organize your persuasive speech.

Michelle was excited. She had recently joined a sorority, and she had an idea that she could not wait to share with the leadership council. Why not have all the sisters participate in meditation twice a week? Michelle had regularly practiced meditation since her junior year of high school, and she believed that it had a big impact on reducing stress and increasing her ability to concentrate. The sisters in her sorority seemed amazingly busy with classes and activities, so surely they would appreciate the chance to lower their stress levels.

Michelle presented her idea to the leadership and explained how beneficial meditation had been for her. She was very disappointed at the response she received. One council member said she was already over-scheduled and so had no time for another activity. Another said that while meditation might work for Michelle, she was sure that it would not help her. A third said that her mother was very religious and would expect her to move out of the sorority house if the sisters adopted "cult" practices. A fourth said that they would become the laughingstock of the campus community—"They'll start calling us 'Tri Zen!'"

Michelle did not realize it, but she had made an error that is all too common among people seeking to persuade others to adopt their ideas. She neglected to explain how her proposal would benefit her listeners—a key element in any persuasive speech.

Michelle might have anticipated council members' concerns and been prepared to address them. For example, she could have presented a brief video of college-age students participating in meditation so that council members could understand how it works. She might have provided research that documents how meditation relaxes college students and improves their focus.[1] With advanced preparation, Michelle would have discovered that other groups on campus (including a faith-based organization) offered meditation sessions, making it unlikely that the sorority would be subject to ridicule. She might have even suggested that they invite other campus groups to participate with them, which could result in some becoming interested in joining the sorority and others wanting to partner on community service activities.

As Michelle discovered firsthand, knowing how to speak persuasively is a vital skill in all areas of life. Consider your own situation: Do you want to get a new policy adopted on campus? Advance in your career? Influence members of your community to support an important cause? Get your roommate to listen to the music you want to hear? Win a major contract for your company from a new customer? Get an extension on the deadline of a paper? In these and many other cases, you'll need to master the art of persuasive speaking if you hope to generate the outcomes you want.

As you read Chapter 17, you will discover that there are many strategies that you can use to become a more persuasive speaker. We start by explaining the nature of a persuasive speech. Then we show you how to select your thesis and supporting content based on your audience analysis. We also discuss ethos (credibility), logos (sound evidence and reasoning), and pathos (emotional appeals)—three building blocks of an effective and ethical persuasive message. Finally, we consider several patterns for organizing a persuasive message.

THE NATURE OF A PERSUASIVE SPEECH

In a **persuasive speech**, your goal is to affect your audience members' beliefs, attitudes, or actions, while also advocating fact, value, or policy claims. Let's take a closer look at these characteristics.

Persuasive Speeches Attempt to Influence Audience Members

Depending on your goal, influencing audience members might mean trying to strengthen their commitment, weaken their commitment, or promote them to take action.

Strengthen audience commitment. If audience members agree with your perspective, you may try to *strengthen their commitment*. For example, your classmates may already believe that there are not enough healthy food and drink options in campus vending machines. In this case, you could seek to convince them to take immediate action to address the problem.

Weaken audience commitment. If audience members disagree with your perspective on an issue, you may try to *weaken their commitment*. For example, suppose you support the removal of all fast-food outlets on campus, but your audience survey reveals that most of your classmates like to eat at those establishments. Your speech is unlikely to succeed if you advocate a ban on campus fast food. Instead, you could try to weaken your audience's commitment to fast food; for instance, you might attempt to persuade them that eating fast food less frequently has many benefits.

Promote audience action. You may also seek to persuade audience members to *take a specific action*. Asking students to drink less caffeine, serve on the campus library's student advisory committee, or vote for an activity fee increase would be examples of this type of speech.

Persuasive Speeches Advocate Fact, Value, or Policy Claims

A **claim** is a statement that you assert is true. In any persuasive speech, your thesis will advance one of three types of claims: a fact claim, a value claim, or a policy claim. A **fact claim** asserts that something is true or false. For example, the thesis "charter schools have (or have not) improved student achievement in our state" makes a fact claim. Conversely, a **value claim** attaches a judgment (such as good, bad, moral, or immoral) to a subject. The thesis "it is better to cut funding for prisons than higher education" is an example of a value claim.

Whereas many people can reach agreement on fact claims when presented with enough evidence, value claims often provide greater challenges. Audience members' ideas of right and wrong may be deeply held and stem from fundamental religious or philosophical beliefs—and thus be difficult to change. If you decide to make a value claim in a persuasive speech, select one that your audience is at least open to considering.

A **policy claim** advocates action by organizations, institutions, or members of your audience. Examples include advocating that the government should increase Pell Grants to students, that your college should offer living-learning programs (in which students are grouped in campus residences based on common interests, such as the arts, world cultures, or health careers),[2] or that your listeners should invest in stocks.

Now that you know typical objectives of persuasive speeches, let's turn our attention to the ways you can tailor your persuasive message.

TAILORING YOUR PERSUASIVE MESSAGE TO YOUR AUDIENCE

Effective persuasive speakers use **strategic discourse**—the process of selecting supporting arguments that will best persuade the audience in an ethical manner. There are many supporting ideas that you could present, typically far more than could be fit into the available time. Your job is to make strategic choices, selecting the ethical arguments that are *most* likely to persuade your particular listeners.

Adapting to Audience Disposition

Your listeners' disposition—their opinions about your topic—should affect the thesis that you select (see Chapter 12 for more on audience analysis). According to **social judgment theory**, audience members make a decision about your thesis by comparing it with their own perspectives on the issue.[3] It is essential to select a thesis that is within or near the audience members' **latitude of acceptance**, which is the range of viewpoints on an issue that they support. Audience members also have a range of viewpoints that they oppose, constituting their **latitude of rejection**.[4] If your thesis falls within their latitude of rejection, your speech may even produce a **boomerang effect**, the act of pushing your listeners to oppose your idea even more vigorously than they previously did.[5] The greater the **ego involvement** (interest and concern) of your listeners on your issue, the narrower their latitude of acceptance is likely to be. If the issue is less important to them, they will be open to a wider range of positions.[6]

How does all this work in practice? Suppose your objective is to increase the purchase of local agricultural products by your campus food service. A campus environmental organization would probably support

THE LAND OF AUDIENCE DISPOSITION

the idea and have a wide latitude of acceptance for plans that help achieve this goal. You might ask this audience not only to support your policy but also to help you with a campaign to build support on campus. Campus food service officials would probably constitute a hostile audience with a narrower latitude of acceptance because they are comfortable working with their existing food suppliers. For this audience, you would advocate a more limited thesis, such as switching to a few local products on a trial basis. Finally, students who rarely eat on campus would probably be a more neutral audience. You could convince them to sign a petition favoring more local products, but a request to give their time to work with you would probably fall outside their latitude of acceptance.

Accounting for Your Audience's Beliefs

Audience members' **beliefs**, or the facts about your topic that they consider to be true, will have a significant effect on their **attitude** (favorable or unfavorable feeling) toward your thesis. For example, suppose you want to persuade audience members to participate in study groups. Relevant beliefs include whether study groups raise student grades, whether there will be students available with matching schedules, and whether other group members will come prepared. If audience members believe that the answer to these questions is no, their attitude toward your topic is likely to be negative. In order to persuade the audience to participate, you can present credible evidence that these beliefs are inaccurate.

Appealing to Your Audience's Needs

Audience members have **needs**—objects they desire and feelings that must be satisfied. Human needs powerfully affect how we behave and how we respond to one another's ideas. As we note in Chapter 14, your message is more likely to succeed when it is relevant to the audience—that is, when it answers their question, "What's in it for me?"[7] Experts from previous eras, such as psychologist Abraham Maslow and social critic Vance Packard,[8] have identified specific sets of needs, which continue to be emphasized in many persuasive appeals.

By focusing on needs that are of concern to audience members, your speech will be more likely to persuade. For example, let's say you want to give a speech convincing your classmates to exercise more often. Exercise fulfills a variety of needs: it can improve people's health, help them perform better at work and in school, increase their self-esteem, mitigate the dangers that come with obesity, and (if done in a social setting) provide opportunities to forge friendships and meet romantic partners. You should determine which of these needs are most important to your audience and emphasize them in your main points and subpoints.

Connecting to Your Listeners' Values

Values are "core conceptions" of what is desirable for our own life and for society.[9] Each of us has values that guide how we live—for example, being helpful, honest, imaginative, or responsible. We also have ideas about what kind of society we want to live in, such as one that offers equality, freedom, happiness, peace, or security.[10] Because values play a central role in guiding our lives, adapting an argument to audience values is one of the most important considerations if your argument is going to be persuasive.[11]

A speech about airline safety provides examples of how a message can be tailored to audience values. Suppose you support more extensive security screening at airports. If national security is an important value for your listeners, you might establish how additional screening could reduce the risk of terrorist attacks on airplanes. On the other hand, suppose you want to persuade your audience that screening is overdone. If punctuality and privacy are important audience values, you could build a strong argument by showing how existing screening practices take up too much time and invade passenger privacy.

Demonstrating How Your Audience Benefits

Audience members weigh the costs and benefits when they are deciding whether to take action in response to a persuasive appeal.[12] They are most likely to support your proposal when you show how they will benefit from doing so and when they feel that the costs involved are minimal—or, at the very least, worth the benefits. For example, one student asking audience members to volunteer their time reading to young children at the campus day-care center emphasized such benefits as sharing stories from students' cultures, earning academic credit for community service, and feeling joy from interacting with young children. She also noted that because the day-care center was right on campus and offered flexible schedules, the sacrifice required was minimal.

Explaining how the costs are low can be particularly important when your listeners are seriously considering your proposal. If this is the case, they probably already recognize the benefits of taking the action you

VALUES GUIDE AUDIENCE JUDGMENTS

advocate. Showing audience members that your proposal has limited disadvantages can be the final step in gaining their support.[13]

Acknowledging Listeners' Reservations

In analyzing your audience, you may discover reasons why your listeners are opposed to your thesis or at least uncommitted or neutral toward it. To address these reservations, consider using a **two-sided argument**. In a two-sided argument, you briefly note an argument *against* your thesis and then use reasoning and evidence to refute that argument.

For example, recall Michelle's idea from the beginning of this chapter—she proposed that her sorority should set aside time for meditation. If her audience analysis revealed that many of her sisters believed they were too busy to commit, she could begin a two-sided argument by noting that the lack of time for meditation is a very reasonable concern for busy college students. Then she could cite evidence that people who meditate actually save time by being more focused and productive.[14]

MAKING A TWO-SIDED ARGUMENT

STEP 1: ACKNOWLEDGE THE
         OPPOSING VIEWPOINT

"I know many of you think that you don't need to wear a seat belt if you've got an airbag, and indeed, an airbag can help protect you in a head-on collision."

STEP 2: REFUTE THE OPPOSING
         ARGUMENT USING REASONING
         AND EVIDENCE

"However, research shows that airbags don't help you in a side or rear crash, only your seat belt can do that—so be safe and buckle up."

A well-presented two-sided argument can help change audience members' attitudes in favor of your thesis and strengthen your credibility.[15] This is because people are more likely to support an idea if they know that its proponent is sensitive to their concerns and understands their views.

BUILDING BLOCKS OF PERSUASION

Now that we have discussed several methods for relating your message to the audience, let's consider three time-honored principles of persuasion—ethos, logos, and pathos. These three principles involve building your own credibility as a speaker, supporting your ideas with sound evidence and reasoning, and evoking audience members' emotions.

Ethos: Your Credibility as a Speaker

Since ancient times, people have recognized that a speaker with **ethos (credibility)** has far more persuasive power than one without. A credible speaker is seen as knowledgeable, honest, and genuinely interested in doing the right thing for his or her audience. But what is credibility, exactly? By taking a closer look at its elements, we can get a deeper understanding of this crucial persuasive tool.

Understanding the elements of credibility. The ancient Greek philosopher Aristotle believed that practical wisdom and virtue are major components of ethos. Modern communication scholars use the term **competence** to refer to practical wisdom and the word **trustworthiness** instead of *virtue*. When audience members perceive a speaker to be both competent (knowledgeable and experienced) about his or her subject and trustworthy (honest and fair), they find it easier to believe the speaker's claims.[16]

Aristotle also urged public speakers to exhibit **goodwill** toward their audiences—by wanting what is best for their listeners rather than what would most benefit themselves.[17] According to contemporary researchers, speakers who exhibit goodwill understand their listeners' needs and feelings, empathize with their audiences' views (even if they don't share them), and respond quickly to others' communication.[18]

Building your credibility. When you're just starting out as a public speaker, your audience members may not immediately recognize your credibility. You will need to build your ethos through what you say during your speech—and how you say it. Here are some helpful strategies:

- Share your qualifications to speak on the subject.
- Present strong evidence from reputable sources.
- Highlight common ground with the audience.
- Choose words that demonstrate understanding of your listeners, and avoid language that your audience might find insensitive or offensive.
- Show respect for conflicting opinions.
- Practice your speech until your delivery is fluent.

Avoiding loss of your credibility. You have many strategies for enhancing your credibility during a speech. But there are just as many ways to make a misstep and erode your ethos while giving a talk. In your speeches, careful preparation can help you avoid credibility-draining mistakes. Here are some common sources of this type of error:

- *Getting your facts wrong.* Your competence and preparation will be questioned if you present factual information that is just plain inaccurate.

- *Pronouncing words incorrectly.* Your experience in a topic area will be questioned if you mispronounce the names of key persons or concepts related to the topic.
- *Failing to acknowledge potential conflicts of interest.* If audience members discover that you have a bias you failed to disclose, your credibility will be seriously damaged.
- *Stretching to find a connection with the audience.* Speakers can get into trouble when they attempt to adopt local or professional slang that they do not understand well or feign interest in audience members' favorite sports team.

Logos: The Evidence and Reasoning Behind Your Message

Reliable facts can further strengthen your credibility and help your audience members make well-informed decisions—key effects of ethical public speaking. When you present trustworthy facts to back your claims and clearly show how those facts have led you to those claims, you use **logos** effectively. In this section, we discuss how to use evidence and reasoning to build a persuasive message. We also discuss how to avoid several common examples of **fallacies** (faulty arguments).

Using evidence. When your audience analysis suggests that listeners may not accept a claim you want to make, you will need to supply proof. One of the best ways to do that is to research evidence from credible sources (see Chapter 13). To use evidence persuasively, apply the following principles:

- *Identify your sources and their qualifications.* Indicate who your source is each time you present evidence, along with his or her qualifications. To ensure your sources' credibility, use facts presented by unbiased experts.[19]

- *Give listeners new evidence.* Use audience analysis to determine what evidence is likely to be new to your listeners. Facts that they're not yet familiar with are more likely to increase their perceptions of your credibility.[20]

- *Provide precise evidence.* Precise evidence consists of specific dates, places, numbers, and other facts. Here's an example of this kind of precision:

  > According to Alyssa Lederer and Susan Middlestadt of the Department of Applied Health Science at Indiana University, "stress was identified as the number one impediment to academic success for college students nationally, with 27.5%

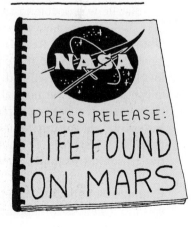

THIS JUST IN...

PRESS RELEASE:
LIFE FOUND
ON MARS

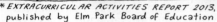

EXTRACURRICULAR ACTIVITIES REPORT 2013, published by Elm Park Board of Education

reporting that stress has negatively impacted their academic performance in the last 12 months."[21]

This citation provides a specific percentage as well as the lead researcher's name and affiliation.

- *Look for compelling evidence.* Audiences are more likely to be persuaded by compelling evidence that includes concrete or detailed examples. Such evidence engages listeners' senses, helps them visualize the point you're presenting, and increases the likelihood that they will remember the information.[22] In the previous example of a speech about college student stress, a speaker might include a compelling anecdote about a student who experienced so much stress that he was unable to study, go to class, or even relax with friends.

Using reasoning. **Reasoning** is the line of thought that connects the facts you present and the conclusions that you draw from those facts. In Chapter 2, we discussed how perceptions of others are formed by taking the details we note about a person and making further assumptions about his or her characteristics. Persuasive speakers typically use **inductive reasoning**, which follows a similar process of generalizing from facts, instances, or examples. Here we discuss four types of inductive reasoning: example, comparison, sign, and causal.[23]

Example Reasoning. When you use **example reasoning**, you present specific instances to support a general claim. Your goal is to persuade the audience that your examples supply sufficient proof of your claim.

For instance, here's how you could use example reasoning to argue that endangered species are making a comeback:

> The Fortymile caribou herd reached a low of 5,000 members in Alaska and the Yukon in 1976. Now, the herd exceeds 46,000 and is growing in range.[24] In California, the breeding population of peregrine falcons has greatly expanded. From a low of two known pairs in the 1970s, there are now active nests in 40 counties.[25] And there are now more than 9,700 breeding pairs of bald eagles in the lower 48 states, far more than the 487 pairs in 1963.[26]

To use example reasoning skillfully, be sure to provide enough instances to persuade your audience that your general claim is reasonable. The more examples you can find, the more confident you can be that your claim is correct.

Of course, in a short speech, you may only have time to present a few examples to back up your argument. In this situation, you'll need to choose the most **representative examples**—that is, examples that

REPRESENTATIVE EXAMPLES

We PEREGRINE FALCONS are enjoying life in California.

We BALD EAGLES are thriving in Maine and North Carolina and...

We CARIBOU are doing well in Alaska.

We PANTHERS are fine in Florida.

CLAIM: FORMERLY ENDANGERED SPECIES ARE THRIVING ACROSS THE U.S.A.

NONREPRESENTATIVE EXAMPLES

We PANTHERS are fine in Florida.

We RED WOLVES are happy in Florida.

We MANATEES are mellow in Florida.

We WHOOPING CRANES are making whoopee in Florida.

CLAIM: FORMERLY ENDANGERED SPECIES ARE THRIVING ACROSS THE U.S.A.

are typical of the class that they represent. To illustrate, if you wanted to present an even more compelling case that endangered species are making a comeback, you should cite different types of species that come from a variety of regions in North America.

Comparison Reasoning. When you use **comparison reasoning** (also known as **analogy reasoning**), you argue that two instances are similar, so that what you know is true for one instance is likely to be true for the other. For example, if you argue that long-term prohibition of marijuana cannot succeed because prohibition of alcohol failed, you would be using this type of reasoning.

For comparison reasoning to work, your audience must agree (or be persuaded) that the two instances are in fact comparable. To illustrate, suppose you can show that marijuana use is similar to alcohol use and that current marijuana law closely resembles earlier alcohol prohibition. By emphasizing these similarities, you can make a more convincing argument that marijuana prohibition will likely fail.

Robert Zubrin, president of the Mars Society (a nonprofit organization), used an analogy to support a proposal to establish a human colony on Mars. He contended that "the frontier environment on Mars will serve as an incubator of innovation, just as it did on the United States," because "you typically have a severe labor shortage and an extremely challenging environment, and so you're forced to innovate."[27]

How strong is this argument about innovation? It would depend on how comparable the circumstances on the American frontier were to the circumstances colonists would face on the red planet in current times. Would the natural resources required for innovation be available on Mars? How would shipping needed items to Mars compare to transporting goods to the frontier? Would the type of people chosen to fly to Mars and establish a settlement have the same interests and capabilities as the earlier pioneers who went west?

Sign Reasoning. When you use **sign reasoning**, you claim that a fact is true because indirect indicators (signs) are consistent with that fact. For example, you might claim that college students are facing serious financial challenges, as evidenced by students working longer hours.

This type of reasoning is most effective if you can cite multiple consistent signs of the fact that you are claiming. For instance, you could strengthen your claim that students' financial challenges are rising by also noting an increase in student loans and a higher rate of students dropping out of school. But as you're researching, look for signs that are *inconsistent* with your argument, too. If you discover that students are spending more money on entertainment and clothes, you may find it difficult to convince your audience that the signs prove that financial struggles are on the rise.

SIGNS THAT STUDENTS ARE FACING FINANCIAL CHALLENGES

Causal Reasoning. When you use **causal reasoning**, you argue that one event has caused another. For instance, you would be using causal reasoning if you claimed that helicopter parenting decreased college students' well-being. (Helicopter parents are highly involved in their child's lives—for example, expecting frequent phone calls or texts, monitoring their child's friendships, trying to solve conflicts with roommates, or calling a professor to try to get a grade changed).

One way to strengthen causal reasoning is to explain the link between cause and effect. For example, you might contend that college students with overinvolved parents may perceive that they are not competent because their parents are frequently second-guessing their decisions or taking actions on their behalf. They also do not develop the ability to take care of their own problems.[28] Another way to use causal reasoning effectively is to support the cause-effect link with evidence. For example, you might cite a study by Holly Schiffrin and her colleagues in the Psychology Department at the University of Mary Washington, which found that "students who reported having over-controlling parents reported significantly higher levels of depression and less satisfaction with life."[29]

Causal reasoning can be tricky, as it is easy to misinterpret the evidence or come to the wrong conclusion. We take a look at errors in causal reasoning and other common reasoning errors in the following section.

Avoiding logical fallacies. Reasoning is fallacious (faulty) when the link between your claim and supporting material is weak. Here we highlight some common fallacies that you'll want to avoid in your speeches.

Hasty Generalization. A **hasty generalization** occurs when a speaker bases a conclusion on limited or unrepresentative examples. For example, it would be fallacious to reason that jobs can be created in any city whose leaders put their mind to it based on the example of Austin, Texas. Austin has a number of unique job-creation advantages that other cities may not be able to match: it is the home of a first-rate university, a highly educated population, the state capitol, and a "robust venture capital scene."[30]

Causal Reasoning Errors. One common error in causal reasoning is the **post hoc fallacy**. This fallacy lies in the assumption that because one event followed another, the first event caused the second. In reality, there could be other factors involved; it might have even been a coincidence. This is why theories that claim that the stock market will go up or down

POST HOC FALLACY

depending on which conference wins the Super Bowl or the change in hemlines during a fashion season are flawed.

It is also important to watch out for **reversed causality**, in which speakers miss the fact that the effect is actually the cause. For example, a speaker might claim that playing violent video games causes crime because statistics show that kids who play such games are more likely to be involved in destructive activities. But this argument could have the link backward. Perhaps kids who have more violent tendencies are more likely to play violent video games.

Ad Populum Fallacy. You've committed the **ad populum (bandwagon) fallacy** if you assume that a statement ("young people are less politically active today than they were fifty years ago," "federal budget deficits cause unemployment," "gun control would reduce the murder rate") is true or false simply because a majority of people say it is.

The problem with basing the truth of a statement on the number of people who believe it is that most people have neither the expertise nor the time to conduct the research needed to arrive at an informed opinion about the big questions of the day. For this reason, it's best to avoid using public opinion polls to prove facts.

Straw Person Fallacy. You commit the **straw person fallacy** if you replace your opponent's real claim with a weaker claim you can more easily rebut. This weaker claim may sound relevant to the issue, but it is not; you're presenting it just because it is easy to knock down, like a person made out of straw.

During the 1999 impeachment trial of former U.S. president Bill Clinton, some of his defenders committed this fallacy when they argued that an extramarital affair is part of private life and not a sufficient justification for impeaching a president. However, Clinton's political opponents maintained that whether the president had an affair was irrelevant: the important thing was that he lied under oath, an action that *did* justify impeachment in their minds.

Slippery Slope Fallacy. You've fallen victim to the **slippery slope fallacy** if you argue against a policy because you assume (without proof) that it will lead to some second policy that is undesirable. Like the straw person fallacy, this type of argument distracts the audience from the real issue at hand. Here's one example of a slippery slope argument:

> We cannot expand background checks on gun purchases. That would lead us down the road to allowing the federal government to confiscate the guns of law-abiding citizens.

In this example, the speaker's argument is based on the assumption that background checks would lead to confiscation of guns. But no evidence is introduced to support that belief.

Pathos: Evoking Your Listener's Emotions

When used with ethos and logos, emotional appeals—known as **pathos**—help you put a human face on the problem you're addressing. When you stir your listener's feelings, you can enhance your persuasive power.

Indeed, some experts have referred to human emotions as "the primary motivating system of all activity."[31] Thus, providing a heartwarming example of a person who benefited greatly from taking an action you're recommending in your speech could be a compelling complement to statistical evidence indicating numbers of those who could benefit. An emotional appeal can be an effective, ethical component of a strong persuasive speech; however, these kinds of appeals can also be abused, so it is important to use them responsibly.

Using emotional appeals. Humans have the capacity to experience a wide range of emotions—including empathy, anger, shame, fear, and pity—and each of these feelings provides an opportunity to enhance your use of pathos in a persuasive speech. For example, you may elicit empathy with a narrative about a young child who is unable to gain access to a quality school, anger with a story about a ninety-five-year-old traveler who is subjected to enhanced airline security screening, or joy with an account of the successful results of a community service trip to help villagers dig a well in Central America.

A **fear appeal**—an argument that arouses fear in the minds of audience members—can be a particularly powerful form of pathos.[32] But to be effective, a fear appeal must demonstrate a serious threat to listeners' well-being.[33] And to be ethical, it must be based on accurate information and not exaggerated to make your argument sound more persuasive.

A fear appeal is also more likely to succeed if your audience members believe they have the power to remedy the problem you're describing.[34] Consider messages by National Park Rangers advocating safe storage of food in parks. The rangers provide statistics showing how often bears have broken into cars or tents when people have left food out. They augment these statistics with videos depicting bears smashing car windows and climbing inside the vehicles to get food. These images usually strike fear into viewers' hearts. But then the rangers show how easy it is to store food safely in lockers or bear-proof canisters. Because audience members realize they *can* readily adopt these practices, they do adopt them.

HOW A FEAR APPEAL SUCCEEDS

Effective *word choice* can also strengthen the power of an emotional appeal. When a speaker's language connects with the values and passions of audience members, the persuasive impact of a message is enhanced. Political consultants on both the right and the left carefully consider the exact words that are used to express an idea to voters. Emory University psychology and psychiatry professor Drew Westen notes that "every word we utter activates what neuroscientists call networks of association—interconnected sets of thoughts, memories and emotions."[35] (As noted in Chapter 2, these networks of association also form perceptions from stimuli we note about others.) The selection of metaphors, for instance, has significant influence in framing how audience members perceive an issue. For example, labeling participants in armed conflict as "freedom fighters" primes the listener to have a more favorable view of the cause for which they are fighting.[36] Referring to young undocumented adults who were brought to the United States as children as "DREAMers" primes the listener to associate these immigrants with the American dream.

While you are unlikely to be able to afford a high-priced political consultant to help you choose the words that will be most compelling to your classmates, you can use your audience analysis to inform the language you select. For example, in a classroom speech, Taja advocated moving the campus's print newspaper to an online-only format. Her audience analysis revealed that many students already read plenty of news and blogs online; however, these same students were concerned that losing the printed newspaper would break a long tradition and result in less reliable reporting. Thus, Taja argued that "the online format we all rely on today could not be a better match for the campus newspaper's long tradition of excellent reporting," framing the change as a move from one medium of communication to an even better one rather than a complete overhaul of the paper's tradition of excellence.

Ensuring ethical use of pathos.
As we've discussed, emotional appeals can be very effective. But emotional appeals can have a dark side, too. If you fail to establish a sound connection between your point and the emotion you are invoking, you may succeed in persuading some audience members, but your appeal will not be logical and will not be ethical. This is unacceptable. History is replete with persuaders who used pathos to achieve unethical and even horrific ends (witness Adolf Hitler's use of racist appeals and false statements to gain power in Nazi Germany). Emotional appeals should never be used to manipulate your audience.

UNETHICAL USE OF AN EMOTIONAL APPEAL

There are numerous examples of emotional appeals that are premised on "facts" that are blatantly untrue. Climate scientists lost credibility after inaccurately stating that the Himalayan glaciers, which feed many rivers in Asia, could melt by 2035.[37] Fear appeals that exaggerate the health consequences of drug use (such as claims that marijuana use is similar to playing Russian roulette) have rarely succeeded;[38] indeed, poorly substantiated claims may even have a boomerang effect.[39] To present a convincing emotional appeal and preserve your own ethos, you must substantiate the consequence you predict with credible evidence.

Ethical speakers must also ensure that the language they select accurately describes the ideas they are discussing. Though compelling word choice can be used as an ethical persuasion tool, it can also cross the line into manipulation, exaggeration, or untruth. The **loaded language fallacy** is committed when emotionally charged words convey meaning that cannot be supported by facts presented by the speaker. For example, one speaker opposing a proposal to tax sugar-sweetened beverages referred to the plan as a "healthy choice tax" and implied that consumers would pay sales tax on orange, apple, and grape juices, which are included in the Agriculture Department's guidelines for healthy eating.[40] The charge evoked anger in many audience members who agreed that taxing such healthy choices was absurd. The ethical problem was that the actual proposal only applied to sugar-sweetened fruit drinks, not to the 100 percent juices included in the guidelines.[41] Audience members were persuaded by the *loaded language* that described the proposal inaccurately, not by a credible argument against the true plan.

ORGANIZING YOUR PERSUASIVE SPEECH

In Chapter 14, we presented several patterns for organizing the main points in the body of your speech. In a persuasive speech, you want to choose a pattern that will clearly convey your message *and* maximize your persuasive impact. There are several patterns that are typically optimal for this rhetorical purpose.

Criteria-Application Pattern

A **criteria-application pattern** has two main points. One establishes standards for the value judgment you are making; the other applies those standards to the subject of your thesis. This pattern is commonly used for a thesis that advances a fact or value claim. Here is how you could use this pattern in a persuasive speech on the value of community service in college.

THESIS   Community service is a valuable part of the college experience

MAIN POINTS
  I. A college education should provide students with several benefits.
      A. New knowledge and skills
      B. Preparation for the workforce
      C. Participation in new experiences
      D. Clarification of students' values and their place in the world
  II. Community service provides college students with the opportunity to gain all these benefits.
      A. It leads to higher grade point averages and stronger communication skills.
      B. It provides valuable work experience and a chance to discover career interests.

CRITERIA–APPLICATION PATTERN

C. It offers an opportunity to experience new situations and work with people from diverse backgrounds.
D. It encourages students to consider their values and see how they can help society.

Categorical Pattern

In Chapter 14, we noted that in a categorical pattern, each main point represents a different but important aspect of your topic. You could use this pattern for a fact or value claim in which each main point reflects a different reason why you believe your claim to be true. Consider the following example for a persuasive speech contending that dinosaur extinction was caused by a giant meteor that hit the earth about 65 million years ago.

THESIS.   Dinosaur extinction was caused by a giant meteor.

MAIN POINTS
 I. Dust and debris kept most sunlight from reaching the earth.
 II. Severe climate change ravaged the earth.
 III. The food chain was significantly disrupted.

Monroe's Motivated Sequence

The **motivated sequence pattern** follows the stages of thinking that people go through while solving a problem or considering new ideas.[42] Developed by Alan Monroe over seventy years ago,[43] it continues to be a popular method for organizing persuasive speeches that advocate action by audience members. The five steps of the motivated sequence are as follows:

- *Attention*: Creating a willingness to listen to your message
- *Need*: Identifying one or more needs that are relevant to your audience
- *Satisfaction*: Showing how your proposal will fulfill the need(s) you identified
- *Visualization*: Helping listeners form a mental picture of the benefits of your proposal
- *Action*: Explaining and advocating the steps you want audience members to take

In addition to being a pattern that is used in persuasive speeches, you can probably identify television commercials in which the motivated sequence has been used. Following is an example of the five stages of a motivated sequence, taken from a speech encouraging students to study abroad.

MAIN POINTS

    I. *Attention*. Few members of our class are looking forward to final exams next month. Do you think it would be more exciting if your finals were happening in Rome, Beijing, or Buenos Aires?

    II. *Need*. Every member of this class plans to get a job after graduation. The job market is highly competitive.

    III. *Satisfaction*. Participation in our college's Study Abroad Program will strengthen your credentials in the job market. Employers report that they are more likely to hire a candidate with international experience.

    IV. *Visualization*. Imagine that you have returned to the United States after an amazing semester in Spain or Japan. At an interview for a great job, the interviewer asks if you have experience with other cultures. You answer yes, and see the interviewer's interest perk up. The next day, the company makes you an offer.

    V. *Action*. Attend an informational session on next year's Study Abroad Program in the Student Union next Wednesday. You can learn more

about the exciting options open to you, hear from past participants, and ask questions. After that, I hope you will decide to make Montreal, Mumbai, or Madrid your home next fall.

Problem-Cause-Solution Pattern

This pattern can be especially helpful if you are advocating a policy change by an organization or institution. It builds to the action you are advocating by noting the existence of a problem, identifying its cause, and finally presenting a solution that minimizes the problem. Following is an example of how a speaker might use this pattern in a persuasive speech advocating the installation of public bike racks near bus stops and train stations.

> **THESIS**   Our local government should install secure bike racks near heavily used bus stops and train stations.

MAIN POINTS

   I. *Problem*: Parking is scarce and traffic is congested near commuter bus stops and train stations in our county.

  II. *Cause*: Many suburban commuters who would take mass transit live more than a mile from the closest bus stop or train station.

 III. *Solution*: Providing secure bike racks will encourage alternative means of transportation to and from stops and stations, opening up parking spaces and alleviating traffic.

CHAPTER REVIEW

In this chapter, you learned about the nature of persuasive speeches, along with strategies for effectively crafting and organizing your message. There are two major attributes of persuasive speeches: they attempt to influence audience members' beliefs, attitudes, or actions, and they advocate fact, value, or policy claims.

Adapting to your audience is one important aspect of strategic discourse. You want to adapt to your audience's disposition and avoid a thesis that is outside the audience's latitude of acceptance. You also want to select arguments based on audience characteristics by relating your speech to their beliefs, needs, and values. In addition, you want to demonstrate how your audience will benefit by taking the action you are promoting. A two-sided argument can be very effective if the audience has reservations about your message.

Three primary building blocks of successful persuasion are ethos, logos, and pathos. Ethos refers to your own credibility as a speaker, which can be established through your competence on the topic, trustworthiness, and goodwill toward the audience. Logos refers to the use of strong evidence and reasoning to construct your supporting arguments. Pathos is invoked through effective and ethical emotional appeals.

To be understood, a persuasive speech must be well organized. For speeches advocating a fact or value claim, a criteria-application or categorical pattern is often effective. Two common approaches for policy claims or calls for action are the motivated sequence pattern and the problem-cause-solution pattern.

LaunchPad
macmillan learning

LaunchPad for *Let's Communicate* offers videos and encourages self-assessment through adaptive quizzing. Go to **launchpadworks.com** to get access to:

 LearningCurve
Adaptive Quizzes

 Video clips that help you understand human communication

Key Terms

persuasive speech 522

claim 523

fact claim 523

value claim 523

policy claim 524

strategic discourse 525

social judgment theory 526

latitude of acceptance 526

latitude of rejection 526

boomerang effect 526

ego involvement 526
beliefs 527
attitude 527
needs 527
values 528
two-sided argument 529
ethos (credibility) 530
competence 531
trustworthiness 531
goodwill 531
◉ logos 533
fallacies 533
reasoning 534
◉ inductive reasoning 534
example reasoning 534
representative examples 535

comparison (analogy)
  reasoning 536
sign reasoning 537
causal reasoning 538
◉ hasty generalization 538
post hoc fallacy 538
reversed causality 539
◉ ad populum (bandwagon)
  fallacy 539
straw person fallacy 539
◉ slippery slope fallacy 540
◉ pathos 540
fear appeal 541
loaded language fallacy 543
criteria-application pattern 544
motivated sequence pattern 546

Review Questions

1. Describe two characteristics of persuasive speaking.
2. Identify six strategies for tailoring your persuasive message to your audience.
3. Define *ethos*, *logos*, and *pathos*.
4. Identify some strategies for building credibility in your speech.
5. What are four types of inductive reasoning that you can use in a persuasive speech?
6. Identify four common patterns for organizing persuasive speeches.

Critical Thinking Questions

1. How is using strategic discourse different from sharing your opinion on an issue?
2. When your audience analysis suggests that audience members may not agree with some of the points you plan to make in your speech, how effective would your message be if you said nothing about opposing viewpoints? Why would a two-sided argument improve your chances of giving a successful persuasive speech?

3. What factors should be considered when determining the ideal mix of logical and emotional appeals for your persuasive speech?
4. Reflect on your position on a controversial issue in society. What evidence could persuade you to adopt a more neutral position or change your mind? Who is a credible source that could lead you to rethink your position? How can the answers to these questions help you in your efforts as a persuasive speaker?
5. As an audience member, how can you identify logical fallacies during a speech? How can you identify weak or misleading evidence?

Activities

1. Review the editorial page in several newspapers (these can be accessed online), and consider their attempts to persuade you. Identify fact, value, and policy claims, and discuss which persuasive strategies they appear to be using.
2. Select a thesis for a persuasive speech that advocates action by the audience. Then rewrite your thesis for three different audiences of your choosing. What aspects of your persuasive message changed, and why?
3. FactCheck.org is a nonpartisan organization that reviews political speeches, advertising, and commentary, and verifies the validity of the claims made in them. In groups of three or four, visit the website, and look at two recent postings. What logical fallacies do they identify? Write down credible sources of evidence that could be used to improve the arguments noted on the website.
4. In small groups, read an online argument written by an expert on a particular topic. Then read the comments written by the public on that same argument (these can usually be found at the bottom of the article). Compare the quality of evidence and reasoning used by the expert and members of the public.
5. Watch an episode of *The Daily Show*. Assess at least three comedic segments, and identify those that focus on pundits' and politicians' use of loaded language and fear appeals. Did you recognize any other fallacies that were exposed?

Apply Your Skills

Go to the illustration on page 520, which depicts the story from the beginning of Chapter 17 (a speaker struggling to persuade her sorority to meditate together twice per week). Working individually or in groups, create your own narrative of a scenario where a speaker was unable to persuade the audience.

Illustrate or write about the scenario. Using persuasive strategies from Chapter 17, discuss how that speaker could improve his or her prospects to convince the audience.

Study Plan

_____

_____

_____

_____

_____

_____

_____

_____

_____

_____

_____

_____

_____

_____

APPENDIX A
Job Interviews

Ned was a recent college graduate who returned home to live with his mother while looking for a job. He hoped to find a position that would allow him to become independent and move into his own place. Allen—a friend of his family—knew Ned was looking for work and offered to help get him a meeting with a new technology company that would soon be hiring.

Although Ned had worked part time in college, he'd never interviewed for a full-time position before. While starting a new job would require many of the skills we've previously discussed (interpersonal, group, inter-cultural, mediated), his first task was making a good impression on the hiring managers. Ned knew there were a lot of factors to con-sider for the interview—including what to prepare beforehand, what to bring, what to wear, how to act dur-ing the interview, and what to do after.

Job interviews are often not very long—the average one lasts just forty minutes.[1] But what you do in that time

can determine whether or not you are ultimately hired. In the following sections, we discuss what to do before, during, and after an interview to navigate it successfully.

PREPARING FOR YOUR JOB INTERVIEW

Finding a job is sometimes the product of things outside your control. For example, a chance resignation might lead to a last-minute job opening, or you might lose a job opportunity because there was already an in-house candidate for the position. However, if you are going to be successful, it's important to treat a job search—and the job interview that comes with it—as part of a process. As with most things, consistency is key. Preparing for the interview during your job search is critical, since it forces you to ask questions and come to some conclusions about what job you're seeking—and why. Preparing for the interview and practicing the interview techniques that work (while avoiding those that don't) can also help you come out of the interview with a real chance at the job. Finally, knowing what you should do *after* your interview can enhance your chances for getting the job as well as provide you with some takeaways for potential future interviews. Let's consider each of these in turn.

Got my suit, practiced my handshake, but... why do I want this job again?

General Questions

Before you actually apply for a specific job and interview for it, you will want to have considered some basic questions. Knowing the answers to these can shape your decisions about which employers to apply to and which interviews you expect to attend. These questions are general in nature because they are intended to encourage some reflection and introspection on your part. For example, you don't want to go into a job interview for a non-profit inner-city organization and then discover halfway through your interview that accumulating more income is important to you because of your sizable student loans. That is something you would want to consider *before* you invest your time (and your interviewer's) in this process. Here are some of these more general questions:

- *What matters most to you in a job?* If this is your first full-time job and you need to earn a living wage—what are you motivated by? Are you most interested in the largest paycheck possible? Do good employee benefits motivate you? Or are money and benefits secondary to the kind of work you aspire to do—meaning you would do this work for the experience even if it paid less? You may keep all these factors in mind as you search for a position, balancing pay, benefits, and interest level in the job.

- *What kind of company would you prefer to work for?* This might mean deciding between the private and the public sector, or between a for-profit and a nonprofit business. It may not surprise you to learn that millennials are very attracted to social causes and seek to link these with the kind of work they would like to do. One study observed that almost three-fourths of millennials want to make a difference in the world, and that more than half of them would take a 15 percent pay cut to work for a company with values like their own.[2] Many would be happy to work at a nonprofit company, and women in the study were twice as likely as men to indicate this preference.

- *Does where you work matter?* All things being otherwise equal for you, are you motivated by where you will do this work? Do you want to be in a big city or a smaller town? Would you prefer to live in a rural area? Do you want to live in a warm climate? Would you prefer to telecommute and work from home?

- *Do you see this job as a stepping-stone for what may become a career, or merely as your first job?* Ask people who have become accomplished and celebrated in their professions (for example, symphony conductors, movie directors, or even veterinarians) and many of them will tell you that they knew they wanted to do this job from a very young age. The late CBS *60 Minutes* reporter Bob Simon recently interviewed James Levine, music director of the Met in New York.[3] Simon asked him, "Was there ever a single moment when you weren't sure you wanted to devote your life to music?" Levine replied, "Never. I knew it was one of my earliest awarenesses, that I loved music, and it was what I was happiest

WRONG WAY TO PREPARE FOR GENERAL QUESTIONS

RIGHT WAY TO PREPARE FOR GENERAL QUESTIONS

doing, always." Are you looking for a job that will be the foundation of a long career? Or are you looking for a good first job—without any assumptions about how long you intend to stay?

If you are unsure of how to answer these and other questions, there are many helpful job search books you could use. One best-selling classic is *What Color Is Your Parachute?*, which comes out with a new edition each year.

Take Stock

In preparation for your job hunt, you will want to take stock of your own motives, qualifications, strengths, and weaknesses. Use the following questions as a starting place.

- *Why do you want this specific job?* What is it about this particular job that attracts you? Is it the chance to learn more about your field? The opportunity to get a solid start at a company you'd like to rise in? The positive working environment? Knowing the answer will help you address the question when it inevitably arises in the interview.

- *What makes you qualified for this job?* What types of experiences or parts of your educational background make you a good fit for this position? For example, many (but not all) communication majors often migrate into public relations jobs because of the communication component required for the work. Some will also have taken an internship—perhaps in a public relations firm—while in school. This combination is a good first step toward being qualified for the job. Again, knowing this answer will help you in the interview.

- *Why should this employer want you?* You already know why you want to work for the company and why you are qualified. Now put yourself in the shoes of your interviewer: Why should the company want you? And, more important, why you instead of somebody else? Before interviewing, it's important to consider what you will be able to bring to the employer or organization—in effect, what you have to offer. What makes you stand out from the list of applicants? Do you have unique qualifications? Do you have an unusual background or a combination of skills (for example, being bilingual) that may add value beyond the usual requirements for the job? Are you particularly detail oriented, hardworking, and passionate about the field? Being able to articulate your strengths will assist you greatly in the job interview. Also, have an answer ready for your greatest weakness—prospective employers often ask this. One strategy is to talk about a weakness you once had, then note how you overcame it.

Résumé

In most cases, you will need to submit a résumé for job postings. Make sure your résumé is up to date and also replete with truthful, verifiable information that shows your qualifications for this job. It's often smart to make a PDF of your résumé (if it is a Word document) to send in, to avoid any formatting issues that can arise in different versions of Word. There are plenty of resources that will show you how to create a résumé; books like *What Color Is Your Parachute?* will include this topic. Your résumé should include your educational background, relevant employment experience, specific job skills (if any), and contact information. If you are close to being hired, you will likely be asked for references, which can be given on a separate page. When going on an interview, bring several printed copies of both.

If you are sending this résumé in advance of being selected for an interview, you will also want to write a cover letter, which is a letter to a specific person at the company that describes your qualifications for the job. When working on a cover letter, try to figure out who you can specifically address your letter to by doing some online research. Job descriptions often say who you'll be reporting to, and you can go from there. You'll likely send both your résumé and your cover letter together, either as file attachments via e-mail or as uploads if you're using a job site. See Figures A-1 and A-2, which show examples of a résumé and a cover letter.

Social Media

Most interviewing opportunities occur because of *networking*—that is, reaching out to people in the field that you know, going on informational interviews, and making it clear to all your contacts (perhaps through social media sites) that you are on the hunt for a job in your field. You can interact with contacts your age on sites like Facebook, Twitter, and Pinterest—but for more professional acquaintances, you will want to connect with them on LinkedIn. Make sure your LinkedIn profile includes your recent résumé. Assume that your interviewers will be looking at this information in advance. Also be aware that interviewers will likely check out your social media presence (Facebook, Instagram, Twitter)—so make sure to limit access or (a better idea) remove photos or posts that could place you in a poor light with prospective employers.

Gene Kwan
240 Round Lane, Oakland, CA 94620
Cell: 510-326-0090
Email: Kwan@CSUEB.edu

Summary:
Motivated, fast-learning, and friendly sales associate with 4+ years of sales experience, earned while also going to school, seeks full-time position at software company.

Skills and Highlights:
- Software Product Knowledge
- Excellent Written Communication
- Self-Starter
- Accurate and Efficient
- Customer Service Focused
- Effective Pipeline Management

Experience:

Sales Associate   *September 2014 to Present*
Rest/Account Software, Inc., *Burlingame, CA*
- Responsible for territory extending from San Francisco to Palo Alto.
- Visited and established customer relationships with CFOs for 23 Rest Homes.
- Assisted customers with purchase of R/A software and upgrades.
- Mined customer base for referrals.

Sales Administrative Assistant   *January 2013 to August 2014*
Senior Horizons, Assisted Living, *Hayward, CA*
- Assisted sales associate with marketing, scheduling, and follow-up.
- Developed knowledge of assisted- and independent-living facilities for seniors.
- Conducted market study of all assisted- and independent-living facilities in Bay Area.

Sales Associate, Women's Department   *January 2012 to December 2012*
Saks Fifth Avenue, Outlet Center, *San Leandro, CA*
- Specialized in working with senior women for clothing.
- Developed skills at assessing their needs and finding the right clothing for a good price.
- Good customer service earned repeat customers.

Education:
- B.A., Communication Studies, Minor in Journalism (2015), California State University, East Bay

Figure A-1
Résumé example

Gene Kwan
240 Round Lane, Oakland, CA 94620
Cell: 510-326-0090
Email: Kwan@CSUEB.edu

July 22, 2016

Roger Murtagh
Director of Human Resources
Xenox Software Inc.
30000 Hillside Road, Suite 404
Palo Alto, CA 94089

Dear Mr. Murtagh:

I am a recent university graduate and an experienced salesperson with interest in your posting for a sales associate. I believe that I possess the experience, knowledge, and special skill set to make a valuable addition to your company.

As my résumé will indicate, I possess more than four years of experience in sales, the last of which has been specific to software as a sales associate. My professional history includes work as a sales associate at Rest/Account Software Inc., as a sales administrative assistant (supporting a sales associate) at Senior Horizons, and as a sales associate for Saks Fifth Avenue.

My current position with Rest/Account Software has helped provide me with the experience and skills you are seeking for your position. These include proficiency in selling software; excellent communication skills; responsibility for a large territory; creation and maintenance of a book of customer business by following up with leads, prospects, and customers; and ability to effectively manage a pipeline of leads and referrals to maintain a steady number of customers.

I have attached my résumé for your review, and I look forward to the opportunity to discuss this position with you. Having just graduated from CSUEB, I am planning to be in your area at the end of next week and would be available to meet with you then, if it is convenient for you. I look forward to discussing how I can benefit your sales team.

Sincerely,

Gene Kwan

Gene Kwan

Figure A-2
Cover letter example

Homework

Depending on the type of work this employer does and how large it is, you can likely get more information in advance by looking through the company's website and Twitter feed, and entering the organization's name in a search engine to find industry-specific news involving the company. As you read through this information, look to answer these questions: Is this a private business or a nonprofit? What is its mission statement? If it is a for-profit business, is it publicly traded? What is the company's reputation? Has it been in the news? What, if any, are its recent stated initiatives, and how could you offer your skills? In addition to the company itself, who are its major players? If you know the name of the interviewer, does he or she have a LinkedIn page? What career path did the interviewer take to get to his or her position? The information you dig up can help you form thoughtful questions when your interviewer inevitably asks, "Do you have any questions for me?"

Practice

As the old adage goes, "Practice makes perfect!" As the day for your interview nears, try practicing with a friend, roommate, or loved one.

For this practice, give your partner the questions you assume the real interviewer will ask about you and your background. Since interviewers often ask the same types of questions (look to your job book or reputable career sites), practice answering these questions until you can do so confidently. When answering, try to showcase your skills and achievements and what would make you a good fit for the company. If you don't have someone to practice with, you can try standing before a mirror—or, better yet, tape yourself with a smartphone, a computer, or another recording device, and then review your performance to see if you come across as confident in the interview.

Attire and Appearance

First impressions are lasting impressions. For that reason, consider how you will appear when the interviewer—your potential employer—first sees you. We advise that you err on the side of dressing up rather than dressing too casually.

Remember Ned, the young man who applied for a job in the introduction to this chapter? This is a real story—and, as it turned out, he did not get the job after his interview. Later, he got the feedback that he'd dressed too casually for the interview. Ned was surprised to hear this. When researching the company, he'd noticed that the employees wore dress shirts and blue jeans. His interviewer—the president of the company—was even dressed this way when they talked. But the president reported back that Ned didn't seem as though he was auditioning for the job—and that his appearance made it look as if he assumed he already had the job. From then on, Ned wore a blazer, slacks, and a tie to each interview—no matter how casual the other employees were dressed.

For men, an interview outfit likely means a suit and tie. If you are looking to build a business casual wardrobe, you would probably want the following items: a good dark blue or gray suit, one blue blazer, two pairs of good quality slacks (brown, tan, or gray), several dress shirts, several ties, and at least one pair of polished black leather shoes. Also invest in one large good-quality umbrella and quality razor blades that you change every few days. For women, an interview outfit might mean a suit or a dress and blazer. If you're applying for a creative position, you could add a colorful scarf or interesting jewelry. For a business casual wardrobe, you might consider a suit, skirts, blouses, slacks, a few nice dresses, and quality shoes (oxfords, flats, heels, and so on). It goes

WHO DO YOU THINK THE BOSS WOULD HIRE? WHY?

without saying that every interviewee should make sure that he or she is properly bathed and groomed.

DURING THE JOB INTERVIEW

If you've made it to the interviewing stage—congratulations! In this section, we share some clear guidelines both to help advance your application for the job and to avoid sabotaging your chances for the same.

Levels of Interviews

For many companies, the HR manager will first do phone interviews to screen out candidates immediately. During this interview, it's necessary to sound lively and relaxed—so make sure to call from a quiet and uninterrupted place. Also make sure to have your résumé and any other pertinent material in front of you.

It's also possible that your initial interview might be via Skype or a company-specific videoconferencing service. If so, make sure you appear in the center of the screen and otherwise comport yourself nonverbally and verbally as if you were in the same room with your interviewer. If you clear these initial interviews, you might meet face-to-face with the hiring manager. On that or a subsequent interview, you might meet other people in the group. You might also meet your possible supervisor's supervisor—but only if you are getting close to the job! Make sure to know or make note of everyone's names (be sure to get their business cards), and bring extra copies of your résumé.

In certain instances, your interview may occur over a meal. Interviewers and prospective employers sometimes do this to see how you interact and socialize in a nonwork environment. These interviews can appear to be less formal—but rest assured, you are still being evaluated. Heed the following tips. First, avoid ordering the most expensive meal on the menu—especially if it is unclear whether you'll pay for your meal or whether your interviewer will pay. Picking something expensive is disrespectful to your host and suggests that you may be cavalier about spending the company's money as an employee. Wait to see what others order, and take your cue from them. If you are still uncertain, it is better to err on the side of choosing something simple and modestly priced. Second, and equally important, if you are over twenty-one, avoid ordering alcohol—especially if your interview meal is for lunch. Employers may be testing to see if new recruits drink during the day—a definite red flag, since that would mean returning to work potentially inebriated.

Third, relax during the meal, but do try to observe the customs for polite conversation at the table—for example, don't talk with your mouth full, and avoid making any potentially inappropriate comments. Instead, be friendly and forthcoming—and communicate that you would be the sort of employee that they would not only be happy to hire but also be happy to take a lunch break with!

Be Prepared

Being punctual leaves a positive first impression. In certain companies, potential employers immediately screen out any late arrivals. We'd suggest doing a practice run before the day of the interview to figure out how long it really takes to get to the building, along with the parking situation. Here you will want to be prepared to answer those basic questions we mentioned previously: (1) Why are you seeking this job with this employer? (2) Why should this employer pick you/What do you have to offer? and (3) In what specific ways are you qualified or experienced? Most common interview questions boil down to these underlying questions. Often these common questions include the following:[4]

- Tell me about yourself.
- What interests you about this job?
- What do you know about our company so far?

On the day of the interview, make sure you get there early—you can always stop at a nearby coffee shop or café beforehand and review your notes on the company. Also, be sure to bring extra copies of your résumé in case multiple people participate in asking you questions. Bring a professional portfolio of your work if you're applying for a creative job.

Act Confident

Remember the chapter on nonverbal communication (Chapter 4)? Most interviewers will understand that you'll be a little nervous, but there are certain nonverbal tricks you can use to project confidence. When greeting each interviewer, shake hands (if the person offers), and do so firmly—like you mean it. Maintain good eye contact throughout the interview, and sit up straight (sitting on the edge of your seat may help). Also, be enthusiastic about the job; if you've done your homework and think that you'd be a good fit for the position, let that passion and interest shine through.

Be a Good Listener

A good interview is a conversation—meaning that you will both talk and listen to your interviewer. Avoid listening in ways that are interruptive, superficial, argumentative, or defeated (see Chapter 5). Instead, listen interactively—maintaining eye contact, nodding, and occasionally asking questions. It's often a good idea to bring a small note pad to take notes on, but don't try to capture everything your interviewer says. Review your notes later, and perhaps mention some of the topics in your thank-you note.

Advocate Honestly

When you do answer questions, always tell the truth. Now is not the time to exaggerate entries on your résumé or any experience you've had. Assume that everything you say or claim may be something the interviewers will try to verify, through your references or by other means.

When asked to explain your qualifications or why you think you may be a good fit for the position, be careful to incorporate your résumé. Focus on explaining how your education, previous work experience, or skill set fit the requirements of the position perfectly. This is where you should be a strong and confident advocate for yourself.

At the same time, make sure that you are learning as much about the company as the interviewer is learning about you. With more information about the position and the work environment, you will be better equipped to evaluate whether this job is a good fit for you. If you are being honest about yourself and your qualifications, maybe you will learn that the job is not what you imagined and wanted. In that case, it's better to know at this stage rather than after you've been hired.

Wrapping Up

Toward the end of the interview, you will likely be asked if you have any questions. Always have a question or two ready—this shows engagement and that you're eager to learn more. You will likely have even more questions, based on your conversation with your interviewer. Be sure to listen to the answers and to jot down notes based on your interviewer's replies. This final question may exponentially help your chances of making it to the next round: "Do you have *any* questions about my qualifications or ability to do the job?" If your interviewer has any hesitations,

he or she will bring them up, thereby giving you an opportunity to alleviate any concerns.

Here are some other questions you could ask your interviewer:

1. Could you please describe what a typical day in this position would look like?

2. How would you describe the culture in this workplace? What type of person really thrives and does well in this culture? What type has more of a challenge?

3. How would the success of a person in this job be measured?

4. If you think back to an individual who did this job very well, what made his or her performance outstanding?

5. Could you share your timeline for getting back to candidates about next steps in the process?

When the interview is over, be respectful of your interviewer's time and take his or her cue to wrap things up. If a hand is offered again, shake it firmly with good eye contact. Be sure to thank your interviewer for the opportunity to meet with him or her.

What to Avoid

Now that we've given you some pointers, let's consider a few things to avoid. First, although we advise you to be confident while interviewing, avoid falling into the trap of trying to oversell yourself or bragging—traits an interviewer may interpret as conceit or the product of desperation. Instead, aim for balance: become a positive advocate for yourself, and project confidence and enthusiasm—but not arrogance. When practicing with a friend, ask how you are coming across. On a related note, be sure to avoid bad-mouthing any former employers (if you've worked in the past), any instructors you've taken classes with, and so on. Even if you've had a bad experience, the hiring manager may see you as a negative or disloyal person, which would set off a red flag against your hire.

Second, remember that you do not have to answer every question—particularly those that are inappropriate or illegal (for example, questions about your marital status, dating life, ethnicity or heritage, sexuality, political affiliation, age, or religious beliefs). Although it is tempting to simply suggest that you might not want to work for someone who would ask such questions, we would counsel you to avoid rushing to judgment about your interviewer's motivations for these questions—and the bias they may suggest. Although some interviewers may indeed be expressing conscious or unconscious bias (prejudice), it is possible that you are dealing with someone who is unaware of the law and is simply acting out of ignorance.

Assuming you want to stay in the interview at this point, you are well within your rights to observe that personal questions about your background (for example, your ethnicity or sexuality) are not the usual or appropriate questions for an interview—and thus you are assuming that this is not what the interviewer meant by his or her question, even if it came out that way. Let a moment pass to allow the interviewer a chance to recover and hopefully to quickly agree with you and refocus the question. If he or she persists in this line of inappropriate questioning and you are uncomfortable, don't be afraid to decline to answer or

WHAT TO AVOID

simply terminate the interview. Although you want and may need a job, you also have rights in this situation.

Third, do not raise the subject of your salary in the first interview—unless the interviewer brings it up first. Ideally, you should hold off on this topic for as long as possible—until the employer makes you an offer. You should also avoid naming a number if possible, since you might pick a number that's lower than what might have been offered. If an interviewer does bring this up early on, you can either attempt to deflect ("I'd be happy to discuss salary after we've discussed the specifics of the job"—since the specifics *would* affect the salary you'd expect) or offer the higher end of a range based on research you've done beforehand.

Finally, and this should go without saying, avoid making inappropriate jokes or comments—or even ones that might be misconstrued as inappropriate. Even if you feel comfortable with an interviewer, or if he or she is your age, you should maintain a professional demeanor. Imagine that your saintly grandmother is listening to the interview; if you would be embarrassed to say something in front of her, you should definitely not say it in the interview.

AFTER THE INTERVIEW

Once the interview is over, it's not yet complete. Here are a few more things you can do to help your chances for getting the job.

Exercise Patience

In a strong economy with lots of employment opportunities, it is likely that you will have to interview for multiple jobs before being offered one of them. In a recession or down economy, that number of interviews only gets larger. Instead of becoming discouraged, remain patient and understand that you should be prepared to keep interviewing, even as you wait to hear about one of the interviews. At the same time, understand that it may take a little time for the interviewer to respond. For example, it can take from twenty-four hours to two weeks for a company to respond after a job interview.[5]

Figure A-3

July 29, 2016

Dear Mr. Murtagh:

I know your time is extremely valuable, and I wanted to express my appreciation that you took the time to meet with me and discuss the Sales Associate position with Xenox Software. As I indicated in our meeting, I believe I am extremely well-qualified for this position and would very much welcome the opportunity to join your team. Please don't hesitate to contact me if you have any other questions. Thank you for your consideration in this matter.

Regards,

Gene Kwan

Thank-You Notes

In the modern era, you can send a note of thanks to each of your interviewers via an e-mail message. We also recommend sending a handwritten note in a card or letter (even if you've already sent an e-mail). Both are acceptable, but a handwritten note will set you apart from the crowd, demonstrating a more personal touch—as well as more effort—on your part. It will also help prospective employers remember you when they receive the card a few days later. Sending a handwritten note leaves a strong impression. Don't forget to ask each interviewer for a business card before you leave the meeting; the card will likely have both an e-mail address and a regular mailing address for you to use. If there's no mailing address, look the address up online or call the front desk and ask. See Figure A-3 for an example of a thank-you note.

Follow Up

If you were asked to provide supplemental material, e-mail (or mail, if asked) it as quickly as possible. If you have not received a response, follow up with an e-mail every few days, politely checking in. If you don't hear back from your e-mails, consider a quick phone call to make sure everything was received. If you interviewed weeks ago and haven't heard anything, you can send a polite e-mail checking in. You could say something like, "I wanted to thank you again for meeting with me on [date] and to ask if there have been any updates on the position. If you need any further information from me, please let me know."

Take Notes

Every interview is an opportunity to learn. After each one, make some notes in which you share your impressions of the interview—that is, what went right and what you might have done better. Use this information to perfect your interviewing skills, and remember that it might take a few (or more) interviews before you land a job. You will likely find yourself interviewing throughout your life—and past experience can be a very good guide for future job hunts!

APPENDIX B
Sample Speeches

◉ EXTRA CREDIT YOU CAN LIVE WITHOUT
(Persuasive)

Anna Martinez
California State University–Fresno

Anna Martinez selected student credit card debt as the topic of her persuasive speech. Based on her survey of the audience, she determined that it would not be feasible to argue that students should not use credit cards. She selected a different thesis that was within their latitude of acceptance: to encourage students to be more careful credit card consumers.

Anna's speech is targeted to an audience of college students, and she refers to information gleaned from her survey to support her points. Anna consistently uses evidence to support her claims. She has a clearly organized speech in a problem-cause-solution format.

Watch the video for this speech in LaunchPad.

There is a dangerous product on our campus. It is marketed on tables outside the student union and advertised on the bulletin board in this classroom. Based on my audience

> Credit card debt on campus is a significant and growing problem...

survey, it is likely that most of you have this product in your possession right now. By the end of my speech, this product may be costing you more than it is right now. The dangerous product is credit cards.

Suspense-building attention-getter

Today, I would like to discuss the problems created by college students' credit cards and hopefully persuade you to be a careful credit card consumer. If your credit card situation is anything like mine—and over two-thirds of this class indicated that they are currently carrying a balance on one or more cards—take note: you can save money.

My husband and I paid for our own wedding. More accurately, we used our credit cards to charge many of our wedding expenses. And thanks to Visa, we are still paying for our wedding every month! We have saved money with some of the suggestions I will present today, and you can do the same.

Anna includes her thesis, connects with the audience, establishes credibility, and previews her main points

To that end, let's cover some of the problems created by students' credit card debt, then analyze causes of the problem, and finally consider steps you can take to be a careful credit card consumer.

We'll start with a look at the problems created by these "hazardous products."

Credit card debt on campus is a significant and growing problem. Many students have credit card debt. According to Matthew Scott in *Black Collegian*, April 2007, "College financial aid provider Nellie Mae reported that 76 percent of undergraduate students had credit cards in 2005, with an average balance of $2,169. An alarming 25 percent of undergraduates had credit card balances totaling $3,000 or more." In *Business Week*, September 5, 2007, Jessica Silver-Greenberg noted that "the freshman 15, a fleshy souvenir of beer and late-night pizza, is now taking on a new meaning, with some freshmen racking up more than $15,000 in credit card debt before they can legally drink." If you are not sure how your own balances compare, you are not alone. The previously mentioned Nellie Mae study found that the average balance reported by students was 47 percent lower than the average balance computed from data provided by credit bureaus.

Anna consistently uses research sources to support her points

High credit card use can change our lives for the worse. According to the April 2007 *Black Collegian* article, Rhonda Reynolds of Bernard Baruch College built up $8,000 worth of debt and was unable to make even the minimum payment. Her account went into collections. *Business Week*, March 15, 1999, provided another example. Jason Britton, a senior at Georgetown University, accumulated $21,000 in debt over four years on sixteen cards! Jason reports that "when I first started, my attitude was 'I'll get a job after college to pay off all my debt.'" Then he realized that he was in a hole because he could not meet the minimum monthly payments. He had to obtain financial assistance from his parents and now works three part-time jobs.

Supporting material: examples

You probably do not owe $20,000 on your credit cards, but even smaller balances take their toll. Robert Frick, associate editor for *Kiplinger's Personal Finance* magazine, March 1997, states that if you make the minimum payments on a $500 balance at an 18% interest rate, it will take over seven years to pay off the loan and cost $365 in interest.

High credit card debt can also haunt your finances after you graduate. Matthew Scott, previously cited, notes that credit bureaus assign you a credit score, which is "your economic report card to the rest of the world." That score will "determine the interest rates you pay for many forms of credit and insurance." He also notes that prospective employers will check your credit score and use that number to decide whether or not you are responsible.

Many people in this class are carrying student loans, which will need to be paid back upon graduation. When you add credit card debt to student loan payments, rent, utilities, food, that payment on the new car you want to buy, family expenses, etc., the toll can be heavy. Alan Blair, director of credit management for the New England Educational Loan Marketing Corporation, in a 1998 report on the corporation's website, noted serious consequences for students who cannot balance monthly expenses and debts, including "poor credit ratings,

Relating the problem to a college audience

inability to apply for car loans or a mortgage, collection activity, and at worst, a bankruptcy filing."

Don't let this happen to you. After all that hard work earning a degree and finally landing a job where you don't have to wear a plastic name tag and induce people to get "fries with that order," the last thing any of us need is to be spending our hard-earned money paying off debt, being turned down for loans, or, worse yet, being harassed by collection agencies.

Transition to main point II

Credit card debt is hazardous to students' financial health, so why are these debts piling up? Let's move on to the causes of this problem.

The reality is that credit card issuers want and aggressively seek the business of students like ourselves. As Jessica Silver-Greenberg writes in her previously cited September 2007 article, "Over the next month, as 17 million college students flood the nation's campuses, they will be greeted by swarms of credit-card marketers. Frisbees, T-shirts, and even iPods will be used as enticements to sign up, and marketing on the Web will reinforce the message."

Card issuers actually troll for customers on campus because student business is profitable. Daniel Eisenberg, writer of the column "Your Money" for *Time* magazine, September 28, 1998, notes that "college students are suckers for free stuff, and many are collecting extra credit cards and heavier debts as a result." Eisenberg refers to a U.S. Public Interest Research Group survey, which found that students who sign up for cards at campus tables in return for "gifts" typically carry higher unpaid balances than do other students. Jessica Silver-Greenberg, in an October 15, 2007, *Business Week* article, writes that "college kids are a potential gold mine—one of the few growing customer segments in the saturated credit-card market. And they're loyal, eventually taking three additional loans, on average, with the bank that gives them their first card."

Supporting material: explanation of why card issuers market to students

Companies use "sucker rates" to induce students to apply for credit. *Business Week*, March 15, 1999, wrote, "Credit card marketers may advertise a low annual percentage rate, but it often jumps substantially after three to nine months. First USA's student Visa has a 9.9% introductory rate that soars to 17.99% after five months. Teaser rates aren't unique to student cards, but a 1998 study by the Washington-based U.S. Public Interest Research Group found that 26% of college students found them misleading."

So it appears that credit card companies will not stop demanding student business any time soon. What can we do about it?

My proposed solution is to be a careful credit card consumer.

Why not get rid of your credit cards before it's too late? All right, maybe you won't go for that solution. My survey indicated that most of you enjoy the flexibility in spending that credit cards provide.

So here are some other ways you should be credit card smart. One practice is to shop carefully for the best credit card deals. The companies that are not spending their money giving away pizzas and iPods on campus may be able to offer you a better deal. In her September 7, 2007, *Business Week* article, Silver-Greenberg recommends that you beware of offers from South Dakota or Delaware corporations. Those states are "considered 'safe harbors' for credit card companies because they have no cap on interest rates or late payment [fees]."

A second solution is to read the fine print on credit card applications to learn what your actual interest rate will be. Alison Barros, a staff writer for the Lane Community College *Torch*, October 29, 1998, quoted Jonathan Woolworth, consumer protection director for the Oregon Public Interest Research Group, who wrote that "students need to read the fine print and find out how long those low interest rates last. Rates that are as low as 3% can jump to 18% within three months, and the credit card company doesn't want the student to know that."

Here is an example of the fine print on an ad that begins at 1.9% and soon rises. If you read the fine print, you note that the rate can rise to more than 20%.

Anna notes that her listeners are likely to reject her strongest suggestion, then advocates a solution within her audience's latitude of acceptance

Anna shows a visual aid here

Second and *third* are examples of signposts

Third, even if you can only make the minimum payment on your cards, pay your bills on time. Silver-Greenberg's September 5 article indicates that students' "credit scores can plunge particularly quickly, with one or two missed payments, because their track records are so short." She further cautions students to be aware of "universal default" provisions in their credit agreements—these provide that if you miss a payment on one card, other credit card companies can also raise your interest rate (even if you have paid those cards on time), perhaps to 30%. *Business Week*, March 15, 1999, cautions that "because students move often and may not get their mail forwarded quickly, bills can get lost. Then the students fall prey to late fees."

Adapting the solution to a college audience

Finally, you can keep money in your pocket and out of the credit card company's by paying attention to your credit report. If any agencies are talking trash about you with inaccurate information, be sure to have it corrected.

To sum up these solutions, even if you do not want to stop using credit cards, there are many ways to be a careful credit card consumer. Shop for a good rate, and be careful to read the fine print so you know what the rate really is. Know what you owe, and take the responsibility to make payments on time.

Internal summary of main point III

This morning, we have learned about a hazardous product on campus—credit cards. We have noted the problem of high student credit card debt, analyzed some of the causes of this problem, and considered several methods for being a careful credit card consumer.

Summary of main points

If your instructor offers you a chance for extra credit in his or her class, take advantage of the opportunity. But when a credit card issuer offers you a free T-shirt or phone card if you sign up for their extra credit, just say no. When you pay off a credit card with a 19.9% interest rate, that "free" T-shirt could turn out to be the most expensive clothing you will ever buy.

Clincher sums up Anna's speech with irony

◎ FREEGANISM: MORE THAN A FREE LUNCH
(Informative)

In this speech about an idea, DJ uses a categorical pattern to cover three elements of the topic: the nature of the freegan lifestyle, the beliefs of its participants, and some reservations about this way of life. DJ uses definitions and explanations to discuss the topic with audience members, who may not be too familiar with it.

Watch the video for this speech in LaunchPad.

How many people in this audience consider themselves—or know someone who is—vegetarian? How about vegan? If you're not familiar with veganism, it's the form of strict vegetarianism in which individuals do not eat food containing any animal products, including dairy, eggs, or honey. Although some vegans choose this dietary lifestyle for health reasons, most do so for ideological reasons, ranging from a commitment to animal

Rhetorical question to get audience's attention

rights to concerns about pollution resulting from animal farming. To many of you, this may seem like an extreme lifestyle choice. However, there are people who take things a step beyond veganism. How many of you are familiar with the term *freegan*?

According to the website Freegan.info, *freegan* is a combination of *free* and *vegan*. Freegans look for free products—from food to furniture—to minimize the impact of human consumerism on both the planet and other people. In fact, not all freegans are vegan; it is the "free" part that is key. Freegans oppose our consumer culture, in which we buy things we don't need and throw away things that are still usable.

During this presentation, I will introduce you to the freegan lifestyle—what the Freegan.info website defines as "living based on limited participation in" capitalism and "minimal consumption of resources." I will first describe a few of the ways that freegans try to minimize their use of resources, then discuss the reasons why some people choose to live this way, and finally explore some legitimate criticisms of the freegan lifestyle.

Preview of main
points

First, the heart of freeganism is a commitment to using fewer resources, and one way to do that is to throw away less trash. As reported in a 2007 article in the *New York Times*, the Environmental Protection Agency found that we throw away nearly 250 million tons of trash per year, which translates to over 4 pounds on average, per person, every single day. Two freegan practices—waste minimization and waste reclamation—specifically deal with trash and seek to reduce the amount of garbage Americans produce every year.

Many of us already support one of the tenets of freeganism—*waste minimization*—through recycling; hopefully everyone in this room today will take the time to throw their empty plastic water bottles and soda cans into a recycling container. But minimizing waste isn't just about recycling. Freegans also reuse everything they can, like using that old mayonnaise jar to hold pens and pencils instead of buying a specially designed pencil holder; this option reduces the demand for resources to make the specialty item and also eliminates the need for energy consumed during recycling.

Waste reclamation is just a formal term for what many of us know affectionately as "Dumpster diving." You've engaged in this truly free acquisition of items that other people have thrown away if you furnished your dorm or apartment with a chair or a bookcase that someone left on the curb or in a Dumpster. But would you consider making your meals out of what other people throw away? Freegans do. In his article on food waste, Robert Fireovid notes a U.S. Department of Agriculture finding: in 2008, the amount of food wasted by restaurants and stores averaged 275 pounds per American, not including what we throw away at home. For freegans, this is unnecessary waste, and so they will reclaim any still-edible food along with other household items. If you think it sounds gross to eat food that has been thrown away by someone else, there are certainly legitimate worries about illness from spoiled food. At the same time, recent research shows that a lot of the food thrown away by grocery stores, for example, is perfectly safe to eat. A 2013 report published by the Natural Resources Defense Council and the Harvard Law School Food Law and Policy Clinic noted that $900 million in food was thrown away by retailers in 2001 because the date listed on the product had expired. Those date labels often refer to the date until which the product will retain its highest quality, not necessarily the date after which the food is no longer safe to eat. That same report confirms that "the FDA's Center for Food Safety and Applied Nutrition (CFSAN) has noted that most foods, when kept in optimal storage conditions, are safe to eat and of acceptable quality for periods of time past the label date."

Yet even if freegans reclaim wasted food safely and are mindful of their health, *why* would people who could afford to buy food *choose* to dig it out of the trash? As defined at the beginning of my presentation, freegans try to avoid participating in capitalism, which they believe to be inherently exploitative. As the Freegan.info

DJ uses definitions and familiar examples to relate abstract concepts to his audience

DJ uses evidence to reinforce a point the audience may doubt—freegan food is safe to eat

Transition to second main point

website puts it, "Instead of avoiding the purchase of products from one bad company only to support another, we avoid buying anything to the greatest degree we are able." Although many health- and environmentally conscious people choose to shop at certain stores so that they can buy organic or fair-trade goods, freegans see even those efforts as problematic choices. Organic and fair-trade products still need to be shipped to stores, consuming fossil fuels and producing exhaust emissions in the process. And given the amount of food wasted unnecessarily in the United States, freegans feel an ethical obligation not to contribute to increased consumer demand when so much of the existing supply is already unused.

Despite their noble commitment to environmentalism and advocacy of a more humane economic system, freegans are not without critics. In some cities, Dumpster diving is illegal under municipal codes against trespassing and vandalism, although those laws are not often enforced against people "reclaiming" waste from Dumpsters, unless the divers create a mess or property owners actively seek to have anti-trespassing laws applied. Harsher objections come from critics who argue that the freegan lifestyle does little to help the truly impoverished and may literally take food out of their mouths. In the words of Jerry Adler in a 2007 *Newsweek* article, "The freegans, most of whom are educated and capable of contributing to the economy, aren't sharing the surplus wealth of the West with those who are destitute by circumstance rather than choice. They are competing with them for it." Given both the small number of Americans who choose to live as freegans and the enormous amount of food wasted in this country, freegans are not very likely to consume all of the still-edible food thrown away by stores and restaurants. But their small numbers also mean they are not likely to have a significant impact on the environmental and economic problems their freegan lifestyle hopes to combat.

During this speech, I have introduced you to the unfamiliar subculture of freegans in the United States.

Through their practices of waste minimization and waste reclamation, freegans hope to avoid the negative impacts of capitalist consumption on both the environment and people. Whether freegans are prophets of a better world or naive idealists living on other people's trash remains an open question, but I hope that the next time you see someone exploring a Dumpster behind a supermarket you remember that some people do so by choice rather than because it is their only option. And so I want to close by introducing you to one woman who made that choice.

As described in the 2007 *New York Times* article by Steven Kurutz, Madeline Nelson lived a life to which many of us aspire, making over $100,000 per year as a communication director for Barnes & Noble bookstores. Frustrated that her job and daily life continued to reinforce the rat race of buying "stuff" only to throw it away before buying more, in 2005 Ms. Nelson sold her posh Manhattan apartment in favor of a small place in Brooklyn and quit her corporate job so she could live as a freegan. When asked if she misses the extravagances that once filled her life, she responds, "Most people work 40-plus hours a week at jobs they don't like to buy things they don't need." We might not wish to become freegans ourselves, but Madeline's life is quite literally food for thought.

DJ uses a narrative as a clincher

▶ PREVENTING CYBERBULLYING (Persuasive)

In this speech, Elijah addresses cyberbullying, a growing problem in society. His first main point establishes the nature and extent of the problem, and his next two points address solutions—what steps can be taken to prevent cyberbullying and how to respond if you are a target of this behavior. As you read this speech, consider how Elijah relates the problem and solution to his college audience, provides evidence to support his main points, and uses compelling language to express his ideas.

You can watch Elijah present his speech by viewing the video in LaunchPad. This presentation is an example of mediated communication, meaning it was transmitted through a mechanical or an electronic medium. Rather than presenting the speech to his audience face-to-face, Elijah's instructor and classmates will view the speech online. As you watch the speech, consider some of the opportunities and challenges that speakers face when using this mode of communication.

Watch the video for this speech in LaunchPad.

On the evening of September 22, 2010, Rutgers University freshman Tyler Clementi updated his Facebook status: "Jumping off the gw [George Washington] bridge sorry." According to Lisa Foderaro's report in the *New York Times*, a few hours later Clementi did just that. But what would cause a bright student and talented musician with a promising future to take his own life? A bully with a webcam.

Compelling narrative to gain audience attention

According to a May 21, 2012, report on CNN, Clementi's roommate was sentenced to thirty days in jail, three years of probation, three hundred hours of community service, and $11,000 in restitution for using a webcam to view and transmit images of Clementi in an intimate encounter with another young man.

Tyler Clementi's story is tragic, but it's not an isolated event. On September 9, 2013, twelve-year-old Rebecca Sedwick jumped to her death after allegedly being tormented by two girls on Facebook. A few months earlier, Rehtaeh Parsons, a seventeen-year-old Canadian high school student, hanged herself after cell phone pictures of her being sexually assaulted were distributed by the alleged attackers. What is going on here? In a word— it's *cyberbullying.*

I'm here today to confront the growing problem of electronic harassment experienced by Tyler Clementi and so many others. I'll start with a look at the various forms cyberbullying takes, and describe the scope of the problem. But I'm not here just to talk about one more social ill; I want to show you how you and your loved ones can stay safe—both by scrupulously guarding your personal information and by actively thwarting cyberbullies. Finally, should you or someone you know become a victim, I want you to be able to respond constructively.

Elijah reveals his topic and previews his main points

As you can imagine from the heartbreaking story I've shared about Tyler Clementi, cyberbullying poses serious mental health risks to the nation's children, teens, and young adults.

Main point I: the problem of cyberbullying

The Cyberbullying Research Center, a leading resource on the topic, defines *cyberbullying* as "willful and repeated harm inflicted through the use of computers, cell phones, and other electronic devices."

Cyberbullying can take many forms, including posting or sending harassing messages via websites, blogs, or text messages; posting embarrassing or private photos of someone without their permission; recording or video-taping someone and sharing it without permission; and creating fake websites or social networking profiles in someone else's name to humiliate them. Often these acts are done anonymously.

Definition of cyberbullying, plus examples to help audience members understand the concept

Recent research paints a chilling picture of the frequency and harm of electronic harassment. According to Hani Morgan—an education professor at the University of Southern Mississippi—the statistics vary widely, but a 2011 report by the National Crime Prevention Council found that 43 percent of teens had been the victims of cyberbullying in the last year. Although most of the research to date has focused on cyberbullying among middle and high school students, a 2012 study published in the *Journal of School Violence* confirmed that the problem of electronic harassment continues into college. Psychologists Allison Schenk and William Fremouw found that nearly 9 percent of university students had experienced cyberbullying; that means that at least two or three people listening to this speech know what I'm describing because they've felt it.

Elijah uses credible evidence to indicate significance of the problem

Connects problem directly to audience

As we have seen with Tyler, Rebecca, Rehtaeh, and too many others, cyberbullying has tragically cut short promising lives. But consequences less dramatic than suicide take a serious toll on cyberbullying's victims. The same study by Schenk and Fremouw reported more symptoms of depression and anxiety, as well as difficulty concentrating, among bullied college students.

Transition to main point II

As Professor Morgan explains, the anonymity of unsigned messages and fake user names marks cyberbullying as a dangerous evolution of a long-standing face-to-face bullying problem, but you can take steps to protect yourself.

For one, you can be vigilant about safeguarding your personal information. Our school's information technology office lists the following advice on its website. First, never, ever, leave your laptops unattended. Second, keep

Use of signposts: first, second, third

your account passwords and Social Security numbers completely private. Third, use the most secure privacy settings on your social networking sites. Finally, think carefully about the types of pictures of yourself and your friends that you post online, and restrict views of them to "friends" only. Each of these steps can minimize opportunities for bullies to harm or embarrass you in some way.

Elijah provides specific audience-centered solutions backed by evidence

In addition to zealously guarding your personal information, you can help combat cyberbullying by being a voice against it whenever you see it happening. Several organizations have websites that provide information you can use to be part of the solution. The Facebook group Don't Stand By, Stand Up! is a student-led organization formed soon after Tyler Clementi's suicide. The group urges Internet users to take a stand against cyberbullying by recognizing that bullies—in all forms—rarely succeed in their harassment without the support and attention of bystanders. The National Crime Prevention Council website gives specific tips on how to thwart a bully's attempts. The first is to refuse to pass bullying messages along to others—whether via text or photo messaging, social networking, or e-mail—and to let the original sender know that you find the message offensive or stupid.

Transition to main point III

Despite your best efforts to keep your personal information private and speak out against cyberbullying, you may still become a victim.

Online safety expert Parry Aftab's website, Stopcyberbullying.org, advises victims to use the "stop, block, and tell" method to respond to bullying behaviors directed against them. Though often taught to younger children, this response makes sense in any case of cyberbullying. After receiving a bullying message, you should first stop. In other words, do nothing. Take five minutes to cool down, take a walk, breathe deeply, or do whatever will help to calm down the understandable anger you are feeling. Then, block: prevent the cyberbully from having any future communication with you. This may mean anything from removing him or her from your

"Stop, block, and tell" sums up advice in four words helps audience remember what to do

social networking site's "friends" list to having your cell phone service provider block the bully from being able to call or text you. The third step is to tell someone about the abuse without embarrassment or shame. For example, you might call campus security or confide in a counselor at the Health and Counseling Center—particularly if the abuse has been going on for a long time and you feel that your self-esteem or relationships have been affected. Similarly, parents of younger children should encourage their children to report any bullying to a trusted adult.

Today we've ventured into the very real—and very dangerous—world of cyberbullying. We've seen cyberbullying's negative impact on people of all ages. We've also seen how you can counter this potentially deadly problem by being vigilant about protecting your personal information and speaking out against cyberbullying. And if you or someone you know experiences cyberbullying, you can react constructively with the "stop, block, and tell" method.

Cyberbullying isn't just someone else's problem. It's very likely something you need to guard against now or in the future—as a student today or as a parent tomorrow. I urge each of you to make a personal commitment to do your part to combat the problem. Refuse to stay silent in the face of cyberbullying. Resolve that you will never send or pass along cyberbullying messages of any kind, no matter how harmless doing so might seem. This act alone can make a world of difference in the life of the intended victim. And wouldn't you want someone to take this simple step for you?

We must never forget Tyler Clementi and the other young lives cut short by unnecessary bullying. Who knows? Your best friend, your younger brother, or your son could just have easily been on that bridge that fateful September evening.

[margin annotations:]

Summary of main points

Clincher reinforces call to action, connects to compelling narrative from introduction

It may surprise you to learn that the last chocolate you ate may well have been tainted with child slavery.

◎ CHILD SLAVERY AND THE PRODUCTION OF CHOCOLATE
(Persuasive)

David Kruckenberg
Santiago Canyon College

Student David Kruckenberg presented this speech in the finals of the Phi Rho Pi National Tournament in 2007. David uses a problem-cause-solution format to address the compelling issue of child labor in the production of chocolate. He uses diverse reasoning strategies and consistently documents his claims with evidence. David's speech is well organized, with a clear preview and transitions between each main point. His audience-centered solution demonstrates how each of us can be personally involved in addressing the problem.

Watch the video for this speech in LaunchPad.

I was forced to stay in a large room with other children from a neighboring plantation. I tried to run away, but I was caught. As punishment they cut my feet; I had to work for weeks while my wounds healed.

Attention-getter: a shocking first-person quotation plus evidence that the problem is growing

This moving testimony may sound like past history, when slavery was prevalent. But these words are not a reminder of the past; they're found in the April 24, 2006, *Forbes* magazine. These are the words of an enslaved boy working in the cocoa fields of the country of Côte d'Ivoire, also known as the Ivory Coast. And he is not alone. UNICEF reports in February 2006 that child trafficking is on the rise in this African region.

It may surprise you to learn that the last chocolate you ate may well have been tainted with child slavery. Despite the promises and agreements made in recent years by chocolate companies, they continue to use child labor in the production of their chocolate. We as consumers must communicate that this is unacceptable.

David states his thesis and previews his main points

To do so, we will first reveal the connection between chocolate and child slavery, second, examine why the problem continues, and finally discover just how much power we have in bringing child slavery to an end.

Main point I: the link between chocolate and child slavery

How are chocolate and child slavery connected?

Cocoa bean production is limited to areas near the equator, such as Central America, Indonesia, and the Ivory Coast. The International Cocoa Initiative website, last updated February 8, 2007, explains that with almost a million acres devoted to growing cocoa, the Ivory Coast accounts for more than 40 percent of world cocoa production. According to a November 10, 2006, report by the *Vancouver Sun*, because growing cocoa is labor intensive, and labor is a significant part of the cost of production, many farmers in the Ivory Coast have turned to using forced child labor to cut costs.

The conditions of these children are beyond comprehension. The International Cocoa Initiative details the hazards they face each day: they must work long hours in the fields in brutal conditions. They clear fields with machetes and apply pesticides without protective gear. After harvesting the cocoa pods, they must split them open with heavy knives. Once the beans are dried and bagged, they must carry these large loads long distances on their young backs.

Even more alarming is just how many children are forced to live this life. The *New York Times* of

October 26, 2006, reports that more than 200,000 children in the Ivory Coast are forced to work in the cocoa fields. The *Chicago Tribune* of May 5, 2006, reports that in contrast to the rest of the world, this region of Africa has the highest rate of child laborers of all children five to fourteen years old; more than one in four are forced to work. EarthSave International, last updated February 14, 2007, says that these children are either enticed with promises of good wages and easy work or outright kidnapped. One example is a boy named Molique, who came to the Ivory Coast at the age of fourteen; despite the promises, he was never paid. When he asked to be paid, he was beaten. He had to scavenge for food and at night was locked up with the other kids. The *New York Times* of October 29, 2006, says that almost twelve thousand children in the Ivory Coast have been trafficked far from their families' homes and into slavery.

Combination of examples to build pathos and statistics to document the extent of the problem

The growing use of child slavery is reprehensible, but why is it allowed to continue? The answer is our widespread and growing demand for chocolate.

Transition to main point II: cause of the problem

Unfortunately, child slavery continues because our demand for chocolate continues, enabling the Ivory Coast and the chocolate companies to ignore the problem. Farmers in the Ivory Coast invest in cocoa for its large profits. In order to maximize their gain, they cut costs by using the forced labor of children. These 600,000 farmers then turn to large export companies in the Ivory Coast to buy their cocoa. The *New York Times* of October 26, 2006, reports that these export companies are able to keep the price that they pay for cocoa low because they have so many farmers to choose from. The exporters then sell their cocoa to large chocolate companies, such as Hershey's, Nestle, M&M/Mars, and Cadbury.

Causal reasoning

The *Calgary Herald* of November 17, 2006, tells us that in 2001, almost all of the big chocolate companies signed the Harkin-Engel Protocol, agreeing that by 2005 they would certify that their chocolate was not tainted with child slavery; however, this deadline passed two years ago, with the companies making excuses and saying they need more time. But the September 20, 2006,

Seattle Post-Intelligencer suggests that they're more concerned about the civil war in the Ivory Coast interfering with their supply of cocoa. Clearly the civil war is also the top priority with the Ivory Coast government. The Associated Press on June 15, 2006, explains that the government doesn't want to interfere with the supply of cocoa because export taxes are its primary source of revenue. The government uses this money to buy military arms and equipment. The Ivory Coast may not have blood diamonds, but [the nation] certainly possesses blood chocolate.

"Blood chocolate": a compelling analogy to blood diamonds

Ultimately, the blame rests on us, because consumer demand for chocolate keeps the industry insulated from pressure. The World Cocoa Foundation website, last updated February 14, 2007, tells us that North America and Europe consume nearly two-thirds of all cocoa products and that demand for confectionary products containing chocolate rises 4 to 5 percent each year. The sad truth is, most consumers are not aware of chocolate's connection to child slavery. Because we continue to buy its chocolate, the industry feels no urgency to change.

Transition to main point III: solution

Now that we understand the problem and why it continues, we must ask what we can do, and the answer is simple. We must stop buying slave-produced chocolate.

But don't worry, I'm not suggesting that we stop buying chocolate altogether. There is an alternative, and it's called fair trade chocolate. TransFair USA, a nonprofit organization, is the only independent third-party certifier of fair trade products in the United States. It allows companies to display the fair trade–certified label on products that meet strict standards. Some of these standards found on the organization's website, last updated November 16, 2006, include a prohibition on forced child labor, safe working conditions, living wages, environmentally safe farming methods, a guaranteed minimum price, and direct trade between the farmers and chocolate companies, thus eliminating the manipulative exporters.

Solution recognizes audience values: you don't need to give up eating chocolate to help

If we as consumers change how we buy chocolate, the industry will have to respond. Currently, companies are trying to distance themselves from the bad press associated with slave labor, and as a result the Ontario *Guelph Mercury*, February 3, 2007, reports that some have begun to buy into the fair trade market. For example, Business Wire, October 11, 2006, reports that Ben and Jerry's is expanding its fair trade–certified ice cream flavors. *Forbes* magazine, previously cited, says that fair trade has even made inroads into the Ivory Coast but still accounts for only about 1 percent of cocoa exports.

Economics teaches us that demand controls supply; they can only sell what we buy. A perfect example of this is the industry's response to the rise in demand for organic food products. The *Boston Herald* on October 16, 2006, reports that organic food sales have risen more than 15 percent in the last two years. According to the September 20, 2006, *Sacramento Bee*, with a multibillion-dollar market, big companies like Wal-Mart and Frito-Lay have made organic food mainstream. If we demand more fair trade chocolate, the industry will have to supply it, and when the chocolate companies start buying more slave-free cocoa, farmers in the Ivory Coast will have to abandon slavery to keep their buyers.

Causal argument shows how solution will reduce problem

Analogy to consumer-generated demand for organic products

Today we have exposed the connection between chocolate and child slavery, examined why the problem continues, and finally discovered how we can bring it to an end.

Summary of main points

The next time you go to buy chocolate, remember the words of a child, quoted in the November 10, 2006, *Toronto Star*: "When the rest of the world eats chocolate, they're eating my flesh." The Ivory Coast may be seven thousand miles away, but we have a responsibility to protect all children. Fair trade chocolate may cost us a little more money, but that's a small price to pay to free thousands of children from slavery.

Clincher includes another compelling quotation that connects to the introduction

NOTES

Chapter 1

1. Office of Adolescent Health, "Teen Media Use Part 1—Increasing and on the Move," November 2013, http://www.hhs.gov/ash/oah/news/e-updates/eupdate-nov-2013 .html.

2. F. E. X. Dance and C. Larson, *The Functions of Human Communication: A Theoretical Approach* (New York: Holt, Rinehart, and Winston, 1976), 171–92.

3. P. Watzlawick, J. H. Beavin, and D. D. Jackson, *Pragmatics of Human Communication: A Study of Interactional Patterns, Pathologies, and Paradoxes* (New York: W.W. Norton, 1967), 51–52.

4. S. J. Drucker and G. Gumpert, "Legal Geography: The Borders of Cyberlaw," in *Real Law@Virtual Space: Regulation in Cyberspace*, 2nd ed. (Cresskill, NJ: Hampton Press, 2005), 2.

5. www.naceweb.org/uploadedFiles/Pages/MyNACE/grab_and_go/students/job-outlook -2014-student-version.pdf.

6. National Association of Colleges and Employers, *Job Outlook 2015,* November 2014, 32.

7. S. Holtz, "The Evolution of the Social Media Manager," *Communication World* 31, no. 1 (2014): 9–11.

8. Center for Community College Student Engagement, *Making Connections: Dimensions of Student Engagement (2009 CCSSE Findings)* (Austin, TX: University of Texas at Austin, Community College Leadership Program, 2009).

9. M.-J. Tsai, "Rethinking Communicative Competence for Typical Speakers: An Integrated Approach to Its Nature and Assessment," *Pragmatics and Cognition* 21, no. 1 (2013): 168.

10. G. D. Bodie and others, "The Temporal Stability and Situational Contingency of Active-Empathic Listening," *Western Journal of Communication* 77, no. 2 (March 2013): 114.

11. C. M. Clark and others, "Is Empathy Effective for Customer Service? Evidence from Call Center Interactions," *Journal of Business and Technical Communication* 27, no. 2 (April 2013): 123–53.

12. E. Root and A. Ngampornchai, "'I Came Back as a New Human Being': Student Descriptions of Intercultural Competence Acquired through Education Abroad Experiences," *Journal of Studies in International Education* 17, no. 5 (November 2013): 513–32.

13. R. M. Berko, A. D. Wolvin, and D. R. Wolvin, *Communicating: A Social and Career Focus,* 3rd ed. (Boston: Houghton Mifflin, 1985), 42.

14. J. Stewart, *Bridges, Not Walls,* 7th ed. (New York: McGraw-Hill, 1999), 16.

15. P. Bizzell and B. Herzberg, *The Rhetorical Tradition* (Boston: Bedford/St. Martin's, 1990), 35.

16. A. Kornet, "The Truth about Lying," *Psychology Today,* May 1, 1997, www .psychologytoday.com/articles/199704/the-truth-about-lying.

17. R. Fournier and S. Quinton, "In Nothing We Trust: Americans Are Losing Faith in the Institutions That Made This Country Great," *National Journal,* April 26, 2012, www .nationaljournal.com/features/restoration-calls/in-nothing-we-trust-20120419.

18. National Communication Association, "NCA Credo for Ethical Communication," 1999, http://www.natcom.org/ethicalstatements/.

19. K. E. Roggensack and A. Sillars, "Agreement and Understanding about Honesty and Deception Rules in Romantic Relationships," *Journal of Social and Personal Relationships* 31, no. 2 (2014): 180.

20. L. Zhou, D. Zhang, and Y. Sung, "The Effects of Group Factors on Deception Detection Performance," *Small Group Research* 44, no. 3 (June 2013): 273.

21. G. R. Stone, *Perilous Times: Free Speech in Wartime from the Sedition Act of 1798 to the War on Terrorism* (New York: W.W. Norton, 2004), 516.

Chapter 2

1. P. R. Hinton, *The Psychology of Interpersonal Perception* (London: Routledge, 1993), 62.

2. Z. Kunda, *Social Cognition: Making Sense of People* (Cambridge, MA: MIT Press, 1999), 18.

3. D. A. Kenny, *Interpersonal Perception: A Social Relations Analysis* (New York: Guilford Press, 1994), 1

4. D. Langdridge and T. Butt, "The Fundamental Attribution Error: A Phenomenological Critique," *British Journal of Social Psychology* 43, no. 3 (2004): 357–69.

5. R. A. Mar, "The Neural Basis of Social Cognition and Story Comprehension," *Annual Review of Psychology,* no. 62 (January 2011): 103–34.

6. W. B. Swann, "Quest for Accuracy in Person Perception: A Matter of Pragmatics," *Psychological Review* 91, no. 4 (1984): 457–77.

7. H. A. Elfenbein and others, "Reading Your Counterpart: The Benefit of Emotion Recognition Accuracy for Effectiveness in Negotiation," *Journal of Nonverbal Behavior* 31, no. 4 (2007): 205–23.

8. M. L. Gunther and others, "Deciphering Spousal Intentions: An fMRI Study of Couple Communication," *Journal of Social and Personal Relationships* 26, no. 4 (2009): 388–410.

9. B. Russell, J. Perkins, and H. Grinnel, "Interviewees' Overuse of the Word 'Like' and Hesitations: Effects in Simulated Hiring Decisions," *Psychological Reports* 102, no. 1 (February 2008): 111–18.

10. A. Todorov, M. Pakrashi, and N. N. Oosterhof, "Evaluating Faces on Trustworthiness After Minimal Time Exposure," *Social Cognition* 27, no. 6 (2009): 813–33; B. A. Nosek, C. B. Hawkins, and R. S. Frazier, "Implicit Social Cognition: From Measures to Mechanisms," *Trends in Cognitive Sciences* 15, no. 4 (April 2011): 152–59.

11. Kunda, *Social Cognition*.

12. H. Shepherd, "The Cultural Context of Cognition: What the Implicit Association Test Tells Us about How Culture Works," *Sociological Forum* 26, no. 1 (March 2011): 121–43.

13. Ibid., 121–43.

14. Ibid., 128.

15. W. W. Wilmot, *Dyadic Communication*, 2nd ed. (Reading, MA: Addison-Wesley, 1980).

16. B. Park and R. Hastie, "Perception of Variability in Category Development: Instance-versus Abstraction-Based Stereotypes," *Journal of Personality and Social Psychology* 53, no. 4 (1987): 621–35.

17. R. K. Goidel, C. M. Freeman, and S. T. Procopio, "The Impact of Television Viewing on Perceptions of Juvenile Crime," *Journal of Broadcasting and Electronic Media* 50, no. 1 (2006): 119–39, 120.

18. J. M. Bonds-Raacke and others, "Remembering Gay/Lesbian Media Characters: Can Ellen and Will Improve Attitudes toward Homosexuals?" *Journal of Homosexuality* 53, no. 3 (2007): 19–34.

19. M. W. Morris and K. Peng, "Culture and Cause: American and Chinese Attributions for Social and Physical Events," *Journal of Personality and Social Psychology* 67, no. 6 (1994): 949–71.

20. R. E. Nisbett and others, "Culture and Systems of Thought: Holistic versus Analytic Cognition," *Psychological Review* 108, no. 2 (2001): 291–10.

21. K. Ishii, T. Tsukasaki, and S. Kitayama, "Culture and Visual Perception: Does Perceptual Inference Depend on Culture?" *Japanese Psychological Research* 51, no. 2 (2009): 103–9.

22. T. V. Pollet and others, "Birth Order and the Dominance Aspect of Extraversion: Are Firstborns More Extraverted, in the Sense of Being Dominant, Than Laterborns?" *Journal of Research in Personality* 44, no. 6 (2010): 742–45.

23. Ibid., 743.

24. D. Langridge and T. Butt, "The Fundamental Attribution Error," 357–69; M. D. Lieberman and others, "Reflexion and Reflection: A Social Cognitive Neuroscience Approach to Attributional Inference," in *Advances in Experimental Social Psychology*, vol. 34, ed. M. P. Zanna, 199–249 (San Diego: Academic Press, 2002), 204–5.

25. Todorov, Pakrashi, and Oosterhof, "Evaluating Faces on Trustworthiness After Minimal Time Exposure," 813–33.

26. Ibid., p. 813.

27. A. Pierro and A. W. Kruglanski, "'Seizing and Freezing' on a Significant-Person Schema: Need for Closure and the Transference Effect in Social Judgment," *Personality and Social Psychology Bulletin* 34, no. 11 (2008): 1492–1503.

28. See, for example, N. Ambady, M. Hallahan, and R. Rosenthal, "On Judging and Being Judged Accurately in Zero-Acquaintance Situations," *Journal of Personality and Social Psychology* 69, no. 3 (1995): 518–29.

29. M. Shaller and others, "The Prejudiced Personality Revisited: Personal Need for Structure and Formation of Erroneous Group Stereotypes," *Journal of Personality and Social Psychology* 68, no. 1 (1995): 544–55.

30. J. P. Forgas, "Can Negative Affect Eliminate the Power of First Impressions? Affective Influences on Primacy and Recency Effects in Impression Formation," *Journal of Experimental Social Psychology* 47, no. 2 (2011): 425–29.

31. A. W. Kruglanski and D. M. Webster, "Motivated Closing of the Mind: 'Seizing' and 'Freezing,'" *Psychological Review* 103, no. 2 (1996): 263–83.

32. C. I. Marek, J. L. Knapp, and M. B. Wanzer, "An Exploratory Investigation of the Relationship Between Roommates' First Impressions and Subsequent Communication Patterns," *Communication Research Reports* 21, no. 2 (2004): 210–20.

33. S. T. Fiske and S. F. Taylor, *Social Cognition*, 2nd ed. (New York: McGraw-Hill, 1991).

34. J. W. Sherman and others, "Attentional Processes in Stereotype Formation: A Common Model for Category Accentuation and Illusory Correlation," *Journal of Personality and Social Psychology* 96, no. 2 (2009): 305–23.

35. Shaller and others, "The Prejudiced Personality Revisited," 544–55.

36. B. A. Martin and C. S. Dula, "More Than Skin Deep: Perceptions of, and Stigma Against, Tattoos," *College Student Journal* 44, no. 1 (March 2010): 200–206.

37. S. M. Lawrence, C. K. Harrison, and J. Stone, "A Day in the Life of a Male College Athlete: A Public Perception and Qualitative Campus Investigation," *Journal of Sport Management* 23, no. 5 (September 2009): 591–614.

38. C. Y. Olivola and A. Todorov, "Fooled by First Impressions? Reexamining the Diagnostic Value of Appearance-Based Inferences," *Journal of Experimental Social Psychology* 46, no. 2 (2010): 315–24.

39. L. P. Naumann and others, "Personality Judgments Based on Physical Appearance," *Personality and Social Psychology Bulletin* 35, no. 12 (2009): 1669.

40. Olivola and Todorov, "Fooled by First Impressions?" 323.

41. Naumann and others, "Personality Judgments Based on Physical Appearance," 1670.

42. Pierro and Kruglanski, "'Seizing and Freezing' on a Significant-Person Schema," 1493.

43. Ibid.

44. D. T. Gilbert, B. W. Pelham, and D. S. Krull, "On Cognitive Busyness: When Person Perceivers Meet Persons Perceived," *Journal of Personality and Social Psychology* 54, no. 5 (1988): 733–40.

45. Pierro and Kruglanski, "'Seizing and Freezing' on a Significant-Person Schema," 1494.

46. Lieberman and others, "Reflexion and Reflection," 224.

47. S. Clarke, "The Fundamental Attribution Error and Harman's Case against Character Traits," *South African Journal of Philosophy* 25, no. 4 (2006): 350–68.

48. W. B. Swann, "Quest for Accuracy in Person Perception: A Matter of Pragmatics," *Psychological Review* 91, no. 4 (1984): 457–77.

49. For examples of the types of questions that could be helpful, see Y. Trope and M. Bassok, "Confirmatory and Diagnosing Strategies in Social Information Gathering," *Journal of Personality and Social Psychology* 43, no. 1 (1982): 22–34.

50. F. C. B. Hansen, H. Resnick, and J. Galea, "Better Listening: Paraphrasing and Perception Checking—A Study of the Effectiveness of a Multimedia Skills Training Program," *Journal of Technology in Human Services* 20, no. 3-4 (2002): 317–31.

51. E. Browning, "Factors Affecting the Self-Concept of Early Adolescent Girls," *Primary and Middle Years Educator* 7, no. 3 (October 2009): 3–9.

52. M. B. Brewer and W. Gardner, "Who Is This 'We'? Levels of Collective Identity and Self Representations," *Journal of Personality and Social Psychology* 71, no. 1 (1996): 83–93.

53. K. Horneffer-Ginter, "Stages of Change and Possible Selves: 2 Tools for Promoting College Health," *Journal of American College Health* 56, no. 4 (2008): 351–58.

54. H. Markus and E. Wurf, "The Dynamic Self-Concept: A Social Psychological Perspective," *Annual Review of Psychology* 38 (1987): 299–337.

55. J. C. Turner and R. S. Onorato, "Social Identity, Personality, and the Self-Concept: A Self-Categorization Perspective," in *The Psychology of the Social Self*, ed. Tom R. Tyler, Roderick M. Kramer, and Oliver P. John, 11–46 (Mahwah, NJ: Lawrence Erlbaum, 1999).

56. C. Sebastian, S. Burnett, and S.-J. Blakemore, "Development of the Self-Concept during Adolescence," *Trends in Cognitive Sciences* 12, no. 11 (2008): 441–46.

57. S. Carpenter and Z. Karakitapoglu-Aygun, "Importance and Descriptiveness of Self-Aspects: A Cross-Cultural Comparison," *Cross-Cultural Research* 39, no. 3 (2005): 293–321.

58. Richard W. Robins and others, "Global Self-Esteem across the Life Span," *Psychology and Aging* 17, No. 3 (2002): 423–34.

59. Turner and Onorato, "Social Identity, Personality, and the Self-Concept," 14.

60. G. M. Houck, "The Measurement of Childhood Characteristics from Infancy to Toddlerhood," *Issues in Comprehensive Pediatric Nursing* 22 (1999): 101–27.

61. G. L. Brown and others, "Young Children's Self-Concepts: Associations with Child Temperament, Mothers' and Fathers' Parenting, and Triadic Family Interaction," *Merrill-Palmer Quarterly* 55, no. 2 (April 2009): 184–216.

62. B. Hart and T. R. Risley, *Meaningful Differences in the Everyday Experience of Young American Children* (Baltimore: Paul H. Brookes, 1995).

63. C. Leaper, T. Farkas, and C. Spears Brown, "Adolescent Girls' Experiences and Gender-Related Beliefs in Relation to Their Motivation in Math/Science and English," *Journal of Youth and Adolescence* 41, no. 3 (March 2012): 268–82.

64. B. Brown, H. Von Bank, and L. Steinberg, "Smoke in the Looking Glass: Effects of Discordance between Self- and Peer Rated Crowd Affiliation on Adolescent Anxiety, Depression and Self-Feelings," *Journal of Youth and Adolescence* 37, no. 10 (2008): 1163–77; R. Wiseman, *Queen Bees and Wannabes: Helping Your Daughter Survive Cliques, Gossip, Boyfriends, and the New Realities of Girl World*, 2nd ed. (New York: Three Rivers Press, 2009).

65. R. Simmons, *Odd Girl Out: The Hidden Culture of Aggression in Girls* (New York: Harcourt Books, 2002).

66. Sunwolf and L. Leets, "Being Left Out: Rejecting Outsiders and Communicating Group Boundaries in Childhood and Adolescent Peer Groups," *Journal of Applied Communication Research* 32, no. 3 (August 2004): 195–223.

67. H. Benzmiller, "The Cyber-Samaritans: Exploring Criminal Liability for the 'Innocent' Bystanders of Cyberbullying," *Northwestern University Law Review* 107, no. 2 (Winter 2013): 927–62.

68. Browning, "Factors Affecting the Self-Concept of Early Adolescent Girls," 3.

69. M. Tarrant, L. MacKenzie, and L. A. Hewitt, "Friendship Group Identification, Multidimensional Self-Concept, and Experience of Developmental Tasks in Adolescence," *Journal of Adolescence* 29, no. 4 (2006): 627–40.

70. R. M. Dailey, "Confirmation from Family Members: Parent and Sibling Contributions to Adolescent Psychosocial Adjustment," *Western Journal of Communication* 73, no. 3 (2009): 273–99.

71. A. J. Krumm and A. F. Corning, "Who Believes Us When We Try to Conceal Our Prejudices? The Effectiveness of Moral Credentials with In-Groups versus Out-Groups," *Journal of Social Psychology* 148, no. 6 (2008): 689–710.

72. D. Oyserman and H. R. Markus, "The Sociocultural Self," in *The Self in Social Perspective*, ed. J. Suls, 187–220 (Mahwah, NJ: Erlbaum, 1993), 187.

73. R. A. Holloway, A. M. Waldrip, and W. Ickes, "Evidence That a Simpático Self-Schema Accounts for Differences in the Self-Concepts and Social Behavior of Latinos versus Whites (and Blacks)," *Journal of Personality and Social Psychology* 96, no. 5 (2009): 1012–28.

74. Ibid., 1013.

75. P. LenkaBula, "Beyond Anthropocentricity: Botho/Ubuntu and the Quest for Economic and Ecological Justice in Africa," *Religion and Theology* 15, no. 3 (2008): 375–94.

76. D. Tutu, "Ubuntu: Putting Ourselves Back Together," http://www.tutufoundationuk.org/ubuntu.

77. LenkaBula, "Beyond Anthropocentricity," 381.

78. T. Devos and others, "The Role of Parenthood and College Education in the Self-Concept of College Students: Explicit and Implicit Assessments of Gendered Aspirations," *Sex Roles* 59, no. 3/4 (2008): 214–28.

79. A. Hatzigeorgiadis, N. Zourbanos, and Y. Theodorakis, "The Moderating Effects of Self-Talk Content on Self-Talk Functions," *Journal of Applied Sport Psychology* 19, no. 2 (2007): 240–51.

80. E. J. Oliver, D. Marklan, and J. Hardy, "Interpretation of Self-Talk and Post-Lecture Affective States of Higher Education Students: A Self-Determination Theory Perspective," *British Journal of Educational Psychology* 80, no. 2 (2010): 307–23.

81. R. B. Levine and others, "Personal Growth during Internship: A Qualitative Analysis of Interns' Responses to Key Questions," *Journal of General Internal Medicine* 21, no. 6 (2006): 564–69.

82. C. Stevic and R. Ward, "Initiating Personal Growth: The Role of Recognition and Life Satisfaction on the Development of College Students," *Social Indicators Research* 89, no. 3 (2008): 523–34.

83. K. McRae and others, "The Neural Bases of Distraction and Reappraisal," *Journal of Cognitive Neuroscience* 22, no. 2 (2010): 248–62.

84. G. Allan, "Flexibility, Friendship, and Family," *Personal Relationships* 15, no. 1 (2008): 1–16.

85. B. Nagy, M. Kacmar, and K. Harris, "Dispositional and Situational Factors as Predictors of Impression Management Behaviors," *Journal of Behavioral and Applied Management* 12, no. 3 (2011): 229–45.

86. B. R. Schlenker and B. A. Pontari, "The Strategic Control of Information: Impression Management and Self-Presentation in Daily Life," in *Psychological Perspectives on Self and Identity*, ed. Abraham Tesser and others, 199–232 (Washington, DC: American Psychological Association, 2000).

87. Ibid.

88. M. R. Leary and A. B. Allen, "Self-Presentational Persona: Simultaneous Management of Multiple Impressions," *Journal of Personality and Social Psychology* 101, no. 5 (2011): 1033–49.

89. R. F. Baumeister, "Motives and Costs of Self-Presentations in Organizations," in *Impression Management in the Organization*, ed. Robert A. Giacalone and Paul Rosenfeld, 57–72 (Hillsdale, NJ: Lawrence Erlbaum, 1989).

90. A. Y. Cole and E. J. Rozell, "Emotional Intelligence and Impression Management: A Theoretical Framework," *Insights to a Changing World Journal*, no. 1 (2011): 93–114.

91. Ibid.

92. E. E. Jones and T. S. Pittman, "Toward a General Theory of Strategic Self-Presentation," in *Psychological Perspectives on the Self*, vol. 1, ed. Jerry Suls, 231–62 (Hillsdale, NJ: Lawrence Erlbaum, 1982).

93. Leary and Allen, "Self-Presentational Persona," 1033.

94. M. Eskritt, J. Whalen, and L. Kang, "Preschoolers Can Recognize Violations of the Gricean Maxims," *British Journal of Developmental Psychology* 26, no. 3 (2008): 436.

95. S. Winter and others, "The Digital Quest for Love: The Role of Relationship Status in Self-Presentation on Social Networking Sites," *Cyberpsychology* 5, no. 2 (2011): 1–10.

96. E. Protalinski, "56% of Employers Check Applicants' Facebook, LinkedIn, Twitter," January 16, 2012, www.zdnet.com/blog/facebook/56-of-employers-check -applicants-facebook-linkedin-twitter/7446.

97. J. L. Gibbs, N. B. Ellison, and C.-H. Lai, "First Comes Love, Then Comes Google: An Investigation of Uncertainty Reduction Strategies and Self-Disclosure in Online Dating," *Communication Research* 38, no. 1 (February 2011): 70–100.

Chapter 3

1. A. Garrett, "The Yurok Language Project at Berkeley: An Online Dictionary with Texts and Pedagogical Tools," *International Journal of Lexicography* 24, no. 4 (2011): 405.

2. S. B. Shimanoff, *Communication Rules: Theory and Research* (Beverly Hills, CA: Sage, 1980), 31–32.

3. S. Pinker, "Language as an Adaptation to the Cognitive Niche," in *Language Evolution*, ed. M. H. Christiansen and S. Kirby, 16–37 (New York: Oxford University Press, 2003), 17.

4. Ibid.

5. J. McWhorter, *The Power of Babel: A Natural History of Language* (New York: Perennial, 2003), 96.

6. D. Lightfoot, *How New Languages Emerge* (Cambridge: Cambridge University Press, 2006), 2.

7. J. McWhorter, *Spreading the Word: Language and Dialect in America* (Portsmouth, NH: Heinemann, 2000), 1–2; National Science Foundation, "Language Change," *A Special Report: Language and Linguistics,* July 12, 2008, www.nsf.gov/news /special_reports/linguistics/change.jsp.

8. National Science Foundation, "Language Change."

9. L. Campbell and M. J. Mixco, *A Glossary of Historical Linguistics* (Salt Lake City: University of Utah Press, 2007), 25–26.

10. J. McWhorter, *The Power of Babel*, 94–96.

11. H. H. Hock and B. D. Joseph, *Language History, Language Change, and Language Relationship: An Introduction to Historical Linguistics* (Berlin: Mouton de Gruyter, 1996), 14.

12. J. McWhorter, *Word on the Street: Debunking the Myth of a "Pure" Standard English* (Cambridge, MA: Perseus, 1998), 55.

13. S. P. Gennari and others, "Context-Dependent Interpretation of Words: Evidence for Interactive Neural Processes," *NeuroImage* 35, no. 3 (2007): 1278.

14. National Science Foundation, "Language Learning," *A Special Report: Language and Linguistics,* July 12, 2008, www.nsf.gov/news/special_reports/linguistics/learn.jsp.

15. Lightfoot, *How New Languages Emerge*, 6.

16. Hock and Joseph, *Language History,* 5.

17. Lightfoot, *How New Languages Emerge*, 13.

18. D. K. Berlo, *The Process of Communication: An Introduction to Theory and Practice* (New York: Holt, Rinehart and Winston, 1960), 175.

19. C. K. Ogden and I. A. Richards, *The Study of Meaning: A Study of the Influence of Language upon Thought and of the Science of Symbolism* (London: Routledge & Kegan Paul, 1923), 9–15.

20. Berlo, *The Process of Communication*, 175.

21. L. Deuster and others, "A Method to Quantify Residents' Jargon Use during Counseling of Standardized Patients about Cancer Screening," *JGIM: Journal of General Internal Medicine* 23, no. 12 (2008): 1947.

22. B. S. Wood, "Oral Communication in the Elementary Classroom," in *Speaking and Writing K–12*, ed. C. Thaiss and C. Suhor, 104–25 (Urbana, IL: National Council of Teachers of English, 1984), 105; J. R. Searle and D. Vanderveken, *Foundations of Illocutionary Logic* (Cambridge, MA Cambridge University Press, 1985), 37.

23. J. Engle, A. Bermeo, and C. O'Brien, *Straight from the Source: What Works for First-Generation College Students* (Washington, DC: Pell Institute for the Study of Opportunity in Higher Education, 2006), 5–6.

24. D. Westen, *The Political Brain: The Role of Emotion in Deciding the Fate of the Nation* (New York: Public Affairs, 2007), 94.

25. Reuters, "Nobel Peace Prize May Recognize Arab Spring," *Jerusalem Post*, September 27, 2011, www.jpost.com/MiddleEast/article.aspx?id=239786&R=R1.

26. Oslo Freedom Forum, "Lina Ben Mhenni," https://oslofreedomforum.com/speakers/lina-ben-mhenni.

27. NBC News, "Mandela Grandchildren: You Tower Over the World Like a Comet," December 10, 2013, www.nbcnews.com/video/nbc-news/53788354#53788354.

28. Wood, "Oral Communication in the Elementary Classroom," 105.

29. W. R. Fisher, "Narration as a Human Communication Paradigm: The Case of Public Moral Argument," *Communication Monographs* 51, no. 1 (March 1984): 6.

30. P. Flynn, "Hollywood and Local College Students Collaborate on Movie," *San Diego Union-Tribune*, June 21, 2011, www.signonsandiego.com/news/2011/jun/21/hollywood-and-local-college-students-collaborate.

31. M. Bluestone, "U.S. Publishing Industry's Annual Survey Reveals $28 Billion in Revenue in 2014," June 10, 2015, http://publishers.org/news/us-publishing-industry's-annual-survey-reveals-28-billion-revenue-2014.

32. MPAA (2015), "2014 Theatrical Market Statistics." http://www.mpaa.org/wp-content/uploads/2015/03/MPAA-Theatrical-Market-Statistics-2014.pdf.

33. J. R. Searle, *Speech Acts: An Essay in the Philosophy of Language* (London: Cambridge University Press, 1969); J. L. Austin, *How to Do Things with Words* (Cambridge, MA: Harvard University Press, 1962).

34. C. R. Lawrence, "If He Hollers Let Him Go: Regulating Racist Speech on Campus," *Duke Law Journal*, (June 1990): 452.

35. M. Matsuda and others, *Words That Wound: Critical Race Theory, Assaultive Speech, and the First Amendment* (Boulder, CO: Westview Press, 1993), 88.

36. D. W. Sue, "Microaggressions, Marginality, and Oppression: An Introduction," in *Microagressions and Marginality: Manifestation, Dynamics, and Impact*, ed. Derald Wing Sue, 3–22 (Hoboken, NJ: John Wiley & Sons, 2010), 3.

37. R. Delgado and J. Stefancic, *Understanding Words That Wound* (Boulder, CO: Westview Press, 2004), 13–14.

38. S. Burn, "Heterosexuals Use of 'Fag' and 'Queer' to Deride One Another: A Contributor to Heterosexism and Stigma," *Journal of Homosexuality* 40, no. 2 (2000): 1, 2.

39. V. Poteat and D. Espelage, "Exploring the Relation between Bullying and Homophobic Verbal Content: The Homophobic Content Agent Target (HCAT) Scale," *Violence and Victims* 20, no. 5 (2005): 513, 525.

40. Delgado and Stefancic, *Understanding Words That Wound*, 13.

41. C. MacKinnon, *Only Words* (Cambridge, MA: Harvard University Press, 1993), 31.

42. D. Gaucher, J. Friesen, and A. C. Kay, "Evidence That Gendered Wording in Job Advertisements Exists and Sustains Gender Inequality," *Journal of Personality and Social Psychology* 101, no. 1 (2011): 110.

43. J. A. Sniezek and C. H. Jazwinski, "Gender Bias in English: In Search of Fair Language," *Journal of Applied Social Psychology* 16, no. 7 (1986): 659.

44. Gaucher, Friesen, and Kay, "Evidence That Gendered Wording in Job Advertisements Exists," 120–21.

45. J. M. Gottman, "A Theory of Marital Dissolution and Stability," *Journal of Family Psychology* 7, no. 1 (1993): 64.

46. D. J. Schneider, *The Psychology of Stereotyping* (New York: Guilford Press, 2004), 337.

Chapter 4

1. M. Lankaster, "The Craziest Ways Daniel Day-Lewis Prepared for Roles," January 28, 2013, *Yahoo UK Movies*, https://uk.movies.yahoo.com/the-craziest-ways-daniel-day-lewis-prepared-for-roles-171013867.html.

2. C. McGrath, "Abe Lincoln as You've Never Seen Him," *New York Times*, October 31, 2012, www.nytimes.com/2012/11/04/movies/daniel-day-lewis-on-playing-abraham-lincoln.html?pagewanted=all&_r=0.

3. M. D'Estries, "Daniel Day-Lewis Plans 5-Year Acting Sabbatical to Live on Farm," February 25, 2013, www.mnn.com/lifestyle/arts-culture/blogs/daniel-day-lewis-plans-5-year-acting-sabbatical-to-live-on-farm#ixzz3W7CL6SRh.

4. A. Mehrabian, *Nonverbal Communication*, 3rd ed. (Piscataway, NJ: Transaction, 1972).

5. N. J. Briton and J. A. Hall, "Gender-Based Expectancies and Observer Judgments of Smiling," *Journal of Nonverbal Behavior* 19, no. 1 (1995): 49.

6. J. A. Hall, *Nonverbal Sex Differences: Communication Accuracy and Expressive Style* (Baltimore: Johns Hopkins University Press, 1984).

7. Ibid.

8. B. Edwards, "Arrests Made in Subway Attack of 2 Transgender Women Allegedly Stripped Naked," *The Root*, June 3, 2014, www.theroot.com/articles/culture/2014/06/arrests_made_in_subway_attack_of_two_trans_women_allegedly_stripped_naked.html.

9. www.now.org.

10. www.equalitynow.org.

11. www.transequality.org.

12. D. Guarini, "More Than 250 Emoji to Be Released, and We Have the List," *Huffington Post*, June 17, 2014, www.huffingtonpost.com/2014/06/17/new-emoji-middle-finger_n_5496856.html; P. Martinez, "New Emojis Coming in July! 250 Emoticons Will Have Texters Live Long and Prosper While Flipping the Bird," *International Digital Times*, June 17, 2014, www.idigitaltimes.com/new-emojis-coming-july-250-emoticons-will-have-texters-live-long-and-prosper-while-flipping-bird.

13. A. Sternbergh, "Smile, You're Speaking Emoji: The Rapid Evolution of a Wordless Tongue," *New York Magazine*, November 16, 2014, http://nymag.com/daily/intelligencer/2014/11/emojis-rapid-evolution.html.

14. P. Ekman and W. V. Friesen, "The Repertoire of Nonverbal Behavior: Categories, Origins, Usage, and Coding," *Semiotica* 1 (1969): 49–98.

15. Ibid.

16. Ibid.

17. Ibid.

18. Ibid.

19. Ibid.

20. R. B. Zajonc, P. K. Adelmann, S. T. Murphy, and P. M. Niedenthal, "Convergence in the Physical Appearance of Spouses," *Motivation and Emotion* 11, no. 4 (1987): 335–46.

21. M. Tomasello, M. Carpenter, and U. Liszkowski, "A New Look at Infant Pointing," *Child Development* 78, no. 3 (2007): 705–22, doi:10.1111/j.1467-8624.2007.01025.x.

22. N. Phyllis Bo-Yuen, "Nonverbal Communicative Behavior in Intercultural Negotiations: Insights and Applications Based on Findings from Ethiopia, Tanzania, Hong Kong, and the China Mainland," *World Communication* 29, no. 4 (2000): 13, 15.

23. Ibid., 13.

24. To access the "Bitchy Resting Face" YouTube video, go to www.youtube.com/watch?v=3v98CPXNiSk.

25. T. R. Wagner, "The Effects of Speaker Eye Contact and Gender on Receiver's Assessments of the Speaker and Speech," *Ohio Communication Journal* 51 (2013): 217–35.

26. R. Lowe and others, "Avoidance of Eye Gaze by Adults Who Stutter," *Journal of Fluency Disorders* 37, no. 4 (2012): 263–74, doi:10.1016/j.jfludis.2012.04.004; M. Wiklund, "Gaze Behavior of Pre-Adolescent Children Afflicted with Asperger Syndrome," *Communication and Medicine* 9, no. 2 (2012): 173–86, doi:10.1558/cam.v9i2.173.

27. Bo-Yuen, "Nonverbal Communicative Behavior," 13.

28. R. Schmidt-Fajlik, "Introducing Non-Verbal Communication to Japanese University Students: Determining Content," *Journal of Intercultural Communication* 15 (2007): 2.

29. F. N. Willis and L. F. Briggs, "Relationship and Touch in Public Settings," *Journal of Nonverbal Behavior* 16, no. 1 (1992): 55–63.

30. R. Feldman, Z. Rosenthal, and A. I. Eidelman, "Maternal-Preterm Skin-to-Skin Contact Enhances Child Physiologic Organization and Cognitive Control Across the First 10 Years of Life," *Biological Psychiatry* 75, no. 1 (2014): 56, doi:10.1016 /j.biopsych.2013.08.012.

31. M. S. Marx, P. Werner, and J. Cohen-Mansfield, "Agitation and Touch in the Nursing Home," *Psychological Reports* 64, no. 3 (1989): 1019–26.

32. E. T. Hall, *The Silent Language* (New York: Doubleday, 1959).

33. S. Rosenbloom, "In Certain Circles, Two Is a Crowd," *New York Times,* November 16, 2006, www.nytimes.com/2006/11/16/fashion/16space.html?pagewanted = all&_r = 0.

34. R. W. Nolan, *Communicating and Adapting across Culture: Living and Working in the Global Village* (Westport, CT: Bergin & Garvey, 1999).

35. L. Fadel and L. Garcia-Navarro, "How Different Cultures Handle Personal Space," *National Public Radio,* May 5, 2013, www.npr.org/blogs/codeswitch/2013 /05/05/181126380/how-different-cultures-handle-personal-space.

36. Ibid.

37. B. R. Sandler, *The Chilly Classroom Climate: A Guide to Improve the Education of Women,* http://sun.iwu.edu/~mgardner/Articles/chillyclimate.pdf.

38. J. Wilson, "Black Women Worry That Their Natural Hair Could Affect Job Employment or Retention," *Huffington Post: Black Voices,* March 5, 2013, www.huffingtonpost .com/2013/03/05/black-women-natural-hair-at-the-workplace_n_2811056.html.

39. K. Steinmetz, "Get Your Creak On: Is Vocal Fry a Female Fad?" *Time,* December 15, 2011, http://healthland.time.com/2011/12/15/get-your-creak-on-is-vocal-fry-a -female-fad.

40. For an example of vocal fry, go to www.youtube.com/watch?v = Ff1JByylQU0.

41. S. Farley, S. Hughes, and J. LaFayette, "People Will Know We Are in Love: Evidence of Differences between Vocal Samples Directed toward Lovers and Friends," *Journal of Nonverbal Behavior* 37, no. 3 (2013): 123–38, doi:10.1007/s10919-013-0151-3.

42. Bo-Yuen, "Nonverbal Communicative Behavior," 16.

43. A. Sorokowska, "Assessing Personality Using Body Odor: Differences between Children and Adults," *Journal of Nonverbal Behavior* 37, no. 3 (2013): 153–63, doi:10.1007/s10919-013-0152-2.

44. "Grooming and Personal Hygiene," *Life in the USA,* accessed June 30, 2014, www .lifeintheusa.com/everyday/grooming.htm.

45. Hall, *The Silent Language.*

46. Y. M. Kalman and S. Rafaeli, "Online Pauses and Silence: Chronemic Expectancy Violations in Written Computer-Mediated Communication," *Communication Research* 38, no. 1 (2011): 54–69, doi:10.1177/0093650210378229.

47. E. Dresner and S. C. Herring, "Functions of the Nonverbal in CMC: Emoticons and Illocutionary Force," *Communication Theory* 20, no. 3 (2010): 249–68, doi:10.1111 /j.1468-2885.2010.01362.x.

Chapter 5

1. R. P. Ramsey and R. S. Sohi, "Listening to Your Customers: The Impact of Perceived Listening Behavior on Relationship Outcomes," *Journal of the Academy of Marketing Science* (Spring 1997): 127–37.

2. B. S. Thomson, "Interpersonal Skills: The Importance of Listening," *Australian Nurses Journal* 16, no. 3 (September 1986): 45–50.

3. R. Emanuel and others, "How College Students Spend Their Time Communicating," *International Journal of Listening* 22 (2008): 13–28.

4. B. D'Ambrosie, "Preparing Teachers to Teach Mathematics within a Constructivist Framework: The Importance of Listening to Children," in *The Work of Mathematics Teacher Educators*, ed. D. Thompson and T. Watanabe (San Diego: Association of Mathematic Teacher Educators, 2004), 135–40.

5. J. Stewart, *Bridges, Not Walls,* 4th ed. (New York: Random House, 1986), 181.

6. K. W. Watson and L. L. Barker, *The Listening Style Inventory* (New Orleans: Spectra, 1985).

7. L. K. Steil, "Listening Training: The Key to Success in Today's Organizations," in *Listening in Everyday Life: A Personal and Professional Approach*, ed. M. Purdy and D. Borisoff (Lanham, MD: University Press of America, 1997), 215.

8. Ibid.

9. O. Hargie, *Skilled Interpersonal Communication: Research, Theory and Practice* (New York: Routledge, 2011), 179–81.

10. Ibid. at 180.

11. J. D. Boudreau, E. Cassell, and A. Fuks, "Preparing Medical Students to Become Attentive Listeners," *Medical Teacher* 31 (2009): 22–29.

12. Study by TCC Consulting (San Francisco) undertaken between 1987 and 1997.

13. K. Watson, L. Barker, and J. Weaver, "The Listening Styles Profile (LPP16): Development and Validation of an Instrument to Assess Four Listening Styles," *International Journal of Listening* 9 (1995): 1–13.

14. M. K. Johnston, J. B. Weaver, K. W. Watson, and L. B. Barker, "Listening Styles: Biological or Psychological Differences?" *International Journal of Listening* 14 (2000): 36.

15. E. Langer, "Rethinking the Role of Thought in Human Interaction," in *New Directions in Attribution Research*, ed. H. Hurvey, W. Ickes, and R. Kidd (Hillside, NJ: Earlbaum, 1980), 2: 35–38.

16. Johnston, Weaver, Watson, and Barker, "Listening Styles," 37.

17. K. Watson, L. Barker, and J. Weaver, "The Listening Styles Profile (LPP16)," 1–13.

18. Johnston, Weaver, Watson, and Barker, "Listening Styles," 37.

19. P. E. King and R. R. Behnke, "The Effect of Time Compressed Speech in Comprehensive, Interpretive and Short-Term Listening," *Human Communication Research* 15 (Spring 1989): 3, 430.

20. J. C. Richards, "Listening Comprehension: Approach, Design Procedure," *Tesol Quarterly* 17 (June 1983): 2, 225.

21. R. Buckley and J. Caple, *The Theory and Practice of Training,* 6th ed. (Philadelphia, PA: Kagen Page, 2009), 145.

22. S. Hygge, E. Borran, and I. Enmarker, "The Effects of Road Traffic Noise and Meaningful Irrelevant Speech on Different Memory Systems," *Scandinavian Journal of Psychology* 44 (2003): 13–21.

23. G. Miller, "The Magical Number Seven, Plus or Minus Two: Some Limits on our Capacity for Processing Information," *Psychological Review* 63 (March 1956): 2, 81–97.

24. K. Cherry, "Multitasking: A Few Reasons Why Multitasking Reduces Productivity," *About.com*, http://psychology.about.com/od/cognitivepsychology/a/costs-of-multi-tasking.htm.

25. T. Klingberg, *The Overflowing Brain: Information Overload and the Limits of Working Memory* (London: Oxford University Press, 2009).

26. S. Yamaguchi, Y. Kato, K. Oimatsu, and T. Saeki, "A Psychological Evaluation Method for Fluctuating Random Noise Based on Fuzzy Set Theory," *Applied Acoustics* 45 (1995): 139–54.

Chapter 6

1. U.S. Census Bureau, "U.S. Census Bureau Projections Show a Slower Growing, Older, More Diverse Nation a Half Century Later from Now," December 12, 2012, www.census.gov/newsroom/releases/archives/population/cb12-243.html.

2. R. Williams, *Culture and Society: 1780–1950* (Columbia University Press, New York: 1958,1983), xvi.

3. A. Tatli, "Discourses and Practices of Diversity Management in the UK," in *International Handbook on Diversity Management at Work: Country Perspectives on Diversity and Equal Treatment*, ed. A. Klarsfeld, 283–303 (Northampton, MA: Edward Elgar Publishers, 2010), 287.

4. These terms do become problematic when we consider their origins. Recall from Chapter 2 the ideas of in-groups and out-groups—social groups you identity with versus those you don't feel a part of. Throughout history, people have deemed others part of an out-group by the use of labels, typically in order to rationalize demonizing or subjugating them (and privileging themselves). This was sometimes based on others' location or even by certain physical characteristics. Researchers have uncovered evidence of this from ancient India, China, and Egypt. See, for example, T. F. Gossett, *Race: The History of an Idea in America* (New York: Oxford University Press, 1997). In the 1700s, Scandinavian researchers took this a step further by attempting to "scientifically" classify races of people, much like plants or animals. For more, see S. J. Gould, *The Mismeasure of Man*, rev. ed. (New York: W.W. Norton, 1996). In modern times, it's become clear that this classification system was not only morally repugnant but also completely without scientific basis. Indeed, modern researchers have conclusively established that if there is such a thing as a race or "species" of people, we are all one human race or species. Contemporary findings in anthropology, genetics, and molecular biology, for example, have demonstrated that all modern humans are *Homo sapiens* and share the same set of twenty-three chromosomes, identical genes, and the equivalent of a six-foot strand of DNA. See S. Olson, *Mapping Human History: Genes, Race and Our Common Origins* (Boston, MA: Houghton Mifflin, 2003). This same research also shows that all modern members of *Homo sapiens* derive from an original source (technically called a female progenitor) that resided in central east Africa millions of years ago. See V. O. Pang and R. Valle, "A Change in Paradigm: Applying Contributions of

Genetic Research to Teaching about Race and Racism in Social Studies Education," *Theory and Research in Social Education* 32, no. 4 (Fall 2004): 508.

5. *Merriam-Webster Online*, s.v. "heritage," www.merriam-webster.com/dictionary/heritage?show = 0&t = 1383588084.

6. E. M. Trauth and others, "Millennials and Masculinity: A Shifting Tide of Gender Stereotyping of ICT?" *Proceedings of the 16th Americas Conference on Information Systems* (Lima, Peru: AMCIS, 2010), 2.

7. R. Jaslow, "Number of Male U.S. Nurses Triple Since 1970," *CBS News*, February 26, 2013, www.cbsnews.com/8301-204_162-57571330/.

8. D. Weiss and F. R. Lang, "The Two Faces of Age Identity," *GeroPsych* 1 (2012): 5–14.

9. Baby boomers are believed to be of the generation of Americans born roughly between 1943 and 1960; the first children of the boomer generation—also known as Generation X—were born between 1961 and 1981, and the group known as millennials came thereafter, roughly between 1982 and 2003—although regarding this last group, there is some disagreement about the exact year this generation began. For this reason, it is more appropriate (and less controversial) to suggest that millennials were born between the early 1980s and the early 2000s. For more, see S. Keeling, "Advising the Millennial Generation," *NACADA Journal* 23, no. 1-2 (Spring/Fall 2003): 30–36; see also A. D. Ross and S. M. Rouse, "Economic Uncertainty, Job Threat, and the Resiliency of the Millennial Generation's Attitudes toward Immigration," *Social Science Quarterly* 96, no. 5 (2015): 1363–79, doi:10.111/ssqu.12168.

10. D. Weiss and A. M. Freund, "Still Young at Heart: Negative Age-Related Information Motivates Distancing from Same-Aged People," *Psychology and Aging* 27, no. 1 (2011): 173–80, doi:10.1037/a0024819.

11. B. A. Nosek, M. R. Banaji, and A. G. Greenwald, "Harvesting Implicit Group Attitudes and Beliefs from a Demonstration Website," *Group Dynamics* 6, no. 1 (2002): 101–15.

12. See, for example, E. T. Hall, *Beyond Culture* (Garden City, NY: Anchor/Doubleday, 1981).

13. For more on this, see G. Hofstede, *Culture's Consequences: Comparing Values, Behaviors, Institutions and Organizations across Nations*, 2nd ed. (Thousand Oaks, CA: Sage, 2001), 145–49.

14. A. Georgakopoulos and L. K. Guerrero, "Student Perceptions of Nonverbal and Verbal Communication: A Comparison of Best and Worst Professors across Six Cultures," *International Education Studies* 3, no. 2 (2010): 3–16.

15. Ibid., 4.

16. Hofstede, *Culture's Consequences*.

17. D. Matsumoto, "Culture and Nonverbal Behavior," in *The Sage Handbook of Nonverbal Communication*, ed. V. Manusov and M. L. Patterson (Thousand Oaks, CA: Sage, 2006): 219–35.

18. G. G. Barker, "Cultural Influences on the News: Portrayals of the Iraq War by Swedish and American Media," *International Communication Gazette* 74, no. 1 (2012): 9, doi:10:1177/174848511426981.

19. G. Hofstede, *Cultures and Organizations: Software of the Mind* (London: Harper Collins, 1991), 97.

20. Ibid., 9.

21. Ibid., 97.

22. For more on this, see O. M. Watson, *Proxemic Behavior: A Cross-Cultural Study* (The Hague: De Gruyter Mouton, 1970).

23. Georgakopoulos and Guerrero, "Student Perceptions of Nonverbal and Verbal Communication," 4.

24. See, for example, P. A. Andersen, *Nonverbal Communication: Forms and Functions*, 2nd ed. (Prospect Heights, IL: Waveland Press, 2008).

25. D. A. Waldman and others, "Cultural and Leadership Predictors of Corporate Social Responsibility Values of Top Management: A GLOBE Study of 15 Countries," *Journal of International Business Studies* 37, no. 6 (2006): 826.

26. Ibid.

27. Georgakopoulos and Guerrero, "Student Perceptions of Nonverbal and Verbal Communication," 4.

28. M. Lara and others, "Acculturation and Latino Health in the United States: A Review of the Literature and Its Sociopolitical Context," *Annual Review of Public Health* 26 (2005): 369.

29. The law was titled Loi n° 2004-228 du 15 mars 2004 encadrant, en application du principe de laïcité, le port de signes ou de tenues manifestant une appartenance religieuse dans les écoles, collèges et lycées publics (literally "Law #2004-228 of March 15, 2004, concerning, as an application of the principle of the separation of church and state, the wearing of symbols or garb which show religious affiliation in public primary and secondary schools").

30. F. J. Collins, "Growing Up Bicultural in the United States: The Case of Japanese Americans," in *Multiple Identities: Race, Gender, Culture, Nationality and Roles*, ed. R. Josselson and M. Harway (New York, NY: Oxford University Press, 2012), 79.

31. C. K. W. DeDreu and others, "Oxytocin Promotes Human Ethnocentrism," *Proceedings of the National Academy of Sciences of the United States of America* 108, no. 4 (2011): 1262.

32. "Gallup Gay Marriage Poll Finds Majority of U.S. Citizens Would Support Nationwide Marriage Equality Law," *Huffington Post*, July 31, 2013, www.huffingtonpost.com/2013/07/31/gallup-gay-marriage-poll-_n_3682884.html.

33. M. E. Williams, "Dick Cheney and Laura Bush Plead for Marriage Equality," Salon.com, February 20, 2013, www.salon.com/2013/02/20/dick_cheney_and_laura_bush_plead_support_for_marriage_equality/.

34. D. Fraleigh and J. Tuman, *Freedom of Expression in the Marketplace of Ideas* (Thousand Oaks, CA: Sage, 2011), 139.

35. K. Clark, *Dark Ghetto: Dilemmas of Social Power* (New York: Harper Row, 1965), 64.

36. R. Delgado, "Words That Wound: A Tort Action for Racial Insults, Epithets and Name Calling," in *Words That Wound: Critical Race Theory, Assaultive Speech, and the First Amendment*, ed. M. J. Matsuda and others, 89–110 (Boulder, CO: Westview Press, 1993), 91.

37. E. Harburg and others, "Socio-Ecological Stress, Suppressed Hostility, Skin Color, and Black/White Male Blood Pressure: Detroit," *Psychosomatic Medicine* 35 (July–August 1973): 276–78.

38. See, for example, J. S. Tuman, "Sticks and Stones Will Break My Bones, but Words Will Never Hurt Me: The Fighting Words Doctrine on Campus," *Free Speech Yearbook* 30, ed. D. Herbeck (1992): 114–28.

39. S. Ting-Toomey, *Communicating across Cultures* (New York: Guilford Press, 1999).

40. For more, see M. Flammia and H. A. Sadri, "Intercultural Communication from an Interdisciplinary Perspective," *U.S.-China Education Review* 8, no. 1 (January 2011): 103–9.

41. T. Pettigrew and L. Tropp, "Allport's Intergroup Contact Hypothesis," in *On the Nature of Prejudice: Fifty Years after Allport*, ed. J. Dovido, P. Glick and A. Rudman (Oxford: Blackwell, 2006), 262–77.

42. S. Steffen, "Successful Women Lose Out in China's Marriage Market," *Deutsche Welle*, September 27, 2013, www.dw.com/en/successful-women-lose-out-in-chinas-marriage-market/a-17115671.

Chapter 7

1. For more, see H. Kennedy, "Tank Man Still Unidentified More Than Twenty Years Later," *New York Daily News*, June 5, 2012, www.nydailynews.com/news/world/tank-man-stood-tall-tiananmen-square-remains-unidentified-20-article-1.1090054.

2. "Tiananmen Square Fast Facts," *CNN*, July 3, 2015, www.cnn.com/2013/09/15/world/asia/tiananmen-square-fast-facts/.

3. "Tiananmen Square Massacre Anniversary: Chinese Activists Call on People to Wear Black," *Huffington Post*, June 3, 2013, www.huffingtonpost.com/2013/06/03/tiananmen-square-massacre-anniversary-activists-wear-black_n_3377635.html.

4. See, for example, Z. Tufecki and C. Wilson, "Social Media and the Decision to Participate in Political Protest: Observations from Tahrir Square," *Journal of Communication* 62, no. 2 (April 2012): 363–79. See also G. Lotan and others, "The Arab Spring! The Revolutions Were Tweeted: Information Flows during the 2011 Tunisian and Egyptian Revolutions," *International Journal of Communication* 5 (2011): 1375–1405.

5. C. O'Donnell, "New Study Quantifies Use of Social Media in Arab Spring," *UW Today*, September 12, 2011, www.washington.edu/news/2011/09/12/new-study-quantifies-use-of-social-media-in-arab-spring/.

6. R. Campbell, *Media and Culture: An Introduction to Mass Communication,* 3rd ed. (New York: Bedford/St. Martin's Press, 2003), 6.

7. Ibid.

8. For example, in *Captain Phillips*, the film condenses the five-day ordeal of the pirate takeover down to a single day for greater dramatic impact. According to litigation by at least one crewmember, it also ignores the heroism of individual crew members by focusing on the efforts of Captain Phillips himself.

9. D. Nuccitelli, "Global Warming: Why Is IPCC Report So Certain about the Influence of Humans?" *The Guardian*, September 27, 2013, www.theguardian.com/environment/climate-consensus-97-per-cent/2013/sep/27/global-warming-ipcc-report-humans.

10. P. Bump, "Fact-Checking the Bill Nye-Marsha Blackburn Climate Change 'Debate,'" *The Wire*, February 17, 2014, www.thewire.com/politics/2014/02/fact-checking-bill-nye-marsha-blackburn-climate-change-debate/358149/.

11. For example, Howard Stern, who commands an audience in the millions for his syndicated radio program, wrote two books, both of which were best sellers based on his life. One of these books was turned a movie—starring Stern as himself—and

did reasonably well at the box office and in video. Although Stern is a funny writer and made a critically well-received acting debut, there is no doubt that the appeal and success of his books and movie owed a lot to his built-in audience and established status as a celebrity in radio.

12. Sales in 2006 were put at 68.2 million PCs in the United States alone. See "Vista Delay Seen Lowering 2006 PC Sales," UPI, March 27, 2006, www.upi.com/Science _News/2006/03/27/Vista-delay-seen-lowering-2006-PC-sales/61071143490301/.

13. B. Garfield, "Slate's 'Minutes to Read' Feature Dumbs Down Journalism," *The Guardian*, November 23, 2013, www.theguardian.com/commentisfree/2013/nov/23/slate -minutes-to-read-dumb-journalism.

14. J. Keller, "Evaluating Iran's Twitter Revolution," *Atlantic* June 18, 2010, www .theatlantic.com/technology/archive/2010/06/evaluating-irans-twitter-revolution /58337/. This was a positive result; sometimes the effects are more negative.

15. S. Ackerman, "Internet Identifies, Threatens Wrong Man as Newtown Shooter," Wired.com, December 14, 2012, www.wired.com/dangerroom/2012/12/newtown -shooter-facebook/.

16. "Trending 20," *Huffington Post*, www.huffingtonpost.com/news/trending-20/.

17. For more on this, see J. S. Tuman, *Political Communications in American Campaigns* (Thousand Oaks, CA: Sage, 2008), 213–15.

18. S. Bennett, "45 Amazing Social Media Facts, Figures and Statistics," *Mediabistro*, September 20, 2013, www.mediabistro.com/alltwitter/45-social-media-stats_b49582.

19. *Merriam-Webster Online*, s.v. "social media," www.merriam-webster.com /dictionary/social%20media.

20. D. L. Hoffman and T. P. Novak, "Social Media Strategy," in *Handbook of Marketing Strategy*, ed. V. Shenkar and G. S. Carpenter (Cheltenham, UK: Edward Elgar, 2012), 205.

21. For more, see N. Kristof, "Bring Back Our Girls," Sunday Review, *New York Times*, May 3, 2014, www.nytimes.com/2014/05/04/opinion/sunday/kristof-bring-back-our -girls.html?_r = 0.

22. For more, go to https://www.khanacademy.org.

23. For example, see P. Glader, "The *Economist* Magazine visits the Khan Academy," *WiredAcademic*, September 16, 2011, www.wiredacademic.com/2011/09/the -economist-magazine-visits-the-khan-academy-in-action/.

24. For more, see www.ted.com.

25. See J. Nicholson, "Pros and Cons of Online Dating," *The Attraction Doctor* (blog), *Psychology Today*, April 30, 2014, www.psychologytoday.com/blog/the-attraction -doctor/201404/pros-and-cons-online-dating.

26. See J. Spira, "Online Dating vs. Offline Dating: Pros and Cons," *Huffington Post*, October 3, 2013, www.huffingtonpost.com/julie-spira/online-dating-vs-offline -_b_4037867.html.

27. "One-Third of Married Couples in U.S. Meet Online: Study," *New York Daily News*, June 4, 2013, www.nydailynews.com/life-style/one-third-u-s-marriages-start-online -dating-study-article-1.1362743.

28. See J. B. Walther, "Computer Mediated Communication: Impersonal, Interpersonal and Hyperpersonal Interaction," *Communication Research* 23, no. 1 (February 1996): 3–43.

29. A. Marcotte, "Rape, Lawsuits, Anonymous Leaks: What's Going On in Steubenville, Ohio?" *Slate*, January 3, 2013, www.slate.com/blogs/xx_factor/2013/01/03 /steubenville_ohio_rape_anonymous_gets_involved_and_the_case_gets_even _more.html.

30. See "Jimmy Soni Explains Why the Huffington Post Is Getting Rid of Anonymous Commenter Accounts," *Huffington Post*, August 23, 2013, www.huffingtonpost.com /huff-tv/jimmy-soni-comments_b_3807521.html.

31. C. Timberg, "Instagram, Facebook Stir Online Protests for Privacy Policy Change," *Washington Post*, December 18, 2012, www.washingtonpost.com/business /technology/instagram-facebook-stirs-online-protests-for-privacy-policy-change /2012/12/18/6c105d92-4948-11e2-b6f0-e851e741d196_story.html.

32. A. Robertson, "One Year of NSA Leaks: Where Are We Now?" *The Verge*, June 5, 2014, www.theverge.com/2014/6/5/5782234/one-year-of-nsa-leaks.

33. D. Rushe, "Edward Snowden Calls for Greater Online Privacy in Reset the Net Campaign," *The Guardian*, June 5, 2014, www.theguardian.com/world/2014/jun/05 /edward-snowden-privacy-reset-the-net.

34. D. Crow, "Net Neutrality: Strife in the Fast Lane," *Financial Times*, November 16, 2014, www.ft.com/intl/cms/s/0/997ad3ee-6b23-11e4-ae52-00144feabdc0 .html#axzz3zuClmrmN.

35. For a broader exploration of this theory as an alternative paradigm, see D. McQuail, *McQuail's Mass Communication Theory* (Thousand Oaks, CA: Sage Press, 2005), 65–70.

36. D. Mandel, "Muslims on the Silver Screen," *Middle East Quarterly* 8, no. 2 (2001): 19–30, www.meforum.org/26/muslims-on-the-silver-screen.

37. Technology and new entertainment media have recently begin to counter these stereotypes. In recent years, it has become more commonplace for witnesses to a confrontation between police officers and young men of color to record the event with their cell phone and then immediately post the video on social media, such as Twitter or Facebook, in the process creating a counternarrative to that offered by news media stories. The film *Fruitvale Station* shares the true story of Oscar Grant, a young man whose death by a BART (Bay Area Rapid Transit) police officer in 2009 was recorded and shared on social media. The video was soon picked up by the news media, sparking protests across the Bay Area and later the nation. The film humanized Grant and worked to counter the stereotypical image of young black males as criminals, while raising questions about a certain population of police officers who may racially profile.

38. L. Steet, *Veils and Daggers: A Century of National Geographic's Representation of the Arab World* (Temple University Press, 2000), 26.

39. P. J. Fourie, *Media Studies: Institutions, Theories and Issues* (Cape Town: Juta, 2004), 247.

40. Ibid., 248.

41. For more on this, see Tuman, *Political Communication in American Campaigns*, 208–13.

42. A. Lutz, "These 6 Corporations Control 90% of the Media in America," *Business Insider*, June 14, 2012, www.businessinsider.com/these-6-corporations-control -90-of-the-media-in-america-2012-6.

43. W. Lippmann, *Public Opinion* (New York: Macmillan, 1921), 16.

44. M. E. McCombs and D. L. Shaw, "The Agenda-Setting Function of Mass Media," *Public Opinion Quarterly* 36 (1972): 176–87.

45. D. L. West and M. E. McCombs, *The Emergence of Political Issues* (St. Paul, MN: West, 1977), 5.

46. For more on how framing works, see E. Goffman, *Frame Analysis* (Boston: New England University Press, 1974); R. M. Entman, "Framing U.S. Coverage of International News," *Journal of Communication* 41, no. 4 (1974): 6–28; R. M. Entman, "Freezing Out the Public: Elite and Media Framing of the U.S. Anti-Nuclear Movement," *Political Communication* 10, no. 2 (1993): 155–73.

47. See T.-N. Coates, "Florida's Self-Defense Laws and the Killing of Trayvon Martin," *Atlantic Monthly*, March 13, 2012, www.theatlantic.com/national/archive/2012/03/floridas-self-defense-laws-and-the-killing-of-trayvon-martin/254396/.

48. J. Dahl, "The Trayvon Martin Case Exposes the Realities of a New Generation of Self-Defense Laws," *CBS News*, July 12, 2013, www.cbsnews.com/news/the-trayvon-martin-case-exposes-the-realities-of-a-new-generation-of-self-defense-laws/.

49. C. M. Blow, "The Curious Case of Trayvon Martin," *New York Times*, March 16, 2012, www.nytimes.com/2012/03/17/opinion/blow-the-curious-case-of-trayvon-martin.html?_r = 0.

50. "Trayvon Martin Shooting Sparks 'Hoodie' Movement," *CBS News*, www.cbsnews.com/pictures/trayvon-martin-shooting-sparks-hoodie-movement/.

51. For more on this, see J. W. Dearing and E. M. Rogers, *Communication Concepts*, vol. 6: *Agenda-Setting* (Newbury Park, CA: Sage Press, 1996).

52. See J. Tuman, *Communicating Terror: The Rhetorical Dimensions of Terrorism*, 2nd ed. (Thousand Oaks, CA: Sage, 2010), 57–61.

53. A. Southall, "A Twitter Message about AIDS, Followed by a Firing and an Apology," *The Lede* (blog), *New York Times*, December 20, 2013, http://thelede.blogs.nytimes.com/2013/12/20/a-twitter-message-about-aids-africa-and-race/.

54. "Study: Facebook Lowers Self-Control," University of Pittsburgh Joseph M. Katz Graduate School of Business, www.business.pitt.edu/katz/faculty/news/facebook.php.

55. S. Khalaf, "The Rise of the Mobile Addict," *Flurry.com*, April 22, 2014, www.flurry.com/bid/110166/The-Rise-of-the-Mobile-Addict#.U5DY6PldU1J.

Chapter 8

1. J. Stewart, K. Zediker, and S. Witteborn, *Together: Communicating Interpersonally: A Social Construction Approach*, 6th ed. (New York: Oxford University Press, 2005).

2. D. L. Kelley, *Marital Communication* (Malden, MA: Polity Press, 2012), 60–92.

3. E. Gilbert, *Committed: A Sceptic Makes Peace with Marriage* (London: Bloomsbury, 2011), 131.

4. L. K. Guerrero, P. A. Andersen, and W. A. Afifi, *Close Encounters: Communication in Relationships*, 3rd ed. (Los Angeles: Sage, 2011), 28–30.

5. A. Aron, M. Paris, and E. N. Aron, "Falling in Love: Prospective Studies of Self-Concept Change," *Journal of Personality and Social Psychology* 69 (1995): 1102–12; Guerrero, Andersen, and Afifi, *Close Encounters*, 28–30.

6. S. Duck, *Rethinking Relationships* (Los Angeles: Sage, 2011).

7. R. S. Weiss, "The Provisions of Social Relationships," in *Doing unto Others*, ed. Z. Rubin (Englewood Cliffs, NJ: Prentice-Hall, 1974), 17–26.

8. B. Brown, *Daring Greatly: How the Courage to Be Vulnerable Transforms the Way We Live, Love, Parent, and Lead* (New York: Gotham Books, 2012).

9. M. Sebastian, "The Psychology of Social Networking," *Ragan's PR Daily*, August 2, 2012, www.prdaily.com/Main/Articles/12304.aspx.

10. W. H. Jones and T. L. Moore, "Loneliness and Social Support," in *Loneliness: Theory, Research and Applications*, ed. M. Hojat and R. Crandall (Newbury Park, CA: Sage, 1989), 145–56.

11. E. Diener and M. E. P. Seligman, "Very Happy People," *Psychological Science* 13 (2002): 81–84.

12. C. Zimmer, "Friends with Benefits," *Time*, February 20, 2012, 34.

13. M. Sebastian, "The Psychology of Social Networking."

14. Ibid.

15. C. Zimmer, "Friends with Benefits."

16. S. Duck, *Understanding Relationships* (New York: Guilford Press, 1991).

17. Z. Rubin, *Liking and Loving: An invitation to Social Psychology* (New York: Holt, Rinehart & Winston, 1973).

18. P. M. Nardi and D. Sherrod, "Friendships in the Lives of Gay Men and Lesbians," *Journal of Social and Personal Relationships* 11 (1994): 185–99; R. B. Hayes, "Friendship," in *Handbook of Personal Relationships: Theory, Research, and Interventions*, ed. S. Duck (Chichester, England: Wiley, 1988), 391–408.

19. W. K. Rawlins, *Friendship Matters: Communication, Dialectics, and the Life Course* (New York: Adeline de Gruyter, 1992).

20. J. Yager, *Friendships* (Stamford, CT: Hannacroix Creek, 1999).

21. W. K. Rawlins, *Friendship Matters*.

22. Nardi and Sherrod, "Friendships in the Lives of Gay Men and Lesbians."

23. K. Floyd, "Gender and Closeness among Friends and Siblings," *Journal of Psychology* 129 (1995): 193–202.

24. G. P. Jones and M. H. Dembo, "Age and Sex Role Differences in Intimate Friendships during Childhood and Adolescence," *Merrill-Palmer Quarterly of Behavior and Development* 35 (1989): 445–62.

25. S. Swain, "Covert Intimacy: Closeness in Men's Friendships," in *Gender and Intimate Relationships*, ed. B. Riseman and P. Schwartz (Belmont, CA: Wadsworth, 1989), 71–86.

26. S. Brandes, "Sex Roles and Anthropological Research in Rural Andalusia," *Women's Studies* 13 (1987): 357–72.

27. P. M. Sias, K. J. Krone, and F. M. Jablin, "An Ecological Systems Perspective on Workplace Relationships," in *Handbook of Interpersonal Communication*, ed. M. L. Knapp and J. A. Daily, 615–42 (Thousand Oaks, CA: Sage, 2002).

28. S. McCornack, *Reflect and Relate: An Introduction to Interpersonal Communication*, 2nd ed. (Boston, MA: Bedford/St. Martin's, 2010).

29. Ibid.

30. Jamie M. Lewis and Rose M. Krieder, U.S. Census Bureau, "Remarriage in the United States: American Community Survey Reports" (March 2015), http://www.census.gov/content/dam/Census/library/publications/2015/acs/acs-30.pdf.

31. M. Lund, "The Development of Investment and Commitment Scales for Predicting Continuity of Personal Relationships," *Journal of Social and Personal Relationships* 2 (1985): 3–23.

32. C. Rosenblum, "Living Apart Together," *New York Times*, September 13, 2013, www .nytimes.com/2013/09/15/realestate/living-apart-together.html.

33. H. Yen, "More Couples Who Become Parents Are Living Together but Not Marrying, Data Show," *Washington Post*, January 7, 2014, www .washingtonpost.com/politics/more-couples-who-become-parents-are-living-together -but-not-marrying-data-show/2014/01/07/2b639a86-77d5-11e3-b1c5- 739e63e9c9a7_story.html.

34. E. Aoki, "Coming Out as 'We Three': Using Personal Ethnography and Case Study to Assess Relational Identity and Parental Support of Gay Male, Three Partner Relationships," *Journal of GLBT Family Studies* 2 (2005): 29–48.

35. S. McCornack, *Reflect and Relate.*

36. J. T. Wood, *Relational Communication: Continuity and Change in Personal Relationships*, 2nd ed. (Belmont, CA: Wadsworth, 2000).

37. K. D. Locke and L. M. Horowitz, "Satisfaction in Interpersonal Interactions as a Function of Similarity in Level of Dysphoria," *Journal of Personality and Social Psychology* 58 (1990): 823–31.

38. J. B. Walther, "Social Information Processing Theory: Impressions and Relationship Development Online," in *Engaging Theories in Interpersonal Communication: Multiple Perspectives*, ed. L. A. Baxter and D. O. Braithwaite, 391–404 (Thousand Oaks, CA: Sage, 2008).

39. S. T. Tong and others, "Too Much of a Good Thing? The Relationship between Number of Friends and Interpersonal Impressions on Facebook," *Journal of Computer-Mediated Communication* 13 (2008): 531–49.

40. H. Fisher, *The Anatomy of Love: The Mysteries of Mating, Marriage, and Why We Stray* (New York: Fawcett/Columbine, 1992).

41. L. O'Connell, "That Loving Feeling: It's All in Your Mind," *Orlando Sentinel*, June 24, 1993, http://articles.orlandosentinel.com/1993-06-24/lifestyle/9306230137_1_brain -chemistry-romantic-love-bowers.

42. E. B. Ebbersen, G. L. Kjos, and V. J. Konecni, "Spatial Ecology: Its Effects on the Choice of Friends and Enemies," *Journal of Experimental Social Psychology* 12 (1976): 505–18.

43. D. L. Molinari, "The Role of Social Comments in Problem Solving Groups in an Online Course," *American Journal of Distance Education* 18 (2004): 89–101.

44. Ibid.

45. L. Acitelli, E. Douvan, and J. Veroff, "Perceptions of Conflict in First Year Marriage: How Important Are Similarity and Understanding?," *Journal of Social and Personal Relationships* 5 (1993): 5–20.

46. S. W. Duck, *Human Relationships* (Newbury Park, CA: Sage, 1992).

47. D. Pillet-Shore, "Doing Introductions: The Work Involved in Meeting Someone New," *Communication Monographs* 78 (2011): 73–95.

48. J. T. Wood, *Relational Communication.*

49. Pillet-Shore, "Doing Introductions."

50. L. Zunin, *Contact: The First Four Minutes* (Los Angeles: Nash, 1972).

51. P. E. Tetlock, "Accountability and the Perseverance of First Impressions," *Social Psychology Quarterly* 46 (1983): 285–92.

52. O. Ybarra, "When First Impressions Don't Last: The Role of Isolation and Adaptation Processes in the Revision of Evaluative Impressions," *Social Cognition* 19, no. 5 (2001): 491–520.

53. B. A. Fisher and K. L. Adams, *Interpersonal Communication: Pragmatics of Human Relationships*, 2nd ed. (New York: Random House, 1994).

54. M. R. Parks, "Ideology in Interpersonal Communication: Off the Couch and into the World," in *Communication Yearbook* 5, ed. M. Burgoon (New Brunswick, NJ: Transaction, 1985), 79–107.

55. J. T. Wood, *Relational Communication*.

56. Knapp and Vangelisti, *Interpersonal Communication and Human Relationships*, 6th ed. (Boston: Pearson, 2009).

57. R. B. Hayes, "The Development and Maintenance of Friendship," *Journal of Social and Personal Relationships* 6 (1984): 75–98.

58. J. K. Kellas, "'The Worst Part Is, We Don't Even Talk Anymore': Post-Dissolutional Communication in Breakup Stories," in *Making Connections: Readings in Relational Communication*, 4th ed., ed. K. M. Galvin and P. J Cooper, 281–90 (Los Angeles: Roxbury, 2006).

59. A. L. Busboom and others, "Can We Still Be Friends? Resources and Barriers to Friendship Quality after Romantic Relationship Dissolution," *Personal Relationships* 9 (2002): 215–23.

60. J. M. Honeycutt, "Memory Structures for the Rise and Fall of Personal Relationships," in *Understanding Relationship Processes*, vol. 1, *Individuals in Relationships*, ed. S. W. Duck (Newbury Park, CA: Sage, 1993), 30–59.

61. J. M. Honeycutt and J. Cantrill, "Using Expectations of Relational Actions to Predict Number of Intimate Relationships: Don Juan and Romeo Unmasked," *Communication Reports* 4 (1991): 14–21.

62. L. A. Baxter and B. M. Montgomery, *Relating: Dialogues and Dialectics* (New York: Guilford, 1996).

63. C. A. Van Lear, "Testing a Cyclical Model of Communicative Openness in Relationship Development: Two Longitudinal Studies," *Communication Monographs* 58 (1991): 337–61.

64. J. Luft, *Of Human Interaction: The Johari Window* (Palo Alto, CA: Mayfield, 1969).

65. A. P. Bochner, "The Function of Human Communication in Interpersonal Bonding," in *Handbook of Rhetorical and Communication Theory*, ed. L. L. Arnold and J. W. Bowers (Boston: Allyn & Bacon, 1984), 554–621.

66. I. Altman and D. A. Taylor, *Social Penetration: The Development of Interpersonal Relationships* (New York: Holt, Rinehart & Winston, 1973).

67. A. W. Gouldner, "The Norm of Reciprocity: A Preliminary Statement," *American Sociological Review* 25 (1960): 161–71; Fisher and Adams, *Interpersonal Communication*.

68. R. L. Heaton, *Abortion as a Taboo Topic: A Network Text Analysis of Abortion Disclosure Decisions and Boundary Coordination* (Ann Arbor, MI: UMI Dissertation Services, 2012).

69. N. L. Collins and L. C. Miller, "The Disclosure-Liking Link: From Meta-Analysis Toward a Dynamic Reconceptualization," *Psychological Bulletin* 116, no. 3 (1994): 457–75.

70. S. Petronio, *Boundaries of Privacy: Dialectics of Disclosure* (Albany, NY: SUNY Press, 2002).

71. Guerrero Andersen, and Afifi, *Close Encounters.*

72. "Robin Thicke Admits to Drug Abuse, Says Paula Patton Left Because He Told Her 'the Truth,'" *ET Online: CBS News*, September 15, 2014, www.cbsnews.com/news /robin-thicke-admits-drug-abuse-says-paula-patton-left-because he-told-her-the -truth/.

73. S. Petronio, *Boundaries of Privacy.*

74. Ibid.

75. S. Petronio and J. N. Martin, "Ramifications of Revealing Private Information: A Gender Gap," *Journal of Clinical Psychology* 42, no. 3 (1986): 499–506.

76. G. N. Hamadeh and S. M. Adib, "Cancer Truth Disclosure by Lebanese Doctors," *Social Science and Medicine* 47, no. 9 (1998): 1289–94.

77. S. Petronio, *Boundaries of Privacy.*

78. Guerrero Andersen, and Afifi, *Close Encounters.*

79. S. Petronio, C. Olson, and N. Dollar, "Privacy Issues in Relational Embarrassment: Impact on Relational Quality and Communication Satisfaction," *Communication Research Reports* 6, no. 1 (1989): 21–27; I. Altman, A. Vinsel, and B. B. Brown, "Dialectical Conceptions in Social Psychology: An Application to Social Penetration and Privacy Regulation," *Advances in Experimental Social Psychology* 14 (December 1981): 107–60.

80. L. A. Baxter and B. M. Montgomery, *Relating: Dialogues and Dialectics.*

81. L. A. Baxter and others, "Everyday Loyalties and Betrayals in Personal Relationships," *Journal of Social and Personal Relationships* 14 (1997): 655–78.

82. Baxter and Montgomery, *Relating.*

83. T. Parker-Pope, "Reinventing Date Night for Long-Married Couples," *New York Times*, February 12, 2008, www.nytimes.com/2008/02/12/health/12well.html? _r = 0.

84. Baxter and Montgomery, *Relating.*

85. E. Sahlstein, "Making Plans: Praxis Strategies for Negotiating Uncertainty-Certainty in Long-Distance Relationships," *Western Journal of Communication* 70 (2006): 147–65.

86. L. A. Baxter and others, "Wives of Elderly Husbands with Dementia," *Journal of Applied Communication Research* 30 (2002): 1–26.

Chapter 9

1. D. J. Canary and L. Stafford, "Maintaining Relationships through Strategic and Routine Interaction," in *Communication and Relational Maintenance*, ed. D. J. Canary and L. Stafford, 3–22 (San Diego, CA: Academic Press, 1994).

2. D. J. Canary and L. Stafford, "Relational Maintenance Strategies and Equity in Marriage," *Communication Monographs* 59 (1992): 239–67.

3. E. L. Miller, V. Hefner, and A. M. Scott, "Turning Points in Dyadic Friendship Development and Termination" (paper presented at the annual meeting of the International Communication Association, San Francisco, CA, May 2007), http://citation.allacademic.com/meta/p_mla_apa_research_citation/1/7/2/4/7/p172478_index.html.

4. Z. Rubin, *Liking and Loving* (New York: Holt, Rinehart, & Winston, 1979).

5. M. Lund, "The Development of Investment and Commitment Scales for Predicting Continuity of Personal Relationships," *Journal of Social and Personal Relationships* 2 (1985): 3–23.

6. Canary and Stafford, "Maintaining Relationships through Strategic and Routine Interaction."

7. Ibid.

8. S. T. Tong and J. B. Walther, "Relational Maintenance and Computer-Mediated Communication," in *Computer-Mediated Communication in Personal Relationships*, ed. K. B. Wright and L. M. Webb, 98–118 (New York: Peter Lang, 2011).

9. N. Cheever and others, "Out of Sight Is Not Out of Mind: The Impact of Restricting Wireless Mobile Device Use on Anxiety among Low, Moderate and High Users," *Computers in Human Behavior* 37 (2014): 290–97.

10. Tong and Walther, "Relational Maintenance and Computer-Mediated Communication."

11. "Couples, the Internet, and Social Media," Pew Research Center: Internet, Science and Tech, February 20, 2014, www.pewinternet.org/2014/02/20/couples-the-internet-and-social-media-2/.

12. Ibid.

13. "How Common Are Long Distance Relationships?" FAQs, www.longdistancerelationships.net/faqs.htm#How_common_are_long_distance_relationships.

14. Tong and Walther, "Relational Maintenance and Computer-Mediated Communication."

15. Ibid.

16. "Couples, the Internet, and Social Media."

17. B. A. Nardi, S. Whittaker, and E. Bradner, "Interaction and Outeraction: Instant Messaging in Action," in *Proceedings of the ACM Conference on Computer-Supported Cooperative Work*, 79–88 (New York: ACM, 2000).

18. Tong and Walther, "Relational Maintenance and Computer-Mediated Communication."

19. Canary and Stafford, "Maintaining Relationships through Strategic and Routine Interaction."

20. R. M. Kowalski and others, "Lying, Cheating, Complaining, and Other Aversive Interpersonal Behaviors: A Narrative Examination of the Dark Side of Relationships," *Journal of Social and Personal Relationships* 20 (2003): 471–90.

21. L. Stafford, "Maintaining Romantic Relationships: Summary and Analysis of One Research Program," in *Maintaining Relationships through Communication: Relational, Contextual, and Cultural Variations*, ed. D. J. Canary and M. Dainton, 51–77 (Mahwah, NJ: Lawrence Erlbaum, 2003).

22. L. Stafford, "Measuring Relationship Maintenance Behaviors: Critique and Development of the Revised Relationship Maintenance Behavior Scale," *Journal of Social and Personal Relationships* 8 (2010): 278–303.

23. M. Dainton and L. Stafford, "Routine Maintenance Behaviors: A Comparison of Relational Type, Partner Similarity, and Sex Differences," *Journal of Social and Personal Relationships* 10 (1993): 255–71.

24. P. McGraw, "Dr. Phil: 3 Ways to Get Stronger Relationships," May 12, 2015, *Oprah.com*, www.oprah.com/relationships/How-to-Improve-Your-Relationship-Dr-Phils-Advice.

25. J. Gottman and S. Carrera, "Why Can't Men and Women Get Along? Developmental Roots and Marital Inequities," *Communication and Relational Maintenance*, ed. D. J. Canary and L. Stafford, 203–26 (San Diego, CA: Academic Press, 1994).

26. D. H. Femlee, "No Couple Is an Island: A Social Network Perspective on Dyadic Stability," *Social Forces* 79 (2001): 1259–87.

27. S. O. Gaines and C. R. Agnew, "Relationship Maintenance in Intercultural Couples: An Interdependence Analysis," *Maintaining Relationships through Communication: Relational, Contextual, and Cultural Variations*, ed. D. J. Canary and M. Dainton, 231–53 (Mahwah, NJ: Lawrence Erlbaum, 2003).

28. S. M. Haas and L. Stafford, "Maintenance Behaviors in Same Sex and Marital Relationships: A Matched Sample Comparison," *Journal of Communication* 5 (2005): 43–60.

29. B. Booth and others, "What We Know about Army Families: 2007 Update, U.S. Army MWR," www.mwrbrandcentral.com/images/uploads/whatweknow2007.pdf.

30. N. B. Ellison, C. Steinfield, and C. Lampe, "The Benefits of Facebook 'Friends': Social Capital and College Students' Use of Online Social Network Sites," *Journal of Computer-Mediated Communication* 12 (2007): 1143–68.

31. Tong and Walther, "Relational Maintenance and Computer-Mediated Communication."

32. "Couples, the Internet, and Social Media."

33. E. Craig and K. B. Wright, "Computer-Mediated Relational Maintenance Development and Maintenance on Facebook," *Communication Research Reports* 29 (2012): 119–29.

34. S. McCornack, *Reflect and Relate: An Introduction to Interpersonal Communication*, 2nd ed. (Boston, MA: Bedford/St. Martin's, 2010).

35. W. K. Rawlins, "Being There and Growing Apart: Sustaining Friendships during Adulthood," in *Communication and Relational Maintenance*, ed. D. J. Canary and L. Stafford, 275–94 (San Diego, CA: Academic Press, 1994).

36. H. Orenstein, "Friendship Quotes from Justin Beiber, Lea Michele, Daniel Radcliffe, and More," *Huffington Post*, August 8, 2008, www.huffingtonpost.com/2012/08/08/friendship-quotes-from-ju_n_1757728.html.

37. Tong and Walther, "Relational Maintenance and Computer-Mediated Communication."

38. Ellison, Steinfield, and Lampe, "The Benefits of Facebook 'Friends.'"

39. M. C. Stewart, M. Dainton, and A. K. Goodboy, "Maintaining Relationships on Facebook: Associations with Uncertainty, Jealousy, and Satisfaction," *Communication Reports* 27 (2014): 13–26.

40. M. Dainton, "Equity and Uncertainty in Relational Maintenance," *Western Journal of Communication* 67 (2003): 164–86.

41. Stewart, Dainton, and Goodboy, "Maintaining Relationships on Facebook."

42. N. Way, *Deep Secrets: Boys' Friendships and the Crisis of Connection* (Cambridge, MA: Harvard University Press, 2011).

43. K. Werking, *We're Just Good Friends: Women and Men in Nonromantic Relationships* (New York: Guilford Press, 1997).

44. S. J. Messman, D. J. Canary, and K. S. Hause, "Motives to Remain Platonic, Equity, and the Use of Maintenance Strategies in Opposite-Sex Friendships," *Journal of Social and Personal Relationships* 17 (2000): 67–94.

45. Werking, *We're Just Good Friends.*

46. Ibid.

47. M. A. Bisson and T. R. Levine Bisson, "Negotiating a Friends with Benefits Relationship," *Archives of Sexual Behavior* 38 (2009): 66–73.

48. Ibid.

49. M. Hughes, K. Morrison, and K. J. K. Asada, "What's Love Got to Do with It? Exploring the Impact of Maintenance Rules, Love Attitudes, and Network Support on Friends with Benefits Relationships," *Western Journal of Communication* 69 (2005): 49–66.

50. P. M. Sias and others, "Narratives of Workplace Friendship Deterioration," *Journal of Social and Personal Relationships* 21 (2004): 321–40.

51. McCornack, *Reflect and Relate.*

52. K. Riach and F. Wilson, "Don't Screw the Crew: Exploring the Rules of Engagement in Organizational Management," *British Journal of Management* 18 (2007): 79–92.

53. McCornack, *Reflect and Relate.*

54. S. R. A. Hovick, R. A. Meyers, and C. E. Timmerman, "E-mail Communication in Workplace Romantic Relationships," *Communication Studies* 54 (2003): 468–80.

55. Canary and Stafford, "Maintaining Relationships through Strategic and Routine Interaction."

56. J. T. Wood, *Relational Communication: Continuity and Change in Personal Relationships*, 2nd ed. (Belmont, CA: Wadsworth, 2000).

57. J. M. Gottman and J. DeClaire, *The Relationship Cure: A Five-Step Guide for Building Better Connections with Family, Friends, and Lovers* (New York: Crown 2001).

58. S. L. Gable and others, "What Do You Do When Things Go Right? The Intrapersonal and Interpersonal Benefits of Sharing Positive Events," *Journal of Personality and Social Psychology* 87 (2004): 228–45.

59. Gottman and DeClaire, *The Relationship Cure.*

60. Ibid.

61. S. K. Whitbourne, "The Top 10 Relationship Myths and Why They're Myths," *Psychology Today*, March, 31, 2012, www.psychologytoday.com/blog/fulfillment-any -age/201203/the-top-10-relationship-myths-and-why-theyre-myths.

62. Canary and Stafford, "Maintaining Relationships through Strategic and Routine Interaction."

63. L. A. Baxter, "A Dialogic Approach to Relationship Maintenance," in *Communication and Relational Maintenance*, ed. D. J. Canary and L. Stafford, 233–54 (San Diego, CA: Academic Press, 1994).

64. K. Flanagan, "The Nine Most Overlooked Threats to a Marriage," *UnTangled* (blog), October 1, 2014, http://drkellyflanagan.com/2014/10/01/the-9-most-overlooked -threats-to-a-marriage/.

65. R. M. Kowalski, S. Walker, R. Wilkinson, A. Queen, and B. Sharpe, "Lying, Cheating, Complaining, and Other Aversive Interpersonal Behaviors: A Narrative Examination of the Dark Side of Relationships," *Journal of Social and Personal Relationships* 20 (2003): 471–90.

66. A. L. Sillars, "(Mis)Understandings," in *The Dark Side of Relationships*, ed. B. H. Spitzberg and W. R. Cupach, 73–102 (Mawah, NJ: Lawrence Erlbaum, 1998).

67. W. W. Wilmot and J. L. Hocker, *Interpersonal Conflict*, 7th ed. (Boston, MA: McGraw-Hill, 2007).

68. Ibid.

69. H. B. Braiker and H. H. Kelley, "Conflict in the Development of Close Relationships," in *Social Exchange in Developing Relationships*, ed. R. L. Burgess and T. L. Huston, 135–68 (New York: Academic Press, 1979).

70. D. R. Peterson, "Conflict," in *Close Relationships*, ed. H. H. Kelley and others, 360–96 (New York: Freeman, 1983).

71. "Couples, the Internet, and Social Media."

72. M. C. Stewart, M. Dainton, and A. K. Goodboy, "Maintaining Relationships on Facebook."

73. B. Hoai-Tran, "Twitter May Kill Your Relationship," *USA Today*, July 9, 2014, www .usatoday.com/story/news/nation/2014/07/09/twitter-romance-relationship-breakup -divorce-cheating/12377979/.

74. W. H. Jones and M. P. Burdette, "Betrayal in Relationships: Essence and Impact," in *Perspectives on Close Relationships*, ed. A. L. Weber and J. H. Harvey, 243–62 (Boston, MA: Allyn and Bacon, 1994).

75. J. K. Alberts, J. N. Martin, and T. K. Nakayama, *Communication in Society* (Boston, MA: Pearson, 2011).

76. S. S. Brehm and S. M. Kassin, *Social Psychology* (Boston, MA: Houghton Mifflin, 1990); Wood, *Relational Communication*.

77. D. J. Canary, W. R. Cupach, and S. J. Messman, *Relationship Conflict* (Thousand Oaks, CA: Sage, 1995).

78. L. A. Coser, *The Function of Social Conflict* (New York: Free Press, 1956).

79. Canary, Cupach, and Messman, *Relationship Conflict*.

80. Alberts, Martin, and Nakayama, *Communication in Society*.

81. Braiker and Kelley, "Conflict in the Development of Close Relationships"; S. Metts, "Relational Transgressions," in *The Dark Side of Interpersonal Communication*, ed. B. H. Spitzberg and W. R. Cupach, 217–39 (Mahwah, NJ: Lawrence Erlbaum, 1998).

82. J. W. Howard and R. M. Dawes, "Linear Prediction of Marital Happiness," *Personality and Social Psychology Bulletin* 2 (1976): 478–80.

83. L. K. Guerrero, P. A. Andersen, and W. A. Afifi, *Close Encounters: Communication in Relationships*, 3rd ed. (Los Angeles: Sage, 2011).

84. A. Sillars, D. J. Canary, and M. Tafoya, "Communication, Conflict, and the Quality of Family Relationships," in *Handbook of Family Communication*, ed. A. Vangelisti, 413–46 (Mahwah, NJ: Lawrence Erlbaum, 2004).

85. M. A. Gross and L. K. Guerrero, "Managing Conflict Appropriately and Effectively: An Application of the Competence Model to Rahim's Organizational Conflict Styles," *International Journal of Conflict Management* 11, no. 3 (2000): 200–26.

86. D. J. Canary and S. G. Lakey, "Managing Conflict in a Competent Manner: A Mindful Look at Events That Matter," in *The Sage Handbook of Conflict Communication*, ed. J. Oetzel and S. Ting-Toomey, 185–210 (Thousand Oaks, CA: Sage, 2006).

87. J. P. Caughlin, A. L. Vangelisti, S. L. Mikucki-Enyart, "Conflict in Dating and Marital Relationships," in *The Sage Handbook of Conflict Communication*, ed. J. Oetzel and S. Ting-Toomey, 161–85 (Thousand Oaks, CA: Sage, 2006).

88. J. L. Hocker and W. W. Wilmot, *Interpersonal Conflict*, 7th ed. (Dubuque, IA: Brown and Benchmark, 2007).

89. D. H. Cloven and M. E. Roloff, "The Chilling Effect of Aggressive Potential on the Expression of Complaints in Intimate Relationships," *Communication Monographs* 60 (1993): 199–219.

90. M. E. Roloff and D. H. Cloven, "The Chilling Effect in Interpersonal Relationships: The Reluctance to Speak One's Mind," in *Intimates in Conflict: A Communication Perspective*, ed. D. D. Cahn, 49–76 (Hillsdale, NJ: Lawrence Erlbaum, 1990).

91. Caughlin, Vangelisti, and Mikucki-Enyart, "Conflict in Dating and Marital Relationships."

92. M. E. Roloff and D. E. Ifert, "Conflict Management through Avoidance: Withholding Complaints, Suppressing Arguments, and Declaring Topics Taboo," in *Balancing the Secrets of Private Disclosures*, ed. S. Petronio, 151–63 (Mahwah, NJ: Lawrence Erlbaum, 2000).

93. L. K. Guerrero and A. G. La Valley, "Conflict, Emotion, and Communication," in *The Sage Handbook of Conflict Communication*, ed. J. Oetzel and S. Ting-Toomey, 69–96 (Thousand Oaks, CA: Sage, 2006).

94. Guerrero Andersen, and Afifi, *Close Encounters*.

95. Canary, Cupach, and Messman, *Relationship Conflict*.

96. C. S. Burggraf and A. L. Sillars, "A Critical Examination of Sex Differences in Marital Communication," *Communication Monographs* 54 (1985): 276–94.

97. Canary, Cupach, and Messman, *Relationship Conflict*.

98. L. Gaelick, G. V. Brodenshausen, and R. S. Wyer, "Emotional Communication in Close Relationships," *Journal of Personality and Social Psychology* 49, no. 5 (1985): 1246–65.

99. D. A. Smith, D. Vivian, and K. D. O'Leary, "Longitudinal Prediction of Marital Discord from Premarital Expressions of Affect," *Journal of Consulting and Clinical Psychology* 58, no. 6 (1990): 790–98.

100. Burggraf and Sillars, "A Critical Examination of Sex Differences in Marital Communication."

101. L. N. Olson and D. O. Braithwaite, "'If You Hit Me Again, I Will Hit Back': Conflict Management Strategies of Individuals Experiencing Aggression during Conflicts," *Communication Studies* 55 (2004): 271–85.

102. M. P. Johnson, "Patriarchal Terrorism and Common Couple Violence: Two Forms of Violence against Women," *Journal of Marriage and the Family* 57 (1995): 283–349.

103. P. Schrodt, P. L. Witt, and J. R. Shimkowski, "A Meta-Analytical Review of the Demand/Withdraw Pattern of Interaction and Its Associations with Individual, Relational, and Communicative Outcomes," *Communication Monographs* 81 (2014): 28–58.

104. Ibid.

105. L. M. Papp, C. D. Kouros, and E. M. Cummings, "Demand-Withdraw Patterns in Marital Conflict in the Home," *Personal Relationships* 16 (2009): 285–300.

106. J. Gottman, *Why Marriages Succeed or Fail* (New York: Simon & Schuster, 1994).

107. E. E. Smith, "Masters of Love," *Atlantic Monthly*, June 12, 2014, www.theatlantic .com/health/archive/2014/06/happily-ever-after/372573/.

108. Gottman, *Why Marriages Succeed or Fail*.

109. C. I. Notarius, "Marriage: Will I Be Happy or Will I Be Sad?" in *A Lifetime of Relationships*, ed. N. Vanzetti and S. Duck, 265–89 (Pacific Grove, CA: Brooks/Cole, 1996).

110. C. E. Rusbult and others, "Accommodation Processes during the Early Years of Marriage," in *The Development Course of Marital Dysfunction*, ed. T. N. Bradbury, 74–113 (New York: Cambridge University Press, 1998).

111. B. Atkinson, "The Love Breakthrough That Could Save Your Relationship," in *O, The Oprah Magazine*, January 2005, www.Oprah.com/APP/O-Magazine.html.

112. C. Carter, "Should You Stay or Should You Go?," *Huffington Post*, February 21, 2011, http://huffingtonpost.com/christine-carter-phd/should-you-stay-or -should_b_824122.html.

113. Gottman, *Why Marriages Succeed or Fail*.

114. A. Weil, "Three Breathing Exercises," www.drweil.com/drw/u/ART00521/three -breathing-exercises.html.

115. E. E. Smith, "Masters of Love."

116. Wood, *Relational Communication*.

117. J. Shotter, *Conversational Realities: The Construction of Life through Language*, (Newbury Park: Sage, 1993).

118. Gottman, *Why Marriages Succeed or Fail*.

119. R. D. Rogge and others, "Is Skills Training Necessary for the Primary Prevention of Marital Distress and Dissolution? A 3-Year Experimental Study of Three Interventions," *Journal of Consulting and Clinical Psychology* 81, no. 6 (2013): 949–61.

Chapter 10

1. L. W. Frey, "Applied Communication Research on Group Facilitation in Natural Settings," in *Innovations in Group Facilitation: Applications in Natural Settings*, ed. Lawrence Frey (Cresskill, NJ: Hampton Press, 1995), 1–26.

2. S. A. Beebe and J. T. Masterson, *Communicating in Small Groups*, 7th ed. (Boston: Allyn & Bacon, 2003), 6–9.

3. E. Salas, D. E. Sims, and C. S. Burke, "Is There a 'Big Five' in Teamwork?," *Small Group Research* 36 (2005): 555–99.

4. T. J. Socha, "Communication in Family Units," in *Handbook of Group Communication Theory*, ed. Lawrence Frey (Thousand Oaks, CA: Sage, 1999), 475–92.

5. S. A. Wheelan and A. R. List, "Cohort Group Effectiveness and the Educational Achievement of Adult Undergraduate Students," *Small Group Research* 31 (2000): 724–38.

6. T. E. Zorn and G. H. Thompson, "Communication in Top Management Teams," in *New Directions in Group Communication*, ed. Lawrence Frey (Thousand Oaks, CA: Sage, 2002), 253–72.

7. B. A. Fisher and D. Ellis, *Small Group Decision Making: Communication and the Group Process*, 3rd ed. (New York: McGraw-Hill, 1990), 20–21.

8. S. A. Wheelan, "Group Size, Group Development, and Group Productivity," *Small Group Research* 40 (2009): 247–62.

9. C. Pavitt and E. Curtis, *Small Group Discussion* (Scottsdale, AZ: Gorsuch Scarisbrick, 1994).

10. C. Anderson, B. Riddle, and M. Martin, "Socialization Processes in Groups," in *Handbook of Group Communication Theory and Research*, ed. Lawrence Frey (Thousand Oaks, CA: Sage, 1999), 139–63.

11. M. Burke, R. Kraut, and E. Joyce, "Membership Claims and Requests: Conversational-Level Newcomer Strategies in Online Groups," *Small Group Research* 41 (2010): 4–40.

12. Salas, Sims, and Burke, "Is There a 'Big Five' in Teamwork?"

13. K. L. Adams and G. J. Galanes, *Communicating in Groups: Applications and Skills*, 9th ed. (New York: McGraw-Hill, 2015).

14. E. Salomon, "60 Minutes Helps Pave Way for Change at NIH, FDA," *60 Minutes: Overtime*, May 15, 2014, www.cbsnews.com/news/60-minutes-helps-pave-way-for-change-at-nih-fda/.

15. W. E. Watson, K. Kumar, and L. K. Michaelson, "Cultural Diversity's Impact on Interaction Processes and Performance: Comparing Homogeneous and Diverse Task Groups," *Academy of Management Journal* 36 (1993): 590–602.

16. Associated Press, "Second Opinion Can Spark Big Changes in Care," August 2, 2011, www.msnbc.msn.com/id/16430071/.

17. D. D. Henningsen and M. L. M. Henningsen, "Examining Social Influence in Information-Sharing Contexts," *Small Group Research* 34 (2003): 391–412.

18. Adams and Galanes, *Communicating in Groups*.

19. K. D. Benne and P. Sheats, "Functional Roles of Group Members," *Journal of Social Issues* 1, no. 4 (1948): 41, 49.

20. J. D. Rothwell, *In Mixed Company: Communicating in Small Groups and Teams*, 5th ed. (Belmont, CA: Wadsworth/Thomson, 2004).

21. B. Tuckman and M. A. Jensen, "Stages of Small-Group Development Revisited," *Group and Organization Studies* 2 (1977): 419–27.

22. C. Gersick, "Time and Transition in Work Teams," in *Small Groups Communication: Theory and Practice*, 8th ed., ed. R. Hirokawa and others, 59–75 (Los Angeles: Roxbury, 2003).

23. D. A. Harrison and others, "Time, Teams, and Task Performance: Changing Effects of Surface and Deep-Level Diversity on Group Functioning," *Academy of Management Journal* 45 (2002): 1029–45.

24. R. Mitchell, S. Nicholas, and B. Boyle, "The Role of Openness to Cognitive Diversity and Group Processes in Knowledge Creation," *Small Group Research* 20 (2009): 535–54.

25. J. G. Oetzel, "Culturally Homogeneous and Heterogeneous Groups: Explaining Communication Processes through Individualism-Collectivism and Self-Construal," *International Journal of Intercultural Relations* 22 (1998): 135–61.

26. D. Matsumoto, *The New Japan: Debunking Seven Cultural Stereotypes* (Yarmouth, ME: Intercultural Press, 2002).

27. M. W. Lustig and L. L. Cassotta, "Comparing Group Communication across Cultures: Leadership, Conformity, and Discussion Procedures," in *Small Group Communication: A Reader*, 6th ed., ed. R. S. Cathcart and L. A. Samovar, 393–404 (Dubuque, IA: Wm. C. Brown, 1992).

28. M. W. Lustig and J. Koester, *Intercultural Competence: Interpersonal Communication across Cultures* (New York: HarperCollins, 1993).

29. S. Ting-Toomey, *Communication across Cultures* (New York: Guilford Press, 1999), 45–54, 261–76.

30. J. K. Alberts, T. K. Nakayama, and J. N. Martin, *Human Communication in Society*, 3rd ed. (Boston, MA: Pearson, 2012), 275–80.

31. J. G. Oetzel, "Effective Intercultural Workgroup Communication Theory," in *Theorizing about Intercultural Communication*, ed. W. B. Gudykunst (Thousand Oaks, CA: Sage, 2005), 351–71.

32. M. S. Poole and J. T. Garner, "Workgroup Conflict and Communication," in *The Sage Handbook of Conflict Communication*, ed. J. G. Oetzel and S. Ting-Toomey (Thousand Oaks, CA: Sage, 2006), 267–92.

33. J. G. Oetzel, "Self-Construals, Communication Processes, and Group Outcomes in Homogeneous and Heterogeneous Groups," *Small Group Research* 32 (2001): 19–54.

34. M. A. Velenti and R. Rockett, "The Effects of Demographic Differences on Forming Intragroup Relationships," *Small Group Research* 39 (2008): 179–202.

35. S. B. F. Paletz and others, "Ethnic Composition and Its Differential Impact on Group Processes in Diverse Teams," *Small Group Research* 35 (2004): 128–58.

36. See, for example, D. F. Crown, "The Use of Group and Groupcentric Individual Goals for Culturally Heterogeneous and Homogeneous Task Groups: An Assessment of European Work Teams," *Small Group Research* 38 (2007): 489–508; D. R. Ilgen and others, "Teams in Organizations: From Input-Process-Output Models to IMOI Models," *Annual Review of Psychology* 56 (2005): 517–43.

37. J. B. Walther, T. Loh, and L. Granka, "Let Me Count the Ways: The Interchange of Verbal and Nonverbal Cues in Computer-Mediated and Face-to-Face Affinity," *Journal of Language and Social Psychology* 24 (2005): 36–65.

38. J. H. Waldeck, P. Kearney, and T. G. Plax, *Business and Professional Communication in a Digital Age* (Boston, MA: Wadsworth, 2013).

39. Ibid.

40. G. J. Galanes and K. L. Adams, *Effective Group Discussion: Theory and Practice*, 14th ed. (New York: McGraw-Hill, 2013).

41. Ibid.

42. Ibid.

43. L. Hambley, T. O'Neil, and T. Kline, "Virtual Team Leadership: Perspectives from the Field," *International Journal of e-Collaboration* 3 (2007): 40–64.

44. Waldeck, Kearney, and Plax, *Business and Professional Communication in a Digital Age*.

45. D. Feldman, "Development and Enforcement of Group Norms," *Academy of Management Review* 9 (1984): 47–53.

46. S. G. Rogelberg, L. R. Shanock, and C. W. Scott, "Wasted Time and Money in Meetings: Increasing Return on Investment," *Small Group Research* 43 (2012): 236–45.

47. M. E. Mayer, "Behaviors Leading to More Effective Decisions in Small Groups Embedded in Organizations," *Communication Reports* 11 (1998): 123–32.

48. D. B. Barker, "The Behavioral Analysis of Interpersonal Intimacy in Group Development," *Small Group Research* 22 (1991): 76–91.

49. S. Zimmerman, "Social Cognition and Evaluation of Health Care Team Communication Effectiveness," *Western Journal of Communication* 58 (1994): 116–41.

Chapter 11

1. B. Handy, "The Daring Genesis of J. J. Abrams's *Star Wars: The Force Awakens*," *Vanity Fair*, June 2015, www.vanityfair.com/hollywood/2015/05/star-wars-the -force-awakens-vanity-fair-cover.

2. D. S. Gouran and R. Y. Hirokawa, "Effective Decision Making and Problem Solving in Groups: A Functional Perspective," in *Small Group Communication: Theory and Practice; An Anthology*, ed. R. Y. Hirokawa and others, 27–38 (Los Angeles: Roxbury, 2003).

3. K. Adams and G. Galanes, *Communicating in Groups: Applications and Skills*, 8th ed. (Boston: McGraw-Hill, 2009): 205–24.

4. Ibid.

5. V. Putnam and P. Paulus, "Brainstorming, Brainstorming Rules and Decision Making," *Journal of Creative Behavior* 43 (2009): 23–39.

6. J. S. Valacich, A. R. Dennis, and T. Connolly, "Idea Generation in Computer-Based Groups: A New Ending to an Old Story," *Organizational Behavior and Human Decision Processes* 57 (1994): 448–68.

7. S. Stone, "Conserve Water in Fresno and Get Up to $1,000," *ABC 30 Action News*, http://abc30.com/news/conserve-water-in-fresno-and-get-up-to-$1000/372571/.

8. Gouran and Hirokawa, "Effective Decision Making and Problem Solving in Groups," 27–38.

9. U. Klocke, "How to Improve Decision Making in Small Groups: Effects of Dissent and Training Interventions," *Small Group Research* 38 (2007): 437–68.

10. G. M. Wittenbaum and J. M. Bowen, "A Social Validation Explanation for Mutual Enhancement," *Journal of Experimental Social Psychology* 40 (2004): 169–84.

11. J. A. Bonito, "An Information-Processing Approach to Participation in Small Groups," *Communication Research* 28 (2001): 275–303.

12. Klocke, "How to Improve Decision Making in Small Groups."

13. M. E. Shaw, *Group Dynamics*, 3rd ed. (New York: McGraw-Hill, 1981).

14. C. Gersick, "Time and Transition in Work Teams," in *Small Group Communication: Theory and Practice,* 8th ed., ed. R. Y. Hirokawa and others (Los Angeles: Roxbury, 2003): 59–75.

15. L. M. Jessup and J. S. Valacich, *Group Support Systems: New Perspectives* (New York: Macmillan, 1993).

16. K. Fisher, *Leading Self-Directed Work Teams: A Guide to Developing New Team Leadership Skills* (New York: McGraw-Hill, 2000).

17. S. K. Johnson, K. Bettenhausen, and E. Gibbons, "Realities of Working in Virtual Teams: Affective and Attitudinal Outcomes of Using Computer-Mediated Communication," *Small Group Research* 40 (2009): 623–49.

18. R. E. Parker, "Distinguishing Characteristics of Virtual Groups," in *Small Group Communication Theory and Practice: An Anthology*, ed. R. Y. Hirwokawa and others (Los Angeles: Roxbury, 2003).

19. G. Galanes and K. Adams, *Effective Group Discussion: Theory and Practice*, 14th ed. (New York: McGraw-Hill, 2013).

20. Ibid.

21. K. W. Hawkins, "Effects of Gender and Communication Content on Leadership Emergence in Small Task-Oriented Groups," *Small Group Research* 26 (1995): 234–49.

22. C. Emery, K. Daniloski, and A. Hamby, "The Reciprocal Effects of Self-View as a Leader and Leadership Emergences," *Small Group Research* 42 (2011): 199–224.

23. K. Wickham and J. Walther, "Perceived Behaviors of Emergent and Designated Leaders in Virtual Groups," *International Journal of e-Collaboration* 3 (January–March 2007): 1–17.

24. L. A. Hambley, T. A. O'Neill, and T. J. B. Kline, "Virtual Team Leadership: Perspectives from the Field," *International Journal of e-Collaboration* 3 (2007): 40–64.

25. Ibid.

26. I. Janis, *Victims of Groupthink* (Boston: Houghton Mifflin, 1972).

27. D. Badie, "Groupthink, Iraq, and the War on Terror: Explaining US Policy Shift toward Iraq," *Foreign Policy Analysis* 6 (2010): 277–96.

28. D. Henningsen and others, "Examining the Symptoms of Groupthink and Retrospective Sensemaking," *Small Group Research* 25 (2006): 36–64.

29. R. J. Welsh Cline, "Detecting Groupthink: Methods of Observing the Illusion of Unanimity," *Communication Quarterly* 38 (1990): 112–26.

30. C. P. Neck and G. Moorhead, "Groupthink Remodeled: The Importance of Leadership, Time Pressure, and Methodical Decision-making Procedures," *Human Relations* 48 (May 1995): 537–57.

31. J. Hall, "Decision, Decisions, Decisions," *Psychology Today* (November 1971): 51–54.

32. R. Y. Hirokawa, "Group Decision-Making Performance: A Continued Test of the Functional Perspective," *Human Communication Research* 14 (1988): 487–515.

33. Galanes and Adams, *Effective Group Discussion*.

34. W. W. Wilmot and J. L. Hocker, *Interpersonal Conflict*, 7th ed. (Boston, MA: McGraw-Hill, 2007).

35. Galanes and Adams, *Effective Group Discussion*.

36. K. J. Behar and others, "Conflict in Small Groups: The Meaning and Consequences of Process Conflict," *Small Group Research* 42 (2011): 127–76.

37. Ibid.

38. Ibid.

Chapter 12

1. National Association of Colleges and Employers, "Job Outlook 2016: Attributes Employers Want to See on New College Graduates' Resumes," November 18, 2015, http://www.naceweb.org/s11182015/employers-look-for-in-new-hires.aspx.

2. Heldrich Center for Workforce Development and Center for Survey Research and Analysis, "Making the Grade? What American Workers Think Should Be Done to Improve Education," June 2000, 14.

3. D. Bodde, *China's First Unifier* (Hong Kong: Hong Kong University Press, 1967), 181.

4. A. Ayres, ed., *The Wisdom of Martin Luther King, Jr.* (New York: Penguin, 1993).

5. K. D. Miller and E. M. Lewis, "Touchstones, Authorities, and Marian Anderson: The Making of 'I Have a Dream,'" in *The Making of Martin Luther King and the Civil Rights Movement*, ed. B. Ward and T. Badger (New York: New York University Press, 1996), 151.

6. E. Rothstein, "A Resonance That Shaped a Vision of Freedom," *New York Times*, June 29, 2006, B7.

7. Ayres, *The Wisdom of Martin Luther King, Jr.*, 62–63.

8. D. Therkelsen and C. Fiebach, "Message to Desired Action: A Communication Effectiveness Model," *Journal of Communication Management* 5, no. 4 (2001): 376.

9. For research that supports Minh's claim, see B. Tuttle, "Survey: Women Are Smarter, More Thorough When Buying Cars," *Time*, January 25, 2012, http://business.time.com/2012/01/25/survey-women-are-smarter-more-thorough-when-buying-cars/.

10. U.S. Census Bureau, "U.S. Census Bureau Projections Show a Slower Growing, Older, More Diverse Nation a Half Century Later from Now," December 12, 2012, www.census.gov/newsroom/releases/archives/population/cb12-243.html.

11. A. R. Williams, "What's in a Surname?" *National Geographic*, January 19, 2011, http://ngm.nationalgeographic.com/2011/02/geography/usa-surnames-interactive.

12. Hillary Rodham Clinton, "Remarks at the Annual State Department Iftar," September 7, 2010, www.state.gov/secretary/20092013clinton/rm/2010/09/146885.htm.

13. P. Russell, "How to Mind Map," www.peterrussell.com/MindMaps/howto.php, accessed January 6, 2011.

14. B. Kirchner, "Mind-Map Your Way to an Idea: Here Is One Approach to Rooting Out Workable Topics That Move You," *Writer* 122, no. 3 (2009): 28–29.

15. J. F. Wilson and C. C. Arnold, *Public Speaking as a Liberal Art* (Boston: Allyn and Bacon, 1974), 70–71.

Chapter 13

1. R. D. Rieke, M. O. Sillars, and T. R. Peterson, *Argumentation and Critical Decision Making*, 7th ed. (Boston: Pearson/Allyn and Bacon, 2009), 163.

2. J. C. Reinard, *Foundations of Argument* (Dubuque, IA: Wm. C. Brown, 1991), 113.

3. Ibid., 115.

4. N. Pastore and M. W. Horowitz, "The Influence of Attributed Motive on the Acceptance of a Statement," *Journal of Abnormal and Social Psychology* 51, no. 2 (1955): 331–32.

5. Natalia Siniavskaia, "Young Adults Living with Parents," Eye on Housing, February 2014, http://eyeonhousing.org/2014/02/young-adults-living-with-parents-up-sharply/.

6. Ibid.

7. K. Ashford, "Parents: Your College Grads Expect You to Support Them Post-College," *Forbes,* May 20, 2015, http://www.forbes.com/sites/kateashford/2015/05/20/post-grad-support/#234f8f7d668c

8. Pew Internet and American Life Project, "The Internet Goes to College: How Students Are Living in the Future with Today's Technology," September 15, 2002, www.pewinternet.org/files/old-media/Files/Reports/2002/PIP_College_Report.pdf .pdf.

9. S. Kolowich, "Study: College Students Rarely Use Librarians' Expertise," *USA Today*, August 22, 2011, http://usatoday30.usatoday.com/news/education/story/2011-08-22 /Study-College-students-rarely-use-librarians-expertise/50094086/1.

10. Primary Research Group, "The Survey of American College Students: Who Goes to the College Library and Why," April 2009, www.researchandmarkets.com /reportinfo.asp?report_id = 888965&t = D&cat_id = .

11. F. Englander, R. A. Terregrossa, and Z. Wang, "Internet Use among College Students: Tool or Toy?" *Educational Review* 62 (February 2010): 93.

12. P. Lyman and H. Varian, "How Much Information? 2003," October 27, 2003, www2 .sims.berkeley.edu/research/projects/how-much-info-2003/.

13. M. de Kunder, "The Size of the World Wide Web (the Internet)," March 10, 2016, www.worldwidewebsize.com.

14. M. J. Metzger, A. J. Flanagin, and L. Zawarun, "College Student Web Use: Perceptions of Information Credibility and Verification Behavior," *Computers and Education* 41, no. 3 (2003): 271–90.

15. L. Holman, "Millennial Students' Mental Models of Search: Implications for Academic Librarians and Database Developers," *Journal of Academic Librarianship* 37, no. 1 (2011): 19–27.

16. W. L. Lym, "Tempting Students with Scholarly Research: Breaking the Fast Food Diet," *College Teaching* 57, no. 4 (2009): 237.

17. C. Chen and Others, "An Assessment of the Completeness of Scholarly Information on the Internet," *College and Research Libraries* 70, no. 4 (July 2009): 386–401.

18. H. Francke and O. Sundin, "Negotiating the Role of Sources: Educators' Conceptions of Credibility in Participatory Media," *Library and Information Science Research* 34, no. 3 (2012): 169–75.

19. A. Brown, "Wikipedia as a Data Source for Political Scientists: Accuracy and Completeness of Coverage," *PS: Political Science and Politics* 44, no. 2 (2011): 339–40.

20. ICANN, "TLD—Top-Level Domain," 2013, www.icann.org/en/about/learning/glossary.

21. J. Newman, "Top-Level Domain Name Grab: ICANN Reveals Results," *PC World*, June 13, 2012, www.pcworld.com/article/257549/top_level_domain_name_grab_icann _reveals_results.html.

22. R. Berkman, "Internet Searching Is Not Always What It Seems," *Chronicle of Higher Education* 46 (July 2000): B9.

23. Virtual Chase, "How to Evaluate Information—Checklist," March 6, 2006, www .virtualchase.com/quality/checklist.

24. C. Heath and D. Heath, *Made to Stick: Why Some Ideas Survive and Others Die* (New York: Random House, 2007), 110–11.

25. C. C. Mann, *1491: New Revelations of the Americas before Columbus* (New York: Alfred A. Knopf, 2005), 345–49.

26. A. Linn, "Big Brother May Not Be Watching, but Your Employer Probably Is," *NBC Today*, May 16, 2013, www.today.com/money/big-brother-may-not-be-watching-your -employer-probably-1C9950793.

27. L. Grossman, "Inside the Code War," *Time*, July 21, 2014, 20–21.

28. M. Tunick, "Privacy in Public Places: Do GPS and Video Surveillance Provide Plain Views?" *Social Theory and Practice* 35, no. 4 (2009): 597–622.

29. "Frequent Fliers, Prepare to Pay More," *New York Times*, March 4, 2013, A20, www .nytimes.com/2013/03/04/opinion/frequent-fliers-prepare-to-pay-more.html?_r = 0.

30. College Board, *Trends in College Pricing 2013*, 11.

31. Reinard, *Foundations of Argument*, 111.

32. W. R. Fisher, *Human Action as Narration: Toward a Philosophy of Reason, Value, and Action* (Columbia: University of South Carolina Press, 1987).

33. W. Brennan, "Google Glass," *Atlantic*, July/August 2014, 88–89.

34. K. E. Rowan, "A New Pedagogy for Explanatory Public Speaking: Why Arrangement Should Not Substitute for Invention," *Communication Education* 44 (July 1995): 236–50.

35. "Science Café: What Is the Higgs Boson?," North Carolina Museum of Natural Sciences, July 13, 2012, http://naturalsciences.org/about-us/news/science-cafe-what -higgs-boson.

36. R. M. Felder and B. A. Soloman, "Learning Styles and Strategies," accessed April 17, 2006, www4.ncsu.edu/unity/lockers/users/f/felder/public/ILSdir/styles.htm.

37. Ibid.

38. New York Civil Practice Law & Rules—Article 70 Habeas Corpus, http://law.onecle .com/new-york/civil-practice-law-rules/CVP0A70_A70.html (site last updated February 15, 2014).

39. C. Siebert, "Should a Chimp Be Able to Sue Its Owner?" *New York Times Magazine*, April 27, 2014, M28.

40. Ibid.

41. Ibid.

Chapter 14

1. J. C. McCroskey, *An Introduction to Rhetorical Communication*, 5th ed. (Englewood Cliffs, NJ: Prentice-Hall, 1986), 185.

2. J. C. McCroskey, "The Effects of Disorganization and Nonfluency on Attitude Change and Source Credibility," *Speech Monographs* 36 (March 1969): 13–21; H. Sharp and T. McClung, "Effect of Organization on the Speaker's Ethos," *Speech Monographs* 33 (June 1966): 182–83.

3. C. S. Hemphill and J. Suk, "The Law, Culture, and Economics of Fashion," *Stanford Law Review* 61, no. 5 (March 2009): 1158, 1168.

4. T. Ferris, "Planet Fever," *Smithsonian* 43, no. 5 (2012): 32–36.

5. P. Bizzell and B. Herzberg, *The Rhetorical Tradition* (New York: St. Martin's Press, 1990); K. Kohrs Campbell, *The Rhetorical Act* (Belmont, CA: Wadsworth, 1996).

6. S. Ride, "Shoot for the Stars," May 25, 2012, http://eloquentwoman.blogspot. com/2012/05/famous-speech-friday-sally-rides-shoot.html.

7. R. Clark, *Einstein: The Life and Times* (London: Hodder and Stoughton, 1973), 26.

Chapter 15

1. More current research indicates that three techniques can reduce speech anxiety. These include desensitization (relaxation, deep breathing, visualization); cognitive restructuring (identifying what causes your anxiety and developing coping strategies); and, most fundamentally, learning and knowing your material and practicing your speech. For more, see T. Docan-Morgan and T. Schmidt, "Reducing Public Speaking Anxiety for Native and Non-Native Speakers: The Value of Systematic Desensitization, Cognitive Restructuring, and Skills Training," *Cross Cultural Communication* 8, no. 5 (2012): 16–19.

2. See, for example, www.merriam-webster.com/dictionary/nuclear.

3. J. S. Tuman and Reverend Paul Levine, personal communication, 1976.

4. D. Matsumoto and H. S. Hwang, "Body and Gestures," in *Nonverbal Communication: Science and Applications*, ed. D. Matsumoto, M. Frank, and H. S. Hwang, 75–96 (Thousand Oaks, CA: Sage, 2013), 75.

5. V. Manusov, "Perceiving Nonverbal Messages: Effects of Immediacy and Encoded Intent on Receiver Judgments," *Western Journal of Speech Communication* 55, no. 3 (1991): 236.

6. J. K. Burgoon and B. A. LePoire, "Nonverbal Cues and Interpersonal Judgments: Participant and Observer Perceptions of Intimacy, Dominance, Composure, and Formality," *Communication Monographs* 66 (1999): 107.

7. Much of the original research on proxemics was pioneered by anthropologist Edward T. Hall; see E. T. Hall, *The Hidden Dimension* (New York: Doubleday, 1966). See also M. L. Patterson, "Spatial Factors in Social Interactions," *Human Relations* 21 (1968): 351–61.

8. Patterson, "Spatial Factors," 351–61.

9. J. K. Burgoon and others, "Relational Messages Associated with Nonverbal Behaviors," *Human Communication Research* 10 (1984): 351–78.

10. E. T. Hall, *Hidden Differences: Doing Business with the Japanese* (New York: Doubleday, 1987).

11. Communication scholars note that other elements of physical appearance, such as physiognomy, hair color, and height, can affect how audiences respond to speakers. For more, see J. K. Burgoon, L. K. Guerrero, and V. Manusov, "Nonverbal Signals," in *The Sage Handbook of Interpersonal Communication*, 4th ed., ed. M. L. Knapp and J. A. Daly, 239–80 (Thousand Oaks, CA: Sage, 2011), 241.

12. L. J. Smith and L. A. Malandro, "Personal Appearance Factors Which Influence Perceptions of Credibility and Approachability of Men and Women," in *The Nonverbal Communication Reader*, ed. J. A. DeVito and M. L. Hecht (Prospect Heights, IL: Waveland Press, 1990), 163.

13. E. Bohn and D. Jabusch, "The Effect of Four Methods of Instruction on the Use of Visual Aids in Speeches," *Western Journal of Communication* 42, no. 3 (1982): 253–65.

14. H. E. Nelson and A. W. Vandermeer, "Varied Sound Tracks on Animated Film," *Speech Monographs* 20 (1953): 261–67.

Chapter 16

1. Flag-folding etiquette is detailed by the American Legion, "Flag-Folding Procedures," www.legion.org/flag/folding (accessed March 23, 2010).

2. U.S. Code, Title 4, Chapter 1 §3, §8(d), via Cornell University Law School, www.law .cornell.edu/uscode/text/4/chapter-1 (accessed March 13, 2016).

3. D. Russakoff, "Building a Career Path Where There Was Just a Dead End," *Washington Post*, February 26, 2007, A1. In 2013, Per Scholas was recognized for inclusion in the S&I (Social Impact) 100 Index, recognizing nonprofits that provide high-impact solutions to America's problems. For more information, see www .socialimpactexchange.org/exchange/si-100.

4. D. M. Fraleigh and J. S. Tuman, *Freedom of Speech in the Marketplace of Ideas* (New York: St. Martin's Press, 1997).

5. J. S. Tuman, *Communicating Terror: The Rhetorical Dimensions of Terrorism* (Los Angeles: Sage, 2004).

6. K. E. Rowan, "A New Pedagogy for Explanatory Public Speaking: Why Arrangement Should Not Substitute for Invention," *Communication Education* 44 (July 1995): 236–50.

Chapter 17

1. A. M. Lederer and S. E. Middlestadt, "Beliefs About Meditating Among University Students, Faculty, and Staff: A Theory-Based Salient Belief Elicitation," *Journal of American College Health,* 62, no. 6 (2014): 360-69.

2. J. E. Fink, "Flourishing: Exploring Predictors of Mental Health within the College Environment," *Journal of American College Health* 62, no. 6 (2014): 380–88.

3. M. Sherif and C. I. Hovland, *Social Judgment, Assimilation, and Contrast Effects in Communication and Attitude Change* (New Haven: Yale University Press, 1961), 188–89.

4. Ibid., 195–96.

5. D. K. O'Keefe, *Persuasion: Theory and Research* (Newbury Park, CA: Sage, 1990), 36–37.

6. Sherif and Hovland, *Social Judgment,* 195–96.

7. R. E. Petty and J. T. Cacioppo, *Communication and Persuasion: Central and Peripheral Routes to Attitude Change* (New York: Springer-Verlag, 1986).

8. A. H. Maslow, "A Theory of Human Motivation," *Psychological Review* 50, no. 4 (1943): 370–96; V. Packard, *The Hidden Persuaders* (New York: Pocket Books, 1964).

9. M. Rokeach, *Understanding Human Values* (New York: Free Press, 1979), 2.

10. M. Rokeach, *Beliefs, Attitudes, and Values: A Theory of Organization and Change* (San Francisco: Jossey-Bass, 1968).

11. J. Hornikx and D. J. O'Keefe, "Adapting Consumer Advertising Appeals to Cultural Values," *Communication Yearbook* 33 (2009): 38–71.

12. M. Fishbein and I. Ajzen, *Belief, Attitude, Intention, and Behavior: An Introduction to Theory and Research* (Reading, MA: Addison-Wesley, 1975).

13. K. Horneffer-Ginter, "Stages of Change and Possible Selves: 2 Tools for Promoting College Health," *Journal of American College Health* 56, no. 4 (2008): 351–58.

14. Lederer and Middlestadt, 366.

15. M. Allen, "Comparing the Persuasive Effectiveness of One- and Two-Sided Messages," in *Persuasion: Advances through Meta-Analysis*, ed. M. Allen and R. W. Preiss, 87–98 (Cresskill, NJ: Hampton Press, 1998), 96.

16. J. C. Reinard, *Foundations of Argument* (Dubuque, IA: Wm. C. Brown, 1991), 353–54.

17. Aristotle, *On Rhetoric*, trans. G. A. Kennedy (New York: Oxford University Press, 1991): 1378a.

18. J. C. McCroskey and J. J. Teven, "Goodwill: A Reexamination of the Construct and Its Measurement," *Communication Monographs* 66, no. 1 (1999): 90–103.

19. J. C. McCroskey, "A Summary of Experimental Research on the Effects of Evidence in Persuasive Communication," *Quarterly Journal of Speech* 55 (April 1969): 169–76.

20. Ibid., 175.

21. Lederer and Middlestadt, 360.

22. R. E. Nisbett and L. Ross, *Human Inference: Strategies and Shortcomings of Social Judgment* (Englewood Cliffs, NJ: Prentice-Hall, 1980).

23. Scholars of rhetoric and argumentation have long described these patterns of reasoning. For example, see W. Brockriede and D. Ehninger, "Toulmin on Argument: An Interpretation and Application," *Quarterly Journal of Speech* 46, no. 1 (1960): 44–53; C. Perelman and L. Olbrechts-Tyteca, *The New Rhetoric: A Treatise on Argumentation* (South Bend, IN: University of Notre Dame Press, 1969), 263–66, 350–57, 371–98.

24. Tr'ondëk Hwëch'in Heritage Sites, "Fortymile Caribou Herd," 2012, http://trondekheritage.com/our-places/forty-mile/what-makes-forty-mile-special/fortymile-caribou-herd/.

25. Desert Renewable Energy Conservation Plan, "American Peregrine Falcon," March 2, 2012, www.drecp.org/meetings/2012-02-24_meeting/species_profiles/American%20Peregrine%20Falcon.pdf.

26. U.S. Fish & Wildlife Service, "Chart and Table of Bald Eagle Breeding Pairs in Lower 48 States," October 16, 2012, www.fws.gov/midwest/eagle/population/chtofprs.html.

27. M. Wall, "Incredible Technology: How to Live on Mars," August 20, 2013, http://news.yahoo.com/incredible-technology-live-mars-111612653.html.

28. H. H. Schiffrin and others, "Helping or Hovering? The Effects of Helicopter Parenting on College Students' Well-Being," *Journal of Child and Family Studies* 23, no. 3 (2014): 554.

29. Ibid., 548.

30. B. Kiviat, "How to Create a Job," *Time*, March 29, 2010, 175.

31. S. Callahan, "The Role of Emotion in Ethical Decision Making," *Hastings Center Report* 18, no. 3 (1988): 9.

32. K. Witte and K. Morrison, "Examining the Influence of Trait Anxiety/Repression-Sensitization on Individuals' Reactions to Fear Appeals," *Western Journal of Communication* 64, no. 1 (2000): 1.

33. P. A. Mongeau, "Another Look at Fear-Arousing Persuasive Appeals," in *Persuasion: Advances through Meta-Analysis*, ed. M. Allen and R. W. Preiss, 53–68 (Cresskill, NJ: Hampton Press, 1998), 66.

34. Ibid.

35. D. Westen, "What We Talk about When We Talk about Health Care," *Washington Post,* June 28, 2009, www.washingtonpost.com/wp-dyn/content/article/2009/06/24/AR2009062403275.html?sid=ST2009062603782.

36. D. Westen, *The Political Brain: The Role of Emotion in Deciding the Fate of the Nation* (New York: Public Affairs, 2007), 94.

37. "Off-Base Camp: A Mistaken Claim about Glaciers Raises Questions about the UN's Climate Panel," *Economist,* January 23, 2010, 76–77.

38. W. DeJong and L. Wallack, "A Critical Perspective of the Drug Czar's Antidrug Media Campaign," *Journal of Health Communication* 4 (1999): 155–60; D. R. Buchanan and L. Wallack, "This Is the Partnership for a Drug-Free America: Any Questions?" *Journal of Drug Issues* 28, no. 2 (1998): 329–56.

39. A. Lang and N. S. Yegiyan, "Understanding the Interactive Effects of Emotional Appeal and Claim Strength in Health Messages," *Journal of Broadcasting and Electronic Media* 52, no. 3 (2008): 432–47.

40. U.S. Department of Agriculture, "What Foods Are in the Fruit Group?" http://fnsweb01.edc.usda.gov/food-groups/fruits.html.

41. Brownell and others, "The Public Health and Economic Benefits of Taxing Sugar-Sweetened Beverages," *New England Journal of Medicine* 361 (October 15, 2009): 1599–1605.

42. R. E. McKerrow and others, *Principles and Types of Public Speaking* (Boston: Pearson Education, 2007), 168.

43. A. Monroe, *Principles and Types of Speech* (New York: Scott, Foresman, 1935).

Appendix A

1. J. Smith, "7 Things You Probably Didn't Know about Your Job Search," *Forbes,* April 17, 2013, www.forbes.com/sites/jacquelynsmith/2013/04/17/7-things-you-probably-didnt-know-about-your-job-search.

2. *Talent Report: What Workers Want in 2012; Executive Summary,* Net Impact, May 2012, https://netimpact.org/sites/default/files/documents/what-workers-want-2012-summary.pdf.

3. "The Maestro: James Levine," interview by Bob Simon, *60 Minutes,* March 8, 2015, www.cbsnews.com/news/maestro-james-levine-bob-simon-60-minutes.

4. A. Green, "The 10 Most Common Interview Questions," *U.S. News and World Report,* April 27, 2015, http://money.usnews.com/money/careers/slideshows/the-10-most-common-interview-questions/1.

5. Smith, "7 Things You Probably Didn't Know."

GLOSSARY

abstract words words that represent the idea that the speaker intends to express, but the words are so broad that they encompass many other possible ideas

accent when nonverbal communication highlights one portion or word of a message

accommodation retaining one's core cultural identity while remaining within the dominant general culture

acculturation the process of learning about other cultures through living within or coming into contact with other cultures

action-oriented listeners listeners who usually focus on getting to the meaning of a message and determining what response is required

ad populum (bandwagon) fallacy assuming that a statement is true or false simply because a majority of people say it is

age identity how people identify themselves based on either chronological age or generational association

agenda a standardized problem-solving plan

agenda-driven listening when one member of a communication dyad is focused on learning or hearing certain information and completely uninterested in—and therefore oblivious to—everything else

agenda-setting the concept through which the news media selects the issues that will make compelling news stories for the public to read, listen to, observe, and discuss

ambiguous (language) the idea that words that have no precise meaning that is understood by all

analogy a comparison based on similarities between two phenomena— one that is familiar to the audience and one that is less familiar

anonymity the state of being unknown

arbitration when a group is at a stalemate, asking an outside person to make a decision for the group

argumentative listening listening to only as much as is needed to fuel one's own argument

arrangement (organization) refers to the structuring of main ideas and supporting material in a manner that will make the message clear and memorable to audience members; one of the classical canons of rhetoric

articulation   the crispness or clarity of one's spoken words

artifact   item or marking we decorate our bodies with to help define ourselves

assimilation   taking on the characteristics of a dominant general culture

assurances   things that encourage, comfort, and meet one's needs; one of the six categories of relational maintenance prosocial behaviors.

attention-getter   material intended to capture an audience's interest

attitude   favorable or unfavorable feeling toward something or someone

audience analysis   the process of learning about an audience's interests and background

avoiding   one of six conflict styles, characterized by a person's refusal to confront their partner

beliefs   the facts about a topic that audience members believe to be true

biased language   words that suggest prejudice or preconceptions about a group of people based on shared characteristics

body   the part of a speech where the main points are presented and supported

body clock time   the time of day or day of the week when a speech will be presented, as it relates to the audience

boomerang effect   the act of inadvertently pushing listeners to oppose an idea even more vigorously than they previously did

borrowing   when words or other features of one language community are adopted by another language community

boundary insiders   those with whom we share information

boundary turbulence   the friction that occurs when privacy rules are threatened or broken

brainstorming   listing every idea that comes to mind without evaluating its merits

brief examples   a set of short instances used to support or illustrate a claim

cascading negativity   a pattern that moves couples from complaints to contempt to defensiveness and finally to stonewalling

categorical (topical) pattern   an organizational pattern in which each main point emphasizes a different but important aspect of the topic

causal pattern   an organizational pattern used in explaining a cause-and-reflect relationship

causal reasoning   the practice of arguing that one event has caused another

centrifugal forces   forces that pull people apart, such as distance, betrayal, coldness, disrespect, and ambivalence

centripetal forces   forces that push people together, such as openness, stability, loyalty, warmth, respect, and caring

channel   the medium of the delivery of a message

chronemics   the study of time

chronological (temporal) pattern   an organizational pattern in which the information is presented in a time-based sequence, from beginning to end

citation   a record that contains information about the author of a piece of evidence and where that evidence can be found

claim   a statement that the speaker asserts is true; the three types of claims are fact, value, and policy

classical canons of rhetoric   five principles to consider when developing a speech: invention, arrangement (organization), style, memory, and delivery

climate   a group's emotional or relational atmosphere

clincher   content that leaves a lasting impression of a speech in listeners' minds

co-cultures   cultures that exist within a larger culture

collaborating   one of six conflict styles, during which two people work toward a solution that is beneficial to both partners

collectivist cultures   cultures that value the group over the individual

collegial peer   a friend who also happens to be a coworker

commitment   one's investment in a relationship

committees   groups formed to serve their larger organizations, such as schools, government agencies, legislatures, and corporations

common couple violence   a pattern involving violence that emerges when partners believe they have no control in the relationship, feel ignored, or want to vent their anger but don't know how

common ground   beliefs, values, and experiences a speaker shares with his or her listeners

communication   the transactional process through which people use symbols to send and receive messages to negotiate, interpret, and create shared meaning

communication competence   the ability to achieve one's communication goals

communication privacy management (CPM) theory   theory built on two ideas: that we "own" our information, and that we have the right to control access to it

communication repertoire   all the skills that we have available for interacting with others, including verbal resources and nonverbal expressions, listening skills, the ability to perceive and empathize with others' perspectives, different communication styles, and channels of communication

comparison (analogy) reasoning   the practice of arguing that because two instances are similar, what is known to be true for one instance is likely to be true for the other

comparison pattern   an organizational pattern that focuses on the major similarities and differences between two events, objects, or situations, with each point discussing one similarity or difference

competence   the quality of being knowledgeable and experienced; one component of credibility

competitive fighting   one of six conflict styles, during which a person takes control to get what they want by accusing, blaming, joking in a hostile manner, and calling their partner names.

compromising   one of six conflict styles, through which partners work together to achieve a solution where both partners get some of what they wanted as a result

computer-mediated communication   communication that occurs using electronic devices, including computers, tablets, cell phones, and smartphones; also known as CMC

concise language   the use of the fewest words necessary to express an idea

concrete words   words that are specific and suggest exactly what is meant

conflict   expressed struggle between group members who see each other as getting in the way of goals, resources, values, and beliefs

conflict patterns   the ways that partners react to each other—and how these reactions affect the conflict

conformity   behaving according to certain standards

conglomeration   the process through which major corporations buy other companies, putting them all under the same umbrella of ownership

connecting bids   the daily overtures of connection we make to our partners

connotative meaning   the associations that come to mind when we hear or read a word

consensus   a group reaching a decision that everyone can support

constructive criticism   feedback a speaker can use to improve his or her skills

content meaning   the literal idea expressed by a message

content-oriented listeners   a type of listener that favors depth and complexity of information and messages

context dependent   the idea that the same word can have different meanings depending on the circumstances in which it is used

contradict   when the message of one's verbal communication does not align with the message of his or her nonverbal communication

convergence   the superimposition of one medium on the platform of another medium; also, the place where two entities meet

coordination   when each main point is at the same level of significance as other main points, each subpoint is at the same level as other subpoints, and so on

credibility   the perception of the audience that the speaker is qualified to speak on the topic

credible sources   sources that can be reasonably trusted to present accurate, objective information

criteria   standards for making a judgment

criteria-application pattern   a speech pattern with two main points: one establishes standards for the value judgment being made, and the other applies those standards to the subject of the thesis

critical media theory   the idea that those who own mass media in its various forms purposely influence the content of mass media messages

cross-cultural   nonverbal behaviors that exist in more than one culture

cultural criticism   the act of examining mass media for potential bias and discrimination

culture   the sum of knowledge, beliefs, values, and patterns of behavior shared by members of a group

cyclical tensions model   one of the more popular models used to depict the turbulent model of relationship progression, this model offers a view of constant and cyclical states of change filled with messy starts and stops, rather than a pattern that holds steady

decision   a choice made between alternative solutions

decode   a receiver's act of processing a source's verbal and nonverbal symbols to form his or her own perception of the message's meaning

defeated listening   when listeners feel overwhelmed by a message and find it too difficult to follow, perhaps because the subject being discussed is too technical or detailed and beyond easy comprehension

definition   a technique for identifying a topic that involves breaking down something by its parts and explaining how those parts add up

delivery   the combination of vocal and nonverbal communication skills used to present a speech; one of the classical canons of rhetoric

delivery reminders   notes jotted down in the margins of a speaking outline to help a speaker handle challenging areas effectively

demand-withdraw   a pattern that occurs when one partner demands a change while the other partner, benefiting from the way things are, withdraws

demographics   listener characteristics, such as age, gender, and ethnicity

demonstration   a technique that typically involves the use of both physical modeling and verbal elements to teach an audience how a process or a set of guidelines works

denotative meaning   a word's exact, literal dictionary definition

description   a technique that involves using words to paint a mental picture for listeners, so that they can close their eyes and imagine what is being said

designated leader   someone selected by an external authority to help a group move quickly forward with its task

dialectical tensions   contradictory forces that push and pull partners in opposing directions

digital divide   the gap between those with access to the Internet and those without access

distracted listening   a type of listening in which the receiver does not pay attention to what he or she is hearing

diversity   differences stemming from traditional categories, including race, ethnicity, gender, age, sexual orientation, disability, and religion

domain-specific self-esteem   one's self-assessment on a specific trait, such as honesty, fitness, or test-taking

dyad   a two-person social unit

ego involvement   personal interest and concern

emergent leader   a group member who comes to be seen as a leader by the group over time

emotional flooding   an instance in which a person's heart rate and blood pressure skyrocket, his or her muscles tense, and he or she finds it difficult to breathe and hard to think

emotional intelligence   the ability to understand one's own as well as others' emotions

encode   the verbal and nonverbal symbols a source uses to express his or her message

enculturation   the process by which we learn about the culture we are born into, including its values, mores and traditions, language, and history

entertainment media   the side of mass media that entertains, made up of novels and short stories, movies, TV shows, and so on

equivocal language   when the speaker uses word(s) with a range of meanings, perhaps in a deceptive manner

ethics the rules and values that a group uses to guide conduct and distinguish between right and wrong

ethnicity cultural background that is usually associated with shared religion, national origin, and language

ethnocentric bias using one's own culture to interpret and evaluate the behavior of others

ethnocentrism the tendency to perceive one's own culture as important and superior to other cultures

ethos (credibility) quality of a speaker who is seen as being knowledgeable, honest, and genuinely interested in doing the right thing for his or her audience

evidence information gained from research sources

example reasoning the presentation of specific instances to support a general claim

examples samples or instances that support or illustrate a general claim

exemplification a communication strategy used to show that a person has a high moral character

expertise knowledge based on reliable facts or opinions about a topic

expert testimony statements made by credible sources who have professional or other in-depth knowledge of the topic at hand

explanation a technique that involves providing an analysis of something for purposes of clarity and specificity by tracing a line of reasoning or a series of causal connections between events

extemporaneous delivery delivering a speech using limited notes

extended examples examples that provide details about the instances being used to give audience members a deeper and richer picture of the point being made

extended self one's perceptions of him- or herself as a participant in a relationship

external one of the two types of challenges; comes from the outside world

external noise additional sensory details in the environment of the communication situation that distract listeners

eye contact looking directly into the eyes of audience members while they do the same

facial expressions one type of nonverbal communication that people notice immediately

fact claim a claim that asserts that something is true or false

facts statements for which there is enough proof to convince almost any reasonable and objective person that they are true

fallacies reasoning patterns for which the link between claim and supporting material is weak

false inference   an incorrect conclusion reached by listeners after being intentionally led there by a speaker's statements

fear appeal   an argument that arouses fear in the minds of audience members

feedback   a receiver's facial or verbal response to a message

feminine cultures   cultures that embrace traditionally feminine values, such as benevolence, caring, interdependence, intuition, and gender equality

flooding   the feeling marked by an intense physiological fight-or-flight response

forum   the location of a speech

four Cs: connect, create, consume, control   the general goals and characteristics of social media and social networking; coined by Hoffman and Novak

framing   featuring a certain attribution of an issue or a story

free media   messages communicated by the news media in a manner that is practically free for the original messenger, such as media coverage of awards shows

friendship   a close dyad defined by strong affinity, warmth, and affection

fundamental attribution error   when we overestimate the impact of others' personal traits and play down the role of circumstances

gender   cultural and behavioral traits related to one's biological sex

gender-neutral term   a word that does not suggest a specific gender

gender stereotypes   oversimplified and often distorted views of what it means to be male or female

Gersick's two-phase model   a model of group development that says that no matter a project's length, groups don't begin to take action until the midpoint of the project

gestures   the use of hand, head, or face movements to emphasize a point, pantomime, demonstrate, or call attention to something

global self-esteem   one's overall self-evaluation

goodwill   the quality of wanting what is best for one's listeners rather than what would most benefit him- or herself; one component of credibility

group decision support system (GDSS)/group support system (GSS)   computer-aided programs designed to quicken the pace of problem solving without sacrificing quality

group socialization   process of adapting to changes in a group by both the new group member and established group members

groupthink   a group's tendency to uncritically accept ideas and information because of strong feelings of loyalty or single-mindedness within the group

half-truth   a statement that includes true facts mixed with false information

haptics   the study of touch

hasty generalization   occurs when a speaker bases a conclusion on limited or unrepresentative examples

hate   intense aversion to and bias against individuals based solely on their membership in a cultural grouping

hate speech   insults, slurs, or epithets directed at individuals based solely on their membership in a cultural grouping

hearing   receiving messages in a passive way

heritage   the traditions, achievements, and beliefs that are part of the history of a group or nation

heterogeneity   member difference (in a group)

heteronormative   the idea that heterosexuality is the normal or preferred sexual orientation

high-contact cultures   cultures in which people feel comfortable expressing themselves both verbally and nonverbally, often standing close to one another and touching frequently

high-context cultures   cultures that rely on information from the situation to help interpret a spoken message

high-power-distance cultures   cultures in which those in superior positions have considerably more power than those in subordinate positions

high uncertainty avoidance   having a low tolerance for uncertainty; those with high uncertainty avoidance prefer making a plan and following a process

homogeneity   member similarity (in a group)

hyperpersonal model   a model for interpersonal communication that suggests that exchanges using computer-mediated communication allow communicators to strategically develop and edit the sense of themselves they present to one another

identity (or impression) management   the process by which people "present information about themselves in order to appear as they wish others to perceive them"

imagined trajectories model   one of the more popular models used to depict the turbulent model of relationship progression, Honeycutt's model states that relationships are composed of periods of stability that are occasionally disrupted by critical events

immutable characteristics   characteristics that are impossible to change or deeply ingrained in one's culture, such as race, ethnicity, gender, sexuality, religion, and mental or physical ability

impromptu delivery   generating speech content in the moment, without time to prepare in advance

improper word choice   when a communicator uses a word that does not have the meaning that he or she intends to express

indirect fighting   one of six conflict styles, during which partners use passive-aggressive tactics to achieve their goals

individualistic cultures   cultures that value the individual over the group

inductive reasoning   form of reasoning used by persuasive speakers that involves generalizing from facts, instances, or examples; the four types are example, comparison, sign, and causal

inferences   the additional assumptions that we make about a person's characteristics based on the sensory information we have already gathered about that person

inflection   the raising or lowering of a voice's pitch

information overload   a condition in which we're no longer capable of effectively processing new information

informative   rhetorical purpose intended to increase an audience's understanding or awareness of a subject

informative presentation   a speech that teaches the audience something and increases listeners' understanding of, awareness of, or sensitivity to the topic

ingratiation   a communication strategy used when a person hopes to be liked

in-group   a social group we feel affiliated with and respect

interactive listening   the act of filtering out distractions, focusing on what the other person or people are saying, and demonstrating that you are listening

intercultural communication   the communication that occurs between people of different cultural backgrounds

interdependence   in relationships, a reliance on each other

internal   one of the two types of challenges; comes from within us

internal noise   thoughts or emotions that make it hard for listeners to concentrate

internal preview   a short list of the ideas that will follow

internal summary   a quick review of the key elements of a main point

interpersonal communication   the communication between two people that includes a deeper level of enjoyment and intimacy

interpersonal conflict   a struggle that occurs when partners reveal what they see as incompatible interests

interpersonal relationship   a special one-on-one connection that can last and change over long periods of time

interruptive listening   a type of listening in which one person consistently interrupts another

intimacy   in a relationship, access to more information about each other and richer insight into the other person

intimidation   a communication strategy used when a person is trying to convince others that he or she is dangerous, using threats or statements that cause discomfort

invention   the generation and selection of ideas for use in a speech; one of the classical canons of rhetoric

jargon   specialized or technical words or phrases familiar to people in a specific field or group; also includes abbreviations, acronyms, and other esoteric expressions

Johari window   a tool for describing the different degrees of what we know about ourselves and what others know about us

kinesics   the study of body language

Knapp's staircase model   one of the most common models used to depict the straightforward model of relationship progression, this stage model follows a linear A-B-C-D-E pattern

language   a standardized use of words that is shared by a community of people

latitude of acceptance   the range of viewpoints on an issue that audience members support

latitude of rejection   the range of viewpoints on an issue that audience members oppose

lay testimony   statements made by persons with no special expertise in the subject they are discussing

leader   a group member who acts in ways that move the group toward its goal

leadership   behavior that moves a group toward its goal

learning groups   popular throughout a person's life, these groups offer a way to understand the world

listening   processing a message to decide on its meaning, and retaining what has been heard and understood

loaded language fallacy   using emotionally charged words that convey meaning that cannot be supported by facts presented by the speaker

logos   quality of a speaker who presents trustworthy facts to back his or her claims and clearly shows how those facts led him or her to those claims

low-contact cultures   cultures in which people tend to be emotionally distant and reserved, generally standing farther apart and touching infrequently

low-context cultures cultures that prefer communication focused on the spoken word rather than on the context or situation in which the words are spoken

low-power-distance cultures cultures in which relationships between those in superior positions and those in subordinate positions are close and more egalitarian

low uncertainty avoidance having a high tolerance for uncertainty; those with low uncertainty avoidance are more casual, informal, and relaxed

main points the ideas that are most important for listeners to remember

marking a special occasion rhetorical purpose intended to honor an occasion by entertaining, inspiring, or emotionally moving the audience

masculine cultures cultures that embrace traditionally masculine values, such as ambition, assertiveness, decisiveness, independence, and differentiated gender roles

mass communication when mediated communication takes place on a very large scale

mass media outlets through which mass communication messages are conveyed, such as television, radio, print media formats, and the Internet

mediated communication messages transmitted through either a mechanical or an electronic medium, such as a television, the Internet, or a cell phone

mediation when a group is at a stalemate, asking an outside person to suggest another alternative

memory refers to the preparation and practice needed to get ready to deliver a speech; one of the classical canons of rhetoric

mental associations (schemas) the subconscious associations that our mind makes between the stimuli we focus on and other ideas stored in our brain

message the ideas that a source conveys

mindful communication characterized by thoughtful reflection, openness, and a willingness to bridge differences

mindful intercultural communication embracing a willingness to learn more about other cultures and to think outside our own cultural biases when communicating

mind mapping writing down a word or phrase in the middle of a piece of paper, then surrounding it with words and images that come to mind

monochronic doing one task at a time

monotone quality of a voice if the tone never varies

motivated sequence pattern follows the five stages of thinking that people go through when solving a problem or considering a new idea: attention, need, satisfaction, visualization, and action

multitasking attending to multiple tasks at the same time

narrative a technique that involves using a story to both share information and capture an audience's attention

narratives anecdotes (brief stories) or somewhat longer accounts that can be used to support a speaker's main points

needs objects that audience members desire and feelings that must be satisfied

negative reciprocity a pattern that results when negativity (name-calling, accusations, yelling, dismissals) triggers more negativity

negotiated permanence the assumption of people in a relationship that they will stay together

nervous listening type of listening in which people feel compelled to talk through silences because they're uncomfortable with lapses in the conversation

net neutrality Internet service providers allowing equal access to all sites, without enacting "fast lanes" for those who pay more

networks patterns of information flow within a group

new media mass communication via newer forms of technology, such as the Internet

news media the side of mass media that informs, made up of newspapers and magazines, journals, news-oriented websites, broadcast and cable news, and so on

noise (interference) a phenomenon that disrupts communication between source and receiver

nonverbal communication the exchange of messages without using words

nonverbal delivery skills skills involving the use of physical behaviors to deliver a speech, such as eye contact, gestures, physical movement, proxemics, and personal appearance

objectivity presenting ideas with no prejudice or partisanship

observational capacity having witnessed a situation firsthand

oculesics the study of eye contact

old media traditional forms of mass communication, such as newspapers and radio

olfactics the study of smell

omission   a source of false inference that occurs when a speaker misleads an audience by making a true statement that omits relevant information

openness   being direct, sharing private thoughts and feelings, giving advice, listening, and discussing the future; one of the six categories of relational maintenance prosocial behaviors

the Other   concept suggesting that people create intergroup identity by focusing on how they're different from other people or outside groups

out-group   a social group we do not feel a part of

outline   a written method of organizing a speech using sentences, phrases, or key words

out-of-context evidence   quotations chosen selectively to support a claim that the author did not make

paid media   paid advertising in any form, such as billboards and TV ads

panning   a technique involving moving the head slowly from one side of an audience to the other; used for making eye contact with large audiences

paralanguage   the tone, pitch, accent, and volume of one's voice

paralinguistics   the study of paralanguage

paraphrase   a restatement of an idea in one's own words

participatory (social) media   online sources in which users both create and access information, making it difficult to determine if the information is credible

pathos   quality of a speaker who uses emotional appeals to put a human face on the problem being addressed

pausing   leaving gaps between words or sentences in a speech

peer review   process in which a work is evaluated by other experts in the field

people-oriented listeners   listeners who, like content-oriented listeners, are willing to invest time and attention to a conversation or discussion, yet who are differentiated by their interest in being supportive of friends and strengthening relationships

perception   the process by which we come to understand the stimuli in our world

perception checking   a conscious, three-step process that allows a person to ask other people about their intentions in a nonthreatening way

periodicals   publications that appear at regular intervals (weekly, monthly, quarterly)

personal appearance   the impression a speaker makes on an audience through his or her clothing, jewelry, hairstyle, and grooming

personal growth   the process of strengthening one's self-awareness and trying to live a life consistent with his or her values and capabilities

person perception   the process of making judgments about others, "deciding what they are like, predicting what they will do, [and] providing explanations for their behavior"

persuasion   the effort to influence people's beliefs, attitudes, or actions

persuasive   rhetorical purpose intended to convince an audience to consider or adopt a new position or belief, strengthen an existing position or belief, or take a particular action

persuasive speech   a speech whose goal is to affect audience members' beliefs, attitudes, or actions, while also advocating fact, value, or policy claims

pervasive   the quality of being everywhere and available at all times

physical appearance   the colors and clothing we wear, our choice of hairstyle, and the **artifacts** we decorate our bodies with to help define ourselves

physical attraction   connecting with others based on outward appearances similar to our own

physical location   one of the factors of a communication event that affects listeners

physical movement   how much or how little a speaker moves around while delivering a speech

plagiarism   presenting another person's words or ideas as if they were one's own

policy claim   a claim that advocates action by organizations, institutions, or audience members

polychronic   doing several tasks at once

positivity   being nice, cheerful, affectionate, and hopeful; one of the six categories of relational maintenance prosocial behaviors.

post hoc fallacy   a causal reasoning error that lies in the assumption that because one event followed another, the first event caused the second

power distance   the extent to which a culture recognizes and tolerates power, particularly the distribution of power among individuals

pragmatic rules   the rules that govern how we use language to accomplish actions

prejudice   the act of showing negative and illogical bias toward that which is different

presentation aid   anything beyond the spoken word employed by a speaker to help audience members understand and remember the message

presentation software   technology that enables users to create, edit, and present information, usually in a slide-show format

presentation time   the length of time available for a presentation

preview   a brief statement of the main points that will be developed in the body of a speech

primary group   a group made up of family members and friends that helps us with our need to both be cared for and connect with others

prior exposure   the extent to which audience members have already heard ideas relating to the topic

private self   the whole picture of how a person sees him- or herself

problem   the realization that reality doesn't match up with what's desired

processing   actively thinking about a message being received from someone else—not only the words but also the nonverbal cues

professional peer   a coworker of equal standing who provides practical as well as personal support

projection   using the air exhaled from the lungs to carry one's voice across a large area to reach all listeners

pronunciation   correctness in the way one says words

prop   something a speaker can use to hide behind while presenting a speech

proxemics   the study of space—particularly the use of space and distance between a speaker and the audience

public self   the self that a person represents to other people

public speaking   the delivery of a message by a speaker to an audience

quality control circles   committees whose goal is to find a way to better their company's performance

race   a commonality based on genetically shared physical characteristics of people in a group

rate of delivery   how fast or how slow an individual speaks

reappraisal   the process of altering one's interpretation of something that happened in his or her life

reasoning   the line of thought that connects the facts presented and the conclusion drawn from those facts

receiver   the person to which the source is communicating his or her message

recency   timeliness

reciprocal altruism   the exchange of favors between non-blood relations

reflected appraisals   based on the metaphor of a looking-glass self—the feedback that allows a person to "see" his or her characteristics, much as a mirror enables a person to see a visual image of him- or herself

regulate when nonverbal communication controls a person's verbal behaviors

relational embarrassment a privacy violation that occurs when a relationship partner acts inappropriately toward his or her partner in front of others

relational maintenance the actions we take to sustain desired levels of mutual control, trust, liking, and commitment in our relationships

relational meaning what a person believes a message has to say about his or her relationship

relational movement how and why our relationships move through time as they do

repeat the act of conveying one's message through verbal and nonverbal communication at the same time in order to emphasize the message

representative examples examples that are typical of the class they represent

research librarians career professionals who are hired to assist students and faculty because of their expertise in tracking down information

research plan a strategy for finding and keeping track of information to use in a speech

retention one's ability to remember what he or she has heard

reversed causality a situation in which speakers miss the fact that the effect is actually the cause

rhetorical purpose a speaker's intended effect on his or her audience

role conflict conflict produced when more than one role played by a group member clash

script a typed or handwritten document containing the entire text of a speech

secondary group a task- or work-oriented group formed to help influence others and solve problems

self our own personal construction of who we are

self-concept all one's perceptions of him- or herself; includes abilities, accomplishments, personality, preferences, and characteristics

self-disclosure the intentional revelation of important information about ourselves that others are not likely to know

self-esteem one's evaluation of the person he or she visualizes when describing him- or herself

self-expansion the opportunity to deepen and broaden one's personal identity

self-fulfilling prophecy when there is a particular outcome that a person expects to occur, the person behaves in a way that makes the outcome more likely

selfish roles roles that accomplish little for a group, as they are motivated by the self-centered, obstructive ends of individual members

self-managed work teams teams in which skilled peers oversee their own schedules and work policies within the boundaries of their parent company with little supervision

self-promotion a communication strategy used to make an individual appear capable

self-serving bias a situation in which we attribute our successes to our own favorable personality traits rather than to circumstances

self-talk the act of talking to ourselves to build ourselves up, through addressing our capabilities, positive traits, and worth as a human being

semantic rules the rules that govern the meaning of words

sensory information the information we receive through our senses of sight, hearing, smell, taste, or touch

separation leading a separate existence while in the midst of a dominant culture

sexist language language with a bias for or against a given gender

sexual orientation a demographic characteristic related to one's sexual identity

shared meaning a common understanding with little confusion and few misinterpretations

sharing activities spending time enjoying each other's company; one of the six categories of relational maintenance prosocial behaviors

sharing tasks doing chore-like tasks together; one of the six categories of relational maintenance prosocial behaviors

signposts words or phrases within sentences that help an audience understand a speech's structure

sign reasoning the practice of claiming that a fact is true because indirect indicators (signs) are consistent with that fact

slippery slope fallacy arguing against a policy because you assume (without proof) that it will lead to a second policy that is undesirable

small group a limited number of people who work toward a common goal and who believe that they can achieve more together than acting alone

small group communication the heart of group dynamics, involving the constant efforts of group members to influence one another

small group dynamics the ways in which group members relate to one another and view one another's functions within the group

small talk polite and usually superficial conversation

social attraction   aligning ourselves with those who we believe are like us

social judgment theory   posits that audience members make a decision about a thesis by comparing it with their own perspectives on the issue

social media   various electronic tools that allow users to create online communities in which to interact with others, share photos, and exchange tips and other information

social networking   interacting through social media

social networks   leaning on friends and family for support; one of the six categories of relational maintenance prosocial behaviors

social penetration theory   a theory explaining that our close relationships are the result of penetrating the more hidden informational layers of the other person

social roles   roles that help sustain and strengthen interpersonal relations within a small group

source   a person with an idea to express

spatial pattern   an organizational pattern in which the main points represent important aspects of a topic that are adjacent to one another in location or geography

speaking outline   shorter than a working outline, a speaking outline expresses a speaker's ideas in brief phrases or key words

special peer   a coworker who fills the role of a best friend at work

specific purpose   the objective of a speech

speech critique   written or oral feedback offered after a speech is presented

speech ethics   the principles and values that should guide a speaker's conduct when preparing and delivering a speech

statistics   information (or data) presented in numerical form

stereotype   an inference that people draw about others simply because they're part of a given social category

stereotyping   making broad generalizations about people based on limited, exaggerated, or even false information

stimuli   any piece of sensory information

strategic discourse   the process of selecting supporting arguments that will best persuade the audience in an ethical manner

straw person fallacy   replacing an opponent's real claim with a weaker claim that is easier to rebut

style   the choice of language that will express a speaker's ideas to audience members in a clear, interesting, and ethical manner; one of the classical canons of rhetoric

subordination   creating a hierarchy of points and their supporting materials in a speech

subpoints supporting materials used to develop a main point

substitute when nonverbal communication replaces verbal communication

sub-subpoints materials that support subpoints

summary a brief review of a speech's main points

superficial listening when listeners pretend to pay attention but are in fact distracted by internal or external noise

supplement nonverbal communication that adds or enhances the meaning of spoken or written words

supplication a communication strategy used when an individual wishes to demonstrate helplessness or dependence on others

supporting materials different types of information used to develop and support a speech's main ideas, such as examples, definitions, testimony, statistics, narratives, and analogies

supporting points materials designed to prove or substantiate main points

symbols words used in communication that arbitrarily represent something else

synergy a collective level of performance greater than that created by any single member

syntactic rules the rules that regulate the order in which words are organized into sentences

task attraction being drawn to those who complete jobs in ways we value and agree with

task forces special committees composed of members with the skills and knowledge necessary to fulfill a particular assignment

testimony information provided by other people

thesis statement a single sentence that captures the overall message a speaker wants to convey in a speech

time a concept that affects effective listening in two ways: the actual time it takes to listen to a message, and the time of day or week with respect to the listener's internal body clock

time-oriented listeners listeners who see time as a precious resource to be conserved and protected and who exhibit impatience in a conversation

tone the highs and lows of a speaking voice, derived from pitch

top-level domain designation at the end of a web address that indicates the sponsor's affiliation, such as .com, .org, or .edu

top management teams (TMTs) teams composed of upper-level managers who focus less on production and more on improving leadership within an organization

transactional   an aspect of communication that includes both sharing one's ideas with others and receiving the ideas that others are sharing with you

transference   when a person's mind triggers inferences about the new person based solely on shared traits

transition   a sentence that indicates a move from one part of a speech to another

trolling   the posting of anonymous comments, sometimes via false identities, solely to stir up controversy and discord

trustworthiness   the quality of being honest and fair; one component of credibility

Tuckman's model   a way to describe the linear stages of a group's development as it sets out to achieve its goal

turning-against response   a response to a connecting bid in which the person displays annoyance and aggression

turning-away response   a response to a connecting bid in which the person recognizes the bid and then quickly shifts to self-centered interests

turning-toward response   a response to a connecting bid in which the person demonstrates how much he or she values and understands the other person

two-sided argument   used by a speaker to address audience members' reservations, a two-sided argument involves noting an argument against the thesis and then using reasoning and evidence to refute that argument

uncertainty avoidance   a society's willingness to tolerate ambiguity or uncertainty

value claim   a claim that attaches a judgment (good, bad, moral, immoral) to a subject

values   "core conceptions" of what is desirable for our own life and for society

verbal clutter   extraneous words that make it hard for others to follow your message

verbal communication   the exchange of messages using language

verbal filler   a word or phrase, such as *you know* or *like*, that speakers use to fill uncomfortable silences

virtual peer   a coworker who communicates only through mediated communication

vocal delivery skills   the effective use of one's voice when delivering a speech

vocal tic   a sound, such as *um* and *ah*, that speakers use when searching for a correct word or when they have lost their train of thought

volume   how loud or soft a speaker's voice is while delivering a speech

word association   listing a single idea, then writing down whatever comes to mind without stopping to evaluate it

working outline   a thorough outline used to craft a speech; also called a detailed or preparation outline

work roles   group member roles that encourage verbal messages having to do with the task at hand or procedures to be followed

works cited list   a list of all the research sources cited in your speech

yielding   one of six conflict styles, where person chooses to pick his or her battles for the sake of the relationship

INDEX

abbreviations, in speaking outlines, 447
Abrams, J. J., 320
abstract language, 78–79
academic journals. *See* periodicals
accenting, nonverbal, 112–13, 123
acceptance, latitude of, 526, 527
accommodation between co-cultures, 177–78
accuracy
    of facts, credibility and, 532, 533
    of perceptions (*see* misperceptions)
acknowledging others' work
    citation information: keeping track of, 384–85; presenting in speech, 394; in working outline, 438, 440
    paraphrasing: spoken word, 394; written word, 395, 408–9
    plagiarism, 381–82, 406–7
    quoting from sources, 395, 407–8, 438
action(s)
    action-oriented listening, 137
    calls to, 523
    language as tool for accomplishing, 85
active learners, 403
ad populum (bandwagon) fallacy, 539
age
    audience demographics and, 359, 511
    diversity spectrum and, 168–69
agency, embracing, 262–63
agenda-driven listening, 143–44
agendas, problem-solving, 322. *See also* problem solving, group
agenda-setting theory, 208–11
agreement, winning, 397
altruism, reciprocal, 222
ambiguous meanings, 74–75
American Psychological Association (APA) style, 440
analogies
    reasoning with, 536–37

simplifying complex material with, 507, 514
supporting evidence with, 400–402
anecdotes. *See* narratives and stories
anonymity, Internet, 205–6, 213
Anonymous (hacktivist group), 205
APA (American Psychological Association) style, 440
appearance, physical. *See* physical appearance
appearances, deceptive, 43–44
apps for group meetings, 308
Arab Spring protests, 192
arbitrary symbol system, communication as, 19–20
arbitration, decision making by, 326
argumentative listening, 144–45, 151
Aristotle, 350, 531
arrangement, in classical canons of rhetoric, 353. *See also* organizing speeches
articles, journal, 366–67, 388, 391
articulation, vocal, 468–69
assignment criteria for speeches, 369
assimilation between co-cultures, 176–77
associations, mental
    to people (schemas): sources of, 39–40; stimuli and, 37–38
    to words (*see also* connotative meanings): emotional appeals and, 542; generating ideas with, 368
assurances, maintaining relationships with, 254, 256
attention-getters, 425–27, 439
attentiveness, listener
    attentiveness curve, 135
    body clock and, 139–40
    modifying message for, 149

attire
  delivering speeches and, 478–79
  job interviews and, 562–63
attitudes, audience, 527
attraction, interpersonal
  factors in: brain chemistry, 227–28;
    proximity, 228–29; similarity,
    228–29
  types of, 226–27
audience analysis
  delivering speeches and: eye contact,
    472; listening skills, 149–50; pre-
    sentation aids, 481
  developing speeches and: main
    points, 417–18; supporting mate-
    rials, 403; topic selection, 370,
    374; word choice, 89–90
  dimensions of: demographics, 357–62,
    481, 508–9; prior exposure,
    364–65, 506–7; psychological
    factors, 526–31; situational
    factors, 356–57
  importance of, 355–56
audioconferencing, 307–8, 309
audio presentation aids
  audience interaction with, 484
  positioning for audibility, 483
  testing volume and clarity, 482
avoiding, as conflict style, 270

background knowledge. See expertise
back-loading main message, 150
back to audience, turning, 151, 456
balance strategy for dialectical
    tensions, 245
balancing positivity and negativity,
    276–77
bandwagon (ad populum) fallacy, 539
BBS (electronic bulletin board services), 308
behavior
  as cause of conflict, 267
  overview of communication behav-
    iors, 15–17
beliefs, audience, 527
belonging, interpersonal relationships
    and, 221

benefits of effective communication. See
    uses of effective communication
benefit to audience, demonstrating,
    427–28, 528–29
bias
  disclosing, 532 (see also objectivity)
  in language: appropriate ethnic refer-
    ences, 93; building credibility and,
    94; effects of, 85–88, 182; gender-
    neutral terms, 92–93; political
    correctness, 94; stereotypes,
    91–92; unnecessary references, 93
  self-serving, 45
bibliographic information. See citation
    information
bigotry, 180
Blair Witch Project, The, 84
blockers, in groups, 297
body clock. See chronemics
body language. See kinesics
body of speech. See main points of
    speech, planning
Boko Haram, 203
books, as research sources, 388, 391
boomerang effect, 526, 543
borrowing, language, 73–74
boundary insiders, 238
boundary turbulence, 240
brain chemistry, attraction and, 227–28
brainstorming, 367
brief examples, 397–98
bulletin board services (BBS), 308
bullying, 24

call of question, thinking about, 462–63
Campbell, Richard, 192–93
canned presentations, 459
canons of rhetoric, classical, 353–54
career, communication and public speak-
    ing in, 10–11, 349
cascading negativity, 272–74
catalogs, library, 388
categorical (topical) pattern of organization
  defined, 420, 545
  informative speeches, 512
  persuasive speeches, 545

causal pattern of organization
   defined, 419–20
   informative speeches, 512
causal reasoning, 538–39
centralized communication networks, 288
centrifugal and centripetal forces, 241.
   See also dialectical tensions
change, language, 72–74
channel, in transactional communication
   model, 18
Chen, Chuanfu, 391–92
Cheney, Dick, 180
Chicago Manual of Style, 440
Chinese, ancient, 350
choosing a speech topic. *See* topics for
   speeches, selecting
chronemics
   attentiveness and, 139–40, 149
   defined, 121
   planning presentations and, 356
chronological (temporal) pattern of organization
   defined, 419
   informative speeches, 512
Cicero, 350, 353
citation information
   keeping track of, 384–85
   presenting in speech, 394
   in working outline, 438, 440
claims (fact, value, policy)
   defined, 523–24
   organizational patterns for: fact and
      value claims, 544–45; policy
      claims, 546–48; clarifiers, in
      groups, 295
clarifying complex information
   in speeches about ideas, 507
   techniques for: making complex
      information seem familiar, 514;
      moving from general to specific,
      513–14; organizational patterns,
      512 (*see also* patterns of organiza-
      tion); presentation aids, 515 (*see
      also* presentation aids); reducing
      quantity of information, 514;
      reiteration, 396–97, 515–16; rep-
      etition, 516

clarity of audio aids, 482
clarity of messages, guidelines for
   audience analysis, 89–90
   concise language, 90
   concrete terms, 78, 90–91
   feedback from audience, 91
classical canons of rhetoric, 353–54
climate, positive group, 313–14
climate change debate, 195–96
clinchers (in speech conclusions)
   emotional messages, 433
   highlighting thesis, 432–33
   stories or anecdotes, 434
   striking sentences or phrases, 432
   tying to introduction, 431
   in working outline, 439–40
Clinton, Bill, 540
Clinton, Hillary, 361–62
clutter, verbal, 90
CMC. *See* computer-mediated
   communication
co-cultures, relations between
   accommodation, 177–78
   assimilation, 176–77
   separation, 178
collaborating, as conflict style, 269
collectivist cultures
   defined, 172–73
   group communication and, 301
   privacy rules and, 239–40
college, communication and public
   speaking in, 11, 349
collegial peers, 224
commitment
   groups and, 293, 313
   interpersonal relationships and, 264–65
   persuasive speaking and, 523
*Committed: A Skeptic Makes Peace with
   Marriage* (Gilbert), 221
committees, 286–87
common couple violence, 272
common ground
   audience analysis and, 362–64
   establishing, in introduction to
      speech, 426, 439
   informative speeches and, 509, 511
   persuasive speeches and, 531, 532

common sense, limitations of, 23–24
communication (overview)
    competence in, 12–17
    contexts for, 5–7
    definition, 5
    goals of, 13–14
    introduction, 3–5
    misconceptions, 22–25
    principles, 17–22
    review materials, 26–29
    uses of, 8–12
communication, interpersonal.
    See interpersonal relationships
communication privacy management
    (CPM) theory, 238–39
community, communication and public
    speaking in, 12, 349
comparison pattern of organization
    defined, 420
    informative speeches, 512
comparison (analogy) reasoning, 536–37
compelling evidence, providing, 534
competence, credibility and, 531
competitive fighting, 269
complete sentences, in working outlines,
    435, 436, 437, 439
complex information, clarifying. *See* clar-
    ifying complex information
complexity, group, 288–89
compromisers, in groups, 296
compromising, as conflict style, 269–70
computer-mediated communication
    (CMC)
    communication theory and: agenda-
        setting theory, 208–11; critical
        media theory, 207–8
    vs. face-to-face communication,
        203–4
    for groups: group work and docu-
        ment sharing, 308–10; meetings,
        305–8, 313
    problem solving, 330–31
    maintaining relationships with,
        254–55, 258
    mass media: critical consumption
        of, 211; defined, 7, 192–93;
        entertainment and news media,

        193–96; free and paid media,
        199–201; mental associations
        and, 39; old and new media,
        197–99
    nonverbal communication and, 107–
        8, 122–25
    online identity management, 60–62
    overview: introduction, 191–92;
        review materials, 215–17; per-
        sonal guidelines, 211–15
    social media: anonymity, free speech,
        and privacy, 205–6, 213; charac-
        teristics of, 201–2; digital divide
        and net neutrality, 206–7; effects
        of, 202–4; job interviews and,
        558; news coverage and, 199; as
        research tool, 392
concise language, 90
conclusions (of speeches)
    audience attentiveness and, 150
    clinchers: emotional messages, 433;
        highlighting thesis, 432–33; sto-
        ries or anecdotes, 434; striking
        sentences or phrases, 432; tying
        to introduction, 431
    in impromptu speeches, 463
    summarizing main points, 430–31
    transitioning to, 430
    in working outline, 439–40
concrete terms, 78, 90–91
conferencing, audio and video, 307–8,
    309, 310
conflict
    dialectical tensions: managing,
        244–45; types of, 241–44
    interpersonal (*see also* interpersonal
        relationships; relational mainte-
        nance): healthy patterns, 274–77;
        overview, 266–68; styles of, 269–
        71; unhealthy patterns, 272–74
    managing, in groups: disruptive emo-
        tions, 341; focusing on tasks vs.
        disagreements, 341; respect,
        340–41; topics vs. people,
        339–40
    in news media, 195
    role conflict, 298

conflicts of interest, 532. *See also* objectivity
conglomeration, media, 208
connecting bids, 263–64
connection/separation dialectic, 241–42, 245
connotative meanings
vs. denotative meanings, 72
loaded language and, 543–44
See also associations, mental
consensus decision making, 326
constructive criticism, 153
contempt, 272–74
content of messages
content-oriented listening and, 137, 138
group communication and, 286
vs. relational meaning, 6
context
communication behaviors and, 17
context-dependent meanings, 74–75
for statistics, 400
contradiction, nonverbal, 110, 474, 475
contrast, in visual aids, 482
convergence, media, 7, 196
conversational delivery style, 461
cooperativeness, as conflict style, 269–71
coordination and subordination of speech subpoints, 422, 437–38
cover letters (for job applications), 558, 560
CPM (communication privacy management) theory, 238–39
creativity, heterogeneous groups and, 303
credibility of sources
evaluating: expertise, 385–86, 399; Internet sources, 392; objectivity, 386; observational capacity, 386–87; recency or timeliness, 387
prioritizing by, 403
credibility of speaker (ethos)
defined, 382–83
establishing, in speech introduction, 428, 439
eye contact and, 472–73
informative speeches and, 509, 511
persuasive speeches and, 530–32
pronunciation and, 469–70, 532

criteria-application pattern of organization
informative speeches, 512
persuasive speeches, 544–45
critical media theory, 207–8
criticism
cultural, 207–8
respectful and gentle, 275–76
speech critiques, 152–54
cross-cultural nonverbal behaviors, 105, 114
cross-sex friendships, 259–60
cultural criticism, 207–8
culture(s)
communication challenges: ethnocentrism and hate, 179–82, 185–86; expressing willingness to learn, 184–85; prejudice, 180–81; respecting variation, 183–84
diversity and: age, 168–69; gender and sexual orientation, 166–67; race, ethnicity, and heritage, 165–66
nonverbal communication and: eye contact, 115–16; handshakes, 114; monochronic and polychronic cultures, 121; olfactics (smell), 121; overview, 16, 104–6; paralanguage (vocal quality), 120; physical appearance, 119; proxemics, 117–18
overview: introduction, 161–64; review materials, 186–89
psychology and: mental associations, 39–40; privacy rules, 239–40; self-concept, 54–55
relations between co-cultures: accommodation, 177–78; assimilation, 176–77; separation, 178
types of: high- vs. low-contact, 174; high- vs. low-context, 171–72, 302; individualistic vs. collectivist, 172–73, 239–40, 301; masculine vs. feminine, 173, 303; power distance, 174–75, 301; uncertainty avoidance, 169–70, 302

cyclical conflict, accepting, 274
cyclical tensions model of interpersonal relationships, 234–35

dating sites, 203–4
Day-Lewis, Daniel, 103–4
decentralized communication networks, 288
deception. *See* truthful communication
deceptive appearances, 43–44
decision making, group, 325–26. *See also* problem solving, group
Declaration of Independence, 83
decoding, in transactional communication model, 18
defeated listening, 151, 467
defensiveness, 272, 274
definition, as informative technique
  overview and types of definitions, 490–92
  speech topics and: ideas, 507–8; objects, 499
  supporting materials and, 396, 398
delivering speeches
  in classical canons of rhetoric, 354
  modes of delivery: extemporaneous (speaking from an outline), 435–36, 460–61; impromptu (speaking without preparation), 461–63; memorizing from a manuscript, 458–60; reading from a manuscript, 456–58
  nonverbal delivery skills: appearance, 478–79 (*see also* personal appearance); eye contact, 472–73 (*see also* eye contact); gestures, 459, 473–75; physical movement, 475–76; proxemics, 117–18, 476–77
  overview: introduction, 455–56; review materials, 485–87
  presentation aids: advantages, 400, 479–80; guidelines for developing, 480–83, 510; informative speeches and, 515; memorized speeches and, 459; software, 482, 484, 510; using during speech, 483–84

speech critiques, 152–54
  vocal delivery skills: articulation, 468–69; pausing, 151, 470–71; projection, 151, 468; pronunciation, 469–70; rate of delivery, 151, 466–68; tone, 458, 465–66; volume, 151, 463–65
delivery notes or reminders, 447
demand-withdraw pattern, 272, 274
demographics, audience
  dimensions of: age, 359, 511; educational level, 506; gender composition, 360; race and ethnicity, 360–61; religious orientation, 361–62; sexual orientation, 361
  importance of, 357, 359
  informative speeches and, 508–9
  presentation aids and, 481
demonstration, as informative technique
  overview, 494–96
  speech topics and: individuals or groups, 500–501; objects, 499; processes, 505
  supporting materials and, 397
denotative (literal) meanings: vs. connotative meanings, 72; dictionary definitions, 491
description, as informative technique
  audience analysis and, 510–11
  overview, 493–94
  speech topics and: events, 502; individuals or groups, 500–501
designated leaders, 332
detailed outlines for speeches.
  See working outlines
detailed phrases, in working outlines, 435, 436, 437, 439
development, group dynamics and, 298–300
dialectical tensions
  managing, 244–45
  types of, 241–44
dictionary definitions (denotative meanings), 491. *See also* denotative meanings
difficult words, 447. *See also* word choice
digital divide, 206

directness, as conflict style, 269–71
direct quotations, 395, 407–8, 438. *See also* acknowledging others' work
disposition, audience, 526–27, 531
distracted listening, 142–43
distracters, in groups, 297
distracting gestures, 151, 474, 475
diverse perspectives, in groups, 291–92
diversity
    dimensions of: age, 168–69; gender and sexual orientation, 166–67; race, ethnicity, and heritage, 165–66
    respect for, 183–84
document sharing, 309
domain-specific self-esteem, 51
dominators, in groups, 297
Douglass, Frederick, 83
dyads
    communication in, 220–21
    types of: friendships, 223, 258–61; romantic relationships, 224–25, 256–58; workplace relationships, 223–24, 261–62
    See also interpersonal relationships
dynamics, group
    development, 298–300, 328–30
    roles: selfish roles, 296–97; social roles, 295–96; work roles, 294–95

educational level, audience, 506
effectiveness, heterogeneous groups and, 303
ego involvement, 526
elaborators, in groups, 295
electronic bulletin board services (BBS), 308
e-mail, 305–6, 309
emergent leaders, 332–33
emojis and emoticons, 108, 123–24, 310
emotional appeals (pathos)
    in conclusions, 433
    persuasive speeches and: ethics and, 542–44; guidelines for use, 540–42
    supporting materials and, 396, 397
emotional flooding, 88, 275
emotional intelligence, 59

emotions
    expressing, with language, 83–84
    managing, in meetings, 341
    monitoring, in relationships, 274–75
    See also feelings
empathy, 155
encoding, in transactional communication model, 18
encouragers, in groups, 296
enjoyment, heterogeneous groups and, 304
entertainment media, 193–94, 196
equivocal language, 80
ethics, communication
    in conversational feedback, 155
    general principles, 20–22
    identity management and, 60
    negative behaviors: deception, manipulation, bullying, 23–24
    recording others without permission, 394
    speech critiques and, 154
    See also ethics, speeches and
ethics, speeches and
    acknowledging others' work: citation information, 384–85, 394, 438, 440; paraphrasing, 394, 395, 408–9; plagiarism, 381–82, 406–7; quoting from sources, 395, 407–8, 438
    emotional appeals and, 542–44
    overview: introduction, 381–82, 403–4; review materials, 409–13
    truthful communication: equivocal language, 80; false inference, 405–6; half-truths, 405; lying, 404–5; misrepresenting another's point of view, 395; omission, 406; out-of-context evidence, 408
    See also ethics, communication; researching a speech; supporting materials for speeches
ethnicity. *See* race and ethnicity
ethnocentrism
    as barrier to communication, 179–80
    combating, 185–86
    group communication and, 300
    media literacy and, 212

ethos, 530–32. *See also* credibility of speaker
etymological definitions, 491
evaluating credibility of sources;
    expertise, 385–86
    Internet sources, 392
    objectivity, 386
    observational capacity, 386–87
    recency or timeliness, 387
evaluators, in groups, 295
events, informative speeches about, 502
evidence
    credibility of speaker and, 531
    defined, 382
    guidelines for presenting; identifying
        sources, 394–95, 533
    persuasive speeches and,
        533–34
    quoting out of context, 408
    in speaking outline, 447
    in working outline, 438
example reasoning, 534–36
examples and exemplification
    as compelling evidence, 534
    hypothetical, 426
    identity management and, 60
    in speech critiques, 153
    in supporting materials, 396,
        397–98
expectations, positive, 276
experience, communication behaviors
    and, 15–16
expert definitions, 398, 491
expertise:
    of audience, 150, 506–7, 510–11
    of sources: credibility and, 385–86;
        expert testimony, 399; identify-
        ing, for credibility, 533; inter-
        viewing experts, 393–94
    of speaker: credibility and, 531; topic
        selection and, 370, 374
explanation, as informative technique
    audience analysis and, 510–11
    overview, 492
    speech topics and: ideas, 507–8; indi-
        viduals or groups, 501; objects,
        499; processes, 504–5

expressions, facial, 114–15, 124
extemporaneous delivery:
    advantages of, 460–61
    building speaking outline, 435–36
extended examples, 398
extended self, 49
external noise, 140–41
eye contact
    delivering speeches and: encouraging
        listening with, 151, 152; extem-
        poraneous delivery, 460; func-
        tions and guidelines, 472–73;
        memorizing from script, 459;
        reading from script, 458
    in job interviews, 565
    in research interviews, 394
    study of (oculesics), 115–16

facial expressions, 114–15, 124
fact claims
    defined, 523, 524
    organizational patterns for, 544–45
facts vs. inferences, 47–48
factual accuracy, credibility and, 532, 533
fallacies, logical. *See* logical fallacies
fallibility, recognizing, 46
false inference, 405–6. *See also* truthful
    communication
family relationships, 222–23
famous quotations, 426–27
fear appeals, 541, 543
feedback
    from audience, 91
    communication behaviors and, 16
    for conversations, 154–55
    self-concept and (reflected appraisals),
        52–53
    speech critiques, 152–54
    in transactional communication
        model, 18
feelings
    expressing with language, 83–84
    taking ownership of, 96–97
    See also emotions
Feminine Mystique, The (Friedan), 55
feminine vs. masculine cultures, 173, 303

fighting, 269–71
figurative analogies, 401
figurative meanings. *See* connotative meanings
fillers, verbal, 471
filtering out distractions, 146–47
first impressions, 41–42, 230
Fisher, Walter, 84
flip charts, 484
flooding, emotional, 88, 275
focus, maintaining
    audience interaction with presentation aids and, 483–84
    in research interviews, 394
formal distance, 117
formatting of news, 198
forum (location)
    analyzing, 356
    informative speeches and, 508, 509
    listening ability and, 140
    presentation aids and, 480–81, 510
four Cs (connect, create, consume, control), 202
Four Horsemen of the Apocalypse model, 272–73
framing, 209
free and paid media, 199–201
Friedan, Betty, 55
friendships, 223, 258–61. *See also* interpersonal relationships
friends-with-benefits (FWB) relationships, 260–61
front-loading main message, 150
fry, vocal, 120
full sentences, in working outlines, 435, 436, 437, 439
functional definitions, 398, 492
fundamental attribution error, 46
FWB (friends-with-benefits) relationships, 260–61

gatekeepers, in groups, 296
GDSS (group decision support systems), 330
gender

audience demographics and, 360
    diversity spectrum and, 166–67
    language and, 92–93, 360
    nonverbal communication and, 106–7
    privacy rules and, 239
    stereotypes and, 360
generalization, hasty, 538
general to specific, moving from, 513–14
generating ideas for speeches
    brainstorming, 367
    invention, in classical canons of rhetoric, 353
    mind mapping, 368–69
    research, 366–67
    word association, 368
    See also topics for speeches, selecting
generational differences. *See* age
Gersick's two-phase model of group development, 299–300
gestures
    distracting, 151, 474, 475
    memorizing speeches and, 459
    See also kinesics
Gettysburg Address (Lincoln), 81
Ghonim, Wael, 83
Gilbert, Elizabeth, 221
global self-esteem, 51
goals, communication, 13–14
goodwill, credibility and, 531
Gorbachev, Mikhail, 350–51
Gottman, John, 272, 277
government documents, as research sources, 388–89
Greeks, ancient, 350, 353, 531
Grimké, Angelina, 350
group advocates, 296
group communication
    advantages of groups: commitment, 293; diverse perspectives, 291–92, 303–5; multiple resources, 292–93
    characteristics of small groups: communication process, 285–86; size of group, 287–91; types of groups, 286–87

group communication (*continued*)
  cultural diversity and: high vs. low context, 171–72, 302; individualism vs. collectivism, 172–73, 301; masculine vs. feminine cultures, 173, 303; mindful communication, 303–5; power distance, 174–75, 301; uncertainty avoidance, 169–70, 302
  group dynamics: development, 298–300, 328–30; roles, 294–98; guidelines for participation; encouraging positive climate, 313–14; fulfilling commitments, 313; listening interactively, 311–12 (*see also* listening skills); participating vs. dominating, 312; preparing for meetings, 311
  leadership (*see* leadership, group)
  overview: introduction, 283–84, 319–20; review materials, 314–17, 342–45
  problem solving in groups: procedures, 321–26; tips and guidelines, 327–31
  technology and: group work and document sharing, 308–10; meetings, 305–8, 313
group decision support systems (GDSS), 330
group dynamics, defined, 6
groups or individuals, informative speeches about, 500–501
group support systems (GSS), 330
groupthink, 337–38
growth, personal, 57
GSS (group support systems), 330

hacktivist groups, 205
half-truths, 405. *See also* truthful communication
Hall, Edward T., 117, 121, 171
Hall, Mildred R., 171
haptics (study of touch), 116–17
harmonizers, in groups, 296
Hart, Betty, 53
hasty generalization, 538

hate and hate speech, 86, 181, 182, 185–86
heritage, 166. *See also* race and ethnicity
heterogeneous groups, 291–92, 303–5
heteronormativity, 167, 180
high-contact cultures, 174
high-context cultures, 171–72, 302
high-power-distance cultures, 174–75, 301
Hitler, Adolf, 542
homogeneous groups, 291–92, 303–5
homo narrans, 84
hooks, for information retention, 396–97
hormones, brain, 227–28
hostile audiences, 527
humor
  in job interviews, 569
  in speeches, 396, 397
hyperpersonal model, 204
hypothetical examples, 426

ideas, generating. *See* generating ideas for speeches
ideas, informative speeches about, 506–8
identity management
  ethics and, 60
  mechanisms of: audience, 58; emotional intelligence, 59; self-disclosure, 58
  objectives of: exemplification, 60; ingratiation, 59; intimidation, 60; self-promotion, 59; supplication, 60
  online activities and, 60–62
  See also self-concept
ignorance, 180
"I Have a Dream" (King), 81, 350, 353
illegal job interview questions, 568–69
imagination, language and, 84–85
imagined trajectories model of interpersonal relationships, 233–34
immutable characteristics, biased language and, 86, 182
impression management. *See* identity management
impromptu speeches, 461–63

improper word choice, 80
indentation, in working outlines,
    434, 437
indexes, library periodical, 367, 384,
    395
indirect fighting, 270–71
individualistic cultures, 172–73, 301
individuals or groups, informative
    speeches about, 500–501
inductive reasoning. *See* reasoning
inferences
    vs. facts, 47–48
    false, 405–6 (*see also* truthful commu-
        nication)
    perceptual process and, 33–34
inflammatory language, 88. *See also* hate
    and hate speech
inflection, vocal, 466
influence, 523. *See also* persuasive
    speeches
information gatherers, in groups, 295
information overload, 141–42
information providers, in groups, 294
informative speeches
    clarifying and simplifying message;
        making complex information
        seem familiar, 514; moving from
        general to specific, 513–14;
        organizational patterns, 512 (*see
        also* patterns of organization);
        presentation aids, 515; reducing
        quantity of information, 514; reit-
        eration, 396–97, 515–16;
        repetition, 516
    developing: audience analysis, 508–9
        (*see also* audience analysis);
        rhetorical purpose and, 511;
        selecting informative techniques,
        509–11
    overview: introduction, 489–90;
        review materials, 516–19
    rhetorical purpose and, 372, 511
    sample speech: "Freeganism: More
        than a free lunch," 579–83
    techniques for informing
        (see informative techniques)
    topic selection and, 372

topics for: events, 502; ideas, 506–8;
    individuals or groups, 500–501;
    objects, 498–500, 501; processes,
    499–500, 501, 503–5
informative techniques
    choosing a technique, 509–11
    definition: overview and types of
        definitions, 490–92; supporting
        materials and, 396, 398; topics
        for, 499, 507–8
    demonstration: overview, 494–96; sup-
        porting materials and, 397; topics
        for, 499, 500–501, 502, 505
    description: audience analysis and,
        510–11; overview, 493–94; topics
        for, 499, 502
    explanation: audience analysis and,
        510–11; overview, 492; topics for,
        499, 501, 504–5, 507–8
    narration: audience analysis and, 511;
        overview, 496–97; supporting
        materials and, 400; topics for,
        499, 501, 502, 505
    See also informative speeches
ingratiation, identity management and,
    59
in-groups, 53
initiating interpersonal relationships
    first impressions, 230
    introductions, 229–30
    small talk, 230–31
initiators, in groups, 294
instant messaging, 306–7, 309
instant relay chat (IRC), 308, 312
intelligence, emotional, 59
interactivity and news coverage, 199
intercultural communication. *See*
    culture(s)
interdependence, 222
interest, listener and audience
    gauging with eye contact, 472
    presentation aids and, 479
    statistics and, 400
    supporting materials and, 395–96
interference, in transactional communi-
    cation model, 18
internal noise, 142–43

internal previews and summaries, 425
Internet research
  benefits and disadvantages, 389–92
  citation information and, 385
  evaluating credibility of online
    sources, 392
interpersonal communication, defined, 6
interpersonal relationships
  choosing: attraction, 226–29; initi-
    ating, 229–31; conflict in (see
    conflict)
  dialectical tensions: managing, 244–
    45; types of, 241–44
  dyads: communication in, 220–21;
    types of, 222–25, 256–62
  maintaining (*see* relational mainte-
    nance)
  overview: introduction, 219–22;
    review materials, 245–49
  pathways for: cyclical tensions model,
    234–35: imagined trajectories
    model, 233–34; stage models,
    232
  privacy: communication privacy man-
    agement (CPM) theory, 238–39;
    openness/closedness dialectic
    and, 242–43, 244–45; rules for,
    239–40; violations of, 240–41
  self-disclosure: disadvantages of, 238;
    identity management and, 58;
    Johari window, 236–37; social
    penetration theory, 237
interruptive listening, 143
interviewing experts for research, 393–94
intimacy, 220–21
intimate distance, 117
intimidation, identity management and,
  60
introductions (personal), 229–30
introductions (to speeches)
  audience attentiveness and, 150
  establishing credibility, 428
  gaining audience attention, 425–27
  previewing main points, 428–29
  showing audience what's in it for
    them, 427–28
  signaling thesis, 427

tying conclusions to, 431
in working outlines, 439
invention, in classical canons of
  rhetoric, 353
IRC (instant relay chat), 308, 312

James, LeBron, 210
jargon, 79–80, 514
job, communication and public speaking
  in, 10–11, 349
job interviews
  sample documents: cover letter, 560;
    follow-up letter, 570; résumé, 559
  step 1: preparing for: attire and
    appearance, 562–63; general
    questions, 554–56; homework,
    561; practicing for, 561–62; résu-
    més, 558; social media, 558; tak-
    ing stock, 556–57
  step 2: during the interview: levels
    of interviews, 563–65; listening
    skills, 566; nonverbal behaviors,
    565; punctuality and prepara-
    tion, 563–65; questions to ask,
    566–68; truthfulness, 566; what
    to avoid, 568–69
  step 3: after the interview: follow-
    up communications, 571–72;
    patience, 570; taking notes, 572;
    thank-you notes, 571
Johari window, 236–37
journal articles, 366–67, 388, 391

Kasdan, Lawrence, 320
keeping track of sources, 384–85
Kennedy, Kathleen, 319–20
keyword searches, 384, 391–92
Khan Academy, 203
kinesics (body language)
  defined, 113–14
  delivering speeches and, 459, 475–76
  distracting gestures, 151, 474, 475
King, Martin Luther, Jr., 42, 81, 350, 353
Knapp's staircase model of interpersonal
  relationships, 232
knowledge. *See* expertise

labeling
  in speaking outlines, 446
  in working outlines, 434, 437
language. *See* verbal communication
latitude of acceptance and rejection, 526,
    527
Lawrence, Charles, III, 86
lay testimony, 399
leadership, group
  challenges, 334
  leaders vs. leadership, 331–32
  leading meetings: assessing effective-
    ness, 339; facilitating decisions,
    338–39; facilitating discussion,
    336; groupthink, 337–38; keep-
    ing members on task, 336;
    modeling behavior, 335–36; pro-
    cedural needs, 334–35
  managing conflict: disruptive emo-
    tions, 341; focusing on tasks vs.
    disagreements, 341; respect,
    340–41; topics vs. people,
    339–40
  types of leaders: designated, 332;
    emergent, 332–33; virtual
    groups, 333
Lean In (Sandberg), 55
learning groups, 286
learning platforms, 308–9
learning styles, 403
lecterns, 476
Lee, Dean, 402
legibility of visual aids, 482
LGBT individuals. *See* sexual orientation
librarians, 384
library research
  books, 388
  government documents, 388–89
  periodicals and newspapers, 366–67,
    388, 395
  usefulness of, 384, 387
life experiences, mental associations and,
    39
Lincoln, Abraham, 81
Lippmann, Walter, 208–9
listening skills
  basics of listening process: listening

styles, 136–38; listening vs. hear-
    ing, 133; processing, 133–34;
    retention, 134–35
  factors affecting listening ability:
    external, 138–41, 151; internal,
    141–46
  improving: in audience, 148–52; in
    conversations, 154–55; in groups,
    311–12; in self, 146–48; speech
    critiques, 152–54
  ineffective listening behaviors:
    agenda-driven listening, 143–44;
    argumentative listening, 144–45;
    defeated listening, 151, 467; dis-
    tracted listening, 142–43; inter-
    ruptive listening, 143; nervous
    listening, 145–46; superficial
    listening, 151–52
  in interviews: job interviews, 566;
    research interviews, 394
  overview: introduction, 131–32;
    review materials, 155–59
  working for accurate understanding,
    95–96
lists
  avoiding long, 403
  of works cited, 440
literal analogies, 400–401
literal (denotative) meanings
  vs. connotative meanings, 72
  dictionary definitions, 491
loaded language fallacy, 543–44
location of speech. *See* forum
logical fallacies
  ad populum (bandwagon) fallacy, 539
  hasty generalization, 538
  loaded language fallacy, 543–44
  post hoc fallacy, 538–39
  reversed causality, 539
  slippery slope fallacy, 540
  straw person fallacy, 539–40
logos (evidence and reasoning), 533–40.
    See also evidence
looking-glass self, 52
low-contact cultures, 174
low-context cultures, 171, 302
low-power-distance cultures, 174–75, 301

Lucas, George, 319
lying, 404–5. *See also* truthful
    communication

magazines, 366–67, 388, 391
main points of speech, planning
    arranging (see patterns of
        organization)
    front- and back-loading, 150 (*see also*
        conclusions; introductions)
    in outlines: speaking outlines, 446,
        447; working outlines, 437–38,
        439–40
    selecting, 417–18
    signaling language: internal previews
        and summaries, 425; signposts,
        424–25; transitions, 423–24,
        430, 438, 447
    subpoints and, 422–23
    summarizing in conclusion: drafting
        and, 430–31; impromptu speak-
        ing and, 463; working outlines
        and, 439–40
maintaining relationships. *See* relational
    maintenance
managing groups. *See* leadership, group
Mandela, Nelson, 84
Mandela, Phumla, 84
manipulation, 24
manuscripts, speech
    memorizing from, 458–60
    reading from, 456–58
Martin, Trayvon, 209–11
masculine vs. feminine cultures, 173, 303
Maslow, Abraham, 527
mass communication, defined, 7
mass media
    critical consumption of, 211
    defined, 7, 192–93
    entertainment and news media,
        193–96
    free and paid media, 199–201
    mental associations and, 39
    old and new media, 197–99
McCombs, Maxwell, 209
media conglomeration, 208

media convergence, 7, 196
mediated communication, 7. *See also*
    computer-mediated
    communication
mediation, decision making by, 326
meetings
    leading: assessing effectiveness, 339;
        facilitating decisions, 338–39;
        facilitating discussion, 336;
        groupthink, 337–38; keeping
        members on task, 336; modeling
        behavior, 335–36; procedural
        needs, 334–35
    technology for: apps, 308; BBS and
        IRC, 308, 312; e-mail, 305–6, 309;
        instant messaging, 306–7, 309;
        text messaging, 306; video and
        audio conferencing, 307–8, 309
    See also group communication
memorizing speeches, 458–60
memory, in classical canons of rhetoric,
    353–54
mental associations (schemas)
    sources of, 39–40
    stimuli and, 37–38
message, in transactional communication
    model, 18
metaphors, 542
Mhenni, Lina Ben, 83
Miller, George, 141–42
mindful communication, 303–5
mind mapping, 368–69
minority-dominated groups, 304
misperceptions
    causes of: deceptive appearances,
        43–44; first impressions, 41–42;
        fundamental attribution error, 46;
        self-serving bias, 45; stereotypes,
        42–43; transference, 44–45
    improving: facts vs. inferences, 47–48;
        perception checking, 48–49;
        recognizing fallibility, 46; seeking
        additional data, 46–47
    See also perceptions
misrepresenting another's point of
    view, 395. *See also* truthful
    communication

mixed-gender audiences, 360
MLA (Modern Language Association)
    style, 440
modeling behavior, 335–36
monochronic cultures, 121
monotone delivery, 458, 465
Moore's motivated sequence, 546–47
multiple resources, in groups, 292–93
multitasking, 142
Myrick, Daniel, 84

narration, as informative technique
    audience analysis and, 511
    overview, 496–97
    speech topics and: events, 502; indi-
        viduals or groups, 501; objects,
        499; processes, 505
    supporting materials and, 400
    See also narratives and stories
narrative pattern of organization, 512
narratives and stories
    as central to human thought, 84
    as compelling evidence, 534
    in conclusion of speech, 434
    in introduction to speech, 426
narrowing a topic
    importance of, 372–73
    specific considerations: assignment
        criteria, 339; audience, 370, 374
        (*see also* audience analysis); own
        knowledge and interests, 370, 374
    sticking to your choice, 370
needs
    of audience, 527–28, 531
    of research process, 384
negative reciprocity, 272
negativity, cascading, 272–74
negotiated permanence, 225
nervous listening, 145–46
net neutrality, 206–7
networks, group communication, 288–89
networks of association. *See* associations,
    mental
neutral audiences, 527
new evidence, providing, 533
new media, 197–99

news media, 193–96, 198–99
newspapers. *See* periodicals
noise
    external, 140–41
    internal, 142–43
    in transactional communication
        model, 18
nonverbal communication
    defined, 18
    functional relationship to verbal com-
        munication: accenting, 112–13,
        123; contradicting, 110, 474, 475;
        regulating, 110–11; repeating,
        109; substituting, 112; supple-
        menting, 108–9
    guidelines for: general, 125–26; job
        interviews, 565
    influences on: culture, 104–6; gender,
        106–7; technology, 107–8
    overview: introduction, 103–4; review
        materials, 126–29
    technology and, 122–25
    types of: chronemics, 121–22, 139–
        40, 149, 356; facial expressions,
        114–15, 124; haptics (touch),
        116–17; kinesics (body language),
        113–14, 459, 473–76; oculesics,
        115–16, 472–73 (*see also* eye
        contact); paralanguage, 119–20;
        physical appearance, 118–19,
        562–63; proxemics, 117–18,
        476–77; smell (olfactics), 120–21
norm facilitators, in groups, 296
notes, taking
    for citation information, 384–85
    job interviews and: after the interview,
        572; during the interview, 566;
        for speech critiques, 152–53
number of points in speech
    main points, 418
    subpoints, 422

objectivity
    credibility and, 532
    informative speeches and, 511
    of research sources, 386

objects, informative speeches about, 498–500, 501
observational capacity, 386–87
oculesics. *See* eye contact
Odd Girl Out (Simmons), 53
Ogden, C. K., 77
old media, 197
olfactics (smell), 120–21
omission, lying by, 406. *See also* truthful communication
online identity management, 60–62
openness
   vs. closedness, 242–43, 244–45
   maintaining relationships with, 254, 259
Orci, Taylor, 115
organizing speeches
   body of speech: arranging main points (see patterns of organization); selecting main points, 417–18; subpoints (supporting materials), 422, 423
   finishing touches: conclusions, 430–34, 463; introductions, 425–29, 431, 463; signaling language, 423–25, 429
   outlining and, 434 (*see also* speaking outlines; working outlines)
   overview: introduction, 415–16; review materials, 450–53
organizing words and sentences. *See* signaling language
Other, the, 207, 212
out-groups, 53
outlining speeches
   mental outlines for impromptu speeches, 462
   overview, 434 (*see also* speaking outlines; working outlines)
out-of-context evidence, 408
overhead transparencies, 484
overused speech topics, 369

pacing, 475
Packard, Vance, 527
paid and free media, 199–201

panning, 473
paralanguage, 119–20
paraphrasing
   spoken word, 394
   written word, 395, 408–9
participatory media. *See* social media
pathos, 540–44. *See also* emotional appeals
patterns of interpersonal conflict
   healthy: accepting cyclical conflict, 274; balancing positivity and negativity, 276–77; criticizing respectfully, 275–76; monitoring emotions, 274–75; positive expectations, 276
   unhealthy: cascading negativity, 272–74; common couple violence, 272; demand-withdraw pattern, 272, 274; negative reciprocity, 272
patterns of organization
   categorical (topical) pattern: defined, 420; informative speeches, 512; persuasive speeches, 545
   causal pattern: defined, 419–20; informative speeches, 512
   chronological (temporal) pattern: defined, 419; informative speeches, 512
   comparison pattern: defined, 420; informative speeches, 512
   criteria-application pattern: informative speeches, 512; persuasive speeches, 544–45
   Moore's motivated sequence (persuasive speeches), 546–47
   narrative pattern (informative speeches), 512
   problem-cause-solution pattern (persuasive speeches), 547–48
   spatial pattern: defined, 418–19; informative speeches, 512
pausing, during speech delivery, 151, 470–71
peer-reviewed journals. *See* periodicals
people, informative speeches about, 500–501

people-oriented listening, 137
perception(s)
    barriers to: causes, 41–46; improving accuracy of, 46–49
    identity management and: ethics and, 60; mechanisms of, 58–59; objectives of, 59–60; online activities and, 60–62
    of others: communication and, 34–36; formation of, 36–40; inferences and, 33–34
    overview: introduction, 31–32; review materials, 62–65
    of self (self-concept): improving, 55–57; nature of, 49–51; sources of, 51–55
periodicals, 366–67, 388, 391
permanence, negotiated, 225
personal appearance. *See* physical appearance
personal distance, 117
personal growth, 57
personality, as cause of conflict, 267–68
personal life, communication in, 8–9
person perception, 33
persuasion, as function of language, 82–83
persuasive speeches
    audience considerations (strategic discourse): beliefs, 527; benefits, 427–28, 528–29; disposition, 526–27, 531; needs, 527–28, 531; reservations, 151, 529–30, 531, 532; values, 528
    building blocks of persuasion: ethos (credibility), 530–32 (*see also* credibility of speaker); logos (evidence and reasoning), 533–40 (*see also* evidence); pathos (emotional appeals), 540–44 (*see also* emotional appeals)
    nature and purpose of: fact, value, and policy claims, 523–24 (*see also* claims); influencing audience members, 523
    organizing: categorical pattern, 545; criteria-application pattern, 544–45; Moore's motivated sequence, 546–47; problem-cause-solution pattern, 547–48
    overview: introduction, 521–22; review materials, 548–52
    sample speeches: "Child slavery and the production of chocolate," 589–93; "Extra credit you can live without," 573–78; "Preventing cyberbullying," 584–88
    topic selection and, 372
pervasiveness of mass media, 193
phrases, in working outlines, 435, 436, 437, 439
physical appearance
    delivering speeches and, 478–79
    job interviews and, 562–63
    as nonverbal communication, 118–19
physical attraction, 226–27
physical movements, delivering speeches and, 475–76. *See also* kinesics
pitch, vocal, 119, 465–66
plagiarism, 381–82, 406–7. *See also* acknowledging others' work
plans, research, 383–85
podiums, 476
pointing, 151, 474
point of view, misrepresenting, 395. *See also* truthful communication
policy claims
    defined, 524
    organizational patterns for, 546–48
political correctness, 94
polychronic cultures, 121
positive expectations, 276
positive self-talk, 55–56
positivity, maintaining relationships with
    friendships, 258–59
    overview, 254
    romantic relationships, 256
post hoc fallacy, 538–39
power distance, 174–75, 301
PowerPoint, 484, 510. *See also* presentation software
pragmatic language rules, 70
precise evidence, providing, 533–34
predictability/novelty dialectic, 243–44, 245

prejudice, 180–81. *See also* stereotypes
preparation outlines for speeches.
    See working outlines
presentation aids
    advantages, 400, 479–80
    audience attentiveness and, 150
    audience size and, 510
    clarifying complex information
      with, 515
    guidelines for developing, 480–83,
      510
    informative speeches and, 515
    memorized speeches and, 459
    using during speech, 483–84
presentation software, 482, 484, 510
presentation time, for speeches, 139, 356
previewing
    as form of signaling language, 425
    in introduction to speech, 428–29,
      439
primary groups, 286
prior exposure, 364–65, 507
privacy
    Internet and, 205, 213
    interpersonal relationships and: com-
      munication privacy management
      (CPM) theory, 238–39; openness/
      closedness dialectic and, 242–43,
      244–45; rules for, 239–40; viola-
      tions of, 240–41
private self, 57
problem-cause-solution pattern of orga-
    nization, 547–48
problem solving, group
    procedures: step 1: defining the prob-
      lem, 322–23; step 2: generating
      possible solutions, 323–24; step
      3: criteria for solutions, 324–25;
      step 4: selecting best solution,
      325–26
    tips and guidelines: clarifying prob-
      lem, 327; eliminating roadblocks,
      328; observing process, 328–30;
      using technology, 330–31
procedural guiders, in groups, 295
procedural needs, addressing,
    334–35

processes, informative speeches about,
    499–500, 501, 503–5
processing
    defined, 133–34
    retention and, 134–35
professional peers, 224
projection, vocal, 151, 468
pronunciation, 469–70, 532
props, speech manuscripts as, 458.
    See also presentation aids
provocative statements, 432, 436
proxemics, 117–18, 476–77
proximity, attraction and, 228–29
public self, 57
public speaking (overview)
    classical canons of rhetoric, 353–54
    defined, 6–7
    history, 350–51
    key elements, 351
    preparing for, 347–48, 354
    review materials, 376–79
    uses of, 349–50
purpose of communication, 13–14
purpose of speech. *See* rhetorical purpose
    of speech; specific purpose of
    speech

qualifications. *See* expertise
quantity of information, reducing, 514
Queen Bees and Wannabes (Wiseman), 53
question, thinking about call of, 462–63
questions
    in job interviews, 568–69
    in research interviews, 393–94
Quintilian, 20–21, 350
quotations, famous, 426–27
quoting from sources, 395, 407–8, 438.
    See also acknowledging others'
    work

race and ethnicity
    appropriate or unnecessary refer-
      ences to, 93
    audience demographics and, 360–61
    culture and, 165–66

rate of delivery
  listening ability and, 139, 151
  speeches and, 466–68
Reagan, Ronald, 350–51
real-time news coverage, 198–99
reappraisal, self-concept and, 57
reasoning
  logical fallacies: ad populum
    (bandwagon) fallacy, 539;
    hasty generalization, 538;
    loaded language fallacy,
    543–44; post hoc fallacy,
    538–39; reversed causality,
    539; slippery slope fallacy,
    540; straw person fallacy,
    539–40
  types of: causal reasoning, 538;
    comparison (analogy)
    reasoning, 536–37; example
    reasoning, 534–36; sign
    reasoning, 537
recall, audience
  compelling evidence and, 534
  presentation aids and, 480
  supporting materials and, 396–97
receivers, in transactional communication model, 18
recency of sources, 387
reciprocal altruism, 222
reciprocity, negative, 272
recorders, in groups, 295
recording conversations, 394
Red Line, 85
reducing quantity of information,
  514
reflected appraisals, 52–53
reflective learners, 403
reframing strategy for dialectical tensions, 245
regulation, nonverbal, 110–11
rehearsing with presentation aids,
  482–83
reinforcing gestures, 474, 475
reiteration, 396–97, 515–16. *See also*
  repetition
rejection, latitude of, 526
relational embarrassment, 240

relational maintenance
  guidelines: acting based on knowl-
    edge, 264; coping with uncer-
    tainty, 265; embracing agency,
    262–63; meeting connecting
    bids, 263–64; nurturing mutual
    commitment, 264–65
  maintenance behaviors: assurances,
    254, 256; openness, 254, 259;
    positivity, 254, 256, 258–59;
    shared activities, 254, 259;
    shared tasks, 254, 257; social net-
    works, 254, 257–58
  overview: introduction, 251–53;
    review materials, 277–81
  technology and, 254–55, 258
  types of relationships and: friend-
    ships, 223, 258–61; romantic
    relationships, 224–25, 256–58;
    workplace relationships, 223–24,
    261–62
  See also conflict; interpersonal rela-
    tionships
relational meaning, 6, 286
relational rules, conflict and, 267
relationships, interpersonal. *See* interpersonal relationships
religion
  audience demographics and,
    361–62
  physical appearance and, 119
  unnecessary references to, 93
repertoire, communication, 14–15
repetition
  nonverbal, 109, 123
  verbal, 516 (*see also* reiteration)
representative examples, 535–36
researching a speech
  evaluating credibility of sources: exper-
    tise, 385–86; objectivity, 386;
    observational capacity, 386–87;
    recency or timeliness, 387
  Internet research: benefits and dis-
    advantages, 389–92; citation
    information and, 385; evaluating
    credibility of online sources,
    392

researching a speech (*continued*)
  interviewing experts, 393–94
  library research: books, 388; government documents, 388–89; periodicals and newspapers, 366–67, 388; usefulness of, 384, 387
  overview: introduction, 382–83; review materials, 409–13; presenting evidence during speech, 394–95
  research plans, 383–85
  for topic selection, 366–67
  See also ethics, speech
research librarians, 384
reservations, acknowledging
  of argumentative listeners, 151
  credibility and, 531, 532
  two-sided arguments, 529–30
responsibility, speech ethics and, 404
résumés
  bringing to interview, 565
  preparing, 558
  sample, 559
retention, 134–35
reversed causality, 539
Rhetoric (Aristotle), 350
rhetoric, classical canons of, 353–54
rhetorical purpose of speech
  speech critiques and, 153
  topic selection and, 371–72, 374
  types of: informative speeches (see informative speeches); persuasive speeches (see persuasive speeches); special-occasion speeches, 349–50, 372
Richards, I. A., 77
Ride, Sally, 432–33
Risley, Todd, 53
role conflict, 298
roles, group
  selfish roles, 296–97
  social roles, 295–96
  work roles, 294–95
Romans, ancient, 20–21, 350, 353
romantic relationships, 224–25, 256–58
rules of language (semantic, pragmatic, syntactic), 69–70

Said, Edward, 207
salience of self-concept, 51
Sam, Michael, 3–4
sample works
  informative speech: "Freeganism: More than a free lunch," 579–83
  job applications: cover letter, 560; follow-up letter, 570; résumé, 559
  persuasive speeches: "Child slavery and the production of chocolate," 589–93; "Extra credit you can live without," 573–78; "Preventing cyberbullying," 584–88
  speech outlines: speaking outline, 447–50; working outline, 440–45
Sánchez, Eduardo, 84
Sandberg, Sheryl, 55
schemas (mental associations)
  sources of, 39–40
  stimuli and, 37–38
school, communication and public speaking in, 11, 349
scripts, speech
  memorizing from, 458–60
  reading from, 456–58
secondary groups, 286–87
selecting a speech topic. *See* topics for speeches, selecting
selection strategy for dialectical tensions, 245
self-concepts
  improving: personal growth, 57; positive self-talk, 55–56; reappraisal, 57; support networks, 57
  nature of: attributes, 50–51; self-esteem and, 51
  sources of: reflected appraisals, 52–53; sociocultural contexts, 54–55
  See also identity management
self-disclosure
  disadvantages of, 238
  identity management and, 58
  Johari window, 236–37
  social penetration theory, 237
self-esteem, 51
self-expansion, 221

self-expression, 83–84, 222
self-fulfilling prophecies, 56
selfish roles, in groups, 296–97
self-managed work teams, 287
self-promotion, 59
self-serving bias, 45
self-talk, positive, 55–56
semantic rules, 69–70
semantic triangle, 77
sensory information (stimuli), 33, 37–38
sentences, in working outlines, 435, 436, 437, 439
separation between co-cultures, 178
separation strategy for dialectical tensions, 244–45
sexist language, 92–93, 360
sexuality. *See* gender
sexual orientation
    audience demographics and, 361
    diversity spectrum and, 167
    prejudice and, 180
    unnecessary references to, 93
shared activities, maintaining relationships with, 254, 259
shared meaning, communication and, 20
shared tasks, maintaining relationships with, 254, 257
Shaw, Donald, 209
signaling language
    internal previews and summaries, 425
    signposts, 424–25, 429
    transitions, 423–24, 430, 438, 447
signposting language, 424–25, 429
sign reasoning, 537
similarity, attraction and, 229
Simmons, Rachel, 53
simplifying complex information. *See* clarifying complex information
single-gender audiences, 360
situational characteristics of speeches, 356–57
size
    of audience, 356, 508, 509–10
    of groups, 288–91
    of visual aids, 482
Skype. *See* videoconferencing
slide shows, 484

slippery slope fallacy, 540
small group communication. *See* group communication
small groups, defined, 6
small talk, 230–31
smell, study of (olfactics), 120–21
Snowden, Edward, 205–6
social attraction, 226–27
social comments, 228–29
social distance, 117
socialization, group, 289–91
social judgment theory, 526
social media
    as research tool, 392; anonymity, free speech, and privacy, 205–6, 213; characteristics of, 201–2; digital divide and net neutrality, 206–7; effects of, 202–4; job interviews and, 558; news coverage and, 199
social networking, 201. *See also* social media
social networks, maintaining relationships with, 254, 257–58
social penetration theory, 237
social roles, in groups, 295–96
sociocultural contexts for self-concepts, 54–55
software
    for group meetings, 308
    for presentations, 482, 484, 510
Sorenson, Gail, 428
sources, research. *See* researching a speech
spatial pattern of organization, 418–19, 512
speaking outlines
    defined, 435–36
    elements of, 446–47
    formatting, 446
    sample, 447–50
special-occasion speeches
    opportunities for, 349–50
    topic selection and, 372
special peers, 224
specific, moving from general to, 513–14

specific purpose of speech
main points and, 417
speech critiques and, 153
thesis statement and, 376
topic selection and, 374
in working outline, 440
stability
of groups, 289–91
of self-concept, 50
stage models of interpersonal relationships, 232
staircase model of interpersonal relationships, 232
statistics, in supporting materials, 399–400
stereotypes
analyzing audience demographics and, 359
gender stereotypes, 360
language and, 91–92
misperceptions and, 42–43
prejudice and, 181
sticking to your speech topic choice, 370
stimuli (sensory information), 33, 37–38
Stone, Tara, 84
stonewalling, 273, 274
stories. *See* narratives and stories
strategic discourse (audience considerations)
beliefs, 527
benefits, 427–28, 528–29
disposition, 526–27, 531
needs, 527–28, 531
reservations, 151, 529–30, 531, 532
values, 528
straw person fallacy, 539–40
striking or provocative statements, 426, 432
student, communication and public speaking as, 11, 349
style, in classical canons of rhetoric, 353.
See also verbal communication
subpoints (supporting points) in speeches
in speaking outlines, 446, 447
subordination and coordination, 422, 437–38
when a subpoint doesn't fit, 423
in working outlines, 437–38

substitution, nonverbal, 112, 123
sub-subpoints, 422, 437, 446, 447
summarizing
of main points, in conclusion:
impromptu speaking and, 463;
organizing speech and, 430–31;
working outlines and, 439–40
as signaling device, 425
superficial listening, 151–52
supplementing, nonverbal, 108–9, 123
supplication, identity management and, 60
supporting materials for speeches
guidelines for use, 403
impromptu speaking and, 463
overview: review materials, 409–13;
uses for supporting materials, 395–97
types of: analogies, 400–402; definitions, 396, 398; examples, 396, 397–98; narratives, 400; statistics, 399–400; testimony, 397, 399
See also subpoints in speeches
support networks, 57
surprising statements, 426, 432
suspense, building, 426
symbol system
language and communication as, 19–20, 71–72
semantic triangle, 77
synergy, 301
syntactic rules, 70
synthesizers, in groups, 295

take-home messages, 153
taping conversations, 394
task attraction, 226–27
team communication. *See* group communication
technology
for group work and document sharing, 308–10
for meetings, 305–8, 313
for presentations, 482, 484, 510
See also computer-mediated communication

TED talks, 203
teleprompters, 457
temporal (chronological) pattern of organization
   defined, 419
   informative speeches, 512
testimony, in supporting materials, 399
text messages, 107–8, 123, 306
thank-you notes (after job interviews), 571
thesis statements
   drafting, 374–76
   highlighting, in conclusion, 432–33
   signaling, in introduction, 427
   in working outline, 439, 440
Thicke, Robin, 238
thinking about call of question, 462–63
Tiananmen Square protests, 191–92
tics, vocal, 471
time
   presentation time, for speeches, 139, 356
   time of day, week, etc. (see chronemics)
timeliness of sources, 387
time-oriented listening, 137, 138
title of speech, 440
tone, vocal, 119–20, 458, 465–66
topic, thinking about call of, 462–63
topical (categorical) pattern of organization
   defined, 420
   informative speeches, 512
   persuasive speeches, 545
topics for speeches, selecting
   overview of public speaking process: introduction, 347–48; review materials, 376–79
   step 1: identifying potential topics: brainstorming, 367; invention, in classical canons of rhetoric, 353; mind mapping, 368–69; research, 366–67; word association, 368
   step 2: narrowing the topic: considering assignment criteria, 369; considering audience, 370, 374

(see also audience analysis); considering own knowledge and interests, 370, 374; importance of narrowing, 372–73; sticking to your choice, 370
   step 3: framing the specific topic: determining rhetorical purpose, 371–72, 374 (see also rhetorical purpose of speech); drafting specific purpose, 374, 376 (see also specific purpose of speech); drafting thesis statement, 374–76 (see also thesis statements)
topic statements, 374–75. See also thesis statements
top level domains, 392
top management teams (TMTs), 287
touch (haptics), 116–17
transactional processes, 5, 17–19
transference, 44–45
transitional words and phrases
   in conclusions of speeches, 430
   signaling with, 423–24
   in speaking outline, 447
   in working outline, 438
transparencies, overhead, 484
"tree trunk" stance, 475
triangle of meaning, 77
trolling, 205
trustworthiness, credibility and, 531
Truth, Sojourner, 350
truthful communication
   in conversational feedback, 155
   equivocal language, 80
   false inference, 405–6
   half-truths, 405
   impact of deception, 23–24
   lying, 404–5
   misrepresenting another's point of view, 395
   omission, 406
   out-of-context evidence, 408
Tuckman's model of group development, 298–99
Tunisian Girl, A (Mhenni), 83
turning-away responses, 263–64
turning-toward responses, 264

Tutu, Desmond, 55
Twitter, 199, 203
two-phase model of group development, 299–300
two-sided arguments, 529–30. *See also* reservations, acknowledging

uncertainty
avoiding, 169–70, 302
coping with, 265
understanding, listener and audience
checking, 151, 155
statistics and, 400
supporting materials and, 396
working for accuracy in, 95–96
uniqueness of self-concept, 50
URLs, 385, 392
uses of effective communication
career, 10–11
community, 12
personal life, 8–9
school, 11

value claims
defined, 534–24
organizational patterns for, 544–45
values, audience, 528
verbal clutter, 90
verbal communication (language)
abuses of: biased language, 85–88, 91–94, 182; inflammatory language, 88; loaded language, 543–44
features of: context dependency, 74–75; dynamic change, 72–74; literal and figurative meanings, 72; rules, 69–70; symbols, 71–72
functions and uses of: accomplishing actions, 85; expressing feelings, 83–84; imagining, 84–85; influence and persuasion, 82–83; sharing information, 82
overview: definition, 18; introduction, 67–68; review materials, 97–101

speech delivery skills: articulation, 468–69; pausing, 151, 470–71; projection, 151, 468; pronunciation, 469–70; rate of delivery, 151, 466–68; tone and inflection, 458, 465–66; volume, 151, 463–65
See also word choice
verbal fillers, 471
verbal learners, 403
videoconferencing, 307–8, 309, 310
violence, common couple, 272
virtual groups, 333
virtual peers, 224
virtue, in classical rhetoric, 531
visual learners, 403
visual presentation aids
audience interaction with, 483–84
positioning for visibility, 483
size, contrast, and legibility of, 482
vocal delivery skills
articulation, 468–69
pausing, 151, 470–71
projection, 151, 468
pronunciation, 469–70
rate of delivery, 151, 466–68
tone and inflection, 458, 465–66
volume, 151, 463–65
vocal fry, 120
vocal tics, 471
volume
of audio aids, 482
of speaking voice, 151, 463–65

Walther, Joseph, 204
"We are all Khaled Saeed" (Ghonim), 83
well-being, interpersonal relationships and, 221
WIIFM (what's in it for me) statements, 427–28, 527
Wikipedia, 392
winning agreement, 397
wisdom, in classical rhetoric, 531
Wiseman, Rosalind, 53
withdrawers, in groups, 297

word choice
  delivering speeches and: emotional appeals, 542; extemporaneous delivery, 461; memorized delivery, 459
  goals of: conciseness, 90; concreteness, 78, 90–91; credibility, 531; respect, 95–97
  misunderstandings: abstract language, 78–79; difficult words, 447; equivocal language, 80; imperfections of language and, 447; improper words, 80; jargon, 79–80
  negative uses: biased language, 85–88, 91–94, 182; inflammatory language, 88; loaded language, 543–44
  signaling language: internal previews and summaries, 425; signposts, 424–25, 429; transitions, 423–24, 430, 438, 447
  See also verbal communication (language)
words, mental associations to
  emotional appeals and, 542
  generating ideas with, 368

See also connotative meanings
working outlines
  body of speech, 437–38
  conclusions, 439–40
  defined, 434–35
  introductions, 439
  list of works cited, 440
  sample working outline, 440–45
  title, specific purpose, or thesis, 440
workplaces
  communication and public speaking in, 10–11, 349
  interpersonal relationships in, 223–24, 261–62
work roles, in groups, 294–95
works cited list, 440
work teams, self-managed, 287

yielding, as conflict style, 270
Yousafzai, Malala, 351

Zimmerman, George, 209–11
Zubrin, Robert, 537

Your Video Choices

launchpadworks.com

LaunchPad offers superior video content organized to work seamlessly with the printed textbook. Go to LaunchPad for *Let's Communicate* to find **key term videos** including full-length speeches and **sample speech resources** that complement the book content. Here is a list of the videos and where their concepts appear in the text. Find even more videos and models of public speaking in LaunchPad.

CHAPTER 1: INTRODUCTION TO COMMUNICATION
Channel — p. 18
Noise — p. 18

CHAPTER 2: PERCEIVING OTHERS, PERCEIVING OURSELVES
Self-fulfilling prophecy — p. 56
Self-disclosure — p. 58
Self-serving bias — p. 45

CHAPTER 3: VERBAL COMMUNICATION
Denotative meaning — p. 72
Connotative meaning — p. 72
Equivocal language — p. 80

CHAPTER 4: NONVERBAL COMMUNICATION
Kinesics — p. 113
Haptics — p. 116
Proxemics — p. 117
Paralanguage — p. 119

CHAPTER 5: LISTENING SKILLS
Action-oriented listeners — p. 137
Content-oriented listeners — p. 137
Time-oriented listeners — p. 137
Argumentative (selective) listening — p. 144

CHAPTER 6: CULTURE AND COMMUNICATION
Low-context cultures — p. 171
High-context cultures — p. 171
Individualistic cultures — p. 172
Collectivist cultures — p. 173
High-contact cultures — p. 174
Low-contact cultures — p. 174
High-power-distance cultures — p. 175
Low-power-distance cultures — p. 175
Assimilation — p. 176

CHAPTER 7: MASS AND MEDIATED COMMUNICATION
Anonymity — p. 205
Trolling — p. 205
Agenda setting and gatekeeping — p. 209

CHAPTER 8: PRINCIPLES OF INTERPERSONAL COMMUNICATION
Integrating — p. 232
Bonding — p. 232
Differentiating — p. 232
Stagnating — p. 232
Dialectical tensions — p. 241

CHAPTER 9: PRACTICES FOR EFFECTIVE INTERPERSONAL RELATIONSHIPS
Relational maintenance — p. 252
Collaborating — p. 269
Compromising — p. 269
Avoiding — p. 270

CHAPTER 10: PRINCIPLES OF GROUP COMMUNICATION
Tuckman's model: forming — p. 299
Tuckman's model: storming — p. 299
Tuckman's model: norming — p. 299
Tuckman's model: performing — p. 299
Tuckman's model: adjourning — p. 299

CHAPTER 12: PUBLIC SPEAKING: FIRST STEPS
Demographics — p. 357
Speech topic — p. 365
Informative speeches — p. 372
Persuasive speeches — p. 372
Special-occasion speeches — p. 372
Thesis statement — p. 374

CHAPTER 13: SPEECH CONTENT: RESEARCH, SUPPORTING MATERIALS, AND ETHICS
Citation — p. 384
Paraphrase — p. 395
Examples — p. 397
Testimony — p. 399
Statistics — p. 399
Analogy — p. 400

CHAPTER 14: ORGANIZING AND OUTLINING YOUR SPEECH
Spatial pattern — p. 418
Chronological pattern — p. 419
Causal (cause-effect) pattern — p. 419
Categorical (topical) pattern — p. 420
Previews, transitions, and summaries — p. 423
Transition — p. 423
Internal previews — p. 425
Internal summaries — p. 425
Preview — p. 428
Summary — p. 430
Clincher — p. 431
Extemporaneous delivery — p. 436

CHAPTER 15: DELIVERING YOUR SPEECH
Manuscript speaking — p. 456
Prop — p. 458
Extemporaneous speaking — p. 460
Impromptu speaking — p. 462
Volume — p. 463
Vocal tone — p. 465
Monotone — p. 465
Rate of delivery (vocal rate) — p. 466
Pronunciation — p. 469
Pausing — p. 470
Verbal filler — p. 471
Immediacy — p. 477
Gestures — p. 474
Presentation aids — p. 479
Presentation software — p. 482

CHAPTER 16: INFORMATIVE SPEAKING
Informative speech — p. 489
Definition — p. 490
Description — p. 493
Demonstration — p. 494
Process or demonstration presentation — p. 494
Narrative presentation — p. 496

CHAPTER 17: PERSUASIVE SPEAKING
Persuasive speech — p. 522
Fact claim — p. 523
Value claim — p. 523
Policy claim — p. 524
Ethos (credibility) — p. 530
Logos — p. 533
Fallacies — p. 533
Inductive reasoning — p. 534
Hasty generalization — p. 538
Ad populum (bandwagon) fallacy — p. 539
Slippery slope fallacy — p. 540
Pathos — p. 540
Motivated sequence — p. 546